Hands-On Microsoft Windows Server 2019

Third Edition

Jason W. Eckert
triOS College

CENGAGE

Australia • Brazil • Mexico • Singapore • United Kingdom • United States

Hands-On Microsoft Windows Server 2019, Third Edition

Jason W. Eckert

SVP, Higher Education Product Management: Erin Joyner

VP, Product Management: Thais Alencar

Product Team Manager: Kristin McNary

Product Manager: Amy Savino

Senior Product Assistant: Anna Goulart

Director, Learning Design: Rebecca von Gillern

Senior Manager, Learning Design: Leigh Hefferon

Learning Designer: Natalie Onderdonk

Vice President, Marketing – Science, Technology, & Math: Jason Sakos

Senior Marketing Director: Michele McTighe

Marketing Manager: Cassie Cloutier

Marketing Development Manager: Samantha Best

Product Specialist: Mackenzie Paine

Director, Content Creation: Juliet Steiner

Senior Manager, Content Creation: Patty Stephan

Senior Content Manager: Brooke Greenhouse

Director, Digital Production Services: Krista Kellman

Digital Delivery Lead: Jim Vaughey

Technical Editor: Danielle Shaw

Developmental Editor: Ann Shaffer

Production Service/Composition: SPi-Global

Design Director: Jack Pendleton

Designer: Erin Griffin

Cover Designer: Joseph Villanova

Cover Image(s): iStockPhoto.com/nadla

For product information and technology assistance, contact us at **Cengage Customer & Sales Support, 1-800-354-9706 or support.cengage.com.**

For permission to use material from this text or product, submit all requests online at **www.cengage.com/permissions**.

Library of Congress Control Number: 2020907519

ISBN: 978-0-357-43615-8

Cengage
200 Pier 4 Boulevard
Boston, MA 02210
USA

Cengage is a leading provider of customized learning solutions with employees residing in nearly 40 different countries and sales in more than 125 countries around the world. Find your local representative at **www.cengage.com**.

Cengage products are represented in Canada by Nelson Education, Ltd.

To learn more about Cengage platforms and services, register or access your online learning solution, or purchase materials for your course, visit **www.cengage.com**.

Notice to the Reader

Printed at CLDPC, USA, 08-22

Brief Contents

iii

Table of Contents

MODULE 2

Configuring Windows Server 2019 65

MODULE 3

Implementing Hyper-V and Rapid Server Deployment ... 149

MODULE 5

Configuring Resource Access 295

MODULE 8

Configuring and Managing Network Services 505

MODULE 9

Configuring and Managing Remote Access Services 577

MODULE 10

Configuring Web Services and Cloud Technologies.......... 655

MODULE 11

Managing and Securing Windows Networks 705

MODULE 12

Monitoring and Troubleshooting Windows Server 2019 781

Introduction

The Microsoft Windows family of operating systems has
dominated both the personal and business computing world for
the past three decades. Within organizations, Windows Server
operating systems support the computing needs of Windows users,
as well as users of other operating systems, such as Linux and
macOS. Windows Server 2019, Microsoft's latest server operating
system, offers a comprehensive set of services and features aimed
to increase user productivity and data security in a wide range of
different environments.

Hands-On Microsoft Windows Server 2019, Third Edition, is the
perfect resource for learning Windows Server 2019 administration
from the ground up. You will learn how to deploy Windows
Server 2019 in a variety of different environments, including
data center and cloud environments that rely on virtualization
and containers. Additionally, you will learn how to configure and
manage server storage, troubleshoot performance issues, as well
as work with common Windows Server technologies and network
services, including Active Directory, Certificate Services, DNS,
DHCP, WSUS, IIS, file sharing, printing, and remote access.

You'll find a focus on quality throughout with an emphasis
on preparing you for valuable real-world experiences. Hands-On
Projects help you practice skills using one of two different lab
environments suitable for both classroom-based and independent
learning, and Discovery Exercises allow you to apply these
skills within real-life environments, as well as explore advanced
topics. Review questions and key terms are provided to reinforce
important concepts. Together, these features give you the
experience and confidence you need to function as a Windows
Server 2019 administrator and provide a solid foundation for
pursuing server- and cloud-focused certification.

Intended Audience

Hands-On Microsoft Windows Server 2019, Third Edition, is intended
for anyone who wants to learn how to configure and support
Windows Server 2019 systems. It also can be used as a starting
point in preparing for the Microsoft Azure certification exam
track. No prior Windows Server experience is required, but some

basic experience with Windows client operating systems, such as Windows 7, 8/8.1, or 10, is helpful. If you are already an experienced Windows Server administrator, this book provides a fast way to upgrade your skills to Windows Server 2019.

Module Descriptions

Module 1, "Getting Started with Windows Server 2019," introduces the features and editions of the Windows Server 2019 operating system, as well as the server configurations available in an on-premises or cloud environment. This module also details the Windows Server 2019 installation process, as well as common post-installation configuration tasks.

Module 2, "Configuring Windows Server 2019," outlines the tools that you can use to configure Windows Server 2019, including Server Manager, Windows Admin Center, Control Panel, Device Manager, Registry Editor, and Windows PowerShell. Additionally, this module introduces the use of PowerShell scripts for automating system configuration tasks.

Module 3, "Implementing Hyper-V and Rapid Server Deployment," discusses the process used to configure and manage Windows Server 2019 virtualization. This module also discusses how to rapidly deploy Windows Server 2019 using virtual machine templates and WDS.

Module 4, "Introduction to Active Directory and Account Management," details how to install and manage Active Directory in an enterprise environment. This module also discusses the procedures used to create and manage Active Directory objects, including users, computers, and groups.

Module 5, "Configuring Resource Access," introduces folder and file attributes, permissions, ownership, and auditing, as well as the process used to share folder contents to users using SMB and NFS. Additionally, this module discusses how to extend the functionality of shared folders using DFS, quotas, and file screens.

Module 6, "Configuring Printing," details the print process, as well as the procedures used to share printers to network users using SMB, and LPD. This module also discusses how to manage print jobs and troubleshoot printer problems.

Module 7, "Configuring and Managing Data Storage," introduces the different data storage configurations available within Windows Server 2019, as well as the procedures used to create and manage simple and software RAID volumes. Additionally, this module discusses the configuration of SAN storage and data deduplication, as well as the tools that can be used to optimize, repair, and back up volumes.

Module 8, "Configuring and Managing Network Services," discusses the procedures used to provide name resolution and IP configuration on a Windows network. More specifically, this module covers the configuration, management, and troubleshooting of DNS, WINS, and DHCP services.

Module 9, "Configuring and Managing Remote Access Services," details the procedures used to configure remote access using VPNs, DirectAccess, and Remote Desktop Services. This module also discusses how RADIUS can be configured to support remote access.

Module 10, "Configuring Web Services and Cloud Technologies," introduces key cloud concepts and configurations, including the role of Web servers, Web apps, and Linux in a cloud environment. Furthermore, this module covers the configuration of the IIS Web server, Windows and Linux containers, and the Windows Subsystem for Linux.

Module 11, "Managing and Securing Windows Networks," discusses the configuration of Group Policy and public key certificates in an enterprise environment. This module also discusses the configuration of 802.1X Wireless, WSUS, Windows Defender, firewalls, and IPSec.

Module 12, "Monitoring and Troubleshooting Windows Server 2019," introduces the processes and tools used to monitor and troubleshoot Windows Server 2019 systems. Additionally, this module discusses common troubleshooting procedures for resolving different hardware, software, operating system, performance, and network problems.

Features

To ensure a successful learning experience, this book includes the following pedagogical features:

- *Module objectives*—Each module in this book begins with a detailed list of the concepts to be mastered within that module. This list provides you with a quick reference to the contents of that module as well as a useful study aid.
- *Illustrations and tables*—Numerous illustrations of server screens and components aid you in the visualization of common setup steps, theories, and concepts. In addition, many tables provide details and comparisons of both practical and theoretical information and can be used for a quick review of topics.
- *End-of-module material*—The end of each module includes the following features to reinforce the material covered in the module:
  - *Summary*—A bulleted list is provided that gives a brief but complete summary of the module.
  - *Key Terms list*—This is a list of all new terms. Definitions for each key term can be found in the Glossary.
  - *Review Questions*—A list of review questions tests your knowledge of the most important concepts covered in the module.
  - *Hands-On Projects*—Hands-On Projects help you to apply the knowledge gained in the module.
  - *Discovery Exercises*—These are additional projects that build upon the Hands-On Projects, as well as guide you through real-world scenarios and advanced topics.

New to this Edition

The content within *Hands-On Microsoft Windows Server 2019, Third Edition,* has been completely revamped from the previous editions to provide several new features and approaches:

- Topics have been reorganized and rewritten to provide a more concise and logical flow.
- Additional focus is placed on new and emerging technologies within Windows Server, such as virtualization, containers, enterprise storage, cloud, and security.
- Inline Activities within each module have been replaced by comprehensive Hands-On Projects designed to work better within a classroom or home environment.
- Two different lab environments are made available in Module 1 that allow students to perform Hands-On Projects within a classroom or home environment using Windows Server 2019 running natively, or within a Hyper-V virtual machine on Windows 10.
- Discovery Exercises have been added to the end of each module to provide additional ways to explore and reinforce key concepts and real-world application.
- Windows PowerShell and server virtualization have been integrated into topics throughout the book.
- A new module has been added to discuss cloud technologies.

Text and Graphic Conventions

Wherever appropriate, additional information and exercises have been added to this book to help you better understand what is being discussed in the module. Special headings throughout the text alert you to additional materials:

Note

The Note heading is used to present additional helpful material related to the subject being described.

Hands-On Project

The Hands-On Project heading indicates that the projects following it give you a chance to practice the skills you learned in the module and acquire hands-on experience.

Discovery Exercise

The Discovery Exercise heading indicates that the projects following it provide additional ways to explore and reinforce key concepts and real-world application.

MindTap

MindTap activities for *Hands-On Microsoft Windows Server 2019, Third Edition*, are designed to help you master the skills you need in today's workforce. Research shows that employers need critical thinkers, troubleshooters, and creative problem-solvers to stay relevant in this fast-paced, technology-driven world. MindTap helps you achieve this goal with assignments and activities that provide hands-on practice and real-life relevance. You are guided through assignments that help you master basic knowledge and understanding before moving on to more challenging problems.

All MindTap activities and assignments are tied to defined learning objectives. Readings support the course objectives, while Networking for Life assignments allow you to explore industry-related news and events. Reflection activities encourage self-reflection and open sharing with your classmates to help improve your retention and understanding of the material.

Labs provide hands-on practice and give you an opportunity to troubleshoot, explore, and try different solutions using the Windows Server 2019 operating system.

Use the interactive Flashcards and PowerPoint slides in each module to help you study for exams. Measure how well you have mastered the material by taking the Review Quizzes and Think Critically Quizzes offered with each module. The Post-Assessment Quiz helps you assess all that you have learned throughout the course, see where you gained deeper knowledge, and identify the skills where you need additional practice!

Instructors can use the content and learning path as they are, or choose how these materials wrap around their own resources. MindTap supplies the analytics and reporting to easily see where the class stands in terms of progress, engagement, and completion rates. To learn more about shaping what students see and scheduling when they see it, instructors can go to *www.cengage.com/mindtap/*.

Instructor Resources

Everything you need for your course in one place! This collection of class tools is available online via *www.cengage.com/login*. Access and download PowerPoint presentations, images, the Instructor's Manual, and more. An instructor login is required.

- *Instructor's Manual*—The Instructor's Manual that accompanies this book includes additional instructional material to assist in class preparation, including items such as overviews, module objectives, teaching tips, quick quizzes, class discussion topics, additional projects, additional resources, and key terms.

- *Test bank*—Cengage Testing Powered by Cognero is a flexible, online system that allows you to do the following:
  - Author, edit, and manage test bank content from multiple Cengage solutions.
  - Create multiple test versions in an instant.
  - Deliver tests from your LMS, your classroom, or wherever you want.
- *PowerPoint presentations*—This book provides PowerPoint slides to accompany each module. Slides can be used to guide classroom presentations, to make available to students for module review, or to print as classroom handouts. Files are also supplied for every figure in the book. Instructors can use these files to customize PowerPoint slides, illustrate quizzes, or create handouts.
- *Solutions*—Solutions to all end-of-module review questions and projects are available.
- *Sample Syllabus*—A sample syllabus is provided to help you plan what objectives you will cover in your course and how you will give your students a sense of what the course will be like, including your criteria for grading and evaluation.
- *MindTap Educator's Guide*—This guide helps you navigate the unique activities that are included in the MindTap, which will better enable you to include the exercises in your curriculum.
- *Transition Guide*—This guide will help you navigate what has changed from the second edition of this book to the third edition of the book and highlight any new materials that are covered in each module.

Author Biography

Jason W. Eckert is an experienced technical trainer, consultant, and best-selling author in the Information Technology (IT) industry. With 45 industry certifications, over 30 years of IT experience, 4 published apps, and 25 published textbooks covering topics such as UNIX, Linux, Security, Windows Server, Microsoft Exchange Server, PowerShell, BlackBerry Enterprise Server, and Video Game Development, Mr. Eckert brings his expertise to every class that he teaches at triOS College, and to his role as the Dean of Technology. For more information about Mr. Eckert, visit *jasoneckert.net*.

Acknowledgments

Firstly, I would like to thank the staff at Cengage for an overall enjoyable experience writing a textbook on Windows Server that takes a fundamentally different approach than traditional textbooks. Additionally, I wish to thank Ann Shaffer, Danielle Shaw, Brooke Greenhouse, Natalie Onderdonk, and Praveen Kumar R.S for working extremely hard to pull everything together and ensure that the book provides a magnificent student experience. I also wish to thank Frank Gerencser of triOS College for providing the necessary project motivation, the Starbucks Coffee Company for keeping me ahead of schedule, and my dog Pepper for continually reminding me that taking a break is always a good idea.

Readers are encouraged to e-mail comments, questions, and suggestions regarding *Hands-On Microsoft Windows Server 2019, Third Edition,* to Jason W. Eckert: jason.eckert@trios.com.

Reviewers

Jeff Riley
Director of Learning Solutions
Box Twelve Communications
Apex, NC

Scott D. Rhine
IT Instructor and Program Coordinator of IT-Network Administration
Lake Land College
Mattoon, IL

Roger Zimmerman, M.Ed.
Instructor, CIS
Portland Community College
Portland, OR

Dedication

This book is dedicated to everyone with a red line under their name in Microsoft Word.

Computer and Lab Setup Guide

The following is the minimum requirement for the Hands-On Projects at the end of each module:

- A 64-bit computer with a recent-generation processor that supports virtualization extensions (Intel VT/AMD-V + SLAT)
- 16 GB of memory
- 500GB hard disk or SSD storage (SSD strongly recommended)
- A DVD or USB flash drive that contains bootable installation media for Windows Server 2019 Datacenter Edition
- A network that provides Internet access

GETTING STARTED WITH WINDOWS SERVER 2019

After completing this module, you will be able to:

Summarize the different ways that Windows Server 2019 can be used within an on-premises or cloud environment

Explain the purpose and function of Windows virtual machines and containers

Outline the key features of Windows Server 2019

Identify the differences between Windows Server 2019 editions

Discuss the considerations necessary to plan for a Windows Server 2019 installation

Describe the concepts and processes used to perform a Windows Server 2019 installation

Outline common post-installation configuration tasks for Windows Server 2019

Identify the different virtualization configurations that can be used to explore Windows Server 2019 within an IT lab environment

Microsoft Windows Server systems serve a critical role in nearly all organizations today, from small businesses to large, multinational corporations. Windows Server 2019, Microsoft's newest server platform, offers even more roles for servers, better security, easier server management, new desktop features, and more reliable computing than its predecessors.

This book is intended to give you a solid grounding in how to install, administer, and support Windows Server 2019 in a wide variety of different environments. In this module, you learn the different ways that Windows Server can be implemented within an organization, in addition to the key features and editions of Windows Server 2019. Additionally, you'll learn how to plan for and install Windows Server 2019, as well as perform post-installation configuration tasks.

> **Note**
>
> Many of the Windows Server 2019 features and supporting topics introduced within this module are properly covered in more depth throughout this book. They are introduced within this module so that you can select the correct Windows Server 2019 edition and installation features to support your environment.

Using Windows Server 2019 within an Organization

Since the introduction of the IBM PC in 1981, Microsoft operating systems have been at the forefront of personal and business computing. By 1990, over three quarters of all personal computers (PCs) ran the Microsoft MS-DOS or Windows operating system on IBM-compatible hardware, and the term PC became synonymous with Microsoft.

During the rise of computer **networks** and the Internet in the 1990s, most organizations started using PCs to connect to other computers across a computer network to obtain access to shared resources such as files, databases, and printers. The PC connecting to the shared resource was called the **client**, and the computer sharing the resource was called the **server**. While any operating system can function as a server if it shares resources with other computers, specialized operating systems geared toward resource sharing on the network also became common during the 1990s. Microsoft released their Windows NT Server operating system in 1993 and it quickly became the standard server operating system that client PCs connected to within organizations. By 2000, Windows NT Server was renamed "Windows Server," with new versions released every three to five years. In 2018, Windows Server operating systems were installed on over 80% of all servers located within organizations worldwide.

> **Note**
>
> Servers that are located within organizations are referred to as **on-premises servers**. Today, many servers exist within data centers outside the organization and are accessed via the Internet. These servers are referred to as **cloud servers** and the collective of servers publicly available on the Internet is referred to as the **cloud**.

Server hardware has a different form factor compared to desktop PCs. Nearly all servers within an organization are housed within a rackmount case that is mounted alongside other servers on a vertical server storage rack. Consequently, we call these servers **rackmount servers**.

Each rackmount server in the rack may contain a different operating system (or multiple operating systems if virtualization software is used) and will connect to a shared monitor/keyboard/mouse. This shared monitor/keyboard/mouse often folds away into the rack for storage and is necessary for initial configuration tasks such as server installation. All other server administration is normally performed remotely from a PC running remote administration tools.

Most racks also contain one or more **storage area network (SAN)** devices, which provide a large amount of hard disk or **solid state disk (SSD)** storage for the servers within the rack, as well as one or more **uninterruptible power supply (UPS)** devices, which provide backup battery power to servers and SANs within the rack in the event of a power loss.

The minimum height of a rackmount server is 1.75 inches. Servers of this size are called **1U servers**. (The letter "U" is short for unit.) Most 1U servers have up to two hard drives (or SSDs) and up to two processors. Other rackmount servers take up more than one spot on the rack and have a height that is a multiple of a 1U server. For example, a 2U server is twice as high as a 1U server and often contains up to four processors and eight hard disks (or SSDs). Rackmount servers rarely exceed 4U, but SAN devices are often 4U or more.

Figure 1-1 shows a sample server rack configuration that hosts three 1U servers (Web server, file server, and firewall server), two 2U servers (database server and email server), a 2U UPS, a 4U SAN, and a management station with a shared monitor/keyboard/mouse.

> **Note** @
>
> A single rackmount server may contain multiple smaller, modular servers. In this case, the modular servers are called **blade servers**.

> **Note** @
>
> If **Non-Volatile Memory Express (NVMe)** SSDs are used, then the number of SSDs within a rackmount server or SAN may be substantially higher due to the small physical size of NVMe devices.

Understanding Windows Server Virtualization

Virtualization is the process of running more than one operating system at the same time on a single computer. It has been used in various capacities since the dawn of computing in the 1960s. To implement virtualization, you must use software that allows the hardware to host multiple operating systems. This software, called a **hypervisor**, serves to handle simultaneous requests for underlying hardware efficiently. **Type 2 hypervisors** are designed to run on top of an existing workstation operating system

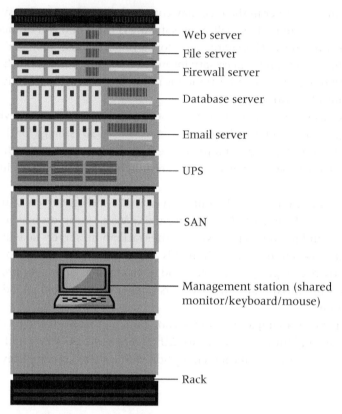

Figure 1-1   A sample server rack

(referred to as the **host operating system**). All additional operating systems (called **guest operating systems** or **virtual machines**) must access the hardware through both the hypervisor and underlying host operating system. Type 2 hypervisors are common today for software testing and development. For example, a software developer can test a specific application or Web app on a variety of operating systems without requiring separate computers. Many college technology courses today also take advantage of Type 2 hypervisors to run multiple operating systems within a classroom or lab environment.

Note

Common Type 2 hypervisors include VMWare Workstation, Oracle VirtualBox, and Parallels Workstation.

By the mid-2000s, a typical server closet or data center contained many individual rackmount servers. To maintain security and stability, each rackmount server contained a single (or small number of) separate server software applications. One rackmount server might host Web server software, while another might host file sharing services, and so on. Unfortunately, most of these server software applications only used a small fraction of the actual rackmount server hardware, and supplying power and cooling to the large number of rackmount servers was expensive. To solve these problems, many IT administrators turned to server virtualization, but with a **Type 1 hypervisor** to ensure that each virtual machine runs as efficiently as possible. A Type 1 hypervisor interacts with the hardware directly, and contains a small operating system to manage the hypervisor configuration and virtual machines. Figure 1-2 shows the difference between Type 1 and Type 2 hypervisors.

Note

Microsoft **Hyper-V** is a Type 1 hypervisor. Other common Type 1 hypervisors used today include VMWare ESX/ESXi and Linux KVM.

Note

Hyper-V is available on Windows Server 2012 and later, as well as on Windows 8 and later (Professional and Enterprise editions).

Note

Nearly all hypervisors today require that your processor supports hypervisor acceleration; this feature is referred to as **Intel VT** (for Intel) or **AMD-V** (for AMD). Most hypervisors, including Hyper-V, also require that your processor supports **Second Level Address Translation (SLAT)** extensions.

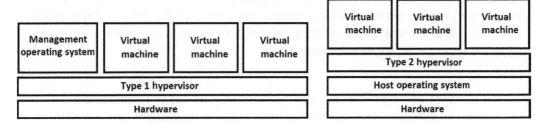

Figure 1-2   Comparing Type 1 and Type 2 hypervisors

Regardless of the hypervisor used, all virtual machines store their configuration within a small configuration file specific to the hypervisor. Meanwhile, they store the actual operating system data for the virtual machine in a virtual hard disk file. When you create a virtual machine, you must choose the size of this virtual hard disk file. You must also choose between allocating a fixed space for the virtual hard disk file when it is created (called **thick provisioning**) or dynamically allocating space as the virtual machine needs it (called **thin provisioning**). For example, if you create a 250 GB fixed-sized virtual disk, then 250 GB is reserved on the storage device immediately. Thin provisioning creates a small virtual disk file that grows up to 250 GB as the virtual machine stores more data. Thin provisioning is often preferred for server virtualization as it conserves space on the underlying server storage hardware.

> **Note** 📎
>
> Hyper-V virtual hard disk files have a `.vhdx` extension, VMWare virtual hard disk files have a `.vmdk` extension, Oracle VirtualBox virtual hard disks have a `.vdi` extension, and KVM virtual hard disks have either a `.qcow2` extension or omit the extension altogether.

> **Note** 📎
>
> Microsoft supports a wide range of operating systems for installation within Hyper-V virtual machines, including Windows 7 and later, Windows Server 2008 and later, Linux, and FreeBSD UNIX. Additionally, Hyper-V can emulate slower, legacy hardware for older operating systems (called a **Generation 1 virtual machine**) instead of modern hardware for newer operating systems (called a **Generation 2 virtual machine**).

> **Note** 📎
>
> Hyper-V also supports virtual machine **checkpoints** (often called **snapshots** in other hypervisors). If you take a checkpoint of a virtual machine, it creates a second virtual hard disk file that stores any changes to the operating system after the time the checkpoint was taken. This is useful before testing a risky software configuration; if the software configuration fails, the checkpoint can be used to roll back the operating system to the state in which it was before the software configuration was applied.

Most on-premises and cloud operating systems today are virtual machines, and the virtual hard disk files that contain each virtual machine operating system are often hosted on a SAN within the organization or cloud data center. This configuration reduces the number of storage devices needed within the rackmount servers on the rack, which in turn reduces the space needed to host the server hardware. Consequently, most servers today that run a hypervisor and virtual machines are 1U, allowing the rack to accommodate more rackmount servers in the same space. For example, virtualization could be used to consolidate the five sample server operating systems shown in Figure 1-1 into two 1U servers running Hyper-V and five virtual machines, as shown in Figure 1-3.

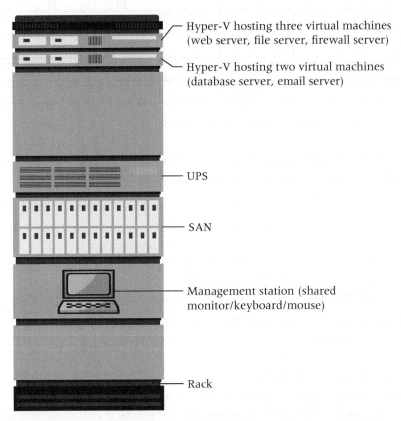

Figure 1-3   A sample server rack that utilizes virtual machines

Unlike most other hypervisors today, Hyper-V allows you to run other virtual machines within an existing virtual machine. This feature, called **nested virtualization**, is shown in Figure 1-4. For nested virtualization to work, both management operating systems illustrated in Figure 1-4 must run either Windows 10, Windows Server 2016, or Windows Server 2019.

Nested virtualization gives cloud data centers the ability to implement a more complex virtualization structure that suits their needs. Additionally, nested virtualization gives software developers and IT administrators the ability to implement a complex virtualization structure on their Windows 10 PCs for learning and testing purposes. For example, you can install a Windows Server 2019 Hyper-V virtual machine on a Windows 10 PC, and then install additional Hyper-V virtual machines within the Windows Server 2019 virtual machine.

Nested virtualization must be enabled in the underlying Hyper-V using a Windows PowerShell command (Windows PowerShell is discussed in the next section). For example, to ensure that the virtual machine named VM1 can install and use Hyper-V

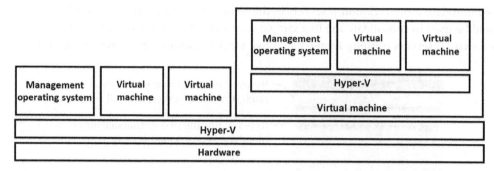

Figure 1-4   Nested virtualization using Hyper-V

to create additional virtual machines, you can power off VM1 and run the following command within Windows PowerShell on the management operating system:

```
Set-VMProcessor -VMName VM1 -ExposeVirtualizationExtensions $true
```

After you power on VM1, you will be able to install and configure Hyper-V on VM1 to host additional virtual machines. To ensure that virtual machines created by VM1 can access the network connected to the underlying Hyper-V hypervisor (to access the Internet, for example), you also need to run the following command within Windows PowerShell on the management operating system to allow MAC address spoofing:

```
Get-VMNetworkAdapter -VMName VM1 | Set-VMNetworkAdapter
-MacAddressSpoofing On
```

Understanding Windows Containers

Although virtualization makes more efficient use of server hardware, each virtual machine running on a hypervisor is a complete operating system that must be managed and secured like any other operating system running exclusively on server hardware.

Unlike virtual machines, **containers** do not have a complete operating system. Instead, a container is a subset of an operating system composed of one or more Web apps and the supporting operating system files needed by those Web apps only. As a result, containers must be run on an existing operating system that has container software installed, as shown in Figure 1-5.

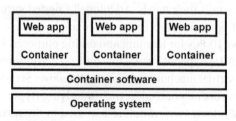

Figure 1-5   Using containers to run multiple Web apps

When you run a container, the enclosed Web apps are executed in a way that is isolated from Web apps running within other containers and the underlying operating system; this type of execution is often called **sandboxing**. To allow each Web app to be uniquely identified on the network, each container functions as a virtual operating system with a unique name and IP address.

Although separate virtual machines could instead be used to run Web apps on the same computer in an isolated fashion, containers are much smaller and use far fewer underlying system resources as a result. This makes containers well-suited for cloud environments, where resource efficiency and scalability are important for controlling data center costs.

Say, for example, that you create an IoT device that can be controlled remotely from a Web app running on a cloud server, and that you plan on selling thousands of these devices to customers. In this case, you don't need to create a large, complex Web app that is designed to connect to thousands of devices simultaneously, and that is hosted within a large virtual machine on a cloud server. Instead, you can create a small, simple Web app that can connect to a single device, and run that Web app within a container that can be run thousands of times on a cloud server. When a customer connects to their device, a new container is run on the cloud server to start a unique copy of the Web app for that customer's device. Similarly, when a customer disconnects from their device, the cloud server stops running the customer's container to free up system resources.

The most common container software used to implement containers on operating systems today is **Docker**, and the underlying component within Windows Server 2016 and later that allows you to install and use Docker is called **Windows Containers**.

Note

Docker is also available for many non-Windows operating systems, including Linux, UNIX, and macOS.

The core component of an operating system that executes all other components of the operating system is called the **kernel**. Containers do not contain a kernel, and thus must rely on the kernel in the underlying operating system to execute Web apps that they host. This means that the three Web apps shown in Figure 1-5 must be written for the Windows operating system and run within a Windows container if they are to use an underlying Windows operating system kernel for execution. It also means that the underlying operating system kernel is a single point of failure; too many containers on a single underlying operating system may slow down the performance of the kernel or cause it to crash. Furthermore, one container could potentially access another container running on the same underlying kernel if a security loophole were exploited.

To solve these problems, Hyper-V can be used alongside containers to provide a separate copy of the underlying kernel to each container. These **Hyper-V containers** use the functionality of Hyper-V alongside Windows containers to provide additional performance and security features to Web apps that are run within containers on Windows Server. Figure 1-6 illustrates the difference between Windows containers and Hyper-V containers.

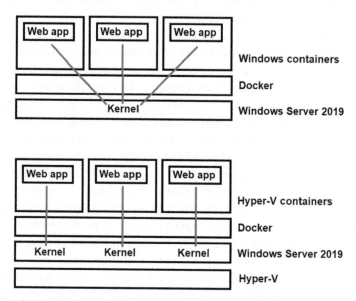

Figure 1-6   Comparing Windows containers and Hyper-V containers

Note

We will examine the configuration of Docker, Windows containers, and Hyper-V containers within Module 10.

Windows Server 2019 Features

Windows Server 2019 offers many features that make it a solid server and network operating system. This section examines the key areas of Windows Server 2019 that deserve special focus, including:

- Active Directory
- Security
- Volume and filesystem features
- Performance and reliability
- Administration tools
- Small footprint installation options

- Hybrid cloud features
- Linux application support

Each of these features is introduced in the sections that follow. You'll learn more about these features as you continue through this book.

Active Directory

When you install any Windows client or Windows Server operating system, your computer is part of a logical grouping of computers on the network called a **workgroup** that is given the default name of WORKGROUP. Workgroups implement **peer-to-peer networking** as each computer (or peer) on the network maintains its own shared resources, users, groups, and security. When connecting to a shared resource on a computer that is part of a workgroup, you are first prompted to supply a valid user name and password on that computer that has permissions to access the resource (a process called **authentication**). If other users on the network want to access those same resources, they must also authenticate with a valid user name and password.

Unfortunately, this means that each user within a workgroup is responsible for the security of their own resources and must know how to set the proper permissions and security. Moreover, client computers are often not designed to handle a growing load of resource requests from other computers on the network. While workgroups are common in home and small office environments of *fewer* than 10 computers, they aren't well suited for most organizations that frequently access resources on servers and other computers on the network.

To coordinate resource access, users, and security on networks today, you normally configure each client and server computer to join a **domain** instead of a workgroup. A domain is a logical grouping of computers that authenticate to a central database of users stored on special servers called **domain controllers**. When users log into a computer that is joined to a domain, their user names and passwords are authenticated on the nearest domain controller, which maintains a central database of users and passwords on the network. Once authenticated, the user receives a token from the domain controller that follows them around the network and automatically proves their identity to other domain-joined servers and clients. Those servers and clients will then allow the user to access resources that specifically grant them access. Because users only need to authenticate once to a domain controller to prove their identity to all domain members, this feature is called **single sign-on**.

The software components that provide for this functionality are collectively called **Active Directory**, and Windows Server can easily be configured as an Active Directory domain controller to provide single sign-on for other computers that are joined to a domain.

In addition to single sign-on for simplified resource access, Active Directory contains many other services and components that can be used to centrally manage and secure the computers that are joined to the domain. When you join a computer to a domain, groups that contain IT administrator user accounts (e.g., Domain Admins) are given administrative access to your computer. This allows IT administrators to easily configure any computer within the domain. **Group Policy** can also be used to configure operating system settings, security, and software for different computers and users in the domain, and **Active Directory Certificate Services** can be used to automate the configuration of deployment of encryption certificates to domain computers and users. Moreover, nearly all Microsoft server products (such as Microsoft Exchange Server and Microsoft SQL Server), as well as many third-party server products (such as Spiceworks) integrate with Active Directory for ease of management.

> **Note** 📎
>
> A single Windows Server computer can host several different roles on the network simultaneously. For example, a single Windows Server 2019 computer could be a domain controller, file server, print server, database server, and email server. Depending on the hardware capabilities, the server can handle hundreds of users at once, providing fast response when delivering the shared resource, and less network congestion when multiple workstations access that resource.

You can also purchase services hosted within Microsoft's Azure cloud to provide Active Directory services to your organization. This is called **Azure Active Directory** and allows easier management of domains that span multiple locations around the world. Windows Server 2019 provides easier integration between Active Directory and Azure Active Directory.

Security

Windows Server 2019 is built to be even more secure than previous Windows Server systems. One important approach built into Windows Server 2019 is implementing security by default. When you install Windows Server 2019, add a feature, or install a Windows component, an essential level of security is automatically implemented. This helps to ensure that no backdoors are left open for an attacker.

Windows Server 2019 also has more protection against malware. Microsoft Defender monitors the server for malware and automatically stops processes that are known to be dangerous. If Microsoft Defender **Advanced Threat Protection (ATP)** is installed, any processes or files that are not known to be dangerous but look suspicious are automatically sent to servers within Microsoft Azure, a cloud computing platform, for deeper inspection. The servers in the Azure cloud use deep learning and sandboxing techniques to determine if a process or file is a new type of malware, and automatically updates ATP on all Windows Server 2019 systems worldwide with new information if it is. This allows Windows Server 2019 to more effectively combat serious security threats, such as zero-day attacks and root kits.

Note 📎

Microsoft Defender ATP requires an additional license beyond Windows Server 2019. Microsoft offers a free 12-month trial which you can access by searching on **Microsoft Azure**.

To ensure that malicious users cannot access the virtual hard disk files used by Hyper-V virtual machines, Microsoft added BitLocker encryption support for these files starting in Windows Server 2016. This feature is called **shielded virtual machines**, and originally required that the virtual machine ran Windows Server 2012 or later (virtual machines running Linux were not supported). With Windows Server 2019, you can now use shielded virtual machines to encrypt virtual machines running Linux, and the data transfer between virtual machines can now also be encrypted.

Windows Server 2019 also places more emphasis on security within the **Internet Information Services (IIS)** Web server software. Additional modules enable IIS to have a lower attack surface (vulnerable openings exposed to network attackers and malicious software), as well as allow modular security updates to quickly repair vulnerabilities that are found in the future.

Windows Server 2019 additionally includes many basic security features, such as:

- File and folder permissions
- Security policies
- Encryption of data
- Event auditing
- Various authentication methods
- Server management and monitoring tools

Volume and Filesystem Features

All servers store data on volumes (e.g., C:\) that are formatted with a filesystem. Like Windows Server 2016, Windows Server 2019 supports both the traditional **New Technology File System (NTFS)** available since Windows NT Server, as well as the new **Resilient File System (ReFS)**.

NTFS is a very mature filesystem in terms of stability and features; it has built-in support for file and folder permissions, compression, **Encrypting File System (EFS)** encryption for individual files and folders, and user quotas that can be used to limit the space users are allowed to consume. It also supports **data deduplication** (or data dedup for short), which saves space by allowing duplicate files on a volume to be stored once on the physical storage device. In Windows Server 2019, you can now create NTFS large disk volumes of up to 8 PB (Windows Server 2016 only supports volumes of up to 256 TB).

NTFS is also a **journaling** file system, which means that it tracks changes to files and keeps a record of these changes in a separate log file. Journaling can be important, for example, when the computer crashes due to a power failure in the middle of updating or changing files. The logged journal information makes it possible to restore a file to its original condition prior to the power failure. Journaling enhances both the security and reliability of a system.

Starting with Windows Server 2008, NTFS volumes are self-healing. This means that when software encounters a damaged disk area, NTFS can heal the area without having to take down the server. NTFS self-heals by generating a "worker thread" that repairs data from the damaged area. The data is not available to the software until the worker thread completes its work. The next time the software wants to access that data, it is available for use. Prior to Windows Server 2008, a damaged disk area meant that you had to reboot the server into Safe Mode (offline to users) and run the chkdsk utility to rebuild the data in the damaged area.

NTFS also works very well in a virtualized environment because of the way that it works with file system cache. File system cache is an area designated in physical computer memory that is used in Windows operating systems to help speed up reading and writing to hard disk. The size of the allocated cache for NTFS operations can affect the speed of reading and writing, which in turn affects how long users have to wait on the server. In Hyper-V virtual machines, file system cache is dynamically allocated so that as memory is released by other applications or operating system processes, that memory is automatically used to increase the size of the NTFS file system cache for faster read and write operations.

ReFS was first offered with Windows Server 2012, but it is still regarded as a filesystem in development. It was originally developed as a filesystem that could fix filesystem writing errors automatically, eliminating the need for utilities such as chkdsk. While some NTFS features, such as EFS encryption, are not supported on ReFS, it excels over NTFS for use within **Storage Spaces**. Storage Spaces is a feature first introduced in Windows Server 2016 that allows you to build large, fault-tolerant volumes that span multiple physical storage devices. The third-generation version of ReFS (ReFS v3) was made available in Windows Server 2019 and comes with additional performance and feature improvements, including support for data deduplication and dramatically improved performance with Storage Spaces.

Windows Server 2016 introduced the ability to replicate data between two different servers seamlessly—a feature called **Storage Replicas**. Storage Replicas now have better performance in Windows Server 2019 and are supported in more editions (discussed in the next section). Microsoft also released a new **Storage Migration Service** in Windows Server 2019 that simplifies the moving of data to newer systems, as well as to systems in the Azure cloud.

Performance and Reliability

Several features make Windows Server 2019 reliable and powerful, including privileged mode, protected processes, multitasking, multithreading, processor scalability, and server clustering.

Privileged Mode and Protected Processes

The Windows kernel runs in **privileged mode**, which protects it from problems created by a malfunctioning program or process. In addition to privileged mode, Microsoft uses protected processes in Windows Server 2012 and later to improve stability and performance. A process is a computer program or portion of a program that is currently running. One large program might start several smaller programs or processes. A **protected process** cannot be influenced by a user or other processes on the system. Key processes on Windows Server 2019, including those that perform system maintenance or update a database, run as protected processes and cannot be interrupted prematurely.

Multitasking and Multithreading

Windows Server 2019 and other recent Windows systems take full advantage of the multitasking and multithreading capabilities of modern computers. **Multitasking** is the ability to run two or more programs at the same time. For example, Microsoft Word can print a document at the same time that a Microsoft Excel spreadsheet can calculate the sum of a column of numbers. Multithreading is the capability of programs written to run several program code blocks (called **threads**) at the same time. For instance, a Microsoft Access database query runs a thread to pull data out of the database, while another thread generates a subtotal of data already obtained.

The multitasking in Windows Server 2019 is called **preemptive multitasking**. This means each program runs in an area of memory separate from areas used by other programs. Early versions of Windows used cooperative multitasking, in which programs shared the same memory area. The advantage of preemptive multitasking is that it reduces the risk of one program interfering with the smooth running of another program, thus increasing reliability.

Processor Scalability

One of the reasons why Windows Server has become such a versatile and powerful operating system is that it can be easily scaled upward in processor capacity. As more capacity is needed, more processors can be added.

A **physical processor** is plugged into a processor socket on the motherboard of the computer. Windows Server 2019 can support up to 64 sockets for individual physical processors. Furthermore, one physical processor can house several **logical processors**. Each logical processor is called a core and can run its own executable threads. A physical processor might consist of eight cores, for example, that enable it to function as eight processors in one. Windows Server 2019 supports an unlimited number of logical processors, providing a large amount of scalability for data center environments.

Additionally, when a computer is functioning as a virtual server, each virtual machine can be set up to use logical processors as **virtual processors**. In this case, a virtual processor is a logical processor that functions for the use of a specific virtual machine.

Server Clustering

Clustering is the ability to increase the access to server resources and provide fail-safe services by linking two or more discrete computer systems so they appear to function as one, as illustrated in Figure 1-7. You can configure a server cluster to provide both increased speed (such that user access is spread evenly across each server in the cluster) and fault tolerance (if one server fails, the other servers in the cluster can still respond to client requests). Alternatively, you can configure a server cluster for fault tolerance only. In this configuration, one server actively responds to client requests, while another one only responds to client requests if the other one fails; a process called **failover**.

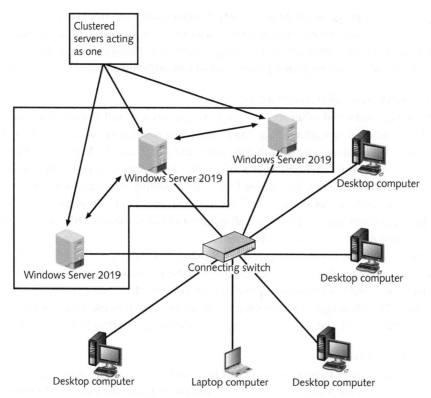

Figure 1-7 A server cluster

Consequently, server clusters are often used for frequently accessed and mission-critical services, such as databases. You can also configure Hyper-V virtual machines to work within a server cluster, or use a server cluster to allow a large amount of disk storage across several different servers to be made available to users (a feature called **Storage Spaces Direct**), with failover for disk storage as well.

The power of clustering is only as good as the tools used to configure it. Windows Server 2019 offers tools to:

- Create a cluster configuration and test to ensure it is set up to accomplish the tasks for which it is intended
- Migrate configuration settings from one cluster to another
- Troubleshoot cluster problems
- Set up and optimize the storage used in a cluster
- Secure a cluster and enable it to use new network capabilities

Administration Tools

Windows Server has several different administration tools that you can use to manage the servers and services on the network. The major administration tools used with Windows Server 2019 include Server Manager, Windows PowerShell, and the Windows Admin Center.

Server Manager

The **Server Manager** tool was originally introduced in Windows Server 2008, with each subsequent version of Windows Server adding even more enhancements. While Server Manager allows you to monitor and manage the configuration of the local server it is running on (as shown in Figure 1-8), it can also be used to centrally manage multiple servers on the network if you choose to add additional servers to the Server Manager interface. When you first log into a Windows Server with administrator privileges, Server Manager automatically starts by default, but can also be started from the Server Manager icon that is pinned to the Windows Start menu. In addition to performing basic server configuration following a Windows Server installation, Server Manager is often used to:

- View computer configuration information
- Add, remove, and configure server roles, features, and system properties
- Configure networking and security (including a firewall)
- Configure Remote Desktop
- Troubleshoot service and performance problems
- Configure and manage storage
- Configure and manage Active Directory objects

While Server Manager is typically used to configure newer components and services introduced in Windows Server 2012 and later (e.g., Storage Spaces), most server

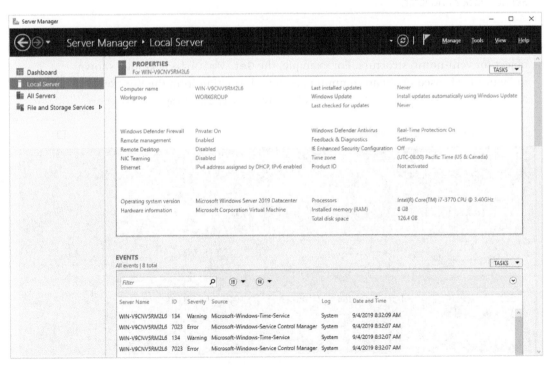

Figure 1-8   Configuring local server properties within Server Manager

configuration is still performed using **Microsoft Management Console (MMC)** snap-in tools that run outside of Server Manager and are specialized for a specific component or service (e.g., the Group Policy Management MMC snap-in tool). Luckily, you can easily access these tools within Server Manager by selecting the Tools menu and choosing the correct MMC snap-in tool from the list.

Windows PowerShell

Microsoft's first operating system, MS-DOS, did not contain a graphical desktop. Instead, MS-DOS users had to type commands within a command line interface called a **shell**. This MS-DOS shell has since been available in every graphical Windows operating system, and is still available within Windows Server 2019 if you execute the Command Prompt app or run the `cmd.exe` command from the Windows Start menu. Unfortunately, the MS-DOS shell doesn't offer the same standardization, rich command set, or advanced scripting functionality that UNIX and Linux shells offer. As a result, Microsoft created a new shell in 2006 called **Windows PowerShell** that provided these features to computers running Windows and Windows Server.

> **Note**
>
> Windows PowerShell is available for Windows Server 2003 and later, as well as Windows XP Service Pack 2 and later.

Commands within Windows PowerShell are called **cmdlets** and have an action-object (or verb-noun) structure. For example, the `Get-WmiObject` cmdlet shown in Figure 1-9 is used to obtain computer system information from the **Windows Management Instrumentation (WMI)** object called `win32_computersystem`.

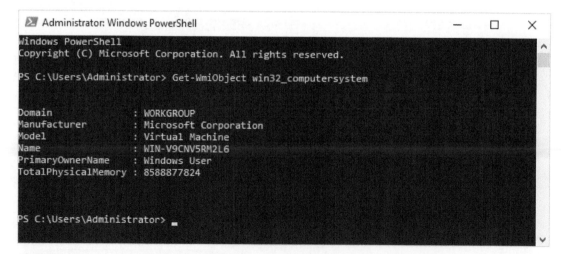

Figure 1-9   Running the Get-WmiObject cmdlet with Windows PowerShell

As shown in the Windows PowerShell title bar in Figure 1-9, Windows PowerShell is run as an Administrator account. While you can start Windows PowerShell by selecting the Windows PowerShell pinned icon from the Windows Start menu, many system configuration tasks that you perform require that you open Windows PowerShell with administrative privileges. To do this, you can right-click the Windows PowerShell pinned icon on the Windows Start menu and choose More, Run as administrator.

Nearly any task (administrative or otherwise) can be performed by cmdlets within Windows PowerShell. When you install additional software, cmdlets are often added to the system that can be used to manage the newly installed software. In fact, some tasks do not have a graphical configuration option and must be performed using cmdlets within Windows PowerShell. If you are logged into an Active Directory domain as a user with administrative privileges in the domain, you can also use Windows PowerShell to perform configuration tasks on other computers in the domain. Common tasks that are performed by administrators within Windows PowerShell include:

- Working with files and folders
- Monitoring and managing disk storage
- Configuring network settings and troubleshooting network connectivity
- Installing and managing software applications and server roles
- Viewing configuration information for auditing and inventory purposes
- Managing services and processes
- Restarting multiple computers within a domain environment
- Managing Active Directory users and groups

Windows PowerShell is also a powerful scripting language. You can also place cmdlets within text files (that have a `.ps1` extension) alongside control structures that modify how the cmdlets are executed. These **PowerShell scripts** can then be executed to perform a series of tasks that can be re-executed periodically in the future as necessary.

> **Note** 📎
>
> Many system administration-related PowerShell scripts are available on the Internet. You can often download and repurpose these scripts to save time when performing system administration.

Windows Admin Center

New to Windows Server 2019 is a Web-based management tool called the **Windows Admin Center**. The Windows Admin Center is not installed on Windows Server 2019 by default, but can be downloaded from `https://aka.ms/WindowsAdminCenter` and installed afterward. Following installation, you can use a Web browser on any networked computer (only Chrome and Edge Chromium are supported at the time of this writing) to connect to the Windows Admin Center. For example, to connect to the Windows Admin

Center installed on a Windows Server 2019 computer named win-v9cnv5rm2l6, you can enter the URL *https://win-v9cnv5rm2l6* in your Web browser, and log in as a user with administrative privileges to obtain access to the Overview page shown in Figure 1-10.

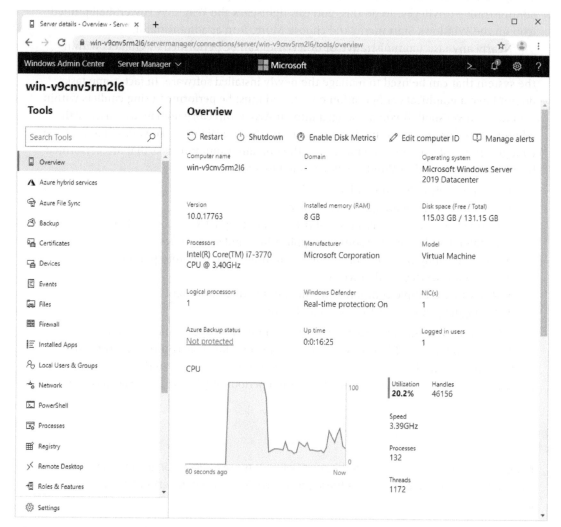

Figure 1-10   The Windows Admin Center tool

Like Server Manager, the Windows Admin Center can be used to manage other Windows Server systems (Windows Server 2008 with limited functionality, and Windows Server 2012 or later with full functionality). However, the Windows Admin Center cannot perform all Windows Server configuration tasks at the time of this writing (e.g., Active Directory configuration). Some of the administrative tasks that you can perform in the Windows Admin Center include:

- Performing system updates
- Displaying resources and resource utilization
- Managing encryption certificates
- Managing hardware devices
- Viewing system events
- Managing files and server storage
- Configuring firewall and network settings
- Managing installed software, processes, and services
- Configuring local user accounts (not Active Directory)
- Editing the Windows registry
- Scheduling tasks
- Managing Hyper-V virtual machines
- Managing clusters
- Managing Azure cloud integration and services
- Obtaining a Windows PowerShell console or Remote Desktop connection

Small Footprint Installation Options

You have the ability to install Windows Server 2019 with a minimal set of services, features, and functionality; this is commonly called a **small footprint** server installation. Because small footprint installations have fewer network services that other computers can interact with, there are fewer ways that a malicious user can use to gain unauthorized access to the server. In other words, small footprint installations have a smaller **attack surface**, and are more secure as a result. Additionally, small footprint installations use far less storage, memory, and processor resources on a server, and can be installed within a virtual machine or used as a container. This makes them more suitable for cloud environments, where thousands of servers are used to respond to client requests across the Internet.

Windows Server 2019 has two small footprint installation options: Server Core and Nano Server. **Server Core** retains much of the core Windows Server operating system but removes most of the graphical frameworks and processes. As a result, you typically configure Server Core using MS-DOS commands, PowerShell cmdlets, or configure remotely from a computer running Server Manager or the Windows Admin Center. To install Server Core, you can choose the appropriate option for your Windows Server edition from the installation wizard. When you boot your Server Core following installation, you will see a graphical login screen. When you log into this screen, you will obtain an MS-DOS command prompt that allows you to start Windows PowerShell

(powershell.exe), or run MS-DOS commands such as the **Windows Server Configuration Wizard** (sconfig.cmd) shown in Figure 1-11. The Windows Server Configuration Wizard is a quick way to configure server settings (network, firewall, computer name, domain, and so on) or perform server administration tasks (reboot, install updates, and so on) from the command line.

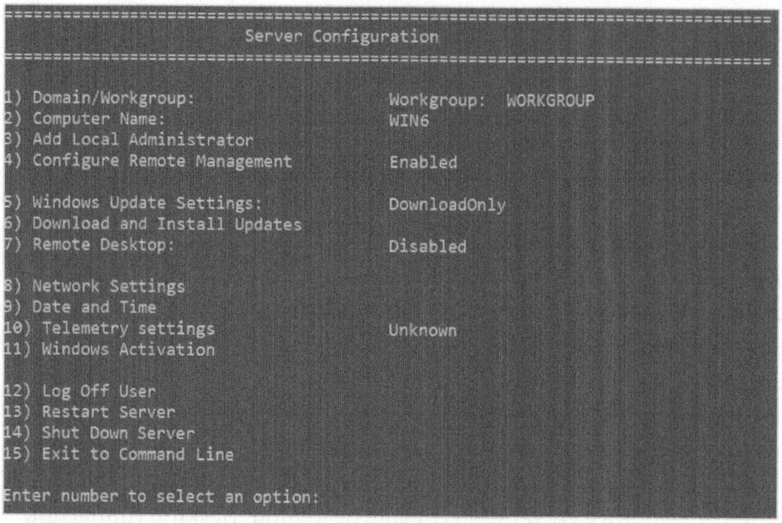

```
================================================================================
                              Server Configuration
================================================================================

1) Domain/Workgroup:                        Workgroup:  WORKGROUP
2) Computer Name:                           WIN6
3) Add Local Administrator
4) Configure Remote Management              Enabled

5) Windows Update Settings:                 DownloadOnly
6) Download and Install Updates
7) Remote Desktop:                          Disabled

8) Network Settings
9) Date and Time
10) Telemetry settings                      Unknown
11) Windows Activation

12) Log Off User
13) Restart Server
14) Shut Down Server
15) Exit to Command Line

Enter number to select an option:
```

Figure 1-11   The Windows Server Configuration Wizard within Server Core

Many Microsoft and third-party software packages cannot be installed on Server Core because they rely on graphical .Net components that are not available in Server Core. However, you can download and install the **Server Core App Compatibility Feature on Demand (FOD)** framework to add many of these .Net components and allow more software to work on Server Core. The FOD framework also adds several graphical management tools back into Server Core, including

- Microsoft Management Console (MMC)
- Event Viewer
- Performance Monitor
- Resource Monitor
- Device Manager
- File Explorer
- Disk Management
- Failover Cluster Manager
- Hyper-V Manager

Nano Server is an even smaller footprint server than Server Core. Without additional software, a base Nano Server consumes less than 500MB of disk space. Nano Server still has fundamental elements, such as the .Net Framework used to develop and execute applications, but it has few other components. As a result, only four server roles are supported on Nano Server:

- DNS server (discussed later in this module)
- DHCP server (discussed later in this module)
- Web server (running custom Web apps)
- File server

Consequently, Nano Server is ideal for use within cloud environments that require the hosting of Web apps and supporting services only. Although it is possible to install Nano Server directly on the hardware of a server, it is designed to be installed within a virtual machine or used as a container. If used as a container, Nano Server does not contain a Windows Server kernel. Moreover, most administration of Nano Server must be done from a remote computer using a subset of the Windows PowerShell cmdlets found in other Windows Server systems.

Note 🖉

To install Nano Server, you use an existing Windows Server to generate a virtual hard disk file that contains Nano Server for use within a virtual machine, or you can download a pre-made Nano Server container from the Internet, as discussed in Module 10.

Hybrid Cloud Features

With Windows Server 2019, Microsoft is adding more integration between on-premises Windows Servers and Windows Servers and services that run within the Azure cloud. This type of integration is often referred to as **hybrid cloud**. The **Windows Server Azure Network Adapter** allows you to easily connect your on-premises Windows Server systems with other virtualized Windows Servers and services in the Azure cloud using a secure connection. You can also use **Azure Backup** to back up important information to storage in the Azure cloud, **Azure Update Management** to centrally manage the updates for on-premises computers and virtual machines running in Azure, as well as **Azure Site Recovery** to ensure that key services that you run on-premises are made automatically available in the Azure cloud if you encounter a failure of an on-premises server. Moreover, hybrid cloud features can be configured and monitored using the Windows Admin Center.

If your organization deploys a large number of Windows Containers, Windows Server 2019 now has support for **Kubernetes**, which is a software product that can coordinate the execution and management of both on-premises containers, as well as containers hosted within the Azure cloud.

Linux Application Support

Most Web apps that run in the cloud run within Linux containers. As a result, Microsoft has made it easier for Web app developers to create and test Linux apps on their Windows 10 PCs using the **Windows Subsystem for Linux (WSL)**. The WSL provides a Linux kernel interface for Linux apps that allows them to execute directly on the Windows kernel within a Linux operating system environment (including a virtual Linux filesystem and directory structure). In short, WSL allows developers to create and test Linux apps on their local PC before deploying those apps to a Linux virtual machine or container in the cloud. Windows Server 2019 now supports WSL, which means that you can run Linux containers on Windows Server, alongside Windows Containers.

Windows Server 2019 Editions

Servers have a wide variety of uses designed to match the needs of a wide variety of different environments, from home offices and small businesses to international corporations and large data centers. Because one size does not fit all needs, Microsoft offers different versions of Windows Server 2019 called **editions**. Each edition is built on the same foundation but offers unique capabilities to suit the size and needs of an organization. Before you deploy Windows Server 2019, it's important to first select the correct edition for your needs. In this section, we'll examine and compare the features of different editions of Windows Server 2019. The major Windows Server 2019 editions include:

- Windows Server 2019 Essentials Edition
- Windows Server 2019 Standard Edition
- Windows Server 2019 Datacenter Edition

However, there are two additional Windows Server 2019 editions, each customized for a specific use:

- Windows Storage Server 2019
- Microsoft Hyper-V Server 2019

Windows Server 2019 Essentials Edition

For a business or organization with up to 25 users, Windows Server 2019 Essentials Edition is a good, cost-effective option for providing most Microsoft server services to users. Windows Server 2019 Essentials Edition also comes with hardware and connection limits; you can't install it on a server with more than 2 processor sockets or more than 64 GB of memory, and only 50 concurrent remote access connections are allowed.

Windows Server 2019 Essentials Edition cannot join an existing Active Directory domain, but can host a single, small Active Directory domain with a single domain controller. Furthermore, Windows Server 2019 Essentials Edition provides most but not all server roles. Most notably, it does not provide the Hyper-V role for hosting and managing virtual machines. However, Windows Server 2019 Essentials Edition can be installed as a virtual machine on an existing hypervisor, such as Hyper-V (included in higher editions).

Microsoft focuses on specific features in Windows Server 2019 Essentials Edition (most of which are also available on higher editions) to make it particularly attractive to small businesses and organizations. These features allow for the following:

- User groups can be created to manage clients and client access to Microsoft Office 365.
- Backups and restores can use file history information for each user instead of only for each device.
- Size and growth of a server folder can be managed through a space quota.
- Installation can be on a standalone physical server or as a virtual machine, which allows you to run Windows Server on an existing hypervisor.
- Server Health Reports are automatically installed to be available at the time Essentials Edition is installed.
- Mobile devices can be managed using Dashboard, which is a tool within Server Manager for simplified management of the server.
- The BranchCache file sharing feature is available to allow fast data access to other Windows and Windows Server computers running an offsite location.

Table 1-1 compares the features found in Windows Server 2019 Essentials Edition to those in other major Windows Server 2019 editions.

Table 1-1   Comparing the major Windows Server 2019 editions

Limitations	Essentials Edition	Standard Edition	Datacenter Edition
Maximum users	25	Limited by number of CALs	Limited by number of CALs
Licensing	Per server	Per processor core	Per processor core
Maximum memory	64 GB	24 TB	24 TB
Maximum processor sockets	2	64	64
Can join a domain	Only to enable migration	Yes	Yes
Maximum file sharing connections	16.8 million	16.8 million	16.8 million
Maximum remote access connections	50	Unlimited	Unlimited
Hyper-V	No	Yes (2 virtual machines)	Yes (unlimited virtual machines)
Containers	No	Yes (unlimited)	Yes (unlimited)
Hyper-V containers	No	Yes (up to 2)	Yes (unlimited)

Windows Server 2019 Standard Edition

Windows Server 2019 Standard Edition is designed to meet the everyday needs of most businesses and organizations. It provides file and print services, secure Internet connectivity, centralized management of users, and centralized management of applications and network resources. It is built on technology from previous editions of Windows Server but includes many new features and security enhancements. Additionally, many features that existed in previous Windows Server versions have been further optimized for performance.

A company might use Windows Server 2019 Standard Edition to host its accounting and payroll software, provide network resources such as shared files and printers, deliver email functionality, or even manage users' access to cloud application software, such as Office 365. Some other key features in Windows Server 2019 Standard Edition include:

- A modern desktop user interface that matches that of the latest Windows 10 builds, including the ability to use virtual desktops
- An improved Windows Defender that configured and enabled by default for malware detection and prevention
- Easier configuration, management, and security options for applications, files, networking, and Active Directory (including the ability to clone domain controllers)
- **Desired State Configuration**, which can be used to quickly configure multiple servers using a template file that lists required software and configuration items
- Intelligent storage features for volumes that use multiple physical storage devices. This includes **storage tiers** (which automatically moves frequently-used data to faster storage devices, such as SSDs) and **storage pinning** (which allows you to force specific data to be stored on a particular device).
- The ability to use Storage Replicas (which previously required Datacenter Edition in Windows Server 2016)
- The ability to create up to two Hyper-V virtual machines under the default Windows Server license
- The ability to create an unlimited number of Windows Containers, and up to two Hyper-V containers

When it comes to purchasing a license for Windows Server 2019 Standard Edition, Microsoft charges based on the number of processor cores that you run it on. In addition, each user connection requires a **Client Access License (CAL)**. Microsoft gives you options to either purchase a set number of CALs per server, or a CAL for each client that accesses the servers within your organization.

Windows Server 2019 Datacenter Edition

Windows Server 2019 Datacenter Edition is designed for environments with mission-critical applications, very large databases, very large virtualization requirements, cloud computing needs, and information access requiring high availability. It shares the same hardware support, features, and licensing requirements as Windows Server 2019 Standard Edition but allows you to create an unlimited number of virtual machines under the default license, as well as an unlimited number of containers (including Hyper-V containers). Because Windows Server 2019 Datacenter Edition is typically used to host a larger number of virtual machines, it also comes with additional **Software Defined Networking (SDN)** features, such as the Network Controller role that can be used to monitor and manage virtual networks used by large numbers of virtual machines.

Windows Storage Server 2019

Windows Storage Server 2019 cannot be purchased directly from Microsoft. Instead, original equipment manufacturers (OEMs) that create storage solutions for organizations can offer Windows Storage Server 2019 on the server-based products they sell. Windows Storage Server 2019 turns a server into a central storage center for data in an organization and takes advantage of the storage utilities offered in Windows Server 2019. To learn more about the storage services, see Module 7, Configuring and Managing Data Storage.

Microsoft Hyper-V Server 2019

Microsoft Hyper-V Server 2019 is the Hyper-V hypervisor. It also installs a small footprint version of Windows Server that contains a PowerShell interface for creating and managing virtual machines. While Microsoft Hyper-V Server 2019 is free to download and use in your environment, each Windows Server virtual machine that you run on it requires a valid license (Linux virtual machines, however, do not).

Preparing for a Windows Server 2019 Installation

Just as a trip goes better with advanced planning, so does an operating system installation. You are likely to work with the operating system for some time, so it makes sense to get off on a solid footing to avoid problems later.

The first step in planning the installation of any operating system is to determine the hardware requirements. Most operating systems come with a list of minimum hardware requirements which must be met for the operating system to run and often a list of recommended requirements. For Windows Server 2019, these requirements are listed in Table 1-2.

In general, you should always exceed the minimum hardware requirements listed for any operating system. Exceeding the minimum requirements also makes your server more scalable, allowing it to meet increased requirements as the organization grows. The amount that you plan to exceed should be determined according to the role the Windows Server 2019 system will play on the network, as well as the number of clients that you

Table 1-2   Minimum hardware requirements for Windows Server 2019

Hardware	Minimum requirements	Additional considerations
Basic Input/Output System (BIOS)	**Unified Extensible Firmware Interface (UEFI)** 2.3.1c BIOS or higher for physical server installation	**Trusted Platform Module (TPM)** is also required for secure boot and encryption features.
Processor	1.4 GHz 64-bit processor (includes support for NX, DEP, CMPXCHG16b, LAHF/SAHF, PrefetchW, EPT, or NPT)	Processor clock speed, amount of processor cache, and number of processor cores should be considered based on planned usage. Hyper-V also requires processor virtualization extensions (Intel VT or AMD-V, with SLAT).
Memory	512 MB (2 GB for a server with the GUI desktop)	Each virtual machine requires 800 MB for setup (although this can be scaled back after setup is complete). ECC memory is recommended for physical (non-virtualized) server installations.
Storage	32 GB	32 GB is the minimum for Server Core, while 36 GB is the minimum for installing a full Windows Server.
Network interface	1 gigabit or faster Ethernet adapter that is compatible with PCI Express architecture and Pre-boot Execution Environment (PXE)	Additional adapters are recommended if you support multiple virtual machines.
Optical drive	DVD drive (optional)	While a DVD drive is needed for installations from DVD media, many administrators install from a USB drive today.
Display	Super VGA at 1024 × 768 or higher resolution	Multiple servers can share one display via the use of a **keyboard-video-mouse (KVM) switch**.
Interactive devices	Keyboard and pointing device	Multiple servers can share a keyboard and pointing device via the use of a KVM switch box.

expect to connect to the server. For example, if your server will function as a file server, hosting things such as home folders and company-shared files and printers, additional storage space will be needed beyond what is required to simply run the operating system. The amount of storage space depends on the number of users that are going to store data on the server as well as the average size of the data per user.

Planning hardware for a specific server given its use within an organization is often called **capacity planning**. Here are some sample questions to consider when performing capacity planning for Windows Server 2019:

- What role or roles will the server have in your organization? For example, is this server limited to file and printer sharing? Are you implementing a Web server, SQL database server, or email server? Will your server offer remote access or will it be a source of applications for users?
- Do you need to deploy virtual machines, and if so, how many?
- How many local and remote users do you need to support?
- What kind of support do you need from the hardware vendor?
- What redundancy features do you need to ensure the server continues running in the event of a hardware failure, such as a failed disk drive, power supply, or network interface?
- What growth in server use and resources do you expect in the next 3 to 5 years?

These questions only provide a starting point for your planning. In a small business, much of the planning can be done with the help of the business owner. In medium and large businesses, the planning will likely require input from management, user departments, technical people, software providers, and hardware vendors. In either case, hardware should be planned based on the server role and projected growth, so as to exceed what is needed to:

- Accommodate the clients that will access the server
- Provide for extra software and services
- Match data storage needs

In terms of processing speed, plan to pay particular attention to the number of processors, as well as their speed and number of cores. For example, a small business using one server with Essentials Edition may consider purchasing a 3 GHz processor with only two cores (two logical processors). A corporation that plans on running several large databases within several virtual machines may consider running Windows Server 2019 Datacenter Edition on a server that has two 4 GHz processors with 12 cores each, as well as a motherboard with two additional processor sockets to allow the server to scale up to a total of four processors in the future.

It's also important to ensure that your server has enough memory for the applications that it will host, as well as free memory slots for future scalability. The small business mentioned earlier might start with 32 GB of memory with room to expand to 128 GB of memory, whereas the corporation mentioned earlier might start with 256 GB of memory with room to expand to 2 TB of memory.

The amount and type of storage is another important consideration. Most servers today come with multiple SSD storage devices for the operating system and core applications, configured to be fault tolerant using **Redundant Array of Independent Disks (RAID)** in the BIOS of the server. You can plan to add additional hard disks (large capacity, slower speed, lower cost) or SSDs (lower capacity, faster speed, higher cost) within the server to store the data used by your applications, or the virtual machine hard disk files used by your virtual machines. Alternatively, if your organization uses a SAN to store data and virtual machine hard disk files, you can simply ensure that your server can connect to the SAN. For iSCSI SANs this will require an additional iSCSI-capable network card, and for Fiber channel SANs this often requires a proprietary PCIe controller card. The size of each storage device is ultimately determined by your estimate of the demand for storage space on the server in the next year. It's also important to ensure that the storage on your server can easily be expanded in the future, as organizations often consume more storage than what is originally planned for.

> **Note** 📎
>
> Before any final decisions are made in selecting hardware, you should check the hardware for the Certified for Windows Server 2019 sticker or consult the **Windows Server Catalog**, which is a list of compatible hardware devices for each version of Windows. You can access the Windows Server Catalog online at *https://windowsservercatalog.com*.

> **Note** 📎
>
> If you are installing Windows Server 2019 on an older server, you may need to first upgrade the BIOS. Consult the server vendor website for the latest BIOS update and update procedure.

Installing Windows Server 2019

A Windows Server 2019 installation can be broken down into three separate tasks:

- Obtaining installation media
- Starting the installation process
- Completing the installation process

Obtaining Installation Media

The most common method used to install Windows Server is by booting a computer or virtual machine from installation media, such as a bootable DVD or USB flash drive (used to install a physical server) or an **ISO image file** that has a `.iso` extension (used to install a virtual machine). Microsoft may have already provided your college or organization with a bootable DVD or USB flash drive that contains the edition or editions of Windows Server 2019. Alternatively, you can download an ISO image file from your Microsoft partner portal and copy it to a DVD using disc burning software such as **Burnaware**, or to a bootable USB flash drive using a program such as **Rufus**. If you plan on installing a virtual machine, there is no need to copy the downloaded ISO image to a DVD or USB flash drive. Instead, you can specify the path to the downloaded ISO image within your virtualization software when configuring the virtual machine.

When downloading an ISO image file, it is important to download the correct one, as Microsoft makes three separate ISO images available for Windows Server 2019, depending on the edition that you wish to install:

- Window Server 2019 Essentials
- Windows Server 2019 Standard and Datacenter (which also includes the associated Server Core versions)
- Microsoft Hyper-V Server 2019

Note

To download a free copy of Burnaware, visit *https://burnaware.com*. To download a free copy of Rufus, visit *https://rufus.ie*.

Note

If your organization does not have access to a Microsoft portal site, you can download the ISO image for Microsoft Hyper-V Server 2019, or a 180-day trial version of the other Windows Server 2019 editions from *https://www.microsoft.com/en-us/cloud-platform/windows-server-trial*.

Starting the Installation Process

After obtaining installation media, you can start the installation process itself. If you are installing a physical server using installation media on a DVD or USB flash drive, you must first ensure that the boot order within your computer BIOS is set to boot an operating system located on the DVD drive or a USB device before other storage devices. To do this, you must access your BIOS configuration program, which is often performed by pressing a function key (such as F2) immediately after powering on your computer, but this will vary by computer manufacturer and model (consult your computer manual for instructions). Within the BIOS configuration program, you can modify the boot order to ensure that the DVD drive and removable USB devices are listed at the top of the boot order (as illustrated in the sample BIOS configuration program shown in Figure 1-12), save your settings and power off your computer. Finally, you can insert your bootable DVD or USB flash drive into your computer and power it on again to start the installation process.

Alternatively, your BIOS may allow you to press a particular key (such as F12) to view a special boot menu at system startup that allows you to choose a specific boot device to boot from (consult your computer manual for instructions). In this case, you don't need to modify the boot order in your computer BIOS to ensure that it boots from a DVD or USB flash drive. Instead, simply access this special boot menu when you power on your computer with the DVD or USB flash drive inserted.

Starting an installation of a virtual machine is similar to starting a physical server. When creating a new virtual machine within a virtualization configuration program

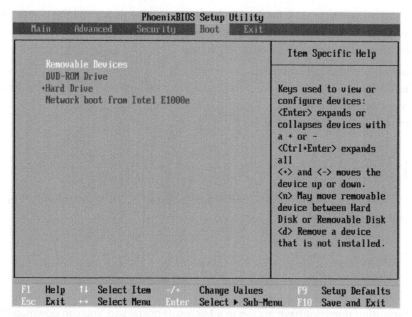

Figure 1-12   Setting the boot order within the BIOS configuration program

(such as **Hyper-V Manager**), you can attach an ISO image file that contains Windows Server 2019 installation media to the virtual DVD drive within the virtual machine (as shown in Figure 1-13), as well as configure the virtual machine BIOS with a boot order that is set to boot from a DVD before the virtual hard disk file (as shown in Figure 1-14).

Finally, when you start your virtual machine within your virtual machine software, it will boot the Windows Server 2019 installation media stored within the ISO image attached to the virtual DVD and start the installation process.

Completing the Installation Process

After you start a Windows Server 2019 installation, the remainder of the installation process is relatively straightforward. The first screen that the installation program displays prompts you for regional locale and keyboard format, as shown in Figure 1-15.

When you click Next in Figure 1-15, you are presented with the option to start an installation of Windows Server 2019 or to use the installation media to repair an already-installed system that is unable to start, as shown in Figure 1-16.

If you click Install now in Figure 1-16, you will then be prompted to choose your Windows Server 2019 edition as shown in Figure 1-17. Standard Edition and Datacenter Edition are often included on the same installation media, and the options available can be misleading because the Server Core small footprint installation option is the default for each edition. For example, you should select the Window Server 2019 Datacenter (Desktop Experience) option if you wish to have a full Windows Server installation

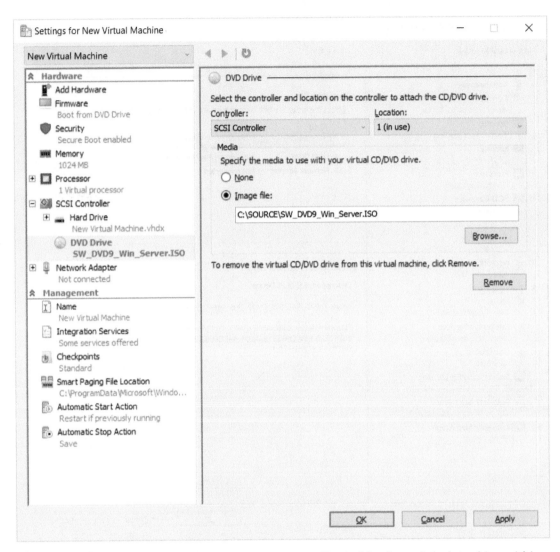

Figure 1-13   Attaching an ISO image file to a virtual DVD drive for a virtual machine within Hyper-V Manager

of Datacenter Edition. If you select the Window Server 2019 Datacenter option, the installation program installs the Server Core small footprint option for Datacenter Edition.

If you click Next in Figure 1-17, you will be prompted to accept the Microsoft license terms for Windows Server 2019. Following this, you will be prompted to choose whether to perform a new installation of Windows Server 2019 or perform an upgrade of an existing Windows Server installation to Windows Server 2019 as shown in Figure 1-18. Windows Server 2012 R2 and Windows Server 2016 can be upgraded to Windows Server 2019 (same edition or higher) while retaining existing applications and data.

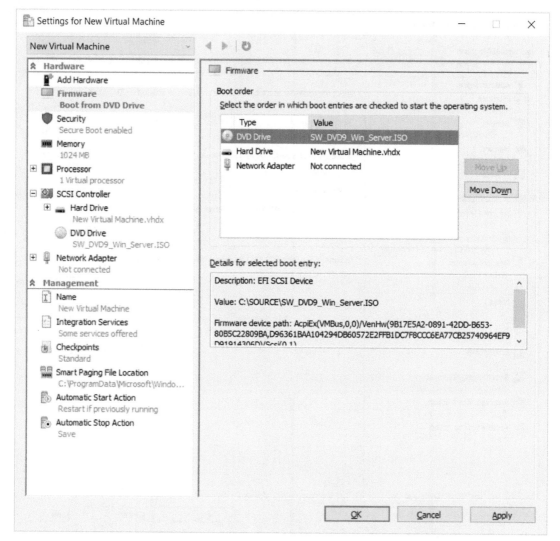

Figure 1-14   Specifying a boot order for a virtual machine within Hyper-V Manager

For example, you can upgrade from Windows Server 2012 R2 Standard Edition to Windows Server 2019 Datacenter Edition using the Windows Server 2019 installation program.

Note

Before performing an upgrade of an operating system, you should first ensure that you install the latest updates, as well as perform a full system backup (in the event of a failure during the upgrade process).

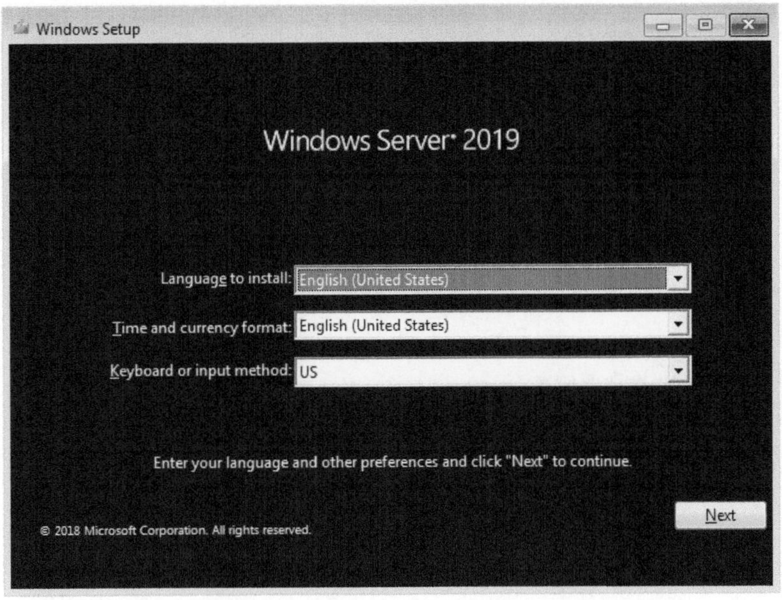

Figure 1-15   Specifying locale and keyboard information

Figure 1-16   Starting a Windows Server 2019 installation

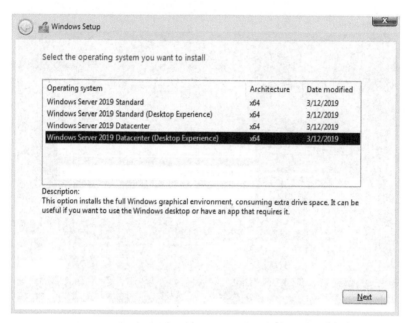

Figure 1-17   Selecting a Windows Server 2019 edition

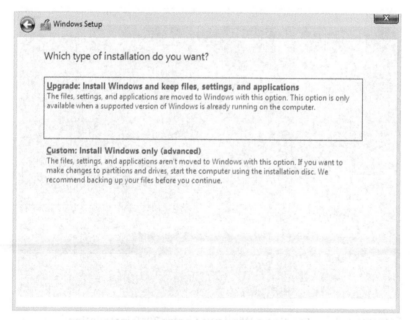

Figure 1-18   Selecting an installation type

Note @

To upgrade versions of Windows Server prior to Windows Server 2012 R2, you must first upgrade them to Windows Server 2012 R2 before performing an upgrade to Windows Server 2019.

On a new server, you normally select the Custom installation option shown in Figure 1-18 to perform a new installation of Windows Server 2019. After selecting this option, you must choose the storage location of the Windows Server operating system. If you select an entire storage device, as shown in Figure 1-19, and press Next, the installation program will automatically create partitions on your device. This typically includes a small hidden partition that stores the recovery environment, as well as a large partition that will be formatted with NTFS and mounted to C:\. If you are installing on a physical server with a UEFI BIOS, the installation program will also create a small UEFI system partition to store the Windows Server boot loader program.

Alternatively, you can choose to create your own partitions by selecting the New button in Figure 1-19 and formatting them with the filesystem of your choice (NTFS or ReFS). If your storage device has existing partitions, you can choose to delete them, re-format them, or extend their size.

Note @

If no storage devices are displayed in Figure 1-19, you may require a device driver for the storage controller on your system. In this case, you can insert a DVD or USB flash drive that has the appropriate driver and choose Load driver from Figure 1-19, followed by Refresh to display your storage devices. This is common for many enterprise-specific storage devices, such as Fiberchannel SANs, or storage class memory devices.

After you press Next in Figure 1-19, the remainder of the installation process copies and configures Windows Server 2019 on your storage, which could take several minutes. When the installation process completes, the system will restart and boot into Windows Server 2019. At this point, you can safely remove any installation media from the computer or virtual machine to ensure that the boot process does not attempt to start another installation.

On the first boot following installation, you will be prompted to specify a password for the local Administrator user account (shown in Figure 1-20) before obtaining a login screen that allows you to log in and access the system (shown in Figure 1-21).

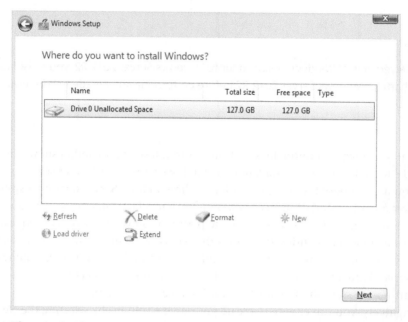

Figure 1-19   Selecting the location of the Windows Server operating system

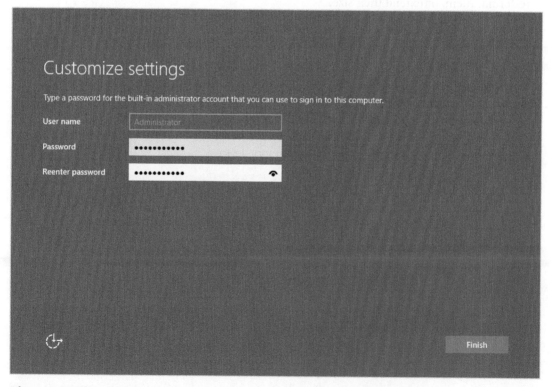

Figure 1-20   Specifying a new password for the local Administrator account

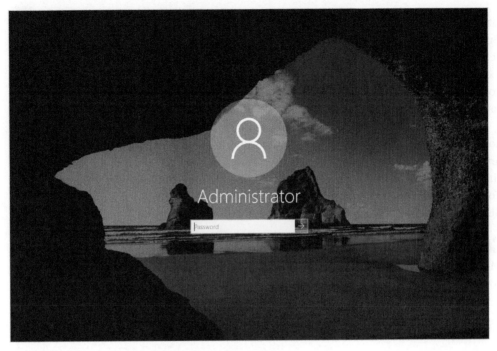

Figure 1-21   The Windows Server login screen

Post-Installation Configuration

As you saw in the previous section, the Windows Server 2019 installation process does not prompt you to specify a great deal of configuration information beyond what is required to get the operating system installed on a storage device. As a result, you must perform some key configuration tasks following any Windows Server 2019 installation, including:

- Setting the correct time and time zone
- Configuring the Internet Protocol (IP) on the server's network interfaces
- Configuring the firewall
- Changing the default computer name and domain membership
- Installing a modern Web browser
- Activating the Windows Server operating system

Note 📎

All of this configuration can easily be performed within the Server Manager tool on a full Windows Server 2019 installation. Alternatively, you can use the Windows Server Configuration Wizard on a Windows Server 2019 Server Core installation.

Setting the Correct Time and Time Zone

Ensuring that your server has the correct time and time zone is required for many services that work with multiple computers on the network, such as Active Directory. For example, if the time on your server is more than five minutes different (after time zone correction) than the time on the nearest domain controller, your server will be unable to join or function within the domain.

By default, Microsoft sets the time to the time listed in your BIOS clock, and the time zone to Pacific Time (the time zone for Microsoft's headquarters). To change your time and time zone for your server within Server Manager, navigate to Local Server and select the hyperlink next to Time zone in the Properties window shown earlier in Figure 1-8. To change your time and time zone within the Windows Server Configuration Wizard on Server Core, select option 9 shown earlier in Figure 1-11.

Configuring the Network

Most functions that computers perform today involve the sharing of information between computers on a network, whether it be the network within your organization or the Internet.

Note

Networks within an organization are often called **Local Area Networks (LANs)**.

Note

The Internet (the name is short for "internetwork") is merely several interconnected public networks. Both home and company networks can be part of the Internet by connecting to public networks maintained by **Internet Service Providers (ISPs)**. Special computers called **routers** transfer information from one network to another.

To connect to a network, your computer must have a network interface that connects to the network media via a cable (e.g., an Ethernet cable) or wireless technology (e.g., Wi-Fi), as well as a **protocol** that breaks information down into **packets** that can be recognized by computers, routers, and other devices on a network. While you can configure many network protocols in Windows operating systems, nearly all Windows computers use the following three protocols by default:

- **Transmission Control Protocol/Internet Protocol (TCP/IP)**, which provides reliable communication of packets across networks and the Internet.
- **User Datagram Protocol/Internet Protocol (UDP/IP)**, which provides fast, yet unreliable communication of packets across networks and the Internet.
- **Internet Control Message Protocol (ICMP)**, which is used to send network-related information and error messages across networks and the Internet.

TCP/IP is actually a set, or suite, of protocols with two core components: TCP and IP. Together, these two protocols ensure that information packets travel across a network as quickly as possible without getting lost or mislabeled.

When you transfer information across a network such as the Internet, that information is often divided into many thousands of small IP packets. Each of these packets may take a different physical route when reaching its destination as routers can transfer information to multiple interconnected networks. TCP ensures that packets can be assembled in the correct order at their destination regardless of the order in which they arrive. Additionally, TCP ensures that any lost packets are retransmitted.

IP is responsible for labeling each packet with the destination address. As a result, each computer that participates on an IP network must have a valid **Internet Protocol (IP) address** that identifies itself to the IP protocol. Nearly all computers on the Internet use a version of the IP protocol called **IP version 4 (IPv4)**. However, a small number of computers use a next-generation IP protocol called **IP version 6 (IPv6)**.

Understanding IPv4

To participate on an IPv4 network, your computer must have a valid IP address as well as a **subnet mask**. Optionally, you can configure a **default gateway** to participate on larger networks such as the Internet.

An IP address is a unique number assigned to the computer that identifies itself on the network, similar to a unique postal address that identifies your location in the world. If any two computers on the same network have the same IP address, it is impossible for information to be correctly delivered to them. Directed communication from one computer to another single computer using IP is referred to as a **unicast**.

The most common format for IPv4 addresses is four numbers called **octets** that are separated by periods. Each octet represents an 8-bit binary number (0–255). An example of an IP address in this notation is 192.168.5.69.

You can convert between decimal and binary by recognizing that an 8-bit binary number represents the decimal binary powers of two in the following order: 128 64 32 16 8 4 2 1.

Thus, the number 255 is 11111111 (128+64+32+16+8+4+2+1) in binary, and the number 69 is 01000101 (64+4+1) in binary. When the computer looks at an IP address, the numbers are converted to binary. To learn more about binary/decimal number conversion, visit *www.wikihow.com/Convert-from-Decimal-to-Binary*.

All IPv4 addresses are composed of two parts: the network ID and the host ID. The **network ID** represents the network on which the computer is located, whereas the **host ID** represents a single computer on that network. No two computers on the same network can have the same host ID; however, two computers on different networks can have the same host ID.

The network ID and the host ID are similar to postal mailing addresses, which are made up of a street name and a house number. The street name is similar to a network ID. No two streets in the same city can have the same name, just as no two networks can have the same network ID. The host ID is like the house number. Two houses can have the same house number as long as they are on different streets, just as two computers can have the same host ID as long as they are on different networks.

Only computers with the same network ID can communicate with each other without the use of a router. This allows administrators to logically separate computers on a network; computers in the Accounting Department could use one network ID, whereas computers in the Sales Department could use a different network number. If the two departments are connected by a router, computers in the Accounting Department can communicate with computers in the Sales Department and vice versa.

Note

If your network is not connected to the Internet, the choice of IP address is entirely up to you. However, if your network is connected to the Internet, you might need to use preselected IP addresses for the computers on your network. IP addresses that can be used on the public Internet are assigned by your ISP.

Note

The IP address 127.0.0.1 is called the **loopback IP address**. It always refers to the local computer. In other words, on your computer, 127.0.0.1 refers to your computer. On your coworker's computer, 127.0.0.1 refers to your coworker's computer.

Each computer with an IPv4 address must also be configured with a subnet mask to define which part of its IP address is the network ID and which part is the host ID. Subnet masks are composed of four octets, just like an IP address. The simplest subnet masks use only the values 0 and 255. An octet in a subnet mask containing 255 is part of the network ID. An octet in a subnet mask containing 0 is part of the host ID. Your computer uses the binary process called **ANDing** to find the network ID. ANDing is a mathematical operation that compares two binary digits and gives a result of 1 or 0. If both binary digits being compared have a value of 1, the result is 1. If one digit is 0 and the other is 1, or if both digits are 0, the result is 0.

When an IP address is ANDed with a subnet mask, the result is the network ID. Figure 1-22 shows an example of how the network ID and host ID of an IP address can be calculated using the subnet mask.

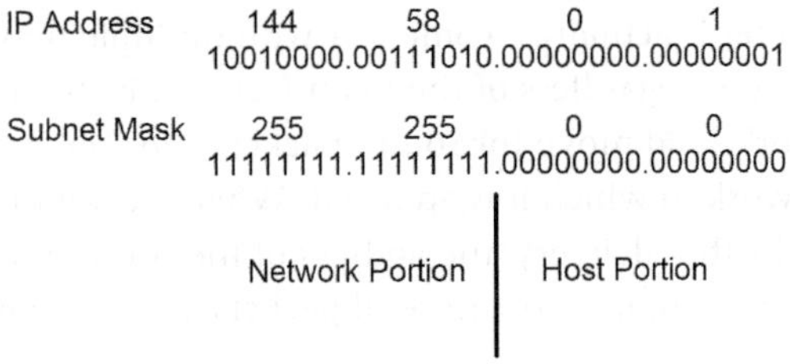

```
IP Address      144       58        0        1
                10010000.00111010.00000000.00000001

Subnet Mask     255       255       0        0
                11111111.11111111.00000000.00000000


                Network Portion  │  Host Portion
                                 │
                                 │
```

Figure 1-22   A sample IP address and subnet mask

Thus, the IP address shown in Figure 1-22 identifies the first computer (host portion 0.1) on the 144.58 network (network portion 144.58).

> **Note**
>
> IP addresses and their subnet masks are often written using the **classless interdomain routing (CIDR) notation**. For example, the notation 144.58.0.1/16 refers to the IP address 144.58.0.1 with a 16-bit subnet mask (255.255.0.0).

The IP addresses 0.0.0.0 and 255.255.255.255 cannot be assigned to a host computer because they refer to all networks and all computers on all networks, respectively. Similarly, using the number 255 (all 1s in binary format) in an IP address can specify many hosts. For example, the IP address 192.168.131.255 refers to all hosts on the 192.168.131 network; this IP address is also called the **broadcast** address for the 192.168.131 network.

> **Note**
>
> A computer uses its IP address and subnet mask to determine what network it is on. If two computers are on the same network, they can deliver packets directly to each other. If two computers are on different networks, they must use a router to communicate.

Typically, all computers on a LAN are configured with the same network ID and different host IDs. A LAN can connect to another LAN by means of a router, which has IP addresses for both LANs and can forward packets to and from each network. Each computer on a LAN can contain the IP address of a router in its IP configuration; any packets that are not destined for the local LAN are then sent to the router, which can forward the packet to the appropriate network or to another router. The IP address of the network interface on the router to which you send packets is called the default gateway.

A router is often a dedicated hardware device from a vendor such as Cisco, D-Link, or HP. Other times, a router is actually a computer with multiple network cards. The one consistent feature of routers, regardless of the manufacturer, is that they can distinguish between different networks and move (or route) packets between them. A router has an IP address on every network to which it is attached. When a computer sends a packet to the default gateway for further delivery, the address of the router must be on the same network as the computer, as computers can send packets directly to devices only on their own network.

Understanding IPv6

As the Internet grew in the 1990s, ISPs realized that the number of IP addresses available using IPv4 was inadequate to accommodate future growth. As a result, the IPv6 protocol was designed in 1998 to accommodate far more IP addresses. IPv6 uses 128 bits to identify computers, whereas IPv4 only uses 32 bits (4 octets). This allows IPv6 to address up to 340,282,366,920,938,463,463,374,607,431,768,211,456 (or 340 trillion trillion trillion) unique computers.

IPv6 IP addresses are written using 8 colon-delimited 16-bit hexadecimal numbers—for example, 2001:0db8:3c4d:0015:0000:0000:adb6:ef12. If an IPv6 IP address contains 0000 segments, they are often omitted in most notation, thus 2001:0db8:3c4d:0015:::adb6:ef12 is equivalent to 2001:0db8:3c4d:0015:0000:0000:adb6:ef12. The IPv6 loopback address is 0000:0000:0000:0000:0000:0000:0000:0001, but it is often referred to as ::1 for simplicity.

> ### Note 📎
>
> Unlike our traditional decimal-numbering scheme, hexadecimal uses an expanded numbering system that includes the letters A through F in addition to the numbers 0–9. Thus, the number 10 is called A in hexadecimal, the number 11 is called B in hexadecimal, the number 12 is called C in hexadecimal, the number 13 is called D in hexadecimal, the number 14 is called E in hexadecimal, and the number 15 is called F in hexadecimal.

Although IPv6 addresses can be expressed several ways, the first half (64 bits) of an IPv6 address identifies your network (the network ID); the first 46 bits are typically assigned by your ISP and identify your organization uniquely on the public Internet, and the following 16 bits can be used to identify unique networks within your organization.

The last 64 bits of an IPv6 address is used to uniquely identify a computer in your LAN (the host ID), and is often generated from the unique hardware address on each computer's network interface.

> **Note** 📎
>
> The hardware address on a network interface is a 48-bit hexadecimal number called the **Media Access Control (MAC) address** that is unique for each network interface manufactured. Your computer translates IPv4- and IPv6-addressed packets into MAC-addressed frames before sending it to the nearest host or router.

Although most operating systems today support IPv6, few networks and computers on the Internet have adopted it. In 2018, Google reported that less than 20 percent of all computers in any country have adopted IPv6. Most computers that have adopted IPv6 are small Internet-connected devices that are collectively referred to as the **Internet of Things (IoT)**. Some example IoT devices include the NEST smart thermostat and the Google Home personal assistant. IoT devices often use an IPv6 address that can be accessed by an online app, and the IPv6 traffic they send is often encapsulated in IPv4 traffic using a protocol such as **Teredo** to allow it to work within IPv4-only networks.

This slow adoption of IPv6 is primarily the result of two technologies that allow IPv4 to address many more computers than was previously possible: **proxy servers** and **Network Address Translation (NAT)** routers.

Proxy servers and NAT routers are computers or hardware devices that have an IP address and access to a network such as the Internet. Other computers on the network can use a proxy server or NAT router to obtain network or Internet resources on their behalf. Moreover, there are three reserved ranges of IPv4 addresses that are not distributed to computers on the Internet and are intended only for use behind a proxy server or NAT router:

- The entire 10.0.0.0 network (10.0.0.0/8)
- The 172.16 through 172.31 networks (172.16–31.0.0/16)
- The 192.168 networks (192.168.0–255.0/24)

Thus, a computer behind a proxy server in Iceland and a computer behind a NAT router in Seattle could use the same IPv4 address—say, 10.0.5.4—without problems because each of these computers only requests Internet resources using its own proxy server or NAT router. A company may use a Cisco NAT router, for example, to allow other networks and computers in the company to gain access to the Internet. Similarly, a high-speed home Internet modem typically functions as a NAT router to allow multiple computers in your home to access the Internet.

Most computers in the world today obtain Internet access via a proxy server or NAT router. Because these computers share IPv4 addresses on a reserved network range, rather than using a unique IP address, the number of available IPv4 addresses has remained high and slowed the adoption of IPv6.

Configuring IP on a Network Interface

While you can manually configure the necessary IP address, subnet mask, and default gateway on a network interface for your network, your network interface can instead receive IP configuration automatically from a **Dynamic Host Configuration Protocol (DHCP)** or **Boot Protocol (BOOTP)** server on the network.

> **Note**
>
> Following a Windows Server 2019 installation, all network interfaces on the server are configured to obtain their IP configuration from a DHCP server on the network.

> **Note**
>
> In addition to receiving IP configuration from a DHCP server, your network interface will often receive the IP address of a **Domain Name Space (DNS)** server on the network that is used to resolve Internet names, such as *www.google.ca* to IP addresses such that you can connect to Internet resources by name. Similarly, when manually configuring IP for a network interface, you should supply the IP address of a valid DNS server on the network to ensure that your computer can resolve Internet names. The proper term for Internet names is **Fully Qualified Domain Names (FQDNs)**.

The process of obtaining an IP address for your network interface varies, depending on whether your computer is on an IPv4 or IPv6 network. If you attempt to obtain IPv4 configuration for your network interface from a DHCP or BOOTP server and no DHCP or BOOTP server exists on your network, your system will assign an IPv4 address of 169.254.*x.x* where *.x.x* is a randomly generated host ID. This automatic assignment feature is called **Automatic Private IP Addressing (APIPA)**. If your network has IPv6-configured routers, an IPv6 address is automatically assigned to each network interface. This is because network interfaces use **Internet Control Message Protocol version 6 (ICMPv6)** router discovery messages to probe their network for IPv6 configuration information. Alternatively, you can obtain your IPv6 configuration from a DHCP server on the network. If there are no IPv6-configured routers or DHCP servers on your network from which you can obtain an IPv6 configuration for your network interface, your system will assign an IPv6 APIPA address that begins with FE80 and ends with the last half of your network interface's MAC address.

> **Note**
>
> A single network interface can have both an IPv4 and an IPv6 address. Each address can be used to access the Internet using the IPv4 and IPv6 protocols, respectively.

Note

In most environments, IPv4 is manually configured on each server network interface to ensure that it does not change over time. For environments that use IPv6, the configuration of IPv6 is typically performed automatically using ICMPv6.

To manually configure IP on a network interface within Server Manager, navigate to Local Server and select the hyperlink next to the associated network interface, such as the Ethernet network interface shown earlier in Figure 1-8. This will open the properties for the network interface as shown in Figure 1-23. You can then select either IPv4 or IPv6 shown in Figure 1-23 and click Properties to modify the associated IP configuration parameters. If you select IPv4 and choose Properties, you can enter an IP address, subnet mask, default gateway, preferred DNS server IP address, and alternate DNS server IP address (used if the preferred DNS server is unavailable), as shown in Figure 1-24. If you are using Server Core, you can modify the same IP configuration for IPv4 and IPv6 by selecting option 8 within the Windows Server Configuration Wizard, shown earlier in Figure 1-11.

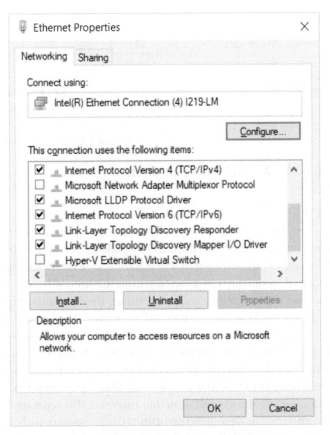

Figure 1-23   **Network interface properties**

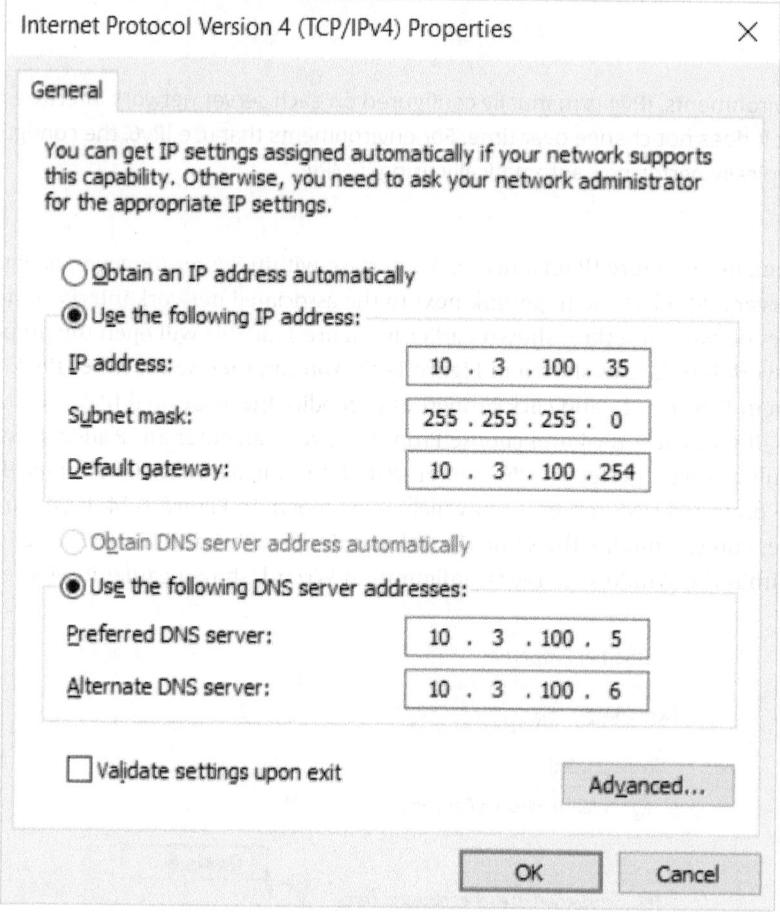

Figure 1-24   A sample IPv4 configuration

Configuring the Firewall

A firewall prevents computers on the network from connecting to software and services that are running on your computer. The firewall in Windows Server 2019 is enabled by default and blocks access to any software or services that have not been configured (only file sharing is configured by default and allowed within the firewall). When you configure software or services that allow network users to connect, the firewall is normally configured automatically to allow users to connect. However, this depends on the software or service that is being configured; sometimes you must manually allow the software or service within the firewall to ensure that users can access it from across the network.

Most servers exist within a separate network that is surrounded by routers that implement advanced firewall capabilities for all traffic that is passing into the network from other computers within the organization and Internet. This separate network is called a **perimeter network** or **demilitarized zone (DMZ)**. Servers within a perimeter network do need to have a firewall configured as they are protected by the network firewalls on the routers surrounding them. Consequently, many server administrators will disable the firewall on these servers to make future troubleshooting of user access easier.

To disable or modify the firewall's configuration within Server Manager, navigate to Local Server and select the hyperlink next to Windows Defender Firewall in the Properties window shown earlier in Figure 1-8.

Changing the Default Computer Name and Domain Membership

When you install Windows Server 2019, the installation process assigns a randomly generated **computer name** for the server, such as WIN-9E7MT5EFTHG. The randomly generated name does not represent the server role and is difficult to type within utilities and commands. As a result, you should change the computer name following a Windows Server 2019 installation to one that follows your organization's server naming convention. For example, a particular organization may have a naming convention that consists of three parts separated by dashes. The first part uses the first letter and last letter of the city (e.g., Toronto would be represented by TO), followed by the server role (e.g., a file server would be represented by FS), followed by a number. Thus, TO-FS-03 would represent the third file server within Toronto.

The computer name can be up to 63 characters and is used to generate the first part of the computer's FQDN, as well as the computer's **NetBIOS name** that is automatically broadcast on the network. NetBIOS names can only be 15 characters long, so you should limit your computer name to 15 characters or less. Additionally, while dash (-) and underscore (_) characters are allowed within a computer name, spaces and other special characters are not.

To change your computer name within Server Manager, navigate to Local Server and select the hyperlink next to Computer name in the Properties window shown earlier in Figure 1-8. This opens the System Properties window, where you can click the Change button and supply a new computer name in the Computer name field as shown in Figure 1-25. To change your computer name within the Windows Server Configuration Wizard on Server Core, select option 2 shown earlier in Figure 1-11.

In most organizations, Active Directory is used to provide single sign-on and central administration for all computers within the organization. However, a newly installed Windows Server 2019 computer is not part of an Active Directory domain by default; instead it is part of a peer-to-peer workgroup network called WORKGROUP. As a result, you will likely need to join a Windows Server 2019 to an Active Directory domain following installation.

Note

Before joining an Active Directory domain, first ensure that the network interface on your computer has a valid IP configuration for your network, as well as a DNS server that contains the records for your Active Directory domain name.

Computer Name/Domain Changes   ✕

You can change the name and the membership of this computer.
Changes might affect access to network resources.

Computer name:

TO-FS-01

Full computer name:
TO-FS-01.myorganization.com

More...

Member of

⦿ Domain:

myorganization.com

◯ Workgroup:

WORKGROUP

OK   Cancel

Figure 1-25   Changing the computer name or
domain membership

To join your server to a domain within Server Manager, navigate to Local Server
and select the hyperlink next to Workgroup in the Properties window shown earlier
in Figure 1-8. This opens the same System Properties window you used to change
your computer name. However, when you click the Change button within the System
Properties window, you can instead select the Domain radio button shown in Figure 1-25
and supply the domain name of your Active Directory domain (e.g., *myorganization.com*).
Following this, you will be prompted to log in as a valid user within the domain. To join
your server to a domain within the Windows Server Configuration Wizard on Server
Core, select option 1 shown earlier in Figure 1-11, supply the Active Directory domain
name, and log in as a valid domain user when prompted.

Note

After changing the computer name or domain membership, the changes will not take effect
until you reboot the computer.

Installing a Modern Web Browser

While the default Web browser that ships with Windows Server 2019 is Internet Explorer, it is included for legacy application support only; most modern Web tools, such as the Windows Admin Center, do not support it. As a result, you should download and install a modern Web browser such as Edge Chromium or Google Chrome following a Windows Server 2019 installation.

Unfortunately, to download a modern Web browser using Internet Explorer will be difficult, as most websites are blocked by **Internet Explorer Enhanced Security Configuration (IE ESC)**. This means that downloading a modern Web browser in Internet Explorer may involve adding over a dozen exceptions within IE ESC, because websites today contain components from several sources. As a result, you should disable IE ESC before using Internet Explorer to download a modern Web browser.

To disable IE ESC within Server Manager, navigate to Local Server and select the hyperlink next to IE Enhanced Security Configuration in the Properties window shown earlier in Figure 1-8. Following this, you will be prompted to either disable IE ESC for all users or just administrators on the system. If Internet Explorer is running during this process, you will need to close and re-open Internet Explorer for the change to take effect.

> **Note** 📎
>
> To download the Chrome Web browser installer, visit *https://google.com/chrome*. To download the installer for the Edge Chromium Web browser (preview build at the time of this writing), visit *https://support.microsoft.com/en-us/help/4501095/download-microsoft-edge-based-on-chromium*.

Activating the Windows Server Operating System

The process of activating a Windows operating system validates that you have a license to use the operating system itself. If your organization has **Key Management Services (KMS)** installed on a server within the network, or the **Active Directory-based Activation role** installed on a domain controller within the domain to which your Windows Server 2019 computer is joined, activation may be automatically performed based on the **Generic Volume License Key (GVLK)** that is stored on the Windows Server 2019 installation media that you received from Microsoft.

Alternatively, if your organization has purchased a retail product key or **Multiple Activation Key (MAK)** that can be used to activate a set number of computers, then you can manually enter this key on your Windows Server 2019 computer to perform the activation if your system is connected to the Internet.

To manually activate a Windows Server 2019 system within Server Manager, navigate to Local Server and select the hyperlink next to Product ID in the Properties window shown earlier in Figure 1-8. Next, enter your license key and click Activate to complete the activation process.

Selecting a Windows Server 2019 Lab Environment

As you progress through the Hands-On Projects within this book, you will configure several different technologies that rely on having multiple Windows Server 2019 systems. To achieve this, we will use Hyper-V to create multiple Windows Server 2019 virtual machines as necessary.

While you can install Windows Server 2019 directly on your computer and use Hyper-V to host these virtual machines (shown in Figure 1-26), this may be impractical in your work, classroom, or home environment if you rely on Windows 10 for productivity. Luckily, Windows 10 Professional, Enterprise, and Education editions support Hyper-V and nested virtualization. This means that you do not need to install Windows Server 2019 directly on your computer to perform the Hands-On Projects within this book. Instead, you can create a virtual machine for Windows Server 2019 that has nested virtualization enabled, and then use Hyper-V on that Windows Server 2019 virtual machine to create additional virtual machines as necessary. This configuration is illustrated in Figure 1-27.

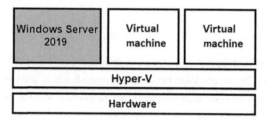

Figure 1-26   Lab Environment 1: Installing Windows Server 2019 directly on your computer

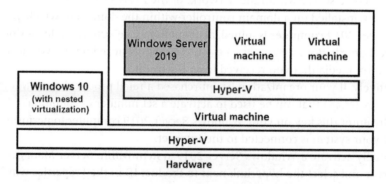

Figure 1-27   Lab Environment 2: Installing Windows Server 2019 within a virtual machine on Windows 10 using nested virtualization

If you choose to install Windows Server 2019 directly on your computer (as illustrated in Figure 1-26), you must perform Hands-on Project 1-1, but you can skip Hands-on Project 1-2. If you choose to install Windows Server 2019 on a Windows 10 host using nested virtualization (Figure 1-27), you can skip Hands-on Project 1-1 and proceed directly to Hands-on Project 1-2. The remaining Hands-On Projects within this book will apply to either lab environment.

Module Summary

- Windows Server 2019 can be installed directly on an on-premises rackmount server or within a virtual machine that is hosted on-premises or within the cloud.

- Although Windows Server 2019 can be installed on any hypervisor, Microsoft's Hyper-V is often used to host Windows Server 2019 virtual machines on-premises. The nested virtualization feature of Hyper-V makes it attractive within cloud environments and IT lab environments.

- Containers are an alternative to virtual machines that may be used to host Web apps that are run on an underlying Windows Server operating system. Hyper-V containers allow each container to access a separate copy of the underlying Windows Server kernel.

- Key features of Windows Server 2019 include additional security, advanced filesystem functionality, enhanced performance and reliability, clustering, greater cloud integration, Linux application support, and the ability to centralize authentication and management using Active Directory.

- The main tools used to configure and manage Windows Server 2019 include Server Manager, Windows PowerShell, and the Windows Admin Center.

- Server Core and Nano Server are two small footprint installation options for Windows Server 2019 that are often used in large data centers and cloud environments.

- There are three major editions of Windows Server 2019. Essentials Edition is designed for small organizations of up to 25 users, Standard Edition is a general-purpose server designed for the majority of organizations, and Datacenter Edition is designed for environments that run a large number of virtual machines.

- Capacity planning should be performed prior to installing Windows Server 2019 and involves determining current and future hardware requirements based on the needs of the users within the organization.

- After obtaining the installation media for Windows Server 2019, you can boot a server or virtual machine from this media to start the installation process. The installation process prompts you to select the locale, edition, storage location, and local Administrator password for Windows Server 2019.

- Following a successful installation, you typically perform several post-installation tasks. These include setting the correct time and time zone, configuring network interfaces with the correct IP settings, verifying firewall configuration, changing the computer name and domain membership, installing a modern Web browser, and activating the Windows Server 2019 operating system.

Key Terms

1U server

Active Directory

Active Directory Certificate
 Services

Active Directory-based
 Activation role

Advanced Threat Protection
 (ATP)

AMD-V

ANDing

attack surface

authentication

Automatic Private IP
 Addressing (APIPA)

Azure Active Directory

Azure Backup

Azure Site Recovery

Azure Update Management

Basic Input/Output System
 (BIOS)

blade server

Boot Protocol (BOOTP)

broadcast

Burnaware

capacity planning

checkpoints

classless interdomain
 routing (CIDR) notation

client

Client Access License (CAL)

cloud

cloud server

clustering

cmdlet

computer name

container

data deduplication

default gateway

demilitarized zone (DMZ)

Desired State Configuration

Docker

domain

domain controller

Domain Name Space (DNS)

Dynamic Host Configuration
 Protocol (DHCP)

edition

Encrypting File System (EFS)

failover

Fully Qualified Domain
 Name (FQDN)

Generation 1 virtual
 machine

Generation 2 virtual
 machine

Generic Volume License Key
 (GVLK)

Group Policy

guest operating system

host ID

host operating system

hybrid cloud

Hyper-V

Hyper-V container

Hyper-V Manager

hypervisor

Intel VT

Internet Control Message
 Protocol (ICMP)

Internet Control Message
 Protocol version 6
 (ICMPv6)

Internet Explorer Enhanced
 Security Configuration (IE
 ESC)

Internet Information
 Services (IIS)

Internet of Things (IoT)

Internet Protocol (IP)
 address

Internet Service Provider
 (ISP)

IP version 4 (IPv4)

IP version 6 (IPv6)

ISO image file

journaling

kernel

Key Management Services
 (KMS)

keyboard-video-mouse
 (KVM) switch

Kubernetes

Local Area Network (LAN)

logical processor

loopback IP address

Media Access Control (MAC)
 address

Microsoft Azure

Microsoft Management
 Console (MMC)

Multiple Activation Key (MAK)

multitasking

Nano Server

nested virtualization

NetBIOS name

network

Network Address
 Translation (NAT)

network ID

New Technology File System
 (NTFS)

Non-Volatile Memory
 Express (NVMe)

octet

on-premises server

packet

peer-to-peer networking

perimeter network

physical processor

PowerShell script

preemptive multitasking

privileged mode

protected process

protocol

proxy server

rackmount server

Redundant Array of
   Independent Disks (RAID)
Resilient File System (ReFS)
router
Rufus
sandboxing
Second Level Address
   Translation (SLAT)
server
Server Core
Server Core App
   Compatibility Feature on
   Demand (FOD)
Server Manager
shell
shielded virtual machines
single sign-on
small footprint
snapshots
Software Defined
   Networking (SDN)
solid state disk (SSD)

storage area network (SAN)
Storage Migration Service
storage pinning
Storage Replicas
Storage Spaces
Storage Spaces Direct
storage tiers
subnet mask
Teredo
thick provisioning
thin provisioning
thread
Transmission Control
   Protocol/Internet Protocol
   (TCP/IP)
Trusted Platform Module
   (TPM)
Type 1 hypervisor
Type 2 hypervisor
unicast
Unified Extensible
   Firmware Interface (UEFI)

uninterruptible power
   supply (UPS)
User Datagram Protocol/
   Internet Protocol (UDP/IP)
virtual machine
virtual processor
virtualization
Windows Admin Center
Windows Containers
Windows Management
   Instrumentation (WMI)
Windows PowerShell
Windows Server Azure
   Network Adapter
Windows Server Catalog
Windows Server Configuration
   Wizard (`sconfig.cmd`)
Windows Subsystem for
   Linux (WSL)
workgroup

Review Questions

1. Servers that exist within a data center that is publicly accessible on the Internet are referred to as on-premises servers. True or False?

2. Which of the following are hardware requirements for Hyper-V?
   a. 64 GB of memory
   b. Two network interfaces
   c. Processor with Intel VT or AMD-V and SLAT
   d. A 32-bit or 64-bit processor

3. Which Hyper-V feature allows you to install a virtual machine within another virtual machine?
   a. Nested virtualization
   b. SLAT
   c. Checkpoints
   d. Hyper-V containers

4. Containers are often used to host Web apps within cloud environments. True or False?

5. What term is used to refer to a logical grouping of computers that participate in Active Directory single sign-on?
   a. Group Policy
   b. Domain
   c. Domain controller
   d. Azure Active Directory

6. Which component of Microsoft Defender can be used to provide cloud-based threat analysis within Windows Server 2019?
   a. Shielded virtual machines
   b. IIS
   c. ATP
   d. Windows Defender Firewall

7. Windows Server 2019 supports up to 64 physical processors and 128 logical processors. True or False?

8. Which filesystem feature of Windows Server 2019 allows you to create large volumes that span multiple physical storage devices?
   a. Storage Spaces
   b. ReFS
   c. Storage Migration Service
   d. Storage Replicas

9. Clustering may be used with multiple Windows Server 2019 systems to enhance speed and fault tolerance for network services. True or False?

10. Which of the following management tools is not installed by default on Windows Server 2019?
    a. Server Manager
    b. MMC
    c. Windows PowerShell
    d. Windows Admin Center

11. Commands within Windows PowerShell are referred to as cmdlets. True or False?

12. Which two small footprint installation options are available for Windows Server 2019? (Choose two answers.)
    a. Nano Server
    b. Microsoft Hyper-V Server
    c. Server Core
    d. Essentials

13. You can start the Windows Server Configuration Wizard within Server Core by running the sconfig.cmd command. True or False?

14. Which Windows Server edition supports Windows Containers and up to two Hyper-V Containers?
    a. Essentials
    b. Standard
    c. Datacenter
    d. Storage Server

15. The minimum memory required for a graphical Windows Server 2019 installation is 512 MB. True or False?

16. Which of the following Windows Server 2019 editions are licensed per processor core? (Choose all that apply.)
    a. Essentials
    b. Standard
    c. Datacenter
    d. Hyper-V Server

17. Which of the following is not a question that should be asked when planning a Windows Server 2019 installation?
    a. What are the storage needs of the server?
    b. Who will be supporting the server?
    c. How many users are expected to connect to the server?
    d. What services will the server run?

18. To install a Windows Server 2019 virtual machine, you typically attach an ISO image file that contains the installation media to a virtual DVD drive within the virtual machine settings. True or False?

19. Which of the following tasks are typically performed following a Windows Server 2019 installation? (Choose all that apply.)
    a. Verify the correct time and time zone information
    b. Activate the Windows Server 2019 operating system
    c. Configure the appropriate computer name and domain membership
    d. Set IP configuration on network interfaces

20. Server Manager is typically used to perform most post-installation tasks on a graphical Windows Server 2019 system. True or False?

Hands-On Projects

The Hands-On Projects presented in this module normally take a total of three hours or less to complete. The software and hardware requirements for this lab include:

- A 64-bit computer with at least 16 GB of memory, a recent-generation processor that supports virtualization extensions (Intel VT/AMD-V + SLAT), and 500 GB of hard disk or SSD storage (SSD strongly recommended)
- For Lab Environment 1 (Figure 1-26), a DVD or USB flash drive that contains bootable installation media for Windows Server 2019 Datacenter Edition
- For Lab Environment 2 (Figure 1-27), Windows 10 (Professional, Enterprise, or Educational) installed on the computer, as well as an ISO image that contains the installation media for Windows Server 2019 Datacenter Edition

Project 1-1: Lab Environment 1

In this Hands-on Project, you configure your system according to Lab Environment 1. More specifically, you use bootable DVD or USB flash drive media to install Windows Server 2019 Datacenter Edition on your computer.

1. Obtain a copy of Windows Server 2019 Datacenter Edition on DVD or USB flash drive media. Alternatively, you can obtain a Windows Server 2019 Datacenter Edition ISO image and write the image to a bootable DVD or USB flash drive as described earlier in this module.
2. Modify the boot order within your computer BIOS (if necessary) to ensure that it first checks for an operating system on your DVD drive and connected USB devices before the hard disk or SSD in your system.
3. Insert the DVD or USB flash drive that contains the installation media for Windows Server 2019 Datacenter Edition into your computer and restart it. If prompted to press a key on your keyboard to boot from the DVD or USB flash drive, press any key within the timeout period.
4. After the Windows Setup screen appears, select the correct language, time and currency format, and keyboard or input type for your locale and click **Next**.
5. Click **Install now**.
6. Select **Windows Server 2019 Datacenter (Desktop Experience)** from the list of Windows Server 2019 editions and click **Next**.
7. Place a check next to **I accept the license terms** and click **Next**.
8. Select **Custom: Install Windows only (advanced)**.
9. Note that the storage devices within your computer are displayed. Highlight any partitions under the storage device that you would like to install Windows Server 2019 on (e.g., Drive 0) and click **Delete** in turn until no more partitions exist under your storage device. Finally, highlight the storage device and click **Next** to install Windows Server 2019 on it.

10. After the installation has completed, click **Restart now**, if necessary.
11. When the Customize settings window appears, supply the password **Secret555** in the Password and Reenter password text boxes and click **Finish**.
12. At the login screen, supply the password **Secret555** for Administrator and press **Enter** to log into the system.
13. Right-click the **Start** menu and click **Shut down or sign out**, **Shut down**. Click **Continue** to shut down your system.
14. Proceed to Project 1-3.

Project 1-2: Lab Environment 2

In this Hands-On project, you configure your system according to Lab Environment 2. More specifically, you install Hyper-V within Windows 10, as well as install Windows Server 2019 within a new virtual machine. Finally, you enable nested virtualization for your new virtual machine.

1. Log into Windows 10 as a user that has administrative privileges.
2. Right-click the **Start** menu and select **Apps and Features**.
   a. In the Apps & features window, scroll down to the Related settings section and click **Programs and Features**.
   b. In the left pane of the Programs and Features window, click **Turn Windows features on or off**.
   c. In the Windows Features window, place a check next to **Hyper-V**, and click **OK**. Click **Restart now** to restart your PC.
3. Log back into Windows 10 as a user that has administrative privileges, right-click the Start menu and select **Run**. In the Run dialog box, type **virtmgmt.msc** and click **OK** to open Hyper-V Manager.
4. In the Actions pane of Hyper-V Manager, click **Virtual Switch Manager**.
   a. In the Virtual Switch Manager window, ensure that **New virtual network switch** is highlighted in the left pane, **External Virtual Switch** is highlighted in the right pane, and click **Create Virtual Switch**. Ensure that the network interface that connects your computer to your network is listed under External network. Finally, modify the default name (New Virtual Switch) to **External Virtual Switch** and click **OK**.
   b. Click **Yes** at the Apply Networking Changes window to complete your virtual switch configuration.

> **Note** 🖉
>
> An external virtual switch allows the virtual network interface in your virtual machine to share the physical network interface in your computer to obtain network access. We'll discuss virtual switches later in Module 3.

5. In the Actions pane of Hyper-V Manager, click **New**, **Virtual Machine** to open the New
   Virtual Machine Wizard.
   a. At the Before You Begin page, click **Next**.
   b. At the Specify Name and Location page, supply the name **WindowsServer2019** (no
      spaces) and click **Next**.
   c. At the Specify Generation page, select **Generation 2** and click **Next**.
   d. At the Assign Memory page, enter **12288** in the Startup memory text box, de-select
      Use Dynamic Memory for this virtual machine, and click **Next**.

Note

If your computer has more than 16 GB of memory, you may specify more than 12288
(12 GB) in the Startup memory text box. However, ensure that you leave at least
4 GB for the Windows 10 operating system. For example, if your system has 32 GB of
memory, you can specify up to 28672 (28 GB) in the Startup memory text box.

   e. At the Configure Networking page, select **External Virtual Switch** from the drop-
      down box, and click **Next**.
   f. At the Connect Virtual Hard Disk page, view the default options that create a 127 GB
      dynamically expanding virtual hard disk, and click **Next**.
   g. At the Installation Options page, select **Install an operating system from a
      bootable image file**, and click **Browse**. Navigate to your Windows Server 2019 ISO
      image file, click **Open**, and then click **Next**.

Note

By specifying the Windows Server 2019 ISO image file in this step, the virtual DVD
within the virtual machine will be attached to this ISO image and the DVD will be
moved to the top of the virtual BIOS boot order.

   h. At the Completing the New Virtual Machine Wizard page, click **Finish**.
6. In the Actions pane of Hyper-V Manager, click **Hyper-V Settings**.
   a. Under the User section, highlight **Keyboard**.
   b. In the Keyboard pane on the right, ensure that **Use on the physical computer** is
      selected and click **OK**.
7. In the Virtual Machines pane of Hyper-V Manager, right-click your **WindowsServer2019**
   virtual machine and choose **Connect**. This will open a remote desktop connection to
   your virtual machine.

8. In the Virtual Machine Connection window, click **Start** to boot your virtual machine, and immediately press any key on your keyboard to boot the installation media from the virtual DVD.

   a. After the Windows Setup screen appears, select the correct language, time format, and keyboard type for your locale and click **Next**.

   b. Click **Install now**.

   c. Select **Windows Server 2019 Datacenter (Desktop Experience)** from the list of Windows Server 2019 editions and click **Next**.

   d. Place a check next to **I accept the license terms** and click **Next**.

   e. Select **Custom: Install Windows only (advanced)**.

   f. Note that your 127 GB virtual hard disk is listed as unallocated space and selected by default. Click **Next** to install Windows Server 2019 on this virtual hard disk.

   g. After the installation has completed, click **Restart now**.

   h. When the Customize settings window appears, supply the password **Secret555** in the Password and Reenter password text boxes and click **Finish**.

   i. At the login screen, supply the password **Secret555** for Administrator and press **Enter** to log into the system. Server Manager will open shortly thereafter. When Server Manager prompts you to try managing servers with Windows Admin Center, select the **Don't show this message again** checkbox and close the window. If the Networks desktop notification screen prompts you to allow your PC to be discoverable by other PCs and devices on the network, click **Yes**.

   j. Right-click the **Start** menu and click **Shut down or sign out**, **Shut down**. Click **Continue** to shut down your system.

9. Click the Windows 10 **Start** menu and type **PowerShell**. Under the Windows PowerShell App, click **Run as Administrator**.

   a. Type `Set-VMProcessor -VMName WindowsServer2019 -ExposeVirtualizationExtensions $true` and press **Enter** to enable nested virtualization for your Hyper-V virtual machine.

   b. Type `Get-VMNetworkAdapter -VMName WindowsServer2019 | Set-VMNetworkAdapter -MacAddressSpoofing On` and press **Enter** to enable MAC address spoofing for your Hyper-V virtual machine.

10. Proceed to Hands-on Project 1-3.

Note

At the beginning of future Hands-On Projects, you will be asked to boot your Windows Server 2019 host. To do this, open Hyper-V Manager (Step 3), connect to your virtual machine (Step 7), and click Start.

Project 1-3: Post-Installation Tasks

In this Hands-on Project, you perform post-installation tasks on your Windows Server 2019 host.

1. Boot your Windows Server 2019 host and log into the system as Administrator using the password **Secret555**. After a few moments, Server Manager will open.

2. Within Server Manager, navigate to **Local Server**. Note the operating system version and hardware information shown.

3. In the Server Manager Properties window, view the hyperlink next to Time zone. If your time and/or time zone are not correct, click the hyperlink to open the Date and Time window.

   a. To change your time, click **Change date and time**, specify the correct time, and click **OK**.

   b. To change your time zone, click **Change time zone**, select the correct time zone, and click **OK**.

   c. Click **OK** to close the Date and Time window.

4. In the Server Manager Properties window, click the **On** hyperlink next to IE Enhanced Security Configuration. Select the **Off** button under the Administrators section and click **OK**.

5. In the Server Manager Properties window, click the **Public: On** hyperlink next to Windows Defender Firewall.

   a. In the Firewall & network protection window, click **Domain network**.

   b. Click the slider under Windows Defender Firewall to turn off the firewall.

   c. Click the back arrow in the upper left of the window to return to the Firewall & network protection window.

   d. Click **Private network** and repeat steps b and c.

   e. Click **Public network** and repeat steps b and c.

   f. Close the Firewall & network protection window.

> **Note** 📎
>
> In most on-premises environments, Windows Server 2019 resides within a DMZ network that is protected by network firewalls. In these environments, it is commonplace to disable the firewall.

6. In the Server Manager Properties window, click the **IPv4 address assigned by DHCP, IPv6 enabled** hyperlink next to your Ethernet network adapter.

   a. In the Network Connections window, right-click your Ethernet adapter and click **Status**.

   b. In the Ethernet Status window, click **Details** and note whether your network environment has successfully assigned IPv4 and IPv6 configuration to your network interface automatically via a DHCP server or ICMPv6. Record this configuration and click **Close**.

c. In the Ethernet Status window, click **Properties**.

d. In the Ethernet Properties window, highlight **Internet Protocol Version 4 (TCP/IPv4)** and click **Properties**. If your network environment requires manual IPv4 configuration, select **Use the following IP address** and supply the correct information. Next, select **Use the following DNS server addresses** and supply the correct DNS server information. Click **OK** when finished.

e. In the Ethernet Properties window, highlight **Internet Protocol Version 6 (TCP/IPv6)** and click **Properties**. If your network environment requires manual IPv6 configuration, select **Use the following IPv6 address** and supply the correct information. Next, select **Use the following DNS server addresses** and supply the correct DNS server information. Click **OK** when finished.

f. Click **OK** to close the Ethernet Properties window, and click **Close** to close the Ethernet Status window. Finally, close the Network Connections window.

7. In the Server Manager Properties window, click the hyperlink next to Computer name.

a. At the System Properties window, click **Change**. Note that your computer received a generated computer name and is part of a workgroup called WORKGROUP.

b. In the Computer name box, type a new computer name of **SERVER*X***, where *X* is a number that is uniquely assigned to you by your instructor, and click **OK**.

c. Click **OK** at the Computer Name/Domain Changes window, and click **Close** in the System Properties window.

d. Click **Restart Now** to restart your Windows Server 2019 server.

8. After your server has rebooted, log into the system as Administrator using the password **Secret555**. After a few moments, Server Manager will open.

9. Within Server Manager, navigate to **Local Server** and note the hyperlink next to Product ID. Depending on the installation media that you used to install your server and the nature of your organization's network environment, you may see that your Windows Server 2019 system is activated. If it is not activated, click the **Not activated** hyperlink and follow the prompts to supply the correct product key and license information for your environment. When finished, close the Settings window and Server Manager.

10. Click the Internet Explorer icon on the Windows taskbar.

a. Click **OK** at the Internet Explorer 11 window.

b. Enter the URL **https://www.google.com/chrome** and follow the prompts to download and install the latest version of the Chrome Web browser.

11. Right-click the **Start** menu and select **Shut down or sign out**, and click **Shut down**. Click **Continue** to shut down your system.

Discovery Exercises

Exercise 1-1

You work for a large manufacturing company which currently hosts several dozen Windows Server systems installed on rackmount servers, some of which host custom Web apps that are used by computers across the entire organization. There are plans to expand in the next year, and the number of servers and clients is expected to double. As part of this expansion, the organization is considering shifting to an environment that involves virtualization for many of its current and future Windows Server operating systems. Additionally, the organization is considering hosting its custom Web apps within containers, possibly within the cloud. The IT manager has asked for your input regarding the benefits of adopting virtualization and containers within the organization. Create a one-page report detailing the benefits that virtualization and containers could bring to your organization over the next year. If possible, relay your ideas within a small group of peers to create the contents of the report.

Exercise 1-2

As the IT administrator for a small organization with 60 Windows clients, you are tasked with introducing a new server running Windows Server 2019. This new server should provide single sign-on for the users in your network, as well as host a third-party app that stores its data within a Microsoft SQL Server database. What considerations must you keep in mind when planning the requirements of this new Windows Server 2019 system from a software and hardware point of view? Create a one-page memo that lists these considerations.

Exercise 1-3

At a local gathering for tech workers, a network administrator asks you are if they should introduce Windows Server 2019 into their existing Windows environment. They suggest that Windows Server 2019 doesn't offer any tangible benefits beyond prior versions of Windows Server. How do you reply? Include new Windows Server 2019 features and examples to demonstrate your points.

Exercise 1-4

You work for a creative startup that creates a Linux Web app that runs within Linux containers in the cloud. Your organization has grown tremendously in the past year, and you now require on-premises servers to support the needs of the users and Linux app developers within the organization. What Windows Server 2019 features can benefit your organization? Prepare a one-page memo that lists key features and benefits, including examples where possible.

Exercise 1-5

The organization you work for deploys hundreds of Windows Server 2016 systems within virtual machines. The Technology Director has mandated that all new virtual machines run the Server Core small footprint installation option of Windows Server 2019. However, your IT

Manager is concerned about the added administrative effort required to manage Server Core, as well as the ability to run many of the existing enterprise applications that the company uses. What can you tell the IT Manager to ease their concerns? Prepare a sample email to your IT Manager that lists your points in a professional manner.

Exercise 1-6

You have recently installed a new Windows Server 2019 system. Following the installation, your server does not have Internet access. You notice that your network interface has an IPv4 address of 169.254.3.29 and an IPv6 address that starts with FE80. What do these indicate, and what steps should you take to remedy the problem? Within a one-page memo, prepare a sample IT support ticket that includes this information.

Exercise 1-7

Research three different vendors of storage solutions that use Windows Storage Server 2019. Compare and contrast their features and costs. After you finish, research the costs of creating a similar Windows Server 2019 Standard Edition installation on a rackmount server to provide the same features. Finally, compare the costs of your rackmount server and Windows Server 2019 Standard Edition license to the Windows Storage Server 2019 products offered by the three different vendors. Which solution would you choose based on the information you researched?

CONFIGURING WINDOWS SERVER 2019

After completing this module, you will be able to:

Use Server Manager to monitor and manage Windows Server systems

Install and use the Windows Admin Center to monitor and manage Windows Server systems

Configure server hardware devices

Use the System File Checker and Sigverif to verify system files

Configure key Windows Server components within Control Panel and Device Manager

Explain the purpose and configuration of the Windows Registry

Identify the components, features, and usage of Windows PowerShell

Use Windows PowerShell to manage a server

Create PowerShell scripts for systems administration

In the previous module, you installed Windows Server 2019 and provided essential post-installation configuration. In this module, you'll examine the different tools that can be used to monitor and manage Windows Server 2019 in more depth, including Server Manager, the Windows Admin Center, Control Panel, and Device Manager. You'll also learn how to check for and repair system files, as well as edit the Windows Registry. At the end of the module, you'll learn how to work within Windows PowerShell, as well as how to create and modify PowerShell scripts to automate system configuration tasks.

Working with Server Manager

As you learned in the previous module, Server Manager is a tool that starts by default when you log into a Windows Server 2019 system. More specifically, it combines several different administrative tools and functions together to make your server easy to manage. Thus, you used the Properties pane within the Local Server section of Server Manager (Figure 1-8) to perform Windows Server 2019 post-installation configuration tasks in Hands-On Project 1-3.

However, Server Manager can be used to monitor and manage several different Windows Server systems on your network as well as the roles that they provide. Because all Windows Server systems provide a basic file server role following installation, you saw the File and Storage Services role listed in the navigation area of Server Manager in Figure 1-8. However, as you add more roles to your server, or more servers to the Server Manager console, you will notice more sections displayed in the navigation area. The navigation area shown in Figure 2-1 displays a total of four server roles that can be monitored and managed by Server Manager: Active Directory Domain Services (AD DS), DHCP, DNS and File and Storage Services.

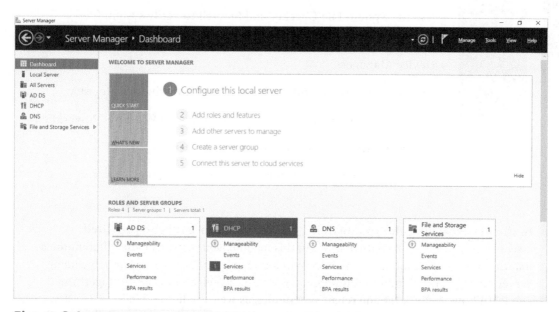

Figure 2-1   Managing servers and roles within Server Manager

The Dashboard section at the top of the navigation area shown in Figure 2-1 allows you to perform common tasks within Server Manager as well as see the state of the servers and roles within your organization. The Welcome to Server Manager pane within the Dashboard section provides options for configuring the local server, adding roles and features, adding other Windows Servers to manage from the Server Manager console, and creating groups to organize other Windows Servers as well as a wizard that allows you to connect Server Manager to servers and roles that you manage within the Microsoft Azure cloud.

Note

If you add additional servers to Server Manager, you should ensure that these servers are joined to an Active Directory domain within your organization. Although it is possible to add a server that is part of a workgroup to Server Manager, the workgroup server will first need to be added to a trusted hosts list, and not all monitoring and management features will be available. Refer to *https://docs.microsoft.com/en-us/windows-server/administration/server-manager/add-servers-to-server-manager* for more information.

Because you can also add roles, features, servers, and server groups from the Manage menu within Server Manager, many administrators choose to hide the Welcome to Server Manager pane so that the Dashboard section only displays the status of roles within your organization, as shown in Figure 2-2.

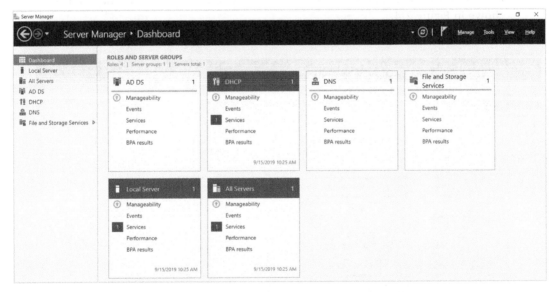

Figure 2-2   Viewing the status of roles and servers within Server Manager

Note

If you hide the Welcome to Server Manager pane, you can navigate to View, Show Welcome Tile to display it again.

The boxes within the Roles and Server Groups pane have a green arrow next to them if they are fully managed by Server Manager. Although you can add other Windows Server 2008 and later servers to Server Manager in Windows Server 2019, not all monitoring and management features are available in Windows Server 2012 R2 and earlier.

Additionally, each box is color coded so you can see right away if there is a problem on a server. Note from Figure 2-2 that there is a problem with one or more services that comprise the DHCP server role within your organization. Because this role is installed on the local server and is part of the All Servers group, the issue is also shown in those two boxes as well. You can click on Services in any of these boxes to see details regarding the problem, or click on the title of the box to navigate to the associated section within the navigation area of Server Manager.

Each section within the navigation area of Server Manager has four additional panes that allow you to monitor and manage the associated server, server group, or server role:

- *Events* (shown in Figure 2-3) lists warning, error, and critical events from all event logs on the associated servers from the past 24 hours. By selecting Configure Event Data from the Tasks menu within this pane, you can modify the time period and event severity levels shown, or choose specific event logs to display events from, as shown in Figure 2-4.

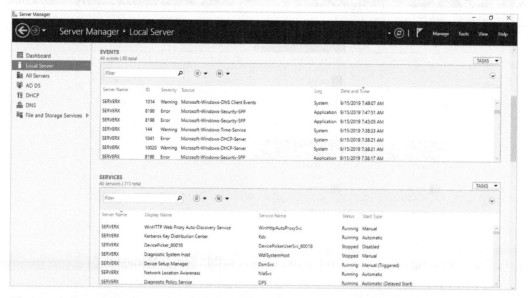

Figure 2-3   Viewing events and services for the local server within Server Manager

- *Services* (shown in Figure 2-3) lists the services that are installed on the associated servers. If you right-click a service listed, you can choose to start, stop, restart, pause, or resume that service.

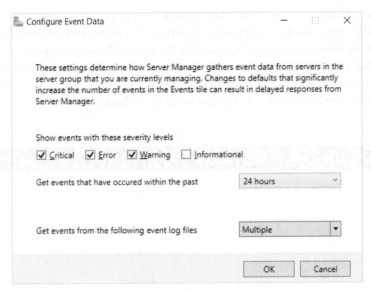

Figure 2-4   Configuring event options within Server Manager

- *Best Practices Analyzer* (shown in Figure 2-5) allows you to scan the associated servers and roles for configuration issues that do not follow Microsoft's recommendations. To perform a **Best Practices Analyzer (BPA)** scan, select Start BPA Scan from the Tasks menu. Following the scan, the results will be listed in the pane for you to view. Because this list is often large, you can use the Filter dialog box within this pane to display only certain results.

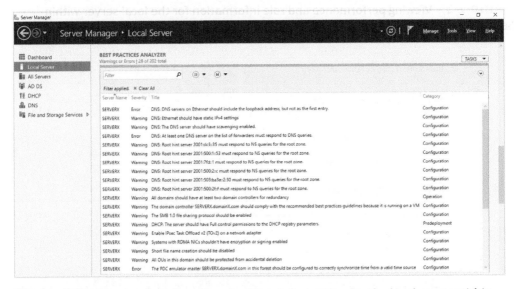

Figure 2-5   Viewing Best Practices Analyzer information for the local server within Server Manager

- *Performance* (shown in Figure 2-6) allows you to see the performance of the associated servers as well as configure processor (CPU) usage and memory alerts. By default, performance data is displayed for the past 24 hours, and you are alerted when processor usage exceeds 85% or less than 2 MB of memory remains available. However, you can modify these values if you select Tasks, Configure Performance Alerts within the Performance pane, as shown in Figure 2-7.

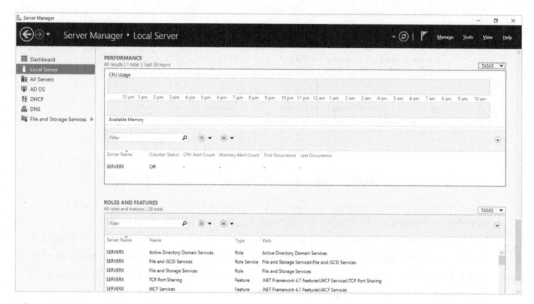

Figure 2-6   Viewing performance and role information for the local server within Server Manager

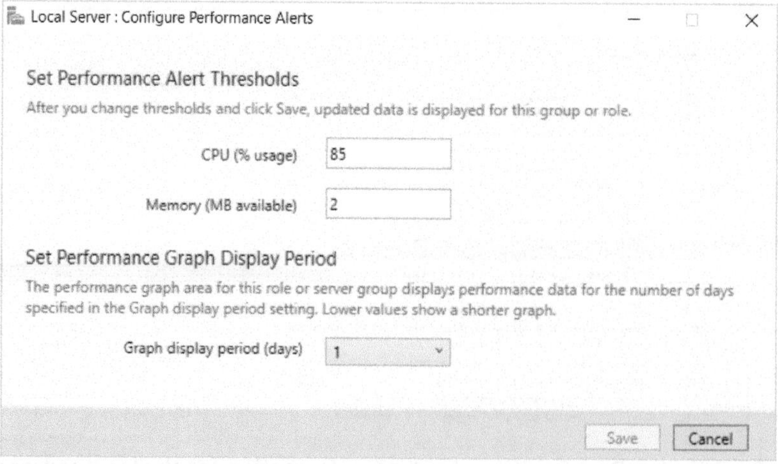

Figure 2-7   Configuring performance options within Server Manager

- *Roles and Features* (shown in Figure 2-6) displays the roles and features that are installed on the associated servers. By selecting Add Roles and Features from the Tasks menu in this pane, you can add additional roles and features to your local server. Alternatively, selecting Remove Roles and Features from the Tasks menu will allow you to remove roles and features that are already installed.

By default, information displayed by Server Manager is refreshed every 10 minutes, but this may be too infrequent when monitoring environments. You can change this interval by selecting Server Manager Properties from the Manage menu in Server Manager and specifying a different data refresh period, as shown in Figure 2-8. Moreover, if you select the Do not start Server Manager automatically at logon option in Figure 2-8, you will need to select Server Manager from the Start menu to start it each time you log into your Windows Server 2019 system.

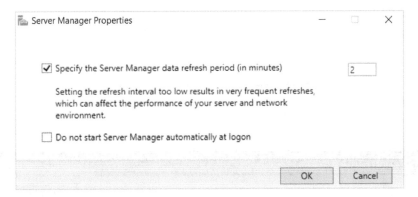

Figure 2-8   **Configuring Server Manager properties**

Some server roles that were introduced starting with Windows Server 2012 have their configuration tools built into the Server Manager interface. One example of this is Storage Spaces, which can be configured on any server that has been added to the Server Manager console by selecting File and Storage Services from the navigation area and selecting the Volumes subsection shown in Figure 2-9. Other server roles often have their own MMC tool for configuration. Although you can select these tools from the Start menu on your local server, it is often easier to select them from the Tools menu as shown in Figure 2-10. To start an MMC tool that connects to another server that is managed by Server Manager, you can navigate to a server group or role section within the navigation area, right-click a server in the Servers pane and choose the appropriate tool (only tools related to the role and server will be shown). For the DHCP server role shown in Figure 2-11, you could right-click SERVERX and select the DHCP Manager to start the DHCP Manager MMC tool on SERVERX. Also note from Figure 2-11 you can perform additional remote management functions on servers that you right-click within Server Manager, including opening a remote Windows PowerShell window, as well as shutting down or rebooting the server itself.

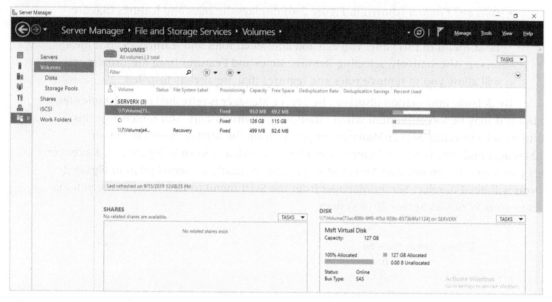

Figure 2-9   Configuring Storage Spaces from within Server Manager

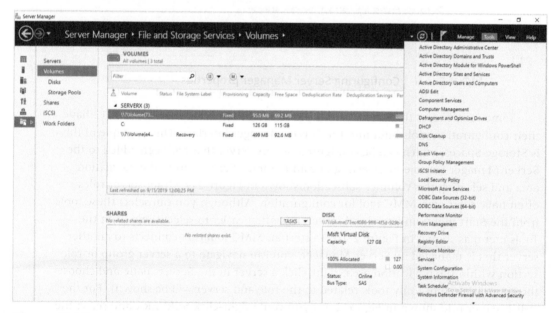

Figure 2-10   The Server Manager Tools menu

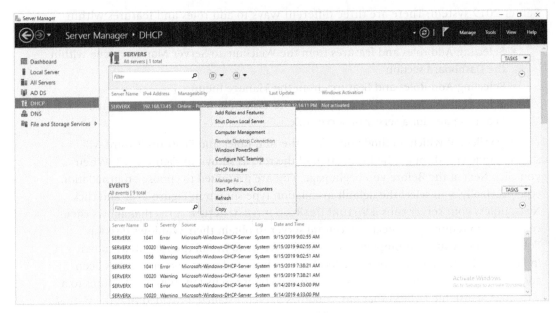

Figure 2-11   The right-click menu for a server within Server Manager

Note

Server Manager in Windows Server 2019 Essentials Edition has some different features targeted for a more simplified introduction to server setup and management. The Server Manager functions you learn in this book relate to the Windows Server 2019 Standard and Datacenter Editions.

Note

You can install the **Remote Server Administration Tools (RSAT)** on a Windows 10 PC that is joined to an Active Directory domain within the organization. This allows you to perform server administration remotely using Server Manager and a wide range of MMC tools from a Windows 10 PC within your IT office. To obtain the RSAT, visit *https://www.microsoft.com/en-ca/download/details.aspx?id=45520*.

Adding Roles and Features Using Server Manager

Throughout this book, you will add several different roles and features to support the technologies that we will discuss as part of different topics. Consequently, it is important to know how to properly install and verify server roles on a Windows

Server 2019 system. There are three different ways to add roles and features within Server Manager:

- Selecting Add roles and features from the Welcome to Server Manager pane within the Dashboard section
- Selecting Add Roles and Features from the Manage menu
- Selecting Add Roles and Features from the Tasks menu within the Roles and Features pane for a server or server role

Regardless of which method you select, the Add Roles and Features Wizard will start to guide you through the installation of the role as shown in Figure 2-12. When you click Next at the Before you begin page, you are prompted to choose an installation type. Normally, you select the default installation type shown in Figure 2-13 and click Next, unless your server runs a **Virtual Desktop Infrastructure (VDI)** that allows client computers to remotely connect to a central server to obtain their Windows desktop. Following this, you are prompted to choose the server to install the role on as shown in Figure 2-14. By default, this is the local server, but can be any server that has been added to Server Manager. Alternatively, you can choose to install roles and features to a virtual hard disk file (.vhdx) that has Windows Server installed, provided that the virtual machine that is using it is powered off. This allows you to install new roles and features on a virtual hard disk file that you use as a template when creating new virtual machines (discussed later in Module 3).

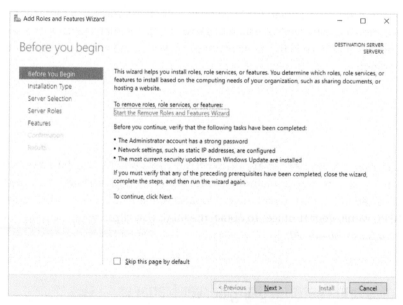

Figure 2-12   The Add Roles and Features Wizard

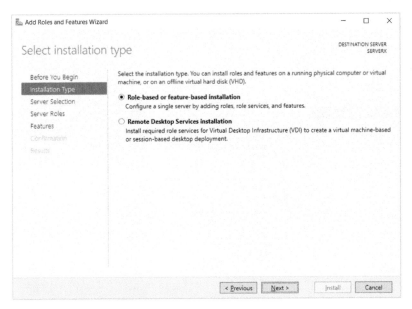

Figure 2-13   Selecting the installation type

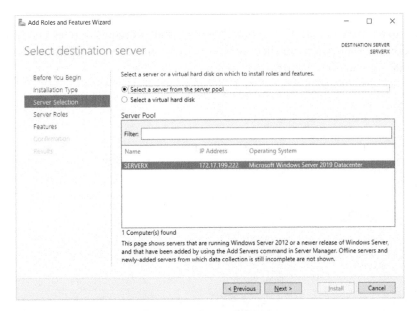

Figure 2-14   Selecting the destination server

After you click Next in Figure 2-14, you are prompted to choose one or more roles that you wish to install as shown in Figure 2-15. To verify whether you have chosen the correct roles, you can highlight each role to view its description. When you place a

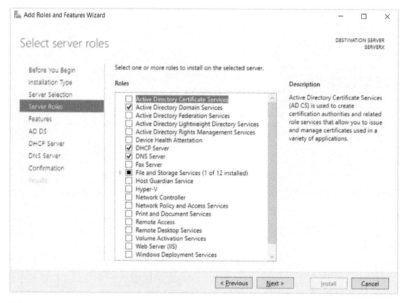

Figure 2-15 Selecting server roles

check next to a role, you may also be prompted to install prerequisite roles and features, depending on the role. After you click Next, you are prompted to select features that you wish to install, as shown in Figure 2-16.

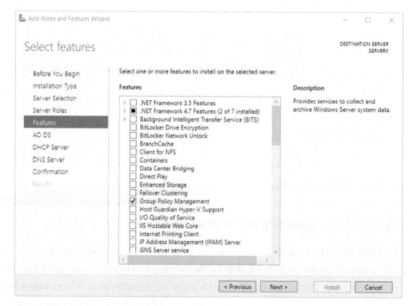

Figure 2-16 Selecting features

Note

In general, server services are displayed under the roles section, and supporting features and programs are displayed under the features section. However, you will find some server services under the features section, such as the iSNS Server Service shown in Figure 2-16.

Depending on the roles and features you selected, when you click Next in Figure 2-16 you may be prompted to provide additional information for the service or view information regarding the service. After following these screens, you can click the Install button in the Add Roles and Features Wizard to install the associated software.

Following the installation of the role or feature, you may also be required to perform specific post-installation tasks. A hyperlink to perform these tasks will be shown on the final screen of the Add Roles and Features Wizard, as shown in Figure 2-17 for the Active Directory Domain Services and DHCP Server roles. If you close the Add Roles and Features Wizard, you can still access these hyperlinks by selecting the yellow warning icon in the notification area within Server Manager (also shown in Figure 2-17).

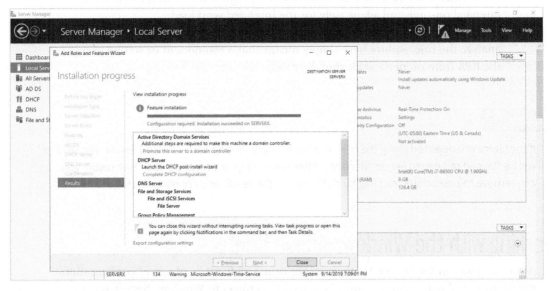

Figure 2-17   Completing the installation of roles and features

Using the BPA to Verify Server Roles

After you have installed a new server role, and periodically afterwards, it's important to run a BPA scan to determine whether your role configuration meets minimum guidelines recommended by Microsoft. When the BPA finds problems, you will see a level of severity as well as a category within the results (shown earlier in Figure 2-5). There are three levels of severity:

- *Information*—The role is in compliance, but a change is recommended. For example, a server's network interface might have a valid IPv4 address temporarily leased by DHCP, but a static address is recommended for the particular role.
- *Warning*—The role complies under current operating conditions, but this may change if the operating conditions change. For example, the Hyper-V role might become noncompliant if another virtual machine is added for which there is no available virtual disk space.
- *Error*—The role does not meet best practices and problems can be expected.

The different categories that you will see for BPA recommendations include the following:

- *Configuration*—Indicates whether role settings are configured for best performance and avoid conflicts with other services
- *Predeployment*— Indicates whether prerequisites for the role are properly installed or configured
- *Postdeployment*— Indicates whether services needed for the role are started and running
- *Performance*— Indicates whether the role can perform the tasks for which it is intended on-time and adequately for the intended workload
- *BPA Prerequisites*— Indicates whether the role is set up in such a way that BPA can analyze the role. Failure here simply means that a component or setting prevented the BPA from properly analyzing the role.

Note

If problems are detected using the BPA, the boxes representing each affected server and service will be flagged red within Server Manager. After remedying or accepting each BPA result, you can remove the associated red flag by right-clicking the result and choosing Exclude Result.

Working with the Windows Admin Center

Although you can use Server Manager to perform a wide range of server configuration, monitoring, and management, you often need to connect to Windows Server system to run it, or install the RSAT on a Windows 10 PC. Alternatively, you can use Windows Admin Center (introduced in Module 1) to remotely manage Windows Server 2019 remotely from any computer that has a modern Web browser. This is often preferred in environments that host a large number of remote Windows Server systems that must be managed centrally, including cloud environments. Although the Windows Admin Center is a relatively new tool, it boasts a wide range of monitoring and management functionality that Microsoft wants to expand to all areas of Windows Server administration. Consequently, when you first open Server Manager on Windows Server 2019, you are prompted to download the Windows Admin Center in an information dialog.

Installing the Windows Admin Center

When you navigate to the Windows Admin Center website (`https://aka.ms/WindowsAdminCenter`), you have the option to download the latest preview version (if you have signed up for the Microsoft Preview channel) or the regular version. Normally, you download the regular version, as it has been validated to be stable by previous administrators. This will download a file called `WindowsAdminCenter<version>.msi` that you can execute to start the installation program.

> **Note** 📎
>
> You cannot install the Windows Admin Center on a Windows Server that has the Active Directory Domain Services (AD DS) role installed and configured as a domain controller for Active Directory.

After you start the installer, you will navigate through several screens, clicking Next each time. More specifically, you will be prompted to accept the license agreement, whether to automatically update the Windows Admin Center with Windows Update (recommended), as well as view information about how the Windows Admin Center functions in different scenarios. When you install the Windows Admin Center on a Windows Server 2016 or 2019 system to provide remote Web access for administrations, it is said to function in **gateway server mode**, as it provides the ability to manage other Windows Server systems on the network. Alternatively, when you install the Windows Admin Center on a Windows 10 PC, it functions similar to the RSAT by connecting to other servers within the Active Directory domain for administration.

Additionally, the installer will prompt you to allow the Windows Admin Center to modify the local computer's trusted host settings as shown in Figure 2-18. This option is necessary if you wish to manage other systems with the Windows Admin Center. Next, you are prompted to either generate an encryption certificate for use with HTTPS (called a **self-signed certificate**), or supply the thumbprint for an existing HTTPS certificate that is already installed on the computer and signed by a public **Certification Authority**, as shown in Figure 2-19. HTTPS traffic normally uses port 443, but you can optionally change this port to a different one if the server already has Web server software installed that provides HTTPS access on port 443. You can also force regular HTTP requests to be automatically redirected to HTTPS.

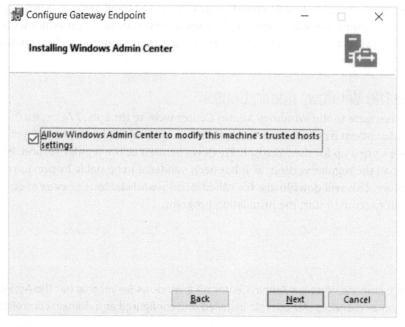

Figure 2-18   Allowing the Windows Admin Center to modify trusted host settings

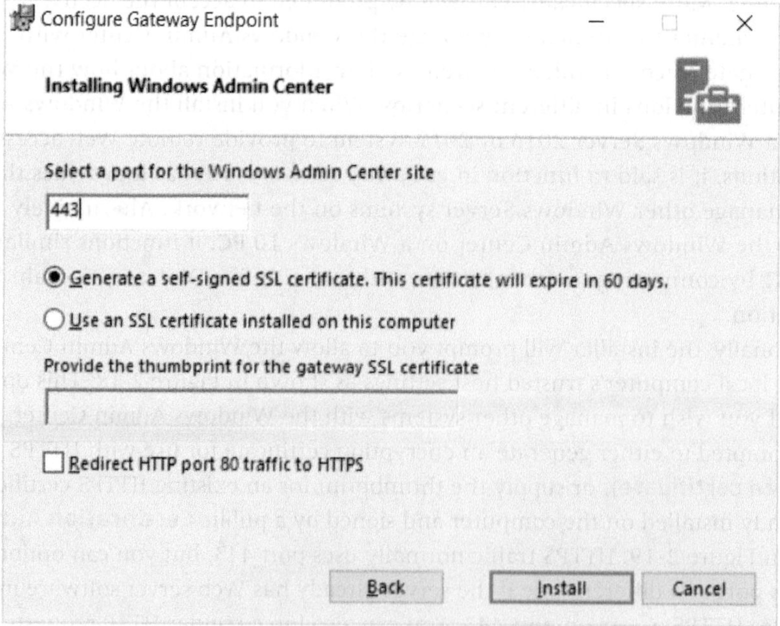

Figure 2-19   Specifying HTTPS options

Note

If you change the port in Figure 2-19, you will need to append `:port` to the URL that you use when connecting to the Windows Admin Center in your Web browser.

When you click Install in Figure 2-19, the Windows Admin Center will be installed on your system. At the end of the installation, the URL that can be used to access it will be shown on the final screen shown in Figure 2-20.

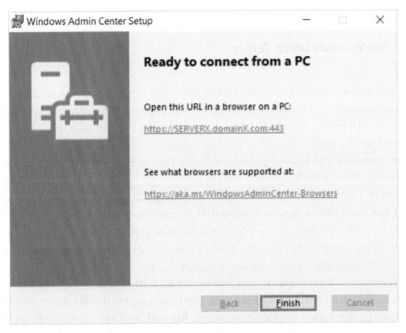

Figure 2-20   **Completing the installation of the Windows Admin Center**

Using the Windows Admin Center

When you navigate to the Windows Admin Center website in a modern Web browser (e.g., Google Chrome) for the first time, you are prompted to log in with valid credentials on the gateway server or Active Directory domain to which the gateway server is joined. Following this, you are prompted to complete a quick tour before being placed at the connections screen within the Windows Admin Center shown in Figure 2-21. The server hosting the Windows Admin Center will be labelled with [gateway] following its

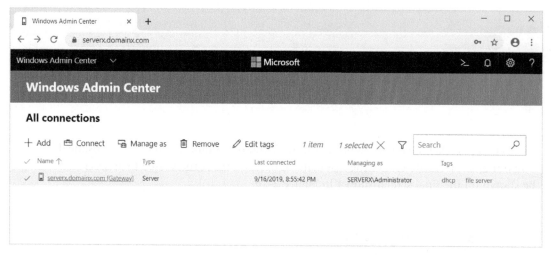

Figure 2-21   **The Windows Admin Center**

name, but you can add other Windows Server 2012 and later systems by clicking Add. If you highlight a server, you can click Manage as to provide specific connection credentials for that system; otherwise, the credentials you used when logging into the Windows Admin Center will be used.

You can also click Edit tags to add one or more tags to each server line that can be searched within the Search dialog box. This is useful if you have many servers added to the Windows Admin Center. For example, the serverx.domainx.com server listed in Figure 2-21 has two custom tags indicating that it contains the DHCP and file server roles. If you click Connect, you will connect to that particular server for server management. For example, selecting serverx.domainx.com in Figure 2-21 and clicking Connect will display the server manager screen shown in Figure 2-22.

When it comes to functionality, you will notice a lot of similarity between the Windows Admin Center and Server Manager. For example, both tools allow you to monitor server performance, configure network, firewall, and system settings, as well as manage services, roles, and features. At the Overview page shown in Figure 2-22, you can see status information, or you can scroll down to see processor (CPU), memory, and network performance information, as well as set alerts (Manage alerts). If you click Enable Disk Metrics, you will also see the performance of storage devices on the system.

Note

Disk metrics are not enabled by default as they cause a slight performance degradation on the server itself.

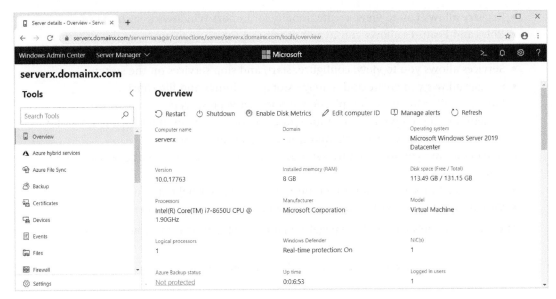

Figure 2-22   Managing *serverx.domainx.com* within the Windows Admin Center

Moreover, you can restart, shut down, or edit the computer name and domain membership (Edit computer ID), just as you can in the Local Server section of Server Manager. Other server configuration, such as remote access, power options, and Windows Admin Center roles, can be handled by clicking the Settings icon below the navigation pane.

Most of the tools within the navigation pane allow you to configure additional areas of the system or access configuration functionality that would normally be provided by MMC tools:

- Certificates allows you to view and import encryption certificates.
- Containers allows you to monitor and manage Windows Containers.
- Devices allows you to configure hardware devices on the system.
- DHCP allows you to monitor and manage DHCP server configuration.
- DNS allows you to monitor and manage DNS server configuration.
- Events allows you to view and search the system event logs.
- Files allows you to upload and download files to and from the filesystems on the server.
- Firewall allows you to view and configure firewall rules.
- Installed Apps allows you to view and remove installed applications.
- Local Users & Groups allows you to create and manage accounts on the system that are not part of Active Directory.
- Network allows you to configure IP on network interfaces as well as add the Azure Network Adapter for cloud integration.
- Processes allows you to manage processes on the system as well as create a process dump file that lists detailed process information (often required by Microsoft Support when a support ticket is created).

- Registry allows you to view, create, modify, or import Windows Registry keys.
- Roles and Features allows you to add or remove roles and features on the system.
- Scheduled Tasks allows you to schedule a command or script to run repetitively.
- Services allows you to view, configure, start, and stop services on the system.
- Storage allows you create and manage storage volumes and file shares.
- Storage Replica allows you replicate volumes between servers.
- System Insights allows you to perform ongoing capacity planning for your server by monitoring processor, network, and storage trends over time.
- Updates allows you to configure Windows Update settings as well as check for and apply updates.
- Virtual Machines allows you to monitor and manage virtual machines.
- Virtual Switches allows you to monitor and manage virtual switches.

There are also tools within the navigation pane for obtaining remote access to your system:

- PowerShell provides access to a PowerShell prompt on the target system as the current user.
- Remote Desktop provides access to a graphical desktop using **Remote Desktop Protocol (RDP)**.

The remaining tools within the Windows Admin Center are focused on providing integration with the Microsoft Azure cloud:

- Azure hybrid services allows you to register your Windows Admin Center within the Azure cloud to perform management of cloud-based systems and services.
- Azure File Sync can be used to synchronize files between on-premises and Azure storage.
- Backup can be used to back up files to Azure storage.
- Storage Migration Service can be used to migrate servers and storage to the Azure cloud.

Note

You can also manage clusters within the Windows Admin Center by selecting Failover Cluster Manager from the Server Manager drop-down menu shown in Figure 2-22.

Configuring Server Hardware Devices

Sometimes you will need to replace existing hardware in a server due to failure of a component, or sometimes you'll need to upgrade the hardware. Alternatively, you might have to add another component such as a second network adapter. Windows Server 2019 offers both automatic and manual methods for installing hardware on a system. Hardware devices can include the following:

- Storage devices such as hard disks, SSDs, and optical drives
- Disk controllers
- Network interface adapters
- Input devices such as keyboards and mice
- Specialized devices

For those times when you add or replace hardware, you'll need to be familiar with how to install and configure new hardware on your server.

Modern hardware, including both computers and peripherals, almost universally support **Plug and Play (PnP)**. PnP allows your operating system to work with hardware devices to automatically detect and configure recently installed hardware to work with the operating system.

Note 📎

Microsoft developed PnP, which has now been supplemented by **Universal PnP (UPnP)**, an open standard that is used in all types of systems and that enables connectivity through networks and network protocols. UPnP supports server-based networking, wireless networking, peer-to-peer networking, and other networking services.

Installing a PnP device is a relatively simple process of attaching the device and then waiting for Windows Server 2019 to detect it and install the appropriate device drivers. In some cases, after the device is installed you might need to configure its properties and settings. You may also need to download the latest device driver from the manufacturer's website. Also keep in mind that you should review the manufacturer's installation instructions before attempting to connect the device to your computer. It might be necessary to power down your computer before installing some types of devices. Even for devices for which this is unnecessary (such as USB devices), you still might have to restart your computer for Windows to detect the new device. Furthermore, some computer manufacturers prefer that you use the device driver that they have supplied on a companion CD, DVD, or website, instead of the generic driver that may be provided by Windows Server 2019.

Adding Hardware Using Control Panel

If Windows Server 2019 does not automatically detect newly installed hardware, or if the device you are installing is not PnP, you can use the **Devices and Printers utility** to manually launch PnP or to manually install the device without PnP.

The Devices and Printers utility can be used to:

- Force the operating system to detect and install new PnP hardware
- Install non-PnP hardware
- Troubleshoot problems you might be having with existing hardware

You start the Devices and Printers utility from Control Panel. By default, information is displayed in Category view, with utilities grouped by general function, as shown in Figure 2-23. If you prefer, you can choose Classic view instead, with individual utilities listed as icons. You can choose the Category drop-down menu shown in Figure 2-23 to select large or small icons.

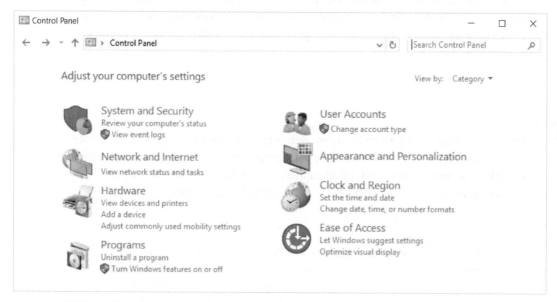

Figure 2-23   **Category view in Control Panel**

To add a new hardware device, you can click Add a device under the Hardware category shown in Figure 2-23. This will probe for both PnP devices that were not previously detected, as well as search for other devices that are not PnP-capable, and prompt you to install the correct driver from a file if one is not found included with Windows Server 2019.

If you click View devices and printers in Figure 2-23, the Devices and Printers utility will display common devices on the system. To troubleshoot a device in this utility, you can right-click the device and select Troubleshoot from the menu. Depending on the issue, Windows Server 2019 may download an updated device driver, prompt you to supply an updated device driver, or advise you to perform certain actions on the hardware device, such as unplugging it and plugging it in again.

Note

If you are installing hardware that is new to the market, you often need to supply a device driver during installation. You can often obtain the latest device driver files from the manufacturer's website.

Using Device Manager

If you install a hardware device that does not have a generic driver provided by Windows Server 2019, or the generic driver provided does not work properly with the hardware device, you may need to open the **Device Manager utility**. To open Device Manager, click the Hardware category within Control Panel and then click Device Manager in the Devices and Printers section. Device Manager shows all devices on the system, including many that are not shown in the Devices and Printers utility. To update the device driver for a device within Device Manager, you can right-click the device and choose Update driver, as shown in Figure 2-24. You will then be prompted to search the Internet for an updated device driver or supply the location of a device driver provided by the manufacturer.

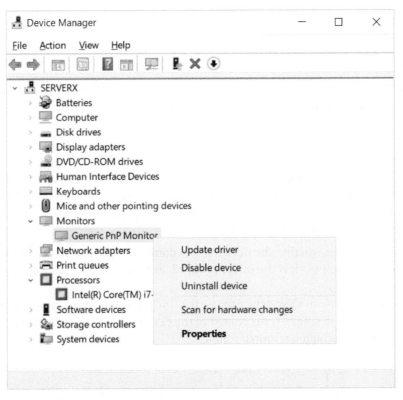

Figure 2-24   Right-clicking a device within Device Manager

Devices that show up with Generic or Unknown within Device Manager will require an updated driver to provide full functionality. Some hardware devices may require that you first remove the existing generic device driver by choosing Uninstall device from the right-click menu shown in Figure 2-24. Following this, you can install the device driver provided by the manufacturer and reboot the system to ensure that Windows Server 2019 detects the hardware and associates it with the manufacturer-provided device driver.

When PnP hardware is installed, the resources that the hardware requires are often coordinated with the system to ensure that there are no conflicts. Hardware resources include the **Interrupt Request (IRQ) line** (which is a channel for communication with the processor) and other elements such as the **Input/Output (I/O) address** and reserved memory range. A computer contains a limited number of IRQ lines. The video display, each disk drive, USB ports, and the sound card each use a dedicated IRQ to communicate with the processor. Each component also needs reserved memory addresses for I/O operations. Resource conflicts can sometimes occur when a network interface, a new storage controller, or some other hardware is added to the system that does not communicate properly with PnP, or is not fully PnP-compliant.

Note 🖉

You can solve most hardware resource conflicts by uninstalling the device driver for a device, rebooting the system, and reinstalling the device driver.

You can use Device Manager to check for a resource conflict as well as examine other properties associated with a device by right-clicking the device and then clicking Properties as shown in Figure 2-24. At minimum, the properties for each device in Device Manager displays four tabs as shown in Figure 2-25:

- General indicates whether the device is functioning properly or not (and why).
- Driver allows you to view the driver installed, as well as update, disable, or uninstall it.
- Details allows you to view device properties, including hardware information.
- Events displays detailed events related to the device that often indicates the nature of a problem, including resource conflicts.

Figure 2-25   **Properties of a device within Device Manager**

Verifying System Files

Device drivers are not the only files on a system that are signed. Many other files that comprise Windows Server 2019 require a signature. Sometimes, drivers and system files can be overwritten, corrupted, or modified by malware. In these cases, the signature on the file will be invalid. Windows Server 2019 offers the **System File Checker** to scan system files for integrity and replace damaged or overwritten files with the proper version. You can run the System File Checker manually from a Command Prompt window (MS-DOS shell) or Windows PowerShell window by executing the `sfc/scannow` command. The scan and repair process could take several minutes to complete and will indicate whether issues were found and repaired, as shown in Figure 2-26. Alternatively, you can use the `sfc/scanfile:`*`filename`* command to scan a single file that you believe is corrupted.

Note

You should use the System File Checker during periods of low server activity, such as after normal business hours.

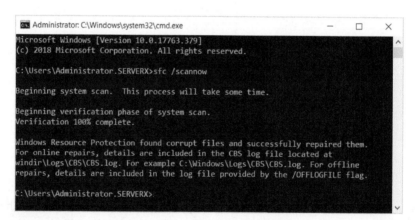

Figure 2-26 Repairing corrupt system files using the System File Checker

Windows Server 2019 includes another tool, called the **File Signature Verification tool (Sigverif)**, which verifies system and critical files to determine if they have a signature, including device drivers. This tool only scans files and does not overwrite inappropriate files, thereby allowing safe use of the tool while the server is active. After the scan is complete, the results are written to a log file, called `sigverif.txt`. If the tool finds a file without a signature that you believe needs to be replaced, you can replace the file using the System File Checker, by obtaining the appropriate file from Microsoft's website, or by reinstalling the associated device driver or program with an updated version.

You can run the System File Checker manually from a Command Prompt or Windows PowerShell window by executing the `sigverif` command. This opens the File Signature Verification window shown in Figure 2-27. You can click the Advanced button to change the location and name of the log file, or Start to start the scan process.

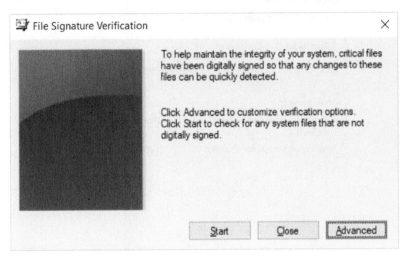

Figure 2-27 The Sigverif tool

Configuring Windows Settings

Using tools included with Windows Server 2019, you can configure many different elements of the operating system, such as performance options, environment variables, startup and recovery options, and power options. The following sections discuss important ways in which you can configure the operating system, focusing on configuration tools accessed from Control Panel.

Configuring Performance Options

Windows Server 2019 allows you to optimize your server for performance. The main areas that you can configure within the operating system to optimize performance include the following:

- Processor scheduling and Data Execution Prevention
- Virtual memory
- File caching and flushing

Configuring Processor Scheduling and Data Execution Prevention

Processor scheduling allows you to configure how processor resources are allocated to programs. You can access the processor scheduling option within Control Panel by navigating to System and Security, System from the Category view. Next, you must select Advanced system settings, click Settings under the Performance section, and highlight the Advanced tab shown in Figure 2-28. The default is set to Background services, which

Figure 2-28   Configuring processor scheduling

means that all programs running will receive equal amounts of processor time. The Programs setting refers to programs you are likely to be running at the server console, such as a backup program. Normally you will leave the default setting for Background services. Sometimes, though, you might need to give programs most of the processor's resources, for instance when you determine that a disk drive is failing and you want to back up its contents as fast as possible using a backup program.

Another performance (and security) option that is good to know about is **Data Execution Prevention (DEP)**. When programs are running on the server, DEP monitors how they use memory to ensure they are not causing memory problems. This is intended to foil malware, such as computer viruses, Trojan horses, and worms. Malware sometimes works by trying to invade the memory space allocated to system functions. If DEP notices a program trying to use system memory space, it stops the program and notifies the system administrator.

Note

Some processors have DEP extensions that can be used to improve the performance of DEP on Windows Server 2019.

Some types of applications might not work well with DEP. For example, applications that use dynamic code generation ("in the moment" code), in which portions of the code are not flagged as executable, might not work well with DEP. Other examples include program code that runs exception handlers, and code requiring executable locations in memory. These programs will often execute on the system, but their performance will be significantly degraded. As a result, you can exclude those programs from DEP to increase performance.

To configure DEP options within Windows Server 2019, you can navigate to the same area in which you configured processor scheduling (shown in Figure 2-28) and highlight the Data Execution Prevention tab, as shown in Figure 2-29. By default, DEP is turned

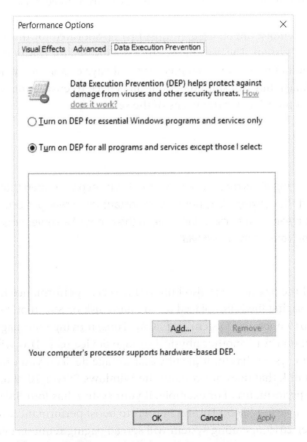

Figure 2-29   Configuring DEP options

on for all programs, but you can click Add to add an exception for a particular program, or select Turn on DEP for essential Windows programs and services only to limit DEP to operating system components.

Configuring Virtual Memory

Virtual memory is disk storage used to expand the capacity of the physical memory installed in the computer. When the currently running programs and processes exceed the physical memory, they treat disk space allocated for virtual memory just as if it were physical memory. The disadvantage of this is that memory activities performed through virtual memory are not as fast as those performed in physical memory (although disk access and data transfer speeds can be quite fast). Virtual memory works through a technique called paging, whereby blocks of information, called **pages**, are moved from physical memory into virtual memory on disk. On a typical computer, data is paged in blocks of 4 KB. For example, if the system is not presently using a 7 KB block of code, it divides the code block between two pages, each 4 KB in size (part of one page will not be completely full). Next, both pages are moved to virtual memory on disk until needed. When the processor calls for that code block, the pages are moved back into physical memory.

Before virtual memory can be used, it must first be allocated for this purpose by tuning the operating system. The area of disk that is allocated for this purpose is called the **paging file**. A default amount of virtual memory is always established when Windows Server 2019 is installed, but you should periodically check to ensure that the amount of virtual memory is appropriate for the needs of the server.

> ### Note 📎
>
> Although having a paging file is theoretically optional, it is recommended that you always have one configured. The paging file is not only important for server performance but also it is necessary for the creation of a crash dump file in the event of a server crash. To learn more, visit *support.microsoft.com/en-us/kb/2860880*.

The location of the paging file is also important. Server performance increases dramatically if the paging file is not placed on the hard disk or SSD that contains the Windows Server 2019 operating system (e.g., C:\). Thus, moving your paging from the default location on C:\ to another physical storage device (e.g., D:\) will improve performance. If your system has multiple physical storage devices, you can create a paging file on each disk that does not contain the Windows Server 2019 operating system to further increase performance. For example, if your system has four SSDs (C:\, D:\, E:\, F:\), you can place a paging file on D:\, E:\ and F:\ to boost performance. In this case, the Windows Server 2019 operating system will spread paging requests evenly across the three storage devices to increase the speed of virtual memory.

Note

For performance reasons, avoid placing a paging file on a RAID volume.

When you tune the size of the paging file, two parameters must be set: initial size and maximum size. A general rule for configuring the initial size is to multiply the amount of installed RAM times 1.5. For a server with 64 GB of RAM, the initial paging file size should be at least 96 GB. Set the maximum size so it affords plenty of room for growth, such as twice the size of your initial paging file setting. For example, if your initial setting is 64 GB, then consider setting the maximum size to 128 GB. Windows Server 2019 always starts using the initial size and only expands the size of the paging file as additional space is needed.

Note

The maximum paging file size on a 64-bit server computer is 256 terabytes.

Note

The paging file size recommendation given here offers a good place to start. As you gain more experience monitoring Windows Server 2019 (discussed later in Module 12), you'll be able to choose a paging file size based on the needs of the applications running on the server.

To configure the paging file options within Windows Server 2019, navigate to the same area where you configured processor scheduling (shown earlier in Figure 2-28), click the Change button in the Virtual memory section, and deselect Automatically manage paging file size for all drives, as shown in Figure 2-30. By default, the paging file is located on the operating system volume (C:\) and set to a default size (System managed size), but you can select Custom size and enter an initial and maximum size of your choice. Following this, you can click Set to set your changes and reboot your system for the change to take effect.

Note

To move a paging file from one volume (e.g., C:\) to another (e.g., D:\) to increase performance, you must first set a paging file on the target volume (e.g., D:\) and reboot to make the change take effect. Next, you can select No paging file for the source volume (e.g., C:\) and reboot for the change to take effect.

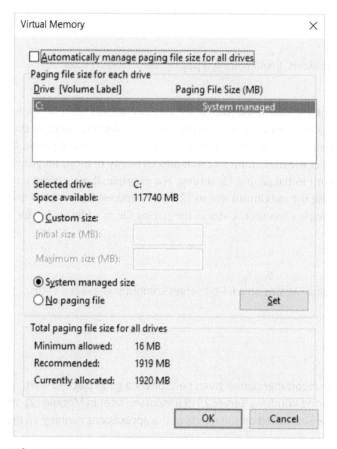

Figure 2-30   Configuring paging file options

Configuring File Caching

Windows operating systems, including Windows Server 2019, cache file data for reading the data from a disk or writing it to disk. This **file caching** is turned on by default and uses an area of memory already established for file caching and controlled by the Windows cache manager. Because file caching uses memory, it can speed up the time it takes to read from or write to a disk.

After data is written to disk, the memory used for that cached data is freed, via a process called **flushing**. On some server systems, administrators choose to turn off file caching and flushing because this enables them to more easily hot swap a disk drive or controller without using the Safety Remove Hardware notification area icon, which warns that a device is in use.

When file caching is turned off, the server can seem slower to users particularly during times of heavy disk read and write operations. When flushing is turned off, less memory is used for file operations, but there may be data loss when a disk drive is hot swapped while the server is in use.

Note

Not all storage devices allow you to disable file caching.

In most cases, server performance is better and disk operations are safer when file caching and flushing are turned on. As you are working to tune a server, consider checking to be sure both capabilities are on. Additionally, you might check this at regular intervals if you work in an environment where there are two or more server administrators, server operators, or system programmers that have access to the servers.

To configure file caching and flushing, you must navigate to the properties of a hard disk or SSD device within Device Manager, and select the Policies tab as shown in Figure 2-31.

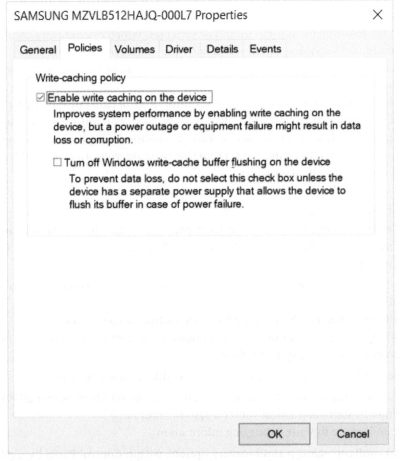

Figure 2-31   Configuring file caching and flushing

> **Note**
>
> When file caching is enabled, it is still possible to lose data after a power outage. For this reason, it is a good idea to have the server connected to a UPS.

Configuring Environment Variables

Environment variables are used to tell the operating system where to find certain programs and program-related information. Environment variables can be broken down into two categories: **system environment variables** and **user environment variables**. System environment variables are defined by the operating system and apply to any user logged into the computer. Administrators can add new system environment variables or change the values of existing ones. User environment variables can be defined on a per-user basis and may be used to provide a wide variety of different information, such as specifying the path where application files are stored. System environment variables are always set first, followed by user environment variables, which override any conflicting system environment variables. Often, server software and developer frameworks require that you manually create a specific system or user environment variable for the software or framework to function correctly.

You can configure environment variables within Control Panel by navigating to System and Security, System from the Category view. Next, you must select Advanced system settings, and click the Environment Variables button to display the Environment Variables window shown in Figure 2-32. From this window, you can create, edit, or delete system and user environment variables.

Configuring Startup and Recovery

Windows Server 2019 enables you to configure parameters that dictate the startup sequence and how the system recovers from errors. You can configure the following system startup options:

- Which operating system to boot by default, if more than one operating system is installed
- How long to display a list of operating systems from which to boot
- How long to display a list of recovery options, if the computer needs to go into recovery mode after a system failure

In the event of a system failure, you can also configure these options:

- Writing information to the system log (mandatory in Windows Server 2019)
- Whether to start automatically after a system failure
- How and where to write debugging information

You can configure startup and recovery options within Control Panel by navigating to System and Security, System from the Category view. Next, you must select

Figure 2-32   Configuring environment variables

Advanced system settings, and click the Settings button in the Startup and Recovery section. Next, you can set the appropriate startup options in the Startup and Recovery window shown in Figure 2-33. Many administrators deselect the Automatically restart option so that the system does not automatically start up after a system failure. This allows the administrator to examine the system before it is rebooted, which is often beneficial if the system stopped functioning and shut down due to a failed storage device.

Configuring Power Options

After installing a new Windows Server 2019 system, you should check the power options to make sure that they are set appropriately for the computer and the way you are using the computer on the network. The power options that you can set are as follows:

- Select a power plan.
- Choose what the power button does.
- Create a power plan.
- Choose when to turn off the display.

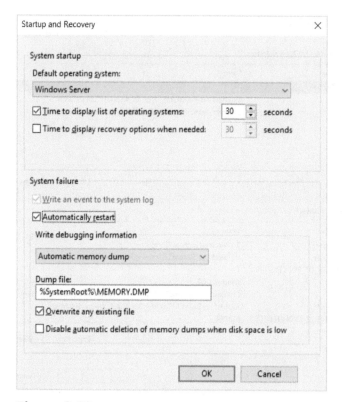

Figure 2-33   Configuring startup and recovery options

 Note

If Windows Server 2019 is installed in a virtual machine, some power options will not be available, such as Require a password on wakeup.

You can configure power options within Control Panel by navigating to Hardware, Power Options from the Category view as shown in Figure 2-34.

Three **power plans** are already created: Balanced, Power saver, and High performance. Each plan consists of a combination of power options including how soon to turn off the display, whether to require a password on wakeup, how soon to turn off the storage devices, sleep/hibernate settings, USB settings, PCI card settings, and processor settings. The Balanced setting offers equal emphasis to energy savings and performance. Power saver favors energy savings over performance, and High performance favors performance over energy savings. For example, with the Balanced and High performance

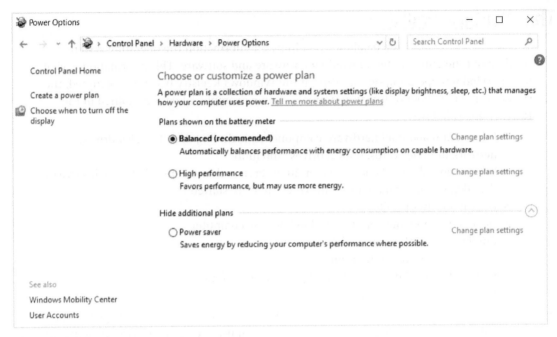

Figure 2-34   Configuring power options

plans, the hard disk and SSD drives are never turned off. However, with the Power saver plan, the hard disk and SSD drives are turned off after 20 minutes of inactivity. Moreover, the processor activity state is set higher (more activity) for the High performance plan than it is for balanced or power saver.

Clicking Change plan settings next to an existing power plan in Figure 2-34 will allow you to change the default settings. However, it is good form to keep the default settings and click Create a power plan to create and use a custom power plan with the settings for your specific server. The option to choose when to turn off the display enables you to turn off the display after a specific period of inactivity, in minutes or hours, or to set the display to never turn off. Because most servers are stored on a rack and connected to a shared KVM switch, it is safe to leave the display on, because most KVM switches require the selection of a server on the KVM switch before the display is activated.

Note

If you install Windows Server 2019 directly on the hardware, you will also see a power option that allows you to choose what happens when the power button is pressed (shut down, hibernate, or do nothing).

The Windows Registry

The **Windows Registry** is a database containing all information the operating system needs about the entire system, including hardware and software. This information is vital for the Windows operating system; thus, if the Windows Registry becomes corrupted, the system may fail to boot or function normally. Some examples of data contained in the Registry are as follows:

- Information about all hardware components, including the CPU, disk drives, network interface cards, optical drives, and more
- Information about Windows Server 2019 services that are installed, which services they depend on, and the order in which they are started
- Data about user profiles
- Data on the previous settings used to boot the computer
- Configuration information about all software in use
- Software licensing information
- Server Manager and Control Panel parameter configurations

When using the Internet to research a potential fix for an application-, service- or Windows Server 2019–related problem, you will often find a solution that requires that you modify the Windows Registry. To do this, you can use the `regedit` command within the Start menu, Run dialog box, Command Prompt or PowerShell window to launch the **Registry Editor** shown in Figure 2-35.

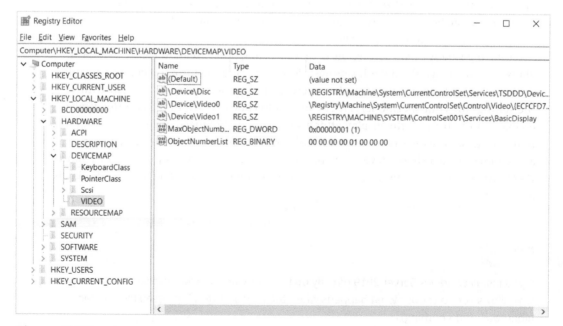

Figure 2-35   The Registry Editor

Making incorrect changes to the Registry can have profound consequences for, and possibly disable, your operating system. As a result, you should always ensure that you back up the Windows Registry before modifying it. To back up the Windows Registry, you can select Computer within the Registry Editor, and then choose Export from the File menu and specify a file name to save to.

Windows Registry Contents

As shown in Figure 2-35, the Windows Registry is hierarchical in structure and is made up of keys, subkeys, and entries:

- **Key**—A folder that appears in the left pane of the Registry Editor and can contain subkeys and entries, for example, HKEY_CURRENT_USER.
- **Subkey**—A part of the Windows Registry that is below a key. A subkey can contain entries or other subkeys.
- **Entry**—An item that appears in the details pane and is the lowest level in the Windows Registry. An entry consists of an entry name, its data type, and its value.

A key is a category or division of information within the Windows Registry. A single key may contain one or more lower-level keys called subkeys, just as a folder may contain several subfolders. An entry is a data parameter associated with a software or hardware characteristic under a key (or subkey). An entry consists of three parts—a name, the data type, and the configuration parameter. For example, in ErrorControl:REG_DWORD:0, ErrorControl is the name, REG_DWORD is the data type, and 0 is the parameter setting. In this entry, the option to track errors is turned off if the parameter is 0, and error tracking is turned on if the value is 1. Entries can have different data formats: DWORD (32 bit) and QWORD (64 bit) are hexadecimal, string (including multistring and expandable string) contains text data, and binary is two hexadecimal values.

The Windows Server 2019 Registry is made up of five root keys:

- HKEY_LOCAL_MACHINE
- HKEY_CURRENT_USER
- HKEY_USERS
- HKEY_CLASSES_ROOT
- HKEY_CURRENT_CONFIG

A root key, also called a subtree, is a primary or highest level category of data contained in the Windows Registry. It might be compared with a main folder, such as the C:\ folder, which is at the root level of folders on C drive. All root keys start with HKEY to show they are the highest level key.

HKEY_LOCAL_MACHINE

Information on every hardware component in the server is provided under the HKEY_LOCAL_MACHINE root key. This includes information about what drivers are loaded and their version levels, what IRQ (interrupt request) lines are used, setup configurations, the BIOS version, and more. Figure 2-35 shows HKEY_LOCAL_MACHINE expanded to display information about video settings.

Under each root key are subkeys, which are BCD00000000, HARDWARE, SAM, SECURITY, SOFTWARE, and SYSTEM for the root key shown in Figure 2-35. Each subkey may have subkeys under it, such as ACPI, DESCRIPTION, DEVICEMAP, and RESOURCEMAP under the HARDWARE subkey shown in Figure 2-35.

A few subkeys are stored as a set, called hives, because they hold related information. This is true for the SOFTWARE subkey, which holds information about installed software.

HKEY_CURRENT_USER

The HKEY_CURRENT_USER key contains profile information about the desktop configuration for the user account currently signed in to the system, as opposed to the HKEY_USERS key, which contains profile settings for all users who have signed in to the server. It contains data on color combinations, font sizes and type, the keyboard layout, the taskbar, clock configuration, and nearly any setup action you have made on the desktop. For example, if you want to change the environment parameter governing where temporary files are stored for applications, you could do it from here. The new path is set by clicking the Environment subkey under the HKEY_CURRENT_USER root key and changing the path shown as the value in the right pane. The sounds associated with a given event can be set by clicking the path \HKEY_CURRENT_USER\AppEvents\ EventLabels and then changing the sound value for a particular event, such as the event to close a window, which is a single value in the Close subkey (\HKEY_CURRENT_USER\ AppEvents\EventLabels\Close).

Another example is to change the delay in the response of the keyboard. For example, if the KeyboardDelay data value under \HKEY_CURRENT_USER\Control Panel\ Keyboard\ is 0, this means there is minimum delay. You could slow down the response a little by setting the delay to 1. This has the same effect as going into Control Panel in Classic View (Large or Small icons), clicking Keyboard, and setting the Repeat delay slider bar one notch to the left of the Short setting.

HKEY_USERS

The HKEY_USERS root key contains profile information for each user who has signed in to the computer. Each profile is listed under this root key. Within each user profile is information identical to that viewed within the HKEY_CURRENT_USER root key. The profile used when you are signed in is one of the profiles stored under HKEY_USERS. You can make the same changes just examined by finding the subkey for your profile and making the changes here instead of under the HKEY_CURRENT_USER root key.

HKEY_CLASSES_ROOT

The HKEY_CLASSES_ROOT key holds data to associate file extensions with programs. This is a more extensive list than the one viewed under HKEY_CURRENT_USER. Associations exist for executable files, text files, graphics files, clipboard files, audio files, and many more. These associations are used as defaults for all users who sign in to Windows Server 2019, whereas the associations in HKEY_CURRENT_USER and HKEY_ USERS are those that have been customized for a given user profile.

HKEY_CURRENT_CONFIG

The last root key, HKEY_CURRENT_CONFIG, has information about the current hardware profile. It holds information about the monitor type, keyboard, mouse, and other hardware characteristics for the current profile. On most servers, there is only one default hardware profile set up. Two or more profiles could be used, but this is more common for a portable computer running Windows 10 that is used with and without a docking station. One profile would have the keyboard and monitor used when on the road, and another would have a larger keyboard and monitor used when the computer is docked.

Using Windows PowerShell

Recall from Module 1 that Windows PowerShell is a modern replacement for the MS-DOS shell, used since the first Microsoft operating system, that provides advanced system configuration and scripting features. In this section, we'll examine how to work with Windows PowerShell, some key commands you can use to perform system administration, how to query system information using WMI, as well as the creation and usage of PowerShell scripts.

Working with Windows PowerShell

After you start Windows PowerShell, you are placed in your home directory on the system and given a PS prompt, where you can type cmdlets as shown earlier in Figure 1-9. If you log into a Windows Server 2019 system as Administrator, you will receive the following prompt:

```
PS C:\Users\Administrator>
```

Note

To perform administrative tasks using PowerShell, ensure that you right-click the Windows PowerShell icon on the Start menu and choose More, Run as administrator. Alternatively, you can right-click the Start menu and choose Windows PowerShell (Admin).

Windows PowerShell can be used to execute most MS-DOS commands, as well as many UNIX/Linux commands. For example, you could run the following MS-DOS command to copy the Windows Calculator executable to the root of C:\:

```
PS C:\Users\Administrator>copy C:\Windows\System32\calc.exe C:\
```

You can also use MS-DOS shell features such as **output redirection** (>>) and **command chaining** (;). For example, you could run the following to save the output of the `ipconfig` command to a file called C:\IPconfig.txt, and then clear the screen using the `cls` command:

```
PS C:\Users\Administrator>ipconfig >> C:\IPconfig.txt ; cls
```

However, most commands that you run within PowerShell will consist of cmdlets that have a specific format describing the function of the cmdlet as well as the object or item that it operates on. In other words, each cmdlet has an action-object or verb-noun structure. For example, when you type `Get-Host` within PowerShell, you "get" (verb) information about your "host" computer (noun).

Note

Cmdlets are case-insensitive, so Get-Host and get-host are equivalent.

Other examples of common cmdlets include `Get-Process`, `Set-Date`, and `Write-Error`. Because cmdlets use descriptive verbs and nouns, you can easily understand their purpose from reading their names. To see a list of all cmdlets within Windows PowerShell, you could run the following command:

```
PS C:\Users\Administrator>Get-Command | more
```

The pipe symbol (|) shown in the previous output sends the results of the `Get-Command` cmdlet to the MS-DOS `more` command within PowerShell. The `more` command then displays the output page-by-page, because the output is too large to fit on one page. Administrators use the pipe symbol extensively within Windows PowerShell as it is one of the most useful ways of sending information between cmdlets to build more complex commands or filter output to display only the output that they wish to see. This process is called **piping**.

Note

You can use multiple pipe symbols within a single Windows PowerShell command to send the output of each cmdlet to another cmdlet or MS-DOS command.

Cmdlets may also have several options available to control their execution as well as accept various arguments that indicate the objects that they need to process. For example, the following command lists all processes on the system:

```
PS C:\Users\Administrator>Get-Process | more
```

You can use the `Get-Help` cmdlet (or simply `help`, which is a shortcut to `Get-Help`) to list the usage of the `Get-Process` cmdlet (including available options and arguments) by running the following command:

```
PS C:\Users\Administrator>help Get-Process
```

To get a full listing of the usage for the Get-Process cmdlet, you could instead run the command `help Get-Process -full`. Alternatively, to get a full help page as well as usage examples, you could run the command `help Get-Process -online`, which will open the help page from Microsoft in your default Web browser. At the bottom of this online help screen, you will notice the names of related cmdlets in a RELATED LINKS section. For example, in the RELATED LINKS section of the `Get-Process` cmdlet, you will notice a reference to the `Stop-Process` cmdlet (which can be used to kill a running process). You can then run the command `help Stop-Process` to get usage information for the `Stop-Process` cmdlet and note that it accepts a process ID (PID) using the `-id` option, or a process name using the `-name` option for the process that you would like to stop. You can view the process ID or process name you would like to stop using the `Get-Process` cmdlet.

Many cmdlets also support the use of the `-whatif` and `-confirm` options to control execution. The `-whatif` option can test to see what would happen if the cmdlet was executed (if there are no errors it would run successfully), and the `-confirm` can be used to prompt you to confirm the execution. Following are some other common options available to most PowerShell cmdlets:

- `-verbose` provides more detail.
- `-debug` provides debugging information.
- `-erroraction` instructs a cmdlet to perform an action, such as continue, stop, silently continue, and inquire, when errors occur.

If you are not sure which cmdlet you would like to use, you can use your knowledge of the verb-noun structure of PowerShell to search for the right one. The easiest way to do this is by using the `Get-Command` cmdlet introduced earlier. For example, the following two commands can be used to display all cmdlets that have a verb that starts with set, and all cmdlets that have a noun that starts with mem:

```
PS C:\Users\Administrator>Get-Command -verb set*
PS C:\Users\Administrator>Get-Command -noun mem*
```

Like `Get-Help`, the `Get-Command` cmdlet can also be used to obtain information on the use of a cmdlet. For example, the `Get-Command -syntax Get-Process` command will return the usage information for the `Get-Process` cmdlet.

PowerShell also supports special navigation keys and key combinations, including:

- Up Arrow/Down Arrow—Cycles through command history
- Home/End—Jumps to the beginning or end of the command line
- Q/q—Quits an interactive command to return to the PowerShell prompt

- Ctrl+LeftArrow/Ctrl+RightArrow—Navigates left/right one word at a time
- Tab–Auto-completes cmdlet and cmdlet options, much like the Tab completion feature available within the MS-DOS, UNIX, and Linux command prompts

Windows PowerShell also has several different features that provide for additional functionality or allow you to be more efficient. For example, you can:

- Customize your Windows PowerShell session
- Use aliases and functions to simplify commands
- Use PowerShell profile scripts to automatically execute commands
- Modify command output to make results easier to read
- Use PowerShell objects to view and manipulate items
- Use PowerShell providers to work with different areas of your system

In the following sections, we'll examine these additional aspects of Windows PowerShell.

Customizing Windows PowerShell Sessions

There may be times when you need to change how your Windows PowerShell session looks or how it is executed to suit your needs or personal preferences.

For example, if you start PowerShell using the `powershell` command, you can provide specific options to the PowerShell executable to control its execution. For example, running `powershell -nologo` will start a Windows PowerShell session without displaying the initial information banner, whereas `powershell -command "&{Get-Process}"` will start a temporary Windows PowerShell session to run the `Get-Process` cmdlet and quit afterwards.

You can also create a customized Windows PowerShell session by creating a **PowerShell console file** that has a `.psc1` extension. You can then double-click this PowerShell console file to open Windows PowerShell. Any changes that you make within the PowerShell Window properties, such as color scheme and font size, are saved to the PowerShell console file and automatically loaded the next time that you double-click the PowerShell console file to open Windows PowerShell. To create a Windows PowerShell console file in your current directory called CustomPowerShell.psc1, you can run the following command:

```
PS C:\Users\Administrator>export-console CustomPowerShell.psc1
```

Aliases and Functions

Windows PowerShell can use UNIX/Linux-style command **aliases**, which are essentially shortcuts to commands. To view all aliases on your system, sorted alphabetically, you can run the following command:

```
PS C:\Users\Administrator>Get-Alias | more
```

Aliases make navigating and using Windows PowerShell easier. For example, when you run the `dir` command in PowerShell, you are actually running an alias to the

`Get-ChildItem` cmdlet, which displays the objects (files and subdirectories) within your current directory on the filesystem by default. Similarly, when you run the `cd` command within PowerShell, you are actually running an alias to the `Set-Location` cmdlet within PowerShell, which changes the directory location on the filesystem by default.

Most Windows users find `dir` and `cd` much easier than their Windows PowerShell counterparts. However, the `Get-ChildItem` cmdlet can also be used to view other objects on the system such as registry keys or certificates. Similarly, the `Set-Location` cmdlet can be used to tell Windows PowerShell to switch from using the filesystem to the Windows Registry or the **Certificate Store** for the current user account.

Note

Switching to other areas of the system within Windows PowerShell is discussed in the next section.

Cmdlets may have several aliases attached to them. For example, the `Get-ChildItem` cmdlet has an alias of `dir` and `gci` and the `Set-Location` cmdlet has an alias of `cd` and `sl`. To view the cmdlet that the sl alias points to, you could run the following command within Windows PowerShell:

```
PS C:\Users\Administrator>Get-Alias sl
```

To create an alias, you can use the `Set-Alias` cmdlet followed by the alias name and the cmdlet that the alias points to. For example, the following example creates an alias called lala that runs the Get-Process cmdlet:

```
PS C:\Users\Administrator>Set-Alias lala Get-Process
```

If you would like to execute multiple cmdlets, you can instead use **functions**. For example, the following example creates a function called c that displays the message "About to clear screen", pauses for 2 seconds, and then clears the screen:

```
PS C:\Users\Administrator>function c {Write-Host "About to
clear screen"; Start-Sleep -s 2; Clear-Host}
```

PowerShell Profile Scripts

Both aliases and functions are essentially **variables**, which are areas of storage within memory in your current Windows PowerShell session. When you exit Windows PowerShell, any aliases and functions that you have created are destroyed.

If you would like to make aliases and functions load into memory each time that you start a PowerShell session, place your alias and function commands within a **PowerShell profile script** for your Windows user account. PowerShell profile scripts are PowerShell scripts that store custom aliases, functions, and any other commands that you want to automatically execute every time you start Windows PowerShell. They are stored within the Documents folder under your Windows profile directory in a file called Microsoft.PowerShell_profile.ps1. For the user bob, this would be:

C:\Users\bob\Documents\WindowsPowerShell\Microsoft.PowerShell_profile.ps1. You can reference your PowerShell profile file at any time using the $profile variable.

Note 📎

Don't confuse PowerShell console files (*.psc1) with PowerShell scripts (*.ps1). PowerShell console files are shortcuts to a customized Windows PowerShell session, whereas PowerShell scripts contain executable Windows PowerShell commands that are run automatically.

By default, no profiles are configured. To see if you have a PowerShell profile, you can use the Test-Path $profile command.

Because a PowerShell profile script is an executable script that runs when you open PowerShell, you must first enable script execution before making the script using the Set-ExecutionPolicy unrestricted command in a Windows PowerShell window that is run as Administrator (Set-ExecutionPolicy will be discussed again later in this module). Next, you can create a new PowerShell profile using the following command:

```
PS C:\Users\Administrator>New-Item -path $profile -itemtype
file -force
```

Finally, you can edit your new PowerShell profile using the command notepad $profile within PowerShell and add any aliases, functions, or other commands that you would like to run each time you open PowerShell.

Modifying Command Output

Many cmdlets such as Get-ChildItem (alias gci), show information regarding the objects (e.g., files, certificates, registry keys, processes) on your system. Quite often, this information needs to be expanded, modified, or reduced to a form that is easy to interpret. There are many ways to modify command output to achieve these actions:

- Pipe output to Format-Table (alias ft), Format-Wide (or fw), Format-List (or fl), or Out-GridView (or ogv).
- Use -recurse option to perform a recursive search (which includes all subfolders or subordinate objects recursively throughout the system).
- Use Sort-Object (alias sort) to sort results.
- Use Group-Object to format output information based on common groups or categories within the output.

- Use `ConvertTo-HTML` to write output in HTML format (to save it to a file, you can use output redirection or pipe the results to the `Out-File` cmdlet).
- Use `Export-CSV` to write output to a comma-separated value file (which can easily be imported into spreadsheet programs such as Microsoft Excel).

Note

The default format for cmdlets within Windows PowerShell is `Format-Table` unless otherwise specified.

For example, to format the output of the `Get-Process` cmdlet using a graphical grid view (`Out-GridView`, or `ogv`), you could use the following command within Windows PowerShell:

```
PS C:\Users\Administrator>Get-Process | ogv
```

PowerShell Objects

Everything in Windows PowerShell can be treated as an **object** that has **attributes** (properties that describe the object) and **methods** (things that the object can do). This is a very powerful feature of Windows PowerShell that can be used to control nearly all aspects of the Windows operating system including processes, files, and network sockets.

You can use the `Get-Member` cmdlet (alias `gm`) to view these attributes and methods. However, the `Get-Member` cmdlet expects to be passed an object to work with. The easiest way to pass an object to Get-Member is to use another cmdlet to view it and send the output to the `Get-Member` cmdlet using a pipe. Information that is passed from one cmdlet to another via a pipe is automatically converted to an object.

For example, to view the attributes and methods for a file called C:\sample.jpg, you could use the following command within Windows PowerShell (`more` is used because there will be several pages of output):

```
PS C:\Users\Administrator>gci c:\sample.jpg | gm | more
```

Another way to create an object is by enclosing an existing Windows PowerShell command within parentheses. For example, you could instead use the following command to view the attributes and methods for the C:\sample.jpg file:

```
PS C:\Users\Administrator>gm –inputobject (gci c:\sample.jpg) |
more
```

You can also create new objects within Windows PowerShell. These objects can be created as references to anything on the system, such as an area of memory, a function, or even a program or service running on the system. Take the following Windows PowerShell command as an example:

```
PS C:\Users\Administrator>$a = new-object -comobject "wscript.
shell"
```

This command creates a variable ($a) that contains a reference to a copy of the wscript.shell object within the Windows **Component Object Model (COM)**. You can think of $a as a variable that contains a Windows shell object.

Now, you can view the attributes and methods available for this object using the following command to send the object to the Get-Member cmdlet (more is used because there will be several pages of output):

```
PS C:\Users\Administrator>$a | gm | more
```

The attributes listed tell you about your Windows shell object. For example, you can use the expandedenvironmentstrings attribute to list variables that the Windows shell object will use. To list an attribute, use the syntax object.attribute. For example, to see the Windows path variable, you could execute the following command:

```
PS C:\Users\Administrator>$a.expandenvironmentstrings("%path%")
```

The methods tell you what you can do with your object. One of those methods available for $a is called run, which can be used to run an executable supplied as an argument. To have your Windows shell object start the Windows calculator (calc.exe), you can execute the following command:

```
PS C:\Users\Administrator>$a.run("calc.exe")
```

After executing calc.exe, PowerShell will display the number 0 in the PowerShell window. This is called the **exit status** and a 0 (zero) exit status means that calc.exe was successfully executed (non-zero numbers denote error messages).

Because everything in PowerShell can be treated as an object, objects are extremely useful for administration. You can easily treat a file or directory (a list of files) as an object and obtain or modify valuable information about them on the system. For example, if you run the gci | gm | more command, you will notice that files have a LastWriteTime attribute. Say that early this morning an accounting database program placed many large files on the file server that are using up too much space. If you wanted to get a listing of the files that were added since yesterday, you could use the following command within Windows PowerShell (assuming yesterday was 01/02/2020):

```
PS C:\Users\Administrator>gci -Path C:\ -Recurse | Where-Object
{$_.LastWriteTime -gt "01/02/2020"}
```

The gci -Path C:\ -Recurse command generates a list of files recursively (in all subdirectories) underneath C:\. This list of files (objects) is sent over the pipe to the Where-Object {$_.LastWriteTime -gt "01/02/2020"} command that only displays items (objects) that have an attribute of LastWriteTime that is greater than (-gt) 01/02/2020.

> **Note** 📎
>
> The $_ is a placeholder that references each object (file) that was sent over the pipe. This allows the command on the right side of the pipe to individually process objects. In the previous example, it processes files to see if the LastWriteTime is greater than 01/02/2020.

PowerShell Providers

PowerShell providers are PowerShell plug-ins that provide functionality within Windows PowerShell (e.g., aliases, functions, variables) or allow PowerShell to interact with other parts of the system (e.g., registry, filesystem, environment variables, certificates). The **filesystem provider** is the default provider, which is why you see PS C:\Users\Administrator> as your prompt when you start PowerShell. You can use the filesystem provider to view and manage the files on your filesystem.

The **variable provider** and **environment provider** are used to view and manage variables. The variable provider works with user-defined variables that exist within your Windows PowerShell session only. Variables created by the variable provider are only valid during the time that your PowerShell window is open. When working with the variable provider, you can use the Get-Variable cmdlet to view existing user-defined variables, or the New-Variable and Set-Variable cmdlets to create them and assign them values. You can also use the Remove-Variable cmdlet to remove user-defined variables.

The environment provider works with environment variables (shown earlier in Figure 2-32) that are normally set within the Windows operating system. When working with the environment provider, you can use Get-ChildItem (alias gci) or Get-Item (alias gi) to obtain information about the environment variables on your Windows system as well as the New-Item, Rename-Item, and Remove-Item cmdlets to create, rename, and remove them, respectively.

The **alias provider** can be used to view and manage aliases, and the **function provider** can be used to view and manage functions within Windows PowerShell. Because you can also manage aliases and functions using the cmdlets discussed earlier in this module, there is no need to use these providers directly. However, if you need additional flexibility when searching for or managing aliases and functions, changing to these providers can be useful.

The **certificate provider** can be used to view and manage encryption certificates issued to user accounts on the system as well as on the local computer. The **registry provider** can be used to view and modify the Windows Registry keys HKEY_LOCAL_MACHINE and HKEY_CURRENT_USER.

You can use Get-PSProvider or Get-PSDrive (alias gdr) to see the available PowerShell providers and Set-Location (alias sl) to change your current PowerShell provider. For example, to switch to the alias provider and view the aliases on the system, you could run the following two commands (note that the Windows PowerShell prompt changes to your current PowerShell provider):

```
PS C:\Users\Administrator>sl alias:\
PS Alias:\>gci | more
```

Although PowerShell providers support different cmdlets within Windows PowerShell, many of the common cmdlets are available in all PowerShell providers, as summarized in Table 2-1.

Table 2-1	Cmdlets that can be used with any PowerShell provider			
Cmdlet	**Alias**	**DOS**	**UNIX/Linux**	**Description**
Get-Location	gl,pwd	pwd	ls	Display current directory/location
Set-Location	sl,cd,chdir	cd,chdir	cd	Change current directory/location
Copy-Item	cpi,copy,cp	copy	cp	Copy files/items from one location to another
Remove-Item	ri,del	del	rm	Remove file/item
Move-Item	mi,move,mv	move	mv	Move file/item
Rename-Item	ren,rni	rn	mv	Rename file/item
New-Item	ni			Create new file/item
Clear-Item	cli			Clears the contents of a file/item
Set-Item	si			Sets the contents of a file/item
Get-Content	gc,type,cat	type	cat	Views the contents of a file/item

System Administration Commands

So far, we have seen how PowerShell Providers can provide useful ways of interacting with our system. However, there are some key PowerShell cmdlets and commands that administrators often use to manage Windows Server 2019. For example, it's much easier to reboot a computer by opening Windows PowerShell and typing `Restart-Computer`. Similarly, it's much easier to power down a computer within Windows PowerShell by typing `Stop-Computer` (or `Stop-` followed by the Tab key to autocomplete the cmdlet).

Many of the post-installation tasks that you examined within Module 1 can be performed easily using Windows PowerShell. For example, you can use `Rename-Computer` *newcomputername* to rename a computer, or `Add-Computer -DomainName` *domainname* to join it to an Active Directory domain following installation.

Windows PowerShell can also be used to view, install, and remove Windows roles and features. For example, `Get-WindowsFeature | ogv` will display installed and available roles and features, including the service name for each one. If the IIS Web server (service name = web-server) is not installed, you can use the following command to install it within Windows PowerShell:

```
PS C:\Users\Administrator>Install-WindowsFeature
-IncludeAllSubfeature -IncludeManagementTools web-server
```

Alternatively, you could use the following command within Windows PowerShell to remove the IIS Web server if it is installed:

```
PS C:\Users\Administrator>Remove-WindowsFeature web-server
```

> **Note** 📎
>
> You can also use the `Get-Hotfix | ogv` command within Windows PowerShell to view installed updates. This is often useful when troubleshooting a problem caused by a recently applied update.

Windows PowerShell can also be used to configure and troubleshoot the network. Perhaps the most useful cmdlet is `Test-NetConnection` (which tests a connection to a Microsoft server on the Internet) to identify problems with IP configuration, firewall configuration, and name resolution. You can optionally specify a host name (e.g., triosdevelopers.com) and port (e.g., 443 for HTTPS), as well as use it to trace the route a packet takes through routers to get to the destination, as shown in the following two examples, respectively:

```
PS C:\Users\Administrator>Test-NetConnection triosdevelopers
.com -Port 443
PS C:\Users\Administrator>Test-NetConnection triosdevelopers
.com -Traceroute
```

Additionally, you can use the `Get-NetIPConfiguration`, `Get-NetAdapter`, and `Get-NetAdapterStatistics` cmdlets to obtain information about your IP configuration, network interfaces, and network statistics, respectively. To configure a network interface called Ethernet with an IPv4 address of 192.168.1.50, 24-bit subnet mask, default gateway of 192.168.1.1, and preferred DNS server of 8.8.8.8, you could run the following commands within Windows PowerShell:

```
PS C:\Users\Administrator>New-NetIPAddress -InterfaceAlias
Ethernet -IPAddress 192.168.1.50 -PrefixLength 24
-DefaultGateway 192.168.1.1
```

```
PS C:\Users\Administrator>Set-DNSClientServerAddress
-InterfaceAlias Ethernet -ServerAddresses 8.8.8.8
```

You can also use Windows PowerShell to configure firewall settings. To disable the firewall for the domain, public, and private profiles, you could run the following command within Windows PowerShell.

```
PS C:\Users\Administrator>Set-NetFirewallProfile -profile
domain,public,private -Enabled false
```

Alternatively, you could configure an exception within the firewall (current profile) to allow inbound traffic on port 80 (TCP) using the following command within Windows PowerShell:

```
PS C:\Users\Administrator>New-NetFirewallRule -DisplayName
"Allow Inbound 80 TCP" -Direction Inbound -Localport 80
-Protocol TCP -Action Allow
```

Managing services and processes is also frequently performed using Windows PowerShell. For example, Get-Service | ogv can be used to list the services on the system (including their service name) and whether they are running or not. To stop, start, or restart the DNS cache service (service name = dnscache), you could then use the Stop-Service dnscache, Start-Service dnscache, or Restart-Service dnscache command, respectively. To ensure that the DNS cache service starts automatically at boot time, you could configure the properties of the service using the following Windows PowerShell command:

```
PS C:\Users\Administrator>Set-Service dnscache -StartupType
Automatic
```

Managing running processes is important when solving performance issues. For example, if your Windows Server 2019 system is running slow, you could use the following Windows PowerShell command to locate the top five processes consuming processor time:

```
PS C:\Users\Administrator>ps | sort -property cpu | select
-last 5
```

If the output shown indicates that the process called iexplore is consuming too many processor resources, you could then use the Stop-Process -name iexplore command within Windows PowerShell to stop it.

Another important feature of Windows PowerShell is that it can be used to perform remote administration of computers within a domain environment. If you log into a system as a user that has domain administrative privileges, you can use Windows PowerShell to view and manage any computer that is joined to the domain.

Some cmdlets allow you to specify the computer name that you wish to perform a particular task on. For example, to restart the computer called TO-FS-03.lala.com, you could run the following Windows PowerShell command from any computer within the domain while logged in as a user with domain administrative privileges:

```
PS C:\Users\Administrator>Restart-Computer -Force -ComputerName
TO-FS-03.lala.com
```

If you wish to run multiple Windows PowerShell commands on a remote system, you can instead obtain a PowerShell session on the remote computer. For example, the following command will open a remote PowerShell session to the computer TO-FS-03.lala.com:

```
PS C:\Users\Administrator>Enter-PSSession TO-FS-03.lala.com
```

When finished performing the remote administration tasks on TO-FS-03.lala.com, you can run the exit command to return to your local Windows PowerShell session.

Moreover, if you create a PowerShell script (discussed in the next section), you can also execute that script on several computers within your domain. For example, to run the C:\script1.ps1 PowerShell script on TO-FS-01.lala.com and TO-FS-02.lala.com, you could run the following command from any computer within the domain while logged in as a user with domain administrative privileges:

```
PS C:\Users\Administrator>Invoke-Command -Computername
TO-FS-01.lala.com, TO-FS-02.lala.com -Filepath C:\script.ps1
```

> **Note** 📎
>
> Remote management with Windows PowerShell requires that the **winRM** component is enabled (the default on Windows Server systems). If winRM is not enabled, you could run winrm -quickconfig from a Command Prompt window, or Set-Service winrm -StartupType automatic ; Enable-PSRemoting -Force from a Windows PowerShell session as Administrator.

Using WMI within Windows PowerShell

Starting with Windows NT 4.0, Microsoft introduced an interface called Windows Management Instrumentation (WMI) that allowed programs and system software to query the hardware and software on the Windows computer. The programs and system software that can query WMI are called **WMI consumers**, and the components that are built into the operating system that respond to WMI queries are collectively called the **WMI infrastructure**.

Windows PowerShell is a WMI consumer that has built-in support for querying WMI. As a result, it is frequently used to obtain system information within Windows

PowerShell. However, before you learn how to query WMI, you must first learn about the structure and nomenclature used to navigate the WMI infrastructure components. The WMI infrastructure consists of three components that work together:

- WMI namespaces
- WMI providers
- WMI classes

WMI namespaces represent/organize different types of WMI data in much the same way that a file cabinet organizes files. There are different namespaces for different purposes, and each namespace holds different WMI providers. The only namespace that is useful to IT administrators within Windows PowerShell is the CIMv2 namespace (Common Information Model version 2), which can query the hardware and software components on systems as well as modify software components as necessary.

WMI providers are like the drawers in a file cabinet. Each provider contains different WMI classes that can be used to obtain/modify different hardware and software information on your system.

WMI classes are individual types of data and are like the files in each drawer of a filing cabinet. It is these classes that we can use within Windows PowerShell to work with different pieces of hardware and software.

The real power of WMI is within the WMI classes that you can query and manipulate. The best way to do this is to run the `Get-WmiObject` (alias `gwmi`) cmdlet with the `–list` option (most of them start with Win32_). You can also use `Get-WmiObject` to query and manipulate WMI classes. For example, the following Windows PowerShell command queries the win32_bios class in the CIMv2 namespace on the local computer ("."):

```
PS C:\Users\Administrator>gwmi –class win32_bios –computer "."
–namespace "root\cimv2"
```

Windows PowerShell has default values for the –computer and –namespace options if you do not supply them. By default, PowerShell assumes the local computer and the CIMv2 namespace. So, the following Windows PowerShell command is equivalent to the previous one:

```
PS C:\Users\Administrator>gwmi win32_bios
```

Instead of specifying the WMI class alongside the `Get-WmiObject` cmdlet, you can instead create a WMI query statement and specify it using the –query option. WMI query statements use a SQL database language called **WQL (WMI Query Language)**. For example, the following command within Windows PowerShell will select all attributes/methods (*) from the win32_share class as shown below:

```
PS C:\Users\Administrator>gwmi –query "select * from
win32_share"
```

Creating PowerShell Scripts

PowerShell scripts are simply text files with a `.ps1` extension that can be executed within Windows PowerShell. Like MS-DOS batch files, the commands within a PowerShell script are executed from top-to-bottom. However, PowerShell scripts can contain both Windows commands and PowerShell cmdlets, as well as complex control structures. PowerShell scripts allow you to do more with Windows PowerShell, including the ability to reuse Windows PowerShell code in different situations, because arguments to the script can be used to accept input that changes how the script works.

In this section, we'll examine how to execute PowerShell scripts as well as use Windows PowerShell ISE to create and test PowerShell scripts. Additionally, we'll learn how to use Windows PowerShell features that are frequently used within PowerShell scripts, including the use of variables and constants, protecting metacharacters, coloring and formatting output, and the use of decision and loop constructs. Finally, we'll discuss some tips that will help you create your own PowerShell scripts as well as locate and reuse PowerShell scripts that are available on the Internet.

Executing PowerShell Scripts

Before you are able to run PowerShell scripts, you must first enable script support in Windows PowerShell (we did this earlier with `Set-ExecutionPolicy unrestricted` as your PowerShell profile is also a script). To see what your current execution policy is, simply run the `Get-ExecutionPolicy` cmdlet. There are five different execution policies that can be set on a Windows system:

- *Restricted* will not run any scripts (script execution is disabled).
- *AllSigned* only runs scripts that are signed by a trusted publisher.
- *RemoteSigned* allows you to run scripts that are downloaded from the Internet only if they are signed by a trusted publisher.
- *Unrestricted* runs all scripts (scripts downloaded from the Internet will prompt you for confirmation before execution).
- *Bypass* runs all scripts (no warnings).
- *Undefined* indicates that a policy is not set.

To execute a PowerShell script in PowerShell, you must use a full path or a "forced" relative path (where "." refers to the current directory):

- Full path: `C:\scripts\myscript.ps1`
- Relative path (within the C:\scripts directory): `.\myscript.ps1` or `./myscript.ps1`

To execute a PowerShell script outside Windows PowerShell, you can use the `powershell` command in the Windows Run dialog box Command Prompt window, and supply the script path as an argument. For C:\scripts\myscript.ps1, you could execute the following command (`-noexit` prevents Windows PowerShell from closing after executing the script):

```
powershell C:\scripts\myscript.ps1 -noexit
```

Using Windows PowerShell ISE

Windows Server 2019 also contains a tool that is very useful for creating, testing, and executing scripts called the **Windows PowerShell Integrated Scripting Environment (ISE)**. When you open the Start menu in Windows Server 2019, Windows PowerShell ISE is listed next to Windows PowerShell. By default, Windows PowerShell ISE opens a Windows PowerShell pane on the left and allows you to search for and execute commands using a Commands pane on the right. However, if you click the Script icon above the Windows PowerShell pane, it opens a new PowerShell script in the upper pane called Untitled.ps1, as shown in Figure 2-36.

After adding content to Untitled.ps1 in the upper pane, you can execute it in the lower Windows PowerShell pane by clicking the green Run script (play button) icon or by pressing the F5 key. After you are satisfied with how your script executes, you can navigate to File, Save As, and choose to save it with a more descriptive file name to a location of your choice (e.g., C:\scripts\myscript.ps1).

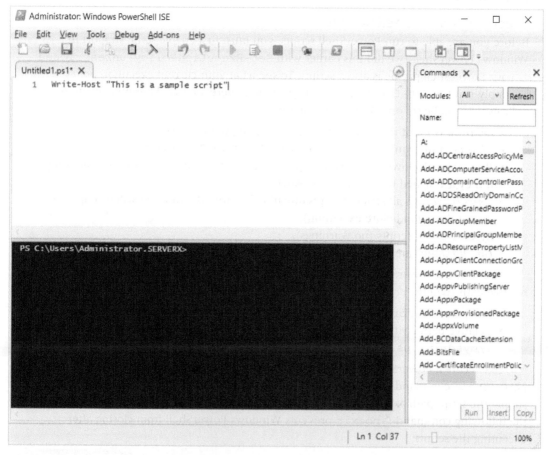

Figure 2-36   **Windows PowerShell ISE**

You can also create and test scripts on remote computers that have winRM started within Windows PowerShell ISE. To do this, navigate to File, New Remote PowerShell Tab and specify the correct computer name. If you are currently logged into an Active Directory domain with domain administrative privileges, you will be allowed to connect to any computer within your domain that has winRM started.

Variables and Constants

Variables and **constants** store a value in memory for later use and are often used within PowerShell scripts. Variables values can be changed after being set, while constant values cannot. Variable names within Windows PowerShell start with $ and are not case sensitive. However, you should avoid using any special characters within a variable name as well as avoid creating variable names that have the same name as reserved keywords within Windows PowerShell (break, continue, do, else, elseif, for, foreach, function, filter, in, if, return, switch, until, where, and while).

Note

To see a complete list of reserved keywords, visit *https://docs.microsoft.com/en-us/powershell/module/microsoft.powershell.core/about/about_reserved_words?view=powershell-6*.

Note

There are many default Windows PowerShell variables that you can use to see information regarding other commands or your system. Visit *https://docs.microsoft.com/en-us/powershell/module/microsoft.powershell.core/about/about_automatic_variables* for a list and description of these variables.

If you type the name of a variable at the PowerShell prompt, it will expand the variable and print its contents for you. For example, if you type $host at a Windows PowerShell prompt, you will see your computer information, as the $host variable contains this information automatically, and the default action in Windows PowerShell on any object (such as a variable) is to display its contents.

Creating variables and assigning values is also very easy within Windows PowerShell. You can use the Set-Variable cmdlet to create variables and set their values. Alternatively, you can create a variable by using the syntax $variablename = value. You can also create an **array variable** that contains multiple values. For example, to create an array variable using three values, you can use the syntax $variablename = value1, value2, value3.

If you want to ensure that the value of the variable cannot be changed after creation, add -option constant to the Set-Variable cmdlet to ensure that it is created as a constant variable. You can also add -option readonly to the Set-Variable cmdlet to ensure that you can't delete the variable.

By default, all information stored within variables and constants in Windows PowerShell are text strings, but this behavior can be changed if you prefix the variable with a **type cast**. For example, [int] $variablename = value will ensure that the value of the variable is treated as a numeric integer (int). By identifying the type of data within the variable using a type cast, you can perform specific operations on the variable using operators. For example, if you use the + operator to add two integer variables together, Windows PowerShell will actually add their values mathematically, rather than combine them into a single text string. Other common mathematical operators that can be used to manipulate integer variables include - (subtract), * (multiply), and / (divide).

The Read-Host cmdlet is quite useful in obtaining information from the user within a PowerShell script. For example, $answer=Read-Host will accept input from the command line and place the output in a new variable called $answer.

Protecting PowerShell Metacharacters

There are several special keyboard characters that have special meaning within Windows PowerShell. We have seen some of these already. For example, the $ refers to variables, the ; can be used to perform command chaining, and the + can be used to combine or add variable contents together. These characters are called **metacharacters**.

There may be times when you do not want Windows PowerShell to interpret the meaning of a metacharacter. In these cases you can protect the metacharacters from being interpreted by PowerShell by using special quote characters:

- Double-quotes (") around text tells Windows PowerShell to treat all characters within (except variables) as a single unit.
- Single-quotes (') can be used instead of double-quotes and protect everything within from special interpretation by Windows PowerShell.
- The back-quote (`) protects only the next character from special interpretation by Windows PowerShell.

Coloring and Formatting Output

When you are writing output to the Windows PowerShell window via a PowerShell script, it is often useful to add different colors to different parts of the output to allow the output to be read easily.

There are many cmdlets that allow you to modify the output color when writing output. For example, the Write-Host cmdlet accepts the -foregroundcolor (or -f) and -backgroundcolor (or -b) options. You must simply supply the name of a color next to these options to change the foreground and background colors respectively.

Similarly, you may wish to print the results of several variables to the Windows PowerShell window using the Write-Host cmdlet. To ensure that the individual pieces of information can be read easily, you can specify a separator character using the

−separator (or −s) option to the Write-Host cmdlet. You can also use special separator characters (called echo **escape characters**) with the −separator option to modify output. These echo escape characters must be preceded by a backquote (`) character. Common escape characters include `n (newline character) and `t (tab character).

Decision Constructs

Decision constructs allow you to modify the flow of your PowerShell script. For example, you may only want a certain part of your PowerShell script to run if there is enough free space on the filesystem, or if the user acknowledges the action. For a decision construct to work, there must be a condition that returns true or false. As a result, we must first explore how to compare data before examining decision constructs.

Comparing Data

It is fairly easy to compare data and return a true or false result within Windows PowerShell. You simply need to use one of several different comparison (Table 2-2) or logical (Table 2-3) operators within a Windows PowerShell command.

Table 2-2 Common comparison operators within Windows PowerShell

Operator	Description
-eq	Equal to (case insensitive if comparing strings)
-ne	Not equal to
-lt	Less than
-gt	Greater than
-ge	Greater than or Equal to
-le	Less than or equal to
-ceq	Equal to (case-sensitive)
-ieq	Equal to (case-insensitive, the default)

Table 2-3 Common logical operators within Windows PowerShell

Operator	Description
-and	And
-or	Or
-not	Not
!	Not

Now that we can compare data, there are two main decision constructs that can be used with a data comparison to modify the flow of your PowerShell script: the if construct, and the switch construct.

The if Construct

The `if` construct uses the following syntax:

```
if   (this returns true)
   {do this}
elseif  (this returns true)
   {do this}
else
   {do this}
```

It is also important to note that `elseif` and `else` statements are optional, and that you can have as many `elseif` statements as you wish. Following is an example that uses the `if` construct:

```
$answer = Read-Host "Would you like to run the analysis?
Yes/No/Quit"
if ($answer -eq "Yes" -or $answer -eq "Y")
      {"Running Analysis - Please Wait"; & C:\analysis.ps1}
elseif($answer -eq "No" -or $answer -eq "N")
   {"Analysis Aborted"}
elseif($answer -eq "Quit" -or $answer -eq "Q")
   {"Quitting Program"; Start-Sleep 2; exit}
else
   {"Invalid Choice - Quitting Program"; Start-Sleep 2; exit}
```

In the first line, the user is prompted to choose whether they wish to run an analysis using the `Read-Host` cmdlet. The result is placed in the $answer variable. Next, an `if` construct is used to alter the flow of the program:

- If the $answer variable contains the string "yes" or "y" (case-insensitive), then it prints "Running Analysis – Please Wait" to the screen and then runs the C:\analysis.ps1 script (the & character tells PowerShell to execute the script within the same memory address space such that it can access all variables and functions from the original script).
- If the $answer variable contains the string "no" or "n" (case-insensitive), then it prints "Analysis Aborted" to the screen and skips to the end of the `if` construct to process the remainder of the script.
- If the $answer variable contains the string "quit" or "q" (case-insensitive), then it prints "Quitting Program" to the screen, waits for 2 seconds (`Start-Sleep 2`) and then quits the script (`exit`).
- If the $answer variable contains anything else, then it prints "Invalid Choice - Quitting Program" to the screen, waits for 2 seconds (`Start-Sleep 2`) and then quits the script (`exit`).

The `switch` Construct

The switch construct uses the following syntax:

```
switch (expression or variable)
{
  value1 {do this}
  value2 {do this}
  value3 {do this}
  default {do this}
}
```

The switch construct simplifies using several elseif statements. Following is an example of using the switch construct to print the meaning of the value that is returned by the win32_processor WMI object ($objCPU) for the architecture of the first logical processor ($objCPU[0].architecture) on the system:

```
$objCPU = get-wmiObject win32_processor
switch ($objCPU[0].architecture)
{
      0 {"This is an x86 architecture"}
      1 {"This is a MIPS architecture"}
      2 {"This is an Alpha architecture"}
      3 {"This is a PowerPC architecture"}
      9 {"This is an x64 architecture"}
default {"This is an alien architecture"}
}
```

Loop Constructs

Another important programming construct that is useful within PowerShell scripts is a **loop construct**. Loop constructs allow you to perform a task several times, such as performing the same operation on each of the files within a particular directory. There are many different types of loop constructs available, including foreach, for, while, do...while, and do...until.

Using `foreach` Loops

ForEach-Object (alias foreach) is the most common loop construct used within a PowerShell script as it works on a predefined list of items. This predefined list (or collection) could come from within the PowerShell script itself via an array variable, from command line arguments on the command line, or from another cmdlet across a pipe. The syntax for a foreach loop is:

```
foreach ($item in $collection) {
do repetitive tasks here
}
```

For example, the following script performs the repetitive tasks within the { } braces for the computers named COMPUTER1, COMPUTER2, and COMPUTER3. More specifically, the first time the loop is run, $i is equal to COMPUTER1, the second time the loop is run, $i is equal to COMPUTER2, and the third time the loop is run, $i is equal to COMPUTER3:

```
$arrayComputers = "COMPUTER1","COMPUTER2","COMPUTER3"
foreach ($i in $arrayComputers){
    Write-Host "Connecting to: " $i ;
    Get-WmiObject -computername $i -class win32_UserAccount |
    Select-Object Name, Domain, Lockout, Disabled |
    Sort-Object -property Name
}
```

During each loop, the script writes "Connecting to: $i" to the screen (the ; denotes the end of a single command), obtains a list of user accounts from the computer using the win32_UserAccount WMI class, pipes that list to the Select-Object cmdlet that obtains the Name, Domain, Lockout, and Disabled properties, and then pipes that information to the Sort-Object cmdlet that sorts the list by the Name attribute. In short, this script displays all of the accounts on COMPUTER1, COMPUTER2, and COMPUTER3 and indicates whether they are locked out or disabled.

However, to make the loop more flexible, you could instead supply a list of computer names as arguments on the command line when executing the PoweShell script (all command line arguments given to a PowerShell script are automatically placed in a special array variable called $args):

```
foreach ($i in $args){
    Write-Host "Connecting to: " $i ;
    Get-WmiObject -computername $i -class win32_UserAccount |
    Select-Object Name, Domain, Lockout, Disabled |
    Sort-Object -property name
}
```

If the script that contained this foreach loop was called C:\myscript.ps1, you could open Windows PowerShell and execute C:\myscript.ps1 COMPUTER1 COMPUTER2 COMPUTER3 to populate the $args array variable with the names of COMPUTER1, COMPUTER2, and COMPUTER3. However, you could later run the same script on COMPUTER4, COMPUTER5, and COMPUTER6 by executing C:\myscript.ps1 COMPUTER4 COMPUTER5 COMPUTER6 at the Windows PowerShell prompt.

Using for Loops

The for construct is similar to foreach, but you define the loop conditions in the argument:

```
for (A; B; C) {
do repetitive tasks here
}
```

- A defines a "counter" variable (e.g., $a=1).
- B specifies the condition that tells us when the loop ends (e.g., when $a reaches the number 10).
- C tells the loop how to increment or decrement the variable after each loop (e.g., after each loop, increment $a by 1).

For example, the following for loop will print the numbers 1 2 3 4 5 to the screen:

```
for ($i=1; $i -le 5; $i++){
  Write-Host $i
}
```

The $i variable is set to 1 at the beginning of the for loop. The loop will keep running while $i is less than or equal to the number 5, and after each loop, the $i variable will be incremented by 1 ($i++).

Note 📎

Incrementing variables using the $i++ syntax has been used by programming languages for decades. The C++ language is named after this useful feature.

Using while, do...while, and do...until Loops

The last three types of loop constructs that we will examine are similar in their syntax and function.

The **while** construct repeats tasks while a certain condition is met:

```
while (this condition remains true) {
do repetitive tasks here
}
```

The do...while construct also repeats tasks while a certain condition is met. Unlike a while construct, a do...while construct is guaranteed to execute at least once as the condition is evaluated at the end of the loop construct rather than at the beginning:

```
do {
repetitive tasks here
} while (this condition remains true)
```

The do...until construct executes until a certain condition is met. Like a do...while construct, it is guaranteed to execute at least once:

```
do {
repetitive tasks here
} until (this condition becomes true)
```

Whether you use a `while`, `do...while`, or `do...until` loop construct is a matter of personal preference. The following example creates a random number generator object (`$random`), and then uses a `do...while` loop construct to display a random number between 1 and 1000 (`$random.Next(1,1000)`) while the value of the $i variable is less than 10:

```
$random = New-Object System.Random
$i=1
do {
    $random.Next(1,1000)
    $i++
} while ($i -le 10)
```

Creating Your Own PowerShell Scripts

Earlier, we examined how to use Windows PowerShell to perform simple administrative tasks using cmdlets and control structures as well as obtain information about hardware and software. On its own, this information is useful in aiding a system administrator, but when placed in a larger script, it can be used to perform several tasks that match the needs of a specific system administrator in a unique environment.

For example, when the following command is executed at a Windows PowerShell prompt, it will display a table that lists specific information regarding the explorer.exe process (Windows Explorer), including:

- The number of file connections (HandleCount)
- The size of the process in virtual memory (VirtualSize)
- The amount of time the process is executing user tasks (UserModeTime)
- The amount of time the process is maintaining itself (KernelModeTime)
- The ID of the process (ProcessID)
- The name of the process (Name)

```
Get-WmiObject win32_process -Filter "name='explorer.exe'" |
Format-Table HandleCount,VirtualSize,UserModeTime,KernelModeTime,
ProcessID,Name
```

The problem with this command is that it is time consuming to type at the PowerShell prompt each time that you wish to use it and much more prone to typographical errors as a result. If you need to list information about the explorer.exe process as part of your system administration job (i.e., because you are troubleshooting an ongoing problem on a Windows 10 client that affects Windows Explorer), then it would be much easier to put the command within a PowerShell script that can be reused again and again. Moreover, you can easily edit the script to change the name of the process used, or use the $args special array variable to accept the name of the process as an argument when running the script.

Say, for example, that you modified the script to accept the $args special array variable as shown below and placed it in a file called C:\scripts\script1.ps1.

```
#
#This script prints process information to the screen for a process
#that is supplied as an argument to the script
#
Get-WmiObject win32_process -Filter "name='$args'" |
Format-Table HandleCount,VirtualSize,UserModeTime,KernelModeTime,
ProcessID,Name
```

The lines that start with a # symbol are **comment** lines; they are effectively ignored during execution, but provide a means for you to document the purpose of your script or any key areas that are difficult to trace. Next, you could execute C:\scripts\script1. ps1 explorer.exe within Windows PowerShell to obtain process information for the explorer.exe process. However, you could instead execute C:\scripts\script1.ps1 winlogon.exe to do the same for the winlogon.exe process. In essence, you have made a complex PowerShell command reusable by ensuring that it is run from a script.

You could instead use the Read-Host cmdlet to obtain the name of the process that should be queried. Say, for example, that you modified your script as shown below and saved it as C:\scripts\script2.ps1.

```
#
#This script prints process information to the screen for a process
#that prompted to supply during script execution
#
$ans=Read-Host "What process would you like to query?"
Get-WmiObject win32_process -Filter "name= '$ans'" |
Format-Table HandleCount,VirtualSize,UserModeTime,KernelModeTime,
ProcessID,Name
```

You could then execute C:\scripts\script2.ps1 within Windows PowerShell to run it and type the name of the process you would like to query when prompted.

Thus, the first step in creating any PowerShell script is to start small. If what you need to do with Windows PowerShell can be accomplished by a single cmdlet (or a few cmdlets), simply add those cmdlets to a PowerShell script that can be run as needed.

Also, ensure that your PowerShell script allows the cmdlets to operate on different objects (e.g., different processes, files, registry keys, etc.) and contains comment lines that describe the function of the script using the techniques shown earlier.

Finding PowerShell Scripts on the Internet

One of the most powerful aspects of computer programming is that you do not need to reinvent the wheel. If you need to perform a task using a PowerShell script, chances are that someone has already created a PowerShell script that will suit your needs, or a PowerShell script that will suit your needs with minor modification.

As an administrator, it is usually not necessary to have an extensive programming background. The focus of the Windows PowerShell sections within this module has been to introduce you to the basic constructs and operation of Windows PowerShell such that you can obtain PowerShell scripts from the Internet and modify them to suit your administrative needs by understanding the basic syntax and function of Windows PowerShell. By this point, you should be able to read and understand most PowerShell scripts on the Internet (a process called **tracing**).

Windows PowerShell can also be used by computer programmers to perform certain tasks that are more difficult to code within other programming languages such as C# or Java. As a result, PowerShell accepts more complex programming constructs that are beyond the scope of this course and require additional programming background in order to understand. Some PowerShell scripts that you will find on the Internet will inevitably contain these advanced constructs and be difficult to trace. It is good practice to avoid using these PowerShell scripts if you feel that you do not grasp their contents and instead look for PowerShell scripts that perform the same tasks, yet written in a fashion that is easier to trace and understand.

There are many websites on the Internet that have plenty of reusable PowerShell scripts organized by function. Some of these include the following:

- *http://pshscripts.blogspot.com/*
- *https://gallery.technet.microsoft.com/ScriptCenter/*
- *http://powershellscripts.com/*
- *http://poshcode.org/*

However, the most effective way to find a PowerShell script that performs a specific function is to search using a search engine such as Google. To do this, ensure that your search begins with the word PowerShell and is followed by any major and minor tasks, in that order. This will allow you to locate a PowerShell script that fits your needs quickly.

Say, for example, that you would like to use a PowerShell script to open up a series of webpages on your desktop automatically. By searching for the phrase PowerShell open web page within a search engine, you will likely find many examples, including the one below that creates a function called Open-WebSiteInDefaultBrowser that accepts an argument (the address of the Web site to open):

```
#
#This function opens a Web site in the default browser.
#If no Web site is supplied as an argument, it opens Google
#
function Open-WebSiteInDefaultBrowser {
Param ([string] $SiteToOpen)

if (! $SiteToOpen)
    {if (! (test-path env:SiteToOpen))
        {$SiteToOpen = "https://google.com"}
    }
```

```
[diagnostics.process]::start($SiteToOpen)
}
#
#The following lines open the https://techcrunch.com,
#https://boingboing.net, and Google (default)
#
Open-WebSiteInDefaultBrowser ("https://techcrunch.com")
Open-WebSiteInDefaultBrowser ("https://boingboing.net")
Open-WebSiteInDefaultBrowser
```

Module Summary

- Server Manager allows you to monitor and manage several Windows Server systems and roles from a single console. To configure roles and features that are not possible within the Server Manager interface, the Tools menu provides a shortcut to the associated MMC tool.

- After installing roles within Server Manager, it is good form to run the Best Practices Analyzer to verify that the configuration of the role and server follows Microsoft best practices.

- The Windows Admin Center can be installed on a Windows Server 2019 system to provide remote Web-based management for several Windows Server systems. In addition to providing Azure cloud integration features, the Windows Admin Center provides much of the same functionality as Server Manager.

- You can use the Devices and Printers tool to add and troubleshoot hardware devices on a system, as well as the Device Manager tool to view and manage detailed hardware configuration.

- The Sigverif tool can be used to detect unsigned system and driver files, and the System File Checker tool can be used to scan system files for integrity and replace them with the correct versions.

- There are many different performance options that can be configured within Windows Server 2019, including processor scheduling, DEP, and virtual memory, as well as file caching and flushing.

- You can use Control Panel to configure system and user environment variables, startup and recovery settings, and power options.

- The Windows Registry stores the hardware and software configuration used by Windows Server 2019 within different entries that are organized into keys and subkeys. You can edit the Windows Registry using the Registry Editor.

- In addition to supporting MS-DOS commands, output redirection, and command chaining, Windows PowerShell offers you the ability to pipe output from one cmdlet to another, obtain detailed cmdlet help, search for cmdlets by keyword, modify cmdlet output, as well as use aliases and functions to simplify the use of cmdlets.

- You can use PowerShell console files to create feature-customized shortcuts to a Windows PowerShell session, as well as PowerShell profile scripts to automatically execute cmdlets after opening a Windows PowerShell session.

- Every item within Windows PowerShell can be treated as an object within a PowerShell provider that represents a specific area of your system. Moreover, detailed system information can be queried using the `Get-WmiObject` cmdlet.

- Windows PowerShell provides a large number of administrative cmdlets that can be used instead of Server Manager or the Windows Admin Center to configure a local or remote system.

- You can create reusable PowerShell scripts that execute cmdlets on one or more Windows system that allows script execution. Alternatively, you can obtain and modify PowerShell scripts available on the Internet to suit your needs.

- Windows PowerShell features that are frequently used within PowerShell scripts include variables, constants, metacharacter protection, decision constructs, loop constructs, as well as the coloring and formatting of output.

Key Terms

alias	environment variables	piping
alias provider	escape character	Plug and Play (PnP)
array variable	exit status	power plan
attribute	file caching	PowerShell console file
Best Practices Analyzer (BPA)	File Signature Verification	PowerShell profile script
certificate provider	tool (Sigverif)	PowerShell provider
Certificate Store	filesystem provider	processor scheduling
Certification Authority	flushing	Registry Editor
command chaining	function	registry provider
comment	function provider	Remote Desktop Protocol
Component Object Model	gateway server mode	(RDP)
(COM)	Input/Output (I/O) address	Remote Server
constant	Interrupt Request (IRQ) line	Administration Tools (RSAT)
Data Execution Prevention	key	self-signed certificate
(DEP)	loop construct	subkey
decision construct	metacharacter	system environment
Device Manager utility	method	variables
Devices and Printers utility	object	System File Checker
driver signing	output redirection	tracing
entry	page	type cast
environment provider	paging file	Universal PnP (UPnP)

user environment variables
variable
variable provider
Virtual Desktop
  Infrastructure (VDI)
virtual memory

Windows PowerShell
  Integrated Scripting
  Environment (ISE)
Windows Registry
winRM
WMI class

WMI consumers
WMI infrastructure
WMI namespace
WMI provider
WQL (WMI Query
  Language)

Review Questions

1. Server Manager can be used to monitor and manage other Windows Server 2008 and later systems. True or False?

2. Which of the following are panes that you will see listed for a server, server group, or server role within Server Manager? (Choose all that apply.)
   a. Services
   b. Events
   c. Roles and Features
   d. Performance

3. Which of the following tools within the navigation pane of the Windows Admin Center can be used to perform capacity planning?
   a. Performance
   b. Services
   c. System Insights
   d. Azure hybrid services

4. The Windows Admin Center allows you to obtain a Windows PowerShell session within your Web browser. True or False?

5. Which of the following utilities can be used to manually install a new device that is not fully PnP-compliant?
   a. Windows PowerShell
   b. Device Manager
   c. Devices and Printers utility
   d. Server Manager

6. Your system has three physical storage devices. Windows Server 2019 is installed on the first physical storage device. What can you do to increase the performance of the system as much as possible?
   a. Move the paging file to the second physical storage device
   b. Move the paging file to the third physical storage device
   c. Create a paging file on the second and third physical storage devices
   d. Create a paging file on the second and third physical storage devices and remove the page file from the first storage device

7. The Sigverif tool can be used to verify and repair corrupt system files. True or False?

8. Which of the following features can be configured within Control Panel? (Choose all that apply.)
   a. File caching and flushing
   b. Environment variables
   c. Power options
   d. Startup and recovery options

9. Some software issues require that you modify the value of an entry within the Windows Registry to fix a system problem. True or False?

10. What should be your first course of action
    when you see a device marked Unknown
    within Device Manager?
    a. Install the manufacturer-provided
       driver package on the system and
       reboot.
    b. Right-click the Unknown device
       within Device Manager and
       choose Update driver. Supply the
       manufacturer-provided driver files
       if prompted.
    c. Right-click the Unknown device
       within Device Manager and choose
       Uninstall device. Reboot your system
       afterwards.
    d. Right-click the Unknown device
       within Device Manager and choose
       Properties. Note whether there is a
       resource conflict.

11. System environment variables apply to
    any user logged onto the system. True or
    False?

12. What command could you execute within
    PowerShell to learn about the syntax of
    the `Get-WMIObject` cmdlet? (Choose all
    that apply.)
    a. `help Get-WMIObject`
    b. `Get-Help Get-WMIObject`
    c. `get-help Get-WMIObject`
    d. `Get-Help Get-WMIObject`
       `-online`

13. PowerShell console files use the `.ps1`
    extension. True or False?

14. Which of the following aliases can be
    used to switch to a different PowerShell
    provider?
    a. `sp`
    b. `ps`
    c. `cd`
    d. `sl`

15. The `Test-NetConnection` cmdlet can
    be used to test network connectivity to a
    target computer. True or False?

16. Which of the following can be used to
    open a new Windows PowerShell prompt
    that is connected to a remote computer
    (provided that winRM is enabled)?
    a. `Enter-PSSession` *computername*
    b. `Invoke-Command` *computername*
    c. `Execute-Shell` *computername*
    d. `Enable-PSRemoting`
       computername

17. Which of the following are valid methods
    for executing the superscript.ps1 file
    within PowerShell, assuming it is in your
    current directory, C:\Scripts? (Choose all
    that apply.)
    a. `C:\Scripts\superscript.ps1`
    b. `superscript.ps1`
    c. `./superscript.ps1`
    d. `.\superscript.ps1`

18. In the following example, three loops will
    be executed. True or False?

    ```
    $args =
    "one","two","three","four"
    foreach ($i in $args)
    {write $i -foregroundcolor
    magenta}
    ```

19. Which of the following PowerShell
    constructs is best to use when you wish
    to perform a specific action based on the
    value of a single variable?
    a. `if`
    b. `switch`
    c. `do...while`
    d. `for`

20. The Tab key can be used to auto complete
    a PowerShell cmdlet as you are typing it.
    True or False?

Hands-On Projects

These Hands-On Projects should be completed in the order given and should take a total of three hours to complete. The requirements for these projects include:

- A system with Windows Server 2019 installed according to Hands-On Project 1-1 (Lab Environment 1) or Hands-On Project 1-2 (Lab Environment 2).

Project 2-1: Server Manager

In this Hands-On Project, you explore the different configuration and management features of Server Manager.

1. Boot your Windows Server 2019 host and log into the system as Administrator using the password **Secret555**. After a few moments, Server Manager will open. If prompted to try the Windows Admin Center, select **Don't show this message again** and close the information window.
2. Within the Server Manager Dashboard, observe the roles and server groups shown. Note that your server is represented by Local Server, a member of the All Servers group and has the File and Storage Services role installed. Also note whether there are any services that are flagged red. If this is the case, click **Services** under your Local Server and note the services that are not started and the reason why.

Note 📎

Many services within Windows Server 2019 are set to Delayed Start, so that they start several minutes following a Windows Server 2019 boot. If you see red flagged services that are listed as Delayed Start, click the Refresh icon in the upper corner of the Server Manager console after a few minutes, and the red flags should disappear.

3. Highlight **Local Server** in the navigation pane of Server Manager.
   a. Observe the default events shown in the Events pane. Next, click **Tasks, Configure Event Data** within the Events pane. At the Configure Event Data window, select **Informational** and click **OK**. Note the additional events that are now shown within the Events pane.
   b. In the Performance pane, click **Tasks, Configure Performance Alerts**. Note the default alert thresholds and graph display period and click **Cancel**.
   c. In the Roles and Features pane, click **Tasks, Add Roles and Features**.
      i. At the Before you begin page, select the **Skip this page by default** checkbox, and click **Next**.
      ii. At the Select installation type page, click **Next**.
      iii. At the Select destination server page, click **Next**.

    iv. At the Select server roles page, select **DHCP Server**, and click **Add Features** when prompted. If prompted to continue after validation errors (because your system has a DHCP-assigned IP address), click **Continue**. Click **Next** when finished.

    v. At the Select features page, select **Telnet Client** and click **Next**.

    vi. At the DHCP Server page, read the information regarding best practices and click **Next**.

    vii. Click **Install** to install the DHCP Server role and Telnet Client feature.

    viii. After the installation has completed, click **Complete DHCP configuration**, click **Commit**, and then click **Close**.

    ix. Click **Close** to close the Add Roles and Features Wizard.

4. Highlight **DHCP** in the navigation pane of Server Manager.

    a. In the Best Practices Analyzer pane, click **Tasks, Start BPA Scan**, and then click **Start Scan**. Note the Warning and Error that you receive.

    b. In the Services pane, right-click the **DHCP Server** service and click **Stop Services**.

5. Click **Dashboard** in the navigation pane of Server Manager. Note that there is one service and one BPA result red flagged for the DHCP, Local Server and All Servers groups.

    a. Click **Services** under Local Server and note that the DHCP Server service is stopped. Right click the **DHCP Server** service, click **Start Services,** and then click **OK**. Click the **Refresh** button in the upper right of Server Manager and note that the service-related red flag disappears.

    b. Click **BPA results** under Local Server and note the Predeployment error shown. Right click the error, click **Exclude Result,** and then click **OK**. Click the **Refresh** button in the upper right of Server Manager and note that the BPA-related red flag disappears.

6. In the upper right of Server Manager, click **Manage**, **Add Servers**. Note that you can add servers within your Active Directory domain, by DNS name, or import them from a file. Because your computer is not domain-joined, you do not see entries under the Active Directory tab. Click **Cancel**.

7. In the upper right of Server Manager, click **Manage**, **Create Server Group**. In the Create Server Group window, specify a name of **Building1** in the Server group name box. Next, highlight **SERVERX** in the Server Pool tab, click the arrow button to move it to the Selected pane, and click **OK**. Note that your new server group appears within the navigation pane.

8. Highlight **Building1** in the navigation pane of Server Manager. Right-click **SERVERX** in the Servers pane and note the options available on the menu. Select the **Windows PowerShell** option to open a Windows PowerShell console as Administrator. Close the Windows PowerShell console when finished.

9. In the upper right of Server Manager, click **Tools** and note the tools that are available. Next, click **Manage, Server Manager Properties**. In the Server Manager Properties window, select **Do not start Server Manager automatically at logon** and click **OK**.

10. Close the Server Manager window.

Project 2-2: Windows Admin Center

In this Hands-On Project, you install and explore the different configuration and management features of the Windows Admin Center.

1. On your Windows Server 2019 host, open the Google Chrome Web browser and navigate to `https://aka.ms/WindowsAdminCenter`. Follow the prompts to download the latest non-preview version of the Windows Admin Center. When finished, the downloaded file will automatically be opened to start the installation.

   a. At the Windows Admin Center Setup screen, select **I accept the terms in the License Agreement** and click **Next**.

   b. At the Use Microsoft Update page, click **Next**.

   c. At the Install Windows Admin Center on Windows Server page, click **Next**.

   d. At the Installing Windows Admin Center page, click **Next**. Note that the installation program will generate a self-signed encryption certificate for use on port 443 (HTTPS) and click **Install**.

   e. Click **Finish**.

2. Navigate to `https://SERVERX:443` within the Chrome Web browser and click **Skip tour** when prompted. Maximize your Chrome Web browser screen.

3. At the All connections page, click **Add, Servers**. Note that you can add servers by server name or import a list of server names. Click **Cancel**.

4. Highlight **serverx** within the All connections page and click **Edit tags**. At the Edit connection tags window, type **2019HOST** and click **Save**.

5. Highlight **serverx** within the All Connections page and click **Connect**. Within the Overview tool, view the information shown and then click **Manage alerts**.

   a. Select **Environment variables** and note that you can create and edit system and user environment variables.

   b. Select **Power configuration**, select the **High performance** power plan and click **Save**.

6. Highlight **Devices** within the Tools pane. Note that you can disable existing hardware devices or update their device drivers.

7. Highlight **Network** within the Tools pane. Select your Ethernet adapter and click **Actions, Settings**. Note that you can configure IPv4 and IPv6 settings for your Ethernet adapter.

8. Highlight **PowerShell** within the Tools pane to open a Windows PowerShell prompt. Type **exit** and press **Enter** to stop your Windows PowerShell session.

9. Highlight **Registry** within the Tools pane. Expand **HKEY_CLASSES_ROOT** and highlight **.ac3**. Note that you can add, modify, and delete values.

10. Highlight **Roles & Features** within the Tools pane. Select **DHCP Server** and click **Remove**. Click **Yes** to remove the role.

11. Optionally navigate to the other tools within the Windows Admin Center and note their functionality. Close Google Chrome when finished.

Project 2-3: Configuration Utilities

In this Hands-On Project, you explore various Windows configuration utilities available within Windows Server 2019.

1. On your Windows Server 2019 host, click **Start** and then click **Control Panel**.

2. Navigate to **System and Security**, **System**, **Advanced system settings**. Under the Performance section of the System Properties window, click **Settings**.

   a. Next, highlight the **Advanced** tab and note the default setting for Processor scheduling.

   b. Click **Change** and note the default size of the paging file that is currently allocated on your system. Because the paging file size is managed by the system by default, this value should be close to the recommended value shown.

   c. Click **OK** to close the Virtual Memory window.

   d. Highlight the **Data Execution Prevention** tab and note the default settings that apply DEP to all programs and services.

   e. Click **OK** to close the Performance Options window.

3. Under the Startup and Recovery section of the System Properties window, click **Settings**. Note the default options and location of the dump file. Click **OK** to close the Startup and Recovery window when finished.

4. At the bottom of the System Properties window, click **Environment Variables**.

   a. In the User variables for Administrator section, click **New**.

   b. At the New User Variable window, supply a Variable name of VAR1 and Variable value of Sample Variable and click **OK**.

   c. In the System variables section, note the values of the Path, TEMP, TMP, and windir variables and click **OK**.

5. In the System Properties window, highlight the **Hardware** tab and click **Device Manager**.

   a. Devices that require attention will be marked with a yellow label and shown by default. If you see any Unknown devices, right-click the device, choose **Update driver** and follow the prompts to search for a driver on the Internet or from removable media supplied by your manufacturer.

   b. Expand **Disk drives**, right-click your storage device, and click **Properties**. Highlight the **Policies** tab and note that write caching is enabled on the device by default but that flushing is not. Click **OK** to close the properties window.

   c. Close Device Manager and click **OK** to close the System Properties window. If you are prompted to restart your computer to apply changes, click **Restart Later**.

6. In the Control Panel window, click **Control Panel** in the navigation bar to switch back to the Category view. Next, click **Add a device** under the Hardware category. Your system will search for devices that may not have been detected by PnP. Follow any prompts to install devices that are found. If no devices were found, click **Cancel**. Close Control Panel when finished.

7. Navigate to **System and Security**, **Power Options**.

   a. Select the **High performance** power plan.

   b. Click **Change plan settings** and note the defaults.

   c. Click **Change advanced power settings**. Navigate through the detailed power plan settings that are available for your computer, making changes that you desire as necessary. Click **OK** when finished.

   d. If you made changes to your power plan, click **Save changes**, otherwise, click **Cancel**.

   e. Close Control Panel.

8. Right-click the Start menu and click **Run**. Type `regedit` in the Run dialog box and click **OK**. Expand **HKEY_CLASSES_ROOT** and highlight **.ac3**. Note that you can add, modify, and delete values. Double-click **(Default)**, supply the value `audio`, and click **OK**. Close the Registry Editor when finished.

9. Right-click the Start menu and click **Run**. Type `sigverif` in the Run dialog box and click **OK**. In the File Signature Verification tool, click **Start** to scan your system for unsigned files. When the scan has completed, click **OK** and then click **Close** to close the File Signature Verification tool.

10. Right-click the Start menu and click **Run**. Type `cmd` in the Run dialog box and click **OK**. At the command prompt, type `sfc /scannow` and press **Enter**. Note whether any system files were replaced with correct versions and close the command prompt window when finished.

Project 2-4: Cmdlets

In this Hands-On Project, you work with common Windows PowerShell administrative cmdlets.

1. On your Windows Server 2019 host, open the Google Chrome Web browser. Next, right-click the **Start** menu and choose **Windows PowerShell (Admin)** to open Windows PowerShell.

2. At the prompt, type `Get-Process | more` and press **Enter**. Note that there are many processes with a ProcessName of chrome that comprise the Google Chrome Web browser. Press q to quit the more command. Next, type `Stop-Process -name chrome` and press **Enter**. Note that the Google Chrome Web browser app was closed.

3. At the prompt, type `Get-Service | ogv` and press **Enter**. Note that the App Readiness service is called AppReadiness and is not started by default. Close the GridView window. Next, type `Start-Service -name AppReadiness` and press **Enter** to start the service. Next, type `Stop-Service -name AppReadiness` and press **Enter** to stop the App Readiness service.

4. At the prompt, type `Get-WindowsFeature | ogv` and press **Enter** to view installed roles and features. Note that the Telnet Client feature that you installed earlier in Hands-On Project 2-1 is given the name Telnet-Client. Close the Out-GridView window. Next, type `Remove-WindowsFeature -name Telnet-Client` and press **Enter** to remove the feature.

5. At the prompt, type `Test-NetConnection` and press **Enter** to test your network connectivity to internetbeacon.msedge.net. Next, execute the following commands at the command prompt, in turn. For each one, note the network configuration information displayed.

   ```
   Get-NetIPConfiguration
   Get-NetAdapter
   Get-NetAdapterStatistics
   ```

6. Close Windows PowerShell.

Project 2-5: Cmdlet Output

In this Hands-On Project, you modify the output of Windows PowerShell cmdlets.

1. Right-click the **Start** menu and choose **Windows PowerShell (Admin)** to open Windows PowerShell.

2. At the prompt, type `cd \` and press **Enter** to switch to the root directory. Next, type `dir` and press **Enter** to list the contents of this directory.

3. At the prompt, type `alias dir` and press **Enter**. Next, type `alias gci` and press **Enter**. Note that dir and gci are aliases to the Get-ChildItem cmdlet. Execute the following commands at the command prompt, in turn. For each one, interpret the output (referencing the aliases and cmdlets within this module, as necessary).

   ```
   Get-ChildItem
   gci | sort -property name
   gci | Format-List
   gci | Format-List -property name,lastwritetime
   gci | Format-Wide
   gci | Format-Wide -column 3
   gci | Format-Wide -column 3 -property length
   gci | Format-Wide -column 3 -property name -groupby length
   gci | Format-Table
   gci | Format-Table -property name,length,lastwritetime
   gci -recurse
   gci -recurse -include *.txt
   ```

4. Other cmdlets that generate a large amount of information may require that you use additional Windows PowerShell features to modify command output for organization and readability. Execute the following commands at the command prompt, in turn. For each one, interpret the output (referencing the aliases and cmdlets within this module, as necessary).

   ```
   Get-EventLog System | more
   Get-EventLog System | Group-Object eventid | more
   Get-EventLog System | Group-Object eventid | Out-GridView
   ```

   (Close the GridView window when finished.)

```
Get-EventLog System | Group-Object eventid | ogv
```
(Close the GridView window when finished.)
```
Get-Process | ogv
```
(Close the GridView window when finished.)
```
Get-Process | ConvertTo-HTML | Out-File C:\PList.html
Invoke-Item C:\PList.html
```
(Choose to open in Google Chrome, and close Chrome when finished.)
```
Get-Process | Export-CSV C:\PList.csv
Invoke-Item C:\PList.csv
```
(Choose to open in WordPad and close WordPad when finished.)

5. Close Windows PowerShell.

Project 2-6: PowerShell Providers

In this Hands-On Project, you work with PowerShell providers.

1. Right-click the **Start** menu and choose **Windows PowerShell (Admin)** to open Windows PowerShell.
2. At the prompt, type Get-PSProvider and press **Enter** to view the available PowerShell providers. Next, type Get-PSDrive and press **Enter** to view the expanded list of PowerShell providers. Note that the filesystem provider is available for each drive letter on the system, and that registry provider is available for HKEY_CURRENT_USER and HKEY_LOCAL_MACHINE.
3. Each PowerShell provider treats each item that it works with as an object. At the prompt, type gci | Get-Member and press **Enter** to view the properties available for the objects within the current directory of the filesystem provider. Note that there is a PSIscontainer property that indicates that the object is a subdirectory. Next, type gci | Where-Object {$_.psiscontainer} and press **Enter** to view only directories. Following this, type gci | Where-Object {!$_.psiscontainer} and press **Enter** to view only non-directories (i.e., files).
4. Within the filesystem provider, you can create, edit, and remove objects, such as files and directories. Execute the following commands at the command prompt, in turn. For each one, interpret the output (referencing the aliases and cmdlets within this module, as necessary).

```
new-item -path C:\ -name mydir -type directory
new-item -path C:\mydir -name lala.txt -type file
get-content c:\mydir\lala.txt
add-content c:\mydir\lala.txt -value "This is line 1"
add-content c:\mydir\lala.txt -value "This is line 2"
add-content c:\mydir\lala.txt -value "This is line 3"
get-content c:\mydir\lala.txt
set-content c:\mydir\lala.txt -value "This is the only line"
get-content c:\mydir\lala.txt
remove-item c:\mydir -recurse
```

5. At the prompt, type `sl env:\` and press **Enter** to switch to the environment provider. Next, type `gci` and press **Enter** to view the environment variables on the system. In many PowerShell providers, you can instead use the Get-Item cmdlet (alias gi) to view items. Type `gi *` and press **Enter** to view all items within the environment provider. Next, execute the following commands at the command prompt, in turn. For each one, interpret the output (referencing the aliases and cmdlets within this module, as necessary).

```
gi * | sort-object -property name
gi windir
gi windir | format-list *
new-item -path . -name lala -value "This is cool!"
gi lala
gi lala | format-list *
rename-item -path env:lala -newname po
gi po
gi po | format-list *
gi * | sort-object -property name
remove-item po
```

6. At the prompt, type `sl variable:\` and press **Enter** to switch to the variable provider. Next, type `gci` and press **Enter** to view the user-defined PowerShell variables on the system. Next, execute the following commands at the command prompt, in turn. For each one, interpret the output (referencing the aliases and cmdlets within this module, as necessary).

```
gci | sort {$_.Name}
get-variable home
get-variable home | format-list
new-variable oobla
set-variable oobla -value "Toast"
get-variable oobla
set-variable tinky -value "Winky"
get-variable tinky
remove-variable tinky
```

7. At the prompt, type `sl alias:\` and press **Enter** to switch to the alias provider. Next, type `gci` and press **Enter** to view the user-defined PowerShell variables on the system. Following this, type `gci | Where-Object {$_.name -like "c*"}` and press **Enter** to view aliases that start with c. Note that "clear" is an alias to Clear-Host.

8. You can also view aliases by their definition. At the prompt, type `gci | Where-Object {$_.definition -like "c*"}` to view aliases that point to cmdlets that start with the letter c.

9. At the prompt, type `sl function:\` and press **Enter** to switch to the function provider. Next, type `gci` and press **Enter** to view the functions on the system. Note that Clear-Host is a function. Next, type `Get-Content Clear-Host` and press **Enter** to view the content of the Clear-Host function.

10. At the prompt, type `sl cert:\` and press **Enter** to switch to the certificate provider. Next, type `gci` and press **Enter**. Note that the certificate provider can manage certificates for the current user and local computer. Next, type `gci -recurse` and press **Enter**. Note the self-signed certificate installed on your system by the Windows Admin Center is displayed in the list.

11. At the prompt, type `sl 'HKLM:\software\microsoft\windows nt\ currentversion'` and press **Enter** to switch to the registry provider for HKEY_LOCAL_MACHINE and navigate to the currentversion subkey for your Windows server system. Next, type `set-itemproperty –path winlogon –name legalnoticecaption –value "Hey!"` and press **Enter** to set a legal notice caption for local logon attempts. Finally, type `set-itemproperty –path winlogon –name legalnoticetext –value "What are you doing on my system?"` and press **Enter** to modify the text message for local logon attempts.

12. Right-click the **Start** menu and click **Shut down or sign out**, **Sign out**. Press Ctrl+Alt+Del (or Ctrl+Alt+End if you are running Windows Server 2019 within a Hyper-V virtual machine on Windows 10). Note your legal notice and click **OK**. Log into the system as Administrator using the password **Secret555**.

Project 2-7: WMI

In this Hands-On Project, you query WMI using Windows PowerShell.

1. Right-click the **Start** menu and choose **Windows PowerShell (Admin)** to open Windows PowerShell.

2. At the prompt, type `alias gwmi` and press **Enter**. Note that gwmi is an alias to Get-WmiObject. Next, execute the following commands at the command prompt, in turn. For each one, interpret the output (referencing the aliases and cmdlets within this module, as necessary).

```
gwmi win32_bios
gwmi win32_processor
gwmi win32_processor | gm
gwmi win32_computersystem
gwmi win32_computersystem | fl *
gwmi win32_logicaldisk
gwmi win32_logicaldisk | fl *
gwmi win32_diskdrive
gwmi win32_diskdrive | fl *
gwmi win32_share
gwmi win32_share | fl *
```

```
gwmi win32_networkadapterconfiguration
gwmi win32_networkadapterconfiguration | fl *
gwmi win32_desktop
gwmi win32_desktop | fl *
gwmi win32_share -filter name="'c$'"
gwmi win32_logicaldisk -filter name="'c$'" |
Measure-Object -property freespace -Minimum -Maximum

gwmi win32_logicaldisk -filter name="'c$'" |
Measure-Object -Property freespace -Minimum -Maximum |
Select-Object -Property freespace, maximum, minimum |
Format-Table -autosize
```

3. You can also query WMI using WQL syntax. Execute the following commands at the command prompt, in turn. For each one, interpret the output (referencing the aliases and cmdlets within this module, as necessary).

```
gwmi -query "Select * from win32_share"
gwmi -query "Select * from win32_share" | gm
gwmi -query "Select name,path,allowmaximum from win32_share"
gwmi -query "Select name,path,allowmaximum from win32_share where name='c$'"

gwmi -query "Select name from win32_share" | Sort-Object -property
name | Format-List -property name

gwmi -query "Select name from win32_share" | Sort-Object -property
name | Format-List -property name > C:\scripts\ShareInformation.txt

notepad C:\scripts\ShareInformation.txt
```

4. Close Notepad and Windows PowerShell.

Project 2-8: PowerShell Customization

In this Hands-On Project, you enable script execution and create a PowerShell profile script that loads a custom alias and function. Next, you create a PowerShell console file to customize your Windows PowerShell experience.

1. Right-click the **Start** menu and choose **Windows PowerShell (Admin)** to open Windows PowerShell.

2. At the prompt, type Set-ExecutionPolicy unrestricted and press **Enter**. Type Y when prompted to confirm. Next, type Test-Path $profile and press **Enter**. Note that you do not have a PowerShell profile script configured.

3. At the prompt, type `New-Item -path $profile -itemtype file -force` and press **Enter** to create a PowerShell profile. Next, type `notepad $profile` to open your PowerShell profile script within Notepad. Add the following lines:

```
Write-Host "Hello"
Set-Alias lala Get-Service
function pro {notepad $profile}
```

4. Click **File, Save** within Notepad to save your changes. Close Notepad when finished.

5. At the prompt, type `cd Desktop` and press **Enter** to switch to your Desktop directory. Next, type `export-console CustomPS` and press **Enter** to create a CustomPS.psc1 file on your Desktop that can be used to open Windows PowerShell. Close Windows PowerShell when finished.

6. Double-click the **CustomPS** file on your desktop to open Windows PowerShell. Note that your PowerShell profile script executed and printed Hello to the screen. Type `lala` and press **Enter** to test your alias. Next, type `pro` and press **Enter** to test your function. Close Notepad when finished.

7. Click the PowerShell icon in the upper left of the Windows PowerShell window and click **Properties**. Navigate through the properties and make some visual changes to your liking (color, font, and so on). Click **OK** to close the Properties dialog box and close Windows PowerShell when finished.

8. Double-click the **CustomPS** file on your desktop to open Windows PowerShell. Note that your customizations are available. Close Windows PowerShell when finished.

9. Right-click the Start menu and choose **Windows PowerShell (Admin)** to open Windows PowerShell. Note that your customizations are not available as PowerShell was not started via the CustomPS.psc1 file.

10. Close Windows PowerShell.

Project 2-9: PowerShell Scripting

In this Hands-On Project, you create and execute a basic PowerShell script using Windows PowerShell ISE, and execute it on the system.

1. Click **Start**. Next, right-click **Windows PowerShell ISE** and click **More, Run as administrator**.

2. Click the **New Script** button above the Windows PowerShell pane, and enter the following contents:

```
#This script prints process information to the screen for
#a process that the user is prompted to supply during
#script execution

$ans=Read-Host "What process would you like to query?"

Get-WmiObject win32_process -Filter "name='$ans'" | Format-Table
HandleCount,VirtualSize,UserModeTime,KernelModeTime,ProcessID,Name
```

3. Click the **Run Script** button (or press **F5**) to test your script in the Windows PowerShell console. Type the value `svchost.exe` and press **Enter** when prompted.

> **Note** 📎
>
> If there are errors in your script, fix the typos in your script and repeat Step 3.

4. After your script executes properly, click **File, Save As**. Type `C:\myscript.ps1` in the File name box and click **Save**.
5. Close Windows PowerShell ISE.
6. Right-click the **Start** menu and choose **Windows PowerShell (Admin)** to open Windows PowerShell.
7. At the prompt, type `cd \` and press **Enter** to switch to the root of C:\. Next, type `./myscript.ps1` and press **Enter** to execute your script again. Type the value `svchost.exe` and press **Enter** when prompted.
8. Close Windows PowerShell.

Discovery Exercises

Exercise 2-1
In most environments, you administer Windows Server systems remotely from a Windows 10 PC running the Remote Server Administration Tools (RSAT). If you use Lab Environment 2, download and install the RSAT on your Windows 10 PC from `https://www.microsoft.com/en-ca/download/details.aspx?id=45520`. Next, explore the tools that are provided by RSAT, including Server Manager. Note any differences in functionality between the Server Manager included with RSAT and the Server Manager that is installed on your Windows Server 2019 system in a short memo.

Exercise 2-2
Search the Internet for problems that others have encountered regarding a hardware device within Windows Server 2019. For three of these issues, write a brief summary that details the nature of each problem, as well as the steps that were taken to remedy it.

Exercise 2-3
Recall that every aspect of a Windows system can be treated as an object within Windows PowerShell, including the Windows PowerShell console window itself. Run the following two commands in turn at a Windows PowerShell prompt and observe the results. Next, explain the actions each command performs, specifically noting the object that is created.

```
$ui = (Get-Host).UI.RawUI
$ui.WindowTitle = "Extreme PowerShell Window!"
```

Exercise 2-4

In Hands-On Project 2-8, you created a script that prompted the user for the name of a process to query. Rewrite this script to instead require that the name of the process be supplied as an argument to the script when executed. Test your results when finished.

Exercise 2-5

Understanding how to interpret (or trace) an existing PowerShell script is vital when searching for PowerShell scripts on the Internet that suit a particular administrative need. Trace the PowerScript script shown in Figure 2-27, and write a short memo describing what it will do after being executed:

```
$list = get-childitem | sort-object


foreach ($objItem in $list) {
      if ($objItem.Attributes -contains "Directory") {
      $fgc="cyan" }
      elseif ($objItem.Extension -eq ".ps1") {
      $fgc="blue" }
      elseif ($objItem.Extension -eq ".exe") {
      $fgc="green" }
      elseif ($objItem.Extension -eq ".zip") {
      $fgc="red" }
      elseif ($objItem.Extension -eq ".rar") {
      $fgc="red" }
      else { $fgc="yellow" }
write-host  $objItem.Name, $objItem.Length, objItem.LastWriteTime
-foregroundcolor $fgc
}
```

Exercise 2-6

You have been tasked with creating two PowerShell scripts. The first PowerShell script should save system documentation information to a file, whereas the second PowerShell script should locate large files on the filesystem and list them in descending order. Search the Internet for two different PowerShell scripts that provide this functionality, and modify them if necessary to suit your needs. Test each script on your system to ensure that it works as expected.

Exercise 2-7

In Project 2-6, you added a legal notice to the Windows logon screen by modifying the Windows Registry using Windows PowerShell. Use the Registry Editor to remove this legal notice.

IMPLEMENTING HYPER-V AND RAPID SERVER DEPLOYMENT

After completing this module, you will be able to:

Install Hyper-V on a Windows Server 2019 host

Explain the purpose and configuration of Hyper-V virtual switches

Create virtual machines within Hyper-V Manager

Modify virtual machine settings

Use virtual machine checkpoints

Outline the process used to configure and perform live migration

Identify the purpose and usage of virtual machine replication

Explain the methods used to perform rapid server deployment with Windows Server 2019

Use virtual machine templates to create new virtual machines

Install and configure WDS

Use WDS to install Windows Server 2019

In this module, you'll learn how to configure Hyper-V to provide virtualization for Windows Server 2019. More specifically, you'll learn how to install Hyper-V on a Windows Server 2019 host operating system, configure virtual switches, as well as create and manage virtual machines. Additionally, you'll learn how to configure Hyper-V checkpoints, live migration, and replication. At the end of this module, you'll learn how to perform rapid server deployment of Windows Server 2019 systems using virtual machine templates and WDS.

Implementing Hyper-V

As you learned in Module 1, virtualization allows you to use server hardware more efficiently by running multiple guest operating systems (virtual machines) simultaneously. This, in turn, allows you to reduce power and server cooling costs within your organization, leading to a reduced energy and carbon footprint that helps the environment. To enable virtualization, a computer must run a hypervisor that emulates a unique set of virtual hardware components for each virtual machine. Hyper-V is a Type-1 hypervisor that is available within the Standard and Datacenter editions of Windows Server 2019, as well as within Microsoft Hyper-V Server 2019.

In the following sections, we'll examine how to install Hyper-V on a Windows Server 2019 Standard or Datacenter edition system, as well as how to create, configure, and manage Hyper-V virtual machines.

> **Note** 📎
>
> The core concepts provided within this section also apply to other hypervisor products on the market, such as Linux KVM, VMWare ESXi, or Oracle Virtualbox.

Installing Hyper-V

Before you install Hyper-V on a Windows Server 2019 system, you must first ensure that your processor supports Intel VT or AMD-V virtualization extensions with SLAT support, as described earlier in Table 1-2. Because these extensions are revised with every generation of Intel and AMD processor to include additional performance and feature improvements, you should additionally ensure that you install Hyper-V on the most recent hardware to guarantee that virtual machines are run as efficiently as possible.

To install Hyper-V on Windows Server 2019, you can select the Hyper-V role when adding a role within Server Manager, as shown in Figure 3-1. This will install the Hyper-V hypervisor, as well as the associated Hyper-V management tools (graphical Hyper-V Manager console and Hyper-V PowerShell cmdlets) on the host operating system. When you click Next in Figure 3-1 and progress through the Add Roles and Features Wizard, you will additionally be prompted to select one or more network interfaces that provide access to the physical network in your organization as shown in Figure 3-2. When you select a network interface at this screen, an external virtual switch (discussed in the next section) will be created within Hyper-V to allow virtual machines access to the physical network using the network interface.

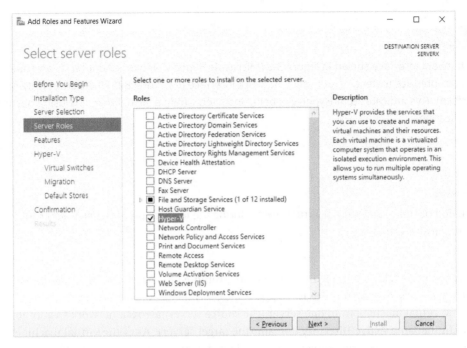

Figure 3-1   Adding the Hyper-V role within Server Manager

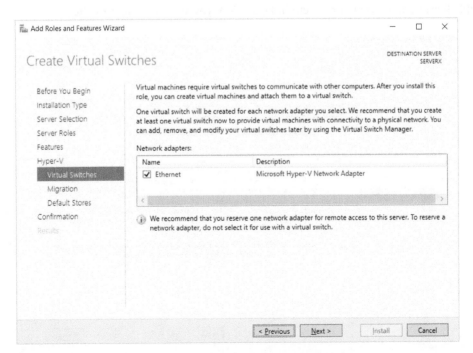

Figure 3-2   Creating an external virtual switch during Hyper-V installation

Note

The network interface shown in Figure 3-2 (Microsoft Hyper-V Network Adapter) is a virtual network interface instead of a physical network interface (e.g., Intel 82579 Ethernet Network Interface). This indicates that Hyper-V is being installed within a virtual machine using nested virtualization.

Note

If you do not create an external virtual switch during the installation of Hyper-V, you can create one afterwards.

When you click Next in Figure 3-2, you are prompted to enable the live migration of virtual machines, as shown in Figure 3-3. **Live migration** allows you to copy a running Hyper-V virtual machine from one server (the source server) across a network to another server in the same Active Directory domain (the target server). After the virtual machine has been copied to the target server, it is started on the target server and stopped on the source server in a coordinated way that does not impact service availability. If you enable live migration on your system in Figure 3-3, you must choose how the

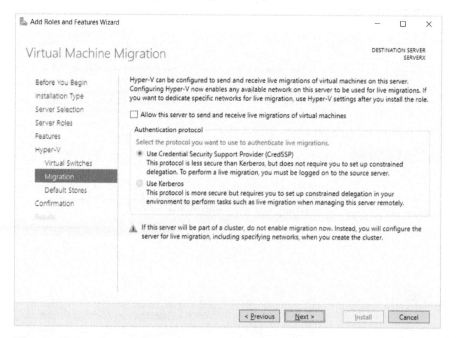

Figure 3-3   Setting live migration options during Hyper-V installation

two servers authenticate to each other during the live migration process. **Credential Security Support Provider (CredSSP)** authentication requires that you start the live migration process while logged into the source server as a user with administrative privileges in the domain. **Kerberos** (the default authentication protocol within Active Directory) allows you to start a live migration from any computer running Hyper-V Manager within an Active Directory domain, but requires that both computer accounts within Active Directory are configured for constrained delegation (discussed later in Module 4).

Note

If you do not configure live migration during the installation of Hyper-V, you can configure it afterwards.

When you click Next in Figure 3-3, you are prompted for the location of the files that comprise each virtual machine, as shown in Figure 3-4. Recall from Module 1 that the operating system installed within a Hyper-V virtual machine is stored within one or more virtual hard disk files. The hardware and feature settings for a particular virtual machine are stored in separate virtual machine configuration files. Many administrators change the default locations for virtual hard disk files and virtual machine configuration files

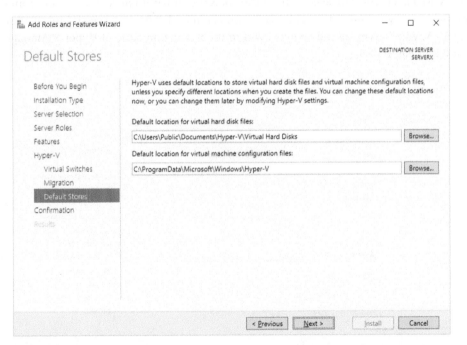

Figure 3-4   Specifying the location for virtual machine configuration

shown in Figure 3-4 to the same location on a separate storage device that represents a large RAID disk array or SAN storage device. For example, if your server is connected to a SAN that is assigned the drive letter D, you could specify D:\VMs as the storage location for both your virtual hard disk and virtual machine configuration files. In this case, virtual hard disk files will be stored within the D:\VMs directory, and virtual machine configuration files will be stored within the D:\VMs\Virtual Machines subdirectory.

After you complete the Add Roles and Features Wizard to install the Hyper-V role, you are prompted to reboot your computer to complete the installation. On most systems, your computer will reboot twice; the first reboot adds Hyper-V in a Type 1 configuration, and the second reboot allows Hyper-V to start the host operating system that is used to manage virtual machines.

Note

You can also install Hyper-V role using the Windows Admin Console, or within Windows PowerShell by running the `Install-WindowsFeature -Name Hyper-V -ComputerName computer_name -IncludeManagementTools -Restart` command.

Following the installation of Hyper-V, you can use PowerShell or the graphical Hyper-V Manager tool to manage Hyper-V and Hyper-V virtual machines. To start Hyper-V Manager, you can select it from the Tools menu within Server Manager, from the Start menu, or by running the `virtmgmt.msc` command. After a successful installation of Hyper-V, your server should be listed within the navigation pane of Hyper-V Manager, as shown in Figure 3-5.

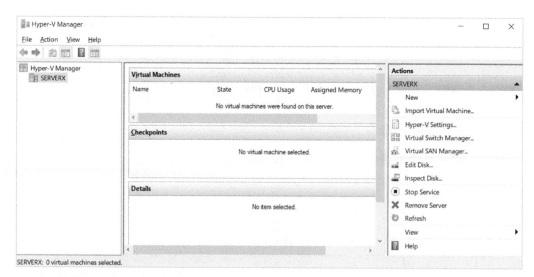

Figure 3-5   Hyper-V Manager

Understanding Virtual Networks

To create a physical network, you often need to use a device that connects to each computer on the network. For wireless networks, this device could be a **wireless access point (WAP)** that sends radio waves to the wireless network interface in each computer on the network. For wired networks, this device is often a physical **switch** that connects to the network interfaces within each computer on the network using an Ethernet cable.

In addition to providing physical network access to virtual machines, most hypervisors allow you to create additional virtual networks that can be used by virtual machines and the host operating systems that manage them. Each virtual network within Hyper-V is called a **virtual switch**, and provides the same capabilities as a physical switch. Virtual machines can connect to a virtual switch by adding a virtual network interface that is associated with the virtual switch. If several virtual machines use the same virtual switch, they will be able to communicate with each other using IP, exactly like computers on a physical switch.

Hyper-V defines three types of virtual switches for use with virtual machines:

- An **external virtual switch** represents an underlying physical switch, and serves to connect virtual machines to an underlying physical network via a physical network interface on the server running Hyper-V.
- An **internal virtual switch** represents a virtual network to which virtual machines and the host operating system can connect.
- A **private virtual switch** represents a virtual network to which only virtual machines can connect.

A single host operating system or virtual machine can have multiple virtual network interfaces that each connect to a different virtual switch. To illustrate this, Figure 3-6 shows a server that is running three virtual machines in addition to the Windows

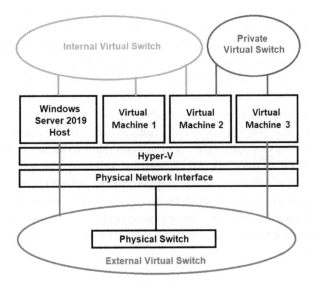

Figure 3-6   An example virtualized network infrastructure

Server 2019 host operating system that manages them. The Windows Server 2019 host and third virtual machine have virtual network interfaces that are associated with the external virtual switch, and will appear as separate servers to other computers connected to the physical switch. The Windows Server 2019 host and first two virtual machines have virtual network interfaces that are associated with the internal virtual switch, and can communicate amongst themselves on the internal virtual network. The second and third virtual machines have virtual network interfaces that are associated with the private virtual switch and can communicate amongst themselves on the private virtual network.

In some environments, the host operating system and all virtual machines are connected only to an external virtual switch, so that they can respond to requests from computers on the physical network.

However, internal and private virtual switches can be used to create an isolated network for specific types of communication (e.g., cluster configuration information), or to provide enhanced security. Say, for example, that the first virtual machine shown in Figure 3-6 hosted a database that contained sensitive information that can only be accessed from a Web app that is running on the Windows Server 2019 host. Clients on the physical network that require access to the data within the database cannot access the database software directly. Instead, they must contact the Web app running on the Windows Server 2019 host to obtain the sensitive information, after satisfying the security measures provided by the Web app. This type of data security design is called **N-tier**, as it requires that users pass through a number of systems (N) that implement security measures before gaining access to sensitive data.

You can create and modify virtual switches by selecting Virtual Switch Manager within the Actions pane of Hyper-V Manager (shown earlier in Figure 3-5). When you open the Virtual Switch Manager, the New virtual network switch option is highlighted by default, as shown in Figure 3-7. To create a new virtual switch, you can select the type of virtual switch, click Create Virtual Switch in the Create virtual switch pane, and supply a virtual switch name, as shown in Figure 3-8 for an internal virtual switch. For an internal or private virtual switch, no other information is necessary. However, if you select External network within Figure 3-8 to create an external virtual switch, you must also select the associated physical network interface from the drop-down menu, and ensure that the *Allow management operating system to share this network adapter* option is enabled to allow multiple virtual machines to use the physical network interface simultaneously. Some PCIe physical network interfaces support **single-root I/O virtualization (SR-IOV)**, which allows the network interface to work closely with Hyper-V to separate network requests from different virtual machines in order to optimize performance. If your physical network interface supports SR-IOV, you should select the option to enable it for the external virtual switch.

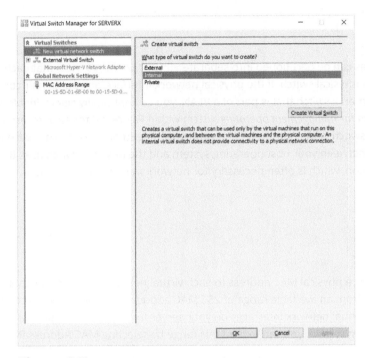

Figure 3-7   Creating a new virtual switch

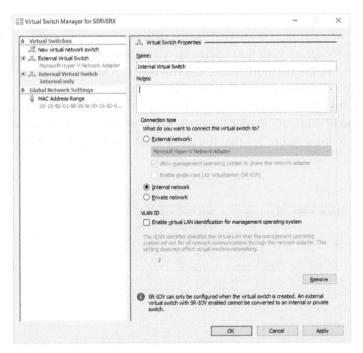

Figure 3-8   Configuring the settings for a new virtual switch

Note 📎

Physical switches can be partitioned into separate **virtual LANs (VLANs)** that each act as an independent physical switch. If the physical network interface on your server connects to an Ethernet port on a switch that is part of a VLAN, you can optionally select *Enable virtual LAN identification for management operating system* within Figure 3-8 for each external or internal virtual switch, and enter the VLAN number for the Ethernet port. This will ensure that network traffic between your host operating system and the physical switch uses the correct VLAN identification, which is often necessary for network management software.

Note 📎

Microsoft assigns a physical MAC address to each virtual network adapter that connects to a virtual switch, from an available range of 256 MAC addresses. If you expect to configure more than 256 virtual network interfaces on your server for use within virtual machines and the host operating system, you can extend this range by selecting MAC Address Range within Figure 3-7.

After you create external and internal virtual switches, you will see the associated virtual network interface on your host operating system within Server Manager, as well as within the Network Connections area of Control Panel, as shown in Figure 3-9. Each virtual network interface starts with vEthernet, and is named for the virtual switch that it connects to by default. You can then access the properties of each virtual network interface to set the IP configuration for the networks to which your host operating system connects. Also note from Figure 3-9 that the physical network interface (Ethernet) is also

Figure 3-9   Viewing physical and virtual network interfaces on a host operating system

shown within the Network Connections area of Control Panel. However, this network interface should not be configured to use IP, because IP functionality must only be provided by virtual network interfaces when Hyper-V is installed. When you access the properties of the physical network interface, as shown in Figure 3-10, you will notice that both IPv4 and IPv6 are not enabled, but that the **Hyper-V Extensible Virtual Switch** protocol is enabled. The Hyper-V Extensible Virtual Switch protocol is automatically enabled on a physical network interface when you create an external virtual switch, and allows Hyper-V the ability to share the physical network interface with multiple virtual machines simultaneously.

Figure 3-10   The properties of a physical network interface on a host operating system running Hyper-V

Note 🖉

You can also manage virtual switches within Windows PowerShell. For example, to create an external virtual switch called ExternalVS that uses the physical network adapter called Ethernet, you can run the `New-VMSwitch -name "ExternalVS" -SwitchType External -NetAdapterName "Ethernet" -AllowManagementOs $true` command.

Creating Virtual Machines

After you have installed Hyper-V and configured the appropriate virtual switches, you can create virtual machines within Hyper-V Manager to host guest operating systems. To create a new virtual machine within Hyper-V Manager, you can select New from the Actions pane and then select Virtual Machine to start the New Virtual Machine Wizard shown in Figure 3-11. If you click Finish in Figure 3-11, a Generation 2 virtual machine called New Virtual Machine with 1 GB of memory and a 127 GB dynamically expanding virtual hard disk will be created. You can then modify this virtual machine to suit your needs. Alternatively, if you click Next in Figure 3-11, you are prompted to supply the appropriate configuration settings, starting with the virtual machine name and path for the virtual machine configuration files, as shown in Figure 3-12. If you do not select *Store the virtual machine in a different location* shown in Figure 3-12, the virtual machine configuration files will be stored within `C:\VMs\Virtual Machines`, and the default location for virtual hard disk files (configured later within the New Virtual Machine Wizard) will be `C:\VMs`. However, if you select *Store the virtual machine in a different location*, the New Virtual Machine Wizard will create a folder structure under `C:\VMs` that is named for your virtual machine:

- `C:\VMs\WindowsServer2019VM1\Virtual Hard Disks` will store virtual hard disk files for the WindowsServer2019VM1 virtual machine.
- `C:\VMs\WindowsServer2019VM1\Virtual Machines` will store the configuration files for the WindowsServer2019VM1 virtual machine.

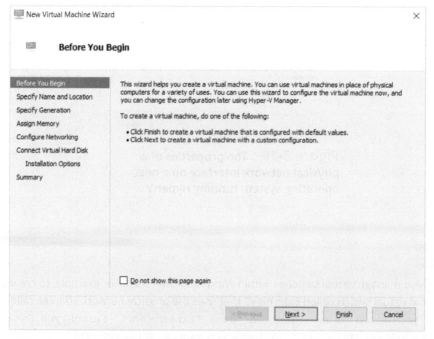

Figure 3-11   The New Virtual Machine Wizard

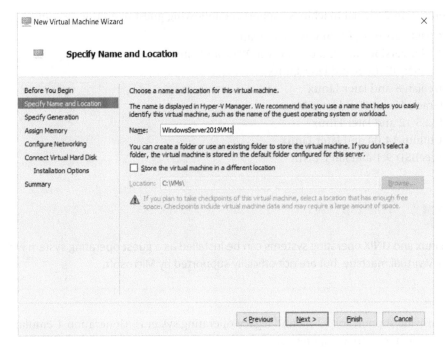

Figure 3-12   Specifying the virtual machine name and configuration file location

After pressing Next in Figure 3-12, you will then be prompted to choose the generation of the virtual machine, as shown in Figure 3-13. Generation 1 virtual machines provide legacy hardware emulation for guest operating systems, whereas Generation 2 virtual machines provide modern hardware emulation for guest operating systems. As a result, Generation 2 virtual machines support different guest operating systems than Generation 1. Because many third-party server apps are only supported by the vendor on specific versions of Windows or Linux operating systems, it is important to choose the correct generation of your virtual machine during creation, as the generation cannot be changed afterwards.

Generation 1 virtual machines support the following guest operating systems:

- 32-bit and 64-bit versions of Windows 7 and later
- 64-bit versions of Windows Server 2008 and later
- CentOS/RHEL 5 and later Linux
- Debian 7 and later Linux
- Oracle Linux 6, UEK R3 QU1 and later Linux
- Open SUSE 12.3 and SLES 11 and later Linux
- Ubuntu 12.04 and later Linux
- FreeBSD 8.4 and later UNIX

Generation 2 virtual machines support the following guest operating systems:

- 64-bit versions of Windows 8 and later
- 64-bit versions of Windows Server 2012 and later
- CentOS/RHEL 6 and later Linux
- Debian 8 and later Linux
- Oracle Linux 7 and later Linux
- SLES 12 and later Linux
- Ubuntu 14.04 and later Linux
- FreeBSD 9.1 and later UNIX

Note

Other Linux and UNIX operating systems can be installed as a guest operating system within a Hyper-V virtual machine, but are not officially supported by Microsoft.

To provide support for 32-bit and legacy operating systems, Generation 1 emulates the following hardware components:

- IDE hard disk (up to 2 TB for the system)
- IDE CD-ROM
- Legacy SCSI hard disk
- Floppy disk
- Standard BIOS
- Legacy network adapter that can boot an operating system from across an IPv4 network using **Preboot Execution Environment (PXE)**
- PS/2 keyboard and mouse
- S3 video card
- Older system components, including a PCI bus, serial (COM) ports, Universal asynchronous receiver/transmitter (UART), i8042 keyboard controller, programmable interrupt controller (PIC), programmable interval timer (PIT), and super I/O device

For faster performance, Generation 2 virtual machines emulate most hardware using software components that are linked directly to an underlying Hyper-V **virtual machine bus (VMBus)**. However, only the supported Generation 2 guest operating systems contain the associated VMBus drivers by default. Additionally, Generation 2 virtual machines emulate a UEFI BIOS that provides a faster boot time (20% on average). More specifically, Generation 2 virtual machines emulate the following hardware:

- Serial Attached SCSI (SAS) hard disk (up to 64 TB for the system)
- SAS DVD-ROM
- UEFI BIOS with support for Secure Boot

- Synthetic VMBus network adapter that can boot an operating system from across an IPv4 or IPv6 network using PXE
- Software-based keyboard, mouse, and video support via the VMBus
- No legacy system components aside from serial (COM) ports

After selecting a generation within Figure 3-13 and clicking Next, you are prompted to select the amount of memory that the virtual machine will use, as shown in Figure 3-14, The default of 1024 MB (1 GB) may be fine for a Server Core, Linux, or UNIX guest operating system, but in most environments, you will want to increase this value to match the needs of the services or applications running on the server. If you select *Use Dynamic Memory for this virtual machine*, the value you specify within the Startup memory box will be automatically increased or decreased based on the needs of the guest operating system. This **dynamic memory** feature of Hyper-V depends largely on the available memory resources on the underlying hardware, and can cause problems if it is enabled on too many virtual machines whose guest operating systems require additional memory at the same time. Additionally, dynamic memory should not be enabled if you use nested virtualization, as memory resource utilization cannot be efficiently managed between two different Hyper-V hypervisors.

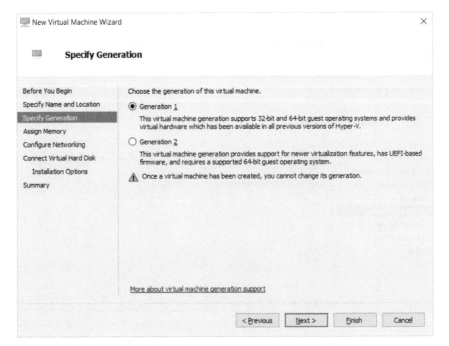

Figure 3-13   Specifying the virtual machine generation

After clicking Next in Figure 3-14, you are prompted to select the virtual switch that your first network adapter will connect to as shown in Figure 3-15. Additional network adapters can be configured after the virtual machine has been created. After you select

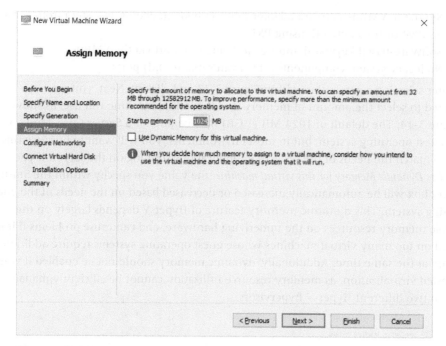

Figure 3-14   Assigning memory to a virtual machine

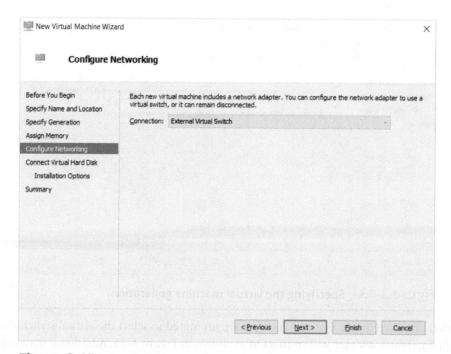

Figure 3-15   Configuring a virtual network connection

a virtual switch and click Next, you are prompted for virtual hard disk configuration as shown in Figure 3-16. By default, the New Virtual Machine Wizard creates a 127 GB dynamically expanding virtual hard disk within the default location with the same name as your virtual machine with a .vhdx extension. However, you can choose to use an existing virtual hard disk file, or assign a virtual hard disk file after creation.

Note

Recall from Module 1 that a dynamically expanding virtual hard disk is often referred to as thin provisioning, as it only consumes the underlying storage space when necessary.

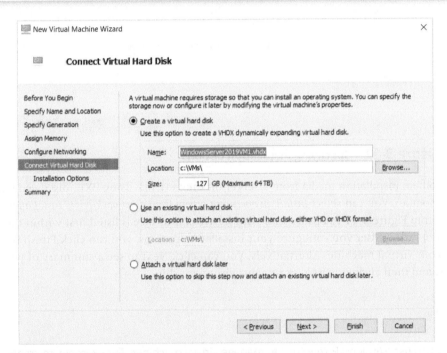

Figure 3-16   Configuring a virtual hard disk

After configuring a virtual hard disk and clicking Next in Figure 3-16, you are prompted for the options needed to install a guest operating system within the virtual machine, as shown in Figure 3-17. If you choose *Install an operating system from a bootable CD/DVD-ROM drive*, you can either choose to associate the physical CD/DVD-ROM drive within the server to the virtual CD/DVD-ROM drive within the virtual machine, or associate an ISO image file that contains the installation image with the virtual CD/DVD-ROM drive within the virtual machine. Choosing this option also modifies the boot order within the BIOS to ensure that the CD/DVD-ROM drive is listed first. For a Generation 1 virtual machine, you can instead choose to boot from a virtual floppy disk image. If you

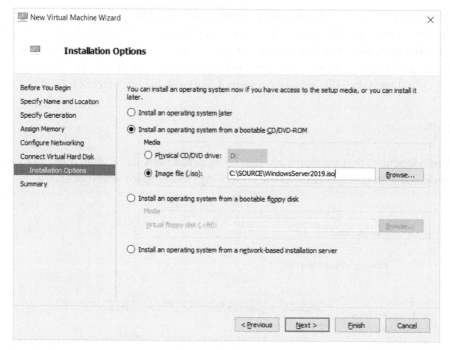

Figure 3-17   Specifying installation options

plan to obtain installation media from a server on the network using PXE (discussed later in this module), you can select *Install an operating system from a network-based installation server* within Figure 3-17 to ensure that your network interface is listed first within the BIOS boot order. After you configure your installation options, you can click Finish to create your virtual machine. Alternatively, you can click Next to see a summary of your choices, and then click Finish to create your virtual machine.

Note

You can also use Windows PowerShell to manage virtual machines. For example, to create a Generation 2 virtual machine called WindowsServer2019VM1 that stores its configuration within the X:\VMs directory, has 4 GB (4294967296 bytes) of memory, contains a new dynamically expanding 127 GB (136365211648 bytes) virtual hard disk file stored within the X:\VMs\WindowsServer2019VM1.vhd file, and uses a virtual network interface connected to the ExtVS virtual switch, you can run the New-VM -Generation 2 -Name "WindowsServer2019VM1" -Path "X:\VMs" -MemoryStartupBytes 4294967296 -VHDPath "X:\VMs\WindowsServer2019VM1.vhdx" -NewVHDSizeBytes 136365211648 -Switchname "ExtVS" command. For a full list of Hyper-V cmdlets, you can run the Get-Command -Module hyper-v | Out-GridView command.

Configuring Virtual Machines

After you create a virtual machine, that virtual machine is displayed within the Virtual Machines pane of Hyper-V Manager, and the Actions pane will list actions that you can take on the virtual machine, as shown in Figure 3-18.

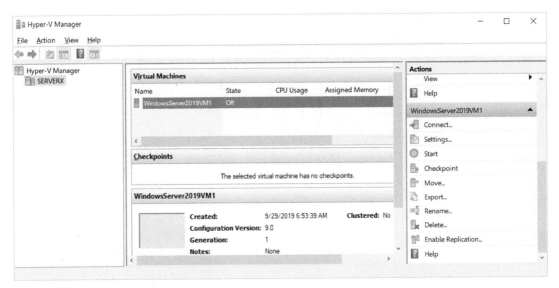

Figure 3-18   Selecting actions for a virtual machine within Hyper-V Manager

You can click Start within the Actions pane to boot the virtual machine. If the virtual CD/DVD-ROM drive is associated with an ISO image that contains Windows Server 2019 installation media, the Windows Server 2019 installer will start and guide you through the remainder of the installation process. Alternatively, you can click Settings within the Actions pane in order to modify the settings for your virtual machine.

Configuring a Generation 2 Virtual Machine

When you access the settings for a Generation 2 virtual machine, you will see a Hardware and Management section similar to that shown in Figure 3-19.

By default, the Hardware section for a virtual machine lists the hardware that was configured during the creation of the virtual machine. In Figure 3-19, this includes 8 GB of memory, one virtual processor, a SCSI controller that is attached to a virtual hard drive, a virtual DVD drive (associated with WindowsServer2019.iso), and a network interface (associated with External Virtual Switch). Additionally, the Generation 2 UEFI BIOS firmware is set to boot from the DVD drive first, and Secure Boot is enabled.

The Add Hardware node within the Hardware section shown in Figure 3-19 can be used to add additional SCSI controllers or network interfaces. If your system has a RemoteFX-capable video card, you can add a virtual RemoteFX 3D video adapter to allow virtual machines to share the processing capabilities of the underlying video card

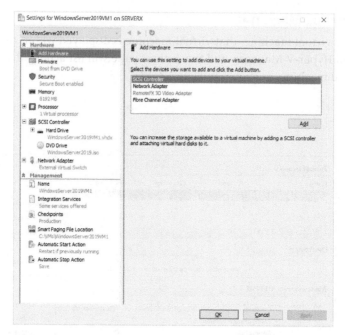

Figure 3-19   Settings for a Generation 2 virtual machine

for 3D graphics accelerations. Alternatively, creating a virtual Fibre Channel adapter that is associated with a physical Fibre Channel adapter in your system will allow the virtual machine to access the SAN that is connected to the physical Fibre Channel adapter.

Selecting Firmware within the Hardware section allows you to change the boot order for hardware devices within the UEFI BIOS (shown in Figure 3-20), and selecting Security within the Hardware section allows you to configure UEFI security settings (shown in Figure 3-21). Secure Boot is enabled by default within Generation 2 virtual machines and serves to protect the system from booting unauthorized operating systems. The Trusted Platform Module (TPM) can optionally be enabled for a virtual machine to store Secure Boot and virtual machine encryption keys. If you enable **Shielding**, BitLocker will be used to encrypt virtual hard disks so that they cannot be used on another virtual machine, using encryption keys that are stored in the TPM.

Note

If you enable the TPM within a virtual machine, you can optionally encrypt live migration traffic by selecting *Encrypt state and virtual machine traffic* within Figure 3-21.

Figure 3-20   Setting the boot order for a Generation 2 virtual machine

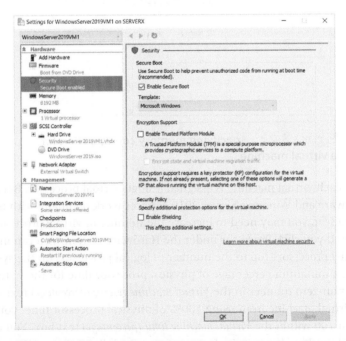

Figure 3-21   Setting UEFI BIOS security settings for a Generation 2 virtual machine

You can modify the memory configuration by selecting Memory under the Hardware section, as shown in Figure 3-22. The RAM text box indicates the memory that will be allocated to the virtual machine when it is started. If *Enable Dynamic Memory* is selected, then you can specify the minimum and maximum values that the virtual machine can utilize, as well as the reserved physical memory buffer that Hyper-V will create to provide for virtual machines that request additional memory (20% by default). You can also increase the Memory weight setting of a virtual machine. This will give the virtual machine more priority compared to other virtual machines when Hyper-V receives requests for additional memory on a system that does not have enough memory to satisfy all running virtual machines.

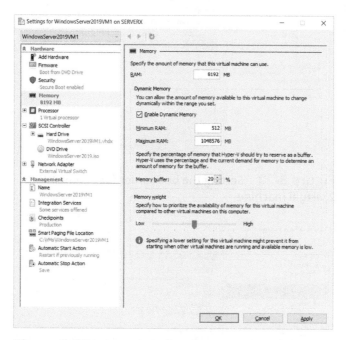

Figure 3-22   Specifying memory configuration for a virtual machine

By default, each virtual machine is assigned a single virtual processor. Because many third-party software and Windows Server 2019 services work optimally with more than one virtual processor, you may need to increase the number of virtual processors for your virtual machine. If you click Processor under the Hardware section, you can increase the number of virtual processors (up to the number of logical processors on the system). You can also reserve a minimum percentage of physical processor time for the virtual machine by specifying a non-zero number in the *Virtual machine reserve (percentage)* text box. To prevent your virtual machine from using 100% of physical processor time, you can specify a value less than 100 within the *Virtual machine limit (percentage)* text box. You can also give your virtual machine less priority for processor scheduling compared to other virtual machines by specifying a number less than 100 in the *Relative weight* text box.

If you expand the Processor node under the Hardware section (also shown in Figure 3-23), you can optionally specify advanced processor capabilities, including:

- *Compatibility*, which allows you to give live migration the ability to move a virtual machine to another Hyper-V host that uses a different processor version.
- *NUMA*, which allows you to define memory settings on multi-physical-processor systems that support **non-uniform memory access (NUMA)** for faster memory sharing between processors.

Figure 3-23   Modifying processor settings for a virtual machine

Recall that Generation 2 virtual machines emulate Serial Attached SCSI (SAS) storage devices. If you select a SCSI Controller under the Hardware section, as shown in Figure 3-24, you can add additional virtual hard disk drives, virtual DVD-ROM drives, or a virtual hard disk that is shared by multiple virtual machines. Alternatively, you can remove the SCSI Controller from the system, which also removes any attached storage devices.

When you highlight a Hard Drive under a SCSI Controller, as shown in Figure 3-25, you will see the associated virtual hard disk file path. You can click:

- *New* to create and associate a new virtual hard disk file with the virtual hard disk.
- *Edit* to compact a dynamically expanding virtual hard disk file (removing unused space), convert a dynamically expanding virtual hard disk file to a fixed size virtual hard disk file (and vice versa), or expand the capacity of an existing virtual hard disk file.
- *Inspect* to display information and usage for a virtual hard disk file.
- *Browse* to replace the current virtual hard disk file with another existing one.

Figure 3-24   Modifying SCSI controller settings within a virtual machine

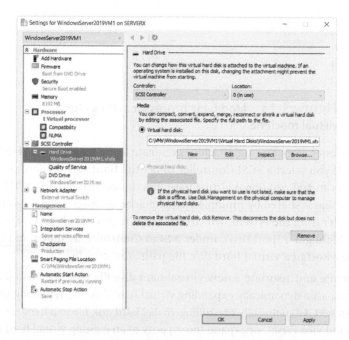

Figure 3-25   Modifying virtual hard drive settings within a virtual machine

If your system has a physical hard disk that is set to an offline state, you can also choose to use this physical hard disk in place of a virtual hard disk file for enhanced performance by selecting *Physical hard disk* in Figure 3-25 and choosing the offline hard disk. This configuration is called a **pass-through disk**.

To remove the virtual Hard Drive altogether, you can click Remove. If you expand a virtual Hard Drive, you will notice a Quality of Service section (also shown in Figure 3-25). **Quality of Service (QoS)** allows you to specify minimum and maximum limits to the number of **Input/Output Operations Per Second (IOPS)** for a virtual hard disk file. Guaranteeing a virtual hard disk file a minimum number of IOPS is recommended if it contains frequently accessed files or databases. Alternatively, you may wish to limit the number of IOPS on virtual hard disks that are not frequently accessed to ensure that they do not dominate the underlying server storage system.

When you highlight a DVD Drive under a SCSI Controller, as shown in Figure 3-26, you can select Image file and click Browse to select an ISO image file that will be associated with the virtual DVD drive, or select None to disassociate an existing ISO image. To remove a DVD drive altogether, you can click Remove.

If you select a Network Adapter under the Hardware section, as shown in Figure 3-27, you can associate the network interface with a virtual switch, and optionally enable and set a VLAN identification number. If you select *Enable bandwidth management*, you can guarantee the virtual network interface a minimum bandwidth in Mbps on the underlying network interface hardware, which is often useful for virtual machines that provide file services to other computers on the network. Alternatively, you can limit the virtual network interface to a maximum bandwidth in Mbps, which can be used to prevent virtual machines that play a non-critical role on the network from running processes inadvertently that saturate the network bandwidth. To remove a virtual network interface, you can click Remove.

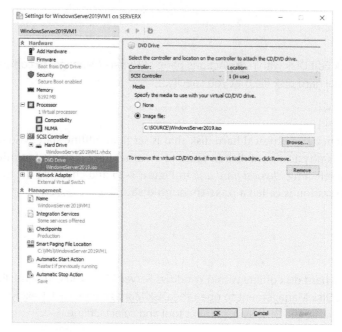

Figure 3-26 Modifying virtual DVD drive settings within a virtual machine

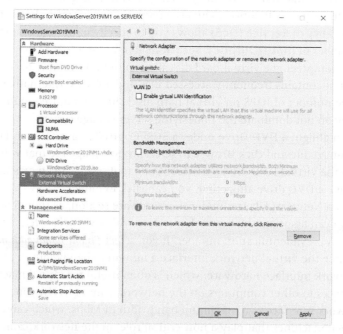

Figure 3-27 Modifying network adapter settings within a virtual machine

If you expand a Network Adapter (also shown in Figure 3-27), you can select Hardware Acceleration or Advanced Features to configure optional network interface components, including:

- **Virtual machine queue** support, which optimizes the transfer of network traffic to a virtual machine (enabled by default).
- **IPsec task offloading**, which performs IPsec calculations within the physical network interface hardware instead of using the virtual processor (enabled by default).
- Single-root I/O virtualization, which separates network traffic for each virtual machine within the network interface hardware. This setting should only be enabled if the underlying network interface hardware supports the feature.
- **MAC address spoofing**, which allows a virtual machine to change its MAC address on outgoing packets. You can also set a static MAC address on the virtual machine in this section.
- **DHCP guard**, which prevents DHCP servers that are not authorized within Active Directory from assigning IP configuration to a network interface.
- **Router guard**, which prevents unauthorized routers from communicating with the network interface.
- **Protected network**, which automatically moves the virtual machine to another Hyper-V system if the virtual machine is part of a cluster (enabled by default).
- **Port mirroring**, which allows all traffic on the virtual switch to be sent to the virtual network interface for monitoring purposes.
- **NIC Teaming**, which allows multiple network interfaces to function together for load balancing and fault tolerance.
- **Device naming**, which allows the name of the underlying physical network adapter to be shown within the virtual network adapter.

All non-hardware-related configuration for a Generation 2 virtual machine is performed within the Management section of virtual machine settings:

- *Name* allows you to modify the name of the virtual machine.
- *Integration Services* allows you to select the services that are provided automatically to the guest operating system from the Hyper-V host operating system. This includes data exchange, time synchronization, backup services, cluster heartbeat information, as well as the ability to shut down the guest operating system automatically when the host operating system is shut down.
- *Checkpoints* lets you allow the use of virtual machine checkpoints, as well as configure the checkpoint type and storage location (checkpoints are discussed later in this module).
- *Smart Paging File Location* allows you to specify the location of a paging file that Hyper-V uses to store memory information if physical memory becomes exhausted. It is good practice to change the location of this **smart paging file** to a fast storage device, such as an SSD to optimize performance.

- *Automatic Start Action* allows you to choose whether to automatically start the virtual machine when Hyper-V is started. This section also allows you to specify a delay in seconds following system startup before the virtual machine is started.
- *Automatic Stop Action* allows you to specify what happens when the system is powered off. You can choose to turn off the virtual machine, safely shut down the guest operating system, or save the virtual machine state (which includes the contents of memory) such that it can be quickly restored when the system starts.

Configuring a Generation 1 Virtual Machine

When you access the settings for a Generation 1 virtual machine, you will see a Hardware and Management section similar to that shown in Figure 3-28.

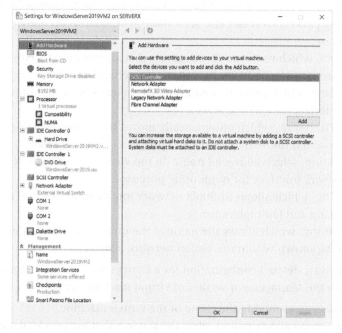

Figure 3-28   Settings for a Generation 1 virtual machine

The Management section is identical for Generations 1 and 2 virtual machines, and is the configuration of the memory, processor, virtual hard disk drive, and network adapter settings within the Hardware section. However, there are some key differences within the Hardware section that you will find when configuring a Generation 1 virtual machine:

- The hard drive and DVD drives are on legacy IDE controllers.
- The CD/DVD-ROM drive can be configured as a pass-through disk to an underlying physical CD/DVD-ROM drive.
- The Add Hardware node allows you to add a legacy network adapter, as well as a synthetic network adapter that uses the VMBus.

- When you add a SCSI Controller in the Add Hardware node, it adds a legacy SCSI Controller (non-SAS). While SCSI disks can be added to the virtual machine, they cannot contain the guest operating system.
- Two serial (COM) ports are emulated for use within the guest operating system, and may be configured to use a **named pipe** (a persistent connection to a process via a file on the filesystem).
- A virtual floppy diskette drive is emulated for use within the guest operating system and may be configured to use a virtual floppy disk image file.
- The boot order also lists the virtual floppy disk drive.
- The Security node does not allow Secure Boot, TPM, or shielded virtual machine support, because the virtual machine emulates a legacy BIOS.

Working with Virtual Machines

If you click Start within the Actions pane for a virtual machine, you will boot the virtual machine itself. Following this, you can click Connect in the Actions pane to obtain a Virtual Machine Connection window that provides a graphical desktop connection to the virtual machine for you to interact with. However, before booting a newly created virtual machine, you should first click Connect in the Actions pane to obtain the Virtual Machine Connection window shown in Figure 3-29, and then click Start within this window to boot the virtual machine. This allows you to see messages at the beginning of the boot

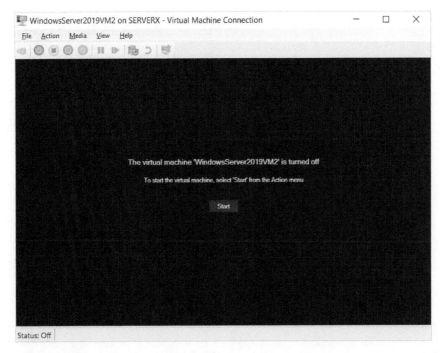

Figure 3-29   The Virtual Machine Connection window

process (e.g., *Press any key to boot from CD or DVD...*) that are necessary to start a Windows Server 2019 installation from installation media associated with a virtual CD/DVD-ROM drive, or from a server on the network. You can then use the associated buttons on the toolbar of the Virtual Machine Connection window, or within the Actions pane of Hyper-V manager (shown in Figure 3-30) to perform key actions within your virtual machine that are normally performed on a physical computer. These actions include:

- *Ctrl+Alt+Del* to unlock a login screen (only available within the Virtual Machine Connection window).
- *Turn Off* to simulate a PC shutdown.
- *Shut Down* to safely shut down.
- *Save* to save the virtual machine state and shut down.
- *Pause* to pause the virtual machine state temporarily.
- *Reset* to simulate a power cycle on an unresponsive system.

You can also view information for a running virtual machine within Hyper-V Manager. For example, selecting the Summary, Memory, Networking, or Replication tabs within the WindowsServer2019VM1 pane shown within Figure 3-30 will display information about the system, memory, network, and replication configuration (replication is discussed in the next section). For ease, you can also click the thumbnail picture within the WindowsServer2019VM1 pane to connect to the WindowsServer2019VM1 virtual machine and obtain a Virtual Network Connection window.

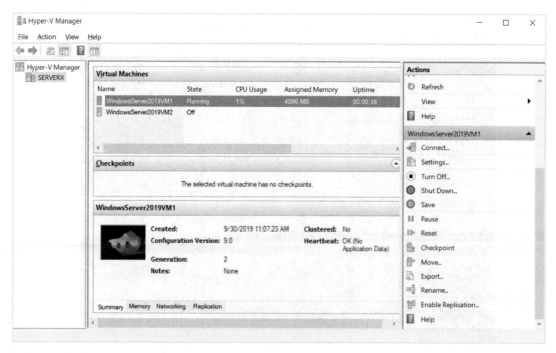

Figure 3-30   Working with a running virtual machine

Managing Hyper-V Features

There are many Hyper-V features that provide extra capabilities beyond running guest operating systems. The most commonly configured Hyper-V features include:

- Checkpoints
- Live Migration
- Replication

Checkpoints

Checkpoints (often called snapshots) is a Hyper-V feature that allows you to revert the state of a virtual machine to a previous point in time. Before making potentially problematic modifications to the operating system (e.g., Windows Registry changes, driver installation), you should create a checkpoint to ensure that you can restore your virtual machine to the previous state should the modification cause problems.

Normally, any modifications you make to your operating system within a virtual machine are stored within the associated virtual hard disk (.vhdx) file. When you create a checkpoint, all modifications that you make to your operating system after that point are instead stored within a checkpoint (.avhdx) file within the same directory as your virtual hard disk file. For example, if you create a checkpoint of your virtual machine at 9:02 am, as shown in Figure 3-31, any modifications that occur after 9:02 am will only be stored within the checkpoint file. All other checkpoint information will be stored within a Snapshots directory under your virtual machine location.

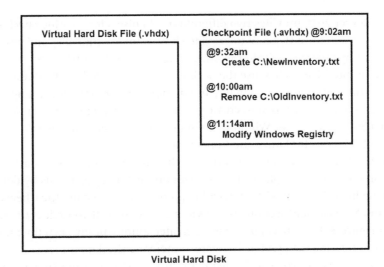

Figure 3-31   A sample checkpoint file configuration

After you create a checkpoint, you can apply it to revert your system to the point in time just prior to when the checkpoint was created. This will also remove the checkpoint file from the system. For example, if you apply the checkpoint shown in Figure 3-31, the C:\NewInventory.txt will be removed, the C:\OldInventory.txt file will be restored, and the modification performed on the Windows Registry will be reversed. Alternatively, if you delete a checkpoint, the modifications within the checkpoint file will be merged into the virtual hard disk file (making the modifications permanent within the operating system), and the checkpoint file will be removed from the system.

> **Note** 📎
>
> You normally apply a checkpoint if the modification that you made to the system proves to be problematic. You normally delete a checkpoint if the modification that you made to the system works as intended.

> **Note** 📎
>
> Writing changes to a checkpoint file requires additional effort from your system. As a result, you should only enable checkpoints for short periods of time to maintain optimal performance. Normally, a checkpoint is taken immediately before a potentially problematic modification, and either applied or deleted shortly thereafter.

Windows Server 2019 provides two different mechanisms for creating checkpoints. **Standard checkpoints** use Hyper-V to provide checkpoint functionality and also save the state of running programs within the Snapshots directory. **Production checkpoints** are less resource-intensive as they use the backup service provided by the guest operating system to perform checkpoint functionality but do not save the state of running programs. The backup service used to create production checkpoints is either the **Volume Shadow Copy Service (VSS)** for Windows guest operating systems, or the **File System Freeze (fsfreeze)** service for Linux guest operating systems.

Because production checkpoints do not save the state of running programs, they cause fewer problems when applied. Hyper-V uses production checkpoints by default, but you can modify this within virtual machine properties by selecting the Checkpoints node under the Management section, as shown in Figure 3-32. If you select *Use automatic checkpoints* in Figure 3-32, a checkpoint will be created automatically each time the virtual machine starts, replacing the previously created automatic checkpoint.

To create a checkpoint, you can highlight a virtual machine within Hyper-V Manager and click Checkpoint in the Actions pane. After the checkpoint has been created, it is displayed within the Checkpoints pane within Hyper-V Manager, as shown in Figure 3-33. To apply a checkpoint, you can highlight the checkpoint shown in Figure 3-33 and click Apply. Alternatively, you can click Delete Checkpoint to delete a checkpoint, or Delete Checkpoint Subtree to delete multiple checkpoints.

Figure 3-32   Modifying checkpoint settings for a virtual machine

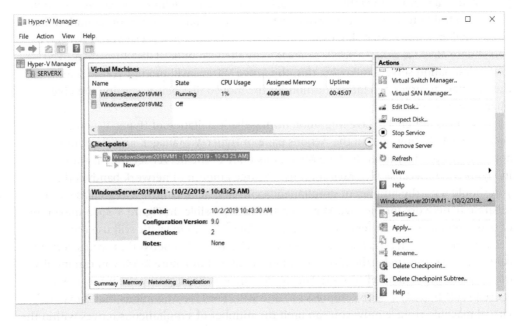

Figure 3-33   Viewing checkpoints within Hyper-V Manager

Note

If you highlight a virtual machine within the Virtual Machines pane, you can select Revert from the Actions pane to apply the most recent checkpoint.

Note

If you apply a production checkpoint, the guest operating system will shut down to perform the action. After you start the virtual machine again, you can safely delete this checkpoint if you do not plan to make other potentially problematic modifications.

Live Migration

If you enabled Live Migration during the installation of Hyper-V, you can move a virtual machine to another server running Hyper-V within the same Active Directory domain. To move a virtual machine using Live Migration, you can select a virtual machine within Hyper-V Manager and click Move within the Actions pane to start the Move Wizard. When you click Next at the Before You Begin screen within the Move Wizard, you are prompted whether to move the virtual machine or virtual machine storage, as shown in Figure 3-34. If you select *Move the virtual machine*, the virtual machine configuration files and virtual machine hard disk files will be moved to the destination server. However, if you choose *Move the virtual machine's storage*, only the virtual hard disk files are moved to the destination server. Following this, the Move Wizard will prompt you to select the destination server and target location for the moved files before starting the Live Migration process.

If you did not enable Live Migration during the installation of Hyper-V, you can click Hyper-V Settings within the Actions pane of Hyper-V Manager, and configure the appropriate options within the Live Migrations node of the Server section, as shown in Figure 3-35. Because Live Migration uses a large amount of network bandwidth, you should limit the number of simultaneous virtual machine moves, as well as use a separate IP network for the Live Migration traffic, if possible. In Figure 3-35, a maximum of two simultaneous transfers are allowed, and Live Migration traffic will use the network interface that has an IP address on the 172.16.0.0/16 network. If you select the Advanced Features under the Live Migrations node within Figure 3-35, you can modify the authentication method (CredSSP or Kerberos), as well as specify the protocol that is used (TCP/IP, TCP/IP with compression, or SMB). For Live Migrations that move the virtual machine storage only, you can limit the number of simultaneous moves within the Storage Migrations node shown in Figure 3-35.

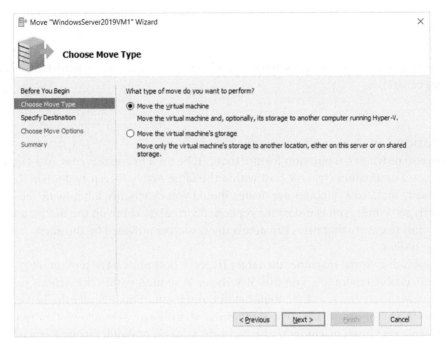

Figure 3-34 Specifying the move type for a live migration

Figure 3-35 Configuring live migration within Hyper-V Settings

> **Note**
>
> Live Migration can only be enabled if the Hyper-V host operating system is joined to an Active Directory domain.

Replication

Hyper-V also provides a replication feature that can be used to create a copy of a virtual machine on a destination Hyper-V host within the same Active Directory domain that is continually updated as changes are made. Should you experience a hardware failure on your Hyper-V host, you can start the replicated virtual machine on the destination Hyper-V host to ensure that users can access the resources provided by the guest operating system.

To replicate a virtual machine, the target Hyper-V host must have replication enabled. To enable replication, you can click Hyper-V Settings within the Actions pane of Hyper-V Manager and select the Replication Configuration node under the Server section, as shown in Figure 3-36. The settings shown in Figure 3-36 allow other Hyper-V hosts to replicate virtual machines to the C:\ReplicatedVMs folder using Kerberos authentication via the HTTP protocol.

Figure 3-36   Enabling replication within Hyper-V Settings

After replication is enabled on the target Hyper-V host, you can replicate a virtual machine by selecting it within Hyper-V Manager and clicking Enable Replication within the Actions pane. This will start the Enable Replication wizard that will prompt you to specify the replication settings for your virtual machine, including the target Hyper-V host, storage location, and replication frequency.

Rapid Server Deployment

Larger organizations today may deploy hundreds, or even thousands, of server operating systems that are installed directly on server hardware or within virtual machines. In these environments, server deployment may be performed multiple times each day, using **rapid server deployment** techniques that minimize the time it takes to install a new server. To perform rapid server deployment of Windows Server 2019 within a virtual machine, you can copy a **virtual machine template**, or perform a network installation using **Windows Deployment Services (WDS)**. WDS can also be used to rapidly deploy Windows Server 2019 to physical servers that are connected to the network.

Using Virtual Machine Templates

A Windows Server 2019 virtual machine template is a virtual machine containing a Windows Server 2019 installation that is saved (exported) to a folder on the file system for future use. This virtual machine template can then be copied (imported) multiple times within Hyper-V Manager to create new virtual machines that contain a Windows Server 2019 installation.

Creating a Virtual Machine Template

To create a virtual machine template, you first create a virtual machine that contains the minimum hardware settings (e.g., memory, virtual hard disk size, virtual processor count) that your organization uses for virtual machines. While this virtual machine can be given any name, you should use a descriptive name such as "WindowsServer2019Template." Next, you perform a normal installation of Windows Server 2019 to the virtual hard disk associated with the virtual machine. Following the installation, you can optionally install server roles and features as well as third party software that you wish to be available on new virtual machines that are created from the virtual machine template.

Next, you must remove all unique information from the Windows Server 2019 operating system installed within the virtual machine, including the computer name, unique system identifiers within the Windows Registry, regional settings, license information, Administrator password, and so on. To do this, you run the **System Preparation Tool** by navigating to the C:\Windows\System32\Sysprep folder within Windows Explorer and executing the sysprep.exe program. Within the System Preparation Tool window, you should select the options shown in Figure 3-37 and click OK. This will remove all unique information from the system (the Generalize option) and shut down the guest operating system when finished. If the virtual machine, or a copy of the virtual machine, is booted again, the **Out-of-Box Experience (OOBE)** wizard will generate a new computer name and unique identifiers within the Windows Registry as well as prompt you to specify regional options, accept the Windows license agreement, and specify a new Administrator password.

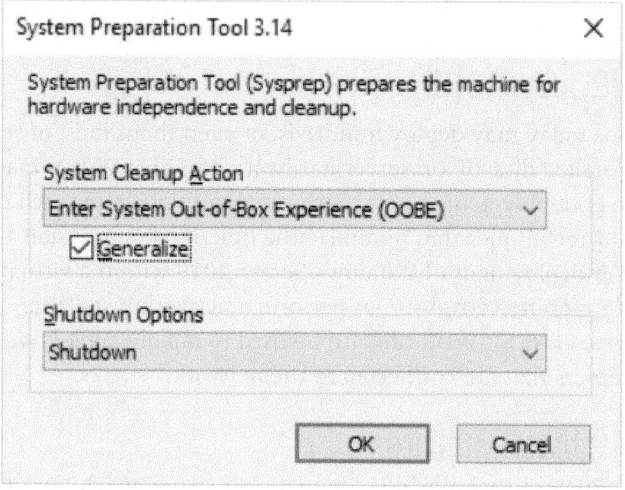

Figure 3-37   **The Sysprep tool**

After the System Preparation Tool shuts down the guest operating system, you can select the virtual machine within Hyper-V Manager and select Export from the Actions menu to create a virtual machine template that can be later imported to create new virtual machines. When you click Export, you must choose a folder in which to store your virtual machine template, such as the `C:\VMTemplates` folder shown in Figure 3-38, and click OK to create the virtual machine template. For a virtual machine called WindowsServer2019Template, this will create a `C:\VMTemplates\WindowsServer2019Template` folder that contains the virtual machine configuration and associated virtual hard disks.

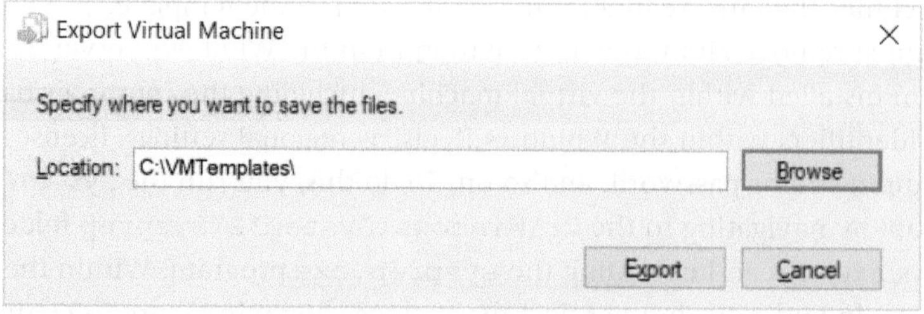

Figure 3-38   **Exporting a virtual machine to create a virtual machine template**

Importing a Virtual Machine Template

After you have created a virtual machine template, you can use it to simplify the creation of new virtual machines. To create a new virtual machine based on your virtual machine template, you can click Import Virtual Machine within the Actions pane of Hyper-V Manager. This will open the Import Virtual Machine wizard. When you click Next at the Before You Begin welcome page in this wizard, you are prompted to specify the folder that contains the virtual machine template to import, as shown in Figure 3-39. After clicking Next, you must select the virtual machine template within the folder that you wish to import, as shown in Figure 3-40.

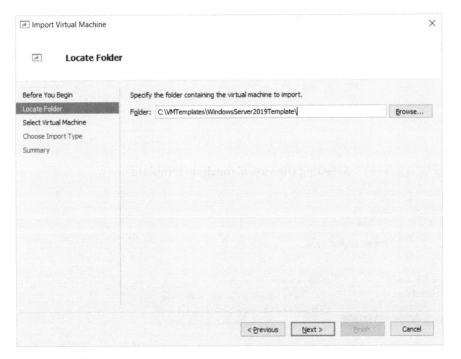

Figure 3-39 Specifying the folder that contains the virtual machine template

After you select a virtual machine template and click Next, you must choose to create a copy of the virtual machine as shown in Figure 3-41 and click Next. You will then be prompted to specify the location for the copied virtual machine configuration files and virtual hard disk files. It is good practice to specify a folder for these configuration files that matches the name that you would like to use for your new virtual machine. For a virtual machine called WindowsServer2019VM2, you could specify the virtual machine configuration folders shown in Figure 3-42, and virtual machine hard disk folder shown in Figure 3-43.

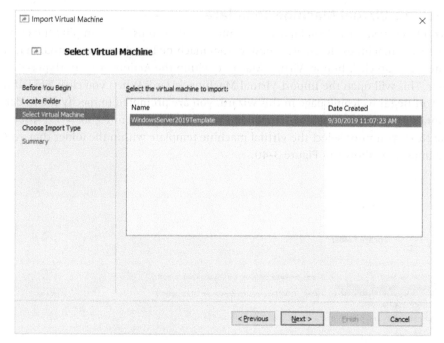

Figure 3-40   Selecting the virtual machine template

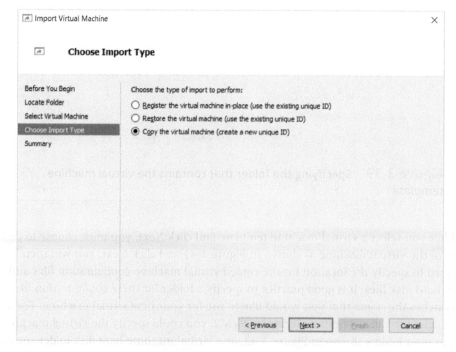

Figure 3-41   Copying the virtual machine template

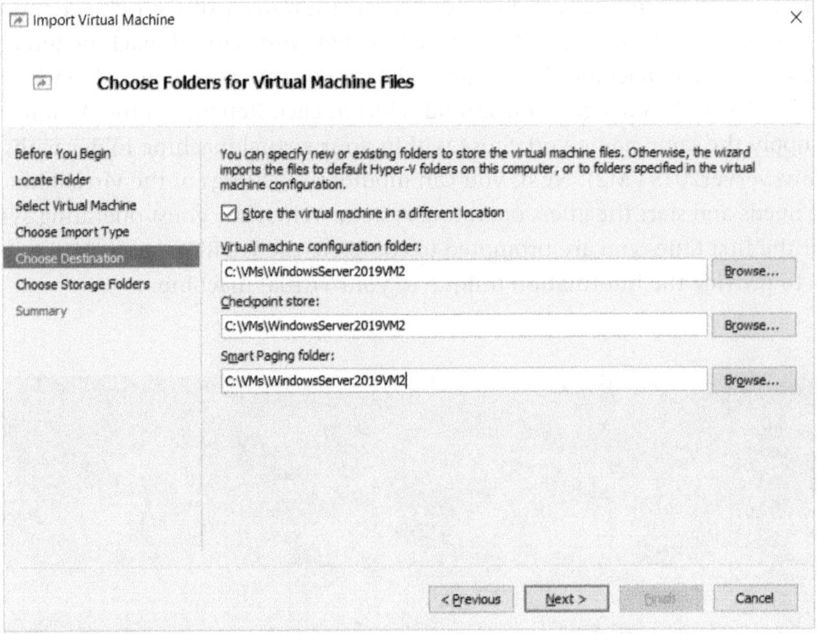

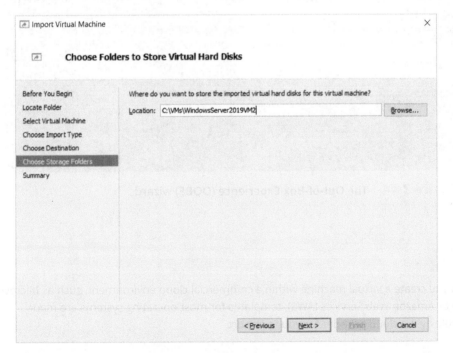

Figure 3-42   Specifying the target folder paths for the virtual machine configuration files

Figure 3-43   Specifying the target folder paths for the virtual hard disk files

When you click Next in Figure 3-43, you will see a summary of your choices and can click Finish to create a new virtual machine based on your virtual machine template. Because this new virtual machine will be given the same name as the virtual machine template within Hyper-V Manager, you should select it, click Rename in the Actions pane, and supply the same name you chose within your virtual machine folder paths (e.g., WindowsServer2019VM2). Next, you can modify the settings of the virtual machine to suit your needs and start the guest operating system. When the guest operating system is started for the first time, you are prompted to complete the OOBE wizard shown in Figure 3-44 to provide the information unique to your virtual machine.

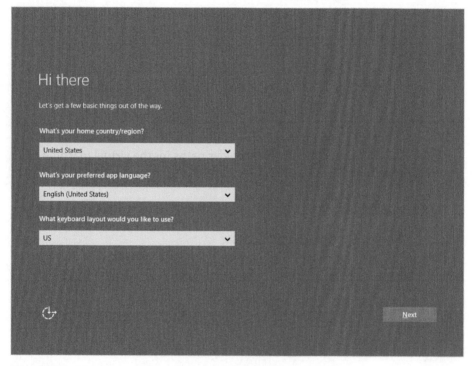

Figure 3-44   **The Out-of-Box Experience (OOBE) wizard**

Note 🔗

When you create a virtual machine within a commercial cloud environment, such as Microsoft Azure or Amazon Web Services (AWS), templates for most operating systems are made available by the cloud provider for you to import.

Using Windows Deployment Services

Starting with Windows Vista and Windows Server 2008, the installation media for Windows client and server operating systems is primarily composed of two large **Windows Imaging Format (WIM)** image files:

- `boot.wim` (called a **boot image**) contains a bootable Windows installation program, and
- `install.wim` (called an **install image**) contains the operating system files that are copied to the hard disk or SSD during the installation process.

These WIM files can be used in conjunction with Windows Deployment Services (WDS) to deploy Windows operating systems to computers that are configured to boot from the network using a PXE-capable network interface. When you boot a computer from the network using PXE, it receives an IP address from a DHCP server, as well as a PXEClient option that refers the computer to a server running WDS. If you acknowledge this option (by pressing a specific key on your keyboard, such as F12 or Enter), your computer then downloads the boot image stored on the WDS server to local memory and executes it to start the Windows installation program. After making your selections, the Windows installation program then obtains the appropriate install image for the version of Windows that you wish to install from the WDS server, and copies the files within to the hard disk or SSD in your computer to complete the installation process.

Furthermore, several computers can simultaneously boot from the network and install an operating system from a WDS server. In this case, the WDS server coordinates the flow of information such that a single copy of the individual files within the WIM images are sent over the network to be processed by each client computer simultaneously using the **multicast** feature of IP. This allows you to install Windows on hundreds of computers using WDS in the same amount of time it takes to install Windows on a single computer. Thus, you can use WDS to perform rapid server deployment of Windows Server 2019 on multiple physical servers or virtual machines that boot from the network using PXE.

To implement rapid server deployment using WDS, you must install WDS as well as configure the WDS to respond to client computers using the appropriate boot and install images. Following this, you can boot physical servers and virtual machines from the network using PXE to perform the installation process.

Installing WDS

To install WDS on Windows Server 2019, you can select the Windows Deployment Services role when adding a role within Server Manager, as shown in Figure 3-45. When you click Next in Figure 3-45 and progress through the Add Roles and Features Wizard, you are prompted to select the two role services that are required for full WDS functionality, as shown in Figure 3-46. The **Deployment Server** provides the core functionality of WDS, while the **Transport Server** responds to PXE requests from the network and uses IP multicast to send the contents of WIM images to each computer.

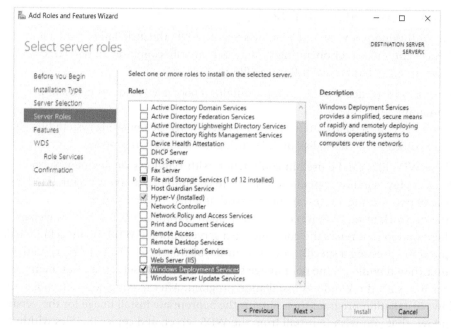

Figure 3-45   Adding the Windows Deployment Services role within Server Manager

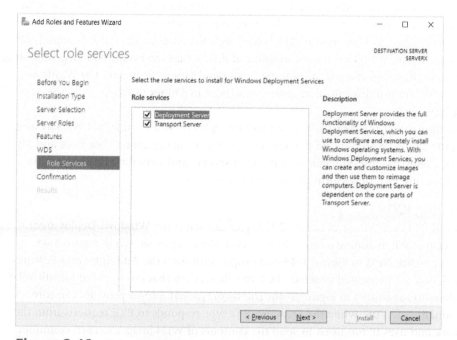

Figure 3-46   Selecting WDS role services within Server Manager

Configuring WDS

The configuration of WDS is performed using the **Windows Deployment Services tool** shown in Figure 3-47. You can start this tool by selecting Windows Deployment Services from the Tools menu within Server Manager. The first time you open the Windows Deployment Services tool, you will see a yellow warning icon on your server object in the navigation pane indicating that the WDS service needs to be configured. To perform the initial configuration of the WDS service, you can right-click your server object and click Configure Server to open the Windows Deployment Services Configuration Wizard. After clicking Next at the Before You Begin page, you are prompted to choose whether to integrate WDS with an Active Directory domain as shown in Figure 3-48. Integrating WDS with Active Directory allows WDS to automatically join Windows systems to the Active Directory domain during the installation process as well as allows any domain user to perform a WDS installation. When you click Next, you are prompted to choose the folder that will be used to store WDS configuration and WIM images as shown in Figure 3-49. For performance reasons, you should change the default folder shown in Figure 3-49 to a folder that is on a separate hard disk or SSD, so that WDS disk operations do not compete with Windows Server 2019 disk operations. Following this, you are prompted to configure the DHCP integration options shown in Figure 3-50. If your network has a DHCP server, you should deselect both options shown in Figure 3-50 and set DHCP option 60 on your DHCP server to the name or IP address of your WDS server. Alternatively, if you install and configure the Microsoft DHCP service on your WDS server, the default options shown in Figure 3-50 will automatically configure this option. If you install a third party DHCP service on your DHCP server, you must deselect the second option and configure DHCP option 60 within the DHCP service.

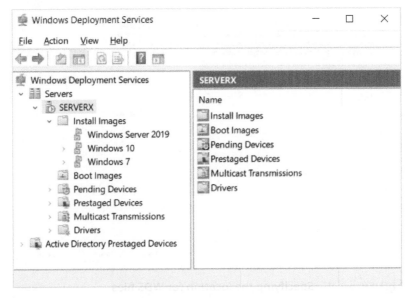

Figure 3-47   The Windows Deployment Services tool

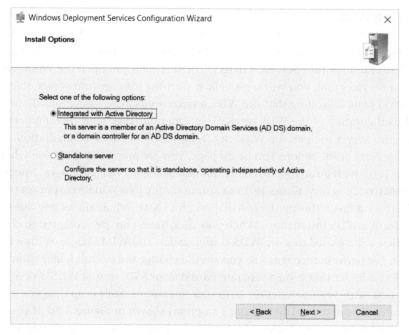

Figure 3-48   Selecting WDS installation options

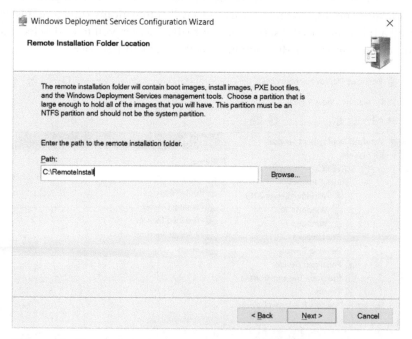

Figure 3-49   Specifying the location for WDS files

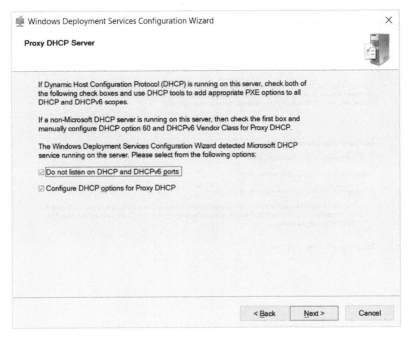

Figure 3-50   Specifying DHCP integration options

Note

The configuration of DHCP is discussed later in Module 8.

When you click Next after configuring DHCP integration options, the Windows Deployment Service Configuration Wizard prompts you to select how the server should respond to PXE requests from computers on the network, as shown in Figure 3-51. Normally, you select the option shown in Figure 3-51 to allow WDS to respond to clients on the network. However, if you select *Respond only to known client computers*, then you will need to pre-create entries for each computer's MAC address within the Prestaged Devices folder shown in Figure 3-47 before WDS will allow the computers to connect. If you select the *Require administrator approval for unknown computers* option, then each PXE request will be listed within the Pending Devices folder shown in Figure 3-47, and you must manually approve each request before the computer is allowed to interact with WDS. If you select *Do not respond to any client computers*, then WDS will not respond to any PXE requests until you choose a different setting on the PXE Response tab within the properties of your WDS server object. After you click Next in Figure 3-51, you will see a summary of your choices and can click Finish to complete the initial WDS configuration.

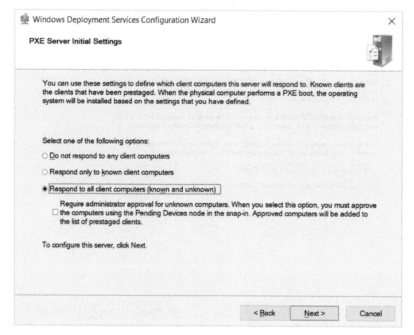

Figure 3-51 Specifying PXE response settings

To add a boot image for Windows Server 2019 to your WDS server, you can right-click the Boot Images folder shown within Figure 3-47 and select Add Boot Image to start the Add Image Wizard shown in Figure 3-52. You can then click Browse and navigate to the boot.wim file within the \sources folder on your installation media. If your installation media is a DVD-ROM or ISO image associated with D drive within Windows, then the path you would supply within Figure 3-52 would be D:\sources\boot.wim. When you click Next in Figure 3-52, you can optionally change the default image name shown in Figure 3-53, and then click Next and Finish to copy the image to the WDS server.

To add an install image for Windows Server 2019 to your WDS server, you can right-click the Install Images folder shown within Figure 3-47 and select Add Install Image to start the Add Image Wizard. Because a WDS server may have several different install image files for different operating systems, you must select an existing image group or create a new one to store any install images, as shown in Figure 3-54. After clicking Next, you are prompted to select the location of the image file as shown in Figure 3-52. As with boot.wim, you can find the install.wim file within the \sources folder on your installation media (e.g., D:\sources\install.wim if your installation media is associated with D drive).

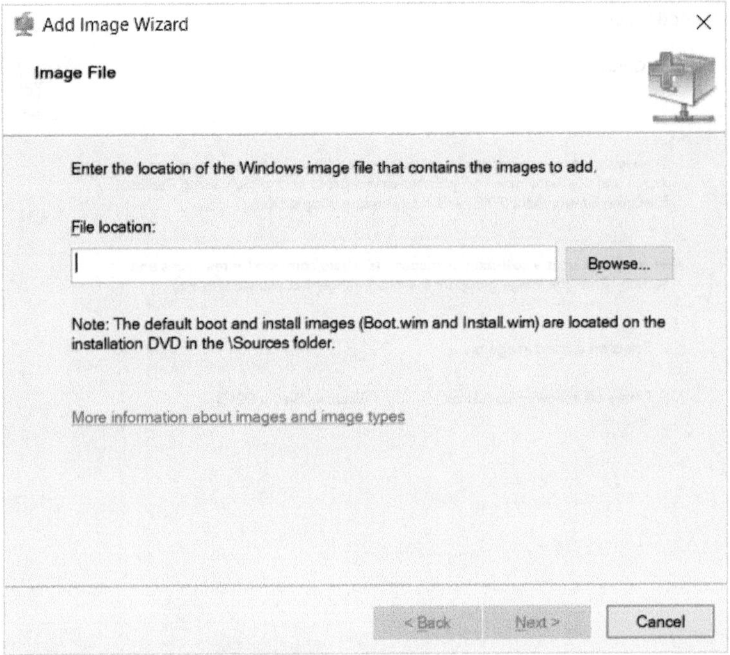

Figure 3-52 Selecting the location of a WIM image

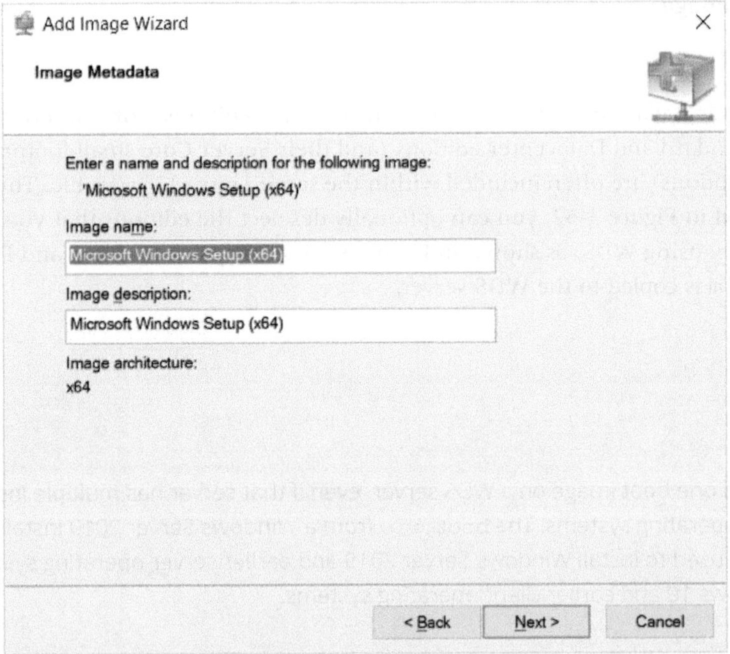

Figure 3-53 Specifying the name for a boot.wim image

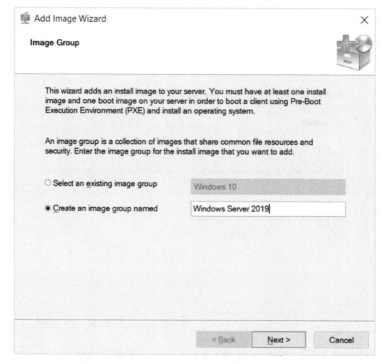

Figure 3-54   Specifying the image group for an install.wim image

Windows installation media often contains multiple editions. For Windows Server 2019, the Standard and Datacenter editions (and their Server Core small footprint installation options) are often included within the same `install.wim` file. Thus, when you click Next in Figure 3-52, you can optionally deselect the editions that you do not wish to deploy using WDS, as shown in Figure 3-55. After you click Next and Finish, the `install.wim` is copied to the WDS server.

Note 📎

You only need one boot image on a WDS server, even if that server has multiple install images for different operating systems. The `boot.wim` from a Windows Server 2019 installation media can be used to install Windows Server 2019 and earlier server operating systems, as well as Windows 10 and earlier client operating systems.

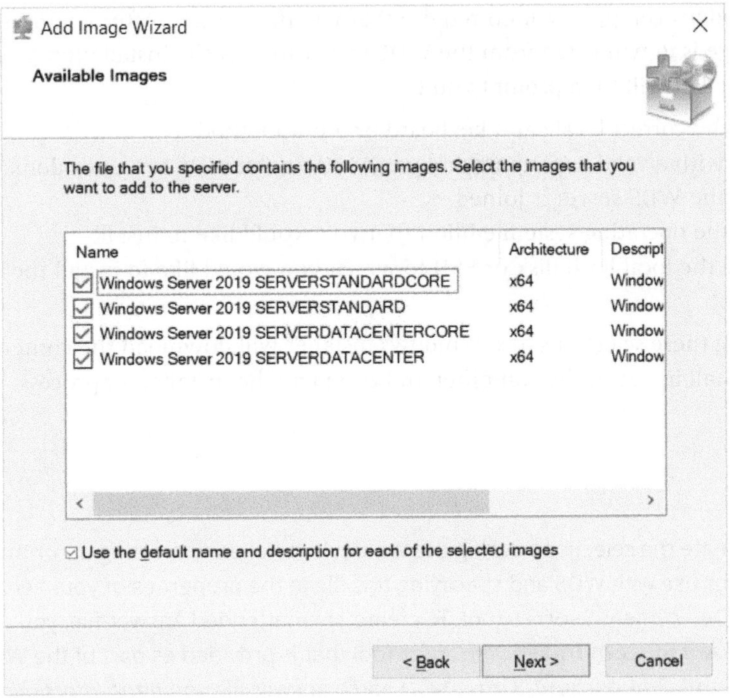

Figure 3-55   Selecting available editions within an install .wim image

Starting a WDS Installation

After you have configured WDS with the appropriate boot and install images, you can right-click your server within the Windows Deployment Services console (shown earlier in Figure 3-47), select All Tasks, and click Start to allow the WDS service to respond to PXE requests.

Next, you can ensure that the network interface is listed at the top of the boot order for computers or virtual machines that you wish to install and proceed to start those systems. If WDS and DHCP are configured properly, you should receive an IP address within a few moments as well as a prompt indicating the key to press in order to start a WDS installation. For legacy computers, this key is typically F12 as shown in Figure 3-56.

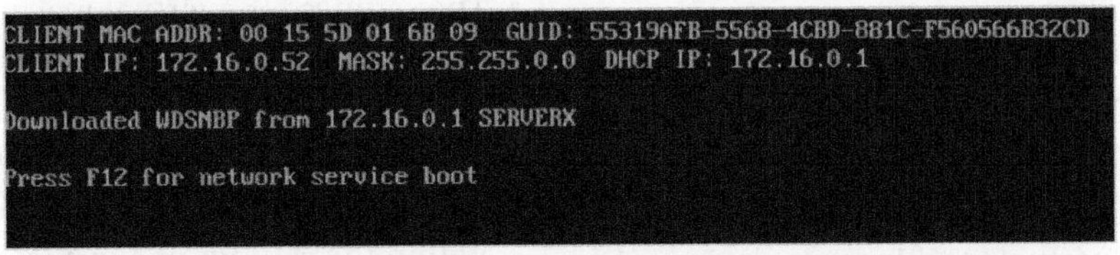

Figure 3-56   Starting a WDS installation from a PXE network boot

However, modern computers often require that you press Enter. After you press this key, the boot image is downloaded from the WDS server to start the installation process. The Windows installer will then prompt you to:

- Select the correct locale and keyboard or input method.
- Log in with a valid user name and password on the WDS server or domain to which the WDS server is joined.
- Select the operating system edition that you would like to install.
- Specify the local hard disk or SSD to which you would like to install the operating system.

Following these selections, the Windows installer will download the contents of the associated install image to the computer and complete the installation process.

> **Note** 📎
>
> You can automate the selections during the Windows installer by creating an **unattended answer file** for use with WDS and specifying this file in the properties of your server within the Windows Deployment Services tool. To create an unattended answer file, you must use the **Windows System Image Manager** tool that is provided as part of the **Windows Assessment and Deployment Kit (ADK)**. Search answer files on *https://docs.microsoft.com* for more information.

Module Summary

- You can add the Hyper-V role using Server Manager or PowerShell. When adding the Hyper-V role using Server Manager, you are prompted to configure several Hyper-V features that can be modified following the installation.

- Hyper-V Manager and PowerShell can be used to create and configure virtual machines as well as start and manage the state of virtual machines.

- Generation 2 virtual machines emulate modern hardware that has direct access to the VMBus as well as a UEFI BIOS that supports Secure Boot and a TPM.

- Generation 1 virtual machines emulate legacy hardware components and a standard BIOS. As a result, Generation 1 virtual machines support a wider range of operating systems compared to Generation 2.

- The settings for a virtual machine are stored independently of the virtual machine hard disk file. You can add virtual hardware components or change the settings for existing virtual hardware components within the settings of a virtual machine in Hyper-V Manager.

- Hyper-V uses virtual switches to create virtual networks. Internal virtual switches can be shared by virtual machines and the host operating system. Private virtual switches can be shared by virtual machines only. External virtual switches allow virtual machines to access the underlying physical network using the Hyper-V Extensible Virtual Switch protocol on a physical network interface.

- Checkpoints store changes made to a virtual hard disk file within a separate checkpoint file after creation. You can apply a checkpoint to revert a virtual machine to a previous point in time or delete a checkpoint to merge the checkpoint and virtual hard disk file contents.

- There are two types of checkpoints available within Hyper-V. Production checkpoints are created by backup software within the guest operating system, whereas standard checkpoints are created by Hyper-V and can additionally store the state of running programs.

- Live migration can be used to move a running virtual machine from one Hyper-V host to another within the same Active Directory domain.

- You can create an updated copy of the contents of a running virtual machine on another Hyper-V host that has replication functionality enabled.

- Rapid server deployment is often used to install operating systems on several servers and virtual machines within large organizations. Virtual machine templates and WDS are two methods that can be used to perform Windows Server 2019 rapid server deployment.

- A virtual machine template is a copy of a virtual machine that can be imported within Hyper-V to quickly create a new virtual machine. To create a virtual machine template, you can install a new virtual machine with Windows Server 2019, run the System Preparation Tool to remove unique system information, and export the virtual machine to a folder on the filesystem.

- WDS can be used to install Windows Server 2019 on multiple computers and virtual machines that boot from the network using PXE. After installing the WDS server role, you must configure WDS settings as well as add the appropriate boot and install images to the WDS server.

Key Terms

boot image
capture image
Credential Security Support Provider (CredSSP)
Deployment Server
Device naming
DHCP guard
differencing disk
dynamic memory
external virtual switch
File System Freeze (fsfreeze)

Hyper-V Extensible Virtual Switch
Input/Output Operations Per Second (IOPS)
install image
internal virtual switch
IPsec task offloading
Kerberos
live migration
MAC address spoofing
multicast

N-tier
named pipe
NIC Teaming
non-uniform memory access (NUMA)
Out-of-Box Experience (OOBE)
pass-through disk
port mirroring
Preboot Execution Environment (PXE)
private virtual switch

production checkpoint

protected network

Quality of Service (QoS)

rapid server deployment

router guard

Shielding

single-root I/O virtualization (SR-IOV)

smart paging file

standard checkpoint

switch

System Preparation Tool

Transport Server

unattended answer file

virtual LAN (VLAN)

virtual machine bus (VMBus)

virtual machine queue

virtual machine template

virtual switch

Volume Shadow Copy Service (VSS)

Windows Assessment and Deployment Kit (ADK)

Windows Deployment Services (WDS)

Windows Deployment Services tool

Windows Imaging Format (WIM)

Windows System Image Manager

wireless access point (WAP)

Review Questions

1. Virtual machine settings are stored within a .vhdx file. True or False?

2. Which of the following commands may be used to start Hyper-V Manager?
   a. hyperv
   b. hyper-v
   c. virtmgmt.msc
   d. new-virtconsole

3. To which of the following virtual switches can a host operating system connect? (Choose all that apply.)
   a. Internal
   b. External
   c. Public
   d. Private

4. The physical network interface used by an external virtual switch is not configured using IP. Instead, it uses the Hyper-V Extensible Virtual Switch protocol to allow virtual network interfaces attached to the external virtual switch to use the physical network interface. True or False?

5. Which of the following operating systems are supported for use within a Generation 2 virtual machine? (Choose all that apply.)
   a. 32-bit versions of Windows 7
   b. 64-bit versions of Windows Server 2008
   c. Ubuntu 14.04
   d. FreeBSD 9.1

6. Which of the following hardware devices does a Generation 1 virtual machine emulate? (Choose all that apply.)
   a. IDE hard disk
   b. SCSI hard disk
   c. UEFI BIOS
   d. Serial ports

7. Guest operating systems require VMBus drivers to support the virtualized hardware within a Generation 2 virtual machine. True or False?

8. Which of the following Hyper-V features allows a virtual machine to use additional physical memory within a server, provided that it is available?
   a. Smart caching
   b. Dynamic memory
   c. Smart paging
   d. Shielding

9. Both Generations 1 and 2 virtual machines support Secure Boot. True or False?

10. Your server has an additional SSD that you wish to use exclusively within a virtual machine as a pass-through disk to increase performance. What must you do to achieve this? (Choose two answers.)
    a. Ensure that the SSD is set to an Online state within the Disk Management tool.

b. Ensure that the SSD is set to an Offline state within the Disk Management tool.

c. In the properties of the virtual machine, create a new virtual hard disk file that is stored on the drive letter that is used by the SSD.

d. In the properties of the virtual machine, select an existing virtual hard disk, choose Physical hard disk, and select the SSD.

11. Which action should you choose for a virtual machine within the Actions pane in order to obtain the Virtual Machine Connection window?

a. Start
b. Connect
c. View
d. Ctrl+Alt+Del

12. Virtual machine checkpoints are often used prior to making an important configuration change within a guest operating system, such as installing software or device drivers. True or False?

13. After creating a production checkpoint of a virtual machine, you would like to revert the virtual machine to the state it was in prior to the checkpoint. What should you select within the Actions pane of Hyper-V Manager after selecting your checkpoint within the Checkpoints pane?

a. Apply
b. Revert
c. Delete
d. Delete Subtree

14. Any changes to a guest operating system made following the creation of a checkpoint are stored within a .avhdx file in the same directory as the associated .vhdx file. True or False?

15. Which of the following Hyper-V features requires that your host operating system be joined to an Active Directory domain? (Choose all that apply.)

a. Live migration
b. Checkpoints
c. Replication
d. Quality of Service (QoS)

16. Replication must be enabled on your Hyper-V host before you are able to copy the contents of a virtual machine to a target Hyper-V host. True or False?

17. To create a virtual machine template, what actions must you perform at minimum? (Choose all that apply.)

a. Create a new virtual machine and install a guest operating system within it
b. Install additional software components within the guest operating system
c. Run the System Preparation Tool within the guest operating system to remove unique identifiers
d. Export the virtual machine to a folder on the filesystem

18. After importing a virtual machine template to create a new virtual machine, you should rename the new virtual machine. True or False?

19. WDS can be used to install multiple physical or virtualized systems at the same time, provided those systems can boot from the network using PXE. True or False?

20. Which two files must you import within the Windows Deployment Services tool to provide for remote installation?

a. `install.wim`
b. `PXE.wim`
c. `bootmgmt.wim`
d. `boot.wim`

Hands-On Projects

These Hands-On Projects should be completed in the order given and should take a total of three hours to complete. The requirements for these projects include:

- A system with Windows Server 2019 installed according to Hands-On Project 1-1 (Lab Environment 1) or Hands-On Project 1-2 (Lab Environment 2).

Project 3-1: Hyper-V Installation

In this Hands-On Project, you install Hyper-V on your Windows Server 2019 system.

1. Boot your Windows Server 2019 host and log into the system as Administrator using the password **Secret555**. Next, click **Start** and then click **Server Manager**.
2. Within Server Manager, click the **Manage** menu and then click **Add Roles and Features**.
3. At the Select installation type page, click **Next**.
4. At the Select destination server page, click **Next**.
5. At the Select server roles page, select **Hyper-V**, and click **Add Features** when prompted.

Note 📎

If your computer does not support virtualization extensions, or the virtualization extensions are disabled in your computer BIOS, a Validation Results page will appear indicating that Hyper-V cannot be installed. You will also see this message if you attempt to install Hyper-V within a Hyper-V virtual machine that does not have nested virtualization enabled.

6. Click **Next**.
7. At the Select features page, click **Next**.
8. At the Hyper-V page, read the information regarding best practices and click **Next**.
9. At the Create Virtual Switches page, select the Ethernet adapter that provides access to your physical network (to place a checkmark next to it), and click **Next**.
10. At the Virtual Machine Migration page, select **Allow this server to send and receive live migrations of virtual machines**, and click **Next**.
11. At the Default Stores page, click the **Browse** button next to Default location for virtual hard disk files. Expand **This PC**, highlight **Local Disk (C:)**, and click **Make New Folder**. Type the name **VMs** in the New folder box to create a C:\VMs folder, and click **OK**. Next, click the **Browse** button next to Default location for virtual machine configuration files. Expand **This PC**, expand **Local Disk (C:)**, click the **VMs** folder and then click **OK**. Verify that C:\VMs is listed in both text boxes on the Default Stores page and click **Next**.
12. On the Confirm installation selections page, select **Restart the destination server automatically if required** and click **Yes** to confirm. Next, click **Install** to install Hyper-V. Your system may reboot twice.

Project 3-2: Virtual Switches

In this Hands-On Project, you explore the external virtual switch created during Hyper-V installation on your Windows Server 2019 system as well as create and configure a new internal virtual switch that will be used in all remaining Hands-On Projects.

1. On your Windows Server 2019 host, log into the system as Administrator using the password **Secret555**. Next, click **Start** and then click **Server Manager**.
2. Within Server Manager, click **Local Server** within the navigation pane and then click the hyperlink next to your vEthernet network interface.
3. In the Network Connections window, note that you have two network interfaces: the original Ethernet network interface and the vEthernet network interface that represents your external virtual switch.
   a. Right-click your Ethernet network interface and click **Properties**. Note that IPv4 and IPv6 are not enabled but that the Hyper-V Extensible Virtual Switch is enabled to allow external virtual switches to share access to this network interface. Click **OK** to close the Ethernet Properties window.
   b. Right-click your vEthernet network interface and click **Properties**. Highlight **Internet Protocol Version 4 (TCP/IPv4)** within the vEthernet Properties window and click **Properties**. Note that the IP configuration that was previously configured within Hands-On Project 1-3 for your Ethernet network interface has been copied to this vEthernet network interface and click **OK**. Click **OK** to close the vEthernet Properties window.
   c. Close the Network Connections window.
4. Within Server Manager, select the **Tools** menu and then click **Hyper-V Manager**.
5. Select your server within the navigation pane of Hyper-V Manager and click **Virtual Switch Manager** within the Actions pane.
   a. Under the Virtual Switches section, click your existing external virtual switch. In the Virtual Switch Properties pane, note that it uses the original Ethernet network interface in your system and allows the management operating system to share it with virtual machines. In the Name text box, type **External Virtual Switch** and click **Apply**.
   b. Under the Virtual Switches section, click **New virtual network switch**. In the Create virtual switch pane, click **Internal** and then click **Create Virtual Switch**. In the Name text box, type **Internal Virtual Switch** and click **Apply**.
   c. Click **OK** to close Virtual Switch Manager.
6. Close Hyper-V Manager.
7. Within Server Manager, click the **Refresh "Local Server"** icon in the top bar and note that you now have vEthernet (External Virtual Switch) and vEthernet (Internal Virtual Switch) network interfaces within the Properties pane. Click the hyperlink next to vEthernet (Internal Virtual Switch).

8. In the Network Connections window, right-click **vEthernet (Internal Virtual Switch)** and click **Properties**.

    a. In the Ethernet Properties window, highlight **Internet Protocol Version 4 (TCP/IPv4)** and click **Properties**.

    b. Select **Use the following IP address**, enter an IP address of **172.16.0.1** and subnet mask of **255.255.0.0**, and click **OK**.

    c. Click **Close** to close the vEthernet (Internal Virtual Switch) Properties window and then close the Network Connections window.

Project 3-3: WDS Configuration

In this Hands-On Project, you install the DHCP and WDS server roles and configure them to provide for rapid deployment of Windows Server 2019 on your internal virtual network.

> **Note** 📎
>
> Note that DHCP is configured within this exercise to support WDS functionality only. The configuration of DHCP will be discussed properly within Module 8.

1. Within Server Manager, select the **Manage** menu and then click **Add Roles and Features**.
    a. At the Select installation type page, click **Next**.
    b. At the Select destination server page, click **Next**.
    c. At the Select server roles page, select **DHCP Server**, and click **Add Features** when prompted. Next, select **Windows Deployment Service** and click **Add Features** when prompted. Click **Next** when finished.
    d. At the Select features page, click **Next**.
    e. At the DHCP Server page, read the information regarding best practices and click **Next**.
    f. At the WDS page, read the information regarding best practices and click **Next**.
    g. At the Role Services page, note that the Deployment Server and Transport Server are selected by default and click **Next**.
    h. Click **Install** to install the DHCP Server and Windows Deployment Service roles.
    i. After the installation has completed, click **Complete DHCP configuration**, click **Commit**, and then click **Close**.
    j. Click **Close** to close the Add Roles and Features Wizard.

2. Within Server Manager, select the **Tools** menu and then click **DHCP**.

3. In the DHCP tool, expand your server within the navigation pane and then expand IPv4. In the Actions pane, click **More Actions** and then click **New Scope**.
    a. In the Welcome page of the New Scope Wizard, click **Next**.
    b. At the Scope Name page, type **Internal Network** in the Name text box and click **Next**.
    c. At the IP Address Range page, supply a Start IP address of **172.16.0.50** and End IP address of **172.16.0.100** and click **Next**.

    d. At the Add Exclusions and Delay page, click **Next**.

    e. At the Lease Duration page, click **Next**.

    f. At the Configure DHCP Options page, select **No, I will configure these options later** and click **Next**.

    g. Click **Finish** to complete the New Scope Wizard.

4. In the DHCP tool, click **Scope [172.16.0.0] Internal Network** within the navigation pane. In the Actions pane, click **More Actions** and then click **Activate**. Close the DHCP tool when finished.

5. Within Server Manager, select the **Tools** menu and then click **Windows Deployment Services**.

6. In the Windows Deployment Services window, expand Servers within the navigation pane. Right-click your server and click **Configure Server**.

    a. At the Before You Begin page, click **Next**.

    b. At the Install Options page, select **Standalone server** and click **Next**.

    c. At the Remote Installation Folder Location page, note the default location and click **Next**. Click **Yes** when prompted.

    d. At the Proxy DHCP Server page, click **Next**.

    e. At the PXE Server Initial Settings page, select **Respond to all client computers (known and unknown)** and click **Next**.

    f. At the Task Progress screen, click **Finish** when available.

7. If you use Lab Environment 1, insert the Windows Server 2019 installation media into the DVD-ROM drive of your computer. If you use Lab Environment 2, attach the ISO image of the Windows Server 2019 installation media to your virtual DVD-ROM within your host operating system virtual machine.

8. In the Windows Deployment Services window, right-click **Boot Images** under your server and click **Add Boot Image**.

    a. At the Image File page of the Add Image Wizard, click **Browse**. Navigate to the **\sources** folder on your DVD-ROM drive, click **boot.wim** and then click **Open**. Click **Next** when finished.

    b. At the Image Metadata page, click **Next**.

    c. At the Summary page, click **Next**.

    d. Click **Finish** to close the Add Image Wizard.

9. In the Windows Deployment Services window, right-click **Install Images** under your server and click **Add Install Image**.

    a. At the Image Group page of the Add Image Wizard, note the default image group name and click **Next**.

    b. At the Image File page, click **Browse**. Navigate to the **\sources** folder on your DVD-ROM drive, click **install.wim,** and then click **Open**. Click **Next** when finished.

    c. At the Available Images page, note the available editions and click **Next**.

    d. At the Summary page, click **Next**.

    e. Click **Finish** to close the Add Image Wizard.

10. In the Windows Deployment Services window, right-click your server in the navigation pane, click **All Tasks,** and then click **Start**. Click **OK** to close the Server window.
11. Close the Windows Deployment Services window.

Project 3-4: WDS Deployment

In this Hands-On Project, you create a new virtual machine called WindowsServer2019VM1 that is connected to the internal virtual switch, and install Windows Server 2019 within it using WDS.

1. Within Server Manager, select the **Tools** menu and then click **Hyper-V Manager**.
2. In the Actions pane of Hyper-V Manager, click **New**, and then click **Virtual Machine** to open the New Virtual Machine Wizard.
   a. At the Before You Begin page, select **Do not show this page again** and click **Next**.
   b. At the Specify Name and Location page, supply the name **WindowsServer2019VM1** (no spaces), select **Store the virtual machine in a different location,** and click **Next**.
   c. At the Specify Generation page, click **Next** to accept the default of Generation 1.
   d. At the Assign Memory page, enter **4096** in the Startup memory text box and click **Next**.
   e. At the Configure Networking page, select **Internal Virtual Switch** from the drop-down box and click **Next**.
   f. At the Connect Virtual Hard Disk page, view the default options that create a 127 GB dynamically expanding virtual hard disk and click **Next**.
   g. At the Installation Options page, select **Install an operating system from a network-based installation server** and click **Next**.
   h. At the Completing the New Virtual Machine Wizard page, click **Finish**.
3. In the Virtual Machines pane of Hyper-V Manager, select your **WindowsServer2019VM1** virtual machine and click **Connect** in the Actions pane.
4. In the Virtual Machine Connection window, click **Start** to boot your virtual machine, and press F12 on your keyboard when prompted to boot from a network server. This will download the boot.wim file from the WDS server to your virtual machine to start the installation process.
   a. After the Windows Setup screen appears, select the correct locale and keyboard or input method and click **Next**.
   b. When prompted to provide a valid user name and password for an account on the WDS server, supply the user name **SERVERX\Administrator** and password **Secret555** and press **Enter**.
   c. At the Select the operating system you want to install page, click **Windows Server 2019 SERVERSTANDARD** and click **Next**.
   d. At the Where do you want to install Windows page, note your virtual hard disk and click **Next**.

e. After the installation has completed, click **Restart now**, if necessary. Your system will reboot twice.

f. When the OOBE wizard appears, select your country/region, preferred app language, and keyboard layout, and click **Next**.

g. At the License terms page, click **Accept**.

h. At the Customize settings page, supply the password **Secret555** in the Password and Reenter password text boxes and click **Finish**.

i. At the login screen, click the Ctrl+Alt+Delete button within the Virtual Machine Connection window, supply the password **Secret555** for Administrator, and press **Enter** to log into the system.

Project 3-5: Templates

In this Hands-On Project, you create a virtual machine template from your WindowsServer2019VM1 virtual machine. Next, you import this virtual machine template to create a new virtual machine called WindowsServer2019VM2.

1. On your WindowsServer2019VM1 virtual machine, click **Start**, and click **File Explorer**. Expand **This PC** and navigate to **C:\Windows\System32\Sysprep** and double-click the **sysprep.exe** application.

2. Within the System Preparation Tool, select **Generalize**. Next, select **Shutdown** from the Shutdown Options drop-down box and click **OK**. After the virtual machine has shut down, close the Virtual Machine Connection window.

3. In Hyper-V Manager, highlight **WindowsServer2019VM1** within the Virtual Machines pane and click **Export** in the Actions pane.

4. In the Export Virtual Machine window, type **C:\VMs\WindowsServer2019Templates** in the location text box and click **Export**.

5. In Hyper-V Manager, click **Import Virtual Machine** within the Actions pane.

   a. At the Before You Begin page of the Import Virtual Machine window, select **Do not show this page again** and click **Next**.

   b. At the Locate Folder page, type **C:\VMs\WindowsServer2019Templates\WindowsServer2019VM1** in the folder text box, and click **Next**.

   c. At the Select Virtual Machine page, note the date that the WindowsServer2019VM1 template was created and click **Next**.

   d. At the Choose Import Type screen, select **Copy the virtual machine (create a new unique ID)** and click **Next**.

   e. At the Choose Destination page, select **Store the virtual machine in a different location**, type the path **C:\VMs\WindowsServer2019VM2** in all three text boxes, and click **Next**.

   f. At the Choose Storage Folders page, type the path **C:\VMs\WindowsServer2019VM2** in the Location text box and click **Finish**.

6. After the import has completed, note that a second WindowsServer2019VM1 virtual machine appears within the Virtual Machines pane of Hyper-V Manager. Highlight this virtual machine and click Rename in the Actions pane. Type **WindowsServer2019VM2** in the Name field for the virtual machine and press **Enter**.

7. In Hyper-V Manager, highlight **WindowsServer2019VM2** within the Virtual Machines pane and click **Connect** in the Actions pane. In the Virtual Machine Connection window, click **Start** to boot your new virtual machine.

   a. When the OOBE wizard appears, select your country/region, preferred app language, and keyboard layout, and click **Next**.

   b. At the License terms page, click **Accept**.

   c. At the Customize settings page, supply the password **Secret555** in the Password and Reenter password text boxes and click **Finish**.

   d. At the login screen, click the Ctrl+Alt+Delete button within the Virtual Machine Connection window, supply the password **Secret555** for Administrator, and press **Enter** to log into the system.

   e. When Server Manager starts and prompts you to try managing servers with Windows Admin Center, select the **Don't show this message again** checkbox and close the window.

   f. Within Server Manager, select the **Manage** menu and click **Server Manager Properties**. In the Server Manager Properties window, select **Do not start Server Manager automatically at logon** and click **OK**.

   g. Close Server Manager.

   h. Right-click the **Start** menu and click **Shut down or sign out**, and then click **Shut down**. Click **Continue** to shut down your system.

Project 3-6: Checkpoints

In this Hands-On project, you create and apply standard and production checkpoints for your WindowsServer2019VM1 virtual machine.

1. In Hyper-V Manager, highlight **WindowsServer2019VM1** within the Virtual Machines pane and click **Connect** in the Actions pane. In the Virtual Machine Connection window, click **Start** to boot your new virtual machine.

   a. When the OOBE wizard appears, select your country/region, preferred app language, and keyboard layout, and click **Next**.

   b. At the License terms page, click **Accept**.

   c. At the Customize settings page, supply the password **Secret555** in the Password and Reenter password text boxes and click **Finish**.

   d. At the login screen, click the Ctrl+Alt+Delete button within the Virtual Machine Connection window, supply the password **Secret555** for Administrator, and press **Enter** to log into the system.

   e. When Server Manager starts and prompts you to try managing servers with Windows Admin Center, select the **Don't show this message again** checkbox and close the window.

   f. Within Server Manager, select the **Manage** menu and click **Server Manager Properties**. In the Server Manager Properties window, select **Do not start Server Manager automatically at logon** and click **OK**.

   g. Close Server Manager.

h. Right-click any area of your desktop background, click **New**, and then click **Text Document**. Type **MyFile** and press **Enter** to create a MyFile text file on your Desktop.

i. Double-click **MyFile** and type a line within the Notepad text editor that reads **This is work in progress**.

2. In Hyper-V Manager, highlight **WindowsServer2019VM1** within the Virtual Machines pane and click **Settings** in the Actions pane. Click **Checkpoints** under the Management section of the Settings window and note that Production checkpoints are enabled by default. Select **Standard checkpoints** and click **OK**.

3. Highlight **WindowsServer2019VM1** within the Virtual Machines pane of Hyper-V Manager and click **Checkpoint** in the Actions pane. After a few moments, you should notice a checkpoint listed in the Checkpoints pane for your WindowsServer2019VM1 virtual machine.

4. In the Virtual Machine Connection window for your WindowsServer2019VM1 virtual machine, close the Notepad program and click **Save** when prompted. Next, right-click **MyFile** on your desktop and click **Delete**. Finally, right-click the Recycle Bin on your desktop, click **Empty Recycle Bin**, and click **Yes**.

5. In Hyper-V Manager, highlight your checkpoint within the Checkpoints pane and click **Apply** in the Actions pane. Click **Apply** to apply the checkpoint.

6. In the Virtual Machine Connection window for your WindowsServer2019VM1 virtual machine, note that **MyFile** is displayed within Notepad on your desktop because Standard checkpoints preserve the state of applications within memory.

7. In Hyper-V Manager, highlight the checkpoint within the Checkpoints pane for your WindowsServer2019VM1 virtual machine and click **Delete Checkpoint** in the Actions pane. Click **Delete** to delete the checkpoint.

8. Highlight **WindowsServer2019VM1** within the Virtual Machines pane of Hyper-V Manager and click **Settings** in the Actions pane. Click **Checkpoints** under the Management section of the Settings window, select **Production checkpoints** and click **OK**.

9. Next, click **Checkpoint** in the Actions pane. After a few moments, you should notice a checkpoint listed in the Checkpoints pane for your WindowsServer2019VM1 virtual machine. Highlight your checkpoint within the Checkpoints pane and click **Apply** in the Actions pane. Click **Apply** to apply the checkpoint. Your WindowsServer2019VM1 virtual machine will be shut down following the creation of the checkpoint.

10. In the Virtual Machine Connection window for your WindowsServer2019VM1 virtual machine, click **Start**.

a. At the login screen, click the Ctrl+Alt+Delete button within the Virtual Machine Connection window, supply the password **Secret555** for Administrator, and press **Enter** to log into the system.

b. Note that **MyFile** is available on the desktop. Double-click **MyFile** to open it within Notepad and note that the contents within notepad were not saved. Close Notepad when finished.

c. Right-click the **Start** menu and click **Shut down or sign out**, and then click **Shut down**. Click **Continue** to shut down your system.

11. In Hyper-V Manager, highlight the checkpoint within the Checkpoints pane for your WindowsServer2019VM1 virtual machine and click **Delete Checkpoint** in the Actions pane. Click **Delete** to delete the checkpoint.

Project 3-7: Virtual Machine Settings

In this Hands-On project, you view and modify hardware and virtual machine settings for your WindowsServer2019VM1 virtual machine.

1. In Hyper-V Manager on your Windows Server 2019 host, highlight **WindowsServer2019VM1** within the Virtual Machines pane and click **Settings** in the Actions pane.

   a. Highlight **BIOS** under the Hardware section. Note the devices that are listed in the boot order.

   b. Highlight **Memory** under the Hardware section. Note that you can modify the startup memory for the virtual machine, or enable dynamic memory (recall that dynamic memory should not be enabled if you use nested virtualization, as with Lab Environment 2).

   c. Highlight **Processor** under the Hardware section. Note the default number of virtual processors is set to 1.

   d. Highlight **Hard Drive** under IDE Controller 0 and click Edit.

       i. On the Locate Virtual Hard Disk page of the Edit Virtual Hard Disk Wizard, click **Next**.

       ii. On the Choose Action page, note that Compact is selected by default and click **Next**.

       iii. Click **Finish** to compact your virtual hard disk file.

   e. Highlight **DVD Drive** under the Hardware section. Note that you can associate an ISO image file or physical CD/DVD drive with your virtual DVD Drive.

   f. Highlight **SCSI Controller** under the Hardware section. Click Add to add an additional hard drive. Next, click New to create a new virtual hard disk file for this additional hard drive.

       i. At the Before You Begin page of the New Virtual Hard Disk Wizard, click **Next**.

       ii. On the Choose Disk Format page, note that VHDX is selected by default and click **Next**.

       iii. On the Choose Disk Type page, note that Dynamically expanding is selected by default and click **Next**.

       iv. On the Specify Name and Location page, type **AdditionalDisk.vhdx** in the Name text box and click **Next**.

       v. On the Configure Disk page, note the default size of 127 GB and click **Next**.

       vi. Click **Finish** to create the new virtual hard disk file and associate it with your new SCSI virtual hard disk.

   g. Highlight **Network Adapter** under the Hardware section. Select **External Virtual Switch** from the Virtual switch drop-down box to connect your virtual network interface to the external virtual network.

   h. Highlight **Integration Services** under the Management section. Note the services that are provided to the guest operating system.

   i. Highlight **Automatic Start Action** under the Management section. Select **Nothing** and click **OK**.

2. Highlight **WindowsServer2019VM1** within the virtual machines pane of Hyper-V Manager and click **Connect** in the Actions pane. In the Virtual Machine Connection window, click **Start** to boot your new virtual machine.

3. At the login screen, click the Ctrl+Alt+Delete button within the Virtual Machine Connection window, supply the password **Secret555** for Administrator, and press **Enter** to log into the system.

4. Right-click **Start** and click **Disk Management**. You will notice a new Disk 1 within your virtual machine that is set to an Offline state.

   a. Right-click Disk 1 and click **Online**. Right-click Disk 1 again, click **Initialize Disk** and then click **OK**.

   b. Right-click the 127.00 GB Unallocated area of Disk 1 and click **New Simple Volume**.

      i. Click **Next** at the Welcome page of the New Simple Volume Wizard.

      ii. At the Specify Volume Size page, click **Next**.

      iii. At the Assign Drive Letter or Path page, note the drive letter that will be assigned and click **Next**.

      iv. At the Format Partition page, note the default NTFS filesystem type and click **Next**.

      v. Click **Finish** to prepare your new virtual disk with a filesystem that will be accessible within Windows.

   c. Close the Disk Management tool.

5. Click **Start** and then click **File Explorer**. Note your new hard drive is displayed under the This PC section and close File Explorer.

6. Right-click Start and click Network Connections. Next, click **Network and Sharing Center**, and then click **Change adapter settings**.

   a. In the Network Connections window, right-click your Ethernet adapter and click **Status**.

   b. In the Ethernet Status window, click **Details** and note whether your network environment has successfully assigned IPv4 and IPv6 configuration to your network interface automatically via a DHCP server or ICMPv6. Record this configuration and click **Close**.

   c. In the Ethernet Status window, click **Properties**.

   d. In the Ethernet Properties window, highlight **Internet Protocol Version 4 (TCP/IPv4)** and click **Properties**. If your network environment requires manual IPv4 configuration, select **Use the following IP address** and supply the correct information. Next, select **Use the following DNS server addresses** and supply the correct DNS server information. Click **OK** when finished.

   e. In the Ethernet Properties window, highlight **Internet Protocol Version 6 (TCP/IPv6)** and click **Properties**. If your network environment requires manual IPv6 configuration, select **Use the following IPv6 address** and supply the correct information. Next, select **Use the following DNS server addresses** and supply the correct DNS server information. Click **OK** when finished.

   f. Click **OK** to close the Ethernet Properties window, and click **Close** to close the Ethernet Status window. Finally, close the Network Connections window.

7. Right-click the **Start** menu and click **Shut down or sign out**, and then click **Shut down**. Click **Continue** to shut down your WindowsServer2019VM1 virtual machine.

Discovery Exercises

Exercise 1-1

In Hands-On Project 2-2, you explored the Windows Admin Center for your Windows Server 2019 host. If Hyper-V is installed, the Windows Admin Center provides a Virtual Machines tool that can be used to provide the same management and monitoring capabilities as Hyper-V Manager. Similarly, the Virtual Switches tool in the Windows Admin Center can be used to manage virtual switches. Open the Windows Admin Center on your Windows Server 2019 host and explore the functionality provided by these two tools.

Exercise 1-2

In heavily virtualized environments, resource efficiency is a key consideration when installing virtual machines. As a result, these environments will often install a small footprint Windows Server 2019 installation option that can host the necessary services. Because small footprint guest operating systems use a smaller number of resources, each server can run a larger number of individual virtual machines. Within Hyper-V Manager on your Windows Server 2019 host, create a new Generation 2 virtual machine called WindowsServer2019VM3 that uses 1 GB of RAM, a 60 GB dynamically expanding virtual hard disk file, and a network interface that is connected to your external virtual switch. Next, install Windows Server 2019 Standard Edition Server Core within this virtual machine using DVD or ISO installation media. Following the installation, perform the post install configuration tasks outlined in Module 1 using the Windows Server Configuration Wizard (`sconfig.cmd`).

Exercise 1-3

While WDS can be used to deploy Windows Server 2019 using source files provided by `install.wim` on the Windows Server 2019 installation media, it can also deploy custom WIM images. In addition to a Windows Server 2019 installation, these custom WIM images can include additional server roles and features, or third-party software. To create a custom Windows Server 2019 WIM image that can be deployed using WDS, you can install a Windows Server 2019 system, add any desired software, and then run the System Preparation Tool (`sysprep.exe`) to remove unique information from the operating system. Next, you can convert an existing `boot.wim` image on your WDS server into a **capture image** (e.g., called `capture.wim`) that contains a modified installation program. If you boot the Windows Server 2019 system that you prepared with the System Preparation Tool from the network and choose the `capture.wim` image instead of the default `boot.wim` image during the boot process, the modified installation program will allow you to create a WIM image (e.g., `custom_install.wim`) of the underlying Windows Server 2019 system on a second local hard disk that is copied to the WDS server afterwards. This `custom_install.wim` image can then be deployed to other systems on the network that boot from the network and select the `boot.wim` image.

Add an additional virtual hard disk to your WindowsServer2019VM2 virtual machine (using the same process described in Hands-On Project 3-7), as well as a server role or feature of your choice. Next, run the System Preparation Tool (`sysprep.exe`) to remove unique information from your installation and shut down the guest operating system.

Next, right-click your existing `boot.wim` image within the Windows Deployment Services tool and choose **Create Capture Image**. Supply an appropriate name and location for your capture image. Following this, boot your WindowsServer2019VM2 virtual machine from the network and select your capture image when prompted. Supply an appropriate custom WIM image name, the image group that it will be uploaded to on the WDS server, and the second hard disk that will be used to store the created WIM image. After the imaging process has completed, add your custom WIM image on the WDS server.

Finally, create a new virtual machine called WindowsServer2019VM4 on the internal virtual switch that is set to boot from the network. Boot your virtual machine and select your `boot.wim` image when prompted. Proceed through the installation process, selecting your newly created WIM image when prompted. Following the installation, ensure that the installed operating system contains the additional role or feature that you chose earlier.

Exercise 1-4

Virtual machine checkpoints are similar to another storage technology called **differencing disks**. Like checkpoint files, differencing disks store changes made to an operating system after creation. However, a differencing disk is a `.vhdx` file that references another `.vhdx` file containing an installed operating system. When you create a new virtual machine, you can attach an existing differencing disk to your virtual machine for storage. When you boot this new virtual machine, the differencing disk will boot the operating system stored in the `.vhdx` file it references. Any changes you make within the operating system will only be stored in the differencing disk and not the `.vhdx` file it references.

In Hyper-V Manager, click **New** in the Actions pane and then click **Hard Disk**. Choose the appropriate options within the New Virtual Hard Disk Wizard to create a differencing disk that references the existing virtual hard disk file for WindowsServer2019VM3. Next, create a new Generation 2 virtual machine called WindowsServer2019VM5 within Hyper-V manager that uses your differencing disk. Boot the WindowsServer2019VM5 virtual machine and note that Windows Server 2019 Standard Edition Server Core is started. Next, add a role or feature of your choice and shut down the WindowsServer2019VM5 virtual machine. Finally, boot your WindowsServer2019VM3 virtual machine and note that the added role or feature is not present, as it was only added to the differencing disk.

INTRODUCTION TO ACTIVE DIRECTORY AND ACCOUNT MANAGEMENT

After completing this module, you will be able to:

Create and manage local user and group accounts

Install and explain the purpose of Active Directory

Outline the purpose of Active Directory objects, forests, trees, and trusts

Describe the different types of Active Directory groups and their use within a forest

Identify the features available within different domain and forest functional levels

Describe how sites can be used to control Active Directory replication

Outline the function of the Active Directory global catalog and UGMC

Identify the different FSMO roles available within a domain and forest

Describe scenarios in which Azure Active Directory can be used within an organization

Use Active Directory Domains and Trusts to raise functional levels and create trust relationships

View and raise functional levels using command line utilities

Use Active Directory Sites and Services to manage sites and global catalog

Use Active Directory Users and Computers to create and manage OU, user, group, and computer objects

Describe the features available within the Active Directory Administrative Center

Explain the purpose of RODCs, as well as the procedures used to install and manage them

In this module, you'll learn how to manage accounts within a workgroup or Active Directory environment. You'll start by examining the management of local users and groups. Next, you'll explore the structure and function of Active Directory, as well as Active Directory components, including trusts, sites, functional levels, global catalog, UGMC, and FSMOs. Afterward, you'll examine the process used to install Active Directory domain controllers as well as the procedures used to configure Active Directory components. Following this, you'll learn how to create and manage Active Directory objects. Finally, you'll examine the features of RODCs as well as the procedures used to install RODCs within an Active Directory domain.

Working with Local Users and Groups

In order to interact with the Windows operating system, you first must prove your identity. Recall from Module 1 that this process is called authentication and is normally performed by providing a valid user name and password at the Windows logon screen that matches an associated **local user account** on the system. After you log into a Windows system, you receive any **rights** to the operating system assigned to your local user account, such as the right to change the system time or shut down the system. After you access resources on the system (e.g., files, directories, and printers), you are granted access to each resource based on the **permissions** that the resource lists for your local user account within its **Access Control List (ACL)**. Moreover, **local group accounts** can be used to simplify assigning rights and permissions to multiple local user accounts. When you assign rights or permissions to a local group account, each member of the group receives those rights and permissions.

When connecting to a shared resource on another computer across a network, you must prove your identity to that computer before it allows you access to the resources based on your permissions within the ACL. Computers that are part of a workgroup (and hence use peer-to-peer networking) maintain their own database of local users and groups. As a result, if you connect to a shared resource on a workgroup computer, you will first be prompted to log into that computer using a local user account that has permissions to the resource.

Local user and group accounts are stored within a **Security Accounts Manager (SAM)** database that is referenced by the Windows Registry. Following installation, a Windows Server 2019 system is part of a workgroup and contains two main local user accounts that are used to authenticate users:

- *Administrator*, which is assigned administrative rights as well as permissions to most resources on the system
- *Guest*, which is assigned a minimal set of rights and permissions to resources on the system (disabled by default as a security measure)

Note

A Windows Server system that is part of a workgroup is often called a **standalone server**.

Note

In addition to Administrator and Guest, you may also see additional local user accounts that are used by applications on the system. For example, the DefaultAccount local user account (used by applications that provide a separate authentication mechanism to users) and WDAGUtilityAccount (used by the Application Guard feature of Windows Defender) are created during a Windows Server 2019 installation. Additional local user accounts may be added by software and server roles that you install.

There are also many local group accounts that are added to a Windows Server 2019 system following installation. By default, the main local group accounts that are used for assigning rights and permissions to users include:

- *Administrators*, which includes the local Administrator user account by default
- *Guests*, which includes the local Guest user account by default
- *Users*, to which all additional local user accounts are added by default. This group allows you to log into the system and perform most non-administrative tasks.

Other default local group accounts are often used by applications or to provide specific rights and permissions. For example, adding local user accounts to the local Print Operators group allows those users the ability to create and manage printers on the system.

To create local user and group accounts, you can use the **Local Users and Groups** MMC snap-in. You can open the MMC by executing the mmc.exe command within a Windows Run dialog box, Command Prompt, or PowerShell window. Next, you can select Add/Remove Snap-in from the File menu, highlight Local Users and Groups, click Add, and then click Finish to add the Local Users and Groups tool for your local computer as shown in Figure 4-1. After you click OK in Figure 4-1, you will be able to access the Local Users and Groups MMC snap-in shown in Figure 4-2.

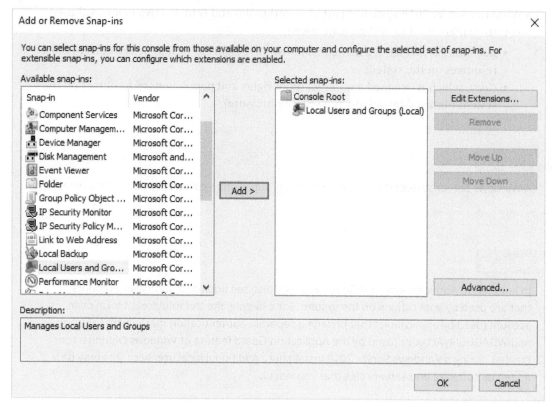

Figure 4-1   Adding the Local Users and Groups MMC snap-in

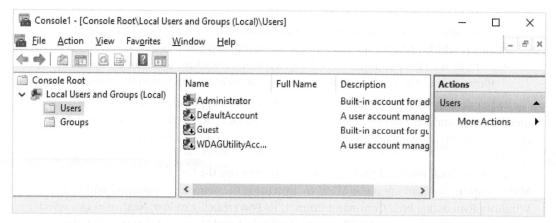

Figure 4-2   The Local Users and Groups MMC snap-in

To create a new local user account, you can select the Users folder shown in Figure 4-2, click More Actions, New User from the Actions pane, and specify the appropriate information in the New User window shown in Figure 4-3. By default, the *User must change password at next logon box* is checked to force users to enter a new password the first time they sign in so that the account creator will not know their password. The other options include:

- *User cannot change password*, which means that only the account administrator can change the user's password
- *Password never expires*, which is used in situations in which an account must always be accessed, such as when a program accesses an account to run a special process
- *Account is disabled*, which provides a way to prevent access to an account with-out deleting it

> **Note** 📎
>
> Symbols that cannot be used in an account name in Windows Server 2019 are [ ] ; : < > = , + / \ | . Also, each account name must be unique so that there are no duplicates. Finally, when you specify a password, it needs to meet the password policy requirements on the local computer. You learn about setting up password requirements in Module 11.

> **Note** 📎
>
> The default Windows Server 2019 password policy requires that passwords be six characters or longer and cannot contain the account name or portions of the user's full name (beyond two characters of the name). Also, a minimum of three of the following four rules apply: includes numbers, includes uppercase letters, includes lowercase letters, includes characters such as $, #, and !.

After you click Create in Figure 4-3, the New User window remains open for creating additional users, until you click Close. After creating a new user, you can select it within the Users folder, click More Actions within the Actions pane, and choose the appropriate task, including:

- *Set password*, which assigns a new password to the account
- *Delete*, to remove the account
- *Rename*, to rename the account
- *Properties*, to configure additional account settings

To create a new local group account, you can select the Groups folder shown in Figure 4-2, click More Actions, New Group from the Actions pane, and specify the appropriate information in the New Group window shown in Figure 4-4. As with the

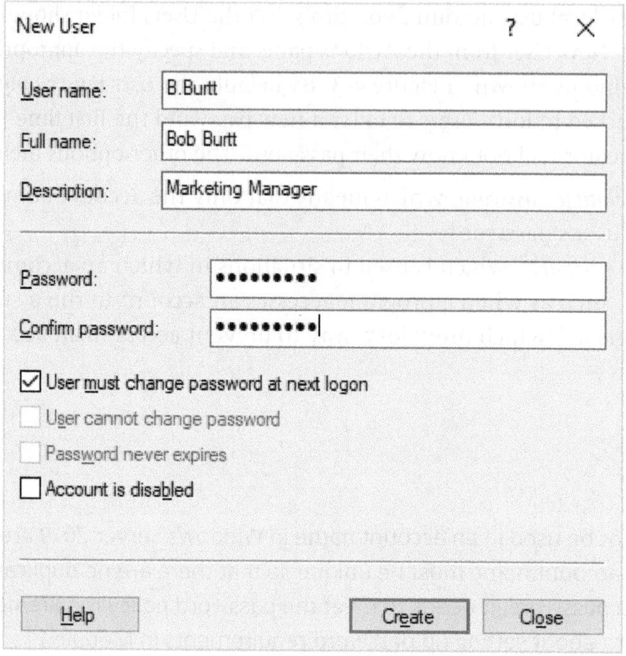

Figure 4-3   Creating a new local user account

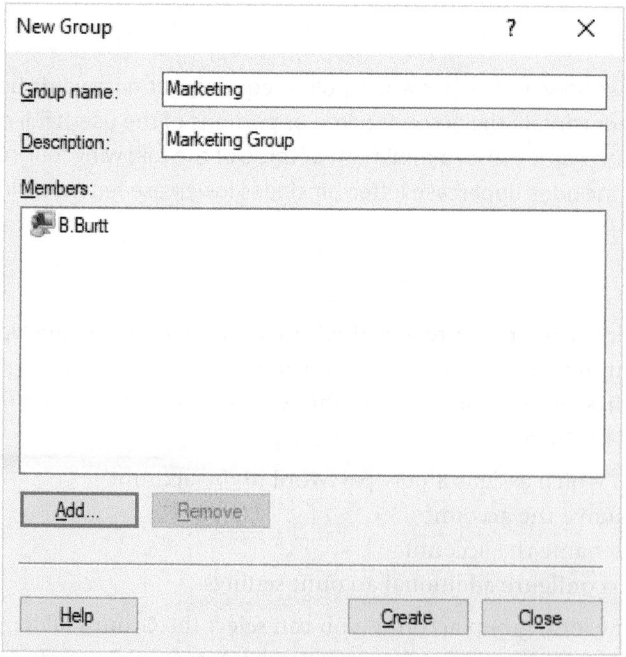

Figure 4-4   Creating a new local group account

New User window, after you click Create within the New Group window, the window will stay open to allow the creation of additional groups until you click Close. If you do not click the Add button within Figure 4-4 to select existing user accounts to add to the local group account, you can add them afterwards. To do this, you can select the local group account within the Groups folder and click More Actions, Add to Group within the Actions pane. You can also select an existing local group account, click More Actions within the Actions pane, and click Delete to remove the account, Rename to assign it a new name, or Properties to manage group membership.

Active Directory Basics

Recall from Module 1 that Active Directory can be used to provide centralized authentication (called single sign-on) to other computers on the network that are joined to an Active Directory domain. When you log into a computer that is joined to an Active Directory domain, you have the option to log into the system using either a local user account or a **domain user account** that is stored in Active Directory. If you log into the system with a local user account, the rights and permissions assigned to your local user account are applied, and you must authenticate to other computers on the network in order to access their shared resources using a peer-to-peer networking model.

However, if you log into the system with a domain user account, your user name and password are authenticated by a domain controller on the network. Each domain controller has a centralized copy of the Active Directory database that contains domain user accounts. After the domain controller validates your user name and password, it issues your computer an encrypted **token** that lists your domain user account, as well as any **domain group accounts** of which you are a member. Tokens can only be decrypted by computers that participate in the same Active Directory domain and are destroyed when you log out of your system (which also logs you out of your domain user account). When you access a shared resource on another computer that is joined to your Active Directory domain, your token is automatically sent with the request to the target computer to verify your identity. You are then granted or denied access to the resource according to the permissions assigned to your domain user and group accounts listed within the resource's ACL.

Note 📎

To locate domain controllers, each computer that participates in an Active Directory domain must be configured to query a DNS server that contains the appropriate **service records** for the Active Directory domain. Normally this DNS server is on a domain controller.

Note

Linux, UNIX, macOS, and Windows 2000 and later clients use the Kerberos ticket-based authentication protocol to authenticate to a domain controller and obtain a token. As a result, these tokens are often called **tickets**.

When you join a computer to an Active Directory domain:

- A **computer account** is created for your computer within the Active Directory database. This computer account contains an encryption key that is used to encrypt the communication between your computer and the domain controllers in the domain during the authentication process.
- The Domain Admins group in Active Directory is added to the local Administrators group. This allows members of the Domain Admins group to log into and administer any system in the Active Directory domain.
- The Domain Users group in Active Directory is added to the local Users group. This allows any user account in the Active Directory domain to log into the computer using a domain user account.
- The Domain Guests group in Active Directory is added to the local Guests group. This allows any accounts within the Domain Guests group to access the computer with the rights and permissions assigned to the local Guests group.

Note

A Windows Server system that is joined to an Active Directory domain but is not a domain controller and does not hold a copy of the Active Directory database is called a **member server**.

Domain user, group, and computer accounts are stored as **objects** within the Active Directory database that conforms to the International Telecommunication Union (ITU) **X.500** standard. Moreover, the Active Directory database can contain an unlimited number of objects and be accessed quickly using the **Lightweight Directory Access Protocol (LDAP)**.

In addition to centralized authentication, the Group Policy feature of Active Directory can be used to automatically deploy software, or configure security, operating system, and application settings on computers within an Active Directory domain based on the location of the user or computer object within the Active Directory database. This reduces the time it takes to administer a domain, as a single Group Policy may apply to hundreds (or even thousands) of different user and computer accounts in the domain.

Note

The configuration of Group Policy will be discussed in Module 11.

Active Directory Objects

Before an object can be created within Active Directory, it must be properly defined as an available object type within the Active Directory database. The Active Directory **schema** stores a list of all available object types (called **classes**) and their associated properties (called **attributes**). In addition, the Active Directory schema can be extended to include additional object classes and attributes. Some server roles and software applications extend the Active Directory schema to add additional attributes to user objects or create new object classes to store software configuration. One example of this is Microsoft Exchange Server, which adds over 100 email-related attributes to user accounts to store mailbox-related configuration information for each user account.

Note

You must be a member of the Schema Admins group within Active Directory to modify the Active Directory schema.

The objects within the Active Directory database that represent a user account, group account, or computer account are called **leaf objects**. Resources that are available on the network, such as shared printers, may also have an associated leaf object if they are published to the Active Directory database.

Some objects can contain leaf objects. These objects are called **container objects** and are primarily used to group leaf objects for ease of administration and the application of Group Policy. There are three main container objects within the Active Directory database:

- domains
- organizational units (OUs)
- sites

A domain object represents an Active Directory domain, and is given a unique DNS domain name, such as domain1.com. Each domain object often represents a separate business unit within your organization and can contain OUs as well as leaf objects.

An **organizational unit (OU)** is similar to a folder on a filesystem. It can contain leaf objects or other OUs (called **child OUs**) much like a folder on a filesystem can contain files or subdirectories. The OU structure you create for each domain should reflect the structure within that particular business unit. For example, the domain1.com domain shown in Figure 4-5 organizes leaf objects into OUs by department (Accounting, Marketing, IT, Production) and sub-department (A/P for Accounts Payable, A/R for Accounts Receivable, R&D for Research and Development, and PA for Product Assembly).

> **Note**
>
> Active Directory domains are often represented by triangles within diagrams, whereas OUs are represented by ovals or circles.

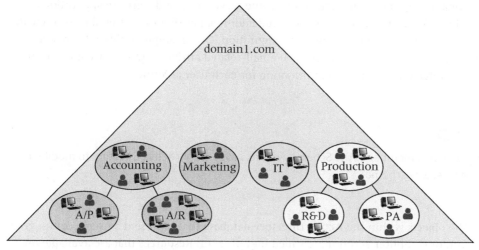

Figure 4-5 **A sample domain and OU structure**

In Figure 4-5, only one level of child OUs exist under the Accounting and Production OUs. Although there is no limit to the number of levels of child OUs that you can place under a single OU, you should limit it to five levels or less to ensure that LDAP can locate leaf objects quickly. Each leaf object is given an LDAP **distinguished name (DN)** that identifies the **common name (CN)** of the object and its position within Active Directory. For example, the DN for a user account called J.Eckert in the R&D OU shown in Figure 4-5 would be CN=J.Eckert,OU=R&D,OU=Production,DC=domain1,DC=com (DC refers to domain component).

Site objects represent physical locations within your organization. Each physical location contains a LAN that communicates with other physical locations over an Internet connection that is often much slower than a LAN. By representing each physical location with a site object, you can create settings that control the replication of Active Directory information across the Internet. Sites will be discussed in more depth later within this module.

Note 🔗

Each leaf and container object in Active Directory is assigned a **security identifier (SID)** attribute that is used to identify the object within an ACL, as well as a **globally-unique identifier (GUID)** attribute that guarantees its uniqueness within the Active Directory database.

Active Directory Forests, Trees, and Trusts

Recall that domains are often used to represent a single business unit within an organization. Although this may be suitable for smaller organizations, larger organizations often have multiple business units, and each business unit may need to access resources within other business units. Consequently, Active Directory **forests** are used to provide for multiple domains within the same organization. When you install the first domain controller within the first domain in an organization, a forest is created with the same name as this first domain. The first domain in a forest is called the **forest root domain**. Additional domain controllers can be added to your forest root domain or be configured to host an Active Directory database for another domain within the same forest. In the sample forest shown in Figure 4-6, the forest root domain is domain1.com, and three additional domains (domain2.com, europe.domain2.com, and asia.domain2.com) have been added to the domain1.com forest. The domain1.com and domain2.com domains are separate business units headquartered in North America, and domain2.com contains

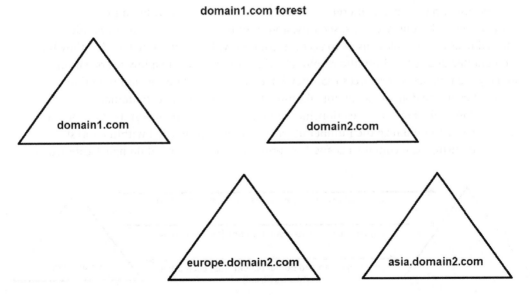

Figure 4-6   A sample Active Directory forest

branch offices within Europe and Asia that function as separate business units. Because the domain2.com, europe.domain2.com, and asia.domain2.com domains share the same core domain name, we refer to them as the domain2.com **tree**. The domain2.com domain is called the **parent domain** within the tree, and the europe.domain2.com and asia.domain2.com domains are called **child domains**. The domain1.com domain is also a tree but without child domains.

> ### Note
>
> A domain is created when at least one domain controller hosts the Active Directory database for that domain. If additional domain controllers are added to a domain, authentication requests will be distributed between the domain controllers to ensure greater performance. Furthermore, you should plan to have a minimum of two domain controllers within each domain to ensure that domain authentication can occur if a domain controller fails.

> ### Note
>
> Different trees in the same forest do not share the same DNS domain name, and are said to have a **disjointed namespace**. Domains within the same tree share the same DNS domain name, and are said to have a **contiguous namespace**.

Because it represents a different business unit, each domain within a forest has its own user and group accounts, security, and resources. **Trust relationships** (often referred to as **trusts**) allow users to access resources within other domains that they have been granted access to within the resource's ACL. For example, to allow users within domain1.com to access resources that they have been granted permission to within domain2.com, the domain2.com domain must trust the domain1.com domain.

In a forest diagram, trust relationships are represented by arrow symbols as shown in Figure 4-7. To minimize the number of trust relationships needed within a forest, trust relationships can contain a **transitive** property. For example, if domain1.com trusts

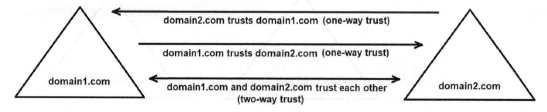

Figure 4-7   Trust relationship types between domain1.com and domain2.com

domain2.com using a transitive trust, and domain2.com trusts the asia.domain2.com using a transitive trust, then domain1.com also trusts asia.domain2.com. This allows users within domain2.com and asia.domain2.com to access resources within domain1.com that they have been granted permissions to.

By default, the first parent domain within each tree trusts the first parent domain within each other tree in the same forest with two-way transitive trust relationships. Moreover, each parent domain within a tree trusts their child domains using two-way transitive trust relationships. These default trust relationships (called **internal trusts**) allow users to access resources in any other domain within the forest that they have been granted permission to. Figure 4-8 shows the default trust relationships for the domain1.com forest shown earlier in Figure 4-6.

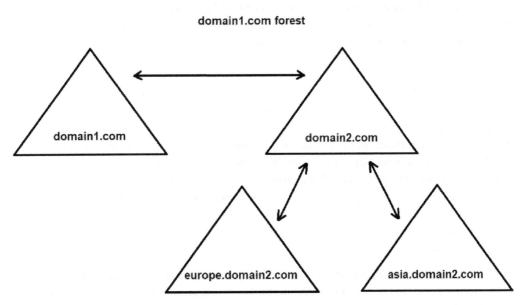

Figure 4-8   Default trust relationships within the domain1.com forest

Although the trusts shown in Figure 4-8 are transitive, users in asia.domain2.com must first contact a domain controller within the domain2.com domain to validate the transitive trust before they can access resources in the domain1.com domain. To speed up resource access, you can manually create a **shortcut trust** directly between the asia.domain2.com and domain1.com domains. You can also create trust relationships to a Windows NT4 or Active Directory domain outside of your forest (called an **external trust**), or to another Active Directory forest (called a **forest trust**). If your organization has a UNIX Kerberos realm, you can create a **realm trust** between an Active Directory domain and the Kerberos realm.

Note 🖉

The two-way transitive features of trust relationships are derived from the Kerberos protocol. Because Windows NT4 does not use Kerberos, external trusts to a Windows NT4 domain must be one-way and non-transitive.

Active Directory Groups

In a workgroup environment, recall that local group accounts are used to simplify the assignment of rights and permissions to multiple local user accounts on a system. Within an Active Directory environment, you can use group account objects to simplify the assignment of rights and permissions to user account objects that are members of the group. Assigning resource permissions to group accounts also minimizes the number of entries within the ACL and results in faster resource access.

There are two main types of group accounts within Active Directory: distribution groups and security groups. **Distribution groups** are designed for use with an email system, such as Microsoft Exchange Server. When you send an email to a distribution group, the email system sends it to all of the user accounts that are members of the distribution group. **Security groups** are the default group type within Active Directory and can be assigned rights and permissions that apply to the members of the group.

Because resources within a forest may be accessed by users in other domains across a trust relationship, Microsoft has defined three **group scopes** that allow administrators to organize the assignment of rights and permissions across multiple domains:

- **Global**
- **Domain local**
- **Universal**

Each group scope places restrictions on the objects that the groups can contain as well as the domains within the forest that can access them. These restrictions are summarized in Table 4-1.

Table 4-1   Active Directory group scopes

Group scope	Allowed members	Domains that can access the group
Global	Objects located within the same domain as the global group	Any domain in the forest
Domain local	Objects located within any domain in the forest	Only the domain where the local group resides
Universal	Objects located within any domain in the forest	Any domain in the forest

Although group scopes apply to both distribution and security groups, we'll limit our discussion to their use with security groups. When assigning rights and permissions to multiple user objects using security groups, keep the following considerations in mind:

- Global security groups may be assigned permissions to resources or added as a member to another group in any domain within the forest. However, they can only contain objects from the same domain in which they were created.
- Domain local security groups can be assigned permissions to resources or added as a member to another group in the same domain, but can contain objects from any domain in the forest.
- Universal security groups can be assigned permissions to resources or added as a member to another group within any domain in the forest. They can contain any object in the forest.

Note

The process of adding a group to the membership list of another group is called **group nesting**.

Note

Universal security groups store their list of members within the global catalog (discussed later in this module). To ensure fast global catalog performance, you should minimize the number of universal groups that you create as well as the number of members within a universal group.

Microsoft recommends using a combination of global, universal, and domain local security groups within a forest to organize the assignment of permissions in a way that is easy to modify and document.

Because rights and permissions are most often assigned by job role within an organization, you should place user objects within global groups in each domain based on job role. For example, you can create a global group called Marketing-G within the domain1.com domain (shown earlier in Figure 4-8) that contains the Marketing department user objects within the domain1.com domain. This Marketing-G group can then be assigned permissions to resources in any domain within the forest. Similarly, you could create Marketing-G groups in the domain2.com, europe.domain2.com, and asia.domain2.com domains that contain the Marketing users from each respective domain.

Universal groups can be used to simplify the assignment of permissions to all users within an organization that are part of a job role. For example, you can create a universal group within the forest called Marketing-U and add the Marketing-G groups from each domain to its membership list. If you assign permissions to the Marketing-U group, all Marketing department users in the forest will receive the permissions.

Domain local groups can be used to make permissions assignments easier to identify or modify. For example, if a printer in your domain called Ricoh4916 must be used by all Marketing department users in the forest, you can create a domain local group called Ricoh4916-DL and add the Marketing-U group as a member. By assigning print permission to the Ricoh4916-DL group within the ACL of the Ricoh4916 printer, you will have given print permission to all Marketing department users within the organization. Moreover, you can add users and groups to the Ricoh4916-DL group to assign them print permission to the Ricoh4916 printer without modifying the ACL on the printer itself.

> **Note** 📎
>
> You can use the letters A, G, U, DL, and P to remember Microsoft's recommended approach to using group membership within a forest: Add users to Global groups based on job role. Then, add these global groups to Universal groups for forest-wide use. Finally, add the appropriate global and universal groups to Domain Local groups that are assigned Permissions to a resource.

Domain and Forest Functional Levels

Microsoft first introduced single sign-on with Windows NT4 Server. However, Windows NT4 domains did not use the Active Directory database. Instead, a **primary domain controller (PDC)** within each Windows NT4 domain stored a read-write copy of a SAM database that could authenticate users within the domain and issue tokens. Additional domain controllers were called **backup domain controllers (BDCs)** and obtained a read-only copy of the SAM database from the PDC so that they could authenticate users. When Active Directory was introduced with Windows 2000 Server, it had to maintain backward compatibility to Windows NT4 domains in order to allow administrators the ability to upgrade or replace Windows NT4 domain controllers with Windows 2000 domain controllers over a long period of time without disrupting user access.

Each version of Windows Server since Windows 2000 contains additional Active Directory features that are unavailable in previous versions. However, it is impractical for most organizations to upgrade or replace all domain controllers with new ones each time a new version of Windows Server is released. Thus, each Active Directory domain contains **domain functional levels** to allow backward compatibility to older versions of Active Directory. Each domain function level defines the oldest version of Windows Server that can be used on domain controllers within a domain. All Active Directory features released since that version of Window Server are disabled automatically on newer domain controllers to ensure backward compatibility. The domain functional levels available for domains that include Windows Server 2019 domain controllers are described in Table 4-2.

Table 4-2   Windows Server 2019 domain functional levels

Functional level	New Active Directory features provided
Windows Server 2008	**Distributed File System (DFS)** replication between domain controllers, **Advanced Encryption Standard (AES)** security for Kerberos authentication, and enhanced user account password policies
Windows Server 2008 R2	**Service Principle Name (SPN)** identification for network services
Windows Server 2012	**Compound authentication**, which creates Kerberos tickets with additional information used by other services, and **Kerberos armoring**, which creates a secure channel for authentication that is protected against network attacks
Windows Server 2012 R2	Additional encryption technologies for Kerberos authentication, as well as the ability to create authentication policies
Windows Server 2016	Additional Kerberos authentication features

You can add a Windows Server 2019 domain controller to an existing Active Directory domain that runs at the Windows Server 2008 or later functional level. As you replace or upgrade legacy domain controllers, you can increase the domain functional level of the domain to enable the new Active Directory features listed within Table 4-2. However, raising a functional level is a one-way operation. You cannot return to the previous functional level after it has been raised.

Note 📎

Domain functional levels only apply to the domain controllers that host the Active Directory database for a domain. A domain at the Windows Server 2016 domain functional level can still contain clients and other servers that are running legacy operating systems such as Windows XP or Windows NT4 Server.

Note 📎

Each domain in a forest can operate at a different functional level.

Some Active Directory features require that all domains within the forest be at a minimum domain functional level. As a result, an Active Directory forest maintains a **forest functional level** that defines the minimum domain functional level required for each domain within the forest. The forest functional levels available for domains that include Windows Server 2019 domain controllers are described in Table 4-3.

Table 4-3   Windows Server 2019 forest functional levels

Functional level	New Active Directory features provided
Windows Server 2008	No additional features beyond those within the Windows Server 2008 domain functional level
Windows Server 2008 R2	The ability to create and use the **Active Directory Recycle Bin** to recover deleted objects
Windows Server 2012	No additional features beyond those within the Windows Server 2012 domain functional level
Windows Server 2012 R2	No additional features beyond those within the Windows Server 2012 R2 domain functional level
Windows Server 2016	The ability to use the **Microsoft Identity Manager (MIM)** to restrict malicious access to Active Directory using **Privilege Access Management (PAM)**

In order to raise your forest functional level, you must ensure that all domains are first raised to the same domain functional level. For example, to obtain the Active Directory Recycle Bin, you can raise each domain within the forest to the Windows Server 2008 R2 functional level and then raise the forest functional level to Windows Server 2008 R2. As with domain functional levels, you cannot return to the previous forest functional level after it has been raised.

Sites and Active Directory Replication

To ensure that the Active Directory database is identical on each domain controller within a domain, objects are replicated between domain controllers when new objects are added to the Active Directory database or existing objects are modified or removed. Moreover, some information is replicated to all domain controllers within the forest.

In order to understand how replication takes place between domain controllers in a domain and forest, you must first understand the three main sections (called **directory partitions**) that make up the Active Directory database:

- Schema
- Configuration
- Domain

The **schema partition** contains the Active Directory schema and must be identical on all domain controllers within the forest to ensure that Active Directory objects from any domain in the forest can be interpreted by any domain controller in the forest. If a change is made to the schema partition, such as the addition of a new object class or attribute, these changes are replicated to all other domain controllers within the forest.

The **configuration partition** stores the structure and layout of the forest, including the names of each domain and the trust relationships between them. As with the schema partition, each domain controller within the forest must share the same configuration partition. Thus, if you add or remove a domain or trust relationship, the configuration partition will be replicated to all other domain controllers in the forest.

The largest section of the Active Directory database is the **domain partition**. It stores all objects within a particular domain, including users, computers, OUs, and groups. Because each Active Directory domain represents a single business unit that is managed separately, the domain partition is only replicated to other domain controllers within the same domain. When a change is made to the domain partition on a domain controller, such as the addition of a user object, that change is replicated to other domain controllers within the same domain only.

Changes to the schema and configuration partitions are relatively infrequent within organizations. However, changes to the domain partition occur regularly each day, as many services modify the properties of objects within Active Directory to store data and configuration information. If all domain controllers within a domain reside on the same LAN, replication of domain partition objects occurs quickly. If, however, domain controllers within a domain are located in separate LANs connected by the Internet, the replication traffic will consume Internet bandwidth and may congest the Internet connection at each location.

To ensure that Active Directory replication does not negatively impact Internet bandwidth, you could design a forest with one domain per location. However, this is impractical in most environments because it is costly to implement and manage multiple domains for a single business unit. A more practical method is to control replication within an organization using objects within Active Directory. A **site object** (or **site**) represents a physical location in your organization and may be associated with one or more **subnet objects** that represent IP networks that contain domain controllers. Site objects are connected to other site objects using **site link objects** that contain attributes that specify when replication is allowed to occur. You can modify site link objects to specify that replication of Active Directory information between domain controllers in different sites only occurs at a specific timed interval or after working hours when Internet bandwidth is more readily available.

Say, for example, that domain1.com contains five domain controllers, as shown in Figure 4-9. Three of these domain controllers (DC1, DC2, and DC3) are located within

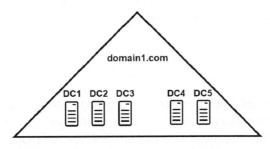

Figure 4-9   A domain with five domain controllers

the Toronto office, while the other two (DC4 and DC5) are located within the Chicago office. If a new user object is created on DC1, it will immediately be replicated to all other domain controllers in domain1.com. The new user will take only a few moments to reach DC2 and DC3 on the Toronto LAN, but will take considerably longer to traverse the Internet from Toronto to Chicago in order to reach DC4 and DC5.

By creating site objects that represent the Toronto and Chicago locations, you can create a site link object between the Toronto and Chicago sites (as shown in Figure 4-10) to specify when replication should occur. Say, for example, that the Toronto-Chicago site link is configured to replicate every hour between 11:00pm and 1:00am (which is after normal business hours in both locations). If you create a new user on DC1, it will immediately replicate to DC2 and DC3, but will not replicate to DC4 and DC5 until 11:00pm.

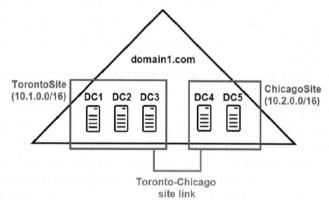

Figure 4-10   **A domain with five domain controllers within two sites**

Moreover, the TorontoSite site object within Figure 4-10 is associated with a subnet object for the 10.1.0.0/16 network, and the ChicagoSite site object is associated with a subnet object for the 10.2.0.0/16 network. Thus, if a new domain controller with an IP address on the 10.2.0.0/16 network is added to the domain, it will be added to the ChicagoSite by default unless you specify otherwise.

Note 📎

To minimize bandwidth, replication between sites only occurs between a single domain controller within each site called a **bridgehead server**. Although Active Directory automatically chooses the bridgehead server in each site, you can choose to manually specify the domain controller that you would like to use as the bridgehead server for each site.

Note

Site link objects can also be used to control the replication of changes to the schema and configuration partitions within the forest.

Note

Large forests may have hundreds of sites that are interconnected with site link objects to form multiple paths from one site to another. In this case, you can lower the cost value on a site link object to encourage Active Directory to use a particular path for replication.

Global Catalog

A single forest can contain an unlimited number of domains. Moreover, each domain can contain an unlimited number of objects. To ensure that you can locate objects quickly within different domains, a list of all object names in the forest (called the **global catalog**) is stored on at least one domain controller in the forest. The global catalog is similar to a telephone book. Whereas a telephone book allows you to quickly locate a telephone number, the global catalog allows you to quickly locate an object in a remote domain. For example, when assigning permissions on a resource, the interface you use will allow you to select users and groups within other domains in the forest from a list that is provided by the global catalog. If a domain controller that holds a copy of the global catalog is located in your LAN, the list of users and groups within other domains will appear quickly. However, if no copies of the global catalog exist within your LAN, it may take several minutes before the list of available users is shown.

For user account objects, the global catalog also stores a unique name that users can use to log into their domain from any computer in the forest. This name is called a **User Principle Name (UPN)** and uses the format username@domainname. To log into a computer as a user account within another domain in the forest, you can specify the appropriate UPN within the user name text box at the Windows logon screen. A global catalog is then contacted to verify the UPN and locate a domain controller that can complete the authentication process.

Recall that universal group membership is stored solely within the global catalog. Because authentication tokens list your group membership, domain controllers must contact a global catalog during the authentication process to determine your universal group membership. Consequently, if a global catalog cannot be contacted, you will not be able to complete the authentication process and log into the domain but may be able to use **cached credentials** to access your system. Moreover, if the nearest global catalog is located in a remote site across the Internet, it may take several minutes for a domain controller to complete the authentication process.

Note 📎

Cached credentials are a list of encrypted passwords stored within the Windows Registry for domain user accounts that have previously logged into the system. If a domain user has logged into a system previously, cached credentials allow that user to log in and access the local resources of the system if a domain controller or global catalog is not available.

Note 📎

To provide fast authentication and browsing of objects within remote domains, each site within Active Directory should contain at least one copy of the global catalog.

The global catalog is updated when objects are added or removed within any domain in the forest, and these updates must be replicated to all other domain controllers that hold a copy of the global catalog. Moreover, global catalog replication is not restricted by site links. Thus, in a large forest, global catalog replication may congest the Internet bandwidth in locations that have a slower Internet connection, such as a small branch office. To solve this problem, you should avoid placing a copy of the global catalog on domain controllers within sites that have limited Internet bandwidth. Unfortunately, this forces domain controllers within these sites to contact a global catalog in another site to complete authentication requests, resulting in slower authentication for users. Fortunately, you can enable **Universal Group Membership Caching (UGMC)** on sites that are unable to hold a copy of the global catalog to provide fast authentication. If UGMC is enabled for a site, domain controllers must contact a remote global catalog the first time each user authenticates to the domain in order to verify their universal group memberships. These universal group memberships are then cached on the domain controller, and subsequent authentication requests use the universal group membership information for the user stored in the cache, eliminating the need to contact a remote global catalog.

FSMO Roles

Certain domain and forest functions must be coordinated from a single domain controller. These functions are called **Flexible Single Master Operations (FSMO)**. A domain controller can be configured to hold a single FSMO role or all FSMO roles for its domain or forest.

Table 4-4 lists the five FSMO roles that are available within Active Directory. Two of these roles are forest-wide, which means that they must be present on a single domain controller in the forest. The other three roles are domain-wide, which means that they must be present on a single domain controller within each domain in the forest.

Table 4-4   Active Directory FSMO roles

FSMO Role	Number per Domain or Forest	Function
Schema Master	1 per forest	Must be contacted in order to modify the Active Directory schema. Any schema changes are then replicated by the Schema Master to all other domain controllers in the forest.
Domain Naming Master	1 per forest	Must be contacted in order to add or remove domains and trust relationships within the forest. Any changes to the domain and trust configuration of the forest are then replicated by the Domain Naming Master to all other domain controllers in the forest. For best performance, the domain controller that holds the Domain Naming Master should also hold a copy of the global catalog.
PDC Emulator	1 per domain	In legacy Active Directory domains, this role emulated a Windows NT4 PDC for backward compatibility. However, in modern Active Directory domains, the PDC Emulator coordinates user password changes and sends time information to each computer within the domain.
RID Master	1 per domain	Issues sequential ranges of **Relative Identifiers (RIDs)** to domain controllers within the domain. RIDs are used to create unique SIDs for newly created objects in the domain. Because the RID Master generates unique ranges of RIDs for each domain controller, SIDs are guaranteed to be unique amongst domain objects. When a domain controller has exhausted its range of RIDs, it contacts the RID Master to obtain another range.
Infrastructure Master	1 per domain	Coordinates group membership, as well as the use of GUIDs and DNs between the current domain and other domains in the forest. Because the global catalog provides similar functionality, the Infrastructure Master should be placed on a domain controller that does not contain the global catalog.

The first domain controller installed within the forest root domain contains all five FSMO roles, including the two forest-wide FSMO roles and the three domain-wide FSMO roles. Furthermore, the first domain controller installed within all other domains in the forest contains the three domain-wide FSMO roles. If one of these domain controllers becomes unavailable (for example, due to a hardware failure), multiple FSMO roles will be unavailable. As a result, you should spread FSMO roles within your forest and domains amongst different domain controllers for fault tolerance.

If a domain controller that holds a FSMO role becomes unavailable, you will notice problems within Active Directory. For example, if the PDC Emulator becomes unavailable, users may receive an incorrect time that prevents them from logging into their domain. This is because Kerberos requires that the time on the computer and domain controller be no more than five minutes different for authentication to succeed. Moreover, if the RID Master becomes unavailable, you could receive an error message when attempting to create a new object in the Active Directory database indicating that a SID could not be generated for the new object. In these cases, you can force another domain controller to assume the FSMO role. This process is called **role seizure**. If the domain controller that originally held the FSMO role becomes available again, it will receive notice that the role has been seized and automatically forfeit the role.

Azure Active Directory

Azure Active Directory is an Active Directory service within the Microsoft Azure cloud. It provides the same single sign-on features of Active Directory, but is designed to allow access to cloud applications, such as Office 365. Office 365 consists of office and productivity applications including Word (word processing), Excel (spreadsheets), PowerPoint (slide presentations), Outlook (email), Publisher (publishable documents), and OneNote (multiuser information gathering and collaboration). An organization can choose to subscribe to Office 365 for its users in Azure Active Directory or in an on-premises Active Directory forest provided by domain controllers located within the organization itself.

Azure Active Directory can be configured to trust an organization's Active Directory forest, or mirror it using a synchronization service. For example, a university with 15,000 students and employees may implement Active Directory on-premises to provide authentication for employee user accounts, but use Azure Active Directory to authenticate student accounts. The employee user accounts can be mirrored to identical accounts within Azure Active Directory to allow access to cloud services, such as Office 365. Moreover, a trust relationship can be configured to allow the student accounts within Azure Active Directory to access on-premises resources within the university forest.

If an organization has a robust Internet connection within each site, Azure Active Directory can even be used to replace an Active Directory forest within an organization. For example, a small office with five users may choose to subscribe to Office 365 and other Microsoft cloud applications, which also creates user accounts for the five users within Azure Active Directory. The five computers within the organization can also be configured to join the Azure Active Directory domain, so that resources on them can be shared to the other four users easily.

The process used to subscribe to Office 365 and integrate an on-premises Active Directory domain with Azure Active Directory is constantly changing and is beyond the scope of this book. However, Microsoft makes this process easy for you. If you visit azure.microsoft.com, documentation and videos describing the current process are available, as well as a free trial.

Installing Active Directory

To install Active Directory on Windows Server 2019, you can select the Active Directory Domain Services role when adding a role within Server Manager, as shown in Figure 4-11. Click Next in Figure 4-11, progress through the Add Roles and Features Wizard, and then click Install. The files necessary to create a domain controller are then installed on your system, along with the associated management tools and Windows PowerShell cmdlets. After this has completed, you can click *Promote this server to a domain controller* on the final page of the Add Roles and Features Wizard (shown in Figure 4-12) to start the Active Directory Domain Services Configuration Wizard discussed in the following sections. This wizard will allow you to configure your server as:

- A domain controller in a new forest (creating the forest root domain)
- A domain controller for a new domain within an existing forest (creating a new domain within the forest)
- An additional domain controller within an existing domain

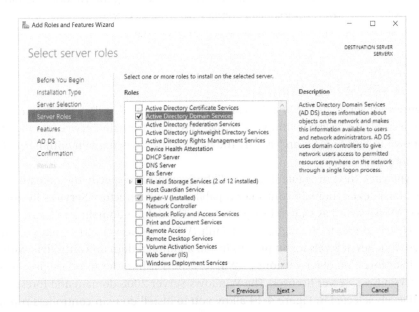

Figure 4-11   **Installing Active Directory Domain Services**

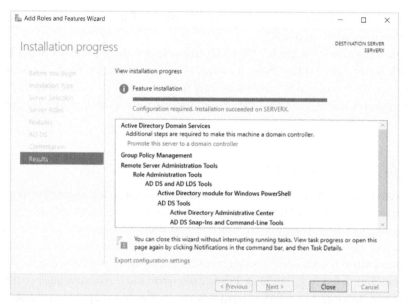

Figure 4-12   Completing the installation of Active Directory Domain Services

Note

You can also install the Active Directory Domain Services role using the Windows Admin Console, or within Windows PowerShell by running the `Install-WindowsFeature AD-Domain-Services -IncludeManagementTools` command.

Installing a Forest Root Domain

To configure your server as the first domain controller for the first domain in a new forest, you can select *Add a new forest* within the Active Directory Domain Services Configuration Wizard shown in Figure 4-13, and specify the name of the new domain within the Root domain name text box.

After you click Next in Figure 4-13, you'll be prompted to specify the domain and forest functional levels, domain controller capabilities, and Directory Services Restore Mode (DSRM) password as shown in Figure 4-14. The default domain and forest functional levels are set to the highest by default (Windows Server 2016), but you should lower these functional levels if you plan to install additional domain controllers within the domain or forest on older versions of Windows Server in order to utilize previously-purchased Windows Server licenses. The Windows Server 2008 domain and forest functional levels selected in Figure 4-14 allow you to install domain controllers running on Windows Server 2008 and later operating systems.

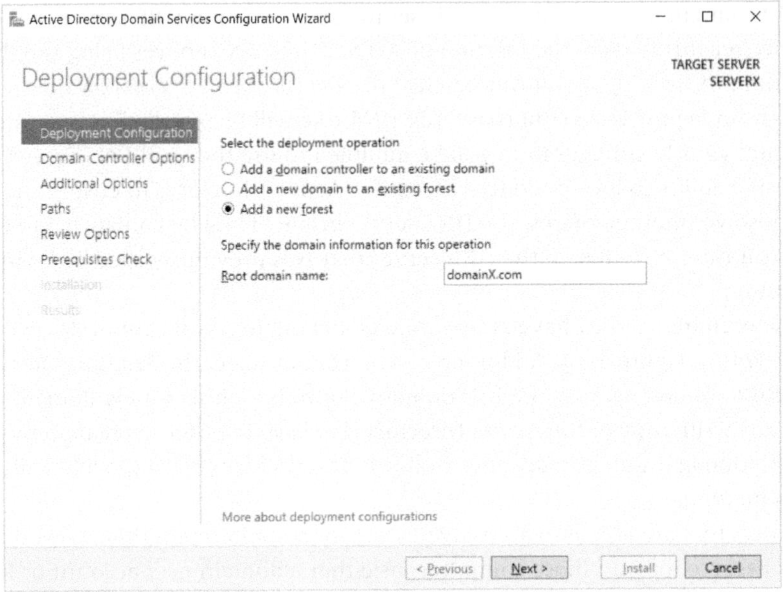

Figure 4-13   Installing a forest root domain

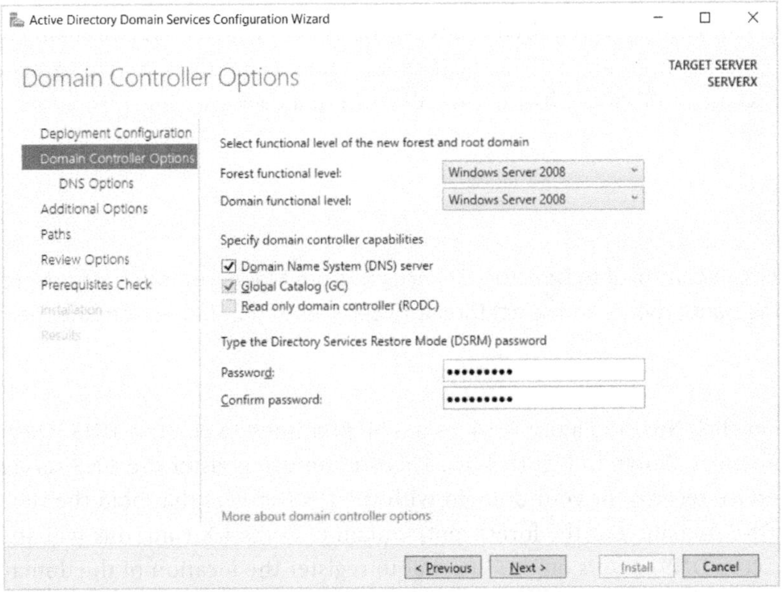

Figure 4-14   Specifying domain controller options

If the IP configuration of your server is set to use an existing DNS server that can create service records to store the location of Active Directory services using the **dynamic update** feature of DNS, then you can deselect the *Domain Name System (DNS) server* checkbox within Figure 4-14. Otherwise, the DNS role will be installed on your domain controller, and your IP configuration will be modified to use the local DNS server to allow your server the ability to locate service records for Active Directory. To ensure that your server can resolve Internet names, the DNS server installed will be configured to forward any requests it cannot resolve to the DNS server that was previously specified within your IP configuration.

Because each forest must have at least one global catalog, you cannot deselect *Global Catalog (GC)* within Figure 4-14. Additionally, you cannot select the *Read only domain controller (RODC)* option because the first domain controller within a new domain must contain a read-write copy of the Active Directory database in order to create new objects. The configuration and use of **Read-only Domain Controllers (RODCs)** will be discussed later in this module.

Computers that are joined to an Active Directory domain retain their SAM database. This allows users to log into those computers as either a domain user account or local user account at the logon screen. However, when you configure a server as a domain controller, the Active Directory database replaces the SAM database and any associated local accounts. Thus, you must specify a password within Figure 4-14 for a special local Administrator account that can be used to access the system if Active Directory becomes unavailable. This account is required to access the system if you boot a domain controller to **Directory Services Restore Mode (DSRM)** to repair a corrupted Active Directory database or restore an Active Directory database from a backup.

Note 📎

To boot a domain controller to Directory Services Restore Mode, you can hold down the F8 key during the boot process and select Directory Services Repair Mode from the menu.

After you click Next in Figure 4-14, you'll be prompted to create a DNS delegation for your domain as shown in Figure 4-15. This attempts to register the DNS server that holds the service records for your domain with the DNS servers that hold the records for the parent DNS domain. For the forest root domain of domainX.com, this will attempt to contact the .com DNS servers on the Internet to register the location of the domainX.com DNS servers, which will fail because .com domain registrations require payment to a **domain registrar** on the Internet. However, if you install a child domain for an existing Active Directory domain that is provided by DNS servers within your organization, then this registration will succeed and allow other computers within the organization to locate the Active Directory services within the child domain.

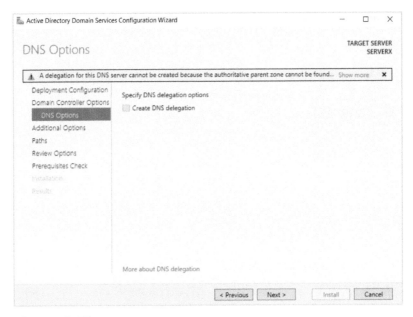

Figure 4-15 Configuring DNS delegation

Recall that you can join legacy computers to an Active Directory domain, regardless of the domain and forest functional level. Computers running operating systems older than Windows 2000 use NetBIOS packets to locate domain controllers instead of service records within DNS. As a result, each Active Directory domain must have a NetBIOS name to allow these legacy clients to join and locate domain controllers to provide authentication. Because NetBIOS names can be up to 15 characters and cannot include period characters, the default NetBIOS name for your domain is taken from the first 15 characters of your domain name before the first period. After you click Next in Figure 4-15, you are allowed to modify this default name, as shown in Figure 4-16.

The Active Directory database is stored in a database file called ntds.dit. Any changes to this file are first written to a transaction log file before they are applied to the ntds.dit file. This increases performance by allowing processes to quickly submit Active Directory changes to the transaction log without having to wait for confirmation that the change has been applied to the ntds.dit database. After you click Next in Figure 4-16, you are allowed to change the default folder path for the database and transaction log folders as well as the SYSVOL shared folder that is used to replicate objects between domain controllers, and distribute Group Policy to domain members. While the default folder paths shown in Figure 4-17 are fine for most domain controllers, choosing a path that is on a separate physical storage device (e.g., D:\) will result in improved performance as the Active Directory files will not need to compete with storage requests from the Windows operating system installed on C:\.

After you click Next in Figure 4-17, you will review a list of your configuration options as shown in Figure 4-18. If you click View script in Figure 4-18, a PowerShell

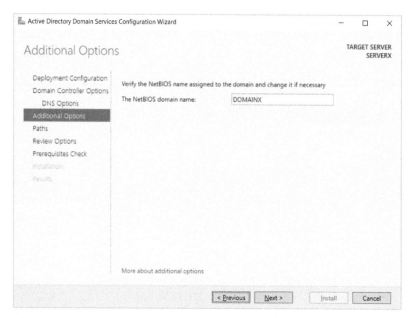

Figure 4-16 Specifying the NetBIOS name of a domain

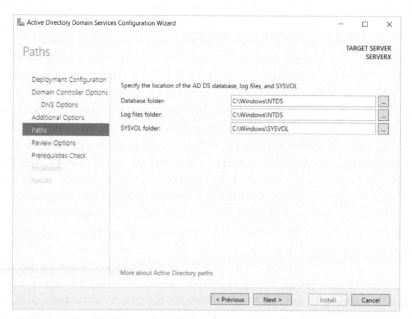

Figure 4-17 Specifying folder paths

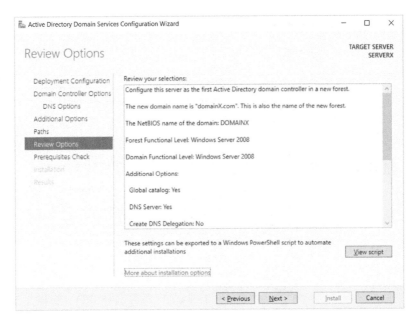

Figure 4-18   Reviewing Active Directory installation options

script that contains your selected configuration items is displayed. You can modify and save this PowerShell script to a file that can be later executed to configure additional domain controllers. After you click Next in Figure 4-18, the Active Directory Domain Services Configuration Wizard will perform a prerequisite check and advise you of any problems or warnings, as shown in Figure 4-19. If you click Install following this prerequisite check, Active Directory will be installed. Following the installation, your system will automatically reboot and you are prompted to log into the system as the Administrator account in the domain with the same password as the previous local Administrator account. For domainx.com, this user will be listed as DOMAINX\ Administrator as shown in Figure 4-20. Alternatively, you can click Other user in Figure 4-20 and specify the UPN of administrator@domainX.com to log into the system.

Installing a Domain within an Existing Forest

Before you install a domain controller for a new domain within an existing forest, you must ensure that the DNS server listed within your server's IP configuration contains the appropriate service records for the existing Active Directory forest. Next, you can start the Active Directory Domain Services Configuration Wizard and select *Add a new domain to an existing forest*, as shown in Figure 4-21.

To add a child domain, you can specify the name of the parent domain as well as the name of the new child domain. For example, to create a child domain called east. domainX.com under the domainX.com parent domain, you would specify the names shown in Figure 4-21. Alternatively, to add a new domain that will be the parent domain

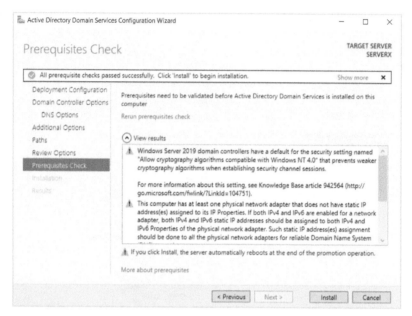

Figure 4-19   Checking prerequisites prior to Active Directory installation

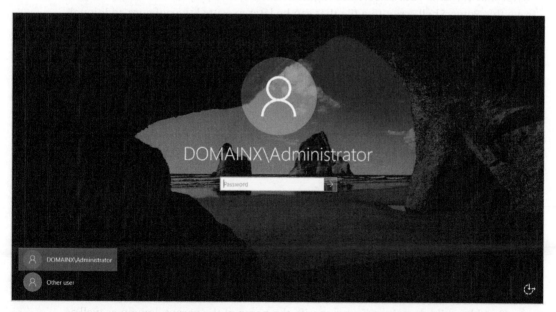

Figure 4-20   Logging into a new domain

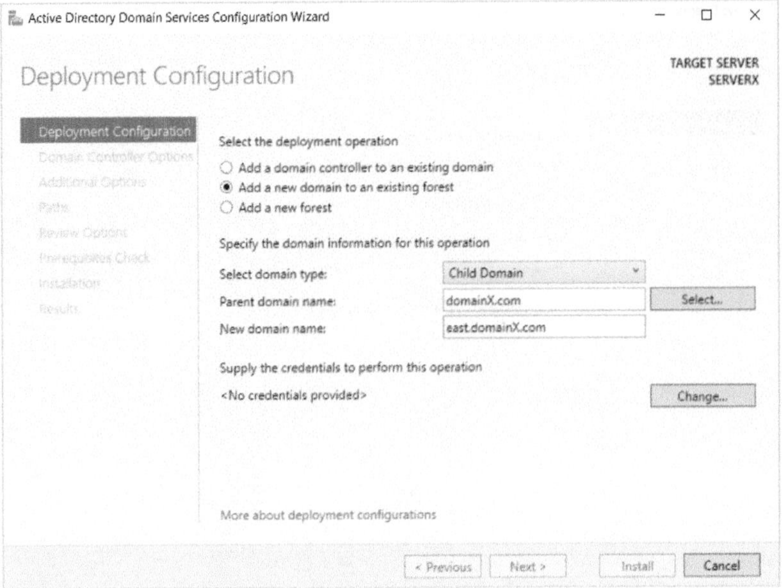

Figure 4-21 Adding a new domain to a forest

for a new tree, you must select Tree Domain from the Select domain type drop-down box in Figure 4-21 and specify the name of the parent domain.

In order to add a new domain to a forest, you must first authenticate as an existing user within the forest that is part of the Enterprise Admins group. To do this, you can click Change in Figure 4-21 and supply the appropriate credentials.

After you click Next in Figure 4-21, you can progress through the remainder of the Active Directory Domain Services Configuration Wizard as you would when configuring a new forest root domain. However, on the Domain Controller Options page shown earlier in Figure 4-14, you will not be prompted to select a forest functional level. Instead, you are prompted to optionally modify the default Active Directory site to which your new domain controller will be placed.

Installing a Domain Controller within an Existing Domain

As with installing a new domain within an existing forest, before you install an additional domain controller within an existing domain, you must ensure that the DNS server listed within your server's IP configuration contains the appropriate service records for the existing Active Directory forest. Next, you can start the Active Directory Domain Services Configuration Wizard, select *Add a domain controller to an existing domain*, and specify the existing domain name within the Domain text box, as shown in Figure 4-22.

In order to add a new domain controller to an existing domain, you must first authenticate as an existing user within the domain that is part of the Domain Admins group. To do this, you can click Change in Figure 4-22 and supply the appropriate credentials.

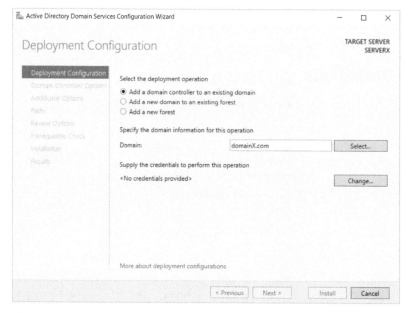

Figure 4-22   Adding a new domain controller to an existing domain

After you click Next in Figure 4-22, the Active Directory Domain Services Configuration Wizard prompts you to supply the same information that you would supply when configuring a new forest root domain, with two exceptions:

- You are not prompted to set the forest or domain functional levels on the Domain Controller Options page shown earlier in Figure 4-14. Instead, you are allowed to modify the default Active Directory site to which your new domain controller will be placed.
- An Additional Options page will prompt you to optionally select the domain controller from which your new domain controller will obtain the initial copy of the Active Directory database. You can instead select *Install from media* on this page to obtain the initial copy of the Active Directory database from a folder on removeable media to save network bandwidth.

Note

You can also configure a new domain controller using Windows PowerShell. For example, you can run the `Install-ADDSForest` cmdlet to install a new forest root domain, the `Install-ADDSDomain` cmdlet to install a new domain within an existing forest, or the `Install-ADDSDomainController` cmdlet to install an additional domain controller within an existing domain. Each of these cmdlets will prompt you for the same information that you supply during the Active Directory Domain Services Configuration Wizard. Installing and configuring a new domain controller with Windows PowerShell is often performed on Server Core.

> **Note** 📎
>
> To rapidly deploy several new domain controllers within the same domain, you can use Windows PowerShell to clone an existing domain controller virtual machine to create additional unique domain controller virtual machines. Search Virtualized Domain Controller Deployment and Configuration on docs.microsoft.com for more information.

Configuring Active Directory

Following the installation of Active Directory, you may need to configure different Active Directory features to meet the needs of your organization. More specifically, you should know how to raise functional levels, create trust relationships, manage FSMO roles, as well as configure sites, replication, global catalog, and UGMC.

Raising Functional Levels

After all domain controllers within your domain have been raised to a common minimum operating system version, you can raise the domain functional level to unlock the features of Active Directory shown earlier in Table 4-2. Similarly, if all domains within the forest have been raised to a common minimum domain functional level, you can raise the forest functional level to match.

> **Note** 📎
>
> You must be logged into your domain as a member of the Domain Admins group within Active Directory to raise a domain functional level. The Administrator user account within each domain is a member of the Domain Admins group by default.

> **Note** 📎
>
> To raise the forest functional level, you must be a member of the Enterprise Admins group. The Administrator user account within the forest root domain is a member of the Enterprise Admins group by default.

To raise functional levels, you can click *Active Directory Domains and Trusts* from the Tools menu of Server Manager to open the **Active Directory Domains and Trusts** tool shown in Figure 4-23. To raise your domain functional level, select your domain within the navigation pane and click More Actions, Raise Domain Functional Level from the Actions pane. This will open the Raise domain functional level window shown in Figure 4-24. You can then select the appropriate functional level from the drop-down box and click Raise to raise your domain to that functional level. Alternatively, to raise your forest functional level, select Active Directory Domains and Trusts within the navigation pane and click More Actions, Raise Forest Functional Level from the Actions pane. This will open the Raise forest functional level window shown in Figure 4-25. After you select the appropriate functional level from the drop-down box and click Raise, it may take several minutes for the process to complete, depending on the size of your forest.

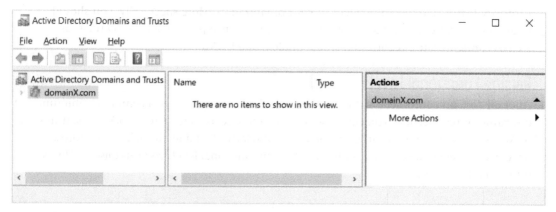

Figure 4-23   The Active Directory Domains and Trusts tool

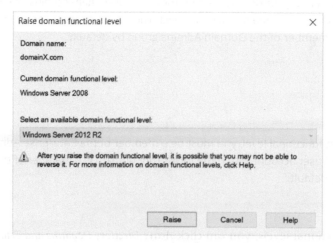

Figure 4-24   Raising the domain functional level

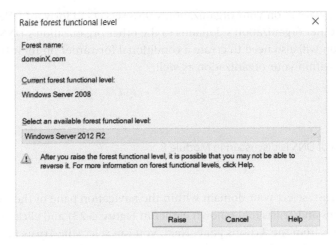

Figure 4-25 Raising the forest functional level

Note

You can also raise domain and forest functional levels using Windows PowerShell. For example, you can run the `Set-ADDomainMode -Identity domainX.com -DomainMode Windows2012R2Domain` command to raise the domain functional level to Windows Server 2012 R2 for the domainX.com domain. If domainX.com is the forest root domain, you can use the `Set-ADForestMode -Identity domainX.com -ForestMode Windows2012R2Domain` command to raise the forest functional level to Windows Server 2012 R2.

Creating Trust Relationships

If your organization purchases or enters a partnership with another organization, you may need to create an external, forest, or realm trust to that organization to allow for resource access between the two organizations. You may also need to create an internal trust from a parent domain in one tree to a child domain in another tree to speed up resource access between those domains.

Note

To create a trust, you must be a member of the Enterprise Admins group.

Prior to creating an external, forest, or realm trust to another organization, you must first ensure that the DNS servers within your organization can resolve the DNS records for the target organization, and vice versa. The most common way to do this is by configuring a **conditional forwarder** on your organization's DNS servers to forward DNS resolution requests for the other organization's domains to the other organization's DNS servers. The other organization will also need to create a conditional forwarder on their DNS servers for the domains within your organization as well.

Note

The configuration of DNS is discussed in Module 8.

To create a trust, select your domain within the navigation pane of the Active Directory Domains and Trusts tool (shown earlier in Figure 4-23) and click More Actions, Properties from the Actions pane. Next, you can select the Trusts tab shown in Figure 4-26 and click New Trust to start the New Trust Wizard. After you click Next at the Welcome screen of the New Trust Wizard, you are prompted to supply the name of the target domain or forest, as shown in Figure 4-27.

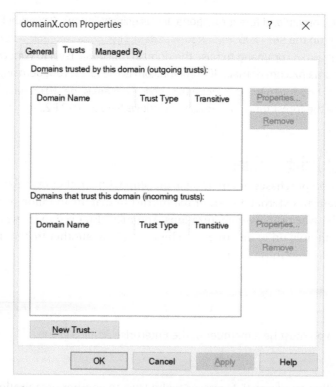

Figure 4-26   The Trusts tab of domain properties

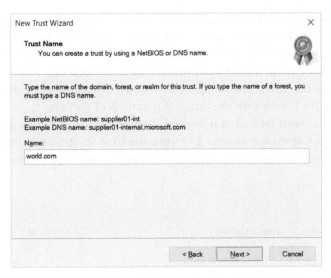

Figure 4-27   Specifying the target domain for a new trust

If the world.com domain shown in Figure 4-27 is within a different forest and your DNS server is able to resolve service records for the target domain, the New Trust Wizard will prompt you to:

- Select the trust type (external or forest)
- Choose whether the trust is one-way outgoing (your domain trusts world.com), one-way incoming (world.com trusts your domain), or two-way
- Complete the creation of the incoming trust relationship in the target domain, if applicable. You will need to specify credentials for a user in the target domain if you choose this option. Otherwise, an administrator in the target domain must create an outgoing trust to your domain.
- Select whether the trust should be transitive or non-transitive
- Determine whether domain controllers should authenticate remote users prior to accessing a resource across the trust (**forest wide authentication**), or authenticate remote users only after determining that the resource is accessible by the user (**selective authentication**). These authentication modes are only available for forest trusts.
- Choose whether to validate the trust to ensure that it is functional

If the world.com domain is a Kerberos realm, the New Trust Wizard will prompt you to:

- Choose whether the trust is one-way outgoing (your domain trusts world.com), one-way incoming (world.com trusts your domain), or two-way
- Select whether the trust should be transitive or non-transitive
- Supply a trust password that can be used to complete the trust on the target Kerberos realm. This password must be entered within the Kerberos realm to complete and validate the trust.

If you specify the name of a domain within your own forest within Figure 4-27, the New Trust Wizard will create up to a two-way transitive internal trust to that domain. Alternatively, if you specify the NetBIOS name of a Windows NT4 domain within Figure 4-27, the New Trust Wizard will prompt you to create a one-way incoming or outgoing non-transitive trust. Incoming trusts require that you specify the credentials for an administrative user within the target Windows NT4 domain.

After a trust has been created, it is displayed within the Trusts tab, as shown in Figure 4-28. You can select the incoming or outgoing trust for the target domain and click Properties to validate or change trust settings. To remove a trust, you can select a trust and click Remove.

Figure 4-28   Viewing trust relationships

You can also use the netdom.exe command within a Windows PowerShell or Command Prompt window to create and validate trusts. Execute netdom /? for more information.

Managing FSMO Roles

In an organization that has multiple domain controllers spanning several domains, it's important to know which domain controllers hold the forest-wide and domain-wide FSMO roles. The easiest way to view all of the FSMO roles held by domain controllers within your forest is to use the `netdom query fsmo` command from Windows PowerShell or a Windows Command Prompt window. You can also run the following two commands within Windows PowerShell to view the domain controllers that hold the forest-wide and domain-wide FSMO roles:

```
Get-ADForest | select SchemaMaster,DomainNamingMaster
Get-ADDomain | select PDCEmulator,RIDMaster,InfrastructureMaster
```

You should ensure that FSMO roles are held by domain controllers that are highly visible on the network. For fault tolerance in the event of a domain controller failure, you should also ensure that a single domain controller does not hold all of the available FSMO roles within a forest or domain. Thus, you may need to move FSMO roles from one domain controller to another. To move the PDC Emulator FSMO to the domain controller serverX.domainX.com, you can run the following command within Windows PowerShell:

```
Move-ADDirectoryServerOperationMasterRole -Identity "serverX.
domainX.com" -OperationMasterRole PDCEmulator
```

To move multiple FSMO roles, you can specify multiple roles separated by commas as an argument to the `-OperationMasterRole` option. For example, to move all FSMO roles to serverX.domainX.com, you can run the following command within Windows PowerShell:

```
Move-ADDirectoryServerOperationMasterRole -Identity "serverX.
domainX.com" -OperationMasterRole PDCEmulator,SchemaMaster,
RIDMaster,InfrastructureMaster,DomainNamingMaster
```

If the source domain controller is offline (e.g., due to a hardware failure), you will need to add the `-Force` option to the `Move-ADDirectoryServerOperationMasterRole` command to perform a role seizure.

Note 📎

To move a forest-wide FSMO role, you must be a member of the Enterprise Admins group. To move a domain-wide FSMO role, you must be a member of the Domain Admins group.

Configuring Sites and Replication

If your domain spans multiple physical locations, it's important to configure sites to control Active Directory replication within your domain. Sites can also be used to control the replication of schema and forest configuration to other domains within the forest. To configure sites, you can click *Active Directory Sites and Services* from the Tools menu of Server Manager to open the **Active Directory Sites and Services** tool shown in Figure 4-29. By default, the only site created within a new forest is called Default-First-Site-Name, and contains the first domain controller object within the forest. However, you can right-click Default-First-Site-Name under the Sites folder shown in Figure 4-29, click Rename, and supply a name that matches your first physical location. Next, you can right-click the Sites folder and click New Site to create additional sites for each physical location within your organization. At the New Object – Site window shown in Figure 4-30, you must supply a name for your site as well as select the appropriate site link before clicking OK to create the site. The DEFAULTIPSITELINK shown in Figure 4-30 is the default site link object created within the forest. It can be changed or replaced after you have configured the sites within your organization. Figure 4-31 shows the Active Directory Sites and Services tool after Default-First-Site-Name has been renamed to TorontoSite, and the ChicagoSite and ParisSite sites have been created.

Note

To move a domain controller from one site to another, you can right-click the associated server object within Active Directory Sites and Services, click Move, and select the target site.

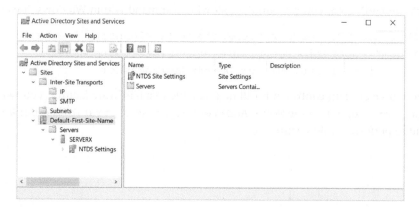

Figure 4-29   The Active Directory Sites and Services tool

Next, you should associate each site with one or more IP networks by creating subnet objects for the sites within your organization. This allows the Active Directory Domain Services Installation Wizard to choose the correct site for new domain controllers by default, as well as allows Group Policy to apply settings to computers that are part of a particular site. To create a new subnet object, right-click the Subnets folder shown in Figure 4-31 and click New Subnet. At the New Object – Subnet window shown in

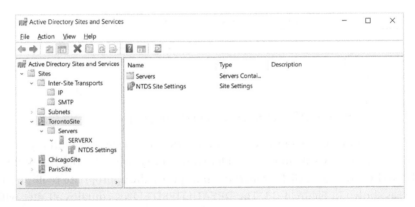

Figure 4-30   Creating a new site object

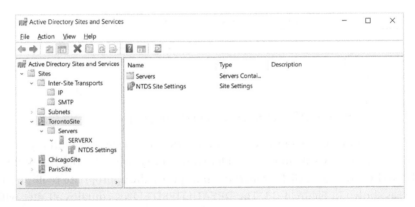

Figure 4-31   A sample site configuration

Figure 4-32, you can specify the appropriate IP network and select the site that it should be associated with. For example, the 10.1.0.0/16 network shown in Figure 4-32 is associated with the TorontoSite site object. There is no limit to the number of subnet objects that can be associated with a single site object.

There are two protocols that can be used to perform Active Directory replication: IP and **Simple Mail Transfer Protocol (SMTP)**. SMTP requires that you first configure an SMTP encryption certificate, and can only be used to replicate schema and configuration changes. As a result, there are no SMTP site links created by default. Instead, all Active Directory replication within your domain and forest uses IP alongside the DEFAULTIPSITELINK object that is stored within the IP folder under the Inter-Site Transports folder (shown in Figure 4-31).

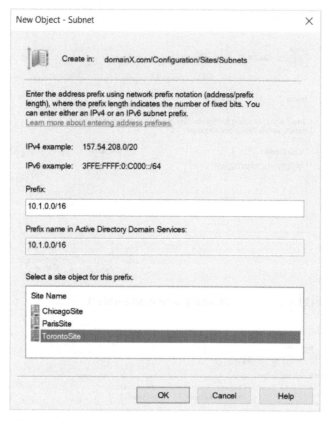

Figure 4-32   Creating a new subnet object

If you wish to provide the same replication restrictions for all sites within your organization, you can navigate to the IP folder shown in Figure 4-31, right-click the DEFAULTIPSITELINK object, click Properties, and specify the appropriate replication restrictions, as shown in Figure 4-33. The DEFAULTIPSITELINK contains all sites within your organization, and ensures that replication between sites only occurs at three-hour (180 minute) intervals by default. The default cost of 100 can be lowered to ensure that the restrictions within this site link are used if other sites links containing the same sites have been configured. To set a time schedule where replication is allowed, click Change Schedule in Figure 4-33 and configure the appropriate times that replication is available. The sample schedule shown in Figure 4-34 prevents replication from occurring during business hours (8:00am to 5:00pm, Monday to Friday).

If you wish to use different replication restrictions between certain sites within your organization, you can create additional site link objects that include the appropriate sites and restrictions and then remove DEFAULTIPSITELINK afterwards. To create a new site link object, right-click the IP folder shown in Figure 4-31, click New Site Link, and specify the sites that the new site link should include. After creating a new site link, you can access its properties to configure replication, as shown earlier in Figure 4-33.

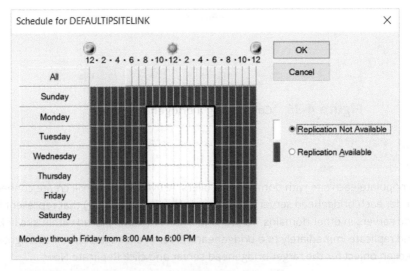

Figure 4-33   Modifying the properties of the DEFAULTIPSITELINK

Figure 4-34   Configuring a replication schedule

If your site has multiple domain controllers, only one domain controller (the bridgehead server) will be used to perform replication to other sites. By default, Active Directory automatically chooses the bridgehead server for each site. However, you may wish to ensure that a particular domain controller with a faster network interface will be used as the bridgehead server for your site to increase replication performance. To do this, right-click the server object under the Servers folder within a site and click Properties. For example, if you right-click SERVERX in Figure 4-31 and click Properties, you can configure SERVERX to be the preferred bridgehead server for the IP protocol, as shown in Figure 4-35.

Figure 4-35 Configuring a bridgehead server

Note

After you populate each site with domain controllers, Active Directory will create connection objects under each bridgehead server object (within the Servers folder) that represent the bridgehead servers in other domains. To override the restrictions placed within site link objects and replicate immediately to a bridgehead server in another site, you can right-click the connection object for the target bridgehead server and click Replicate Now.

Note 📎

There are many cmdlets within Windows PowerShell that can be used to create and manage site, subnet, and site link objects. For example, the `New-ADReplicationSite` cmdlet can be used to create a new site object, whereas the `Set-ADReplicationSiteLink` cmdlet can be used to configure the replication settings within a site link object.

Configuring Global Catalog and UGMC

During the Active Directory Domain Services Configuration Wizard, you are prompted to select whether the domain controller will contain a copy of the global catalog. It is important to ensure that each site has at least one copy of the global catalog to provide fast logon and object search. Configuring two or more copies of the global catalog in a site will ensure that the global catalog is available in the event of a domain controller failure. However, configuring too many global catalog servers within a site could impact the bandwidth of your Internet connection as global catalog is replicated forest-wide and does not adhere to site link restrictions. Thus, you may need to add or remove the global catalog from existing domain controllers following installation.

To configure a domain controller to host a copy of the global catalog, right-click NTDS Settings under the server object for the domain controller within Active Directory Sites and Services and click Properties. Next, you can select the Global Catalog option shown in Figure 4-36 to place a copy of the global catalog on the domain controller, or deselect it to remove the existing copy of the global catalog.

If your site cannot host a copy of the global catalog due to replication concerns, you can instead enable UGMC for your site to allow universal groups to be cached on domain controllers within the site to allow for fast logon. To enable UGMC for a site within Active Directory Sites and Services, highlight the site within the navigation pane, right-click NTDS Site Settings within the right pane, and choose Properties. Next, you should select *Enable Universal Group Membership Caching*, and choose the nearest site that contains the global catalog within the Refresh cache from drop-down box, as shown in Figure 4-37.

Note 📎

You can also use Windows PowerShell to configure global catalog and UGMC. For example, to configure UGMC on ParisSite with the settings shown in Figure 4-37, you can run the `Set-ADReplicationSite -Identity ParisSite -UniversalGroupCachingEnabled 1 -UniversalGroupCachingRefreshSite TorontoSite` command.

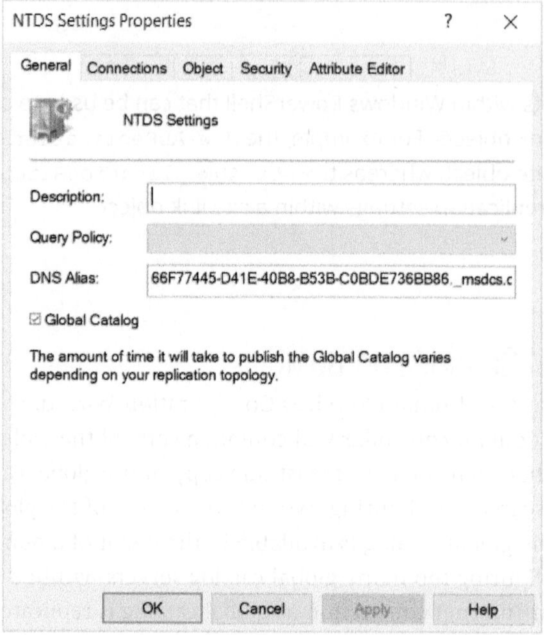

Figure 4-36   Configuring global catalog

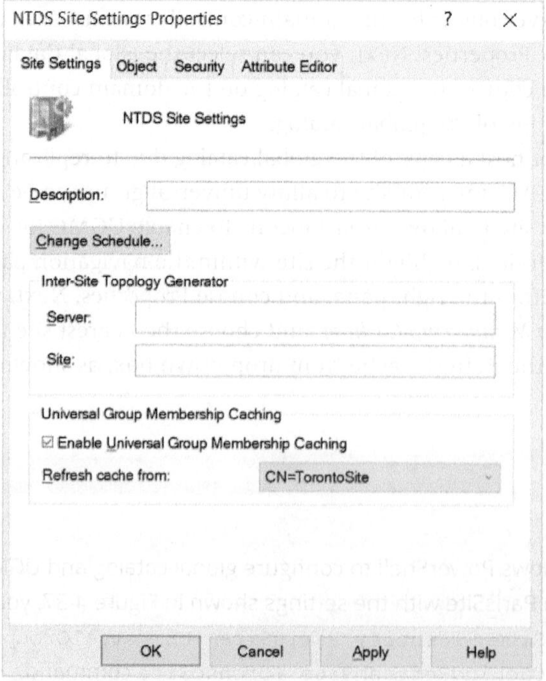

Figure 4-37   Enabling UGMC for a site

Managing Active Directory Objects

Most of the day-to-day tasks that you perform within Active Directory involve creating and managing the objects within the Active Directory database that allow computers on the network to authenticate users and provide access to resources. More specifically, you'll need to know how to create and manage OU, user, group, and computer objects.

Working with Organizational Units

The most common utility used to create and manage OUs within an Active Directory domain is the **Active Directory Users and Computers** tool shown in Figure 4-38. You can start this tool by selecting *Active Directory Users and Computers* from the Tools menu of Server Manager.

By default, a new domain only has one OU called Domain Controllers that contains the computer accounts for the domain controllers within the domain. Other folders exist to organize the default objects within the domain:

- *Builtin* contains domain local security groups that were previously local groups within the SAM database on the computer that was promoted to become the first domain controller in the domain (e.g., Administrators, Users, and Guests).
- *Computers* contains computer accounts for computers that join the Active Directory domain. Normally, these accounts are moved to the appropriate OU afterward.

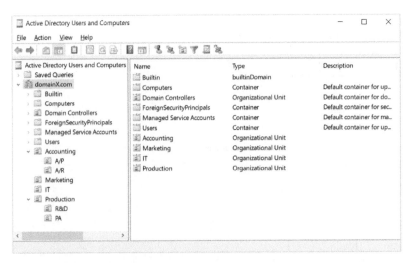

Figure 4-38   The Active Directory Users and Computers tool

- *ForeignSecurityPrincipals* contains users, groups, and computers from other domains that are members of groups within the local domain.
- *Managed Service Accounts* contains user accounts within Active Directory that represent one or more services on a computer.
- *Users* contains the default Administrator and Guest domain user accounts (Guest is disabled by default as a security measure), as well as the default security groups within the domain (e.g., Domain Admins, Domain Users, and Domain Guests). For the forest root domain, this folder also contains the Schema Admins and Enterprise Admins groups.

The domainX.com domain shown in Figure 4-38 contains additional OUs that reflect the OU structure shown earlier in Figure 4-5. The process of creating an OU is similar to the process for creating a folder. You can right-click the folder under which you wish to create the OU and click New, Organizational Unit. To create an OU underneath the domain, right-click the domain object and click New, Organizational Unit. This will open the New Object – Organizational Unit window shown in Figure 4-39, where you can supply the name of the OU. The *Protect container from accidental deletion* option is selected by default and prevents you from deleting the OU accidentally within the Active Directory Users and Computers tool. In order to delete the OU, you must first remove this option. To do this, you must first select Advanced Features from the View menu within Active Directory Users and Computers. Next, you must right-click the target OU, click Properties, highlight the Object tab, and deselect the *Protect container from accidental deletion* option.

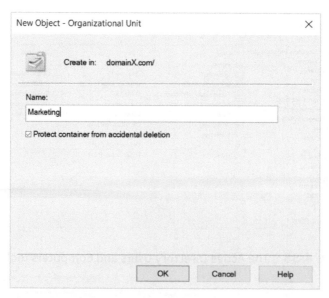

Figure 4-39 **Creating a new OU**

Note

You can also create and manage OUs within Windows PowerShell. For example, to create an OU called Marketing under the domainX.com domain that is protected from accidental deletion, you run the `New-ADOrganizationalUnit -Name "Marketing" -Path "DC=domainX,DC=com" -ProtectedFromAccidentalDeletion $True` command.

Working with User Objects

Before a user is able to log into an Active Directory domain, you must create a domain user account object for them in the appropriate OU. To do this, right-click the appropriate OU within Active Directory Users and Computers and click New, User. This will open the New Object – User wizard shown in Figure 4-40, where you can supply the appropriate information. The *User logon name* represents the UPN for the user, while the *User logon name (pre-Windows 2000)* represents the standard naming convention used at the Windows logon screen, including the Windows logon screen on legacy clients that do not support UPNs. The name that you supply within these sections should reflect the user naming convention within your organization. For example, b.burtt shown in Figure 4-40 reflects a naming convention of first letter of first name, followed by a period, followed by the last name.

After you click Next in Figure 4-40, you are prompted to supply the password for the new user as well as the same account options that you configure for a local user account, as shown in Figure 4-41. After clicking Next in Figure 4-41, you can click Finish to create the user object.

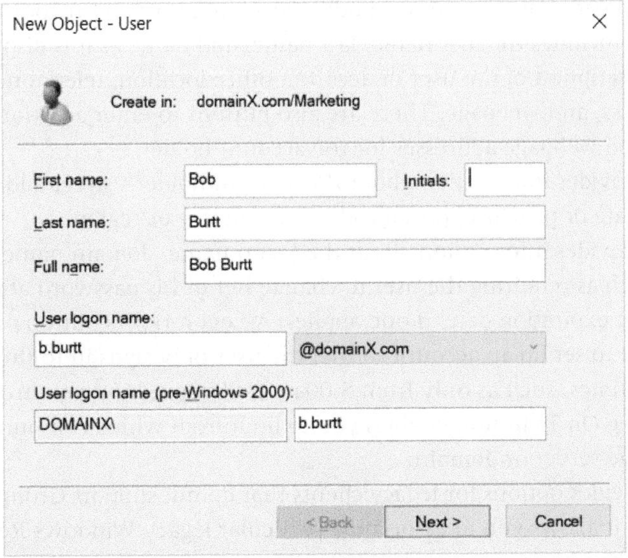

New Object - User			✕
	Create in:	domainX.com/Marketing	
First name:	Bob	Initials:	
Last name:	Burtt		
Full name:	Bob Burtt		
User logon name:			
b.burtt		@domainX.com	
User logon name (pre-Windows 2000):			
DOMAINX\		b.burtt	
	< Back	Next >	Cancel

Figure 4-40   Creating a new user

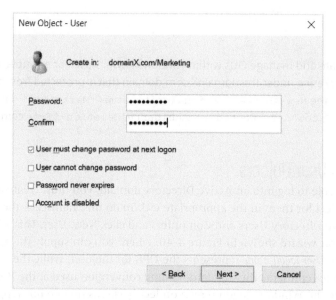

Figure 4-41   Specifying password and account options

After creating a new user object, you should add the appropriate user attributes. To do this, right-click the user object, and click Properties to access the attributes for the user as shown in Figure 4-42 for the Bob Burtt user. Following is a brief summary of the tabs available within the properties of a domain user object:

- *General*—Enables you to enter or modify personal information about the account holder that includes the first name, last name, and name as it is displayed in the console, description of the user or account, office location, telephone number, email address, and webpage. There are also buttons to enter additional telephone numbers and webpage addresses for the account holder.
- *Address*—Provides information about the account holder's street address, post office box, city, state or province, postal code, and country or region.
- *Account*—Provides information about the logon name, domain name, and account options, such as requiring the user to change her or his password at next logon, and account expiration date, if one applies. A Logon Hours button on this tab enables you to set up an account so that the user only signs in to the domain at designated times, such as only from 8:00am to 7:00pm Monday through Friday. Also, the Log On To button enables you to limit from which computer a user can sign in to the server or domain.
- *Profile*—Provides options for legacy clients that do not support Group Policy. More specifically, it allows you to associate a particular legacy Windows Registry profile with a user or set of users, to provide options such as a common desktop. This tab is also used to associate a logon script and a home folder (directory) with an account.

Figure 4-42   Setting attributes for a user object

A **logon script** is a file of commands that are executed at logon, and a home folder is disk space on a particular server given to a user to store his or her files.

- *Telephones*—Allows you to associate specific types of telephone contact numbers for an account holder, which include one or more numbers for home, pager, mobile, fax, and IP phones.

- *Organization*—Provides a place to enter the account holder's title, department, company name, and the name of the person who manages the account holder.

- *Remote Control*—Allows you to set up remote control parameters for a client who uses Remote Desktop Services. The remote-control capability enables you to view and manipulate the client session while it is active, in order to troubleshoot problems.

- *Remote Desktop Services Profile*—Allows you to set up a user profile for a client who uses Remote Desktop Services.

- *COM+*—Specifies the COM+ partition set of which the user is a member.

- *Member Of*—Allows you to add the account to an existing group.
- *Dial-In*—Allows you to control remote access from dial-in modems or from **virtual private networks (VPNs)**.
- *Environment*—Allows you to configure the startup environment for clients who access one or more servers using Remote Desktop Services (for running programs on the server).
- *Sessions*—Allows you to configure session parameters for a client using Remote Desktop Services, such as a session time limit, a limit on how long a session can be idle, what to do when a connection is broken, and how to reconnect.

If you right-click a user object within the Active Directory Users and Computer console, you can perform other common user management functions, as shown in Figure 4-43. The most common of these functions are listed below:

- *Copy*—Creates a new user object that contains many of the same attributes (such as department and group membership). Some administrators create a **template user account** for each department that they copy to create new user accounts with common properties.
- *Add to a group*—Allows you to add the user as a member of a group object you specify.
- *Disable Account*—Disables the account from authenticating. This option changes to *Enable Account* for a currently disabled account.
- *Reset Password*—Allows you to enter a new password for the user, or unlock the user account if it was locked using an account policy (discussed in Module 10).
- *Move*—Allows you to move the user account to an OU you specify. This is normally performed when a user transfers to a different department within the organization.
- *Delete*—Removes the user account.

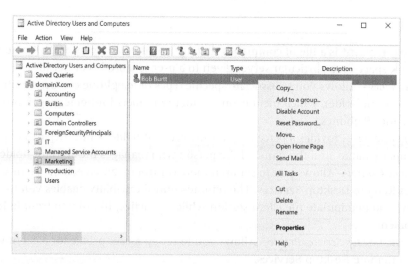

Figure 4-43   The right-click menu for a user object

Note

After you delete a user object, the SID cannot be reused. Thus, when a user leaves the organization, most administrators disable the associated user object to prevent the user from logging into the domain. If this user returns to the organization, their user object can be enabled again to provide them with previously-assigned rights and permissions.

Note

There are many Windows PowerShell cmdlets that can be used to create and manage user objects. For example, the `New-ADUser` cmdlet can be used to create a user object, the `Set-ADUser` cmdlet can be used to modify its attributes, and the `Remove-ADUser` cmdlet can be used to delete it. To disable or enable a user object, you can use the `Disable-ADAccount` or `Enable-ADAccount` cmdlets, respectively.

Working with Group Objects

To simplify the assignment of rights and permissions to users within your organization, you will need to create group objects and manage their membership. To create a group object within Active Directory Users and Computers, right-click the appropriate OU and click New, Group. This will open the New Object – Group window shown in Figure 4-44,

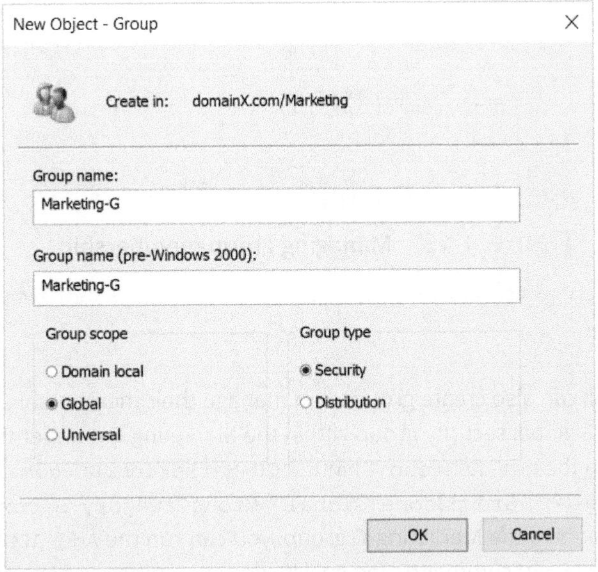

New Object - Group	✕

Create in: domainX.com/Marketing

Group name:

Marketing-G

Group name (pre-Windows 2000):

Marketing-G

Group scope	Group type
○ Domain local	● Security
● Global	○ Distribution
○ Universal	

OK   Cancel

Figure 4-44   Creating a new group object

where you can supply the group type, scope, and name. As with users, you will need to ensure that the group name follows your organization's group naming convention. For example, the Marketing-G global security group shown in Figure 4-44 follows a convention of department-scope, where letter codes represent the scope (G for global group, U for universal group, and DL for domain local group).

After creating a group object, you can right-click it within Active Directory Users and Computers, click Properties, and highlight the Members tab to manage group membership. The Members tab shown for the Marketing-G group shown in Figure 4-45 indicates that the Bob Burtt, John Lavigne, and Mary Stewart user objects are members of the group. You can also highlight the Member Of tab in order to add the Marketing-G group as a member of another group object.

Figure 4-45   Managing group membership

Note

Windows PowerShell can also create groups and manage their membership. For example, to create a Marketing-G global security group within the Marketing OU under the domainX.com domain, you can run the `New-ADGroup -Path "OU=Marketing,DC=domainX,DC=com" -Name "Marketing-G" -GroupScope Global -GroupCategory Security` command. To add group members to the Marketing-G group, you can run the `Add-ADGroupMember -Identity Marketing-G` command, and specify group members when prompted.

Working with Computer Objects

Recall from earlier that when a computer joins an Active Directory domain, a computer account object is automatically created within the Computers folder under the domain. However, computer accounts should normally be located within an OU for ease of management, as well as the application of Group Policy. To move a newly created computer account within Active Directory Users and Computers, right-click the computer account within the Computers folder, click Move, and select the target OU.

Alternatively, you can pre-create computer accounts for computers within the appropriate OUs prior to joining the computer to the domain (a process called **prestaging**). This eliminates the need to move the computer account after the computer joins the domain. However, the name of the computer account must match the computer name of the computer that is about to join the domain. To prestage a computer account, right-click the appropriate OU within Active Directory Users and Computers and click New, Computer. This will open the New Object – Computer window shown in Figure 4-46, where you can supply a computer name that follows your organization's computer naming convention. By default, only users that are members of the Domain Admins group are able to join computers to a domain using a prestaged computer account, but you click Change to select a different user or group. Because Group Policy applies to Windows 2000 and later computers only, you should select *Assign this computer account as a pre-Windows 2000 computer* if the operating system on the computer is older than Windows 2000. This prevents Group Policy from attempting to contact the computer.

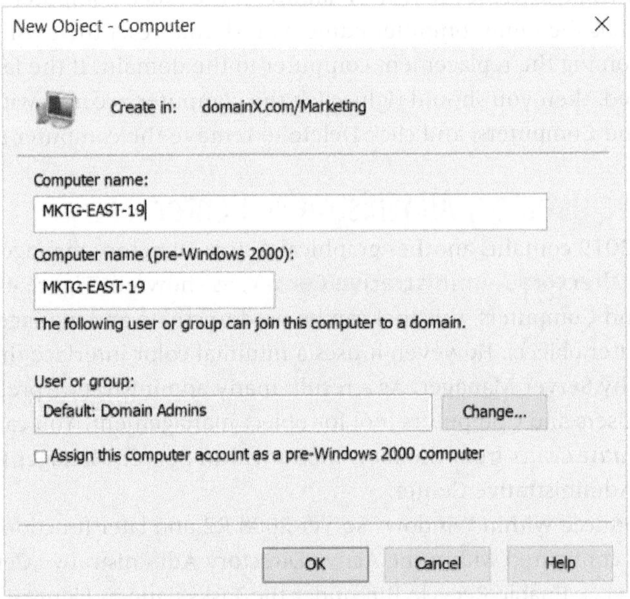

Figure 4-46   **Prestaging a computer account**

> **Note** 🔗
>
> You can also prestage computer accounts within Windows PowerShell. For example, to create the computer account shown within Figure 4-46, you could run the `New-ADComputer -Name "MKTG-EAST-19" -SamAccountName "MKTG-EAST-19" -Path "OU=Marketing, DC=domainX, DC=com"` command.

Recall that each computer account contains an encryption key that is used when the computer communicates with a domain controller. This same encryption key is also stored within the Windows Registry on the computer. To maintain security, the domain controller creates a new encryption key every 14 days and communicates this key to the client for use within the Windows Registry. If this process fails, the client computer will no longer be able to log users into the domain, regardless of the domain user account used. If the computer is running Windows 7 or Windows Server 2008 or later, you can run the `Test-ComputerSecureChannel -Repair` command within Windows PowerShell on the computer to renegotiate a new encryption key within the computer account in Active Directory. However, for older computers, you will need to reset the computer account, join the computer to a workgroup, and then rejoin the computer to the Active Directory domain again. To reset a computer account, right-click the computer account within Active Directory Users and Computers and click Reset Account.

Occasionally, computers within your organization that are joined to an Active Directory domain will experience hardware failure. If the failed computer is replaced with another one that has the same computer name, you should reset the existing computer account prior to joining the replacement computer to the domain. If the failed computer will not be replaced, then you should right-click the computer account within Active Directory Users and Computers, and click Delete to remove the computer account.

Using the Active Directory Administrative Center

Windows Server 2019 contains another graphical Active Directory management tool called the **Active Directory Administrative Center**, as shown in Figure 4-47. Like Active Directory Users and Computers, this tool can be used to create and manage OU, user, group, and computer objects. However, it uses a minimal color interface that is similar to the one provided by Server Manager. As a result, many administrators prefer using the Active Directory Users and Computers tool for object management. You can select *Active Directory Administrative Center* from the tools menu within Server Manager to open the Active Directory Administrative Center.

Features introduced within Windows Server 2008 R2 and later functional levels are often enabled and configured within the Active Directory Administrative Center. For example, you can click Enable Recycle Bin under the Tasks pane in Figure 4-47 to enable the Active Directory Recycle Bin, provided that your forest functional level is at least

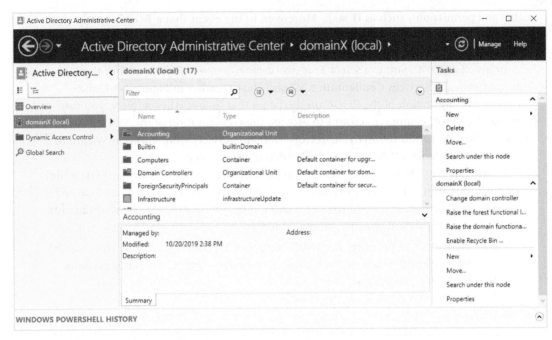

Figure 4-47 The Active Directory Administrative Center

Windows Server 2008 R2. If you delete a user account object after the Active Directory Recycle Bin has been enabled, you can easily restore it within the Active Directory Administrative Center. To do this, navigate to the Deleted Objects folder under your domain object, select your deleted user account object and click Restore within the Tasks pane.

Read-Only Domain Controllers

In addition to large office locations, many organizations contain smaller branch office locations. Often, these branch office locations do not have dedicated IT staff or the physical security features found in large offices, such as security guards and secure server closets. To provide secure domain authentication within these branch offices, you can install a Read-only Domain Controller (RODC). Because RODCs contain a read-only copy of the Active Directory database for the domain, the creation and management of objects (such as user accounts) must be performed on a domain controller within a larger office and replicated to the RODC in the branch office. Because security is the primary concern within branch offices, when user account objects are replicated to a RODC, the password attribute is only included for users that you specify. Normally, you replicate password attributes for users that work within the branch office only. Thus, if the RODC is stolen by a malicious user, the Active Directory database on the domain controller only contains passwords for branch office users, and not users within the organization that have greater rights and permissions, such as IT staff. Moreover, in the event that a RODC is stolen, you can force Active Directory to reset the passwords for all user account objects that contain a password attribute on the RODC by deleting the RODC computer account itself.

To install a RODC, you can select *Read only domain controller (RODC)* within the Active Directory Domain Services Configuration Wizard shown earlier in Figure 4-14, and specify the configuration of the RODC on the pages that follow. Alternatively, you can prestage the RODC computer account to provide the configuration of the RODC and delegate the right to run the Active Directory Domain Services Configuration Wizard to a user within the branch office, such as the branch office manager.

To prestage a RODC computer account, right-click the Domain Controllers OU under your domain within Active Directory Users and Computers and click *Pre-create Read-only Domain Controller account*. This will start the Active Directory Domain Services Installation Wizard. During this wizard, you are prompted to specify:

- User credentials to prestage the RODC computer account. By default, you must be a member of the Domain Admins group to prestage a RODC computer account.
- The RODC computer name
- The site that should contain the RODC
- Whether the RODC should contain the DNS service and global catalog
- A user (or group) that will be delegated permission to complete the installation of the RODC using the Active Directory Domain Services Installation Wizard (optional if a member of the Domain Admins group will perform the installation)

Next, you can install a Windows Server 2019 system that has the same computer name as the prestaged RODC computer account and install Active Directory Domain Services. When you run the Active Directory Domain Services Installation Wizard afterward, it will obtain the remaining information from the prestaged RODC computer account and complete the installation of Active Directory.

Note

By default, only users that are members of the *Allowed RODC Password Replication Group* domain local security group within the Users folder under the domain will have their password attribute replicated to the RODC. Thus, you should add branch office user accounts to this group before running the Active Directory Domain Services Installation Wizard on the RODC.

In the event that a RODC is stolen, you can right-click the RODC computer account within Active Directory Users and Computers and click Delete. After you click OK to confirm the deletion, you are presented with the Deleting Domain Controller window shown in Figure 4-48. By default, any user accounts that had a password attribute stored on the RODC will be reset to ensure that malicious users cannot log into the domain

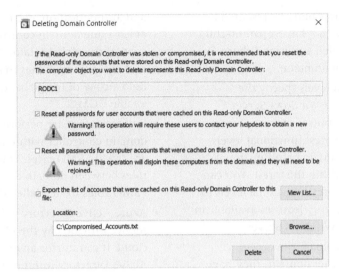

Figure 4-48 Deleting a RODC computer account

using their user account, and the list of affected users will be exported to the file name that you specify in the Location text box. If other computers within the branch office were stolen, you can also select the *Reset all passwords for computer accounts that were cached on this Read-only Domain Controller* option to reset each computer account within the branch office site. This will ensure that any stolen computers will not be able to log into the domain using any valid user account. However, this will require that any remaining computers rejoin the domain again.

Module Summary

- You can log into a system with a local user account to obtain rights and permissions to local resources. Local group accounts can be used to simplify the assignment of local rights and permissions. Each local user and group account is stored within a SAM database on the system.

- Alternatively, you can use a domain user account to log into a system that is joined to an Active Directory domain. After authenticating to a domain controller, you receive a token that automatically

authenticates you to computers within the domain for resource access. Each token also lists any domain group accounts of which you are a member.

- Domain user, group, and computer accounts are stored as leaf objects within the Active Directory database. Leaf objects are often located within OUs that represent departments or functional units within an organization.

- Each organization is represented by a forest within Active Directory. Each forest contains one or more business units represented by domains. Domains that have a parent-child relationship are called a tree, and share a common DNS domain name.

- Domain functional levels specify the minimum version of Windows Server that each domain controller must possess within a domain. Forest functional levels specify the minimum domain functional levels supported within the forest. You can raise domain and forest functional levels to unlock Active Directory features available in newer versions of Windows Server.

- Users within one domain can access resources within other domains they have been granted permission to using trusts relationships.

- To organize the assignment of permissions to resources within a forest, Active Directory provides three group scopes: global, domain local, and universal. At minimum, users are typically added to global groups within their domain by job role.

- The Active Directory database contains three partitions. Domain objects are stored within the domain partition and replicated to other domain controllers within the same domain. The schema partition (list of object types and attributes) and configuration partition (domain and trust structure) are replicated to all domain controllers within the forest.

- If you create sites to represent different physical locations within your organization, you can configure site links to control replication between domain controllers in different sites.

- The global catalog lists all objects within the forest and is used to store universal group membership. To ensure fast search

and authentication, each site should have at least one domain controller that holds a copy of the global catalog. To provide fast authentication for sites that are unable to hold a copy of the global catalog, you can enable UGMC.

- Functions that are performed by a single domain controller within a domain or forest are called FSMO roles. You can move FSMO roles between domain controllers or seize FSMO roles from a failed domain controller.

- Azure Active Directory is an Active Directory service provided by the Microsoft Azure cloud. It can mirror an existing on-premises Active Directory forest or be configured to trust it for resource access.

- After installing Active Directory Domain Services on a Windows Server system, you can run the Active Directory Domain Services Configuration Wizard to configure it as a domain controller within an existing or new domain.

- In addition to Windows PowerShell cmdlets, there are many graphical tools that can be used to manage Active Directory. The Active Directory Domains and Trusts tool can manage functional levels and trust relationships, whereas the Active Directory Sites and Services tool can manage sites and global catalog. The Active Directory Users and Computers tool or Active Directory Administrative Center tool can be used to manage objects within a domain.

- RODCs can be used to provide authentication within smaller branch offices that lack adequate physical security. They contain a read-only copy of the Active Directory database that is configured to store password attributes for user accounts within the branch office only.

Key Terms

Access Control List (ACL)
Active Directory
  Administrative Center
Active Directory Domains
  and Trusts
Active Directory Recycle Bin
Active Directory Sites and
  Services
Active Directory Users and
  Computers
Advanced Encryption
  Standard (AES)
attribute
backup domain controller
  (BDC)
bridgehead server
cached credential
child domain
child OU
class
common name (CN)
compound authentication
computer account
conditional forwarder
configuration partition
container object
contiguous namespace
directory partition
Directory Services Restore
  Mode (DSRM)
disjointed namespace
distinguished name (DN)
Distributed File System
  (DFS)
distribution group
domain functional level
domain group account
domain local
Domain Naming Master
domain partition
domain registrar

domain user account
dynamic update
external trust
Flexible Single Master
  Operations (FSMO)
forest
forest functional level
forest root domain
forest trust
forest wide authentication
global
global catalog
globally-unique identifier
  (GUID)
group nesting
group scope
Infrastructure Master
internal trust
Kerberos armoring
leaf object
Lightweight Directory
  Access Protocol (LDAP)
local group account
local user account
Local Users and Groups
logon script
member server
Microsoft Identity Manager
  (MIM)
object
organizational unit (OU)
parent domain
PDC Emulator
permission
prestaging
primary domain controller
  (PDC)
privileged access
  management (PAM)
Read-only Domain
  Controller (RODC)

realm trust
Relative Identifier (RID)
RID Master
right
role seizure
schema
Schema Master
schema partition
Security Accounts Manager
  (SAM)
security group
security identifier (SID)
selective authentication
Service Principle Name
  (SPN)
service record
shortcut trust
Simple Mail Transfer
  Protocol (SMTP)
site
site link object
site object
standalone server
subnet object
template user account
ticket
token
transitive
tree
trust
trust relationship
universal
Universal Group
  Membership Caching
  (UGMC)
User Principle Name (UPN)
virtual private network
  (VPN)
X.500

Review Questions

1. Domain controllers store local user accounts within a SAM database and domain user accounts within Active Directory. True or False?

2. Which of the following occurs when you join a computer to an Active Directory domain? (Choose all that apply.)
   a. The Domain Users group is added to the local Users group
   b. A computer account is created within Active Directory, if one has not been prestaged
   c. The Domain Admins group is added to the local Administrators group
   d. The SAM database is replaced by the Active Directory database

3. You can use the `Install-ADDSDomain` cmdlet within Windows PowerShell to configure a new forest root domain. True or False?

4. Which of the following trust relationships can be created between two domains in separate Active Directory forests?
   a. Forest trust
   b. Shortcut trust
   c. Realm trust
   d. External trusts

5. Which of the following group scopes can contain objects from any domain within the forest? (Choose all that apply.)
   a. Global
   b. Domain local
   c. Distribution
   d. Universal

6. You must be a member of the Enterprise Admins group in order to add a trust relationship. True or False?

7. Which of the following domain functional levels provides Kerberos armoring? (Choose all that apply.)

   a. Windows Server 2008 R2
   b. Windows Server 2012
   c. Windows Server 2012 R2
   d. Windows Server 2016

8. The schema and configuration partitions of the Active Directory database are replicated forest-wide. True or False?

9. Your domain consists of two separate physical locations. Each location contains several domain controllers, and you have noticed that domain controller replication traffic consumes a large amount of your Internet bandwidth. What can you do within Active Directory Sites and Services to ensure that replication occurs outside of business hours? (Choose all that apply.)
   a. Create a site object for each physical location, and ensure that domain controller objects are placed within the correct site object.
   b. Create subnet objects for each site. Ensure that the properties of each subnet object contains a schedule that excludes business hours.
   c. In the properties of a site link object, configure a replication schedule that excludes business hours.
   d. Modify the NTDS Site Settings for each site to include a replication schedule that excludes business hours.

10. Which functions does the global catalog provide? (Choose all that apply.)
    a. Fast object searching
    b. Time synchronization
    c. Universal group membership
    d. Domain authentication using UPNs

11. If a global catalog cannot be placed within a branch office site, you can enable UGMC on the site to ensure branch

office domain controllers provide fast authentication. True or False?

12. Which of the following FSMO roles are stored on one domain controller within each domain? (Choose all that apply.)

    a. Schema Master
    b. PDC Emulator
    c. RID Master
    d. Domain Naming Master

13. Before installing Active Directory on a Windows Server system to function as an additional domain controller within a forest, you must first ensure that the Windows Server is configured to contact a DNS server that contains the appropriate service records for the forest. True or False?

14. You wish to add a copy of the global catalog to a domain controller within Active Directory Sites and Services. For which object must you right-click and select Properties?

    a. Server
    b. NTDS Settings
    c. NTDS Site Settings
    d. Site link

15. The Active Directory Recycle Bin can be enabled using the Active Directory Domains and Trusts tool. True or False?

16. Which default folder under a domain within Active Directory Users and Computers contains the Administrator user account and Domain Admins group?

    a. Builtin
    b. Default
    c. Users
    d. ForeignSecurityPrinciples

17. Which of the following PowerShell cmdlets can be used to move or seize a FSMO role?

    a. `Move-FSMORole`
    b. `Move-ADDirectoryServerOperation MasterRole`
    c. `Transfer- ADOperationMasterRole`
    d. `Set-DirectoryServerOperation Master`

18. Creating OUs within the Active Directory database is also called prestaging. True or False?

19. You have created a template user account within Active Directory Users and Computers. What must you do to create additional user accounts based on this template user account?

    a. Create a new user account and select the template user account when prompted
    b. Create a new user account and specify the name of the template user account in the User Principle Name text box
    c. Right-click the template user account, and click Copy
    d. Right-click the template user account, and click Import

20. If a RODC is stolen, you can delete the computer account to reset affected user and computer accounts. True or False?

Hands-On Projects

These Hands-On Projects should be completed in the order given and normally take a total of three hours or less to complete. The requirements for these projects include:

- A system with Windows Server 2019 installed according to Hands-On Project 1-1 (Lab Environment 1) or Hands-On Project 1-2 (Lab Environment 2).

Project 4-1: Cleanup

In this Hands-On Project, you perform cleanup tasks on your Windows Server 2019 host in preparation for the installation of Active Directory. More specifically, you remove the Windows Admin Center installed in Hands-On Project 2-2, as well as remove the DHCP Server and Windows Deployment Services roles installed in Hands-On Project 3-3.

1. Boot your Windows Server 2019 host and log into the system as Administrator using the password **Secret555**. Next, click **Start** and then click **Server Manager**.
2. Within Server Manager, click the **Manage** menu and then click **Remove Roles and Features**.
3. At the Select destination server page, click **Next**.
4. At the Remove server roles page, de-select **DHCP Server** and click **Remove Features** when prompted. Next, de-select **Windows Deployment Services** and click **Remove Features** when prompted.
5. Click **Next**.
6. At the Remove features page, click **Next**.
7. On the Confirm removal selections page, select **Restart the destination server automatically if required** and click Yes to confirm. Next, click **Remove** to remove the DHCP Server and Windows Deployment Services roles. Your system will reboot when finished.
8. After your Windows Server 2019 host has started, log into the system as Administrator using the password **Secret555**. Next, click **Start** and then click **Server Manager**.
9. Click **Close** on the Removal progress page of the Remove Roles and Features Wizard to confirm the successful removal of the DHCP Server and Windows Deployment Services roles, and close Server Manager when finished.
10. Right-click **Start** and then click **Apps and Features**.
11. In the Apps and Features section of the Settings window, select **Windows Admin Center** and click **Uninstall**. Click **Uninstall** when prompted to uninstall the Windows Admin Center and close the Settings window when finished.

Project 4-2: Active Directory Installation

In this Hands-On Project, you install Active Directory Domain Services on your Windows Server 2019 host and configure it as a forest root domain. Following the installation, you examine your DNS configuration and FSMO roles.

1. On your Windows Server 2019 host, log into the system as Administrator using the password **Secret555**. Next, click **Start** and then click **Server Manager**.
2. Within Server Manager, click the **Manage** menu and then click **Add Roles and Features**.
3. At the Select installation type page, click **Next**.
4. At the Select destination server page, click **Next**.
5. At the Select server roles page, select **Active Directory Domain Services** and click **Add Features** when prompted.
6. Click **Next**.
7. At the Select features page, click **Next**.

8. At the Hyper-V page, read the information regarding best practices and click **Next**.

9. At the Active Directory Domain Services page, read the information provided and click **Next**.

10. On the Confirm installation selections page, click **Install** to install the files needed for Active Directory Domain Services.

11. On the Installation progress page, click **Promote this server to a domain controller** to start the Active Directory Domain Services Configuration Wizard.

    a. At the Deployment Configuration page, select **Add a new forest**. In the Root domain name text box, type **domainX.com**, where *X* is a number that is uniquely assigned to you by your instructor, and click **Next**.

    b. At the Domain Controller Options page, select a Forest functional level of **Windows Server 2008**, and then select a Domain functional level of **Windows Server 2008**. Type **Secret555** in the Password and Confirm password text boxes and click **Next**.

    c. At the DNS Options page, click **Next**.

    d. At the Additional Options page, note the NetBIOS name of your domain and click **Next**.

    e. At the Paths page, note the default folders displayed and click **Next**.

    f. At the Review Options page, click **Next**.

    g. At the Prerequisites Check page, click **Install**. Your computer will automatically reboot following installation.

12. After your Windows Server 2019 host has started, log into domainX.com as Administrator using the password **Secret555**. Next, click **Start** and then click **Server Manager**.

13. Within Server Manager, click **Local Server** within the navigation pane, and then click the hyperlink next to your vEthernet (External Virtual Switch) network interface.

    a. In the Network Connections window, right-click **vEthernet (External Virtual Switch)** and click **Properties**.

    b. Highlight **Internet Protocol Version 4 (TCP/IPv4)** within the vEthernet (External Virtual Switch) Properties window and click **Properties**. Note that the Preferred DNS server has been set to 127.0.0.1 to ensure that your domain controller can locate Active Directory services using the locally-installed DNS service.

    c. Click **OK**. Click **OK** again to close the vEthernet (External Virtual Switch) Properties window.

    d. Close the Network Connections window.

14. Within Server Manager, click the **Tools** menu and then click **DNS**.

    a. In the DNS Manager window, right-click the **SERVERX** object within the navigation pane and click **Properties**.

    b. In the SERVERX Properties window, highlight the **Forwarders** tab. Note that the DNS service on your computer is set to forward requests it cannot resolve to the DNS servers that were previously used by your vEthernet network interface, and click **OK**.

    c. Close the DNS Manager window.

15. Right-click the **Start** menu and choose **Windows PowerShell (Admin)** to open Windows PowerShell.

   a. At the prompt, type `netdom query fsmo` and press **Enter**. Note that your domain controller holds all FSMO roles.

   b. Type `Get-ADForest | select SchemaMaster,DomainNamingMaster` and press Enter to view the forest-wide FSMO roles.

   c. Type `Get-ADDomain | select PDCEmulator,RIDMaster,InfrastructureMaster` and press **Enter** to view the domain-wide FSMO roles.

   d. Close Windows PowerShell.

Project 4-3: Functional Levels

In this Hands-On Project, you raise your domain and forest functional levels to Windows Server 2016.

1. Within Server Manager, click the **Tools** menu and then click **Active Directory Domains and Trusts**.

2. Highlight **domainX.com** in the navigation pane of the Active Directory Domains and Trusts window, and click **More Actions**, **Raise Domain Functional Level** in the Actions pane.

   a. Note that the current functional level is set to Windows Server 2008 from Hands-On Project 4-2.

   b. Select **Windows Server 2016** from the drop-down box and click **Raise**.

   c. Click **OK** to confirm. Click OK again to close the Raise domain functional level window.

3. Highlight **Active Directory Domains and Trusts** in the navigation pane of the Active Directory Domains and Trusts window, and click **More Actions**, **Raise Forest Functional Level** in the Actions pane.

   a. Note that the current functional level is set to Windows Server 2008 from Hands-On Project 4-2.

   b. Select **Windows Server 2016** from the drop-down box and click **Raise**.

   c. Click **OK** to confirm. Click **OK** again to close the Raise forest functional level window.

4. Close the Active Directory Domains and Trusts window.

Project 4-4: Trusts

In this Hands-On Project, you work with a partner to create a forest trust relationship between your forest and your partner's forest.

Note

Steps 1 and 2 should be completed by both you and your partner.

1. Within Server Manager, click the **Tools** menu and then click **DNS**.

   a. In the DNS Manager window, expand the **SERVERX** object within the navigation pane, right-click **Conditional Forwarders** and click **New Conditional Forwarder**.

b. In the New Conditional Forwarder window, type the name of your partner's domain in the DNS Domain text box.

c. Under the IP addresses of the master servers section, click the **<Click here to add a...** link, type the IP address of your partner's DNS server and press **Enter**.

d. Click **OK** to create the conditional forwarder entry, and close the DNS Manager window.

2. Within Server Manager, click the **Tools** menu and then click **Active Directory Domains and Trusts**.

Note 📎

Step 3 should be completed by you and not your partner.

---

3. Highlight **domainX.com** in the navigation pane of the Active Directory Domains and Trusts window, and click **More Actions**, **Properties** in the Actions pane.

a. In the domainX.com Properties window, click the **Trusts** tab. Note that no incoming or outgoing trusts have been defined.

b. Click **New Trust**.

c. At the New Trust Wizard, click **Next**.

d. On the Trust Name page, type your partner's domain name in the Name text box and click **Next**.

e. On the Trust Type page, select **Forest trust** and click **Next**.

f. On the Direction of Trust page, ensure that **Two-way** is selected and click **Next**.

g. On the Trust Type page, select **Forest trust** and click **Next**.

h. On the Sides of Trust page, **select Both this domain and the specified domain** and click Next.

i. On the User Name and Password page, type **Administrator** in the User name text box. Next, supply the password for your partner's Administrator account in the Password text box and click **Next**.

j. On the Outgoing Trust Authentication Level-Local Forest page, ensure that **Forest-wide authentication** is selected and click **Next**.

k. On the Outgoing Trust Authentication Level-Specified Forest page, ensure that **Forest-wide authentication** is selected and click **Next**.

l. On the Trust Selections Complete page, click **Next**.

m. On the Trust Creation Complete page, click **Next**.

n. On the Confirm Outgoing Trust page, select **Yes, confirm the outgoing trust** and click **Next**.

o. On the Confirm Incoming Trust page, select **Yes, confirm the incoming trust** and click **Next**.

p. Click **Finish** to close the New Trust Wizard. Note that your trust appears as both an incoming and outgoing trust.

q. Click **OK** to close the domainX.com Properties window.

r. Close the Active Directory Domains and Trusts window.

> **Note** 📎
>
> Step 4 should be completed by your partner.

4. Highlight **domain*X*.com** in the navigation pane of the Active Directory Domains and Trusts window, and click **More Actions**, **Properties** in the Actions pane.

   a. In the domain*X*.com Properties window, click the **Trusts** tab. Note that the trust that your partner configured is present.

   b. Click **OK** to close the domain*X*.com Properties window.

   c. Close the Active Directory Domains and Trusts window.

Project 4-5: Sites

In this Hands-On Project, you configure site, subnet, and site link objects. This configuration will be used in Hands-On Projects 4-6 and 4-9, as well as Discovery Exercises 4-3 and 4-4.

1. Within Server Manager, click the **Tools** menu and then click **Active Directory Sites and Services**.

2. Under the Sites folder within the navigation pane of Active Directory Sites and Services, right-click **Default-First-Site-Name** and click **Rename**. Type **TorontoSite** and press **Enter**.

3. Expand **TorontoSite**, **Servers** within the navigation pane. Note that SERVER*X* is listed within the TorontoSite.

4. Right-click the **Sites** folder within the navigation pane, and click **New Site**. Type **ChicagoSite** in the Name text box, select **DEFAULTIPSITELINK** and click **OK**. Click **OK** again to close the Active Directory Domain Services information window.

5. Right-click the **Sites** folder within the navigation pane and click **New Site**. Type **ParisSite** in the Name text box, select **DEFAULTIPSITELINK,** and click **OK**.

6. Right-click the **Subnets** folder within the navigation pane and click **New Subnet**. Type the CIDR notation for the IP network that you use on your External Virtual Switch within the Prefix text box. Next, select **TorontoSite** and click **OK**.

7. Right-click the **Subnets** folder within the navigation pane and click **New Subnet**. Type 172.16.0.0/16 within the Prefix text box. Next, select **ChicagoSite** and click **OK**.

8. Right-click the **Subnets** folder within the navigation pane and click **New Subnet**. Type 172.17.0.0/16 within the Prefix text box. Next, select **ParisSite** and click **OK**.

9. Highlight the **Subnets** folder and note that each site is associated with a subnet object.

10. Expand the **Inter-Site Transports** folder and highlight the **IP** folder.

    a. Right-click **DEFAULTIPSITELINK** and click **Properties**. Note that all three sites are included within this site link and that replication between sites will only occur at 3 hour (180 minute) intervals.

    b. Click **Change Schedule**.

    c. At the Schedule for DEFAULTIPSITELINK window, select a range of times from 8:00am Monday to 6:00pm Friday, and click **Replication Not Available**.

  d. Click **OK** to close the Schedule for DEFAULTIPSITELINK window.

  e. Click **OK** to close the DEFAULTIPSITELINK Properties window.

11. Close the Active Directory Sites and Services window.

Project 4-6: Global Catalog

In this Hands-On Project, you view your global catalog configuration as well as configure UGMC for ParisSite.

1. Within Server Manager, click the **Tools** menu and then click **Active Directory Sites and Services**.

2. Under the Sites folder within the navigation pane of Active Directory Sites and Services, expand **TorontoSite**, **Servers**, **SERVERX**.

3. Under SERVERX, right-click **NTDS Settings** and click **Properties**. Note that your server is configured with a copy of the global catalog and click **OK**.

4. Highlight **ParisSite** within the navigation pane. In the right pane, right-click **NTDS Site Settings** and click **Properties**.

   a. At the NTDS Site Settings Properties window, select **Enable Universal Group Membership Caching**.

   b. In the Refresh cache from drop-down box, select **TorontoSite**.

   c. Click **OK** to close the NTDS Site Settings Properties window.

5. Close the Active Directory Sites and Services window.

Project 4-7: Objects

In this Hands-On Project, you create and explore OU, user, group, and computer objects within the Active Directory Users and Computers tool.

1. Within Server Manager, click the **Tools** menu and then click **Active Directory Users and Computers**.

2. Expand **domainX.com** within the navigation pane of the Active Directory Users and Computers window. Note the default folders and Domain Controllers OU.

3. Right-click **domainX.com** and click **New**, **Organizational Unit**. Type **Marketing** in the Name text box and click **OK**.

4. Right-click the **Marketing** OU and click **New**, **Group**. Note that the default options create a global security group. Type **Marketing-G** in the Group name text box and click **OK**.

5. Right-click the **Marketing** OU and click **New**, **Group**. Select **Universal** in the Group scope section. Type **Marketing-U** in the Group name text box and click **OK**.

6. Right-click the **Marketing-U** group within the Marketing OU and click **Properties**.

   a. In the Marketing-U Properties window, highlight the **Members** tab and click **Add**. Note that objects are searched from your domain by default.

   b. Click **Locations** and note that the trust relationship you created in Hands-On Project 4-4 allows you to select members from your partner's domain as well as your own. Click **Cancel**.

c. Type **Marketing-G** in the *Enter the object names to select (examples)* text box and click **Check Names** to validate the name.

d. Click **OK** to add the Marketing-G group to the membership list of the Marketing-U group.

e. Click **OK** to close the Marketing-U Properties window.

7. Right-click **domainX.com** and click **New**, **Group**. Select **Domain local** in the Group scope section. Type **Ricoh4916-DL** in the Group name text box and click **OK**.

8. Highlight **domainX.com** within the navigation pane. Next, right-click the **Ricoh4916-DL** group within the right pane and click **Properties**.

a. In the Ricoh4916-DL Properties window, highlight the **Members** tab and click **Add**.

b. Type **Marketing-U** in the *Enter the object names to select (examples)* text box and click **Check Names** to validate the name.

c. Click **OK** to add the Marketing-U group to the membership list of the Ricoh4916-DL group.

d. Click **Add**.

e. Type **Administrator** in the *Enter the object names to select (examples)* text box and click **Check Names** to validate the name.

f. Click **OK** to add the Administrator user to the membership list of the Ricoh4916-DL group.

g. Click **OK** to close the Ricoh4916-DL Properties window.

9. Right-click the **Marketing** OU and click **New**, **User**.

a. In the New Object – User window, type the following values within associated text boxes and click **Next**.

- First name: **Marketing Template**
- User logon name: **marketing.template**

b. Type **Secret555** in the Password and Confirm text boxes and click **Next**.

c. Click **Finish** to create the Marketing Template user account within the Marketing OU.

10. Highlight the **Marketing** OU within the navigation pane. Next, right-click the **Marketing Template** user within the Marketing OU and click **Properties**.

a. In the Marketing Template Properties window, highlight the **Organization** tab, and type **DomainX** in the Company text box.

b. Highlight the **Member Of** tab. Note that new users are automatically added to the Domain Users group by default.

c. Click **Add**.

d. Type **Marketing-G** in the *Enter the object names to select (examples)* text box and click **Check Names** to validate the name.

e. Click **OK** to add the Marketing Template user to the membership list of the Marketing-G group.

f. Click **OK** to close the Marketing Template Properties window.

11. Right-click the **Marketing Template** user and click **Copy**.
    a. In the Copy Object – User window, type the following values within associated text boxes and click **Next**.
       i. First name: **Bob**
       ii. Last name: **Burtt**
       iii. User logon name: **b.burtt**
    b. Type **Secret555** in the Password and Confirm text boxes and click **Next**.
    c. Click **Finish** to create the Bob Burtt user account within the Marketing OU.

12. Right-click the **Marketing Template** user and click **Copy**.
    a. In the Copy Object – User window, type the following values within associated text boxes and click **Next**.
       i. First name: **John**
       ii. Last name: **Lavigne**
       iii. User logon name: **j.lavigne**
    b. Type **Secret555** in the Password and Confirm text boxes and click **Next**.
    c. Click **Finish** to create the John Lavigne user account within the Marketing OU.

13. Right-click the **Marketing Template** user and click **Copy**.
    a. In the Copy Object – User window, type the following values within associated text boxes and click **Next**.
       i. First name: **Mary**
       ii. Last name: **Stewart**
       iii. User logon name: **m.stewart**
    b. Type **Secret555** in the Password and Confirm text boxes and click **Next**.
    c. Click **Finish** to create the Mary Stewart user account within the Marketing OU.

14. Right-click the **Mary Stewart** user and click **Properties**.
    a. In the Mary Stewart Properties window, highlight the **Organization** tab, and note that Domain*X* is listed in the Company text box.
    b. Highlight the **Member Of** tab. Note that Mary Stewart has been added to the Marketing-G group.
    c. Click **Cancel** to close the Mary Stewart Properties window.

15. Right-click the **Mary Stewart** user and note the options available. Click **Reset Password**. Type **Secret555** in the New password and Confirm password text boxes and click **OK**. Click **OK** to close the Active Directory Domain Services information window.

16. Right-click the **Marketing** OU and click **New**, **Computer**. Type **MKTG-PC-01** in the Computer name text box and click **OK**.

17. Right-click the **MKTG-PC-01** computer account and note the options available. Click **Reset Account**. Click **Yes** to confirm the reset, and then click **OK** to close the Active Directory Domain Services information window.

18. Close the Active Directory Users and Computers window.

Project 4-8: Active Directory Admin Center

In this Hands-On Project, you enable the Active Directory Recycle Bin, as well as use it to recover a deleted user object.

1. Within Server Manager, click the **Tools** menu and then click **Active Directory Administrative Center**.
2. Highlight **domainX (local)** within the navigation pane of the Active Directory Administrative Center window and click **Enable Recycle Bin** within the Tasks pane. Click **OK** when prompted to confirm and then click **OK** again to close the Active Directory Administrative Center information window.
3. Click the **"Refresh domainX (local)"** button in the upper right of the Active Directory Administrative Center window.
4. Under the domainX (local) pane, double-click **Marketing**. Highlight the **John Lavigne** user account and click **Delete** within the Tasks pane. Click **Yes** to confirm the deletion. Note that the John Lavigne user account no longer appears within the Marketing OU.
5. Highlight **domainX (local)** within the navigation pane of the Active Directory Administrative Center window and double-click **Deleted Objects** within the domainX (local) pane. Note that the John Lavigne user account is listed, alongside the time that the user account was deleted.
6. Highlight the **John Lavigne** user account and click **Restore** within the Tasks pane to restore the John Lavigne user account to the Marketing OU.
7. Click **Marketing** under domainX (local) within the navigation pane. Note that the John Lavigne user has been restored successfully.
8. Close the Active Directory Administrative Center window.

Project 4-9: RODCs

In this Hands-On Project, you prestage a computer account for a RODC within ParisSite. Next, you allow a user's password to be stored within the Active Directory database on the RODC. Finally, you examine the options available when a RODC computer account is deleted.

1. Within Server Manager, click the **Tools** menu and then click **Active Directory Users and Computers**.
2. Right-click the **Domain Controllers** OU within the navigation pane of the Active Directory Users and Computers window and click **Pre-create Read-only Domain Controller account**.
   a. At the welcome page of the Active Directory Domain Services Installation Wizard, click **Next**.
   b. At the Network Credentials page, click **Next**.
   c. At the Specify the Computer Name page, type **RODC1** in the Computer name text box and click **Next**.
   d. At the Select a Site page, click **ParisSite** and click **Next**.
   e. At the Specify the Computer Name page, type **RODC1** in the Computer name text box and click **Next**.

Note 📎

At this point, it may take several minutes for the Active Directory Domain Services Installation Wizard to examine the DNS configuration.

    f. At the Additional Domain Controller Options page, deselect **Global catalog** and click **Next**. Recall that you configured ParisSite to use UGMC within Hands-On Project 4-6 to allow for fast authentication in the absence of a local global catalog.

    g. At the Delegation of RODC Installation and Administration page, click **Next**. This requires that a member of the Domain Admins group perform the configuration of Active Directory Domain Services on the RODC.

    h. At the Summary page, click **Next**.

    i. Click **Finish** to close the Active Directory Domain Services Installation Wizard.

3. Highlight the **Domain Controllers** OU within the navigation pane. Right-click the **RODC1** computer account within the Domain Controllers OU and click **Properties**.

    a. At the RODC1 Properties window, highlight the **Password Replication Policy** tab. Note that members of the Allowed RODC Password Replication Group will have password attributes replicated to the Active Directory database on RODC1.

    b. Click **Cancel** to close the RODC1 Properties window.

4. Highlight the **Users** folder within the navigation pane. Right-click the **Allowed RODC Password Replication Group** domain local security group within the Users folder and then click **Properties**.

    a. At the Allowed RODC Password Replication Group Properties window, highlight the **Members** tab.

    b. Click **Add**.

    c. Type **John** in the *Enter the object names to select (examples)* text box and click **Check Names** to validate the name.

    d. Click **OK** to add the John Lavigne user to the membership list of the Allowed RODC Password Replication Group group.

    e. Click **OK** to close the Allowed RODC Password Replication Group Properties window.

5. Highlight the **Domain Controllers** OU within the navigation pane. Right-click the **RODC1** computer account within the Domain Controllers OU and click **Delete**.

    a. Click **Yes** to confirm the deletion. At the Deleting Domain Controller window, note that passwords for user accounts that were cached on RODC1 will be reset, including John Lavigne, if RODC1 was in operation.

    b. Click **Cancel**.

6. Close the Active Directory Users and Computers window.

Discovery Exercises

Exercise 4-1

In Hands-On Project 4-7, you used the Active Directory Users and Computers tool to create the Marketing OU within your domain and populated it with user and group objects. Create the remaining OUs shown earlier in Figure 4-5 within your domain, using either Windows PowerShell, Active Directory Users and Computers, or the Active Directory Administrative Center. Next, create global and universal security groups for each OU, using the same naming convention you used for groups within Hands-On Project 4-7. Finally, populate the OUs with the user accounts listed in Table 4-5, ensuring that each user has appropriate attributes and is added to the appropriate global security group.

Table 4-5   User accounts for Discovery Exercise 4-1

Account Name	User logon name	Department
Bryan Griffiths	b.griffiths	Accounting
David Swimmer	d.swimmer	Product Assembly (PA)
Bill Pigeon	b.pigeon	Accounts Payable (A/P)
Lori Fast	l.fast	Accounts Payable (A/P)
Mary Xi	m.xi	Information Technology (IT)
Harvey Lipshitz	h.lipshitz	Accounts Receivable (A/R)
Taziva Morei	t.morei	Research & Development (R&D)
Loretta Ritu	l.ritu	Information Technology (IT)
Jeff Smith	j.smith	Accounting
Dan Kerr	d.kerr	Production
Roberta Power	r.power	Production
Jason Eckert	j.eckert	Information Technology (IT)
Sahar Ali	s.ali	Research & Development (R&D)
Dave McKelvey	d.mckelvey	Accounts Receivable (A/R)
Uzma Beretti	u.beretti	Product Assembly (PA)
Larry Van Goozen	l.vangoozen	Accounts Payable (A/P)
Tom Woods	t.woods	Product Assembly (PA)
Arlene Mahood	a.mahood	Product Assembly (PA)
Patrick Steffler	p.steffler	Research & Development (R&D)

Exercise 4-2

In Hands-On Project 3-4, you installed a virtual machine called WindowsServer2019VM1 that communicates on the External Virtual Switch within Hyper-V. Configure the IP settings for the network interface on WindowsServer2019VM1 to use the IP address of your Windows Server 2019 host, to ensure that it can access the service records for domain*X*.com. Next, install Active Directory Domain Services on WindowsServer2019VM1, and configure it as an additional domain controller within domain*X*.com. Ensure that WindowsServer2019VM1 is located within TorontoSite and contains a DNS service as well as a copy of the global catalog.

Exercise 4-3

In Hands-On Project 4-5, you configured three sites for domain*X*.com (TorontoSite, ChicagoSite, and ParisSite), as well as modified the DEFAULTIPSITELINK object to ensure that replication between sites occurs at 180-minute intervals after working hours. In Discovery Exercise 4-2, you added, within TorontoSite, a second domain controller (WindowsServer2019VM1) to domain*X*.com. To test the replication restrictions within your site configuration, perform the following tasks:

a. Open the Active Directory Users and Computers tool on both your Windows Server 2019 host and your WindowsServer2019VM1 virtual machine. Create a user called **replicationtest1** on your Windows Server 2019 host and verify that it has replicated immediately to WindowsServer2019VM1.

b. Use the Active Directory Sites and Services tool on your Windows Server 2019 host to move the domain controller object for WindowsServer2019VM1 to ChicagoSite.

c. Create a user called **replicationtest2** within the Active Directory Users and Computers tool on your Windows Server 2019 host and verify that it has not replicated to WindowsServer2019VM1.

d. Right-click the connection object for WindowsServer2019VM1 within the Active Directory Sites and Services tool on your Windows Server 2019 host and choose **Replicate Now**.

e. Within the Active Directory Users and Computers tool on WindowsServer2019VM1, verify that the replicationtest2 user account is available.

Exercise 4-4

Hardware resource utilization is a key consideration in heavily virtualized environments. As a result, these environments often install Active Directory on Server Core. In Discovery Exercise 3-2, you installed a virtual machine called WindowsServer2019VM3 with Server Core, and configured it to communicate on the External Virtual Switch within Hyper-V. Configure the IP settings of the network interface for WindowsServer2019VM3 to use the IP address of your Windows Server 2019 host to ensure that it can access the service records for domain*X*.com. Next, install Active Directory Domain Services on WindowsServer2019VM3 and configure it as an additional domain controller within domain*X*.com. Ensure that WindowsServer2019VM3 is located within TorontoSite and contains a DNS service as well as a copy of the global catalog. Finally, move the Infrastructure Master and Schema Master FSMO roles to WindowsServer2019VM3 and verify your results.

CONFIGURING RESOURCE ACCESS

After completing this module, you will be able to:

Describe the use and configuration of folder and file attributes

Identify the permissions available for NTFS and ReFS folders and files

Configure file ownership, permissions, and auditing

Share folders using SMB and NFS

Publish shared folders to Active Directory

Implement DFS namespaces to simplify shared folder access

Configure DFS replication to synchronize folder contents

Restrict content using user quotas, folder quotas, and file screens

Files are one of the most frequently accessed network resources within organizations today. As a result, providing secure access to folder and file resources is a key aspect of many IT administrator jobs. In this module, you'll learn how to configure and manage folder and file attributes, permissions, ownership, and auditing. Following this, you'll learn how to share folder contents to network users using the SMB and NFS file sharing protocols, as well as publish shared folders within Active Directory. Next, you'll explore how DFS can be used to simplify shared folder access and keep folder content synchronized between file servers. At the end of this module, you'll learn how to limit the space that content can consume using quotas, as well as how to limit the types of files that can be stored on your file server using file screens.

Configuring Folder and File Attributes

Attributes are features of a folder or file that are used by a filesystem. They have been used within Microsoft filesystems since the FAT filesystem was introduced in 1977. Each folder and file that is stored on a filesystem contains a **metadata** component that stores information about the folder or file. Attributes are stored within this metadata component, along with other characteristics including ownership, permissions, date of creation, and time of last access.

Working with Basic Attributes

The main filesystems supported by Windows Server 2019 include NTFS and ReFS. Additionally, Windows Server 2019 supports the FAT32 filesystem for use on local storage and removable media, as well as the newer exFAT filesystem for use on large-capacity removable media. Each of these filesystems contains two basic attributes that are compatible with the original FAT filesystem: read-only and hidden. To view and set these attributes, you can right-click a folder or file within a **File Explorer** window and click Properties. Both attributes are listed at the bottom of the General tab, as shown for the SampleFile.rtf file in Figure 5-1.

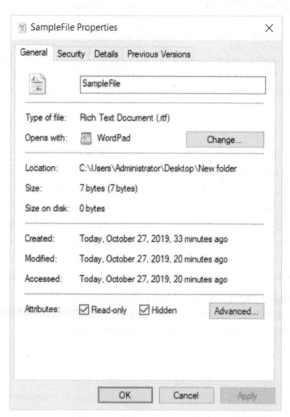

Figure 5-1   The General tab of file properties

The File Explorer in Windows was originally called **Windows Explorer**, but was renamed to avoid confusion with the Internet Explorer Web browser. You will still find Windows Explorer referenced within documentation and websites on the Internet.

When you enable the read-only attribute for a file, changes to its contents cannot be saved to the same file name, and it cannot be deleted by using a command within a Windows PowerShell or Command Prompt window. However, it can be deleted within File Explorer. Moreover, when you enable the read-only attribute for a folder, it applies to existing files within the folder only, and not the folder itself.

Note

Most Windows Server 2019 administrators ignore the read-only attribute box and set the equivalent protection using permissions instead, because permissions apply to the folder and can be inherited by its files.

Folders and files can be assigned the hidden attribute to prevent users from listing their names. However, you can add an option to a command to view the folder or file. For example, the `dir /ah` MS-DOS command and the `Get-ChildItem -hidden` Windows PowerShell command will display folders and files that have the hidden attribute. Similarly, you can configure File Explorer to view hidden folders and files by clicking the View menu and enabling the Hidden items checkbox shown in Figure 5-2.

Figure 5-2   Viewing hidden folders and files within File Explorer

Note

If you modify an attribute on a folder, you will be prompted whether to apply that change to only the folder, or to the files and subfolders within that folder as well.

Working with Advanced Attributes

In addition to the read-only and hidden attributes, NTFS offers four advanced attributes for folders and files: archive, index, compress, and encrypt. You can access these attributes by clicking the Advanced button on the General tab for a folder or file (shown earlier in Figure 5-1). This will open the Advanced Attributes window shown in Figure 5-3.

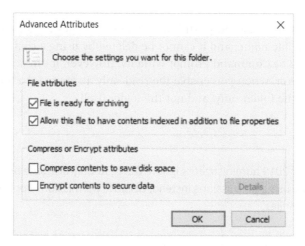

Figure 5-3   The Advanced Attributes window for a file

 Note

The FAT32 and exFAT filesystems only support the archive and encrypt advanced attributes, whereas the ReFS filesystem only supports the archive advanced attribute. Moreover, the encrypt attribute is only available for FAT32 and exFAT filesystems within Windows 10, Windows Server 2016, and later.

Archive Attribute

The archive attribute (*File is ready for archiving* in Figure 5-3) indicates that the folder or file needs to be backed up. This attribute is automatically enabled on files, but not folders, when they are newly created or changed. If you wish to manually set the archive attribute on all files within a folder, you can enable the archive attribute on the folder, and select the option *Apply changes to this folder, subfolders and files* when prompted. File backup software can then be configured to detect files with the archive attribute to ensure that modified files are backed up. The backup software often removes the archive attribute following the backup process.

Index Attribute

When you search for files within File Explorer, the legacy **Windows Indexing Service** is used to obtain a list of files whose name or content matches your search based on a pre-created list called an **index**. The **Windows Search Service** is a faster replacement for the Windows Indexing Service that is available on Windows Server 2019 if you install the Windows Search Service server feature. Moreover, Windows 10 clients can directly access the Windows Search Service on a Windows Server 2019 file server when searching for shared files.

While commonly accessed user folders on a Windows Server 2019 system are indexed by default, system folders are excluded to help reduce the size of the index in order to keep searches as fast as possible. You can access the Indexing Options tool within Control Panel to rebuild an index, as well as specify additional folders or file types to index.

Moreover, only files that have the index attribute (*Allow this file to have contents indexed in addition to file properties* in Figure 5-3) are indexed by the Windows Indexing Service or Windows Search Service. By default, all new files have the index attribute. To ensure that a certain file is not indexed, you can deselect the index attribute for that file. Similarly, to ensure that the files within a certain folder are not indexed, you can deselect the index attribute for that folder, and select the option *Apply changes to this folder, subfolders and files* when prompted.

Compress Attribute

In order to conserve space, the contents of a file can be stored on the filesystem in compressed format. If you enable the compress attribute on a file (*Compress contents to save disk space* in Figure 5-3), the system compresses the file on the filesystem, and automatically decompresses it when you access it. Any changes you make to the file are then compressed before being written to the filesystem. Similarly, to compress all of the files within a certain folder, you can enable the compress attribute for that folder, and select the option *Apply changes to this folder, subfolders and files* when prompted. Moreover, enabling the compress attribute on a folder ensures that new files created within the folder, or copied to the folder, are assigned the compress attribute.

> **Note** 📎
>
> Because compression and decompression results in additional processor calculations, the compress attribute is not enabled by default and is typically enabled only on files that are accessed infrequently, such as accounting documents from a previous fiscal year. If you set the compress attribute on a large number of frequently accessed files, your server performance may degrade significantly.

Encrypt Attribute

If a file that contains sensitive data is stolen or inadvertently copied to an insecure location, the data within may be accessed by others that shouldn't have access to it. To prevent this, you can use an encryption algorithm to protect the data before it is stored on the filesystem. An **encryption algorithm** uses a series of mathematical steps in sequence to scramble data. Because the steps within encryption algorithms are widely known, nearly all encryption algorithms use a random component called a **key** to modify the steps within the algorithm. **Symmetric encryption** algorithms are reversible; data can be decrypted by reversing the algorithm using the same key that was used to encrypt it. **Asymmetric encryption** uses a pair of keys that are uniquely generated for a system or user account: a **public key** and a **private key**. You can think of a public key as the opposite of a private key. If you encrypt data using a public key, that data can only be decrypted using the matching private key.

If you enable the encrypt attribute on a file (*Encrypt contents to secure data* within Figure 5-3), the system symmetrically encrypts the data within the file using a randomly-generated symmetric key that is stored in the file's metadata. Next, the public key within your user account is used to asymmetrically encrypt the symmetric key stored within the file's metadata. If your user account does not have public and private keys, they will be generated and stored within your user account at this point.

Note ⬛

Because the encrypt and compress attribute use the same metadata section, you cannot enable the encrypt and compress attributes on the same file. If you attempt to enable the encrypt attribute on a compressed file, the compress attribute will be deselected automatically.

Note ⬛

To encrypt all of the files within a certain folder, you can enable the encrypt attribute for that folder, and select the option *Apply changes to this folder, subfolders and files* when prompted. Moreover, enabling the encrypt attribute on a folder ensures that new files created within the folder, or copied to the folder, are assigned the encrypt attribute.

Note ⬛

Because sensitive documents are often stored within the same folder, when you encrypt a file, you are prompted whether to encrypt the file, or the parent folder.

When other users try to open the file, they will not be able to decrypt the data within. This is because they do not have the private key to match the public key used to encrypt the symmetric key within the metadata. And without this symmetric key, the data within the file cannot be decrypted.

However, when you open the file, your private key is used to successfully decrypt the symmetric key stored within the file's metadata, because your public key encrypted it in the first place. Next, the decrypted symmetric key is used to decrypt the file's contents. If you make changes to the file, the symmetric key encrypts the file's contents again to keep the data secure.

This filesystem feature is called **Encrypting File System (EFS)**, and works within a workgroup or Active Directory domain environment. In a workgroup, your local user account stores your EFS public and private keys. However, within an Active Directory domain, these keys are stored within your domain user account such that you can access them from any computer within the forest. As a safety precaution, the EFS private key is integrated into the password attribute of your user account. If a malicious user attempted to clear or reset your password using another utility, the private key is lost, and all EFS-encrypted files will not be readable. This also means that if you reset a password for a local or domain user account, that user will not be able to access any of their EFS-encrypted files.

To prevent data from being lost in an Active Directory environment in the event of a password reset, each time you encrypt a file using a domain user account, a second copy of the symmetric key is added to the file's metadata and encrypted with a **recovery agent** public key. The default recovery agent is the Domain Admins group in your domain. Thus, any member of the Domain Admins group will be able to decrypt your EFS-encrypted files in the event that your password is reset. You can then encrypt them again to secure their contents.

> **Note** 📎
>
> There is no recovery agent within a workgroup environment. As a result, you should back up your EFS public and private keys to removable media using the Certificates MMC snap-in for your user account. You can start this snap-in by running the `certmgr.msc` command within a Windows Run, Command Prompt or PowerShell window. After you are in the Certificates MMC, expand the Personal folder in the tree and click Certificates. In the middle pane, right-click the EFS certificate for your user account, click All Tasks, Export, and follow the steps in the Certificate Export Wizard.

> **Note** 📎
>
> As with the compress attribute, the encrypt attribute requires additional processor calculations. If you set the encrypt attribute on a large number of frequently accessed files, your server performance may degrade significantly.

After encrypting a file using EFS, you can optionally allow other users to decrypt its contents. This is useful if you must work on a sensitive file with other people in your organization. To do this, you can access the Advanced Attributes window, shown earlier in Figure 5-3, and click the Details button. For SampleFile.rtf, this will open the User Access to SampleFile.rtf window shown in Figure 5-4, where you can add additional users, remove existing users, or even back up your EFS keys. Because SampleFile.rtf was encrypted in an Active Directory environment, Administrator (the default member of the Domain Admins group) is listed as the recovery agent.

Figure 5-4 Allowing multiple users to access an EFS-encrypted file

When you copy or move an encrypted file to another folder within an NTFS, FAT32, or exFAT filesystem on the same computer or removable media, that file remains encrypted, even if you rename it. The same holds true for copying or moving the file to a different NTFS, FAT32, or exFAT filesystem on another Windows 10, Windows Server 2016, or Windows Server 2019 system within the same Active Directory domain. However, if you copy or move the file to a filesystem that does not support EFS (such as ReFS, or FAT32 on a Windows 7 system), the file is automatically decrypted.

Note

You can also use the `Set-ItemProperty` cmdlet within Windows PowerShell to configure basic and advanced attributes on folders and files. At a Command Prompt window, you can also use the `compact.exe` command to configure the compress attribute, or the `cipher.exe` command to configure the encrypt attribute.

Managing Folder and File Security

Recall from the previous module that creating user and group accounts are the initial steps for sharing resources, such as folders, files, and printers. The next steps are to modify the access control lists (ACLs) on each resource and then to set them up for sharing.

Windows Server 2019 uses two types of ACLs: discretionary and system. A **discretionary access control list (DACL)** lists the permissions given to user and group accounts and is used to grant or deny access to the resource. A **system access control list (SACL)** contains information used to audit the access to the resource. For example, a soft drink company may decide to audit files that contain the secret recipes for their products. By configuring a SACL for each file containing a recipe, the company can monitor who has successfully viewed the file's contents and who has tried to view the contents but failed because of DACL restrictions. If no SACL is configured, auditing is disabled for the resource.

Note

A user or group that is listed within a DACL or SACL is often called a **security principal**.

When you create a resource, such as a file, folder, or printer, you become the owner of that resource by default. By default, the owner of a resource, the local Administrator user account (within a workgroup), and members of the Domain Admins group (within a domain) can change folder and file ownership as well as configure DACLs and SACLs.

Folders and files on an NTFS or ReFS filesystem support both DACLs and SACLs. To provide security for folders and files on these filesystems, you should understand how to configure permissions and ownership, troubleshoot permission assignments, as well as enable and configure auditing.

Configuring Folder and File Permissions

To view and configure the DACL for a folder or file on an NTFS or ReFS filesystem, you can right-click the folder or file within a File Explorer window and click Properties. Next, you can highlight the Security tab, as shown in Figure 5-5 for the SampleFile.rtf file. Table 5-1 lists the folder and file permissions supported by NTFS and ReFS.

Note from Figure 5-5 that the built-in SYSTEM group (that represents operating system components) is allowed Full control permission to SampleFile.rtf, which includes all other permissions on the file. These permissions are grey, which indicates that they were not set on the SampleFile.rtf directly but instead were inherited from the parent

Figure 5-5   The Security tab of file properties

Table 5-1   NTFS/ReFS folder and file permissions

Permission	Description	Applies to
Full control	Can read, add, delete, execute, and modify files, change permissions and attributes, and take ownership	Folders and files
Modify	Can read, add, delete, execute, and modify files; cannot change permissions or take ownership	Folders and files
Read and execute	Implies the capabilities of both List folder contents and Read (traverse folders, view file contents, view attributes and permissions, and execute files)	Folders and files
List folder contents	Can list (traverse) files in the folder or switch to a subfolder, view folder attributes and permissions, and execute files; cannot view file contents	Folders only

Table 5-1	NTFS/ReFS folder and file permissions *(continued)*	
Permission	Description	Applies to
Read	Can view file contents, as well as view file and folder attributes and permissions; cannot traverse folders or execute files	Folders and files
Write	Can create files, write data to files, append data to files, create folders, and modify folder and file attributes; cannot delete files	Folders and files
Advanced permissions	Advanced permissions apply (see Table 5-2)	Folders and files

folder that contains SampleFile.rtf. To add additional permissions for users or groups, you can click Edit in Figure 5-5. This will open the Permissions window shown in Figure 5-6, where you can add or remove existing users or groups as well as set their permissions. The Bob Burtt user shown in Figure 5-6 was added to the DACL and granted Read & execute permission (which also grants Read permission).

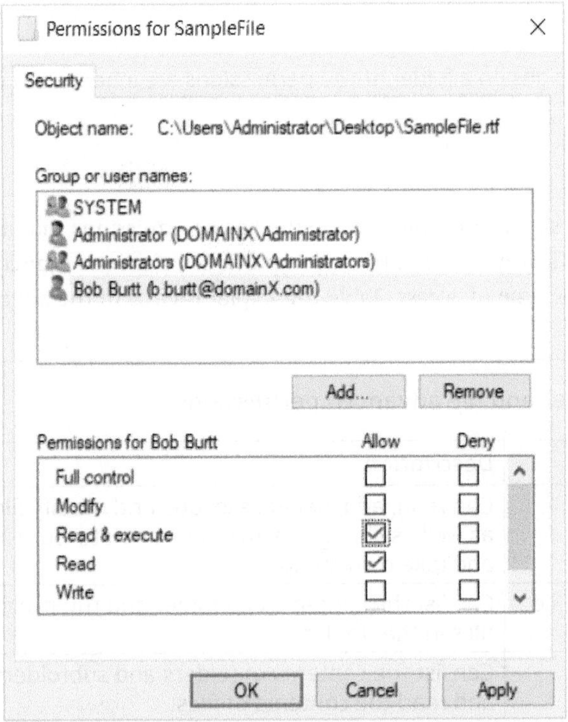

Figure 5-6   Configuring file permissions

Note 📎

You receive the permissions on a folder or file that are assigned to your user account as well as any group accounts that you belong to. For instance, if your user account is granted Read permission to a file and a group that your user account belongs to is granted Full control to the same file, you effectively receive Full control when accessing the file.

Note 📎

If none of the Allow or Deny boxes are checked in Figure 5-6, then the associated user or group has no access to the folder. If the Deny box is checked, this overrides any other access. For instance, if your user account is granted Read permission to a file, and a group that your user account belongs to is denied Read permission to the same file, you are denied Read access to the file.

Note 📎

When you set permissions on a folder, those permissions are inherited by default to files and subfolders.

The permissions shown in Table 5-1 are the basic permissions that are normally set on folders and files. However, they are made up of one or more advanced permissions that provide a specific type of access. Table 5-2 explains each of the advanced permissions.

Table 5-2   NTFS folder and file advanced permissions

Permission	Description	Applies to
Full control	Can read, add, delete, execute, and modify files, as well as change permissions and attributes, and take ownership	Folders and files
Traverse folder/execute file	Can list the contents of a folder and run program files in that folder	Folders and files
List folder/read data	Can list the contents of folders and subfolders and read the contents of files	Folders and files

Table 5-2 NTFS folder and file advanced permissions *(continued)*

Permission	Description	Applies to
Read attributes	Can view the read-only and hidden attributes	Folders and files
Read extended attributes	Can view extended attributes (archive, index, compress, and encrypt)	Folders and files
Create files/write data	Can add new files to a folder and modify, append to, or write over file contents	Folders and files
Create folders/append data	Can add new folders and add new data at the end of files, but otherwise cannot delete, write over, or modify data	Folders and files
Write attributes	Can add or remove the read-only and hidden attributes	Folders and files
Write extended attributes	Can add or remove the archive, index, compress, and encrypt attributes	Folders and files
Delete subfolders and files	Can delete subfolders and files (the following Delete permission is not required)	Folders and files
Delete	Can delete the specific subfolder or file to which this permission is attached	Folders and files
Read permissions	Can view the permissions (DACL) associated with a folder or file, but cannot change them	Folders and files
Change permissions	Can change the permissions associated with a folder or file	Folders and files
Take ownership	Can take ownership of the folder or file (read permissions and change permissions automatically accompany this permission)	Folders and files

If the basic permissions do not suit your needs, you can modify the DACL to set advanced permissions. To do this for SampleFile.rtf, you can click Advanced in Figure 5-5 to open the Advanced Security Settings window shown in Figure 5-7. When you click Add in Figure 5-7, you will access the Permission Entry window shown in Figure 5-8. At this window, you can select a security principal, whether to allow or deny permissions to the security principal, as well as the associated permissions (you must click *Show advanced permissions* to assign advanced permissions). For example, the Bob Burtt user shown in Figure 5-8 is only allowed the *List folder / read data* special permission.

You can also click Disable inheritance in Figure 5-7 to prevent parent folder permissions from being inherited to the SampleFile.rtf file. When you click this button, you will be prompted to either remove the inherited permissions or convert any previously inherited permissions to explicit permissions on the SampleFile.rtf file that you can modify afterwards.

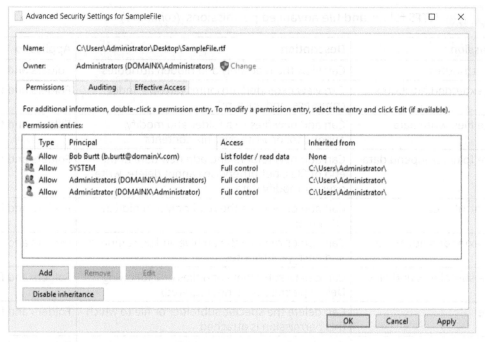

Figure 5-7   Configuring advanced security settings

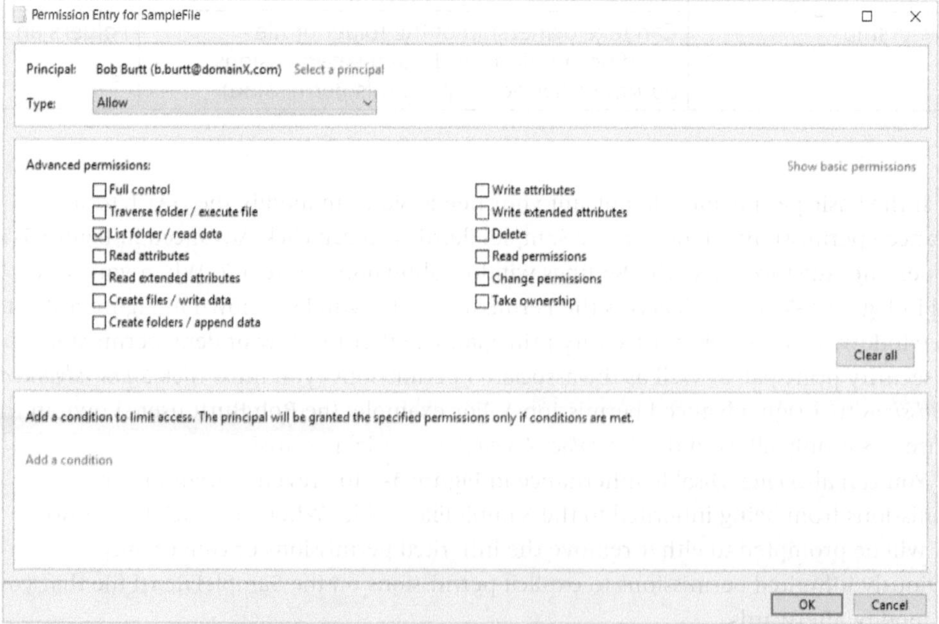

Figure 5-8   Configuring advanced file permissions

> **Note** 📎
>
> Always err on the side of too much security. It is easier, in terms of human relations, to give users permissions later than it is to take away existing permissions.

> **Note** 📎
>
> When removing groups and users from confidential folders and files, make sure you do not remove all access for SYSTEM or administrative groups (such as Domain Admins or Administrators) to ensure that the operating system and IT staff can obtain access to the file in a support situation. For the same reason, you should also avoid using Deny on any folder or file for these groups.

Configuring Folder and File Ownership

Each folder and file on a system must have an owner, which, by default, is the user that created the file. The owner of a folder or file is able to change the ownership to another user. Moreover, if you are granted the Take ownership advanced permission or Full control permission (which includes Take ownership) to a folder or file, you can change the owner of it to yourself. After you are the owner of that folder or file, you have the ability to change the permissions on it.

To modify the owner of a folder or file, you can access the Advanced Security Settings window (shown in Figure 5-7), click Change next to the current owner, and specify the new owner.

> **Note** 📎
>
> The Administrators group always has the right to take ownership of any folder or file, regardless of the permissions set. This ensures that IT staff can always take ownership of a file and modify the permissions when necessary.

> **Note** 📎
>
> If you create a folder or file as the Administrator user, the Administrators group automatically becomes the owner of it.

Note

User quotas (discussed later in this module) use file ownership to determine how much storage each user consumes on a filesystem and applies restrictions accordingly.

Troubleshooting Folder and File Permissions

Sometimes you configure folder or file access for a user but find that the user does not actually have the type of access you set up. Say, for example that a user within your organization requires the ability to maintain all files within the C:\Blueprints folder. As a result, you grant the user Modify permission to the folder. However, when that user attempts to access the C:\ Blueprints folder, they receive an access denied message because their user account is also a member of a group that has been denied Modify permission to the C:\Blueprints folder.

To troubleshoot this problem, you should review the permissions that have been assigned on the C:\Blueprints folder to the user, as well as all groups to which the user belongs, taking permission inheritance into consideration. Alternatively, you can access the Advanced Security Settings window for the C:\Blueprints folder and highlight the Effective Access tab, as shown in Figure 5-9. Next, you can click *Select a user* to choose the appropriate user account, and then click *View effective access* to list the effective permissions

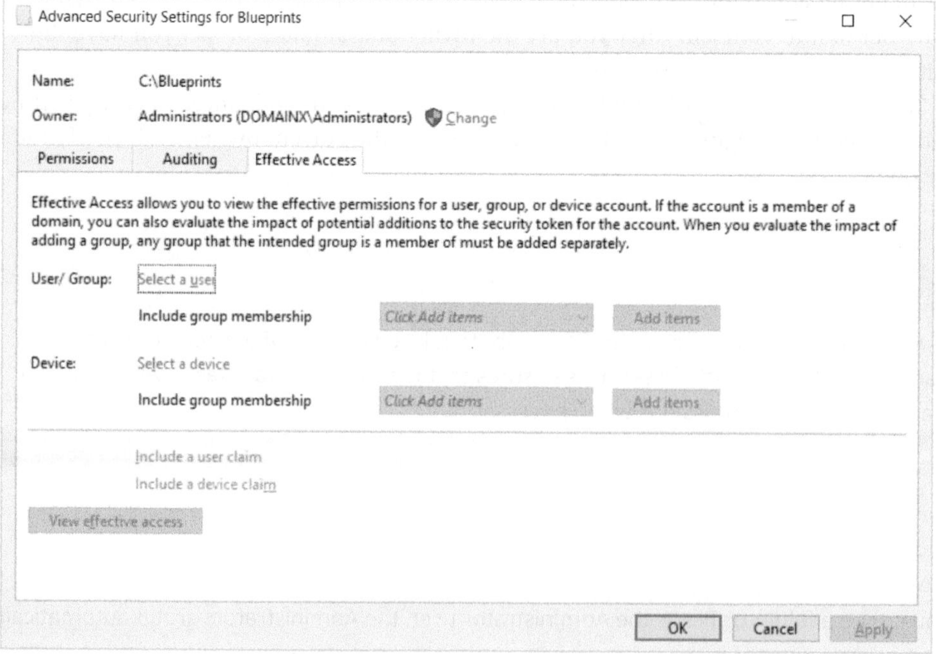

Figure 5-9   **The Effective Access tab**

that the user has to the C:\Blueprints folder after permissions (including inherited permissions) for the user and all groups that they are a member of have been applied.

Other permission-related problems can occur after a file or folder is copied or moved. When a file is copied, the original file remains intact and a copy is made in another folder. Moving a file to a folder on the same volume does not create a copy of the file; it only renames the file to reflect the new path. Moving a file to a folder on a different volume creates a copy of the file in the target folder, and removes the original file. Copying and moving works the same for a folder, but the entire folder contents (files and subfolders) are also copied or moved. When a file or folder is created, copied, or moved, the file and folder permissions are affected in the following ways:

- A newly created file inherits the permissions configured on its folder.
- A file that is copied from one folder to another on the same volume inherits the permissions configured on the folder to which it is copied.
- A file or folder that is moved from one folder to another on the same volume retains its original permissions. For example, if a file assigns Read permission to the Accounting group, and it is moved to a folder that assigns Modify to the Accounting group, that file will continue to assign Read permissions to the Accounting group.
- A file or folder that is moved or copied to a folder on a different volume inherits the permissions of the folder to which it is moved or copied.
- A file or folder that is moved or copied from an NTFS or ReFS volume to a folder on a FAT32 or exFAT volume, all permissions are removed because FAT32 and exFAT do not support NTFS/ReFS permissions.
- A file or folder that is moved or copied from a FAT32 or exFAT volume to a folder on an NTFS or ReFS volume inherits the permissions of the folder to which it is moved or copied.

Configuring Folder and File Auditing

Folder and file auditing allows you to track activity on a folder or file, such as read or write activity. Some organizations choose to implement auditing on folders and files that involve financially sensitive information, such as those involving accounting and payroll. Other organizations configure auditing to see which users access information, such as a folder containing files of employee guidelines and announcements, to determine if it is being used. Windows Server 2019 allows you to audit successful and failed attempts to access folders and files using a combination of any or all of the basic or advanced permissions listed previously in Table 5-1 and Table 5-2. This audit configuration is stored within the SACL on the folder or file.

Consider a situation in which your organization's financial auditors require you to record each time any files in the C:\Accounting folder are changed by a user within the Accounting-G group that has access to them. In this case, you could configure the folder's security to audit each successful type of write event, including those that require the *Create files / write data* and *Create folders / append data* advanced permissions. For extra information, you could also track permission, attribute, and ownership changes by monitoring successful attempts to use the *Write attributes, Write extended attributes, Change permissions,* and *Take ownership* advanced permissions.

To configure this auditing, you could access the Advanced Security Settings window (shown earlier in Figure 5-7) for the C:\Accounting folder, highlight the Auditing tab, and click Add. This will open the Auditing Entry window, where you can make the selections shown in Figure 5-10 (you must first click *Show advanced permissions* to select advanced permissions).

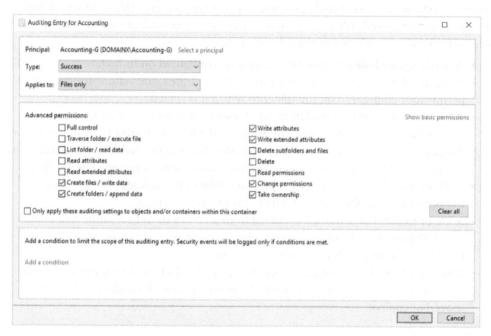

Figure 5-10   Configuring an audit entry

Note 🖉

Audited events are recorded in the Windows Server 2019 **Security log**. You can access the Security log using the `Get-EventLog Security` command within Windows PowerShell, or by using the **Event Viewer** tool. To open Event Viewer, right-click Start and click Event Viewer.

Note 🖉

Be cautious about how much you choose to audit on a server. Auditing a large number of folders or files will require additional processor calculations and use additional space within the Security log, making individual audit events more difficult to locate.

Because auditing requires additional processor calculations and storage, it is not enabled on Windows Server 2019 by default. To enable auditing functionality, you must edit the **audit policy** within a Group Policy object that applies to your computer. Within an Active Directory environment, you can edit the settings of the Default Domain Policy object to enable auditing functionality on every computer within the domain. To do this, you can select Group Policy Management from the Tools menu within Server Manager. Within the **Group Policy Management** tool, you can navigate to, and expand, your domain object, right-click *Default Domain Policy*, and click *Edit*. This will open the **Group Policy Management Editor** tool, where you can navigate to the Audit Policy section shown in Figure 5-11. Finally, you can right-click the *Audit object access* policy setting in the right pane and click Properties to enable auditing for success or failure events, or both. The *Audit object access* policy setting shown in Figure 5-11 enables auditing functionality for both success and failure events.

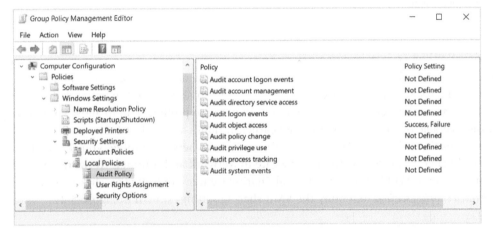

Figure 5-11   Enabling file and folder auditing functionality

Note

If your Windows Server 2019 system is part of a workgroup, you can run the `gpedit.msc` command to open the local Group Policy object. Next, you can navigate to the same Audit Policy section shown in Figure 5-11 to enable auditing functionality for your computer.

Note

You can also use the `Set-ACL` cmdlet within Windows PowerShell to configure permissions, ownership, or auditing for folders or files on an NTFS or ReFS filesystem.

Configuring Shared Folders

To allow users to access the files within a folder on your Windows Server 2019 system from across a network, you must share the folder. Furthermore, there are two different protocols that can be used to share folders on Windows Server 2019 systems: **Server Message Block (SMB)** and **Network File System (NFS)**. Originally developed by IBM, SMB is the default file sharing protocol used by Windows systems. NFS is a UNIX file sharing protocol that was introduced by Sun Microsystems and can be installed on Windows Server 2003 and later systems. Regardless of the protocol used, shared folders can also be published within Active Directory for easy access.

Note

SMB is also called **Common Internet File System (CIFS)**.

Sharing Folders Using SMB

After you install Windows Server 2019, SMB sharing is enabled by default. Additionally, your Windows Server 2019 system is visible to other computers on the network if you click Yes when the Networks desktop notification screen prompts you to allow your PC to be discoverable by other PCs (performed earlier in Hands-On Project 1-2).

To enable or disable SMB sharing for your current network profile, you can open Control Panel in category view and navigate to Network and Internet, Network and Sharing Center. Within the Network and Sharing Center, you can then click *Change advanced sharing settings* to modify the SMB sharing settings shown in Figure 5-12.

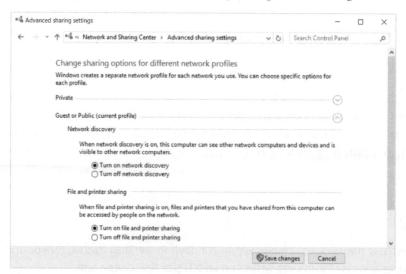

Figure 5-12   Configuring SMB sharing settings

The *Turn on file and printer sharing* setting allows your system to share folders and printers using SMB, while the *Turn on network discovery* setting makes your system and shared folders visible to other computers on the network that search for network resources.

If SMB sharing is enabled on your system, you can easily share a folder by accessing the properties of the folder or by using Server Manager.

Sharing a Folder Using Folder Properties

To share a folder using SMB, you can right-click the folder, click Properties, and highlight the Sharing tab. Figure 5-13 shows the Sharing tab for the C:\CompanyForms folder on SERVERX. If you click the Share button in Figure 5-13, you will see the Network access window shown in Figure 5-14. You can then type a user or group name within the text drop-down box, click Add, and specify the level of permission that they have to the shared folder.

SMB requires that you have a **shared folder permission** in order to connect to a shared folder. The permissions available in Figure 5-14 include the following:

- *Read*—Allows groups or users to read and execute files.
- *Read/Write*—Allows groups or users to read, execute, delete, and modify the contents of files, as well as add and delete subfolders.
- *Owner*—Automatically assigned to the owner of the folder, it allows the owner to read, execute, delete, and modify the contents of files, as well as add and delete subfolders and modify share permissions.

Figure 5-13   **The Sharing tab of folder properties**

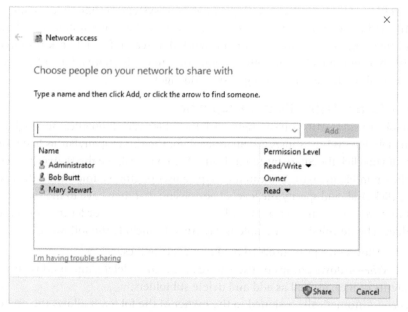

Figure 5-14   Sharing a folder

In Figure 5-14, Bob Burtt is the owner of the folder and receives Owner permissions to the shared folder as a result. Administrator is granted Read/Write permission to the shared folder, while Mary Stewart is granted Read. If you click Share in Figure 5-14, the C:\CompanyForms folder will be shared with these shared folder permissions. You can then connect to the shared folder from another computer on the network by searching for the server within File Explorer, or by entering \\SERVERX\CompanyForms within the navigation bar of File Explorer or the Windows Run dialog box. Within a domain environment, the user name and groups listed within your token will be used to grant you the appropriate access to the shared folder. Within a workgroup environment, you will be prompted to log into SERVERX as a valid local user account that provides access to the shared folder.

Note 📎

The \\servername\sharedfoldername syntax is called a **Universal Naming Convention (UNC)**, and is used when connecting to shared SMB resources. You can instead specify the IP address of a server instead of the server name within a UNC (e.g., \\IPaddress\ sharedfoldername).

Note

You can use the graphical file browsing app on a UNIX, Linux, or macOS system to connect to SMB shared folders. However, you will need to specify the format `smb://servername/sharedfoldername`.

Note

You receive the shared folder permissions that are assigned to your user account as well as any group accounts that you belong to. Moreover, permissions that are denied to your user or group accounts override permissions that are allowed.

Note

You must be granted both shared folder permissions and NTFS/ReFS permissions in order to access files within a shared folder on an NTFS or ReFS filesystem. This is because file sharing and filesystem DACLs are two separate components within the Windows operating system and they maintain their own security restrictions. For example, if you are granted Read/Write share permission to a shared folder and attempt to access a file within the shared folder that grants you Read NTFS/ReFS permission, you will only be able to read the contents of the file. Alternatively, if you are granted Read share permission to a shared folder, and attempt to access a file within the shared folder that grants you Modify NTFS/ReFS permission, you will only be able to read the contents of the file.

Note

If you share a folder on a FAT32 or exFAT filesystem, the level of access each user obtains to the folders and files within is determined solely by the shared folder permissions that you configure.

Instead of clicking the Share button in Figure 5-13, you can instead click the Advanced Sharing button, and then select *Share this folder* within the Advanced Sharing window shown in Figure 5-15. You can then specify the share name, limit the number of simultaneous connections to the shared folder (the default value is 16777216) or supply a description within the Comments text box. If you click the Permissions button,

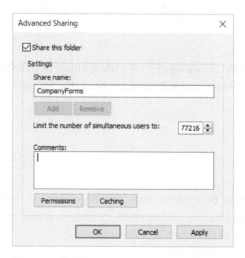

Figure 5-15   **The Advanced Sharing window**

you can configure advanced shared folder permissions for groups and users, as shown in Figure 5-16. The three advanced shared folder permissions shown in Figure 5-16 are:

- *Read*—Allows groups or users to read and execute files.
- *Change*—Allows groups or users to read, execute, delete, and modify the contents of files, as well as add and delete subfolders.
- *Full Control*—Allows groups or users to read, execute, delete, and modify the contents of files, as well as add and delete subfolders and modify share permissions.

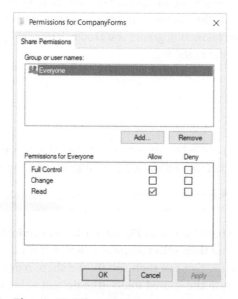

Figure 5-16   **Configuring advanced shared folder permissions**

Note 📎

By default, the special Everyone group (which includes all authenticated users by default) has Read permission to a new share when configuring advanced shared folder permissions. However, to simplify the management of shared folder permissions for folders that reside on an NTFS or ReFS filesystem, many administrators assign the Everyone group Full Control shared folder permission. While this allows all authenticated users to connect to the shared folder to perform all actions, those users are still restricted by the NTFS/ReFS permissions they are assigned on the underlying filesystem.

Note 📎

If you specify a share name that ends with $ in Figure 5-15 (e.g., CompanyForms$), that share will be hidden from searches on the network. In this case, users must specify the UNC (e.g., \\SERVERX\CompanyForms$) in order to connect to the shared folder.

The Caching button in Figure 5-15 allows you to configure the **offline file caching** feature of SMB, as shown in Figure 5-17. The default option shown in Figure 5-17 allows users to right-click files and programs within the shared folder and select *Make available offline* to ensure that a copy is downloaded to a cache folder on their local computer. This prevents a network disruption from impacting the editing of files or execution of a program within the shared folder. When the user disconnects from the shared folder, any modified files within the cache folder are then uploaded to the shared folder. If two or more users attempt to cache the same file, they have the option of choosing whose version to use or of saving both versions.

You can disable the offline file caching feature for the shared folder by selecting *No files or programs from the shared folder are available offline* in Figure 5-17. Alternatively, you can select *All files and programs that users open from the shared folder are automatically available offline* to force users to cache all files and programs within the shared folder, and *Optimize for performance* to ensure that Windows XP and older operating systems use minimal bandwidth for offline file caching.

Note 📎

BranchCache is an optional performance enhancement to offline file caching for Windows 7 and later clients that is not installed or configured by default. Search BranchCache at docs.microsoft.com for more information.

Figure 5-17 Configuring offline file caching

Sharing a Folder Using Server Manager

You can also manage SMB shared folders within Server Manager. To do this, you can click File and Storage Services within the navigation pane of Server Manager, and then highlight Shares as shown in Figure 5-18. The NETLOGON and SYSVOL shares shown in Figure 5-18 are automatically created during the installation of Active Directory Domain Services, whereas the REMINST share is automatically created during the configuration of WDS.

To share a folder, you can select the Tasks drop-down box in the Shares section of Figure 5-18 and click New Share. This will start the New Share Wizard shown in Figure 5-19. Normally, you select *SMB Share – Quick* from Figure 5-19. However, you can

Figure 5-18 Managing shared folders using Server Manager

instead select *SMB Share – Advanced* to additionally configure file classifications and folder quotas if the **File Server Resource Manager** is installed (discussed later in this module), or *SMB Share – Applications* to automatically configure NTFS/ReFS permissions on the folder that are compatible with most applications.

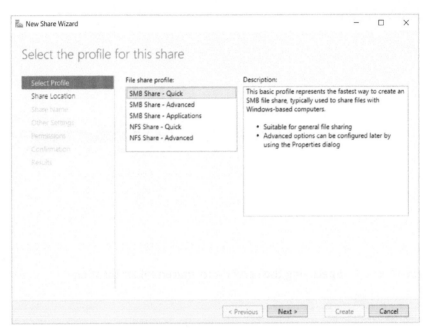

Figure 5-19   The New Share Wizard

If you select *SMB Share – Quick* and click Next in Figure 5-19, you will be prompted to select the server, and the volume that should contain the shared folder, as shown in Figure 5-20. This will create a \Shares parent folder on the volume (if one does not already exist) that will include a subfolder for your new shared folder. Alternatively, you can select *Type a custom path* and specify the path to an existing shared folder that you wish to share.

When you click Next in Figure 5-20, you will be prompted to supply the share name and optional share description, as shown in Figure 5-21. After clicking Next in Figure 5-21, you can configure the optional share features shown in Figure 5-22:

- *Enable access-based enumeration* prevents users from viewing shared folders (and subfolders and files) for which they do not have at least Read share and NTFS/ReFS permissions. The **access-based enumeration** feature prevents users from receiving an access denied error message when opening a folder or file that they can see within File Explorer but are not granted sufficient permission to access.
- *Allow caching of share* enables offline file caching and is equivalent to the *Only the files and programs that users specify are available offline* option shown earlier in Figure 5-17.
- *Encrypt data access* allows Windows 8, Windows Server 2012, and later systems to encrypt SMB packets when accessing the shared folder.

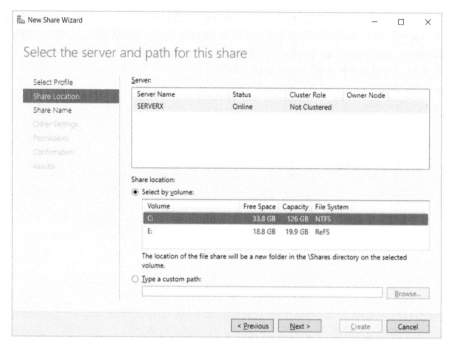

Figure 5-20   Specifying the server and shared folder location

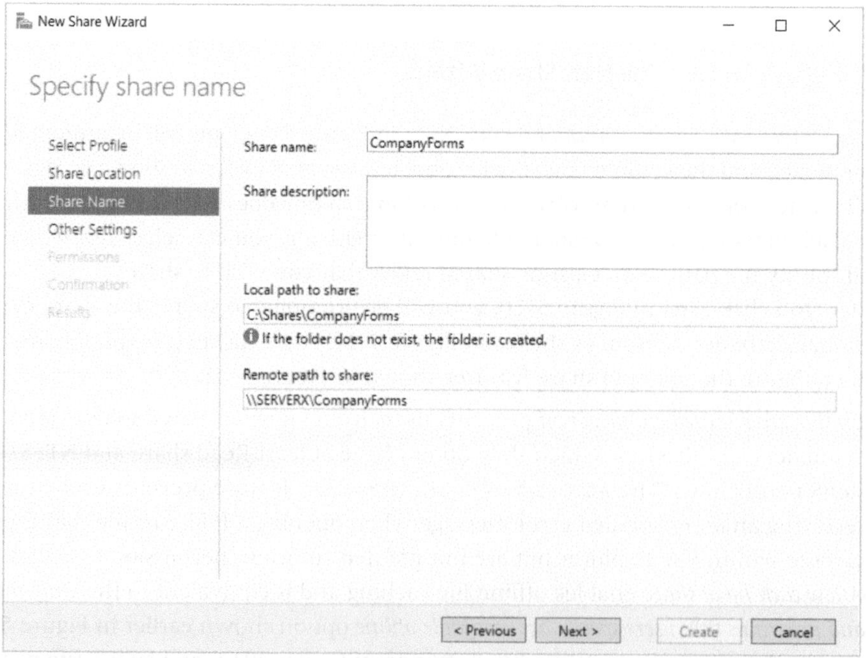

Figure 5-21   Specifying the share name

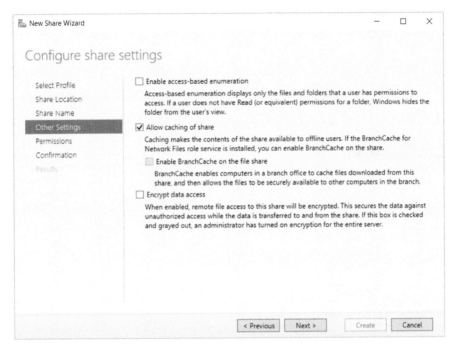

Figure 5-22   Configuring optional share features

To simplify the permissions associated with sharing folders on NTFS and ReFS filesystems, the New Share Wizard automatically assigns the Everyone group Full Control advanced share permission. When you click Next in Figure 5-22, you will be able to modify the NTFS/ReFS permissions on the folder to match the desired level of access for groups and users, as shown in Figure 5-23. Following this, you can click Next and then Create to create the new shared folder.

Note

After creating a shared folder, you can right-click it within the Shares section of Server Manager (shown in Figure 5-18) and click Properties to modify shared folder settings, or Stop Sharing to discontinue folder sharing without removing the folder on the filesystem.

Note

In addition to folder properties and Server Manager, you can use the `New-SmbShare` cmdlet within Windows PowerShell to share a folder with SMB.

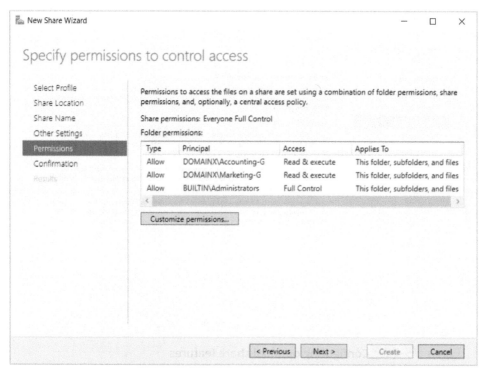

Figure 5-23   Configuring NTFS/ReFS permissions for a shared folder

Sharing Folders Using NFS

To share folders using NFS on Windows Server 2019, you must first install the **Server for NFS** server role. To select this role within the Add Roles and Features Wizard in Server Manager, you must first expand File and Storage Services, and then expand File and iSCSI Services, as shown in Figure 5-24.

Note

To connect to NFS shared directories from a Windows Server 2019 system, you must also install the **Client for NFS** feature.

Note

Windows Server 2019 requires that any NFS shared folders reside on an NTFS or ReFS filesystem.

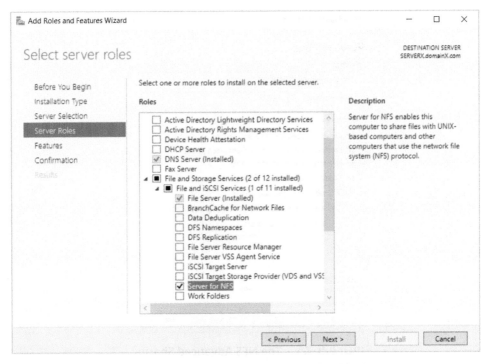

Figure 5-24   Installing the Server for NFS server role

As with SMB, you can share a folder using NFS by accessing the properties of the folder or by using Server Manager.

Sharing a Folder Using Folder Properties

To share a folder using NFS, you can right-click the folder, click Properties, highlight the NFS Sharing tab, and click Manage NFS Sharing. This will open the NFS Advanced Sharing window shown in Figure 5-25, where you can enable NFS file sharing, specify the share name, and configure the appropriate NFS options.

NFS was designed for UNIX systems that shared the same user database, either by coordinating the **user ID (UID)** and **group ID (GID)** numbers assigned to each UNIX user in the UNIX user database stored on each system, or by providing centralized authentication for users on the network using Kerberos. Because Active Directory provides centralized user authentication using Kerberos, NFS works well within an Active Directory environment for sharing files between UNIX, Linux, macOS, and Windows systems.

The three Kerberos v5 options selected in Figure 5-25 allow all forms of Kerberos authentication for UNIX, Linux, macOS, and Windows users within the Active Directory domain. The *No server authentication, Enable unmapped user access,* and *Allow unmapped user Unix access (by UID/GID)* options allow UNIX, Linux, and macOS users to access the NFS shared folder by passing their UID and GID to the server, instead of using Kerberos. In this case, the user accounts within Active Directory for each UNIX, Linux, and macOS user

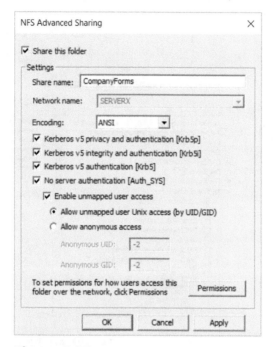

Figure 5-25   **The NFS Advanced Sharing window**

must contain the same UID and GID that is stored within the UNIX user database on that user's system. Alternatively, you could select *Allow anonymous access* to force UNIX, Linux, and macOS users that are not configured to use Kerberos to connect as the Guest account.

Note

You can set the UID and GID for a user account within Active Directory using Windows PowerShell. For example, to set the UID to 1053 and the GID to 1002 for the Bob Burtt user account within your Active Directory domain, you could run the `Set-ADUser -Identity "Bob Burtt" -Replace @{uidNumber="1053",gidNumber="1002"}` command.

Note

The Encoding value shown in Figure 5-25 refers to the character set that is used when accessing an NFS-shared folder from a command line terminal. The default of ANSI is supported by most modern systems, but you can modify it to match an encoding type necessary for older UNIX systems, if necessary.

As with SMB shared folders, shared folder permissions are required to connect to an NFS shared folder. However, NFS shared folder permissions are granted to computers instead of users. If you click the Permissions button in Figure 5-25, you can add entries for computers (by DNS name) that are granted access to the NFS shared folder, as shown in Figure 5-26. There are only two levels of access that you can grant to computers:

- *Read-Only*—Allows computers to read and execute files.
- *Read-Write*—Allows computers to read, execute, delete, and modify the contents of files, as well as add and delete subfolders.

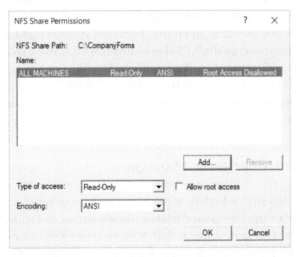

Figure 5-26   Setting permissions on an NFS share

The default permission listed in Figure 5-26 assigns Read-Only NFS share permission to all computers. Selecting the *Allow root access* option will also allow the root user (the equivalent of Administrator on a UNIX, Linux, or macOS system) to access the NFS share.

Note

After a computer connects to an NFS shared folder successfully, the identity of the user (using Kerberos or UID/GID) is used to obtain access to the folder and files within according to the associated NTFS/ReFS permissions.

Note

NFS shared folder permissions and NTFS/ReFS permissions must both be satisfied in order to gain access to an NFS shared folder. For example, if your computer is granted Read/Write permission to an NFS shared folder, and you attempt to access a file within the shared folder that grants you Read NTFS/ReFS permission, you will only be able to read the contents of the file. Alternatively, if your computer is granted Read permission to an NFS shared folder, and you attempt to access a file within the shared folder that grants you Modify NTFS/ReFS permission, you will only be able to read the contents of the file.

After you have configured the appropriate shared folder permissions in Figure 5-26 and click OK, you can click OK at the NFS Advanced Sharing window in Figure 5-25 to share the folder using NFS. UNIX, Linux, and macOS users will be able to use the mount command or their graphical file browsing app to connect to the shared folder using the syntax servername:/sharedfoldername. Windows systems that have the Client for NFS installed can connect to the NFS shared folder within File Explorer using UNC syntax (\\servername\sharedfoldername) or by using the mount command to associate a drive letter with the NFS shared folder. For example, to connect G:\ to the CompanyForms NFS shared folder on SERVERX, you could run the mount -t nfs \\SERVERX\CompanyForms G: command. Following this, you can access your G:\ within File Explorer to connect to the CompanyForms NFS shared folder on SERVERX.

Sharing a Folder Using Server Manager

The Shares section of Server Manager (shown earlier in Figure 5-18) can also be used to create and manage NFS shared folders, using the same general process as SMB shared folders. When you start the New Share Wizard (shown earlier in Figure 5-19), you can select *NFS Share – Quick* to share a folder with NFS, or select *NFS Share – Advanced* to additionally configure file classifications and folder quotas if the File Server Resource Manager is installed. If you select *NFS Share – Quick* and progress through the New Share Wizard, you will be prompted to select the location of the shared folder (shown earlier in Figure 5-20), as well as the share name (shown in Figure 5-27). When you click Next in Figure 5-27, you are prompted to select the authentication methods that clients can use when connecting to the NFS share, as shown in Figure 5-28. After clicking Next in Figure 5-28, you are prompted to add NFS shared folder permission entries for computers on the network, as shown in Figure 5-29. The options selected in Figure 5-28 and Figure 5-29 match those described earlier in Figure 5-25 and Figure 5-26.

After you click Next in Figure 5-29, you will be able to modify the NTFS/ReFS permissions on the folder to match the desired level of access for groups and users, as shown earlier in Figure 5-23. Following this, you can click Next and then Create to create the new shared folder.

Note

In addition to folder properties and Server Manager, you can use the New-NfsShare cmdlet within Windows PowerShell to share a folder with NFS.

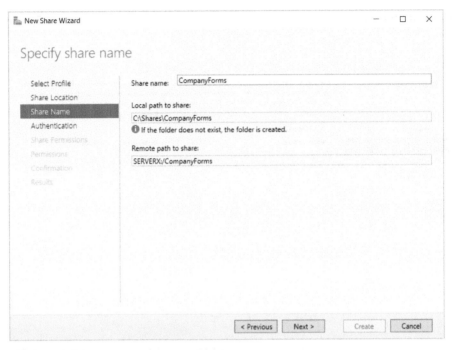

Figure 5-27   Specifying the share name

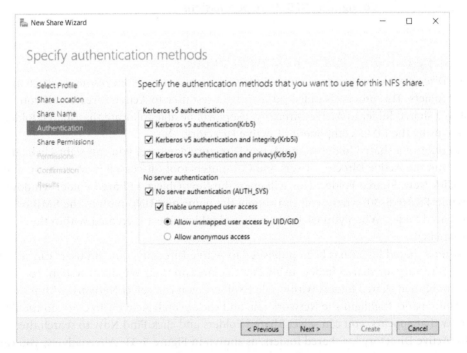

Figure 5-28   Configuring NFS authentication methods

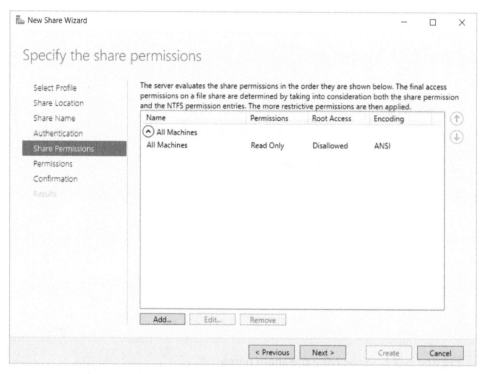

Figure 5-29 Configuring NFS share permissions

Publishing a Shared Folder in Active Directory

Active Directory allows you to create objects that represent network resources, such as shared folders. This process is called **publishing** a resource to Active Directory. If you publish a shared folder to Active Directory, users will be able to locate that shared folder quickly using the LDAP component of Active Directory.

To publish a shared folder to the Active Directory database, you can right-click an OU within the Active Directory Users and Computers tool (discussed in Module 4), and then click New, Shared Folder. This will open the New Object – Shared Folder window shown in Figure 5-30, where you can supply the name and UNC path to the SMB or NFS shared folder. When you click OK, a shared folder object is created within the associated OU.

After a shared folder has been published to Active Directory, domain users can search Active Directory for shared folders using File Explorer on their Windows system. To locate published shared folders within File Explorer, you can select Network within the navigation pane, highlight the Network tab, and click Search Active Directory. In the Find window that appears, you can select Shared Folders and click Find Now to search the entire Active Directory for shared folders, as shown in Figure 5-31. Alternatively, you can narrow the search results by specifying additional criteria. For example, you can supply

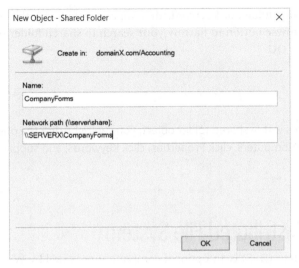

Figure 5-30   Publishing a shared folder to Active Directory

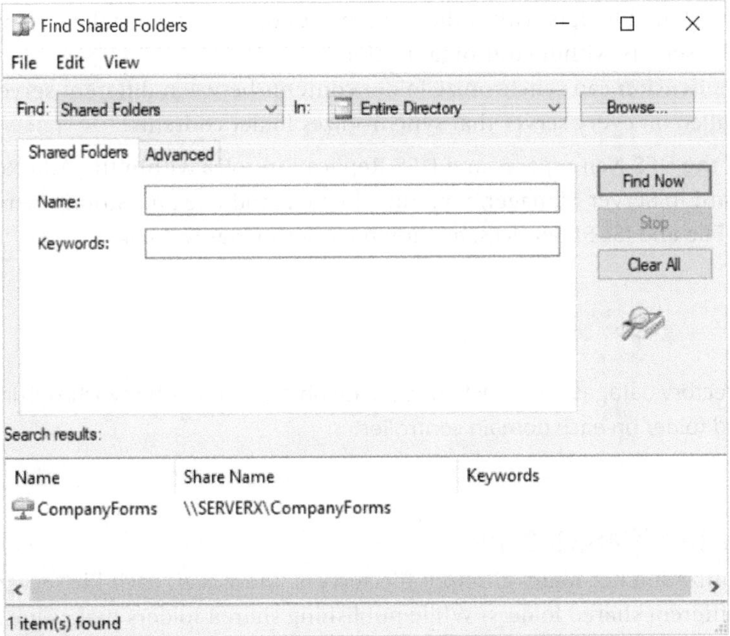

Figure 5-31   Searching for published shared folders within File Explorer

the name of the shared folder, or keywords that are associated with the shared folder. You can also click the Browse button to narrow your search to shared folder objects within a particular domain or OU.

> **Note**
>
> To associate keywords with a shared folder object, you can right-click the object within Active Directory Users and Computers, click Properties, click Keywords, and supply the appropriate keywords.

Implementing Distributed File System

Distributed File System (DFS) is an optional component provided by Windows Server 2019 that delivers additional functionality for accessing and managing content on file servers. Two separate server roles comprise DFS; each of these roles work independently of the other but can be managed using the same **DFS Management** tool:

- **DFS Namespaces** provides a central location from which users can access the different shared folders within their organization. It can be installed on one or more file servers within your organization.
- **DFS Replication** can synchronize folder contents between different servers. It must be installed on every server that synchronizes folder contents.

To install the DFS Namespaces and DFS Replication roles within the Add Roles and Features Wizard in Server Manager, you must first expand File and Storage Services, and then expand File and iSCSI Services, as shown earlier in Figure 5-24.

> **Note**
>
> The Active Directory database uses DFS to replicate object changes by synchronizing the SYSVOL shared folder on each domain controller.

Configuring DFS Namespaces

A typical organization has many different file servers. Moreover, each file server usually hosts many different shared folders. While publishing shared folders makes it easier for users to locate a specific shared folder, it does not provide an easy way to browse the available shared folders within the organization. By installing DFS namespaces on a Windows Server 2019 system, you can create a **DFS namespace** shared folder that users can access. After accessing the DFS namespace folder, users will see subfolders (called **targets**) that represent the shared folders on the file servers within the organization.

In this way, the DFS namespace folder provides a visual representation of multiple shared folders on the network. When users navigate to a target, they are automatically forwarded to the associated shared folder on the network.

> **Note** 📎
>
> You can think of a DFS namespace as a home page for some or all of the shared folders within your organization. Just as users can navigate to a home page within their Web browser and click hyperlinks that take them to different websites on the Internet, they can access a DFS namespace within File Explorer and double-click targets that connect them to different shared folders on the network.

> **Note** 📎
>
> You can have multiple DFS namespaces within an organization that each provide a unique list of targets. By default, you can create up to 5000 targets within a single DFS namespace.

To configure a DFS namespace, you can select DFS Management from the tools menu of Server Manager to start the DFS Management tool shown in Figure 5-32. Next, you can click New Namespace within the Actions pane and specify the name of the server that will host the DFS namespace within the New Namespace Wizard, as shown in Figure 5-33.

When you click Next in Figure 5-33, you will be prompted for the shared folder name for the DFS namespace, as shown in Figure 5-34. Most organizations choose a name that includes their business unit name, or the word *public*, *common*, *root*, or *warehouse*

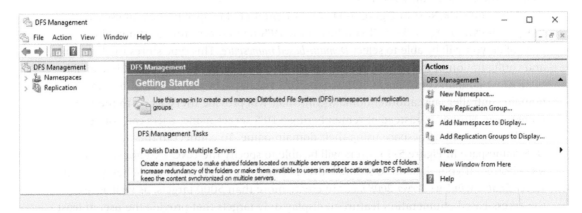

Figure 5-32   **The DFS Management tool**

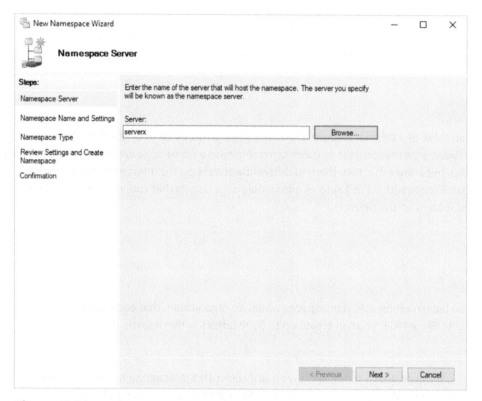

Figure 5-33   The New Namespace Wizard

(which represents "data warehouse"). By default, the path for the warehouse shared folder shown in Figure 5-34 is C:\DFSRoots\warehouse, and users will receive read-only permission to it, such that they cannot add content directly underneath the DFS namespace. However, you can click Edit Settings in Figure 5-34 to modify the path and share permissions to suit your needs.

After you click Next in Figure 5-34, you are prompted to specify the namespace type, as shown in Figure 5-35. If you install the DFS namespaces role on a domain controller, you will be able to select *Domain-based namespace*. This type stores the location and configuration of the DFS namespace within Active Directory, such that it is available to all other domain controllers that have the DFS namespaces role installed. If a single domain controller fails, another domain controller will provide users access to the DFS namespace. Moreover, instead of remembering a DFS server name, users can connect to a domain-based namespace using their domain name. To connect to the warehouse DFS namespace in Figure 5-35, users will be able to specify the UNC \\domainX.com\ warehouse. If your domain functional level is Windows Server 2008 or higher, you can select *Enable Windows Server 2008 mode* to create more than 5000 targets, as well as use the access-based enumeration feature to display only targets that provide the user at least Read share and NTFS/ReFS permission.

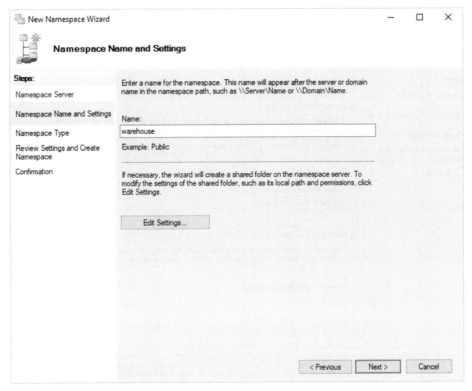

Figure 5-34   Specifying the shared folder name and settings

The *Stand-alone namespace* option in Figure 5-35 stores the namespace configuration on the local file server and is the only option available if the file server is not a domain controller. In this case, users will need to specify the server name within a UNC (e.g., \\serverx\warehouse in Figure 5-35) in order to access the DFS namespace shared folder.

Note @

The access-based enumeration feature is not enabled by default after you create a DFS namespace. To enable it, you can highlight the DFS namespace within the DFS Management tool and click Properties from the Actions pane. Next, you can highlight the Advanced tab and select Enable access-based enumeration for this namespace.

After you click Next in Figure 5-35, you can click Create to create the DFS namespace. Next, you can add targets to the DFS namespace that represent the shared folders within your organization. To add a target to your DFS namespace within the DFS Management tool, you can highlight your DFS namespace and click New Folder in the Actions pane. This will display the New Folder window shown in Figure 5-36, where you

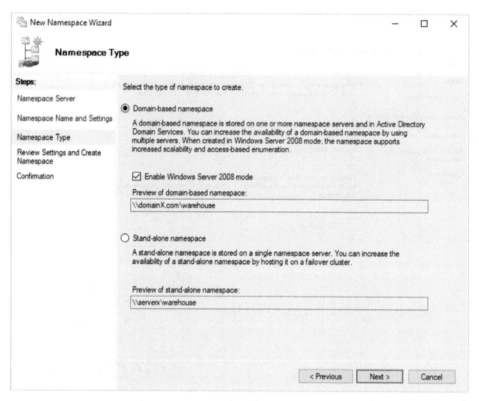

Figure 5-35   Specifying the namespace type

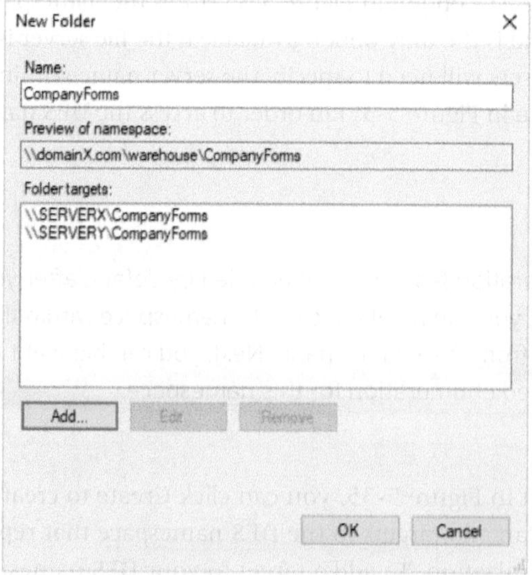

Figure 5-36   Adding a target to a DFS namespace

can specify a target name and the UNC of one or more shared folders on the network that contain the associated content. The CompanyForms target shown in Figure 5-36 will only appear once under the DFS namespace. However, users that select the CompanyForms target will be forwarded to the CompanyForms share on the server (either SERVERX or SERVERY) that is within their Active Directory site, or closer to their Active Directory site after site link costs are calculated. If both SERVERX and SERVERY are located in the same Active Directory site, the target will alternate the forwarding of clients to the CompanyForms share on SERVERX and SERVERY to distribute the load.

Configuring DFS Replication

To configure folders on two or more file servers to synchronize contents, you must first create a **DFS replication group**. To create a DFS replication group, you can click New Replication Group within the DFS Management console shown in Figure 5-32 and specify the appropriate settings within the New Replication Group wizard. However, if you add a target that contains more than one UNC to a DFS namespace, the DFS Management tool will give you the option to automatically create a replication group that keeps the content within each shared folder synchronized using DFS replication. Thus, if you click OK in Figure 5-36 and then click Yes when prompted to create a replication group, the Replicate Folder Wizard shown in Figure 5-37 will create a replication group and prompt you for

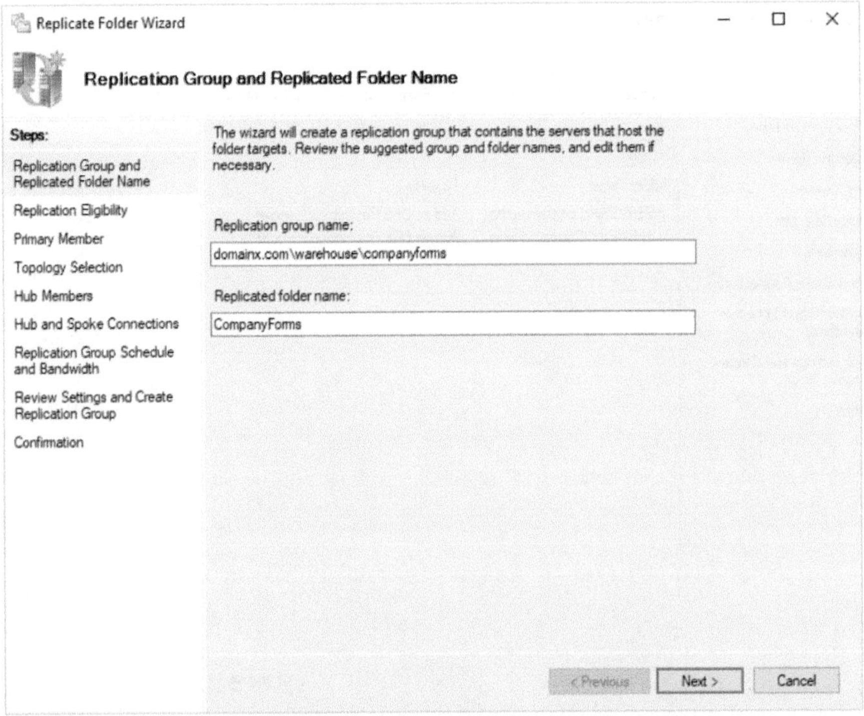

Figure 5-37   The Replicate Folder Wizard

the remaining configuration. The replication group and folder name shown in Figure 5-37 are provided by default, but you have the option to change their values.

When you click Next in Figure 5-37, the replicated folders on each server will be displayed, as shown in Figure 5-38. If the folders on each server contain files with identical names and different contents, the initial DFS replication will need to ensure that one copy overwrites the other. When you click Next in Figure 5-38, you can select the server whose file contents should overwrite other copies during the initial DFS replication, as shown in Figure 5-39.

After clicking Next in Figure 5-39, you will be prompted to select the DFS replication topology as shown in Figure 5-40. The *Full mesh* topology selected in Figure 5-40 allows each server within the replication group to replicate directly to all other members, consuming additional network bandwidth as a result. If you have three or more members within the replication group, selecting *Hub and spoke* will force replication to occur via a central member to minimize network traffic.

To ensure that replicated folder contents are updated immediately, the DFS replication service runs at all times of the day on each server within the replication group by default. Moreover, the DFS replication service is permitted by default to use all

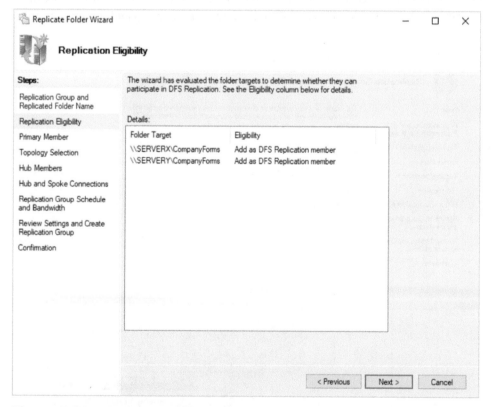

Figure 5-38   **Verifying replicated folders**

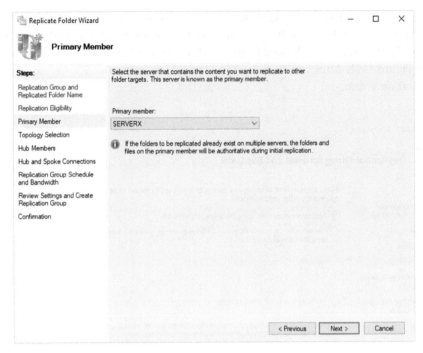

Figure 5-39   Selecting the primary member

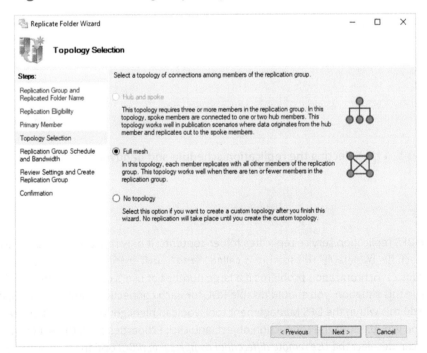

Figure 5-40   Selecting the replication topology

available network bandwidth provided by the network interface of each system. However, when you click Next in Figure 5-40, you can optionally restrict the days and times that the DFS replication service is allowed to run, and the network bandwidth it can use, as shown in Figure 5-41. After you click Next in Figure 5-41, you can click Create to create your replication group.

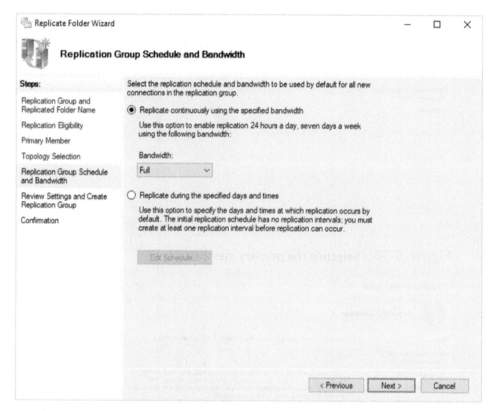

Figure 5-41   Selecting the replication schedule and bandwidth

Note

When the DFS replication service replicates folder contents, it only replicates the changes made to each file by default. This feature is called **remote differential compression (RDC)**, and can cause synchronization problems if a large number of users continually modify the same file. In this situation, you should disable RDC for each connection within the replication group. To do this within the DFS Management tool, you can highlight the Connections tab for a replication group, select the connection object, and click Properties from the Actions pane. Next, you can deselect the *Use remote differential compression (RDC)* option.

> **Note** 📎
>
> The DFS replication service uses a temporary folder called the **DFS staging folder** to store files that need to replicate to other systems. By default, the size of this folder is limited to 4 GB on each system. To prevent poor replication performance, you should ensure that the DFS staging folder limit can accommodate the 32 largest files within the replicated folder. To change the size limit for the DFS staging folder within the DFS Management tool, you can highlight the Memberships tab for a replication group, select the folder, and click Properties from the Actions pane. Next, you can select the Staging tab and supply the correct value within the Quota text box.

> **Note** 📎
>
> You can use the `dfsutil.exe` MS-DOS command to configure and manage DFS. Additionally, there are a large number of Windows PowerShell cmdlets that can be used to manage DFS. Search PowerShell DFSN (for DFS Namespace) and PowerShell DFSR (for DFS Replication) on docs.microsoft.com for more information.

Implementing Quotas and File Screens

When you share folders on an NTFS filesystem that provide permissions for users to add files and subfolders, you may need to configure additional restrictions on the size and type of files that users can add. These restrictions can prevent users from consuming too much space on your file server, or block users from adding the wrong type of files to shared folders. NTFS provides three features that allow you to restrict the content that users can store within folders on the filesystem:

- **User quotas** can be configured to limit the space that users can consume within the filesystem.
- **Folder quotas** can be configured to limit the space consumed by a folder on the filesystem.
- **File screens** can be configured to prevent certain types of files (such as audio and video files) from being stored within a folder on the filesystem.

Before configuring folder quotas and file screens, you must first install the File Server Resource Manager server role on your file server. To install this server role within the Add Roles and Features Wizard in Server Manager, you must first expand File and Storage Services, and then expand File and iSCSI Services, as shown earlier in Figure 5-24.

Configuring User Quotas

NTFS user quotas are not enabled on each filesystem by default. To enable NTFS quotas for a filesystem, you can right-click the root folder of a filesystem (e.g., C:\) within File Explorer, click Properties, highlight the Quota tab, and select the appropriate options. The options shown in Figure 5-42 prevent users from storing more than 2 GB on the C:\ filesystem. Furthermore, users receive a warning when they reach 1.5 GB of storage, and an event will be logged to the Windows Server 2019 **System log**.

You can also click the Quota Entries button to provide specific quota options for individual users and groups that override the default options shown in Figure 5-42. By default, members of the Administrators group receive no limits.

Figure 5-42   Configuring user quotas

Note

You can access the Windows Server 2019 System log using the `Get-EventLog System` command within Windows PowerShell, or by using the Event Viewer tool.

Configuring Folder Quotas

Folder quotas can be configured to prevent users from storing files after a limit has been reached (called a **hard quota**) or allow the limit to be surpassed (called a **soft quota**). Moreover, when a percentage of the limit has been reached, folder quotas can be configured to email a user, log an event to the Windows Server 2019 System log, run a command, or generate a report. To configure folder quotas, you can select File Server Resource Manager from the Tools menu within Server Manager to start the File Server Resource Manager tool shown in Figure 5-43. The Quota Management section within the navigation pane of the File Server Resource Manager tool contains two subfolders:

- *Quotas* stores quota entries for folders on NTFS filesystems. There are no quota entries configured in this folder by default.
- *Quota Templates* stores templates that contain quota settings that can be used to simplify the creation of new quota entries. There exist several default quota templates within this folder.

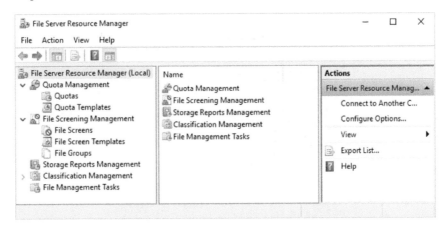

Figure 5-43   The File Server Resource Manager tool

To create a new folder quota, you can highlight the Quotas folder with the File Server Resource Manager tool, click Create Quota within the Actions pane, and specify the appropriate folder path and settings, as shown in Figure 5-44. The quota for the C:\ CompanyForms folder shown in Figure 5-44 prevents the folder from storing more than 5 GB of content, emails a warning to the user who reaches 85% and 100% of the 5 GB limit, as well as logs an event to the Windows Server 2019 System log when the 5 GB limit has been reached. To modify these settings, you can click the Custom Properties button and select the appropriate options. If you select *Derive properties from this quota template (recommended)* in Figure 5-44, you can select a pre-configured template from the drop-down box to copy the quota settings from that template. Additionally, you can select *Auto apply template and create quotas on existing and new subfolders* to create folder quotas on existing and new subfolders of C:\CompanyForms based on the template you chose. When you click Create in Figure 5-44, you can optionally save your quota settings in a new quota template for future use, as shown in Figure 5-45.

Note

Because folder quotas consume few system resources, most IT administrators prefer them to user quotas.

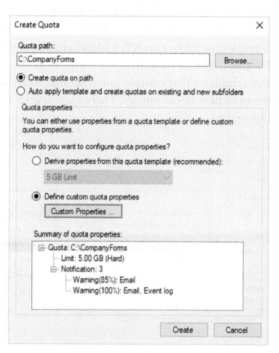

Figure 5-44 Configuring a new folder quota

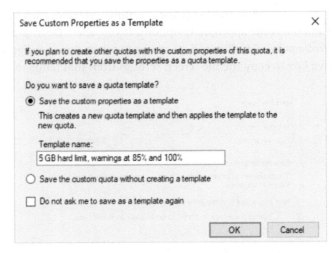

Figure 5-45   Creating a folder quota template from folder quota settings

Configuring File Screens

File screens can be used to prevent users from storing files of a certain category within folders on an NTFS volume (called an **active screening**), or log an event when this occurs (called **passive screening**). Each category is called a **file group**, and consists of one or more filename extensions. For example, the default Text Files file group consists of files that end with .asc, .text, and .txt. Moreover, when an active or passive screening event occurs, file screens can be configured to email a user, log an event to the Windows Server 2019 System log, run a command, or generate a report.

As with folder quotas, you configure file screens within the File Server Resource Manager tool. The File Screening Management section within the navigation pane of the File Server Resource Manager tool (shown in Figure 5-43) contains three subfolders:

- *File Screens* stores file screen entries for folders on NTFS filesystems. There are no file screen entries configured by default.
- *File Screen Templates* stores templates that contain file screen settings that can be used to simplify the creation of new file screens. There exist several default file screen templates within this folder.
- *File Groups* stores file groups that identify file categories by filename extension. The default file groups stored within this folder include Audio and Video Files, Backup Files, Compressed Files, E-mail Files, Executable Files, Image Files, Office Files, System Files, Temporary Files, Text Files, and Web Page Files.

To create a new file screen, you can highlight the File Screens folder with the File Server Resource Manager tool, click Create File Screen within the Actions pane, and specify the appropriate folder path and settings, as shown in Figure 5-46. The file screen for the C:\CompanyForms folder shown in Figure 5-46 prevents the folder from storing audio, video, and executable files. To modify these settings, you can click the Custom Properties button and select the appropriate options. If you select *Derive properties from this file screen template (recommended)* in Figure 5-46, you can select a pre-configured template from the drop-down box to copy the file screen settings from that template.

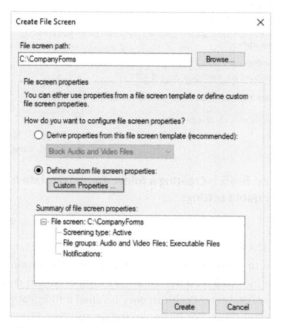

Figure 5-46   Configuring a new file screen

 Note

As when creating folder quotas, you will be prompted to optionally save your file screen settings in a new file screen template for future use when you click Create in Figure 5-46.

Note

User quotas can also be created and managed using the `fsutil.exe` MS-DOS command. There also exist many Windows PowerShell cmdlets that can be used to configure and manage folder quotas and file screens. Search PowerShell FsrmQuota (for file quotas) and PowerShell FsrmFileScreen (for file screens) on docs.microsoft.com for more information.

Module Summary

- Folders and files on filesystems can contain attributes that provide for different filesystem features. All filesystems support the read-only, hidden, and archive attributes. The FAT32, exFAT, and NTFS filesystems support the encrypt attribute, and NTFS additionally supports the index and compress attributes.

- Windows Server 2019 uses discretionary access control lists (DACLs) for managing access to folders and files on NTFS and ReFS volumes and system access control lists (SACLs) for auditing access to folders and files.

- DACLs grant or deny permissions to groups and users. Users receive the basic or advanced permissions assigned to their user account as well as any group accounts to which they belong. Deny permissions take precedence over allow permissions.

- Members of the Administrators group, users that have Full Control permission, and the owner of a folder or file are able to modify ownership and permissions.

- If an audit policy is enabled, folders and files will log events to the Security log according to the audit entries configured within the SACL.

- To allow network users to access files on a file server, the folder that contains the files must be shared using SMB or NFS, and shared folder permissions must be configured. SMB shared folder permissions are assigned to groups and users, whereas NFS shared permissions are assigned to computers.

- After connecting to a shared folder on an NTFS/ReFS filesystem, users are further restricted by the permissions within the DACL on each folder and file.

- DFS namespaces can be configured to provide a central location for users to access the shared folders on your network. If integrated with Active Directory, domain users can use their domain name within a UNC to connect to DFS namespaces.

- By configuring a replication group, DFS replication can be used to keep the contents of folders on different file servers synchronized for ease and fault tolerance.

- Quotas can be used to limit the amount of space that files can consume. User quotas limit the space user files can consume on an NTFS filesystem, whereas folder quotas limit the space consumed by specific folders on an NTFS filesystem.

- File screens can be applied to folders on an NTFS filesystem to limit the type of files that can be stored.

Key Terms

access-based enumeration
active screening
asymmetric encryption
attribute
audit policy
BranchCache

Client for NFS
Common Internet File
  System (CIFS)
DFS Management
DFS namespace
DFS Namespaces

DFS Replication
DFS replication group
DFS staging folder
discretionary access control
  list (DACL)
Encrypting File System (EFS)

encryption algorithm	metadata	shared folder permission
Event Viewer	Network File System (NFS)	soft quota
File Explorer	offline file caching	symmetric encryption
file group	passive screening	system access control list
file screens	private key	(SACL)
File Server Resource	public key	System log
Manager	publishing	target
folder quota	recovery agent	Universal Naming
group ID (GID)	remote differential	Convention (UNC)
Group Policy Management	compression (RDC)	user ID (UID)
Group Policy Management	Security log	user quota
Editor	security principal	Windows Explorer
hard quota	Server for NFS	Windows Indexing Service
index	Server Message Block	Windows Search Service
key	(SMB)	

Review Questions

1. Which of the following occurs when you encrypt a file using EFS within a domain environment? (Choose all that apply.)
   a. An asymmetric private key is generated and used to encrypt the file contents
   b. A copy of the symmetric encryption key is stored within the file metadata and asymmetrically encrypted with your public key
   c. A symmetric encryption key is generated and used to encrypt the file contents
   d. A copy of the symmetric encryption key is stored within the file metadata and asymmetrically encrypted with recovery agent's public key

2. Only the NTFS filesystem supports all of the basic and advanced attributes for folders and files. True or False?

3. Which of the following can be used to set the compress attribute for an NTFS file? (Choose all that apply.)
   a. `Set-ItemProperty`
   b. `cipher.exe`

   c. `compress.exe`
   d. `compact.exe`

4. Which of the following basic NTFS/ReFS permissions allows you to delete a file? (Choose all that apply.)
   a. Full control
   b. Modify
   c. Write
   d. Read and execute

5. You wish to grant a specific user the ability to view the read-only attribute on files within a particular folder on the system, but do not wish to grant any other access. What advanced permission should you assign to this user?
   a. Traverse folder/execute file
   b. Read attributes
   c. Read extended attributes
   d. Read permissions

6. You can use the `Set-ACL` cmdlet within Windows PowerShell to configure entries within a DACL or SACL. True or False?

7. Your organization maintains a shared folder called PrivateHR that only the

HumanResources-G and Domain Admins groups have access to. You wish to audit each time a member of the HumanResources-G group successfully modifies or deletes a file within this folder. What must you do? (Choose all that apply.)

a. Configure an audit entry within the SACL of the PrivateHR folder that allows the Modify permission for the HumanResources-G group

b. Configure the audit attribute on the PrivateHR folder

c. Configure an audit entry within the SACL of the PrivateHR folder that audits the Modify permission for the HumanResources-G group

d. Enable success auditing for the system using an audit policy

8. Which of the following Windows logs stores auditing events?

a. System

b. Application

c. Security

d. Auditing

9. You are about to move an EFS-encrypted file called SecureData.xml from a folder on an NTFS volume to a folder on a ReFS volume. Which of the following statements are true regarding the permissions and encryption on the file following the move operation? (Choose all that apply.)

a. SecureData.xml will retain its original permissions following the move operation

b. SecureData.xml will remain encrypted following the move operation

c. SecureData.xml will inherit the permissions from the target folder following the move operation

d. The SecureData.xml will be not be encrypted following the move operation

10. The *View effective access* tab within the Advanced Security Settings window for a folder or file can be used to view the groups that have access to a particular folder or file. True or False?

11. You have shared a folder using SMB and assigned members of the Accounting group Full Control shared folder permission. One of the members of the Accounting group complains that they get an access denied message when attempting to access files within the shared folder. What are two possible causes of this issue? (Choose two answers.)

a. The shared folder is on an FAT32 or exFAT volume, and the DACL on the files denies access to a group to which the user belongs

b. The shared folder is on an FAT32 or exFAT volume, and the DACL on the files does not allow the user access

c. The shared folder is on an NTFS or ReFS volume, and the DACL on the files denies access to a group to which the user belongs

d. The shared folder is on an NTFS or ReFS volume, and the DACL on the files does not allow the user access

12. Windows systems that have the Client for NFS installed can access an NFS shared folder by browsing the network or specifying the shared folder's UNC. True or False?

13. You would like to share a folder that uses the access-based enumeration feature. What must you do?

a. Share the folder using SMB by accessing folder properties

b. Share the folder using SMB using Server Manager.

c. Share the folder using NFS by accessing folder properties.

d. Share the folder using NFS using Server Manager.

14. Which of the following NFS shared folder permissions allows computers to access an NFS shared folder and modify content?

a. Full Control

b. Change

c. Read-Write

d. Modify

15. Both NFS and SMB shared folders can be published to Active Directory. True or False?

16. You would like to provide a central shared folder that users can access to view all other shared folders within the organization. What must you do? (Choose all that apply.)

a. Install the DFS Namespaces role and configure a DFS namespace

b. Configure a replication group

c. Add targets to the DFS namespace for each shared folder

d. Install the DFS Replication role on each file server

17. You are configuring a DFS replication group to synchronize folder contents between four file servers. To minimize the network bandwidth used by DFS replication, you should choose a Full mesh topology for your replication group. True or False?

18. You have a large number of users that access the same files within a shared folder that is replicated to another shared folder on the network using DFS replication. Users often report problems with missing content in the files that they access within the shared folder, and that changes take a long time to propagate from one shared folder to the other. What two actions can you take to address these issues? (Choose two answers.)

a. Add a shared folder on a third file server to the replication group

b. Disable remote differential compression (RDC) on the connections within the replication group

c. Increase the size limit of the DFS staging folder for each member of the replication group

d. Modify the replication group settings to use a Full mesh topology for replication

19. Which of the following features are provided by the File Server Resource Manager server role? (Choose all that apply.)

a. File screens

b. Access-based enumeration

c. Folder quotas

d. User quotas

20. You can use soft quotas to provide warnings to users that exceed folder quotas, while not restricting their ability to add content to a folder. True or False?

Hands-On Projects

These Hands-On Projects should be completed in the order given and normally take a total of three hours or less to complete. The requirements for these projects include:

- A system with Windows Server 2019 installed according to Hands-On Project 1-1 (Lab Environment 1) or Hands-On Project 1-2 (Lab Environment 2).
- A WindowsServer2019VM2 virtual machine installed according to Hands-On Project 3-5.

Project 5-1: Host Setup

In this Hands-On Project, you install the server roles and features on your Windows Server 2019 host required for the remaining Hands-On Projects within this module, including the Server for NFS, Client for NFS, File Server Resource Manager, DFS Namespaces, and DFS Replication.

1. Boot your Windows Server 2019 host and log into domain*X*.com as Administrator using the password **Secret555**. Next, click **Start** and then click **Server Manager**.
2. Within Server Manager, click the **Manage** menu and then click **Add Roles and Features**.
3. At the Select installation type page, click **Next**.
4. At the Select destination server page, click **Next**.
5. At the Select server roles page, expand **File and Storage Services**, and then expand **File and iSCSI Services**.

   a. Select **Server for NFS** and click **Add Features** when prompted.

   b. Select **File Server Resource Manager** and click **Add Features** when prompted.

   c. Select **DFS Namespaces** and click **Add Features** when prompted.

   d. Select **DFS Replication**.

6. Click **Next**.
7. At the Select features page, select **Client for NFS** and click **Next**.
8. At the Confirm installation selections page, click **Install** to install the Server for NFS, File Server Resource Manager, DFS Namespaces, and DFS Replication server roles, as well as the Client for NFS feature.
9. At the Installation progress page, click **Close**.

Project 5-2: Member Server Setup

In this Hands-On Project, you configure your WindowsServer2019VM2 virtual machine as a member server within your Active Directory domain, and then install the DFS Replication role required for Hands-On Project 5-7.

1. Within Server Manager on your Windows Server 2019 host, select the **Tools** menu and then click **Hyper-V Manager**.
2. Highlight **WindowsServer2019VM2** within the Virtual Machines pane and click **Settings** in the Actions pane.

   a. Highlight **Legacy Network Adapter** under the Hardware section.

   b. Select **External Virtual Switch** from the Virtual switch drop-down box to connect your virtual network interface to the external virtual network.

   c. Click **OK**.

3. Highlight **WindowsServer2019VM2** within the virtual machines pane of Hyper-V Manager and click **Connect** in the Actions pane. In the Virtual Machine Connection window, click **Start** to boot your new virtual machine.
4. At the login screen, click the **Ctrl+Alt+Delete** button within the Virtual Machine Connection window, supply the password **Secret555** for Administrator and press **Enter** to log into the system.

5. Click **Start** and then click **Server Manager**. Within Server Manager, click **Local Server** within the navigation pane.

  a. Click the hyperlink next to your Ethernet network interface.

  b. In the Network Connections window, right-click **Ethernet** and click **Properties**.

  c. Highlight **Internet Protocol Version 4 (TCP/IPv4)** within the Ethernet Properties window and click **Properties**. If your network environment requires manual IPv4 configuration, select **Use the following IP address** and supply the correct IP address, subnet mask, and default gateway.

  d. Next, select **Use the following DNS server addresses** and supply the IP address of your Windows Server 2019 host in the Preferred DNS server input area. Click **OK** when finished.

  e. Click **OK**. Click **OK** again to close the Ethernet Properties window.

  f. Close the Network Connections window.

  g. Click the **WORKGROUP** hyperlink within the Properties pane of Server Manager.

  h. At the System Properties window, note your computer name. Next, click **Change**.

  i. At the Computer Name/Domain Changes window, select **Domain**, type **domainX.com** in the text box and click **OK**.

  j. At the Windows Security window, supply the user name **administrator@domainX.com** and password **Secret555** and click **OK**.

  k. Click **OK** at the Computer Name/Domain Changes information window, and then click **OK** again when prompted that you must restart your computer to complete the domain join.

  l. Click **Close** to close the System Properties window and click **Restart Now** when prompted to reboot your virtual machine.

6. After your virtual machine has rebooted, click the **Ctrl+Alt+Delete** button within the Virtual Machine Connection window and then click **Other user**. Supply the user name **administrator@domainX.com** and password **Secret555** for the Administrator user within **domainX.com** and press **Enter** to log into the system.

> **Note** 🔗
>
> Recall from Module 4 that domain-joined computers retain their SAM database. If you log in as the Administrator account after joining a computer to a domain, you will be logging into the system using the local Administrator account and will not be able to access domain resources. As a result, the first time you log into a member server after joining a domain, you must click Other user and supply the appropriate UPN to log in as a domain user account.

7. At the Server Manager information window, select **Don't show this message again** and close the window.

8. Within Server Manager, click the **Manage** menu and then click **Server Manager Properties**. Select **Do not start Server Manager automatically at logon** and click **OK**.

9. Within Server Manager, click the **Manage** menu and then click **Add Roles and Features**.

a. At the Select installation type page, click **Next**.

b. At the Select destination server page, click **Next**.

c. At the Select server roles page, expand **File and Storage Services** and then expand **File and iSCSI Services**. Select **DFS Replication** and click **Add Features** when prompted.

d. Click **Next**.

e. At the Select features page, click **Next**.

f. At the Confirm installation selections page, click **Install** to install the DFS Replication role.

g. At the Installation progress page, click **Close**.

10. Close Server Manager.

Project 5-3: Permissions

In this Hands-On Project, you configure and verify NTFS permissions on your Windows Server 2019 host.

1. On your Windows Server 2019 host, click **Start** and then click **File Explorer**.

2. In the navigation pane of File Explorer, expand **This PC** if necessary and highlight **Local Disk (C:)**.

3. Click the **Home** menu and then click **New folder**. Type **MarketingMaterials** and press **Enter**.

4. Right-click the **MarketingMaterials** folder and click **Properties**.

a. Highlight the **Security** tab within the MarketingMaterials Properties window and note the default permissions assigned to the different groups on the system.

b. Click **Advanced**. At the Advanced Security Settings for MarketingMaterials window, note that the owner of the folder is the Administrators group.

c. Click **Disable inheritance** and then click **Remove all inherited permissions from this object** when prompted. Click **OK** and then click **Yes** when prompted to close the Advanced Security Settings for MarketingMaterials window.

d. In the MarketingMaterials Properties window, note that all default permissions inherited from C:\ have been removed and click **Edit**.

e. At the Permissions for MarketingMaterials window, click **Add**. Type **Domain Admins** and click **OK**. Select **Full control** under the Allow permissions column. Click **Add** again. Type **Marketing-G** and click **OK**. Select **Modify** under the Allow permissions column and click **OK**.

f. Click **Advanced**. At the Advanced Security Settings for MarketingMaterials window, highlight the **Marketing-G** permission entry and click **Edit**. Next, click **Show advanced permissions**, note the advanced permissions that comprise the basic Modify permission, and click **OK**. Click **OK** to close the Advanced Security Settings for MarketingMaterials window.

g. Click **OK** to close the MarketingMaterials Properties window.

5. Double-click the **MarketingMaterials** folder. Next, click the **Home** menu, select the **New item** drop-down box, and click **Text Document**. Type **File1** and press **Enter** to create a File1.txt file within the MarketingMaterials folder.

6. Click the **Home** menu, select the **New item** drop-down box, and click **Text Document**. Type **File2** and press **Enter** to create a File2.txt file within the MarketingMaterials folder.

7. Right-click **File2** and click **Properties**.

   a. Highlight the **Security** tab within the File2 Properties window and note the default permissions inherited from the MarketingMaterials folder.

   b. Click **Edit**. At the Permissions for File2 window, click **Add**. Type **Bob Burtt** and click **OK**. Select **Modify** under the Deny permissions column and click **OK**. Read the contents of the Windows Security window and click **Yes**.

   c. Click **OK** to close the File2 Properties window.

   d. Click **Advanced**. At the Advanced Security Settings for File2 window, highlight the **Effective Access** tab. Recall that both Bob Burtt and Mary Stewart are both members of the Marketing-G group (configured within Hands-On Project 4-7).

   e. Click **Select a user**, type **Bob Burtt,** and click **OK**. Next, click **View effective access** and note that Bob Burtt is denied all access because the permissions denied to the Bob Burtt user account override the permissions granted to the Marketing-G group.

   f. Click **Select a user**, type **Mary Stewart,** and click **OK**. Next, click **View effective access** and note that Mary Stewart receives the advanced permissions that comprise the basic Modify permission granted to members of the Marketing-G group.

   g. Click **OK** to close the Advanced Security Settings for File2 window.

   h. Click **OK** to close the File2 Properties window.

8. Right-click the Start menu and choose **Windows PowerShell (Admin)** to open Windows PowerShell. Next, type `Add-ADGroupMember -Identity "Backup Operators" -Members "Marketing-G"` and press **Enter** to add the Marketing-G global group as a member of the Backup Operators built-in group. Close Windows PowerShell when finished.

Note 📎

While any member of the Domain Users group is assigned the right to log in locally to any computer that is joined to an Active Directory domain, domain controllers receive a Group Policy that restricts users from logging in locally to a domain controller computer unless they are a member of a group that has administrative rights in the domain, such as Backup Operators. To ensure that you can log in locally to your Windows Server 2019 host as Bob Burtt to test permission assignments, you added the Marketing-G group to the Backup Operators group in this step.

9. Right-click the **Start** menu and click **Shut down or sign out** and then click **Sign out**.

   a. Press **Ctrl+Alt+Delete** (or the Ctrl+Alt+Delete button within the Virtual Machine Connection window if you use Lab Environment 2) and then click **Other user**.

   b. Supply a user name of **b.burtt@domainX.com** and password of **Secret555** and press **Enter**.

   c. When prompted to change your password, click **OK**. Type **NewPassword555** in both password text boxes and press **Enter**.

   d. Click **OK** to continue to log into the system.

10. Click **Start** and then click **File Explorer**.

    a. In the navigation pane of File Explorer, expand **This PC**, **Local Disk (C:)** and highlight **MarketingMaterials**.

    b. Double-click **File1** to open it within Notepad. Type a line of your choice, click the **File** menu and then click **Save**. Close Notepad when finished.

    c. Double-click **File2** and note the error message that you receive. Click **OK** and close Notepad.

11. Right-click the **Start** menu and click **Shut down or sign out** and then click **Sign out**.

    a. Press **Ctrl+Alt+Delete** (or the Ctrl+Alt+Delete button within the Virtual Machine Connection window if you use Lab Environment 2) and then click **Other user**.

    b. Supply a user name of **administrator@domainX.com** and password of **Secret555** and press **Enter** to log into the system.

Project 5-4: Auditing

In this Hands-On Project, you enable, configure, and test file auditing on your Windows Server 2019 host.

1. On your Windows Server 2019 host, click **Start** and then click **Server Manager**.

2. Within Server Manager, click the **Tools** menu and then click **Group Policy Management**.

   a. Within the navigation pane of the Group Policy Management window, expand **Forest: domainX.com**, **Domains**, **domainX.com**.

   b. Right-click **Default Domain Policy** and click **Edit**.

   c. In the navigation pane of the Group Policy Management Editor window, expand **Computer Configuration**, **Policies**, **Windows Settings**, **Security Settings**, **Local Policies**, and highlight **Audit Policy**.

   d. Double-click **Audit object access** in the right pane. In the Audit object access Properties window, select **Define these policy settings**. Next, select **Failure** and click **OK**.

   e. Close the Group Policy Management Editor window and then close the Group Policy Management window.

3. Click **Start** and then click **File Explorer**.

4. In the navigation pane of File Explorer, expand **This PC**, **Local Disk (C:)** and highlight **MarketingMaterials**.

5. Right-click **File2** and click **Properties**.

   a. Highlight the **Security** tab within the File2 Properties window and click **Advanced**.

   b. At the Advanced Security Settings for File2 window, highlight the **Auditing** tab. Note that no auditing entries are created by default.

   c. Click **Add**. In the Auditing Entry for File2 window, click **Select a principle**, type **Marketing-G,** and click **OK**. Next, select **Fail** from the Type drop-down box, select **Full control** permission within the Basic permissions section, and click **OK**. This will create an auditing entry that records failures of any permission level on File2 for members of the Marketing-G group.

   d. Click **OK** to close the Advanced Security Settings for File2 window.

   e. Click **OK** to close the File2 Properties window.

6. Right-click the **Start** menu and click **Shut down or sign out** and then click **Sign out**.

   a. Press **Ctrl+Alt+Delete** (or the Ctrl+Alt+Delete button within the Virtual Machine Connection window if you use Lab Environment 2) and then click **Other user**.

   b. Supply a user name of **b.burtt@domainX.com** and password of **NewPassword555** and press **Enter** to log into the system.

7. Click **Start** and then click **File Explorer**.

   a. In the navigation pane of File Explorer, expand **This PC**, **Local Disk (C:)** and highlight **MarketingMaterials**.

   b. Double-click **File2** to generate an error message due to denied permissions. Click **OK** and close Notepad.

8. Right-click the **Start** menu and click **Shut down or sign out** and then click **Sign out**.

   a. Press **Ctrl+Alt+Delete** (or the Ctrl+Alt+Delete button within the Virtual Machine Connection window if you use Lab Environment 2) and then click **Other user**.

   b. Supply a user name of **administrator@domainX.com** and password of **Secret555** and press **Enter** to log into the system.

9. Right-click the Start menu and choose **Windows PowerShell (Admin)** to open Windows PowerShell. Next, type `Get-EventLog Security -EntryType FailureAudit -Newest 3 | Format-List` and press **Enter** to view the details for the most recent three failure audit entries within the Security log. Note that Bob Burtt's failed attempt to access File2.txt using Notepad was recorded.

10. Close Windows PowerShell.

Project 5-5: Attributes

In this Hands-On Project, you configure and test file attributes on your Windows Server 2019 host.

1. On your Windows Server 2019 host, click **Start** and then click **File Explorer**.

2. In the navigation pane of File Explorer, expand **This PC**, **Local Disk (C:)** and highlight **MarketingMaterials**.

3. Right-click **File1** and click **Properties**.

   a. On the General tab of File1 Properties, select **Read-only** and **Hidden** and click **Advanced**.

   b. At the Advanced Attributes window, note the attributes selected by default. Select **Compress contents to save disk space** and click **OK**.

   c. Click **OK** to close the File1 Properties window. Note that File1 disappears from view after a few moments.

4. Click the **View** menu within File Explorer and select **Hidden items**. Note that File1 appears again, but has a grey icon with a blue compression arrow symbol.

5. Double-click File1 to open it within Notepad. Type a line of your choice, click the **File** menu, and then click **Save**. Instead of saving the changes, Notepad displays a Save As window that will allow you to save the file to a different file name, because File1 has the read-only attribute. Click **Cancel**, close Notepad, and click **Don't Save** when prompted.

6. Right-click **File1** and click **Properties**.

   a. On the General tab of File1 Properties, deselect **Read-only** and **Hidden** and click **Advanced**.

   b. At the Advanced Attributes window, select **Encrypt contents to secure data**, note that the compression attribute was automatically deselected, and click **OK**.

   c. Click **OK** to close the File1 Properties window. Select **Encrypt the file only** when prompted and click **OK**. Note that the File1 icon now has a yellow lock symbol.

7. Double-click File1 to open it within Notepad. Type a line of your choice, click the **File** menu, and then click **Save**. Close Notepad when finished.

8. Right-click the **Start** menu and click **Shut down or sign out** and then click **Sign out**.

   a. Press **Ctrl+Alt+Delete** (or the Ctrl+Alt+Delete button within the Virtual Machine Connection window if you use Lab Environment 2) and then click **Other user**.

   b. Supply a user name of **b.burtt@domainX.com** and password of **NewPassword555** and press **Enter** to log into the system.

9. Click **Start** and then click **File Explorer**.

   a. In the navigation pane of File Explorer, expand **This PC**, **Local Disk (C:)** and highlight **MarketingMaterials**.

   b. Double-click **File2** and note the error message. Click **OK** and close Notepad.

   c. Click the **Home** tab, select the **New item** drop-down box, and click **Text Document**. Type **File3** and press **Enter** to create a File3.txt file within the MarketingMaterials folder.

   d. Double-click **File3** to open it within Notepad. Type a line of your choice, click the **File** menu and then click **Save**. Close Notepad when finished.

   e. Right-click **File1**, click **Properties**, and then click **Advanced**.

   f. At the Advanced Attributes window, select **Encrypt contents to secure data** and click **OK**.

   g. Click **OK** to close the File1 Properties window. Select **Encrypt the file only** when prompted and click **OK**.

10. Right-click the **Start** menu and click **Shut down or sign out** and then click **Sign out**.

    a. Press **Ctrl+Alt+Delete** (or the Ctrl+Alt+Delete button within the Virtual Machine Connection window if you use Lab Environment 2) and then click **Other user**.

    b. Supply a user name of **administrator@domainX.com** and password of **Secret555** and press **Enter** to log into the system.

11. Click **Start** and then click **File Explorer**.

    a. In the navigation pane of File Explorer, expand **This PC**, **Local Disk (C:)** and highlight **MarketingMaterials**.

    b. Double-click **File3** and note that you were able to access it even though Bob Burtt encrypted it. Close Notepad.

    c. Right-click **File3**, click **Properties**, and then click **Advanced**.

    d. At the Advanced Attributes window, click **Details**, note that Administrator is listed as a recovery agent within the domain by default, and click **OK**.

    e. Click **OK** to close the Advanced Attributes window and click **OK** to close the File3 Properties window.

    f. Right-click **File1**, click **Properties**, and then click **Advanced**.

    g. At the Advanced Attributes window, click **Details**.

    h. At the User Access to File1 window, click **Add**, select **b.burtt@domainX.com,** and click **OK** to allow Bob Burtt to access File1 using EFS.

    i. Click **OK** to close the User Access to File1 window, click **OK** to close the Advanced Attributes window, and click **OK** to close the File1 Properties window.

    j. Close File Explorer.

Project 5-6: Sharing Folders

In this Hands-On Project, you share folders using SMB and NFS.

1. On your Windows Server 2019 host, click **Start** and then click **File Explorer**.

2. In the navigation pane of File Explorer, expand **This PC** and highlight **Local Disk (C:)**.

3. Right-click the **MarketingMaterials** folder and click **Properties**.

    a. Highlight the **Sharing** tab within the MarketingMaterials Properties window and click **Advanced Sharing**.

    b. In the Advanced Sharing window, select **Share this folder** and note the default share name and number of simultaneous connections allowable.

    c. Click **Permissions** and note that the Everyone group has Read shared folder permission by default. Select **Full Control** under the Allow column and click **OK**.

> **Note** 📎
>
> Recall that assigning the special Everyone group Full Control shared folder permission is common practice on NTFS and ReFS volumes that already provide appropriate restrictions for groups and users on the system.

   d. Click **Caching**, note that manual offline file caching is enabled by default, and click **OK**.

   e. Click **OK** to close the Advanced Sharing window and click **Close** to close the MarketingMaterials Properties window.

   f. Close File Explorer.

4. Right-click **Start** and click **Run**. Type **\\serverX\MarketingMaterials** in the Run dialog box and click **OK**. Note that you have access to File1, File2, and File3 using SMB. Optionally modify the content of each file, saving your changes when finished.

5. Highlight **Local Disk (C:)** within the navigation pane of File Explorer.

6. Click the **Home** menu and then click **New folder**. Type **MarketingTemplates** and press **Enter**.

7. Right-click the **MarketingTemplates** folder and click **Properties**.

   a. Highlight the **Security** tab within the MarketingTemplates Properties window and click **Advanced**.

   b. Click **Disable inheritance** and then click **Remove all inherited permissions from this object** when prompted. Click **OK** and then click **Yes** when prompted to close the Advanced Security Settings for MarketingTemplates window.

   c. In the MarketingTemplates Properties window, click **Edit**.

   d. At the Permissions for MarketingTemplates window, click **Add**. Type **Domain Admins** and click **OK**. Select **Full control** under the Allow permissions column. Click **Add** again. Type **Marketing-G** and click **OK**. Note the default assigned permissions and click **OK**.

   e. Highlight the **NFS Sharing** tab within the MarketingTemplates Properties window and click **Manage NFS Sharing**.

   f. In the NFS Advanced Sharing window, select **Share this folder** and note the default share name, encoding, and authentication options.

   g. Click **Permissions** and note the default permission entry that grants all computers Read-Only access to the NFS shared folder. Select **Read-Write** from the Type of access drop-down box and click **OK**.

   h. Click **OK** to close the NFS Advanced Sharing window and click **Close** to close the MarketingTemplates Properties window.

   i. Close File Explorer.

8. Double-click the **MarketingTemplates** folder. Next, click the **Home** menu, select the **New item** drop-down box, and click **Text Document**. Type **File4** and press **Enter** to create a File4.txt file within the MarketingTemplates folder.

9. Right-click **Start** and click **Run**. Type **\\serverX\MarketingTemplates** in the Run dialog box and click **OK**. Note that you have access to File4 using NFS. Optionally modify the content of File4, saving your changes when finished.

10. Close File Explorer.

11. Within Hyper-V Manager on your Windows Server 2019 host, highlight **WindowsServer2019VM2** within the virtual machines pane and click **Connect** in the Actions pane. Click the **Ctrl+Alt+Delete** button within the Virtual Machine Connection

window, supply the password **Secret555** for administrator@domain*X*.com, and press **Enter** to log into the system.

12. Click **Start** and then click **File Explorer**.

13. In the navigation pane of File Explorer, expand **This PC** and highlight **Local Disk (C:)**.

14. Click the **Home** menu and then click **New folder**. Type **MarketingMaterials** and press **Enter**.

15. Right-click the **MarketingMaterials** folder and click **Properties**.

   a. Highlight the **Security** tab within the MarketingMaterials Properties window and click **Advanced**.

   b. At the Advanced Security Settings for MarketingMaterials window, click **Disable inheritance** and then click **Remove all inherited permissions from this object** when prompted. Click **OK** and then click **Yes** when prompted to close the Advanced Security Settings for MarketingMaterials window.

   c. In the MarketingMaterials Properties window, click **Edit**.

   d. At the Permissions for MarketingMaterials window, click **Add**. Type **Domain Admins** and click **OK**. Select **Full control** under the Allow permissions column. Click **Add** again. Type **Marketing-G** and click **OK**. Select **Modify** under the Allow permissions column, and click **OK**.

   e. Highlight the **Sharing** tab within the MarketingMaterials Properties window and click **Advanced Sharing**.

   f. In the Advanced Sharing window, select **Share this folder** and note the default share name and number of simultaneous connections allowable.

   g. Click **Permissions** and note that the Everyone group has Read shared folder permission by default. Select **Full Control** under the Allow column and click **OK**.

   h. Click **OK** to close the Advanced Sharing window and click **Close** to close the MarketingMaterials Properties window.

16. Right-click **Start** and click **Run**. Type ***name*\\MarketingMaterials** in the Run dialog box, where *name* is the computer name of your WindowsServer2019VM2 virtual machine and click **OK**. Note that you have access to the shared folder on the server but there are no contents. We will use this shared folder in the following Hands-On Project.

17. Close File Explorer.

Project 5-7: DFS

In this Hands-On Project, you configure a DFS namespace shared folder to provide access to the MarketingMaterials and MarketingTemplates shared folders, as well as configure DFS replication for the MarketingMaterials shared folder available on your Windows Server 2019 host and WindowsServer2019VM2 virtual machine.

   1. On your Windows Server 2019 host, click **Start** and then click **Server Manager**. Within Server Manager, click the **Tools** menu and then click **DFS Management**.

2. In the navigation pane of the DFS Management tool, highlight **Namespaces** and note that no namespace shared folder exists by default. Click **New Namespace** within the Actions pane.

   a. On the Namespace Server page of the New Namespace Wizard, type **serverX** within the Server text box and click **Next**.

   b. On the Namespace Name and Settings page, type **warehouse** within the Name text box and click **Edit Settings**. Note the default path and permissions for the shared folder, click **OK**, and then click **Next**.

   c. On the Namespace Type page, note the default options and UNC for the shared folder and click **Next**.

   d. On the Review Settings and Create Namespace page, click **Create**.

   e. On the Confirmation page, click **Close**.

3. In the navigation pane of the DFS Management tool, expand **Namespaces** (if necessary) and highlight **\\domainX.com\warehouse**.

4. Click **Properties** in the Actions pane.

   a. In the \\domainX.com\warehouse Properties window, highlight the **Advanced** tab.

   b. Select **Enable access-based enumeration for this namespace** and click **OK**.

5. Click **New Folder** within the Actions pane.

   a. In the New Folder window, type **MarketingTemplates** within the Name text box.

   b. Click **Add**, type **\\serverX\MarketingTemplates** within the Path to folder target text box, and click **OK**.

   c. Click **OK** to close the New Folder window.

6. Click **New Folder** within the Actions pane.

   a. In the New Folder window, type **MarketingMaterials** within the Name text box.

   b. Click **Add**, type **\\serverX\MarketingMaterials** within the text box, and click **OK**.

   c. Click **Add**, type **\\name\MarketingMaterials** within the text box, where *name* is the computer name of your WindowsServer2019VM2 virtual machine, and click **OK**.

   d. Click **OK** to close the New Folder window. When prompted to configure a replication group (to keep the contents of the two shared folder locations within the MarketingMaterials target synchronized using DFS replication), click **Yes**.

   e. At the Replication Group and Replicated Folder Name page of the Replicate Folder Wizard, note the default names and click **Next**.

   f. At the Replication Eligibility page, click **Next**.

   g. At the Primary Member page, select **SERVERX** from the Primary member drop-down box and click **Next**.

   h. At the Topology Selection page, note the default option and click **Next**.

   i. At the Replication Group Schedule and Bandwidth page, note the default options and click **Next**.

   j. At the Replication Settings and Create Replication Group page, click **Create**.

   k. At the Confirmation page, click **Close**. Click **OK** at the Replication Delay information window.

7. In the navigation pane of the DFS Management tool, expand **Replication** and highlight **Domain System Volume**. Note that the SYSVOL share (which provides Active Directory object replication using DFS) is shown within the DFS Management console because your system is a domain controller.

8. Under Replication in the navigation pane of the DFS Management tool, highlight **domainX.com\warehouse\marketingmaterials** and note the two paths and servers shown on the Memberships tab.

   a. Highlight the **C:\MarketingMaterials** path for SERVERX and click **Properties** in the Actions pane. Highlight the **Staging** tab and note the default location and maximum size of the DFS staging folder. Click **Cancel** when finished.

   b. Highlight the **Connections** tab, select **SERVERX,** and click **Replicate Now** in the Actions pane.

   c. Click **OK** at the Replication Now window to perform the replication immediately and click **OK** to close the Resume Schedule Successful information window.

   d. Click **Properties** in the Actions pane. Note that replication is enabled and uses remote differential compression. Highlight the **Schedule** tab and click **View Schedule**. Note that replication occurs at all times of the day. Click **Cancel** and click **Cancel** again when finished.

9. Close the DFS Management window.

10. Right-click **Start** and click **Run**. Type **\\domainX.com\warehouse** in the Run dialog box and click **OK**. Note that you have access to the MarketingMaterials and MarketingTemplates targets.

11. Double-click **MarketingMaterials** and note that you can access File1, File2, and File3. Optionally modify the content of each file, saving your changes when finished.

12. Click **warehouse** in the navigation bar of File Manager to return to the warehouse share. Double-click **MarketingTemplates** and note that you have access to File4. Optionally modify the content of File4, saving your changes when finished.

13. Right-click **Start** and click **Run**. Type **\\name\MarketingMaterials** in the Run dialog box, where *name* is the computer name of your WindowsServer2019VM2 virtual machine, and click **OK**. Note that File1, File2, and File3 are available because they were replicated from the MarketingMaterials share on serverX using DFS.

14. Close File Manager.

Project 5-8: Quotas and File Screens

In this Hands-On Project, you explore the configuration of user quotas, folder quotas, and file screens.

1. On your Windows Server 2019 host, click **Start** and then click **File Explorer**.

2. In the navigation pane of File Explorer, expand **This PC**, right-click **Local Disk (C:),** and click **Properties**.

   a. Highlight the **Quota** tab within the Local Disk (C:) Properties window and select **Enable quota management**. Note the default limit and warning level settings.

   b. Select **Deny disk space to users exceeding quota limit**, **Log event when a user exceeds their quota limit**, and **Log event when a user exceeds their warning level,** and click **OK**.

   c. At the Disk Quota window, note the warning and click **OK**.

   d. Click **OK** to close the Local Disk (C:) Properties window.

3. Click **Start** and then click **Server Manager**. Within Server Manager, click the **Tools** menu and then click **File Server Resource Manager**.

   a. In the navigation pane of the File Server Resource Manager tool, expand **Quota Management** and highlight **Quota Templates**. Note the default templates available, including their limits and type.

   b. Highlight **Quotas** in the navigation pane and click **Create Quota** in the Actions pane.

   c. At the Create Quota window, type **C:\MarketingTemplates** in the Quota path text box, select **Define custom quota properties,** and click **Custom Properties**.

   d. At the Quota Properties of c:\MarketingTemplates window, select **2 GB Limit** from the *Copy properties from quota template (optional)* drop-down box and click **Copy**. Note the default quota type and warning thresholds and click **OK**.

   e. Click **Create**.

   f. At the Save Custom Properties as a Template window, type **Marketing Quota** in the Template name text box and click **OK**.

   g. Expand **File Screening Management** and highlight **File Groups**. Note the default file groups available, including the related file extensions.

   h. Highlight **File Screen Templates** in the navigation pane and note the default templates available, including their screening type and the file groups that they contain.

   i. Highlight **File Screens** in the navigation pane and click **Create File Screen** in the Actions pane.

   j. At the Create File Screen window, type **C:\MarketingTemplates** in the Quota path text box, select **Define custom file screen properties** and click **Custom Properties**.

   k. At the File Screen Properties of c:\MarketingTemplates window, note that Active screening is the default type. Within the File groups section, select all file groups except for Office Files and click **OK**.

   l. Click **Create**.

   m. At the Save Custom Properties as a Template window, type **Marketing Screen** in the Template name text box and click **OK**.

4. Close the File Server Resource Manager and Server Manager windows.

5. In the navigation pane of File Explorer, expand **This PC**, expand **Local Disk (C:)**, and highlight **MarketingTemplates**. Note that File4.txt is available within the folder as it was created prior to applying the file screen. Click the **Home** menu and then click **New item**, **Text Document**. Note the error that you receive and click **Cancel**. Close File Manager when finished.

Discovery Exercises

Exercise 5-1

In Hands-On Project 5-6, you shared the C:\MarketingMaterials and C:\MarketingTemplates folders by accessing folder properties within File Explorer. Use Server Manager to create the following SMB shared folders on your C:\ volume:

- UserGuides
- HelpDeskKnowledgebase
- EquipmentRequestForms

For each shared folder, ensure that the Domain Admins group is assigned Full Control permission and that the Domain Users group is assigned Read permission. Next, create some sample file content within each shared folder. Finally, log into your WindowsServer2019VM2 virtual machine as Bob Burtt and verify that you can connect to each shared folder but not modify or create files.

Exercise 5-2

To provide fault tolerance for the shared folders that you created in the previous Discovery Exercise, the IT department head has requested that you:

- Create the same shared folders on another file server
- Synchronize the contents of both shared folders using DFS replication
- Add targets that allow users to access the shared folder that is closest to their PC

Use Server Manger to create the same shared folders listed in the previous Discovery Exercise on your WindowsServer2019VM2 virtual machine. Next, update the DFS namespace that you created in Hands-On Project 5-7 to include targets that users can use to access the shared folders on either your Windows Server 2019 host or your WindowsServer2019VM2 virtual machine. Finally, ensure that folder contents for each of these shared folders is synchronized between your Windows Server 2019 host or your WindowsServer2019VM2 virtual machine using DFS replication, and validate that each replicated folder has identical contents. To test fault tolerance, shut down your WindowsServer2019VM2 virtual machine and ensure that you can still access and modify the files within each replicated folder. Next, boot your WindowsServer2019VM2 virtual machine and verify that your modifications were replicated to the shared folders on WindowsServer2019VM2.

Exercise 5-3

In organizations that have many shared folders, access-based enumeration helps reduce the list of shares that can be seen by users when accessing a DFS namespace. Modify the permissions on the HelpDeskKnowledgebase shares on both your Windows Server 2019 host and WindowsServer2019VM2 virtual machine to remove the Domain Users group (leaving only the Domain Admins group). Access the DFS namespace you configured in Hands-On Project 5-7 to verify that the HelpDeskKnowledgebase share is shown. Next, log into your

WindowsServer2019VM2 virtual machine as Bob Burtt and connect to the same DFS namespace to verify that the HelpDeskKnowledgebase share is not shown.

Exercise 5-4

DFS replication does not require that the replicated folder on each file server is shared using SMB or NFS. Create a C:\Test folder on both your Windows Server 2019 host and your WindowsServer2019VM2 virtual machine. Add sample content to the C:\Test folder on your Windows Server 2019 host. Next, use the DFS Management console to create a replication group that synchronizes the content of these two folders and verify that replication has occurred to the C:\Test folder on your WindowsServer2019VM2 virtual machine.

Exercise 5-5

In Hands-On Project 4-4, you created a forest trust relationship between your forest and a partner's forest. Modify the permissions on your MarketingMaterials and MarketingTemplates shared folder to allow the Domain Users group within your partner's domain to read file contents within each shared folder. Next, have your partner connect to your MarketingMaterials and MarketingTemplates shared folders using the appropriate UNC and access the files within.

CONFIGURING PRINTING

After completing this module, you will be able to:

Describe the process for printing documents to a print device or shared printer

Configure and monitor a print server using the Print and Document Services role

Use the Print Management tool to add and configure shared printers

Deploy shared printers using Group Policy

Manage print jobs

Troubleshoot common printing problems

Printers are one of the most common shared network resources within environments today. Consequently, server administrators must have a solid understanding of how to configure print servers and support print clients. In this module, you'll learn how a document is printed to a local and shared printer, as well as the process used to connect to a print server using the SMB, IPP, and LPD print-sharing protocols. Following this, you'll learn how to configure a Windows Server 2019 print server to provide shared printers on the network. Next, you'll learn how to configure printer properties, enable Branch Office Direct Printing, and deploy shared printers using Group Policy. At the end of this module, you'll learn how to manage print jobs, monitor printers, and troubleshoot printing problems.

Windows Printing Basics

Setting up a physical printer on a Windows client or server system is a relatively straightforward process. Physical printers that are PnP-capable typically connect to your system using a physical port (e.g., USB, parallel, or serial), and are configured by the system automatically the first time they are connected, prompting you for the correct **printer driver**, if necessary. Printers that are not PnP-capable, as well as printers that have a network interface and connect to your system using a network connection (e.g., Ethernet, Wi-Fi, Bluetooth) require that you add them manually using the Devices and Printers utility discussed in Module 2. After being installed, each printer will be represented by a printer name and icon within the Devices and Printers utility, as shown with HPLaserJet_6MP in Figure 6-1. You can then select this same printer name within the Print window of a software application to print a document to the physical printer.

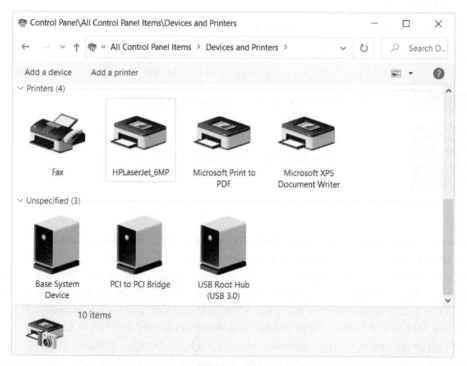

Figure 6-1   **Viewing installed printers within the Devices and Printers utility**

Note 🔗

To avoid confusion, Microsoft calls each physical printer a **print device**, and uses the word **printer** to refer to the printer name (e.g., HPLaserJet_6MP) that represents the physical printer within software on the system. We'll use these terms accordingly from this point onward.

Note

Printers that print to a print device connected to a physical port (e.g., USB) on your computer are called **locally attached printers**, whereas printers that print to the network interface of a print device across a network connection (e.g., Ethernet) are called **network-attached printers**. Similarly, print devices that provide a physical port connection are called **locally attached print devices**, while print devices that contain a network interface are called **network-attached print devices**.

As with folders, you can configure printers on a Windows Server 2019 system as a shared resource that grants access to users on the network. This allows a single print device to be shared by multiple users within the organization, as well as provides a way to restrict the users that are allowed to print. In order to configure, share, and troubleshoot printers, you must first understand the print process on a system, as well as the process used to print documents to a shared printer.

The Printing Process

After a locally attached or network-attached printer has been configured on a Windows system, several events must occur before a document can be successfully printed. The following steps outline this printing process:

1. The user of a software application, such as Microsoft Word, chooses to print their document to a printer that is installed on the system.
2. The software application contacts a print **application programming interface (API)** within the Windows operating system that stores the document within a **spool folder** located under C:\Windows\System32\spool\PRINTERS.
   Two different print APIs are available:

   - **Graphics Device Interface (GDI)** is supported by both legacy and modern Windows systems and applications. It normally stores documents within a spool folder using **Enhanced Metafile (EMF)** format, which contains document content as well as formatting instructions (e.g., font, color, positioning).
   - **XML Paper Specification (XPS)** is supported by Windows Vista and later systems that print from applications that use the **Windows Presentation Foundation (WPF)** framework. It stores documents within a spool folder using XPS format, which provides a standard graphical layout format similar to **Portable Document Format (PDF)**.

Note

The spool folder is also called the **print queue**.

> **Note**
>
> The process of converting a document to EMF or XPS format and storing it within a spool folder is called **spooling** or **queuing**.

> **Note**
>
> While the GDI API uses EMF format by default, it can also be configured to use RAW or TEXT format for legacy printers and applications.

> **Note**
>
> XPS in Windows 8 and later is often called Open XPS.

3. The documents within the spool folder are converted to a format that the print device can accept using instructions within the printer driver. This process is called **rendering**, and often results in a much larger file within the spool folder compared to the original document. At this point, the document is called a **print job**.

> **Note**
>
> Because XPS provides a standard graphical layout, printers that support XPS-formatted documents do not need to convert the XPS document to a different format within the spool folder, saving time, storage, and processor calculations. In this case, the rendering process merely adds any printer-specific features to the XPS-formatted document, according to the information within the printer driver.

> **Note**
>
> If a software application uses the XPS API to print a document to a print device that does not support XPS, the XPS-formatted document within the spool folder is first converted to EMF before being rendered at this step. Alternatively, if a software application uses the GDI API to print a document to a print device that supports XPS, the EMF-formatted document within the spool folder is converted to XPS before being rendered at this step.

4. The print job is then sent to the locally attached or network-attached print device after the print device acknowledges that it is ready to receive it.

5. The print device proceeds to print the document and notifies you when the print job has completed.

> **Note** 📎
>
> Print devices have a limited amount of storage to store print jobs. Moreover, print jobs that exceed print device storage need to be divided into smaller parts and sent to a print device sequentially. Before sending a print job (or part of a print job) to a print device, instructions within the printer driver are used to communicate with the print device to determine if the printer is ready to accept the next portion of a print job.

> **Note** 📎
>
> The **Print Spooler** service within Windows provides for the functionality described within steps 1 through 5.

Printing to a Shared Printer

While network-attached print devices are common within organizations today, they have limited storage for print jobs and are not designed to handle simultaneous print jobs from large numbers of computers. As a result, nearly all network-attached print devices within organizations are configured to only accept print jobs from a **print server**. Each print server creates a **shared printer** for each print device that users can submit print jobs to from across the network, and has the storage capacity and processor capabilities to handle print jobs from a large number of users. Moreover, print servers can be used to share locally attached print devices to users across the network that would otherwise not be able to contact the print device. Ensuring that users submit print jobs to a print server also allows your organization to manage and control access to the network-attached and locally attached printers that are shared by the print server.

Configuring a new printer on a client computer to print to a shared printer across a network is similar to accessing a shared folder on a file server. You must specify the print server that is sharing the printer, as well as the name of the shared printer to which you have permission to print. Moreover, the format you specify when connecting to a shared printer depends on the protocol that is used. Windows systems support three printer sharing protocols:

- Server Message Block (SMB) is the default protocol used to print documents to shared printers hosted on Windows print servers. As with SMB shared folders, you can use a UNC to connect to a SMB shared printer using either the server name or IP address:

```
\\servername\sharedprintername
\\IPaddress\sharedprintername
```

- **Internet Printing Protocol (IPP)** uses HTTP or HTTPS to print documents to a shared printer on a server that has IPP installed. You can use one of three different formats when connecting to a shared printer using IPP:

```
http://servername/printers/sharedprintername/.printer
http://servername:631/printers/sharedprintername
ipp://servername/printers/sharedprintername
```

- **Line Printer Daemon (LPD)** is a UNIX printer sharing protocol that uses TCP/IP to print documents to a shared printer on a server that has the LPD print service installed. When printing to an LPD shared printer, you must specify a **Line Printer Request (LPR)** port type and supply the server name and shared printer name when prompted.

Your computer must have the **Internet Printing Client** feature installed in order to print to a shared IPP printer, and the **LPR Port Monitor** feature installed in order to print to a shared LPD printer. These features can be installed within the Add Roles and Features wizard on a Windows Server 2019 system. To install these features on a Windows 8 or later system, you can access the Programs and Features tool within Control Panel, click *Turn Windows features on or off* and select them under the Print and Document Services, as shown in Figure 6-2 for a Windows 10 system.

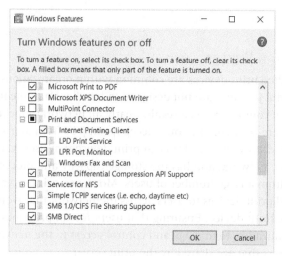

Figure 6-2   Installing the Internet Printing Client and LPR Port Monitor on Windows 10

You can use the Devices and Printers utility on a Windows system to add a printer that prints to a shared printer on the network. If you click *Add a printer* in Figure 6-1, the Add a device wizard will first attempt to locate a locally attached print device, a network-attached print device that advertises its presence on the network, or a shared printer that is published in Active Directory. If the print device or shared printer is listed, you can select it from the list to start the Add Printer wizard. However, if the shared printer is not listed, as shown in Figure 6-3, you can click *The printer that I want isn't listed* to manually specify the location to the shared printer. This will open the Add Printer wizard, as shown in Figure 6-4. To add an

SMB or IPP shared printer, you can select *Select a shared printer by name* and supply the correct format in the text box for the shared printer. The UNC shown in Figure 6-4 accesses an SMB shared printer named HPLaserJet_6MP on serverX.domainX.com. To add an LPD shared printer, you must select *Add a local printer or network printer with manual settings* in Figure 6-4, click Next, and create a new LPR port using the options shown in Figure 6-5. When you click Next in Figure 6-5, you will be prompted for the LPD server name and printer name, as shown in Figure 6-6 for the HPLaserJet_6MP printer on serverX.domainX.com.

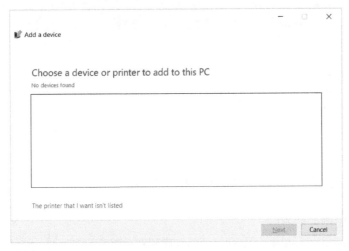

Figure 6-3 Searching for a shared printer using the Devices and Printers tool

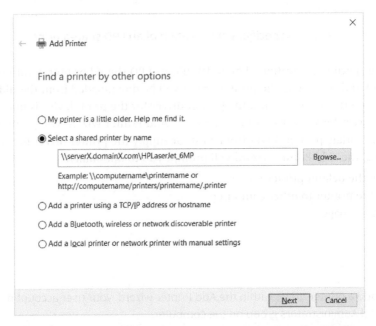

Figure 6-4 Specifying the location of an SMB shared printer

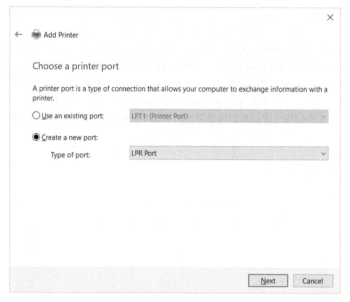

Figure 6-5   Adding an LPR port

Figure 6-6   Specifying the location of an LPD shared printer

After you specify the location of an SMB, IPP, or LPD shared printer within the Add Printer wizard and click Next, the printer driver will be downloaded from the hidden PRINT$ share on the print server. If the printer driver for the print device is not available on the print server for your operating system, the Add Printer wizard will prompt you to select the appropriate printer driver from a list, or supply the printer driver files manually. Following this, the Add Printer wizard will prompt you to optionally:

- Modify the default printer name
- Share the printer to other computers
- Print a test page

Note

To manually add a printer driver within the Add Printer wizard, your user account must be part of the local Administrators group on the computer.

Note

Computers that print to a shared printer on a print server are commonly called **print clients**.

The Printing Process for a Shared Printer

The process used by a print client when printing to a shared printer across the network starts with the same three steps used when printing to a locally attached or network-attached printer. However, after the print job has been rendered, it is sent to, and spooled on, the print server before being sent to the print device. The following steps outline this printing process:

1. On the print client, the user of a software application, such as Microsoft Word, chooses to print their document to a shared printer.
2. The software application contacts a print API (GDI or XPS) on the print client, which stores the document within a spool folder (under C:\Windows\System32\spool\PRINTERS) using the appropriate format, such as EMF or XPS.
3. The documents within the spool folder on the print client may be converted between EMF and XPS formats (to match the requirements of the print device) and rendered using the printer driver to produce a print job.
4. The print job is sent from the print client to the print server across the network using the correct protocol (SMB, IPP, or LPD).
5. The print server stores the print job within a spool folder under C:\Windows\System32\spool\PRINTERS.
6. The print server sends the print job to the locally attached or network-attached print device after the print device acknowledges that it is ready to receive it.
7. The print device proceeds to print the document and notifies the print server that the print job has completed.
8. The print server notifies the print client that the print job has completed.
9. The print client notifies the user that the print job has completed.

Note

The Print Spooler service on the print client provides for the functionality described within steps 1 through 4 and 9, whereas the Print Spooler service on the print server provides the functionality described within steps 5 through 8.

Configuring a Windows Server 2019 Print Server

By default, all Windows client operating systems have the ability to add locally attached or network-attached printers, as well as share them to other computers on the network using SMB. You can perform this in Windows 10 using the Devices and Printers utility discussed earlier. While you can also use the Devices and Printers utility on Windows

Server 2019 to add and share locally attached or network-attached printers, you should instead use the **Print Management** tool that is part of the **Print and Document Services** server role. The Print Management tool allows you to add, share, and manage several locally attached or network-attached printers on one or more print servers within an Active Directory environment, and it contains print server configuration options that are not available within the Device and Printers utility.

Installing Print and Document Services

To install the Print Management tool, as well as the IPP and LPD printer sharing protocols, you must first install the Print and Document Services server role. When you select this role within the Add Roles and Features Wizard in Server Manager and progress through the wizard, you will be prompted to choose the Print and Document Services components that you wish to install, as shown in Figure 6-7. These components include:

- *Print Server*—Installs the Print Management tool.
- *Internet Printing*—Allows Windows Server 2019 to share printers using IPP. This component will install and configure IIS to provide the HTTP or HTTPS functionality required by IPP.
- *LPD Service*—Allows Windows Server 2019 to share printers using LPD.

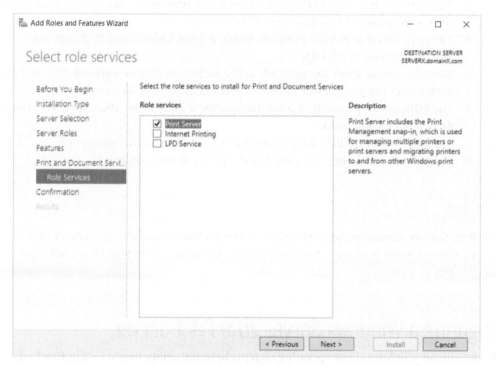

Figure 6-7   Selecting Print and Document Services components

Note

If you do not select Internet Printing or LPD Service in Figure 6-7, all printers you configure will be shared using SMB only.

Configuring a Print Server

After the Print Server component of the Print and Document Services server role has been installed, you can select Print Management from the tools menu of Server Manager to start the Print Management tool shown in Figure 6-8.

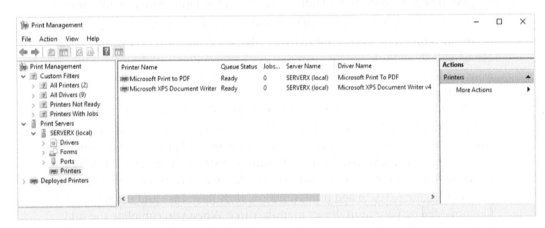

Figure 6-8   The Print Management tool

By default, your local server is listed under the Print Servers section within the navigation pane. To add other print servers that are part of your Active Directory domain to the Print Management tool, highlight Print Servers within the navigation pane and click More Actions, Add/Remove Servers from the Actions pane.

The Printers node under a new print server within the navigation pane of the Print Management tool lists two printers by default, as shown for SERVERX in Figure 6-8:

- *Microsoft Print to PDF* allows users to save their document as a PDF file when they print to this printer. PDF files can be read by most applications that have the ability to view documents.
- *Microsoft XPS Document Writer* allows users to save their document as an XPS file when they print to this printer. XPS files can be read by certain applications, such as Microsoft Word.

> **Note** 📎
>
> If you are configuring a print server on a virtual machine within the Virtual Machine Connection window, you will additionally see printers that have been configured on the Hyper-V host operating system under the Printers node. This is because Hyper-V allows printers within the host operating system to be accessed by Windows 10, Windows Server 2016, and later guest operating systems. To disable this feature, click Hyper-V Settings within the Actions pane of Hyper-V Manager, select *Enhanced Session Mode* under the User section, and then de-select *Use enhanced session mode*.

Before you add additional printers that are shared to users on the network, you should first configure the other nodes under your server within the Print Management console:

- *Drivers* stores printer drivers for ARM, 32-bit Intel (x86), and 64-bit Intel (x64) processor-based systems on your network. Before adding printers on your print server, you should first add any manufacturer-supplied printer drivers for the associated print devices. To do this, highlight this node and click More Actions, Add Driver from the Actions pane to open the Add Printer Driver Wizard. When you click Next at this wizard, you will be prompted for the processor type, as shown in Figure 6-9. It is good practice to select all processor types, in case you add systems with new processors in the future that need to download printer drivers from your print server (e.g., ARM-based Microsoft Surface systems). When you click Next in Figure 6-9, you will be prompted to select the associated printer driver files, as shown in Figure 6-10. To add printer drivers, click Have Disk and navigate to the files provided by your print device manufacturer. When you complete the Add Printer Driver Wizard, the printer drivers will be added to the print server and made available to print clients using the PRINT$ share.

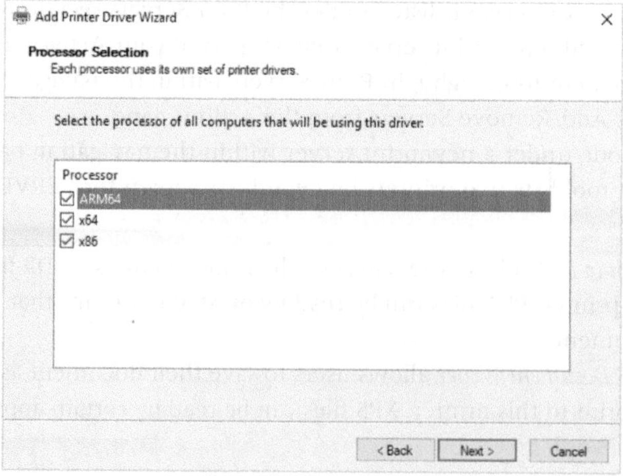

Figure 6-9   Selecting the processor type for drivers

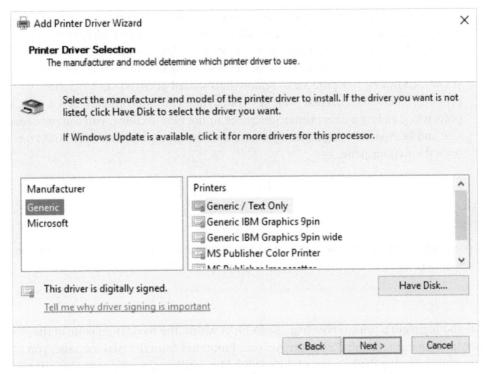

Figure 6-10   Adding printer drivers to a print server

Note

Windows 8, Windows Server 2012, and later systems can use a new type of printer driver that relies on core Microsoft components, with optional extensions provided by print device manufacturers. These drivers will display a Type 4 driver type when displayed in the Print Management console, whereas legacy printer drivers will display a Type 3 driver type. Windows Server 2019 print servers support both Type 4 and Type 3 printer drivers for print devices.

Note

Print clients check the printer driver each time they connect to a shared printer. If an updated printer driver is available on the PRINT$ share of the print server, the updated printer driver will automatically be downloaded to the print client and configured for use.

- *Forms* stores supported paper sizes and formats for use by printers on the system. While most sizes and formats are provided by default, you can highlight this node and click More Actions, Manage Forms to define additional ones.
- *Ports* lists the available printer ports on the system, including parallel (LPT), serial (COM), USB, LPR (for printing to remote LPD shared printers), and TCP (for printing to network-attached print devices). While you can configure LPR and TCP ports when adding a new printer (discussed in the next section), you can pre-create LPR and TCP ports by highlighting this node and clicking More Actions, Add Ports from the Actions pane.

Note 📎

USB ports are added automatically when a USB print device is connected to the system. The first USB port is called USB001, the second USB port is called USB002, and so on.

If you highlight a print server (e.g., SERVERX) within the navigation pane of the Print Management tool and click More Actions, Properties from the Actions pane, you will be able to modify the location of the spool folder, or display notifications for printers, as shown in Figure 6-11. Notifications are displayed when the state of a printer changes due to information received by the associated print device, such as an *out of toner* message, or *paper jam* message.

Note 📎

Because print servers use a large amount of storage when processing print jobs, it is good practice to ensure that the spool folder is located on a separate storage device (e.g., D:\) that has a large capacity for storing print jobs.

If you highlight the Security tab, as shown in Figure 6-12, you can allow groups and users the ability to view or configure the print server, manage print jobs or printer settings for printers on the print server, as well as submit print jobs to printers on the print server. Table 6-1 lists the permissions that are available to the printers on the print server, as well as to the print server itself. Permissions that apply to printers are stored within the DACL of the printer object within the Print Management console, whereas permissions that apply to the print server are stored within the DACL of the print server object.

Table 6-1   Printer and print server permissions

Permission	Description	Applies to
Print	Allows users to submit print jobs to printers on the system as well as manage their own print jobs within the spool folder (pause, restart, resume, and cancel). By default, the Everyone group is granted this permission.	Printers
Manage Printers	Allows users to configure printer settings, pause and restart the printer, as well as submit print jobs to the printer. By default, members of the Administrators, Server Operators, and Print Operators group are granted this permission.	Printers
Manage Documents	Allows users to manage print jobs (pause, restart, resume, and cancel) that other users have submitted to the spool folder only. By default, CREATOR OWNER (the user that added the printer) and members of the Administrators group are granted this permission.	Printers
View Server	Allows users to view the shared printers available on the print server. By default, the Everyone group is granted this permission.	Print server
Manage Server	Allows users to configure print server settings within the Print Management tool. By default, members of the Administrators, Server Operators, and Print Operators group are granted this permission.	Print server

Note

Normally, you provide printer permissions to groups and users within an Active Directory environment. Workgroup users can also submit print jobs to a print server but will first be prompted to log into the print server as a local or domain user account that has Print permission to the shared printer.

Figure 6-11   The Advanced tab of print server properties

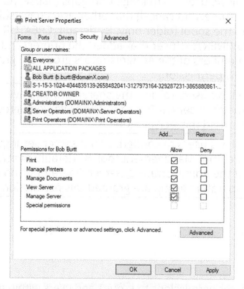

Figure 6-12   The Security tab of print server properties

If your organization has an email account configured for your print server on an email server, you can configure the Print Management console to email printer notifications to an email address, or run a script. To do this, you can highlight a print server (e.g., SERVERX) within the navigation pane of the Print Management tool and click More Actions, Set Notifications from the Actions pane to open the Set Notifications window. The Set Notifications window shown in Figure 6-13 is configured to email printer notifications to jason.eckert@trios.com with a subject line *Notification from Print Service on serverX.domainX.com* using the email account for printserver@domainX.com on the email server called exchange.domainX.com.

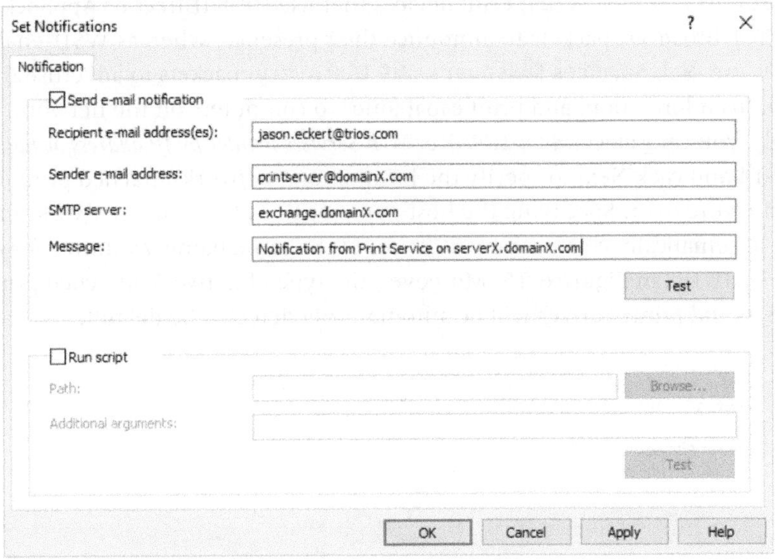

Figure 6-13   Configuring email notifications

Adding Printers to a Print Server

To add a new printer to a print server within the Print Management tool, highlight the Printers node under a server within the navigation pane and click More Actions, Add Printer from the Actions pane to open the Network Printer Installation Wizard shown in Figure 6-14.

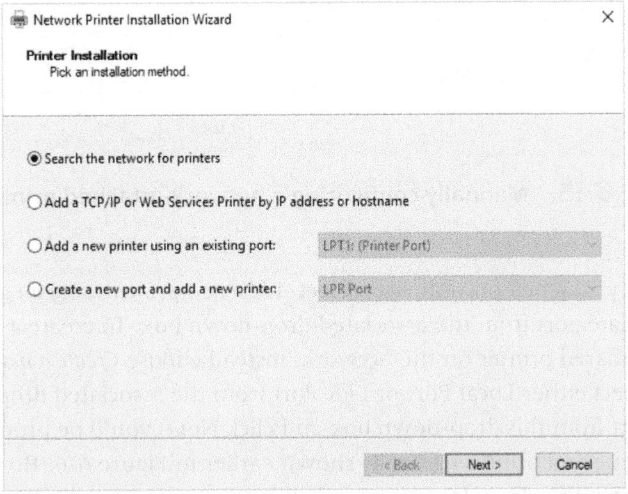

Figure 6-14   The Network Printer Installation Wizard

The default option shown in Figure 6-14 will search the network for shared printers that are published within Active Directory, network-attached print devices that use the **HP JetDirect** or **AppSocket** protocols, as well as network-attached printers that support **Web Services for Devices (WSD)**. Print devices that use HP JetDirect or AppSocket respond to TCP broadcast packets to announce their presence, whereas WSD-enabled print devices use **Web Services Discovery (WS-Discovery)** packets to advertise their presence, status information, and print capabilities to computers on the network. Alternatively, you can select *Add a TCP/IP or Web Services Printer by IP address or hostname* in Figure 6-14 and click Next to specify the location of a network-attached print device, as shown in Figure 6-15. Specifying the host name or IP address for a network-attached printer will automatically create a new TCP port of the same name, as shown for the IP address 10.3.101.188 in Figure 6-15. Moreover, the type of network-attached printer (TCP or WSD) and printer driver will be automatically detected by default.

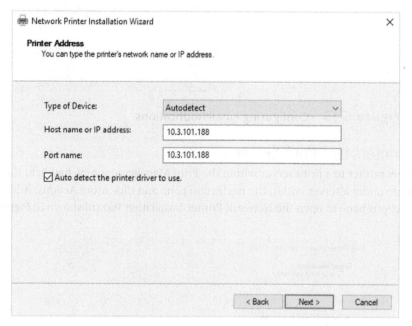

Figure 6-15 Manually configuring a network-attached printer

To add a locally attached print device, select *Add a new printer using an existing port* and select the appropriate port from the associated drop-down box. To create a printer that prints to another shared printer on the network, instead choose *Create a new port and add a new printer* and select either Local Port or LPR Port from the associated drop-down box. If you select LPR Port from this drop-down box and click Next, you'll be prompted to supply the LPD server name and printer name, as shown earlier in Figure 6-6. However, if you select Local Port from this drop-down box and click Next, you can supply the location of an existing SMB or IPP printer, as shown in Figure 6-16. For example, the UNC shown in Figure 6-16 would create a new port that would use SMB to print to the shared printer called HPLaserJet_6MP on the print server named serverX.

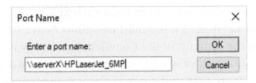

Figure 6-16   Adding a local port to print to an existing shared printer

After you have selected or specified the location of the print device within the Network Printer Installation Wizard, you will be prompted for the printer driver. If you have previously added the correct printer drivers to the Drivers node under your print server within the Print Management console, the Printer Installation Wizard will automatically select the correct driver. Alternatively, the Network Printer Installation Wizard will prompt you to supply the correct driver, as shown in Figure 6-17. You can click Windows Update in Figure 6-17 to search for available drivers online, or click Have Disk to supply the appropriate drivers from files obtained by your print device manufacturer.

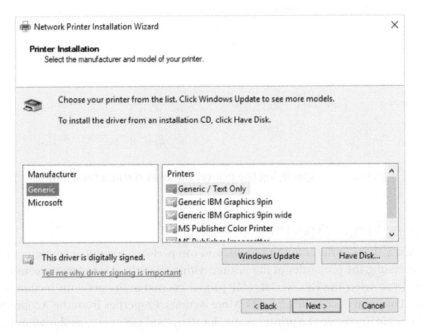

Figure 6-17   Specifying the correct printer driver

After printer driver information has been detected or specified, the Network Printer Installation Wizard prompts allow you to specify the printer name and sharing settings, as shown in Figure 6-18. If you have installed the Internet Printing and LPD Service components (shown earlier in Figure 6-7), the printer will be shared using SMB, IPP, and LPD. Moreover, specifying a value within the Location text box allows users to search for the printer by location or keyword if it is published within Active Directory (discussed in the next section), and the contents of the Comment text box will be shown to users who view the properties of a printer within the Print dialog box of a software application. When you click Next in Figure 6-18 and progress through the remaining confirmation pages of the Network Printer Installation Wizard, you will be prompted whether to print a test page or add another printer before clicking Finish to add the printer to the print server.

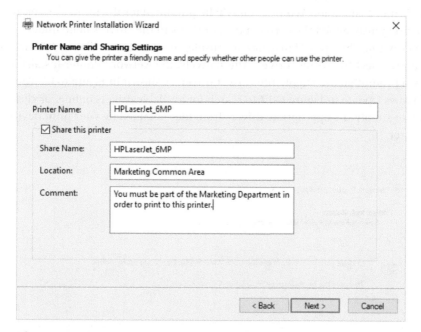

Figure 6-18   Specifying the printer name and share information

Configuring Printer Properties

After adding a shared printer to the system, you can perform additional configuration tasks by accessing the properties of the printer within the Print Management console. For example, if you select the HPLaserJet_6MP printer created in the previous section within the Print Management console and click More Actions, Properties from the Actions menu, you will be able to change the printer name, location, and comment, as shown in Figure 6-19. You can use the Preferences button to specify additional information such as the default paper size, layout (portrait or landscape), paper source, or print resizing options. You can also click the Print Test Page button to print a sample print job to the printer in order to verify that the print process is working.

Figure 6-19   **The General tab within the properties of a printer**

The other tabs shown in Figure 6-19 that are common to other printers include:

- Sharing
- Ports
- Advanced
- Security
- Device Settings

Note

The Printer Commands, Font Selection, and Color Management tabs shown in Figure 6-19 are unique to the printer driver selected when the printer was created. They are often omitted or replaced by tabs with different names that provide configuration options that are specific to the print device. Refer to the print device manufacturer's website for more information.

The Sharing Tab

If you highlight the Sharing tab in Figure 6-19, you can control whether the printer is shared to other systems on the network and the share name that is used for the SMB, IPP, and LPD sharing protocols, as shown in Figure 6-20. By default, print jobs are rendered on print clients before being forwarded to the print server. However, if print clients have limited processor and storage for rendering print jobs, you can deselect *Render print jobs on client computers* to ensure that documents are directly forwarded to, and rendered by, the print server. If you select *List in the directory*, the shared printer will be automatically published in Active Directory. This will allow domain users to search Active Directory for the shared printer within the Print window of a software application, as well as ensure that it appears in the list of available printers at the beginning of the Add Printer wizard. To add additional printer drivers for the printer, click Additional Drivers, select the appropriate processor type, and supply the associated printer driver files.

Note

When you share a printer, that printer is shared using all available protocols on the print server (SMB, IPP, LPD) using the shared printer name configured in Figure 6-20.

Note

If you publish a printer by selecting *List in the directory* in Figure 6-20, you will not see an object representing a published shared printer object within Active Directory Users and Computers. Instead, a printQueue object for the printer is created under the computer object of the print server. To see this printQueue object, you must use a tool that can examine the structure of Active Directory, such as **ADSI Edit**.

Note

To publish an SMB shared printer on a UNIX, Linux, or pre-Windows 2000 print server within Active Directory, you can use the Active Directory Users and Computers tool. To do this, right-click the appropriate OU, and click New, Printer. Next, supply the shared printer UNC and click OK to create a shared printer object within that OU that can be searched by domain users.

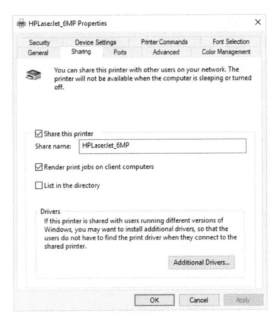

Figure 6-20   **The Sharing tab within the properties of a printer**

The Ports Tab

To configure the ports used to contact the print devices, highlight the Ports tab in Figure 6-19. This will allow you to add, delete, and configure the properties of ports, as shown in Figure 6-21. If the HPLaserJet_6MP printer connected to the first parallel port (LPT1) in Figure 6-21 experiences a failure that prevents print jobs from being sent to the print device, you can redirect print jobs within the spool folder to another shared printer (with the same print device model) on the network by changing the port. For example, to redirect print jobs to the SMB shared printer called HPLaserJet_6MP on serverX, you can click Add Port, select Local Port, click New Port, and supply the UNC shown earlier in Figure 6-16.

If the print device supports **bidirectional printing**, select *Enable bidirectional support* to ensure that the print device is able to send notifications to the print server. If you select *Enable printer pooling*, you will be able to select multiple ports for use with the printer. A **printer pool** allows multiple print devices (of the model) to be used by a single printer to increase the speed at which print jobs are printed. For example, if you select *Enable printer pooling* in Figure 6-21, and then select LPT1, LPT2, and LPT3, you will create a printer pool that sends print jobs for the HPLaserJet_6MP printer to the first available print device on LPT1, LPT2, or LPT3 (assuming there are three HP LaserJet 6MP print devices connected to the associated ports). Printer pools are commonly used within office environments where users pick up print jobs from a print room, or a common print area that contains the associated print devices in close physical proximity.

Figure 6-21   The Ports tab within the properties of a printer

The Advanced Tab

If you highlight the Advanced tab in Figure 6-19, you can configure the times that a printer is available to users, the printer priority, the printer driver, and spooling options. The default values on the Advanced tab are shown in Figure 6-22.

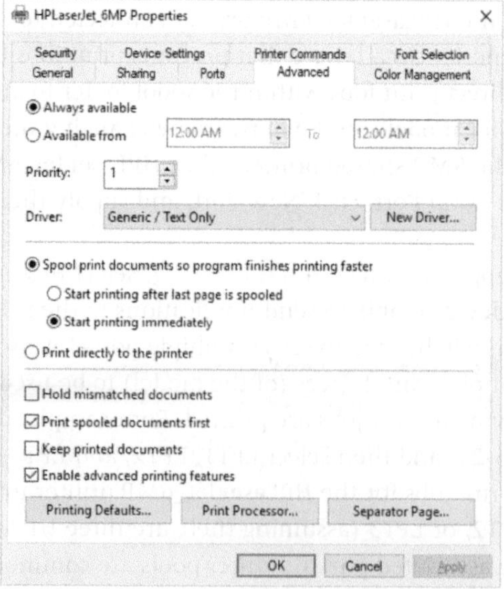

Figure 6-22   The Advanced tab within the properties of a printer

By default, printers are available to accept print jobs at all times of the day, but they can be limited to certain hours by selecting *Available from* and specifying the time range. The Priority value specified in Figure 6-22 can be set from 1 (low priority) to 99 (high priority), and is only used if multiple printers are configured to print to the same port and associated print device. Say, for example, you have a printer called HPLaserJet_6MP_IT_STAFF on the print server that prints to the same port and print device as the HPLaserJet_6MP printer shown in Figure 6-22. However, the HPLaserJet_6MP_IT_STAFF printer has a priority of 99 and only allows members of the Domain Admins group Print permission. In this case, when members of the Domain Admins group submit print jobs to the HPLaserJet_6MP_IT_STAFF printer, their jobs will be printed before print jobs submitted by other users to the HPLaserJet_6MP printer.

The default spooling options shown in Figure 6-22 starts sending pages within a print job to the print device after the first page has been submitted to the spool folder on the print server. However, this may result in large print jobs being interrupted by a one-page print job on the print device itself. To prevent this, select *Start printing after last page is spooled*; this ensures that pages of a print job are sent to the print device only after all pages within the print job have finished spooling. To disable spooling altogether, you can select *Print directly to the printer*. However, this can cause problems if the print device does not have adequate storage for the print jobs (most print devices contain only a small amount of storage). You can use the remaining spooling options to further configure how spooled documents are processed:

- *Hold mismatched documents* causes the system to compare the document layout of the printer with the document layout within the print job. For example, if the printer is configured with a standard paper layout (8.5″ × 11″), but the document within the print job is formatted for a legal format paper layout (8.5″ × 14″), the print job is placed on hold. The job does not print until the document is resumed by the user, or a member of the Administrators, Server Operators, or Print Operators group (discussed in the next section). If this option is not set, users that submit print jobs may find that the contents on each page of their print job is spread across multiple pieces of paper, once it is printed by the print device. This wastes paper resources and forces the user to submit the print job again using the correct format.
- *Print spooled documents first* only applies if multiple printers are configured with the same port and associated print device. This option allows print jobs that have completed spooling to be printed, regardless of their priority. In high-volume printing situations, this speeds the printing process by ensuring that low priority small print jobs that have already spooled are submitted to the print device before higher priority large print jobs from another printer that take much longer to spool.
- *Keep printed documents* retains documents in the spool folder after they have printed, until a notification of successful print job completion is received from the print device, or the Print Spooler service is restarted. This allows the printer to restart the submission of a print job to a print device following a printer jam or other problem.

- *Enable advanced printing* features option allows you to make use of special features associated with a particular printer, such as the ability to print booklets or to vary the order in which pages are printed (e.g., back to front).

The Printing Defaults button in Figure 6-22 allows you to specify default settings for print jobs. These can include the print layout, page print order (e.g., front to back, or back to front), and paper source, depending on the print device. Alternatively, the Print Processor button allows you to modify the default format used by print APIs when storing documents within the spool folder. The formats available depend on your print device capabilities, and include the following:

- *RAW*—Does not format documents from software applications before they are spooled. It is often used by legacy Windows, UNIX, Linux, and macOS print clients, as well as when printing to **PostScript** print devices.
- *RAW (FF appended)*—Equivalent to *RAW*, but with form-feed code placed at the end of the document to ensure that the last page of the file is printed.
- *RAW (FF auto)*— Equivalent to *RAW (FF appended)*, but a form-feed code is only added at the end of the document if one is not there already.
- *NT EMF* (different versions)—The default format used to store documents received by the GDI API for modern print devices. Because EMF is not printer-specific, it requires less processor calculations from the Print Spooler service and also allows for background printing of documents.
- *XPS* or *OXPS*—The default format used to store documents received by the XPS API for modern print devices. XPS and OXPS documents are not rendered after they are spooled.
- *TEXT*—Used for printing text files formatted with the ANSI character set. This format is often used when printing to specialized print devices such as carbon-copy forms and plotters.
- *XPS2GDI*—This format converts XPS documents to GDI for printing on GDI-compatible printers.
- *GDI2XPS*—This format converts GDI documents to XPS for printing on XPS-compatible printers.

Note 📎

Since Windows NT, Microsoft has allowed third-party print device vendors to add to Windows their own software components that provide for the formatting of documents within the spool folder. These software components are called **print processors**. However, this practice is rare today, and most third-party print device vendors use the default WinPrint print processor that you will see if you click the Print Processor button shown in Figure 6-22.

> **Note** 📎
>
> A PostScript print device is one that has special firmware to print using a **page description language (PDL)**. Most non-PostScript print devices use a version of the **Printer Control Language (PCL)**, which was developed by Hewlett-Packard.

> **Note** 📎
>
> The optimal format for your print device is normally selected by default when you add a printer. However, when troubleshooting a printer problem, a solution listed on the print device manufacturer's website may instruct you to change the spooling format.

The Separator Page button in Figure 6-22 allows you to select a separator page file. A **separator page** is used to place an information page at the beginning of each printed document that lists the document name and user that printed it. This helps designate the end of one printout and the beginning of another so that users do not take the wrong print job on a print device that accepts a large number of print jobs. In small offices, a separator page is often unnecessary, because users can quickly identify their own printouts. Windows Server 2019 has four separator page files from which to choose, located in the C:\Windows\System32 folder:

- *Pcl.sep*—Used to print a PCL separator page on a print device that supports PCL or PostScript.
- *Pscript.sep*—Used to print a PostScript separator page on a printer that supports PCL or PostScript.
- *Sysprint.sep*—Used to print a PostScript separator page on a printer that supports PostScript only.
- *Sysprtj.sep*—Used in the same way as *Sysprint.sep*, but for documents printed in the Japanese language.

> **Note** 📎
>
> The contents of separator pages can also be customized to suit your organization. Search Custom Separator Pages on docs.microsoft.com for more information.

> **Note** 📎
>
> You should first consider the added cost of separator pages before implementing them within an organization. If a separator page is used, each print job will consume an additional piece of paper.

The Security Tab

By default, printer permissions applied to the print server (shown earlier in Figure 6-12) are inherited by each printer added to the print server. If you highlight the Security tab in Figure 6-19, you will be able to configure the three permissions (described earlier within Table 6-1) that apply to the HPLaserJet_6MP printer, as shown in Figure 6-23:

- Print
- Manage this printer (equivalent to the Manage Printers permission within Table 6-1)
- Manage documents

You can modify or remove these inherited permissions or click Add to add additional groups and users to which you can assign permissions to the HPLaserJet_6MP printer.

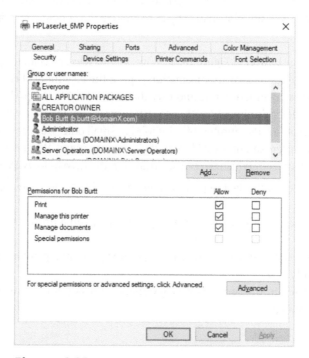

Figure 6-23   **The Security tab within the properties of a printer**

Like folders, printers contain a SACL that provides auditing capabilities, provided that the *Audit object access* policy setting (shown earlier in Figure 5-11) has been configured within a Group Policy that applies to the print server. This allows you to log an event to the Security log on the print server each time a user successfully (or unsuccessfully) prints a print job, manages another user's document within the spool folder, or modifies the settings of a printer. To edit the SACL on the HPLaserJet_6MP printer shown in Figure 6-23, you can click the Advanced button and add the appropriate entries to the Auditing tab, as shown in Figure 6-24. The entries shown in Figure 6-24 log an event to the Security log when a user within the Marketing-G group successfully submits a print job, or when Bob Burtt successfully manages another user's print job within the spool folder for the HPLaserJet_6MP printer.

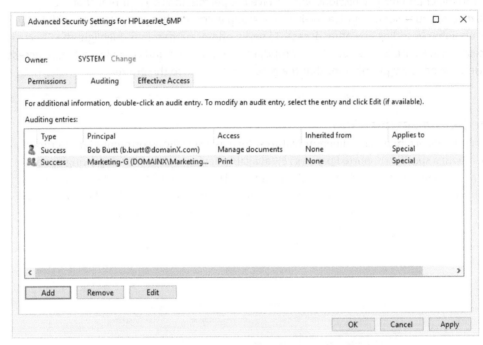

Figure 6-24   The Advanced Security Settings window for a printer

Although you can click Change in Figure 6-24 to modify the printer owner, you should normally leave the default SYSTEM owner in place to ensure proper print server operation. However, if your organization installs third-party print tracking or management software, you may need to change the ownership of each printer to match the domain user that the third-party software runs as.

Note

The printer permissions shown in Figure 6-23 are made up of advanced permissions of the same names, with the Read advanced permission added to allow users to view the printer. The *Manage this printer* permission additionally includes the *Change permissions* and *Take ownership* advanced permissions. You can configure these advanced permissions by highlighting the Permissions tab shown in Figure 6-24.

Note

As with folder and file permissions, you receive the permissions on a printer that are assigned to your user account, as well as any group accounts that you belong to, with Deny permissions overriding any other access. To verify printer permissions, highlight the Effective Access tab in Figure 6-24, select the appropriate group or user, and click View effective access to view the effective permissions that the group or user has to the printer.

The Device Settings Tab

Each print device may have different features, such as a specific assortment of printer trays (each with a specific supported paper size), available device memory, or duplexing options. If you highlight the Device Settings tab in Figure 6-19, you can configure the standard features that are provided by your printer driver, as shown in Figure 6-25. The *Generic/Text Only* printer driver used for the HPLaserJet_6MP printer shown in Figure 6-25 supports few standard features, but provides the Color Management, Font Selection, and Printer Commands tabs that allow you to configure additional features provided by the printer driver.

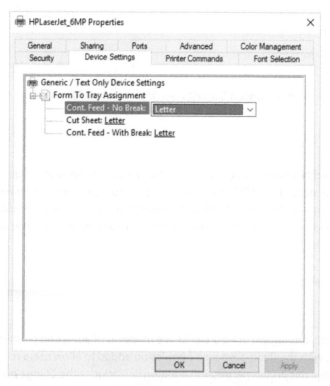

Figure 6-25 The Device Settings tab within the properties of a printer

Some printer drivers do not provide any configurable options on the Device Settings tab and instead provide additional tabs for all print device-specific configuration options.

Using Group Policy to Deploy Shared Printers

While users can use the Add Printer wizard to add shared printers provided by print servers within your organization, they will first need to know the server and printer name as well as the correct format used to connect to the shared printer. To simplify the addition of printers on client computers within your organization, you can use Group Policy to automatically add SMB shared printers to computers that are joined to the domain, provided that the appropriate printer drivers for the computers are installed on the print server. To do this, right-click a printer within the Print Management console and select *Deploy with Group Policy*. This will open the Deploy with Group Policy window shown in Figure 6-26, where you can select an existing Group Policy and whether to add the shared printer to user or computer objects that receive the group policy. The settings shown in Figure 6-26 automatically install the HPLaserJet_6MP shared printer on SERVERX to each computer within the domain that receives the Default Domain Policy Group Policy.

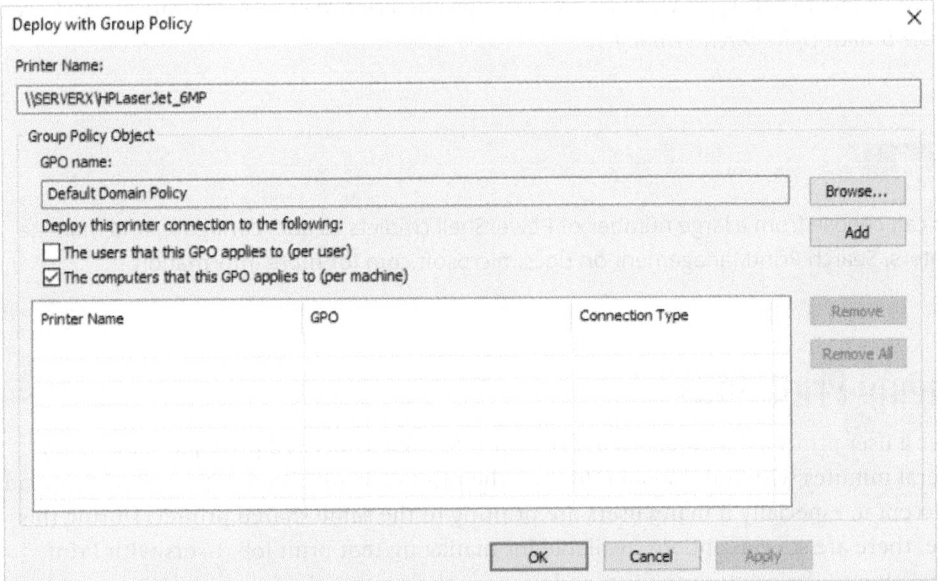

Figure 6-26   Deploying a shared printer using Group Policy

> **Note** 📎
>
> You can highlight the Deployed Printers node within the navigation pane of the Print Management tool (shown earlier in Figure 6-8) to view printers that have been deployed using Group Policy.

Configuring Branch Office Direct Printing

Some organizations have branch offices that contain a network-attached print device that users within the branch office can print to after contacting the associated shared printer on a print server within the main office. This structure allows the organization to restrict access to the print device, because users must have Print permission to the shared printer on the print server in order to print to the network-attached print device. However, each print job must be forwarded across the Internet to the main office before being forwarded back across the Internet to the network-attached print device in the branch office. This slows the printing process and may congest the Internet connection for the branch office. To solve this problem, you can enable **Branch Office Direct Printing (BODP)** on the shared printer. When branch office users connect to a shared printer across the Internet that has BODP enabled, the print server does not spool the print job. Instead, the print server validates that they have Print permission to the printer and then directs the Print Spooler service on the print client to forward the print job directly to the network-attached print device after the network-attached print device is ready to accept the print job. To enable BODP, right-click a printer within the Print Management console and click *Enable Branch Office Direct Printing*.

> **Note** 📎
>
> You can choose from a large number of PowerShell cmdlets to add, configure, and manage printers. Search PrintManagement on docs.microsoft.com for more information.

Managing Print Jobs

After a user prints a document to a shared printer, the associated print job may spend several minutes within the spool folder on the print server before the print device is ready to accept it, especially if many users are printing to the same shared printer. During this time, there are several options available for managing that print job. Users with Print permission to the printer can view and manage their own print jobs, while users with Manage Documents permission can view and manage the print jobs of other users.

On a print client, users can view and manage their print jobs by clicking the printer icon within their notification area (the right side of the Windows taskbar). This will open the print queue window for the associated printer, as shown in Figure 6-27 for the HPLaserJet_6MP printer. Administrators can right-click the HPLaserJet_6MP printer within the Print Management console and select *Open Printer Queue* to obtain the same print queue window shown in Figure 6-27.

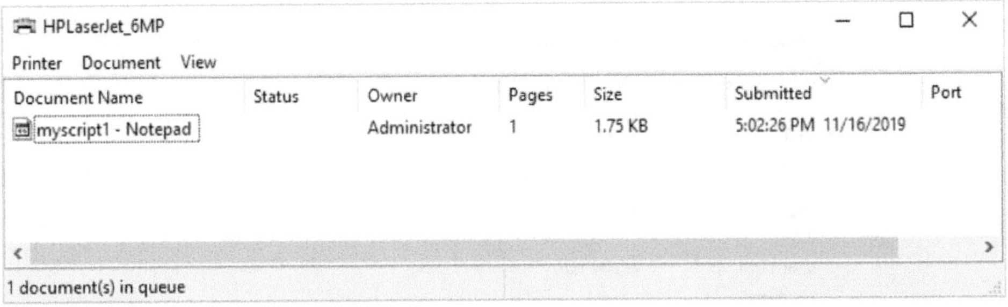

HPLaserJet_6MP						— □ ✕
Printer Document View						
Document Name	Status	Owner	Pages	Size	Submitted	Port
myscript1 - Notepad		Administrator	1	1.75 KB	5:02:26 PM 11/16/2019	

1 document(s) in queue

Figure 6-27   **The print queue window**

If you select the myscript1 document (printed with Notepad) shown in Figure 6-27 and click the Document menu, you can select:

- *Pause* to hold the print job within the print queue until you choose to resume it.
- *Resume* to resume a print job that has been previously paused by the user or Print Spooler service. The Print Spooler will pause documents that do not match the page dimensions configured on the printer if the *Hold mismatched documents* option has been configured on the printer.
- *Restart* to restart printing the print job from the first page. This is often performed after a printer malfunction that causes the print job to be printed improperly, or after the user notices that the wrong paper type or color was used in the print device paper tray.
- *Cancel* to remove the print job. If the print job has already started printing on the print device, this option will stop printing and prevent the remainder of the print job from being sent to the print device.
- *Properties* to view the print job properties, as well as modify the print job layout, paper type, user to notify upon print job completion, print job priority, and schedule (to prevent a print job from being printed until a certain time), as shown in Figure 6-28.

Note

Increasing the priority of a print job will allow that print job to print before other print jobs submitted by other users. As a result, users must have Manage Documents permission to modify the priority of a print job.

Note

Depending on the amount of memory in the print device, a print job might not stop printing immediately after you cancel it.

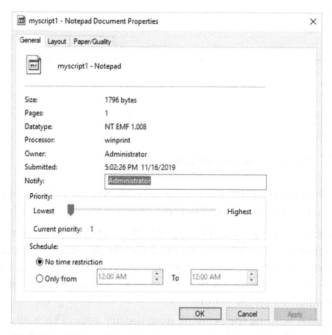

Figure 6-28   The properties of a print job

If you have Manage Documents permission to the HPLaserJet_6MP printer, you can also click the Printer menu in Figure 6-27 and select:

- *Pause Printing* to hold all documents within the print queue. Documents will be placed on hold until this option is deselected.
- *Cancel All Documents* to stop printing and remove all print jobs from the print queue.

Note

Pausing all documents within a print queue is often performed prior to performing routine maintenance on a print device, such as changing toner or refilling paper trays. After the maintenance has been completed, the printer can be configured to resume printing the documents within the print queue.

If you have the Internet Printing component of Print and Document Services installed on your print server, users can instead access a website (`http://printservername/printers`) to manage their print jobs. For example, to view the list of printers available on SERVERX, you can navigate to the URL `http://serverx/printers` within your Web browser. Clicking on the HPLaserJet_6MP printer on this webpage will display the associated print queue webpage, as shown in Figure 6-29. If you are granted Print permission to HPLaserJet_6MP, you can select your own documents and click the links under the DOCUMENT ACTIONS section (*Pause, Resume, Cancel*) to manage them. If you are granted Manage Documents permission, you can click the links under the PRINTER ACTIONS section (*Pause, Resume, Cancel All Documents*) to perform the same actions for all print jobs within the print queue for HPLaserJet_6MP. Under the VIEW section, you can click:

- *Document List* to refresh the list of print jobs within the print queue.
- *Properties* to view printer properties, such as location, comment, IPP name format, and features.
- *All Printers* to return to the website that lists all available printers on the print server.

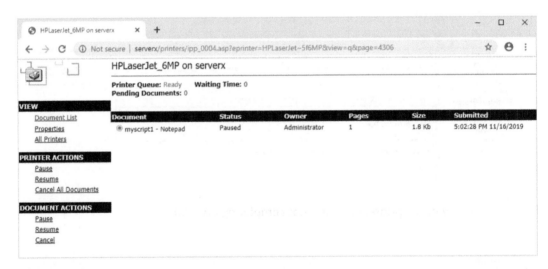

Figure 6-29   The print queue webpage

Note

You can also use the `Get-PrintJob`, `Remove-PrintJob`, `Restart-PrintJob`, `Suspend-PrintJob`, and `Resume-PrintJob` cmdlets within Windows PowerShell to view and manage print jobs within the print queue for a printer.

Monitoring and Troubleshooting Printers

Printing is a necessary and common process within nearly all organizations today. Most organizations deploy multiple print servers that accept print jobs from many users within the organization and print them to a wide range of different print device models. Consequently, printing problems will occur periodically. As a server administrator, you will need to troubleshoot printing problems within your organization, as well as monitor shared printers to identify printing problems before they affect users.

The Print Management tool provides **custom filters** that you can use to quickly check the status of printers, in order to identify any problems. The *Printers Not Ready* custom filter shown in Figure 6-30 displays printers that cannot complete the print process and provides the status of the printer within the Queue Status column. The Queue Status column may indicate that the printer is offline or paused, or it may display a notification from the print device (e.g., paper jam, out of paper, out of toner, door open, or out of memory). The Queue Status column for the HPLaserJet_6MP printer shown in Figure 6-30 is Paused, which is why print jobs are not completing. In this case, you could highlight the HPLaserJet_6MP printer in Figure 6-30 and select More Actions, Resume Printing to resolve the problem.

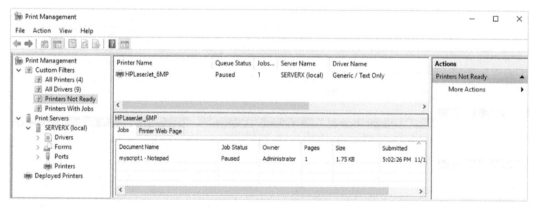

Figure 6-30   Viewing printers that are not completing print jobs

Note

Printers must have bidirectional printing enabled in order to display notifications from the print device within the Queue Status column shown in Figure 6-30.

If the Queue Status column displays *Processing* or *Waiting*, a print job destined for the associated print device may be pausing the print process because it is not formatted correctly, corrupted, or was interrupted by a print device action (such as a toner replacement). In this case, you can highlight the Printers Not Ready node, and select

More Actions, Show Extended View to display the Jobs tab (also shown in Figure 6-30). If the status listed within the Job Status column of the Jobs tab is:

- *Paused*, the print job was placed on hold. You can right-click the print job and click Resume to process the print job.
- *Stopped*, the print job was interrupted by the print device. You can right-click the print job and click Restart to restart the print job.
- *Error*, the print job is not formatted correctly, or corrupted. You can right-click the print job and click Cancel to remove the print job. Following this, the user will need to print their document again.

> **Note** 📎
>
> If all documents from a single user repeatedly become corrupted within the print queue for a printer, you should update or reinstall the printer driver on the print client, or remove and re-add the printer on the print client. If documents from all users become corrupted within the print queue for a printer, you should update or reinstall the printer driver on the print server.

If the Queue Status column displays *Attention Required, Not Available, Error*, or *Ready* (but no print jobs are printing), you may need to restart the Print Spooler service on the print server to remedy the problem. To do this use the `Restart-Service spooler` command within Windows PowerShell. If the LPD Service is installed on your print server, it is dependent on the Print Spool service. In this case, you will need to use the `Restart-Service spooler-force` command within Windows PowerShell to restart the Print Spooler service and all dependent services, including the LPD Service.

> **Note** 📎
>
> You can also use the `net stop spooler` and `net start spooler` MS-DOS commands to restart the Print Spooler service. However, if the LPD Service is installed on your print server, it must be started afterward using the `net start lpdsvc` MS-DOS command.

> **Note** 📎
>
> Recall from Module 2 that you can also use Server Manager or the Windows Admin Center to restart services, including the Print Server service. Alternatively, you can use the graphical **Services tool** to restart the Print Spooler service. To start the Services tool, you can select Services from the Tools menu of Server Manager. Next, right-click Print Spooler and click Restart. If the LPD Service is installed on your print server, you will be prompted to restart it as well.

> **Note**
>
> Restarting the Print Spooler service will remove any corrupt or incomplete print jobs from the print queue, as well as remove the error status from printers and their print jobs, if applicable.

The other custom filters available by default within the Print Management console can be used to list all printers and printer drivers as well as printers that have jobs within their print queue. You can also create additional custom filters that display printers that have different criteria, such as a specific location, print server, or status (value within the Queue Status column) in order to simplify printer monitoring and troubleshooting. To do this, highlight Custom Filters within the navigation pane of the Print Management console and select More Actions, Add New Printer Filter from the Actions pane. This will start the New Printer Filter Wizard shown in Figure 6-31. After specifying a name for your custom filter and clicking Next, you will be prompted to select the custom filter criteria, as shown in Figure 6-32. The criteria shown in Figure 6-32 will display all printers that have a *Toner/Ink Low* status. After you click Next in Figure 6-32, you can optionally configure email notifications or script execution and then click Finish to create the custom filter.

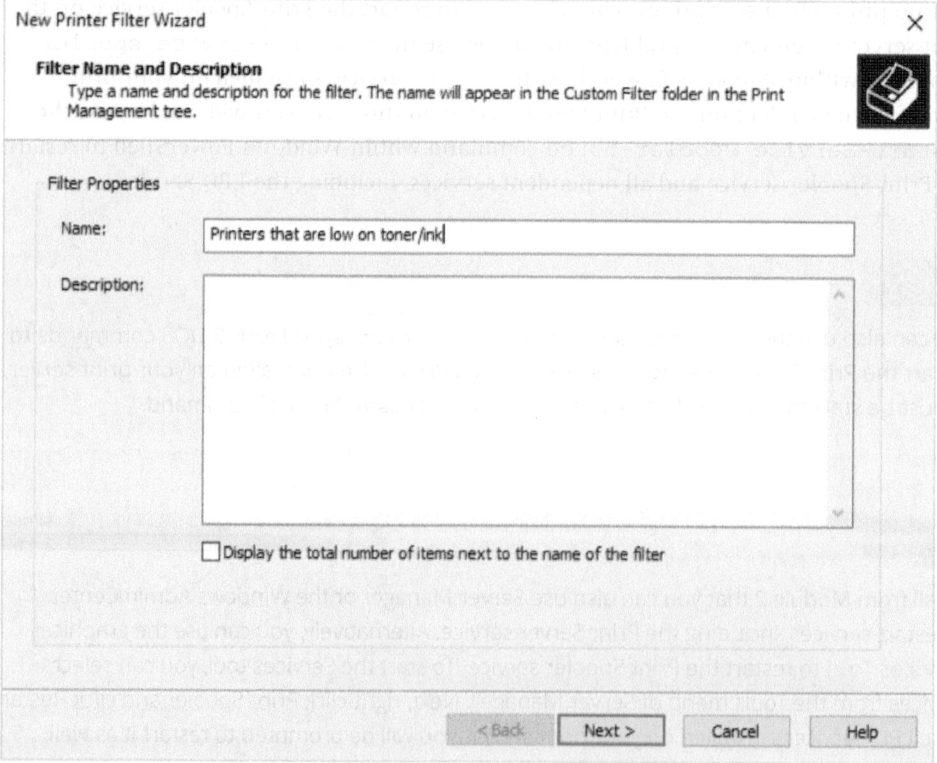

New Printer Filter Wizard	×
Filter Name and Description	
Type a name and description for the filter. The name will appear in the Custom Filter folder in the Print Management tree.	

Filter Properties

Name: Printers that are low on toner/ink|

Description:

☐ Display the total number of items next to the name of the filter

< Back   Next >   Cancel   Help

Figure 6-31   The New Printer Filter Wizard

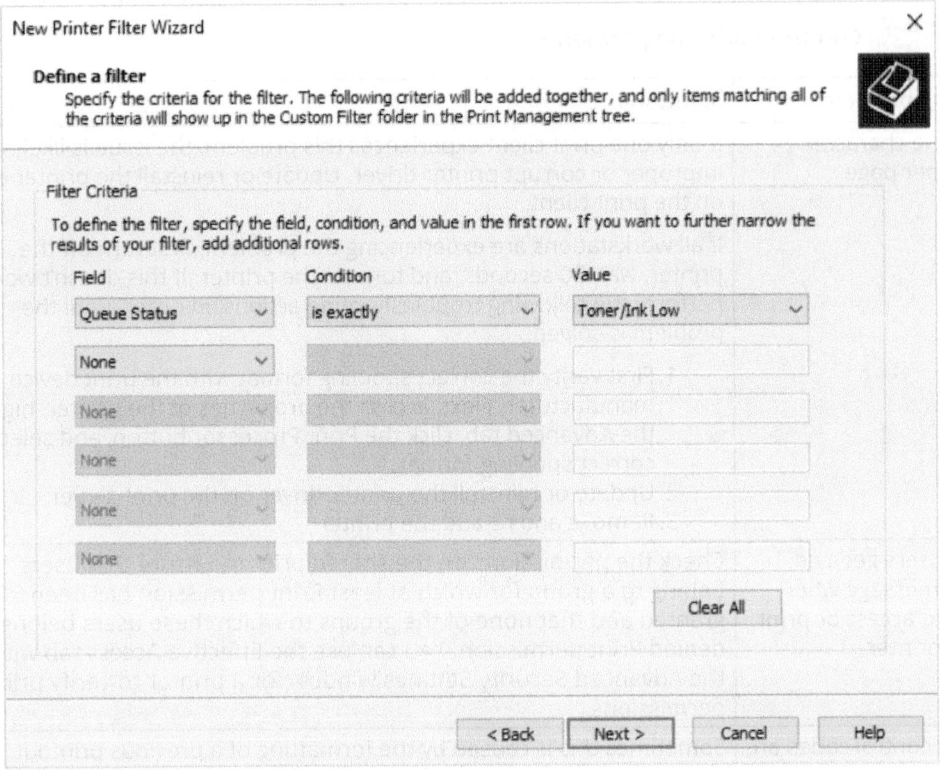

Figure 6-32   Specifying custom filter criteria

Viewing the status of printers and print jobs using the custom filters within the Print Management console may not always help identify and troubleshoot printer problems. This is because some problems are specific to the document that is printed, the hardware capabilities of the print server, or the print device model. Solving these problems may involve researching error codes on a print device manufacturer's website, configuring the print settings within third-party software, modifying print device settings, restarting the Print Spooler service on the print server and print clients, trying different printer settings, or reinstalling printer drivers. As a result, server administrators within two different organizations will likely use different printer troubleshooting steps that correlate to the documents, print servers, and print devices within their respective environments. However, there are some common printing problems that you may encounter that have solutions that work in most environments. These printing problems and their solutions are summarized in Table 6-2.

Table 6-2 Common printing problems

Printing problem	Solutions
Only one character prints per page	If only one print client experiences this problem, the issue is likely an improper or corrupt printer driver. Update or reinstall the printer driver on the print client.
	If all workstations are experiencing the problem, first turn off the printer, wait 30 seconds, and turn on the printer. If this doesn't work, perform the following troubleshooting actions, in order, until the problem is solved: 1. First verify the correct spooling format with the print device manufacturer. Next, access the properties of the printer, highlight the Advanced tab, click the Print Processor button, and select the correct spooling format. 2. Update or reinstall the printer driver on the print server 3. Remove and re-add the printer
Some users get a *no access* message when trying to access or print to the printer	Check the permissions on the shared printer. Ensure that users belong to a group for which at least Print permission has been granted and that none of the groups to which these users belong are denied Print permission. You can use the Effective Access tab within the Advanced Security Settings window for a printer to verify printer permissions.
Printer control codes are on the printout	Sometimes this is caused by the formatting of a previous printout. In this case, turn the printer off, wait for 30 seconds, and turn it back on.
	Some software applications are designed to print using RAW format to a specific print device. In this case, ensure that the software application is configured correctly for the print device model.
	Improper or corrupt printer drivers can also cause this issue. If only one print client experiences the problem, update or reinstall the printer driver on the print client. If all print clients are experiencing the problem, update or reinstall the printer driver on the print server.
A print job shows it is printing, and the printer status does not report an error, but nothing is printing	Sometimes, a problematic print job can prevent other jobs from printing. View the status for the print job at the top of the print queue for the printer. If the status indicates that the job is printing, but the print device is not printing, cancel that print job to allow other print jobs to be sent to the print device. In this case, the user of the problematic print job will need to print their document again.
	If a problematic print job is not the issue, restart the Print Spooler service and advise users to print their documents again.
Some clients find that only the first part of a large print job is printed	The rendering process may require a large amount of storage space to complete for certain document types, such as graphic design files. Verify that the print client has adequate storage available for the document to be spooled and rendered and that the print server has adequate storage available for the document to be spooled.

Table 6-2 Common printing problems *(continued)*

Printing problem	Solutions
On some long print jobs, pages from other print jobs are found in the printout	Configure the printer to start printing only after all pages are spooled. To do this, access the properties of the printer, highlight the Advanced tab, and ensure that *Spool print documents so program finishes printing* and *Start printing after last page is spooled* are selected.
Extra separator pages are printed or print jobs are stuck in the print queue for all users	This is often due to an improper spooling format. First, verify the correct spooling format with the print device manufacturer. Next, access the properties of the printer, highlight the Advanced tab, click the Print Processor button, and select the correct spooling format.
Print jobs print garbled text on hundreds of pages	Improper or corrupt printer drivers can cause this issue. If only one print client experiences the problem, update or reinstall the printer driver on the print client. If all print clients are experiencing the problem, update or reinstall the printer driver on the print server. This problem can also be caused by software applications that choose the wrong document layout options. To prevent these options from causing the issue, access the properties of the printer, highlight the Advanced tab, and select the *Hold mismatched documents* option.
No documents are printing from the printer	Look for warning lights on the print device indicating a printer jam or other problem. Follow the instructions within the print device manual to remedy the issue. If the print device is functional, verify that the cable or network connection is seated properly and functional. Next, turn off the printer, wait 30 seconds, and restart the printer.

Module Summary

- To print to a locally attached or network-attached print device, you must configure a printer that has the appropriate printer driver. Print servers can share printers to print clients using the SMB, IPP, or LPD protocols.

- Windows applications use the GDI or XPS print API to submit documents for printing. These documents are spooled and rendered using the instructions within the printer driver before being sent as a print job to a print device or print server on the network. Print servers spool print jobs from print clients before sending them to a print device.

- The Print and Document Services server role on Windows Server 2019 provides the Print Management tool, as well as the optional IPP and LPD printer sharing protocols.

- The Print Management tool can be used to add, configure, and manage shared printers on multiple servers within an Active Directory environment. Server administrators that have Manage Printers permission can access the properties of the printer within the Print Management tool to perform most printer configuration tasks.

- Shared printers can be published in Active Directory or deployed automatically using Group Policy. Users must have Print permission to a shared printer in order to submit print jobs.

- Branch Office Direct Printing is used to minimize network traffic when branch office users print to network-attached

print devices via a print server within a main office.

- Users can open the print queue window or print server website to manage their own print jobs as well as print jobs for other users if they are granted the Manage Documents permission.

- Custom filters can be used within the Print Management tool to locate printers that have a problem status.

- Printing problems are diverse within most environments but can often be solved by restarting the Print Spooler service, turning a print device off and on again, or by updating or reinstalling a printer driver.

Key Terms

ADSI Edit

application programming
 interface (API)

AppSocket

bidirectional printing

Branch Office Direct
 Printing (BODP)

custom filters

Enhanced Metafile (EMF)

Graphics Device Interface
 (GDI)

HP JetDirect

Internet Printing Client

Internet Printing Protocol
 (IPP)

Line Printer Daemon (LPD)

Line Printer Request (LPR)

locally attached print
 devices

locally attached printers

LPR Port Monitor

network-attached print
 devices

network-attached printers

page description language
 (PDL)

Portable Document Format
 (PDF)

PostScript

Print and Document
  Services

print client

print device

print job

Print Management

print processor

print queue

print server

Print Spooler

printer

Printer Control Language
 (PCL)

printer driver

printer pool

queuing

rendering

separator page

Services tool

shared printer

spool folder

spooling

Web Services Discovery
 (WS-Discovery)

Web Services for Devices
 (WSD)

Windows Presentation
 Foundation (WPF)

XML Paper Specification
 (XPS)

Review Questions

1. Windows 10 PCs can be configured to print directly to a network-attached print device, or to a shared printer on print server that prints directly to a network-attached print device. True or False?

2. Which of the following spooling formats can be used by the GDI print API? (Choose all that apply.)
   a. EMF
   b. XPS
   c. RAW
   d. TEXT

3. Documents are rendered into print jobs on the print client by default. True or False?

4. Which of the following formats can be used to print to a shared printer using IPP?
   a. `servername:\sharedprintername`
   b. `servername:/sharedprintername`
   c. `\\servername\sharedprintername`
   d. `http://servername/printers/sharedprintername/.printer`

5. Which of the following features must you install on a Windows print client in order to print to a shared printer using SMB?
   a. Internet Printing Client
   b. LPR Port Monitor
   c. SMB Printer Client
   d. None of the above

6. You wish to configure a Windows Server 2019 print server using the Print Management tool to share printers using SMB and LPD. What components must you select when installing the Print and Document Service server role? (Choose all that apply.)
   a. Print Management
   b. Print Server

   c. LPD Service
   d. Internet Printing

7. Which of the following are print server configuration tasks that you normally perform before adding shared printers within the Print Management tool? (Choose all that apply.)
   a. Add manufacturer-supplied printer drivers for the print devices within your organization
   b. Add a PRINT$ shared folder
   c. Verify the ports and forms available on your print server, and add additional ones, if necessary
   d. Configure default printer and print server permissions

8. Which of the following settings within printer properties allows print device notifications to be sent to the print server?
   a. Enable printer pooling
   b. Enable bidirectional support
   c. Enable notifications and logs
   d. Allow printer notifications

9. When you select the *List in the directory* option within printer properties, a shared printer object is created within the OU that you specify within Active Directory. True or False?

10. You notice that printouts from small print jobs are inserted within the printouts of large print jobs on a print device within your organization. What option can you select within printer properties to resolve the issue?
    a. Start printing after last page is spooled
    b. Hold mismatched documents
    c. Print directly to the printer
    d. Keep printed documents

11. Separator pages can be configured to reduce the cost of printing for an organization. True or False?

12. The manager of the Accounting department needs to be able to print to the shared printer within the Accounting department, as well as manage other user's print jobs within the print queue. What printer permissions must you assign to the manager on the shared printer at minimum?
    a. Print
    b. Manage Documents
    c. Print and Manage Documents
    d. Manage Documents and Manage Printers

13. You can configure auditing for a shared printer provided that the *Audit object access* policy setting is configured within a Group Policy that applies to the print server. True or False?

14. You would like to ensure that an SMB shared printer is automatically configured on client computers within your organization. What must you do?
    a. Access the Sharing tab of the printer, and select *List in the directory*.
    b. Create a shared printer object within Active Directory Users and Computers.
    c. Access the Advanced tab of the printer and select *Auto deploy printer to client computers*.
    d. Select the printer within the Print Management tool and click *More Actions, Deploy with Group Policy* from the Actions menu.

15. To allow users within a branch office to print to a network-attached printer within a main office, you must enable Branch Office Direct Printing. True or False?

16. You have submitted a print job to a shared printer that uses a different layout than is supported by the print device. After noticing that your print job was not printed, you open the print queue and see your print job with a Paused status. What action can you select from the Documents menu to ensure that the print job is printed, even if the layout is not ideal?
    a. Resume
    b. Unhold
    c. Restart
    d. Cancel

17. Users can access a webpage to view and manage their own print jobs provided that the Internet Printing component of the Print and Document Services role is installed on the print server. True or False?

18. Several users are complaining that a particular printer is not printing their documents. What should be your first course of action?
    a. Restart the Print Spooler service on the print server
    b. Advise each user to restart the Print Spooler service on their print client and re-print their document
    c. View the Queue Status column for the printer within the Printers Not Ready custom filter within the Print Management console
    d. Update or replace the printer driver for the printer within the Print Management console

19. Which of the following commands can be used to restart the Print Spooler service within Windows PowerShell?
    a. `Net-Restart PrintSpooler`
    b. `Restart-Service spooler -force`
    c. `Restart-PrintSpooler`
    d. `Set-Printer` ***printername*** `-restart`

20. A single user complains that their print job is printing garbled text on hundreds of pages on the printer. What are two possible causes of this issue?

  a. The user selected wrong document layout options within their software application when printing the document

  b. The printer driver has become corrupted on the print client

  c. The printer driver has become corrupted on the print server

  d. The shared printer is configured with an improper spooling format

Hands-On Projects

These Hands-On Projects should be completed in the order given. They normally take a total of three hours or less to complete. The requirements for these projects include:

- A system with Windows Server 2019 installed according to Hands-On Project 1-1 (Lab Environment 1) or Hands-On Project 1-2 (Lab Environment 2).
- A WindowsServer2019VM2 virtual machine installed according to Hands-On Project 3-5 and configured as a member server according to Hands-On Project 5-2.

Project 6-1: Enhanced Session Mode Removal

If your system is configured according to Lab Environment 2, you will configure the Hyper-V virtual machine for your Windows Server 2019 host to prevent Windows 10 print devices from being made available within Windows Server 2019.

1. On your Windows 10 system, log in as a user that has administrative privileges, right-click the Start button, and select **Run**. In the Run dialog box, type **virtmgmt.msc** and click **OK** to open Hyper-V Manager.
2. In the Actions pane of Hyper-V Manager, click **Hyper-V Settings**.
3. In the Hyper-V Settings window, select **Enhanced Session Mode** under the User section within the navigation pane. Deselect **Use enhanced session mode** and click **OK**.

Project 6-2: Print Server Installation

In this Hands-On Project, you install, on your Windows Server 2019 host, the server roles and features required for the remaining Hands-On Projects in this module. These include the Print and Document Services role as well as the Internet Printing Client and LPR Port Monitor features.

1. Boot your Windows Server 2019 host and log into domain*X*.com as Administrator using the password **Secret555**. Next, click **Start** and then click **Server Manager**.
2. Within Server Manager, click the **Manage** menu and then click **Add Roles and Features**.
3. At the Select installation type page, click **Next**.
4. At the Select destination server page, click **Next**.
5. At the Select server roles page, select **Print and Document Services** and click **Add Features** when prompted. Click **Next**.

6. At the Select features page, select **Internet Printing Client** and **LPR Port Monitor** and click **Next**.

7. At the Print and Document Services page, click **Next**.

8. At the Select role services page, note that Print Server is automatically selected.
   a. Select **Internet Printing** and click **Add Features** when prompted.
   b. Select **LPD Service** and click **Next**.

9. At the Web Server Role (IIS) page, click **Next**.

10. At the Select role services page, click **Next**.

11. At the Confirm installation selections page, click **Install** to install the Print and Document Services role, as well as the Internet Printing Client and LPR Port Monitor features.

12. At the Installation progress page, click **Close**.

Project 6-3: Print Server Configuration

In this Hands-On Project, you examine the configuration of your Windows Server 2019 print server and then add two sample shared printers (SamplePrinter1 and SamplePrinter2).

1. Within Server Manager on your Windows Server 2019 host, click the **Tools** menu and then click **Print Management**.

2. In the navigation pane of the Print Management tool, expand **Print Servers**, and then expand **SERVERX**.

3. Highlight **Drivers** in the navigation pane and note the default printer drivers that are installed on your print server. For each driver, scroll to the right and note whether the printer driver is an XPS driver. Next, click **More Actions**, **Add Driver** from the Actions pane.
   a. At the Add Printer Driver Wizard, click **Next**.
   b. At the Processor Selection page, note the default architecture listed and click **Next**.
   c. At the Printer Driver Selection page, note the default selection (Generic/Text Only) and click **Next**.
   d. At the Completing the Add Printer Driver Wizard page, click **Finish**.
   e. For your newly added driver, scroll to the right and note whether the printer driver is an XPS driver.

4. Highlight **Forms** in the navigation pane and note the default forms installed on your print server.

5. Highlight **Ports** in the navigation pane and note the default ports available on your print server.

6. Highlight **Printers** in the navigation pane and note the two default printers available on your print server.
   a. Click **More Actions**, **Add Printer** from the Actions pane.
   b. At the Network Printer Installation Wizard, select **Add a new printer using an existing port**, ensure that **LPT1: (Printer Port)** is listed in the associated drop-down box, and click **Next**.

   c. At the Printer Driver page, select **Use an existing printer driver on the computer**, ensure that **Generic/Text Only** is listed in the associated drop-down box and click **Next**.

   d. At the Printer Name and Sharing Settings page, note that printer sharing is enabled by default, type **SamplePrinter1** in both the Printer Name and Share Name text boxes. Next, type **Marketing Department** in the Location text box, type **Sample Marketing Printer for Module 6** in the Comment text box and click **Next**.

   e. At the Printer Found page, click **Next**.

   f. At the Completing the Network Printer Installation Wizard, select **Add another printer** and click **Finish**.

   g. At the Printer Installation page, ensure that **Add a new printer using an existing port** is selected, that **LPT1: (Printer Port)** is listed in the drop-down box, and click **Next**.

   h. At the Printer Driver page, ensure that **Use an existing printer driver on the computer** is selected and that **Generic/Text Only** is listed in the associated drop-down box and click **Next**.

   i. At the Printer Name and Sharing Settings page, type **SamplePrinter2** in both the Printer Name and Share Name text boxes. Next, type **Accounting Department** in the Location text box, type **Sample Accounting Printer for Module 6** in the Comment text box and click **Next**.

   j. At the Printer Found page, click **Next**.

   k. At the Completing the Network Printer Installation Wizard, click **Finish**.

   l. Note that SamplePrinter1 and SamplePrinter2 have been added to the Printers node. Scroll to the right and note that each printer uses a Type 3 printer driver.

7. Highlight **SERVERX** in the navigation pane and click **More Actions**, **Properties** from the Actions pane. Note the default location of the spool folder and that notifications are enabled by default.

   a. Highlight the **Security** tab and note the default printer and print server permissions are granted to the Everyone, CREATOR OWNER, and Administrators groups.

   b. Click **Add**, type **Bob Burtt,** and click **OK**.

   c. Note that Bob Burtt is assigned Print and View Server permissions by default. Select **Manage Documents** and click **OK**.

8. Click **More Actions**, **Properties** from the Actions pane. Note the email and script options available notifications and click **OK**.

Project 6-4: Printer Properties

In this Hands-On Project, you explore and configure various properties and features for SamplePrinter1 as well as verify that it was published successfully to Active Directory.

1. In the navigation pane of the Print Management tool on your Windows Server 2019 host, highlight **Printers** under SERVERX. Next, select **SamplePrinter1** and click **More Actions**, **Pause Printing** from the Actions pane to ensure that documents printed to SamplePrinter1 are held in the print queue.

2. Click **More Actions**, **Properties** from the Actions pane.

   a. On the General tab, note the name, location, comment, features, and paper information for SamplePrinter1.

   b. Click **Preferences** and note the default options on the Layout tab. Highlight the **Paper/Quality** tab, note the default paper source setting, and click **OK**.

   c. Click **Print Test Page** to submit a test page document to SamplePrinter1, and click **Close** at the confirmation window.

   d. Highlight the **Sharing** tab, note the default sharing options render print jobs on client computers, and select **List in the directory**.

   e. Highlight the **Ports** tab and note that SamplePrinter1 prints to the print device located on LPT1. Select **Enable printer pooling** and then select **LPT2** and **LPT3**. Next, select **Add Port**, note the default port types available, and click **Cancel**.

   f. Highlight the **Advanced** tab and note the default time, priority, driver, and spooling options. Select **Start printing after last page is spooled** and then select **Hold mismatched documents**.

      i. Click **Print Processor**, note the available spooling formats available for a non-XPS print device, and click **OK**.

      ii. Click **Separator Page** and then click **Browse**. Select **pcl.sep** from the System32 directory and click **Open**. Click **OK** to add the separator page to SamplePrinter1.

   g. Highlight the **Security** tab, highlight **Bob Burtt**, and note the permissions you assigned on the print server were inherited to SamplePrinter1.

      i. Select **Manage this printer** under the Allow column and click **Apply** to ensure that Bob Burtt has all printer permissions.

      ii. Click **Advanced**, highlight the **Bob Burtt** entry that grants *Manage this printer,* and click **Edit**. Click **Show advanced permissions**, note the advanced permissions that make up the *Manage this printer* print permission, and click **OK**.

      iii. Highlight the **Auditing** tab and click **Add**.

      iv. Click **Select a principal**, type **Domain Admins** in the text box, and click **OK**. Note that Print permission is audited by default. Select **Manage this printer** and **Manage documents** to additionally audit printer and document management events, and click **OK**.

      v. Highlight the **Effective Access** tab and note the information message. Click **Apply**. Next, click **Select a user**, type **Bob Burtt** in the text box, and click **OK**. Click **View effective access**, note that Bob Burtt is granted all printer permissions, and click **OK**.

   h. Highlight the **Device Settings** tab, note the default paper options, and click **OK**. Note that SamplePrinter1 has a status of Paused and that there is 1 print job within the queue that contains the test page you printed.

3. Click **More Actions**, **Enable Branch Office Direct Printing** from the Actions pane. Because Branch Office Direct Printing only applies to printers that print to network-attached print devices, click **More Actions**, **Disable Branch Office Direct Printing** from the Actions pane to remove this setting.

4. Close the Print Management tool.

5. Within Server Manager, click the **Tools** menu and then click **ADSI Edit**.

   a. In the ADSI Edit tool, select **More Actions**, **Connect to** within the Actions pane.

   b. At the Connection Settings window, click **OK** to add the domain partition of the Active Directory database (Default naming context).

   c. In the navigation pane, expand **Default naming context**, **DC=domainX, DC=com**, **OU=Domain Controllers**, and then highlight **CN=SERVERX**. Note the printQueue object that represents SamplePrinter1.

   d. Close ADSI Edit.

Project 6-5: Adding Shared Printers

In this Hands-On Project, you add SamplePrinter1 and SamplePrinter2 on your WindowsServer2019VM2 virtual machine. Then you submit print jobs to both SamplePrinter1 and SamplePrinter2.

1. Within Server Manager on your Windows Server 2019 host, select the **Tools** menu and then click **Hyper-V Manager**.

2. Highlight **WindowsServer2019VM2** within the virtual machines pane of Hyper-V Manager and click **Connect** in the Actions pane. In the Virtual Machine Connection window, click **Start** to boot your new virtual machine.

3. At the login screen, click the **Ctrl+Alt+Delete** button within the Virtual Machine Connection window, supply the password **Secret555** for Administrator and press **Enter** to log into the system.

4. Click **Start** and then click **Control Panel**. Click **View devices and printers** under the Hardware section, and note the default printers shown.

   a. Click **Add a printer** to start the Add Printer wizard. Note that SamplePrinter1 on SERVERX was automatically detected because it was published in Active Directory.

   b. Ensure that **SamplePrinter1** is selected and click **Next**. The printer driver for SamplePrinter1 is automatically downloaded and configured on your system during this process. When the process has completed, note the shared printer called *SamplePrinter1 on SERVERX.domainX.com* within the Devices and Printers section of Control Panel. Click **Finish**.

   c. Click **Add a printer** to start the Add Printer wizard. Next, click **The printer that I want isn't listed**.

   d. Select **Select a shared printer by name** and type \\serverX\SamplePrinter2 in the text box and click **Next**.

   e. Click **Next**.

   f. Click **Print a test page** and note that Windows Server 2019 indicates that there was an error printing the test page. Click **Close**.

   g. Click **Finish**. Note the shared printer *SamplePrinter2 on serverX* within the Devices and Printers section of Control Panel.

   h. Right-click **SamplePrinter1 on SERVERX.domainX.com** and click **Printer properties**. Click **Print Test Page** and note that Windows Server 2019 indicates that the printer is in an error state. Click **Close** to close the information window and click **OK** to close the *SamplePrinter1 on SERVERX.domainX.com* Properties window.

Project 6-6: Print Job Management

In this Hands-On Project, you view and manage the print jobs that you have submitted to SamplePrinter1 and SamplePrinter2 on your WindowsServer2019VM2 virtual machine and Windows Server 2019 host.

1. Within the Devices and Printers section of Control panel on your WindowsServer2019VM2 virtual machine, double-click **SamplePrinter1 on SERVERX.domainX.com** to open the associated print queue. Note the two Test Page print jobs and their submission times. The first one was submitted in Project 6-4, and the second one was submitted in Project 6-5. Also note the absence of a Status value.

2. Highlight the second (most recent) print job, select the **Document** menu, and note the options available. Click **Properties**, drag the Priority slider to the right side to set a value of **99** and click **OK**.

3. Highlight the first (oldest) print job, select the **Document** menu, click **Cancel,** and click **Yes** when prompted.

4. Select the **Printer** menu and note that printing is paused for all documents within the SamplePrinter1 print queue. Click **Close** to close the print queue window for SamplePrinter1.

5. Double-click **SamplePrinter2 on serverX** to open the associated print queue. Note the Test Page print job that was submitted in Project 6-5. Also note that the Test Page print job has a status of *Error - Printing* since the print queue for SamplePrinter2 was not paused, and the print server attempted to print the Test Page to a non-existent print device.

6. Select the **Printer** menu and click **Close** to close the print queue window for SamplePrinter2.

7. Close Control Panel.

8. Within Server Manager on your Windows Server 2019 host, select the **Tools** menu and then click **Print Management**.

   a. Highlight **Printers** under SERVERX and note the value in the Queue Status column for SamplePrinter1 and SamplePrinter2.

   b. Select **SamplePrinter1** and select **More Actions**, **Open Printer Queue**. Note that the print queue for SamplePrinter1 indicates the same information shown within the same print queue on your WindowsServer2019VM2 virtual machine.

   c. Highlight the Test Page print job, select the **Document** menu, and note the options available.

   d. Select the **Printer** menu, note the options available, and click **Close** to close the print queue window for SamplePrinter1.

   e. Select **SamplePrinter2** and select **More Actions**, **Open Printer Queue**. Note that the print queue for SamplePrinter2 indicates the same information shown within the same print queue on your WindowsServer2019VM2 virtual machine.

   f. Close the Print Management tool.

9. Open the Google Chrome Web browser, and navigate to the URL `http://serverX/printers`. Note the status, location, and comment for SamplePrinter1 and SamplePrinter2.

   a. Click **SamplePrinter1** to open the SamplePrinter1 print queue. Note your Test Page and view the document and printer actions available.

   b. Click **All Printers** to return to the printer list.

   c. Click **SamplePrinter2** to open the SamplePrinter2 print queue. Select the **Test Page** print job and click **Pause** under the DOCUMENT ACTIONS section to place the print job on hold. Note the new status of *Paused – Error – Printing*.

   d. Close the Google Chrome Web browser.

Project 6-7: Printer Troubleshooting

In this Hands-On Project, you use custom filters within the Print Management tool to examine printer and print job errors, as well as restart the Print Spooler service on your Windows Server 2019 host.

1. Within Server Manager on your Windows Server 2019 host, select the **Tools** menu and then click **Print Management**.

   a. Expand **Custom Filters** in the navigation pane and highlight **Printers Not Ready**. Note the status of SamplePrinter1 and SamplePrinter2 within the Queue Status column.

   b. Highlight **SamplePrinter1** and click **More Actions**, **Resume Printing** from the Actions pane. Note that the status of SamplePrinter1 now reports Error.

   c. Click **More Actions**, **Show Extended View** under the Printers Not Ready section of the Actions pane. Note that the Test Page job for SamplePrinter1 lists *Error – Printing* within the Job Status column.

   d. Highlight **SamplePrinter2** and note that the Test Page job for SamplePrinter1 lists *Paused - Error – Printing* within the Job Status column.

2. Right-click **Start** and click **Windows PowerShell (Admin)**. Type `Restart-Service spooler -force` at the Windows PowerShell prompt and press **Enter**. Close Windows PowerShell when finished.

3. In the Print Management tool, highlight **Printers Not Ready** in the navigation pane and click **More Actions**, **Refresh**. Note that the SamplePrinter1 and SamplePrinter2 are no longer visible within the Printers Not Ready custom filter.

4. Highlight **Printers With Jobs** in the navigation pane. Note that SamplePrinter1 and SamplePrinter2 are shown and that each one has a status of Ready within the Queue Status column and 1 print job listed within the Jobs In Queue column.

   a. Highlight **SamplePrinter1** and note that the Test Page print job has a status of *Sent to Printer* in the Job Status column.

   b. Highlight **SamplePrinter2** and note that the Test Page print job has a status of *Paused* in the Job Status column.

c. Right-click the **Test Page** print job in the SamplePrinter2 print queue and click **Resume**. Note that the status returns to *Error – Printing*.

d. Right-click the **Test Page** print job in the SamplePrinter2 print queue and click **Cancel**. After a few moments, SamplePrinter2 should disappear from the Printers With Jobs custom filter.

e. Close the Print Management console.

Discovery Exercises

Exercise 6-1

Some print device problems may involve the failure of the print device itself. In this case, users may need to wait several hours or days for the print device to be repaired. In this case, you can redirect print jobs that are waiting in the print queue for the failed printer to another shared printer within the organization that prints to the same print device model. Assume that SamplePrinter1 has failed. Access the properties of SamplePrinter1 within the Print Management tool and create a new local port that prints to \\SERVERX\SamplePrinter2. Next, submit a new print job to SamplePrinter1 and verify that it is stored within the print queue for SamplePrinter2.

Exercise 6-2

In Hands-On Project 6-5, you added the shared SamplePrinter1 and SamplePrinter2 printers to your WindowsServer2019VM2 virtual machine using the Add Printer wizard. Create another shared printer on your Windows Server 2019 host called SamplePrinter3 that is shared to systems on the network. Next, deploy the printer automatically to all computers within your Active Directory domain using a Group Policy. Finally, reboot (or boot) your WindowsServer2019VM2 virtual machine and verify that SamplePrinter3 was automatically added.

Exercise 6-3

While SMB is the most common print-sharing protocol on Windows networks, the SamplePrinter1 and SamplePrinter2 printers that you created within Hands-On Project 6-3 were shared using all protocols available on your print server, including SMB, IPP, and LPD. Use the Print Management tool on your Windows Server 2019 host to create two new shared printers called SamplePrinter4 and SamplePrinter5. On your WindowsServer2019VM2 virtual machine, use the appropriate options within the Add Printer wizard to add SamplePrinter4 using the IPP protocol. Next, use the appropriate options within the Add Printer wizard to add SamplePrinter5 using the LPD protocol. Test your configuration by submitting print jobs to SamplePrinter4 and SamplePrinter5.

Exercise 6-4

In Hands-On Project 6-7, you explored default custom filters available within the Print Management tool. Custom filters are often used by server administrators to view shared printers that exhibit a recurring problem. Say, for example, that your organization frequently experiences *Out of Memory* errors on a particular brand of print device. The solution you have found for this problem involves turning the print device off and on again and then restarting the Print Spooler service on the associated print server. To respond quickly to these errors, you would like to have a custom filter within the Print Management tool that alerts you to *Out of Memory* errors before users create a help desk ticket. Create a custom filter within the Print Management tool on your Windows Server 2019 host that only displays shared printers within your organization that have a Queue Status of *Out of Memory*.

Exercise 6-5

In Hands-On Project 6-4, you configured auditing for SamplePrinter1. View the Security log on your Windows Server 2019 host by running the `Get-EventLog Security -EntryType SuccessAudit | Format-List` command within Windows PowerShell and search the output for the events that you performed within Hands-On Projects 6-5, 6-6, and 6-7.

Exercise 6-6

To practice the configuration of a print server without a physical print device, you used a generic print driver for the SamplePrinter1 and SamplePrinter2 printers that you created within Hands-On Project 6-3. Use the Internet to search for print drivers for a print device of your choice and add those drivers to your print server within the Print Management tool on your Windows Server 2019 host. Note whether the drivers are Type 3 or Type 4. Next, use the Print Management tool to create a new shared printer called SamplePrinter6 that uses one of the drivers that you added. Afterwards, access the properties of SamplePrinter6 and note the driver-provided options on the General, Advanced, and Device Settings tabs as well as any additional tabs that have been added.

CONFIGURING AND MANAGING DATA STORAGE

After completing this module, you will be able to:

Describe local storage options available for Windows Server 2019

Create and manage simple and software RAID volumes

Configure and connect to SAN storage

Configure data deduplication

Optimize and repair volumes

Backup and restore data

A wide variety of different storage options are available to servers. As a server administrator, you must know how to configure these storage options as well as manage stored data. In this module, you'll explore the local storage options available for a server as well as learn how to configure and manage simple and software RAID volumes. Following this, you'll explore the methods used to connect a Windows Server 2019 system to SAN storage. Next, you'll learn how to provide iSCSI SAN storage to other systems, configure data deduplication, and optimize and repair volumes. At the end of this module, you'll learn how to use Windows Server Backup to back up and restore data.

Windows Server 2019 Local Storage Options

Before configuring local storage on a Windows Server 2019 system, it is important to understand the storage device types available and the ways they can be configured to provide access to data.

Storage Devices

As discussed in Module 1, you can install two types of storage devices inside rackmount servers: hard disks and SSDs. While SSDs are a newer technology that offers very fast transfer speeds, they are far more expensive per GB of storage capacity compared to hard disks. As a result, a server administrator may choose to use a combination of hard disks and SSDs in a rackmount server to stay within budget. For example, SSDs may be configured to store the operating system and applications, while hard disks may be used to provide storage for data. This configuration provides fast performance for the operating system and applications while allowing for a large storage capacity for data at a low cost. In another example, SSDs may be configured to store the operating system, applications, and frequently accessed data (e.g., databases and shared folders that store user documents), while hard disks may be used to store data that is not accessed frequently (e.g., archive databases and shared folders that store backups).

Note 📎

If multiple hard disks are used, they can be configured as a Redundant Array of Independent Disks (RAID) to provide faster data transfer speeds than a single hard disk as well as fault tolerance in the event of a hard disk failure. This allows organizations to provide fast, high-capacity storage for data at a much lower cost than SSDs.

Before the introduction of SSDs, legacy rackmount servers typically used **IDE (Integrated Drive Electronics)** or **Small Computer Systems Interface (SCSI)** hard disks. However, modern rackmount servers often use **Serial Advanced Technology Attachment (SATA)** hard disks or SSDs, **Serial Attached SCSI (SAS)** hard disks or SSDs, or Non-Volatile Memory Express (NVMe) SSDs. Because SATA storage devices are commonly used on PCs, they are the least expensive and widely supported storage option for a rackmount server. SAS storage devices offer greater transfer speeds compared to SATA, but at an increased cost per GB of storage capacity. NVMe SSDs are much faster than SATA and SAS SSDs as they provide an SSD-only architecture that directly connects to the PCIe interconnect on the system. However, NVMe SSDs are the most expensive per GB of storage capacity and, because they are a recent technology, may not be supported by some rackmount servers in an organization.

Partitions, Filesystems, and Volumes

Regardless of type, each storage device is divided into sections called **partitions**. Before you can store files in a partition, you must format it with a filesystem. **Filesystems** provide a structure that specifies how data should reside on the storage device itself.

Filesystems also define storage-related features that operating systems can use, including folder and file permissions, compression, encryption, and journaling. A **journaling** filesystem uses a journal to keep track of the information written to the storage device. If you copy a file on the filesystem from one folder to another, that file must pass into memory and then be written to the new location. If the power to the system is turned off during this process, information might not be transmitted as expected and data might be lost or corrupted. With a journaling filesystem, each step required to copy the file to the new location is first written to a journal. This allows the system to automatically retrace the steps taken prior to a power outage and complete the file copy, after the power is restored. NTFS and ReFS are journaling filesystems, while FAT32 and exFAT are not.

Note

Creating a filesystem on a storage device is commonly referred to as **formatting**.

Note

Due to their lack of storage-related features, FAT32 and exFAT are only used for removable media storage devices, not on permanent storage devices in servers.

A filesystem may reside on one partition on your storage device or span multiple partitions on different storage devices using RAID. You typically access a filesystem using a drive letter (e.g., C: or D:) in the Windows operating system. This drive letter and the associated filesystem is collectively referred to as a **volume**. For example, *the C: volume* represents the filesystem that can be accessed via C:, whereas *the D: volume* represents the filesystem that can be accessed via D:. Moreover, if D: represents a filesystem stored on a single partition, then D: is called a **simple volume**. However, if D: represents a filesystem stored on three different storage devices using RAID, then D: is called a **RAID volume**.

Note

Since the introduction of MS-DOS on the IBM PC, the A: and B: drive letters have been reserved for representing filesystems on floppy disks. While floppy disks are no longer used on modern systems, their drive letters still remain reserved.

> **Note** 📎
>
> Rather than using a drive letter to represent a filesystem, volumes can instead use an existing folder to represent a filesystem. For example, if you use the C:\Data folder to represent a filesystem on a partition, users can access the folders and files on the filesystem by navigating to the C:\Data folder. UNIX and Linux systems use this same structure when accessing filesystems.

> **Note** 📎
>
> The term **mounting** refers to the process of associating a drive letter or folder to a filesystem so that the drive letter or folder can be accessed by the operating system.

Partition Types and Strategies

In addition to creating a partition that is mounted to C:, the Windows Server 2019 installation program creates a **recovery partition** formatted with NTFS. A recovery partition contains tools you can use to repair a Windows Server 2019 installation that is unable to boot. On systems that use a UEFI BIOS, the Windows Server 2019 installation program also creates a **UEFI system partition** (also called an **EFI system partition**) formatted with FAT32 to store the **boot loader** program used to load the Windows Server 2019 operating system after the system is powered on. Because the recovery and UEFI system partitions are not made accessible to the Windows Server 2019 operating system via a drive letter or folder, they are not considered volumes.

> **Note** 📎
>
> On systems that have a standard (non-UEFI) BIOS, the boot loader for Windows Server 2019 is stored on the recovery partition, and the recovery partition is assigned an *active* label. The standard BIOS will search this **active partition** for an operating system boot loader after the system is powered on.

> **Note** 📎
>
> The partition that contains the boot loader is called the **system partition** on Microsoft systems, while the partition that contains the operating system is called the **boot partition**. The UEFI system partition is the system partition on systems that have a UEFI BIOS, whereas

the recovery partition is the system partition on systems that have a standard BIOS. Unless configured otherwise during the Windows Server 2019 installation, the boot partition is the partition that hosts the C: volume.

The table of all partition information for a storage device is located at the beginning of the storage device itself. The traditional partition table is called the **Master Boot Record (MBR)**, and is limited to storage devices that are equal to or less than 2 TB in size. Newer storage devices and storage devices larger than 2 TB use a **GUID Partition Table (GPT)** instead of an MBR.

Note

The MBR and GPT are functionally equivalent.

There are limits to the number and types of partitions into which a storage device can be divided. On storage devices that use an MBR, you can create a maximum of four major partitions (called **primary partitions**). To overcome this limitation, you can optionally label one of these primary partitions as *extended*; this **extended partition** can then contain an unlimited number of smaller partitions called **logical drives**. Each logical drive in the extended partition and all other primary partitions can contain a filesystem and be used to store data. On storage devices that use a GPT, you can create up to 128 primary partitions, with no extended partitions or logical drives allowed.

To demonstrate the difference between MBR and GPT partitioning, Table 7-1 shows an example MBR partition layout for the first storage device on a system that uses a standard BIOS, while Table 7-2 shows an example GPT partition layout for the first storage device on a system that uses a UEFI BIOS.

Table 7-1   Example MBR partition layout for the first storage device on a system with a standard BIOS

Partition	Filesystem	Volume name	Description
First primary partition	NTFS	None	Recovery partition Active partition System partition
Second primary partition	NTFS	C:	Boot partition
Third primary partition	NTFS	D:	
Fourth primary partition (extended)	None	None	Extended partition

(continues)

Table 7-1   Example MBR partition layout for the first storage device on a system with a standard BIOS *(continued)*

Partition	Filesystem	Volume name	Description
First logical drive in the extended partition	ReFS	E:	
Second logical drive in the extended partition	NTFS	F:	
Third logical drive in the extended partition	NTFS	G:	

Table 7-2   Example GPT partition layout for the first storage device on a system with a UEFI BIOS

GPT partition	Filesystem	Volume name	Description
First primary partition	NTFS	None	Recovery partition
Second primary partition	FAT32	None	UEFI system partition System partition
Third primary partition	NTFS	C:	Boot partition
Fourth primary partition	NTFS	D:	
Fifth primary partition	ReFS	E:	
Sixth primary partition	NTFS	F:	
Seventh primary partition	NTFS	G:	

Note

If your system has a DVD drive, the D: drive letter is often reserved for it following the creation of the C: volume during the Windows Server 2019 installation process, and additional volumes will use the E: drive letter onwards.

Note

Drive letters do not need to be contiguous. When creating a volume, you can choose the drive letter that you wish to use for a filesystem.

Not all server administrators will create additional volumes on storage devices, as shown with the D:, E:, F:, and G: volumes in Table 7-2. Many server administrators prefer to configure a single volume on each storage device that uses the maximum available capacity. In this case, the C: volume shown in Figure 7-2 would use the remaining available space on the first storage device, the D: volume would represent the filesystem in the first primary partition on the second storage device, the E: volume would represent the filesystem in the first primary partition on the third storage device, and so on. However, creating additional volumes on a single storage device allows you to do the following:

- Segregate different types of data—for example, configuring an application to store its log files on the D: volume in Table 7-2 will make locating the log files easier, as well as ensure that they cannot consume all available space on the C: volume, which can slow or halt the performance of the Windows Server 2019 operating system.
- Allow for the use of more than one type of filesystem on a single storage device— for example, if a database application performs faster when installed on an ReFS filesystem, you could install that application on the E: volume in Table 7-2.
- Reduce the chance that filesystem corruption will render all data on the storage device unusable; if the NTFS filesystem in the F: volume in Table 7-2 becomes corrupted, it does not affect the data stored on other volumes or the operating system installed on the C: volume.
- Speed up access to stored data by keeping filesystems as small as possible. This process is similar to searching for a penny in a 20,000-square-foot warehouse. It takes much less time to find the penny if that warehouse is divided into four separate departments of 5,000 square feet each and you know in which department the penny is located. Searching and maneuvering is much quicker and easier in a smaller, defined space than in a larger one.

RAID Types and Strategies

While creating several volumes on a storage device will decrease the likelihood that the failure of a single filesystem will affect data on other volumes, it does not protect data in the event that the storage device fails. To protect data against storage device failure, you can spread filesystems across several storage devices using a fault tolerant RAID volume. In addition to using RAID to implement filesystem fault tolerance, you can use RAID to speed up access to storage devices and to combine multiple storage devices into a single volume.

Note ☍

Fault-tolerant RAID volumes are not a replacement for performing regular data backups. If files become corrupted, or are inadvertently deleted from a fault-tolerant RAID volume, you will need to restore those files from a backup. Backing up and restoring data is discussed later in this module.

One type of RAID-like configuration, known as **spanning** or **Just a Bunch of Disks (JBOD)**, consists of two or more storage devices that the system sees as one large volume. Using this technology, you could, for example, combine two 1 TB storage devices into a single 2 TB volume. Spanning is useful when you need a large amount of storage space in a single volume without fault tolerance. In addition to spanning, seven basic RAID configurations are available, ranging from level 0 to level 6. RAID level 0 configurations are not fault tolerant.

In RAID level 0, called **striping**, an individual file is divided into sections and saved concurrently on two or more storage devices, one section per storage device. For example, suppose you have a striping configuration made up of three storage devices. In that case, when you save a file, it is divided into three sections, with each section written to separate storage devices concurrently, in a third of the amount of time it would take to save the entire file on one storage device. Note that the system can also read the same file in one-third the time it would take if the file were stored on a single storage device. Striping is useful when you need to speed up storage device access (e.g., with hard disks), but it is not fault tolerant. If one storage device fails in a striping configuration, all data is lost.

RAID level 1, which is often referred to as **mirroring**, provides fault tolerance in the event of a storage device failure. In this RAID configuration, the same data is written to two separate storage devices at the same time. This results in two storage devices with identical information. If one fails, the copy automatically replaces the failed storage device. The only drawback to RAID level 1 is the cost, because you need to purchase twice the storage device space needed for a given computer.

Note 📎

If the two storage devices in a RAID level 1 configuration are stored on separate storage controllers on the system, it is called **duplexing**. In this configuration, data remains available in the event that a single storage controller fails on the system.

Note 📎

Three-way mirroring can also be configured if you have five or more storage devices. In this configuration, data is stored on three different storage devices. This allows data to be available in the event that two storage devices fail at the same time.

RAID level 2 is no longer used and was a variant of RAID 0 that allowed for error and integrity checking on storage devices. Modern storage devices do this intrinsically.

RAID level 3 is striping with a parity bit, or marker, which indicates what data is where. It requires a minimum of three storage devices to function, with one of the storage devices used to store the parity information. Should one of the storage devices containing data fail, you can replace the storage device and regenerate the data using the parity information stored on the parity storage device. If the parity storage device fails, the system must be restored from a backup device.

RAID level 4 is only a slight variant on RAID level 3. RAID level 4 offers greater access speed than RAID level 3 because it can store data in blocks and, thus, does not need to access all storage devices at once to read data.

RAID level 5 replaces RAID levels 3 and 4; it is the most common RAID configuration used today and is called **striping with parity**. As with RAID levels 3 and 4, it requires a minimum of three storage devices; however, the parity information is not stored on a separate storage device but is intermixed with data on the storage devices that make up the set. This offers better performance and fault tolerance; if any storage device in the RAID configuration fails, the information on the other storage devices can be used to automatically regenerate the lost information such that users can still access their data. After the failed storage device has been replaced, the data can easily be rebuilt on the new storage device, returning the RAID configuration to its original state. However, if two storage devices fail at the same time, the data must be restored from a backup copy. Figure 7-1 uses a simple example to demonstrate using parity information to calculate data on a RAID level 5. The parity bits shown in Figure 7-1 are a sum of the information on the other two storage devices (22 + 12 = 34). If the third storage device fails, the information can be regenerated because only one element is missing from each equation:

$$22 + 12 = 34$$

$$68 - 65 = 3$$

$$13 - 9 = 4$$

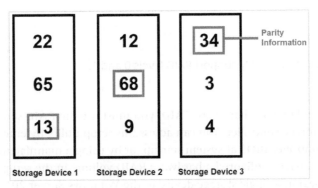

Figure 7-1   Organization of data on RAID level 5

RAID level 6 is fundamentally the same as RAID level 5, but it adds a second set of parity bits for added fault tolerance and allows up to two simultaneous storage device failures while remaining fault tolerant. While RAID level 6 requires a minimum of four storage devices, at least seven storage devices are required for acceptable performance.

> **Note**
>
> RAID levels 0, 1, and 5 are widely implemented today.

> **Note**
>
> RAID levels are often combined; for example, RAID level 10 refers to a striping configuration (RAID level 0) that is mirrored (RAID level 1) to another striping configuration. Similarly, RAID level 15 refers to a striping with parity configuration (RAID level 5) that is mirrored (RAID level 1) to another striping with parity configuration.

RAID configurations can be handled by software running on an operating system (called **software RAID**, by the hardware contained on a storage controller (called **hardware RAID**), or by the system BIOS (called **firmware RAID**).

> **Note**
>
> To ensure that the processor performance of the system is not impacted following a RAID level 5 storage device failure, storage controllers that provide hardware RAID level 5 contain a small processor that is used to perform the calculations needed to provide data to users.

> **Note**
>
> Most firmware RAID devices only support RAID levels 0 and 1.

To configure and manage hardware RAID, you must use the RAID setup utility for your specific storage controller. You can access this setup utility by entering the system BIOS or controller BIOS at system startup, or by using a manufacturer-supplied program. After you have configured a hardware RAID volume in the setup utility, it will automatically appear as a single storage device to the Windows Server 2019 operating system, or Windows Server 2019 installation program if you are installing Windows Server 2019 to a RAID volume. For example, if you configure three storage devices in a RAID level 5 volume using the RAID setup utility prior to installing Windows Server 2019, the Windows Server 2019 installation program will see the RAID level 5 configuration as a single storage device. You can then create volumes on this storage device as you would any other storage device.

> **Note** 📎
>
> While firmware RAID functions identically to hardware RAID, you must configure and manage firmware RAID using the RAID setup utility in the system BIOS.

Unlike hardware or firmware RAID, software RAID is performed entirely by the Windows Server 2019 operating system. As a result, it can only be configured following the installation of Windows Server 2019.

> **Note** 📎
>
> Most rackmount servers ship from the manufacturer with two storage devices pre-configured using hardware or firmware RAID 1. This allows server administrators to install Windows Server 2019 on a fault tolerant RAID volume. Additional storage devices can then be configured using hardware, firmware, or software RAID.

Creating and Managing Local Volumes

After adding local storage devices to a system, you must create the volumes that will store data. The two main tools in Windows Server 2019 that you can use to create and manage local volumes are Disk Management and Server Manager. Disk Management can be used to create and manage partitions, simple volumes, and software RAID volumes that include up to 32 storage devices. You can use Server Manager to create and manage partitions and simple volumes, as well as create software RAID volumes on an unlimited number of storage devices using the built-in Storage Spaces component of Windows Server 2019. Using Storage Spaces Direct, you can also create RAID volumes in Server Manager that access storage on multiple servers.

Using Disk Management

While the **Disk Management** tool has been available in the Windows operating system since Windows 2000, the version of Disk Management in Windows Server 2019 includes additional support for modern storage devices, such as NVMe SSDs, as well the latest versions of NTFS, ReFS, FAT32, and exFAT filesystems. You can right-click the Start menu and select Disk Management to open the Disk Management tool shown in Figure 7-2.

All storage devices, regardless of type, are labeled as disks in the Disk Management tool. The first disk (Disk 0) shown in Figure 7-2 contains three primary partitions: a 499 MB recovery partition, a 99 MB EFI system partition, and a 126.40 GB boot partition that is configured as the C: volume. Because Disk 0 is not configured as a software RAID volume, it is called a **basic disk** in the Disk Management tool, and the

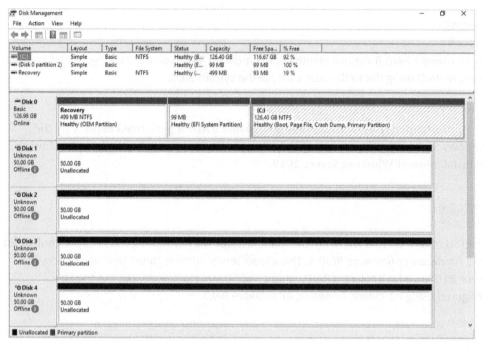

Figure 7-2   The Disk Management tool

word *Basic* is displayed under Disk 0 as a result. Newly added disks are disabled (*Offline*) by default, as shown with Disk 1 through Disk 4 in Figure 7-2. Before you create volumes on a disk, you must first enable the disk. To enable Disk 1, you can right-click Disk 1, and click Online. If the newly enabled disk displays a status of *Not Initialized*, you must also create an MBR or GPT on the disk. To create a GPT on Disk 1, you can right-click Disk 1, click Initialize Disk, and supply the options shown in Figure 7-3. After you click OK in Figure 7-3, Disk 1 is displayed as a basic disk in the Disk Management tool.

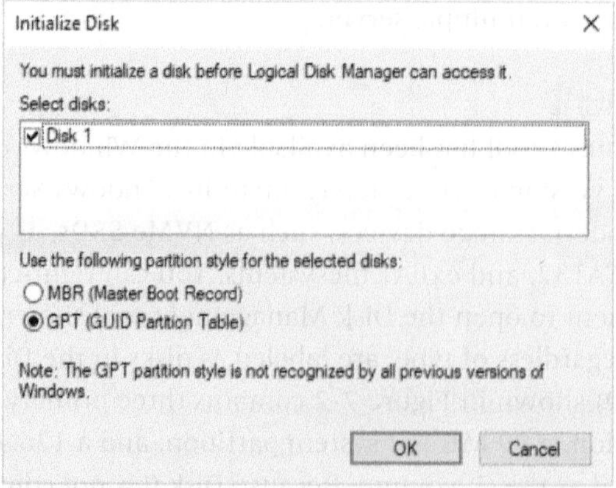

Figure 7-3   Creating a GPT on a new disk

Note

Provided that no partitions exist on the disk, you can right-click a disk in the Disk Management tool and click *Convert to GPT* to create a GPT on a disk that has an MBR, or click *Convert to MBR* to create an MBR on a disk that has a GPT.

Creating and Managing Simple Volumes

To create a simple volume on Disk 1 in Figure 7-2, you can right-click the Unallocated section next to Disk 1, and then click New Simple Volume to open the New Simple Volume Wizard. When you click Next at the first page of the New Simple Volume Wizard, you are prompted to select the size of the volume, as shown for the 5000 MB (4.88 GB) volume in Figure 7-4. When you click Next in Figure 7-4, the New Simple Volume Wizard will automatically assign the next available drive letter (E:) by default, as shown in Figure 7-5. Alternatively, you can select *Mount in the following empty NTFS folder* and supply the path to a folder on an existing NTFS volume, or *Do not assign a drive letter or drive path* to create a partition that is not made available to the system. After you click Next in Figure 7-5, you are prompted to select formatting options. The formatting options shown in Figure 7-6 perform a quick format of the NTFS filesystem on the partition using the default allocation unit size and a volume label of New Volume. If you select the *Enable file and folder compression* option shown in Figure 7-6, the compress attribute is enabled on the root folder of the volume (E:\) to ensure that folders and files created on the volume automatically receive the compress attribute.

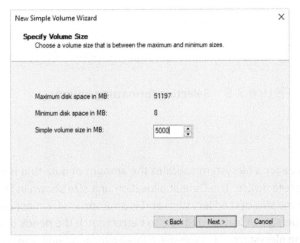

Figure 7-4 Specifying the simple volume size

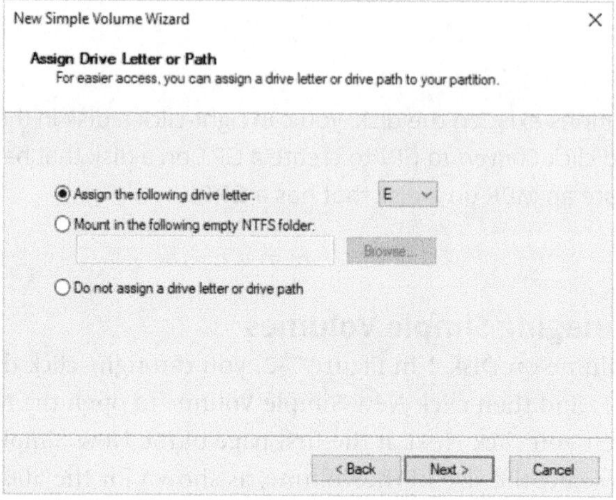

New Simple Volume Wizard   ✕

Assign Drive Letter or Path
For easier access, you can assign a drive letter or drive path to your partition.

● Assign the following drive letter: E   ▾
○ Mount in the following empty NTFS folder:
                                          Browse...
○ Do not assign a drive letter or drive path

                              < Back   Next >   Cancel

Figure 7-5   Choosing a drive letter or path

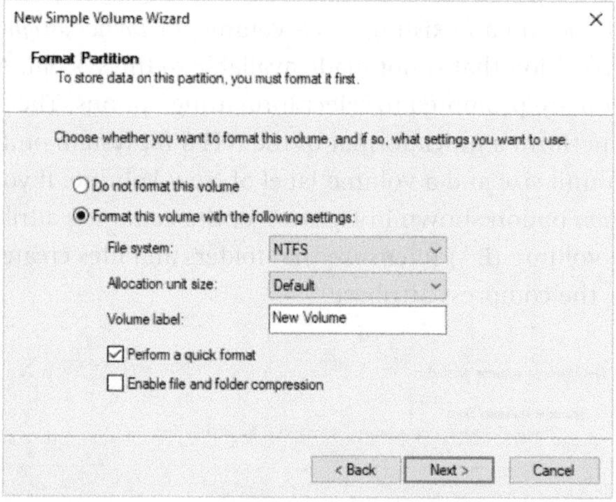

New Simple Volume Wizard   ✕

Format Partition
To store data on this partition, you must format it first.

Choose whether you want to format this volume, and if so, what settings you want to use.

○ Do not format this volume
● Format this volume with the following settings:
   File system: NTFS   ▾
   Allocation unit size: Default   ▾
   Volume label: New Volume
   ☑ Perform a quick format
   ☐ Enable file and folder compression

                              < Back   Next >   Cancel

Figure 7-6   Selecting formatting options

Note

The allocation unit size for a filesystem specifies the amount of data that is written as a single unit to the storage device. The Default allocation unit size shown in Figure 7-6 is calculated based on the size of the filesystem and is appropriate for most uses. However, you can modify the default allocation unit size to better match the needs of applications that store data on the filesystem. For example, a large allocation unit size will increase the performance of file sharing applications, whereas a smaller allocation unit size will increase the performance of database applications.

After you click Next in Figure 7-6, you can click Finish to create the E: simple volume. Because it is the first volume on the storage device, the New Simple Volume Wizard created a primary partition to host it, as shown in Figure 7-7. After creating a simple volume, you can right-click it in the Disk Management tool and then click:

- *Shrink Volume* to reduce the size of volume, provided there is adequate unused space in the filesystem. The reclaimed space can then be used to create additional simple volumes.
- *Extend Volume* to increase the size of the volume, provided there is unallocated space on the storage device.
- *Delete Volume* to remove the volume. This also removes the partition as well as all data on the associated filesystem.
- *Format* to reformat the volume with the same or a different filesystem, removing all existing data in the process.
- *Change Drive Letters and Paths* to modify the existing drive letter or folder path used to access the filesystem, or specify an additional one.

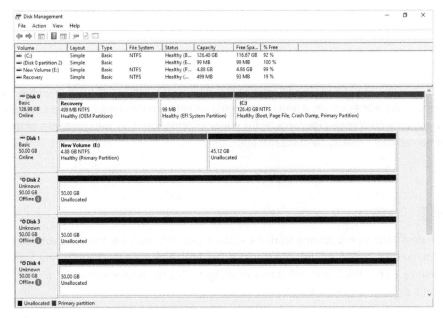

Figure 7-7   The E: simple volume on Disk 1

 Note

If you create multiple simple volumes on a disk that has an MBR, the Disk Management tool will automatically create primary partitions for the first three simple volumes. Additional simple volumes will automatically be created as logical drives in an extended partition.

Creating and Managing RAID Volumes

To create a software RAID volume in the Disk Management tool, you right-click one of the disks that you wish to configure as a RAID volume and then click:

- *New Spanned Volume* to create a spanned volume with 2–32 disks
- *New Striped Volume* to create a RAID level 0 (striping) volume with 2–32 disks
- *New Mirrored Volume* to create a RAID level 1 (mirroring) volume with 2 disks (three-way mirroring is not supported in the Disk Management tool)
- *New RAID-5 Volume* to create a RAID level 5 (striping with parity) volume with 3–32 disks

Regardless of the RAID volume chosen, the process is very similar to creating a simple volume. For example, to create a RAID level 5 volume from Disk 2, Disk 3, and Disk 4 in Figure 7-7, you can right-click Disk 2 and select New RAID-5 Volume to start the New RAID-5 Volume wizard. When you click Next at the first page of the New RAID-5 Volume wizard, you are prompted to select the disks that will make up the RAID volume, as shown in Figure 7-8 for Disk 2, Disk 3, and Disk 4. While each disk is 51197 MB, the total volume size is two thirds (102394 MB) of the total combined disk capacity (153591 MB) because one third of the capacity (51197 MB) is reserved for parity information.

> **Note** 📎
>
> The parity overhead for a RAID level 5 volume reduces as the number of disks used for the volume increases. For example, a RAID level 5 volume with ten disks will only use one tenth (10%) of the total combined disk capacity for parity information. This will leave 90% of the total combined disk capacity for data storage.

> **Note** 📎
>
> If you create a RAID level 0 volume from the disks shown in Figure 7-8, the total volume size will reflect the total combined disk capacity (153591 MB). Alternatively, if you create a RAID level 1 volume using Disk 2 and Disk 3 shown in Figure 7-8, the total volume size will reflect the size of a single disk (51197 MB).

> **Note** 📎
>
> When creating a RAID level 0, RAID level 1, or RAID level 5 volume, you should ensure that the associated storage devices have the same storage capacity. If one of the storage devices has a lower capacity than the others, then only that lower capacity is utilized on the other storage devices that make up the RAID volume, with the remaining space unusable.

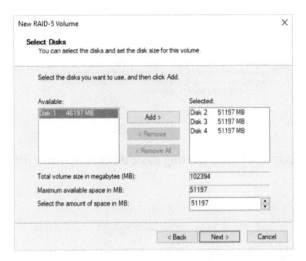

Figure 7-8   Selecting disks for a RAID volume

When you click Next in Figure 7-8, the remaining pages of the New RAID-5 Volume wizard are identical to the New Simple Volume Wizard. You are prompted to choose a drive letter or path (shown in Figure 7-5) as well as select formatting options (shown in Figure 7-6). Because NTFS and ReFS are the only filesystems that support software RAID volumes, they are the only filesystems available from the *File system* drop-down box shown in Figure 7-6. When you click Finish at the end of the New RAID-5 Volume wizard, you are prompted to convert Disk 2, Disk 3, and Disk 4 from basic disks to **dynamic disks** to complete the RAID configuration, as shown in Figure 7-9. Dynamic disks include a 1 MB table at the end of the storage device that contains the associated software RAID configuration. After you click Yes in Figure 7-9, blocks used to coordinate the striping of data are written to each disk, which could take several minutes depending on the size of the volume. During this process, the status of the RAID volume in the Disk Management tool will display *Resyncing*. After the resyncing process has completed, the word *Dynamic* is displayed under Disk 2, Disk 3, and Disk 4, and the status of the RAID volume displays *Healthy*, as shown in Figure 7-10.

Note 📎

When you partition a storage device during the Windows Server 2019 installation, or afterward using a Windows tool, the last 1 MB of storage on the device is automatically reserved to ensure that it can be converted to a dynamic disk, if necessary.

If a storage device that is part of the RAID level 5 volume shown in Figure 7-10 fails, the status for the volume will display *Failed Redundancy* and the failed disk will display the word *Missing* or *Foreign*. Because users can still access the data on the fault tolerant

Figure 7-9   Converting basic disks to dynamic disks

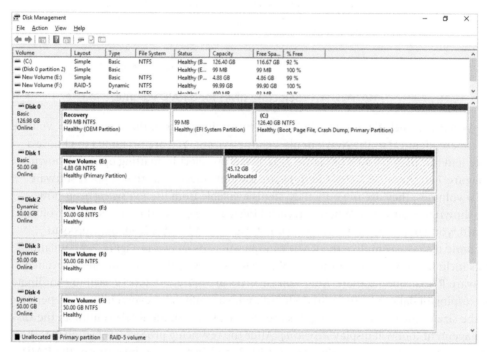

Figure 7-10   The F: RAID level 5 volume on Disk 2, Disk 3, and Disk 4

volume, you can wait until after working hours to replace the failed storage device. After the storage device has been replaced with a new one, you can right-click the RAID volume, click Repair Volume, and select the new storage device. This will regenerate the data and parity information on the new storage device. After this process has completed, the status for the RAID volume will indicate *Healthy* again.

Alternatively, if a storage device that is part of a RAID level 5 volume becomes temporarily unavailable (e.g., due to a temporary storage controller issue), the status for the volume will indicate *Failed Redundancy*, even after the affected storage device returns to normal operation and the associated disk displays the word *Online*. In this case, you can right-click the RAID volume and click Reactivate Volume to perform the resyncing process again and return the status of the volume to *Healthy*.

The options available in the Disk Management tool for managing spanned and other RAID volumes depend on the RAID level:

- You can right-click a spanned volume for a disk and click Shrink Volume to reduce the size of the volume, freeing space on the disk. Alternatively, if there is unallocated space on one of the disks that contains a spanned volume, you can right-click the volume on that disk and click Extend Volume to increase the size of the volume using the unallocated space.
- If a storage device that is part of a RAID level 0 volume becomes temporarily unavailable, you can right-click the volume and click Reactivate Volume once the storage device is available again.
- You can right-click a RAID level 1 volume and click Remove Mirror to remove the volume, while retaining the data from one disk you specify. The disk that you specify will retain the data in a simple volume using the same drive letter or path.
- You can right-click a RAID level 1 volume and click Break Mirrored Volume to remove the mirroring configuration, while retaining the data on both disks. The data on each disk is contained in two simple volumes that are assigned the next two available drive letters.

Note 📎

If a storage device that is part of a RAID level 1 volume fails, the status for the volume will display *Failed Redundancy* and the failed disk will display the word *Missing* or *Foreign*. In this case, you should replace the failed storage device after working hours with a new one. Next, you can right-click the existing RAID volume and click Break Mirrored Volume to remove the mirroring configuration. Finally, you can right-click the functioning disk that contains the data, click Add Mirror, and select the new storage device to re-add the mirroring configuration.

Note 📎

The system and boot partitions cannot be configured as part of a software RAID level 0 or RAID level 5 volume. However, you can configure the system and boot partitions as part of a software RAID level 1 volume following the installation of Windows Server 2019. To do this, you can right-click the system or boot partition in the Disk Management tool, click Add Mirror, and select the second storage device.

To remove a RAID volume, you can right-click it in the Disk Management tool and click Delete Volume. This process will remove all data on the volume, as well as convert the associated disks to basic disks.

The Disk Management tool cannot be used to add more storage devices to an existing RAID volume in order to increase the total available storage capacity. Thus, to add storage capacity to an existing RAID volume, you must remove and recreate the volume. For example, to add a fourth storage device to an existing RAID level 5 volume that uses three storage devices, you must first back up the data and then remove the volume. Next, you can recreate the RAID level 5 volume with four storage devices, and then restore the data from backup.

Note

You can also use the `diskpart` command at a Command Prompt window to perform the same tasks available in the Disk Management tool. For more information, search *diskpart* on *docs.microsoft.com*.

Using Server Manager

You can also use the File and Storage Services component in Server Manager to create and manage volumes on the storage devices in your system. To do this, first expand File and Storage Services in the navigation pane of Server Manager, expand Volumes, and then select Disks, as shown in Figure 7-11.

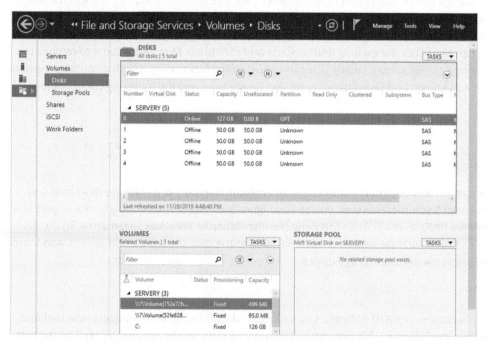

Figure 7-11   Viewing disks and volumes in Server Manager

All storage devices are assigned a number in Server Manager. Because the first storage device (0) is selected in the DISKS pane in Figure 7-11, the VOLUMES pane displays the same recovery partition, EFI system partition, and boot partition (C: volume) shown earlier in Figure 7-2. By default, newly added storage devices are disabled and labeled *Offline* in the Status column of the DISKS pane, as shown with storage devices 1 through 4 in Figure 7-11. To enable these storage devices, right-click each one in turn and click Bring Online. If a storage device does not have an MBR or GPT, *Unknown* is displayed in the Partition column. To add a GPT to a storage device, right-click it and click Initialize. Alternatively, to remove an MBR or GPT from a storage device, as well as all existing partitions, you can right-click it and click Reset Disk.

Note @

While Server Manager can create and manage simple volumes on storage devices that use an MBR or GPT, Server Manager can only be used to create a GPT on new storage devices.

Note @

Because Server Manager uses the Storage Pools feature of Windows Server 2019 to implement software RAID, it can only manage basic disks. Dynamic disks must be managed using the Disk Management tool.

Creating and Managing Simple Volumes

The process used to create a simple volume in Server Manager is similar to the process used to create a simple volume in the Disk Management tool. To add a simple volume to a storage device in Server Manager, you can select the TASKS drop-down box in the VOLUMES pane shown in Figure 7-11 and click New Volume to start the New Volume Wizard. When you click Next at the first page of the New Volume Wizard, you are prompted to select the storage device to host the simple volume, as shown with Disk 1 in Figure 7-12. When you click Next in Figure 7-12, you are prompted to specify the size of the volume, as shown with the 5 GB volume in Figure 7-13. After clicking Next in Figure 7-13, the New Volume Wizard will assign the next available drive letter (e.g., E:) to the volume, as shown in Figure 7-14. However, you can instead choose to assign a folder path to the volume, or create a partition that is not assigned a drive letter or folder path. When you click Next in Figure 7-14, you are prompted to select formatting options for the volume. The formatting options shown in Figure 7-15 will place an NTFS filesystem on the partition using the default allocation unit size and a volume label of New Volume. If you select *Generate short file names* in Figure 7-15, MS-DOS-compatible filenames will be generated for files created on the filesystem that have a name longer than 8 characters

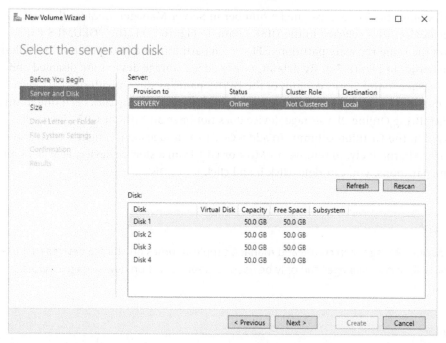

Figure 7-12 Selecting the storage device for a new volume

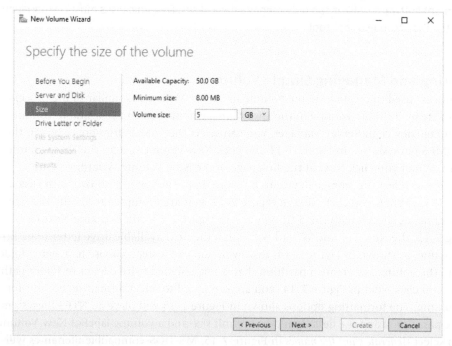

Figure 7-13 Specifying the volume size

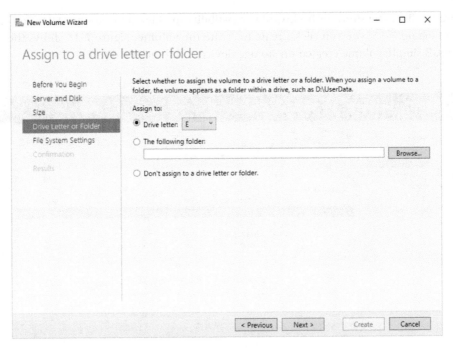

Figure 7-14   Choosing a drive letter or path

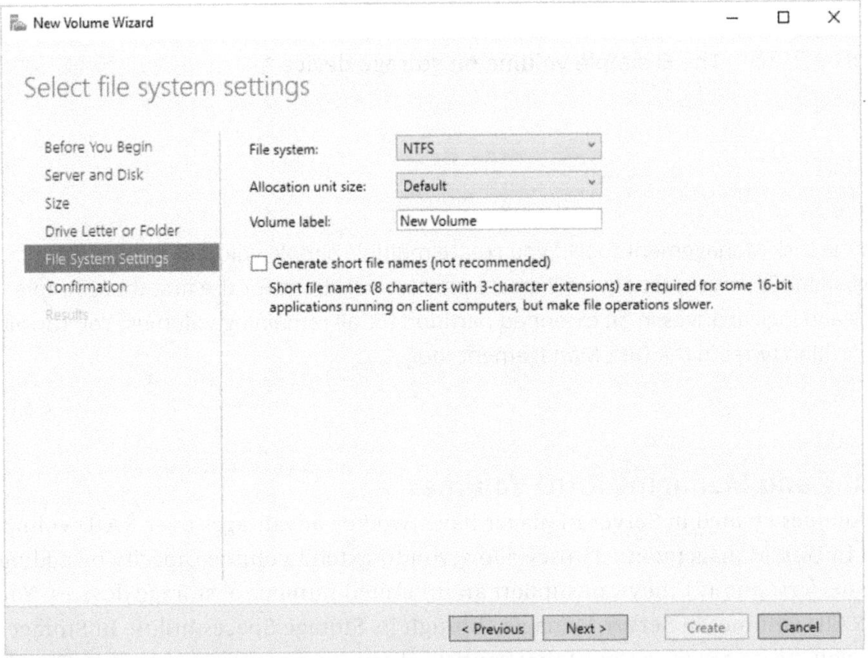

Figure 7-15   Selecting formatting options

(before the file extension) for backward compatibility to older applications. After you click Next in Figure 7-15, you can click Create to create the volume. Figure 7-16 shows the new 5 GB simple volume created on storage device 1 and mounted to E:.

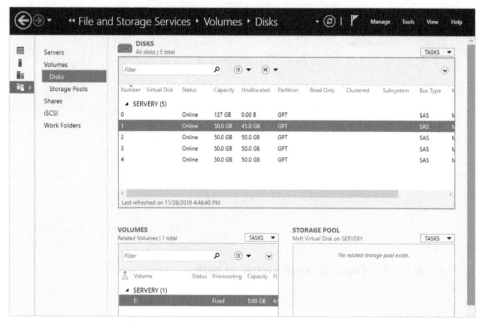

Figure 7-16 The E: simple volume on storage device 1

Note

As with the Disk Management tool, if you create multiple simple volumes on a storage device that has an MBR, Server Manager will create primary partitions for the first three simple volumes and logical drives in an extended partition for all remaining volumes. You can view these partition types in the Disk Management tool.

Creating and Managing RAID Volumes

RAID volumes created in Server Manager have two key advantages over RAID volumes created in Disk Management: (1) they allow you to extend volume capacity by adding storage devices; and (2) they can support an unlimited number of storage devices. You create RAID volumes in Server Manager through its Storage Spaces utility. In Storage Spaces, you create a **storage pool** that consists of one or more storage devices. The size of the storage pool is equivalent to the combined size of all the storage devices in the pool, and you can easily add storage devices to the storage pool. After you create the storage pool, you create virtual disks to define the space within the storage pool that implements a level of software RAID. **Virtual disks** are similar to virtual hard disk files in that they can be configured to use available space from the storage pool as necessary (thin provisioning), or be configured to use a fixed amount of space from the storage pool (thick provisioning). If the storage pool contains both hard disk and SSD storage devices, you can also enable storage tiers on virtual disks to ensure that frequently accessed data is stored only on faster SSD storage devices. After creating virtual disks from the available space in a storage pool, you create RAID volumes on them using the same procedure used to create simple volumes.

To configure storage pools and virtual disks, you can select Storage Pools in the navigation pane shown in Figure 7-16. The **primordial storage pool** (*Primordial*) in the STORAGE POOLS pane shown in Figure 7-17 is a placeholder that serves to list the four available local storage devices in the PHYSICAL DISKS pane.

> **Note** 🖉
>
> The storage device that contains the boot and system partitions is not included in the primordial storage pool and excluded from use by Storage Spaces as a result.

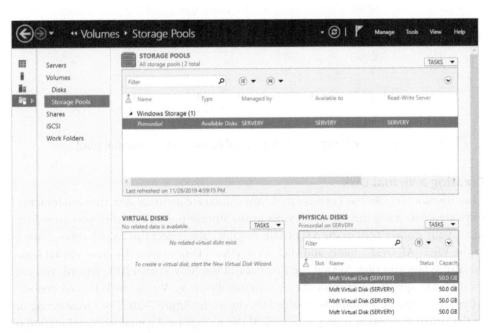

Figure 7-17   The Primordial storage pool

Creating a Storage Pool

To create a new storage pool, you can select the TASKS drop-down box in the STORAGE POOLS pane shown in Figure 7-17 and click New Storage Pool to start the New Storage Pool Wizard. When you click Next at the first page of the New Storage Pool Wizard, you are prompted to specify a name for your new storage pool (e.g., Storage Pool 1), as well as select the primordial storage pool from which storage devices are obtained, as shown in Figure 7-18. When you click Next in Figure 7-18, you are prompted to select the storage devices that you wish to add to the storage pool. The three 50 GB storage devices selected in Figure 7-19 provide a storage pool capacity of 150 GB. After you click Next in Figure 7-19, you can click Create to create the storage pool.

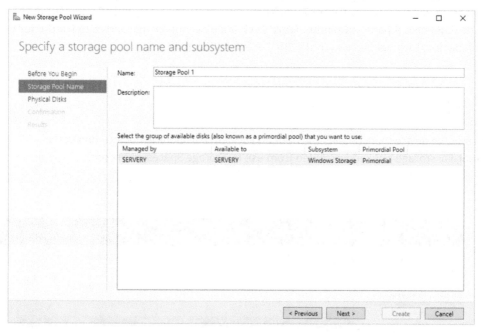

Figure 7-18   Specifying the storage pool name and primordial pool

Creating a Virtual Disk

After the storage pool has been created, you can create a virtual disk that implements software RAID using the storage devices in the storage pool. To do this, you must first select your storage pool in the STORAGE POOLS pane, select the TASKS drop-down box in the VIRTUAL DISKS pane, and click New Virtual Disk to start the New Virtual Disk Wizard. When you click Next at the first page of the New Virtual Disk Wizard, you are prompted to specify a name for the new virtual disk (e.g., Virtual Disk 1), and choose whether storage tiers should be enabled, as shown in Figure 7-20. The *Create storage tiers on this virtual disk* option is only selectable if the storage pool contains a combination of hard disk and SSD storage devices.

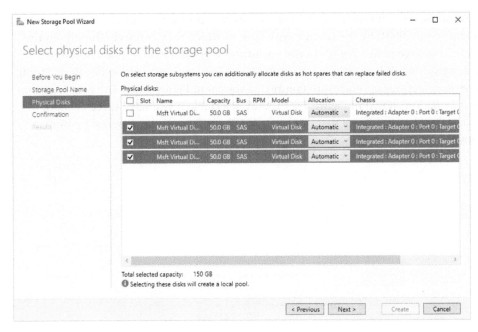

Figure 7-19   Adding storage devices to the storage pool

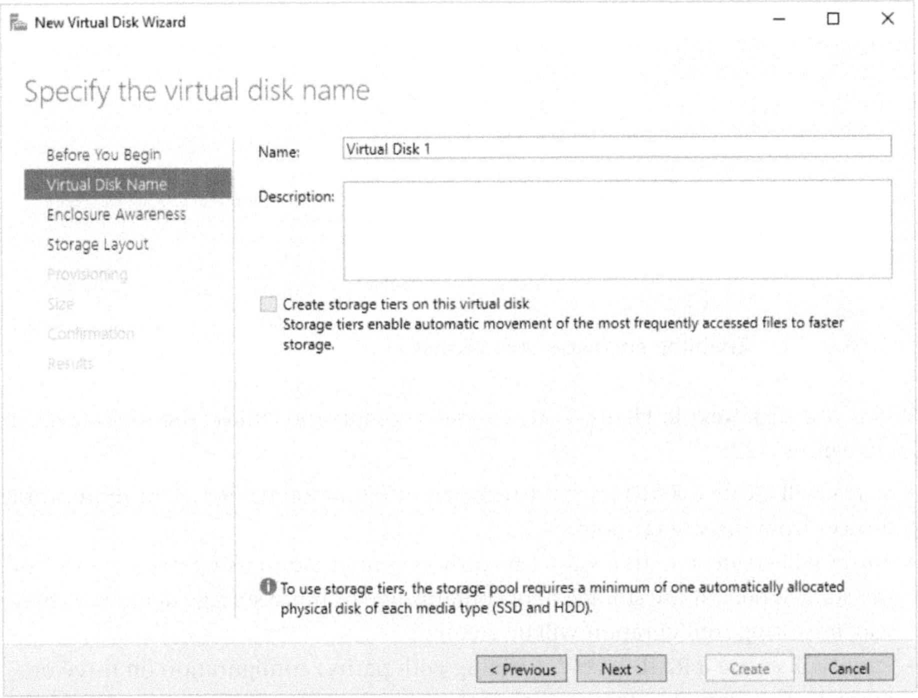

Figure 7-20   Specifying the virtual disk name and storage tier functionality

Some rackmount servers contain one or more sets of storage devices that are configured as a JBOD by the storage enclosure to which they connect. This allows the combined storage of the devices in the enclosure to be shown as a single unit to the operating system. When you click Next in Figure 7-20, you can optionally allow Storage Spaces to detect storage enclosure failures, as shown in Figure 7-21. The *Enable enclosure awareness* option shown in Figure 7-21 is only selectable if you have three or more devices in your storage pool that represent JBOD configurations provided by storage enclosures.

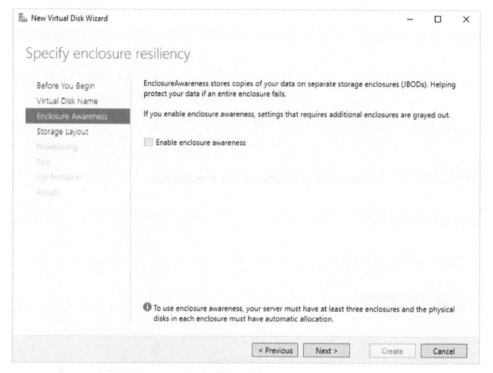

Figure 7-21   Enabling enclosure awareness

When you click Next in Figure 7-21, you are prompted to choose the RAID level, as shown in Figure 7-22:

- *Simple* will create a RAID level 0 (striping) configuration using two or more storage devices from the storage pool.
- *Mirror* will create a RAID level 1 (mirroring) configuration using two devices from the storage pool. If the storage pool contains five or more storage devices, a three-way mirroring configuration will be created.
- *Parity* will create a RAID level 5 (striping with parity) configuration on three or more devices from the storage pool. If the storage pool contains seven or more storage devices, a RAID level 6 configuration will be created.

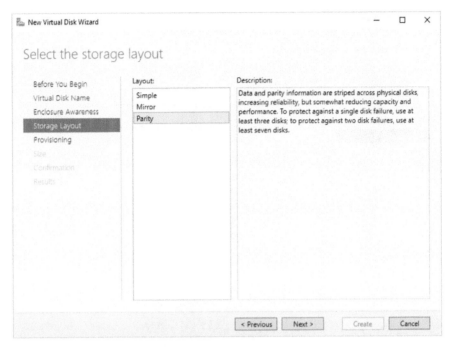

Figure 7-22   Selecting the virtual disk RAID level

After you select the appropriate RAID level in Figure 7-22 and click Next, you are prompted to choose thin or thick (fixed) provisioning, as shown in Figure 7-23. It is possible to create several thin-provisioned virtual disks with a combined capacity larger than the storage pool from which they were created. However, if you do, then you must monitor the storage consumed by each virtual disk to know when additional storage devices should be added to the storage pool. When you click Next in Figure 7-23, you are prompted to choose the size of the virtual disk as shown in Figure 7-24. If thin provisioning is used, the 100 GB size shown in Figure 7-24 will not be immediately allocated to storage devices in the storage pool. Instead, the virtual disk will grow until it consumes 100 GB of storage from storage devices in the storage pool. After you click Next in Figure 7-24, you can click Create to create the virtual disk. Figure 7-25 shows a 100 GB, thin provisioned, virtual disk (Virtual Disk 1) created from a storage pool (Storage Pool 1) that is composed of three 50 GB storage devices.

Creating a RAID Volume

After you create a virtual disk, it is listed as a new storage device in the DISKS pane of the Disks section of Server Manager, as shown with storage device 5 (Virtual Disk 1) in Figure 7-26. Before creating a RAID volume on Virtual Disk 1, you must right-click it and click Bring Online to enable it. Next, you can right-click Virtual Disk 1 and click New Volume to start the New Volume Wizard. When you click Next at the first page of the New Volume Wizard, you can select Virtual Disk 1 as the location for your RAID volume, as

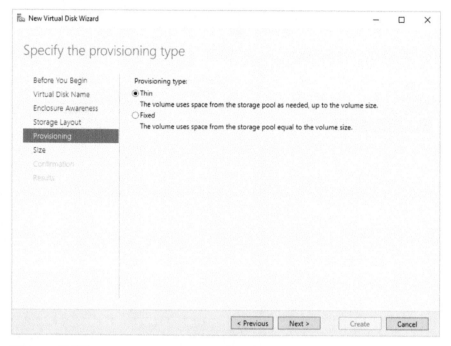

Figure 7-23   Choosing the provisioning type

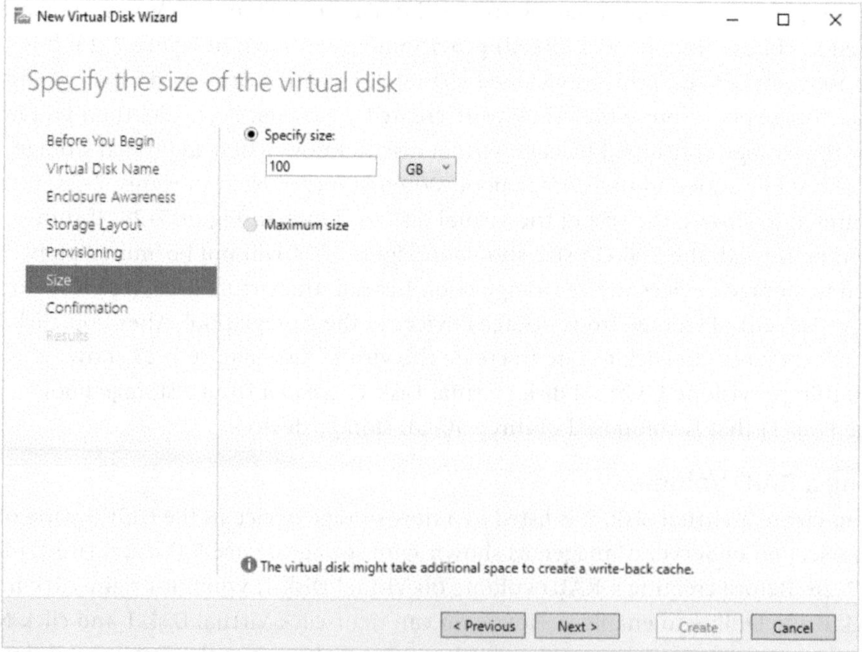

Figure 7-24   Specifying the virtual disk size

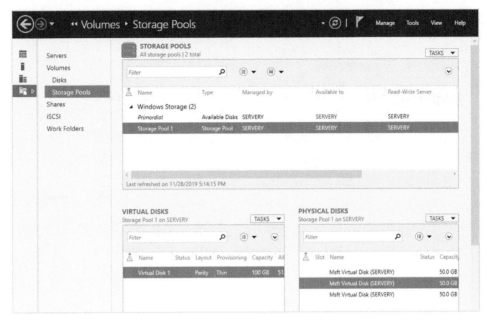

Figure 7-25   Viewing virtual disks and storage pools

Figure 7-26   Virtual Disk 1 in the DISKS pane

shown in Figure 7-27. After you click Next in Figure 7-27, you can progress through the remaining pages of the New Volume Wizard normally, as shown earlier in Figures 7-13 through 7-16. While you can select NTFS or ReFS as the filesystem type during the New Volume Wizard (Figure 7-15), ReFS was designed to perform faster with Storage Spaces. Figure 7-28 shows the 100 GB F: RAID volume created from Virtual Disk 1.

Configuring Storage Tiers and Storage Pinning

Storage tiers modify the implementation of each RAID level to automatically store frequently accessed files on SSDs and infrequently accessed files on hard disks. If you select the *Create storage tiers on this virtual disk* option when creating a virtual disk, storage tier functionality does not take effect until you define hard disk and SSD storage tiers

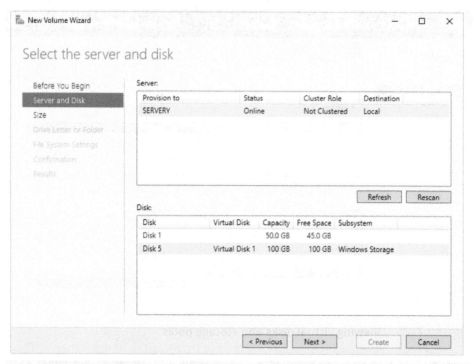

Figure 7-27 Creating a RAID volume on Virtual Disk 1

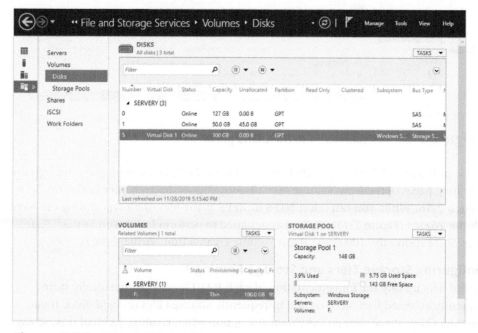

Figure 7-28 The F: RAID volume on Virtual Disk 1

for your storage pool. To define a hard disk storage tier called HDDTier for a storage pool called Storage Pool 1, you can run the `New-StorageTier -FriendlyName HDDTier -MediaType HDD -StoragePoolFriendlyName "Storage Pool 1"` command in Windows PowerShell. Similarly, to define an SSD storage tier called SSDTier for Storage Pool 1, you can run the `New-StorageTier -FriendlyName SSDTier -MediaType SSD -StoragePoolFriendlyName "Storage Pool 1"` command in Windows PowerShell.

After storage tiers has been enabled, you may want to ensure that a particular file is stored on a hard disk or SSD, regardless of how frequently it is accessed. This is called storage pinning and can be configured using a Windows PowerShell command. For example, to ensure that the F:\Databases\OnlineOrders.mdb file is always stored on SSD storage devices using the SSDTier storage tier, you can run the `Set-FileStorageTier -FilePath "F:\Databases\OnlineOrders.mdb" -DesiredStorageTier SSDTier` command in Windows PowerShell. Alternatively, to ensure that the F:\Databases\Archive.mdb file is always stored on a hard disk storage device using the HDDTier storage tier, you can run the `Set-FileStorageTier -FilePath "F:\Databases\Archive.mdb" -DesiredStorageTier HDDTier` command in Windows PowerShell.

Adding Storage Capacity

If the RAID volumes on your system have exhausted the available capacity provided by a storage pool on your system, you can add storage devices to the existing storage pool to provide additional space for creating new RAID volumes or for extending existing ones. Say, for example, that you want to add an additional storage device to Storage Pool 1 shown in Figure 7-25, as well as extend Virtual Disk 1 and the associated F: volume to use the additional capacity. To do this, you can select Storage Pool 1 in the STORAGE POOLS pane, select the TASKS drop-down box in the PHYSICAL DISKS pane, click Add Physical Disk, and select the new storage device. Following this, you can right-click Virtual Disk 1 in the VIRTUAL DISKS pane and click Extend Virtual Disk to increase the capacity of your existing virtual disk. Next, you can access the Disks section shown in Figure 7-28, select the Virtual Disk 1 in the DISKS pane, right-click the F: volume in the VOLUMES pane and click Extend Volume to increase the capacity of your RAID volume.

Managing Storage Device Failure

If a storage device that is part of Storage Pool 1 in Figure 7-25 experiences a failure, the storage device will display a *Lost Connection* status in the PHYSICAL DISKS pane. In this case, you can replace the failed storage device with a new one. After the failed storage device has been replaced, you can right-click the failed storage device in the PHYSICAL DISKS pane, and click Remove Disk. Next, you can select the TASKS drop-down box in the PHYSICAL DISKS pane, click Add Physical Disk, and select the new storage device. The storage device that you add must have a capacity equivalent to or greater than the failed storage device to ensure the recovery of RAID volumes.

After the failed storage device in Storage Pool 1 has been replaced, the process used to return the F: RAID volume (shown in Figure 7-28) back to normal operation depends on whether Virtual Disk 1 was created using a fault tolerant RAID level (mirror or parity) or a non-fault tolerant RAID level (simple):

- If Virtual Disk 1 was created with a mirror or parity RAID level, you can right-click Virtual Disk 1 in the VIRTUAL DISKS pane in Figure 7-25 and click Repair Virtual Disk to ensure that the data is redistributed to the new storage device.
- If Virtual Disk 1 was created with the simple RAID level, then you must right-click Virtual Disk 1 in the VIRTUAL DISKS pane in Figure 7-25 and click Delete Virtual Disk. Following this, you can recreate Virtual Disk 1 and the associated F: volume, as well as restore the data that was previously on the F: volume from backup.

> **Note** 📎
>
> You can also use Windows PowerShell to perform the same storage-related tasks that you can perform in Server Manager. For example, you can use the `New-StoragePool` cmdlet to create a storage pool, whereas you can use the `New-Volume` cmdlet to create a new volume on a storage device or virtual disk. For a list of all storage-related cmdlets, search *PowerShell storage* on *docs.microsoft.com*.

Using Storage Spaces Direct

Normally, the RAID volumes created in Server Manager store data on a virtual disk that consumes space from a storage pool made up of local storage devices. However, you can also configure Storage Spaces to create storage pools that include storage devices from up to 16 servers on the network using Storage Spaces Direct. Storage Spaces Direct uses the **Failover Clustering** feature on each server to create a **clustered storage pool** that includes the combined local storage devices from all of the servers. After you create a clustered storage pool, you can create virtual disks and RAID volumes as you normally would using Storage Spaces, with each RAID volume accessible by all servers. Storage Spaces Direct distributes data between the storage devices on the servers in a way that ensures that RAID volumes remain available in the event that an entire server fails.

To provide this server fault tolerance, Storage Spaces Direct requires that each server have a minimum number of storage devices. In addition to the storage device used to host the system and boot partitions, each server that you configure with Storage Spaces Direct must have a minimum of six SATA, SAS, or NVMe storage devices, and at least two of these storage devices must be SSDs. Moreover, each server must be joined to the same Active Directory domain and have a fast network connection. Microsoft only supports Storage Spaces Direct on systems that have a 10 Gb or greater Ethernet network interface that supports **remote-direct memory access (RDMA)**.

Configuring Storage Spaces Direct

To configure Storage Spaces Direct, you must first install the Failover Clustering feature on each server. Next, you use Windows PowerShell to create a cluster between the servers. For example, to create a cluster called StorageCluster1 that includes SERVERX and SERVERY, you can log into either SERVERX or SERVERY as a domain administrator account and run the `New-Cluster -Name StorageCluster1 -Node SERVERX, SERVERY` command in Windows PowerShell.

After you create the cluster, you can create a clustered storage pool that includes the available storage devices on each server. To create a clustered storage pool called Clustered Storage Pool 1, you can run the `Enable-ClusterStorageSpacesDirect -PoolFriendlyName 'Clustered Storage Pool 1'` command in Windows PowerShell and click Yes at the confirmation window. After Clustered Storage Pool 1 has been created, it will be displayed in the STORAGE POOLS pane under the Storage Pools section of Server Manager (Figure 7-25), and will list the storage devices from both SERVERX and SERVERY in the PHYSICAL DISKS pane. You can then create virtual disks using the space from Clustered Storage Pool 1, as well as create RAID volumes on the virtual disks.

Adding Servers to Storage Spaces Direct

Just as you can add storage to an existing storage pool, you can add servers to an existing Storage Spaces Direct configuration to expand the storage capacity of the clustered storage pool. For example, to add SERVERZ to StorageCluster1, you must first install the Failover Clustering feature on SERVERZ. Next, you can log into either SERVERX or SERVERY as a domain administrator account and run the `Add-ClusterNode -Name SERVERZ` command in Windows PowerShell. After SERVERZ is added to the cluster, the storage from SERVERZ will automatically be made available to Clustered Storage Pool 1, and the data in existing virtual disks is distributed evenly across the storage devices on SERVERX, SERVERY, and SERVERZ. Finally, you can extend the capacity of existing virtual disks and RAID volumes or create new ones from the additional storage in Clustered Storage Pool 1.

Accessing and Configuring SAN Storage

Some modern rackmount servers contain only enough storage to host the Windows Server 2019 operating system and associated server programs. All other data files, databases, Web content, virtual hard disk files, and so on are stored on a high-capacity external storage area network (SAN) device on the server rack that is connected to the Windows Server 2019 operating system via a SAN protocol. The two most common SAN protocols today include iSCSI and Fibre Channel. You can configure Windows Server 2019 to connect to both iSCSI and Fibre Channel SAN devices, access multiple SAN devices using MPIO, or provide storage to other servers using iSCSI.

Note

SAN devices use hardware RAID internally to provide fault tolerance for the storage devices that they contain.

Note

SAN devices only provide storage to other systems using a SAN protocol and do not format or manage filesystems on this storage. Instead, the operating system that connects to the SAN device provides this functionality. As a result, a SAN device is functionally similar to an external USB drive.

Note

SAN devices are not the same as **network-attached storage (NAS)** devices. Although NAS devices often contain several storage devices configured using hardware RAID, they run an operating system and function as a file server on the network that clients connect to using SMB, NFS, or File Transfer Protocol (FTP).

Connecting Windows Server 2019 to an iSCSI SAN Device

Internet SCSI (iSCSI) is a technology that uses Ethernet network cables to transfer data to and from a SAN device, either on the local network or across the Internet, using the SCSI protocol at speeds of up to 40 Gb/s. The software component in the operating system that connects to the SAN device via iSCSI is referred to as an **iSCSI initiator**, and the storage on the SAN device that is made available to the iSCSI initiator is called the **iSCSI target**. A single iSCSI target is normally composed of multiple storage devices combined together using fault tolerant hardware RAID (e.g., RAID level 5) on the SAN device itself. As a result, the iSCSI initiator and Windows Server 2019 operating system will see the iSCSI target as a single storage device. You can then create volumes on this storage device as you would on any other storage device.

Note

iSCSI is simply a transfer protocol used between a server and a SAN device. The SAN device itself can use different storage technologies to physically store the data itself, including NVMe SSDs, or SATA/SAS hard disks or SSDs.

> **Note** 📎
>
> A single iSCSI SAN device can be accessed by multiple servers. The servers that access an iSCSI SAN device are said to be part of a "storage area network."

To connect a Windows Server 2019 system to an iSCSI SAN, you must first ensure that the appropriate iSCSI target has been configured on the iSCSI SAN device and that your server is allowed to connect to it. These tasks must be performed using the configuration tools provided by the iSCSI SAN device manufacturer. Next, you must connect an iSCSI-compatible Ethernet cable from an iSCSI-compliant network interface on your rackmount server to an Ethernet port on your iSCSI SAN device. Finally, you must configure the iSCSI initiator on your Windows Server 2019 system to connect to the name or IP address of the SAN device.

All Windows Server 2019 editions contain a **Microsoft iSCSI Initiator Service** that can be used to connect to an iSCSI target. To configure a Windows Server 2019 system to connect to an iSCSI target, click the Tools menu in Server Manager and click iSCSI Initiator. The first time that you click iSCSI Initiator, you are prompted to start the Microsoft iSCSI Initiator Service and configure it to start automatically at boot time, as shown in Figure 7-29. Next, supply the name or IP address of the iSCSI SAN device in the Target text box of the iSCSI Initiator Properties window shown in Figure 7-30 and click Quick Connect. This will establish a persistent connection to the iSCSI target on the SAN device that is automatically reestablished each time the system is booted.

> **Note** 📎
>
> When you click Quick Connect in Figure 7-30, you may be prompted to enter a user name and password to complete the initial SAN connection, depending on the configuration of the iSCSI SAN device.

> **Note** 📎
>
> A single Windows Server 2019 system can connect to multiple iSCSI targets to access storage on multiple different SAN devices. To do this, first connect to each target individually in Figure 7-30. Then, highlight the Volumes and Devices tab and click Auto Configure to ensure that connections to all available iSCSI targets are automatically established at boot time.

> **Note**
>
> You can also use the `Connect-IscsiTarget` cmdlet in Windows PowerShell to connect a Windows Server 2019 system to an iSCSI target.

Figure 7-29   Starting the Microsoft iSCSI Initiator Service

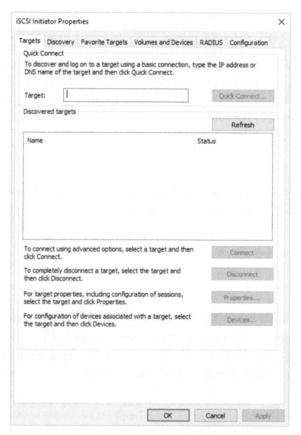

Figure 7-30   Connecting to an iSCSI target

After you have connected your Windows Server 2019 system to the iSCSI target, the iSCSI target should be identified by the Windows Server 2019 system as a new storage device that you can create volumes on in Server Manager or the Disk Management tool.

> **Note** 📎
>
> Most server administrators create simple volumes on storage devices that are provided by iSCSI targets, because the iSCSI target uses fault tolerant hardware RAID on the underlying storage devices. However, if your Windows Server 2019 system connects to multiple iSCSI targets, you can create software RAID volumes from the storage provided by the iSCSI targets for added fault tolerance.

> **Note** 📎
>
> You can configure the iSCSI initiator on Windows Server 2019 running in a Hyper-V virtual machine to connect to an iSCSI target. To do this, you must ensure that the virtual machine is connected to an external virtual switch associated with the iSCSI-compliant network interface on your rackmount server that has a physical connection to the iSCSI SAN device.

> **Note** 📎
>
> Some rackmount servers include an iSCSI initiator in the system BIOS. In this case, you can configure the iSCSI initiator in the system BIOS to connect to the iSCSI target before installing Windows Server 2019. This allows you to create the system and boot partitions on the iSCSI target during the Window Server 2019 installation, eliminating the need for local storage devices in the rackmount server.

Connecting Windows Server 2019 to a Fibre Channel SAN Device

Fibre Channel (FC) is a technology that can be used to transport SCSI data to a remote FC SAN device, across an Ethernet or fiber optic cable at speeds of up to 128 Gb/s. A rackmount server uses a hardware-based FC controller called an FC **Host Bus Adapter (HBA)** that connects to an FC SAN device. Each FC SAN device contains FC-capable storage devices connected via an FC switch. FC-capable storage devices are normally SAS hard disks or SSDs that contain additional FC circuitry, or NVMe SSDs that have an FC-capable memory controller.

> **Note** 📎
>
> An FC HBA can also be an FC-capable 10 Gb Ethernet network interface if the FC SAN device uses **FC over Ethernet (FCoE)**.

To configure FC SAN storage on a Windows Server 2019 system, you must first configure the appropriate storage and hardware RAID on an FC SAN device using the configuration tools provided by the FC SAN device manufacturer. Next, you must install an FC HBA in the rackmount server, as well as obtain and install the device driver for the FC HBA on your Windows Server 2019 system. The FC HBA provides the same functionality as an iSCSI initiator; if connected properly, the FC HBA should automatically detect and make any FC storage available to Windows Server 2019. This storage is represented by a new storage device in Server Manager or the Disk Management tool on which you can create volumes.

> **Note** 📎
>
> You can also configure FC HBAs during a Windows Server 2019 installation. To do this, you must click *Load driver* at the *Where do you want to install Windows?* screen (shown previously in Figure 1-19) and supply the path to the FC HBA driver. Following this, you can choose to install Windows Server 2019 entirely on FC SAN storage, eliminating the need for local storage devices in the rackmount server.

> **Note** 📎
>
> After installing the driver for an FC HBA in the host operating system, you can make the FC HBA available to Hyper-V virtual machines. To do this, you can add a virtual Fibre Channel Adapter in virtual machine Settings, as shown previously in Figure 3-19. After it is added, you must associate the virtual Fibre Channel adapter with the physical FC HBA on the system.

Using MPIO to Connect to Multiple SAN Devices

Data center server environments often have several iSCSI or FC SAN devices. Each server in a data center can have multiple connections to a single SAN for fault tolerance in case a single connection becomes unavailable, or to load balance requests across multiple connections for greater speed. Larger data centers often have multiple SANs that host the same information. In this case, servers can have multiple connections to different

SANs to provide fault tolerance in case a single SAN becomes unavailable, or to load balance requests across multiple SANs for greater speed. These configurations are called **Multipath Input Output (MPIO)**.

On Windows Server 2019, MPIO is implemented by the **Multipath I/O** feature that can be installed using the Add Roles and Features Wizard. After you install this feature, you can click the Tools menu in Server Manager and then click MPIO to open the MPIO configuration tool shown in Figure 7-31.

Figure 7-31   The MPIO configuration tool

To configure multiple FC SAN connections using MPIO, click Add in Figure 7-31 and enter the hardware ID of each FC HBA that you have installed on your system. You can locate these hardware IDs by examining the label on each physical FC HBA or by viewing the properties of the associated FC HBA device drivers in Device Manager. To configure multiple iSCSI SAN connections using MPIO, click the Discover Multi-Paths tab in Figure 7-31, select *Add support for iSCSI devices* and click Add to automatically add all available iSCSI targets on the system.

If your FC HBA or iSCSI target cannot be added to the MPIO tool, you may need to obtain an MPIO support file from the SAN device manufacturer. This MPIO support file is called a **Device Specific Module (DSM)**. To add the DSM to your system, you can click the DSM Install tab in Figure 7-31, supply the path to the DSM and click Install. Next, you can add the associated FC HBAs or iSCSI targets to the MPIO tool.

Configuring Windows Server 2019 as an iSCSI SAN Device

Instead of purchasing an iSCSI SAN device, you can instead configure an existing Windows Server 2019 system that has a large storage capacity as an iSCSI SAN device. To do this, you install the **iSCSI Target Server** server role using the Add Roles and Features Wizard. This server role is located under the File and iSCSI Services section of File and Storage Services, as shown in Figure 7-32. To allow backup programs to use the Volume Shadow Copy Service (VSS) to back up open files stored in volumes on the iSCSI SAN device, you should also select the **iSCSI Target Storage Provider** server role in Figure 7-32. This server role also allows you to manage the iSCSI Target Server using legacy management tools that use the **Virtual Disk Service (VDS)**.

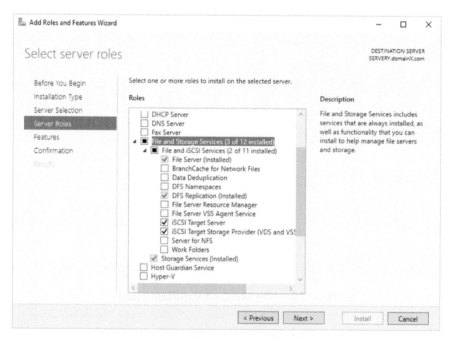

Figure 7-32   Installing the iSCSI Target Server

After the iSCSI Target Server has been installed, you can create a special .vhdx file (called an **iSCSI virtual disk**) that contains the storage you wish to make available to other systems via an iSCSI target. To create and manage iSCSI virtual disks and targets, select the iSCSI section of File and Storage Services in the navigation pane of Server Manager, as shown in Figure 7-33.

To create an iSCSI virtual disk, select the TASKS drop-down box from the iSCSI VIRTUAL DISKS pane in Figure 7-33 and click New iSCSI Virtual Disk. This will start

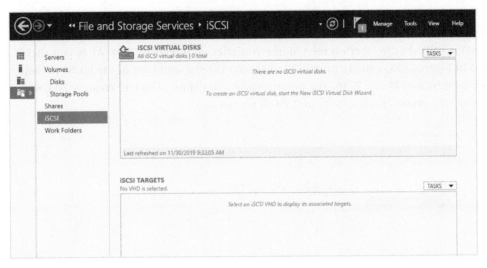

Figure 7-33   The iSCSI section of Server Manager

the New iSCSI Virtual Disk Wizard and prompt you to select the volume on which the iSCSI virtual disk will be stored, as shown in Figure 7-34. While the iSCSI virtual disk can be stored on any existing volume on the system, you should store it on a fault tolerant RAID volume to provide protection against storage device failure. When you click Next

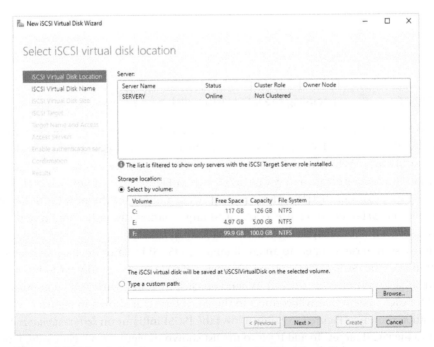

Figure 7-34   Selecting a volume for the iSCSI virtual disk

in Figure 7-34, you must specify a name for the iSCSI virtual disk, as shown for iSCSI Virtual Disk 1 in Figure 7-35. The associated iSCSI virtual disk file will be stored in the iSCSIVirtualDisks directory on the volume you selected in Figure 7-34. After you click Next in Figure 7-35, you are prompted to choose the size and type of the iSCSI virtual disk, as shown in Figure 7-36. The options shown in Figure 7-36 will create a 70 GB thin provisioned (dynamically expanding) iSCSI virtual disk.

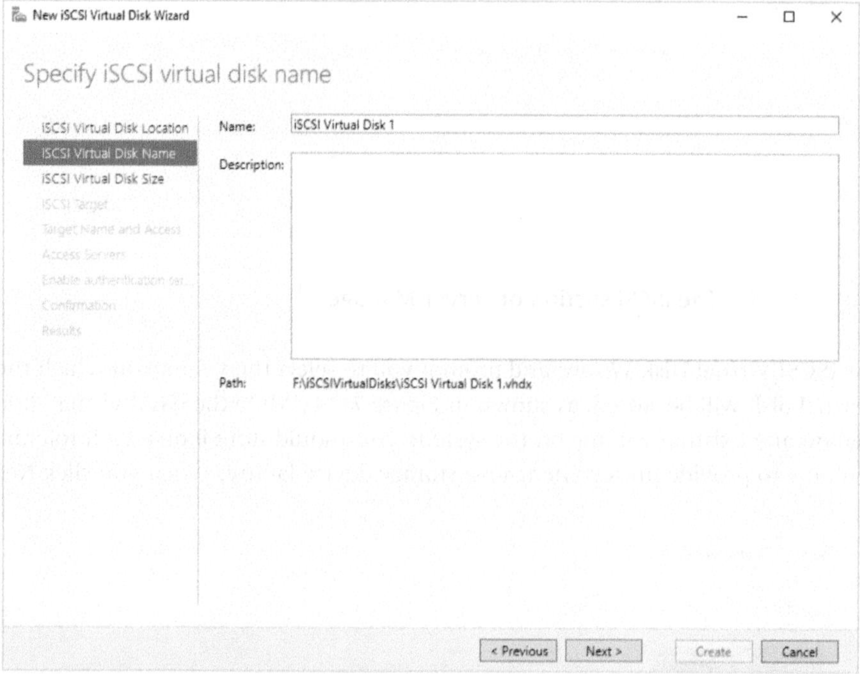

Figure 7-35 Specifying the iSCSI virtual disk name

To ensure that the iSCSI virtual disk is made available to systems on the network using iSCSI, the New iSCSI Virtual Disk Wizard will associate the new iSCSI virtual disk with an iSCSI target. When you click Next in Figure 7-36, you are prompted to select an existing iSCSI target or create a new one, as shown in Figure 7-37. If you select *New iSCSI target* in Figure 7-37 and click Next, you must provide a name for the new iSCSI target, as shown for iSCSITarget1 in Figure 7-38. iSCSI target names can only contain letters and numbers; spaces and other special characters are not allowed.

Before a system can connect to an iSCSI target, its iSCSI initiator must be allowed in the configuration of the iSCSI target on the SAN device. iSCSI targets identify iSCSI initiators using an **iSCSI Qualified Name (IQN)**. When you click Next in Figure 7-38, you must add the IQN for each system that will connect to the iSCSI target, as shown in Figure 7-39. The configuration shown in Figure 7-39 only allows the iSCSI initiator on *serverx.domainx.com* to connect to the iSCSI target. To add IQNs to the list shown in Figure 7-39, click Add, type the FQDN of the system in the *Query initiator computer for ID* text box and click OK.

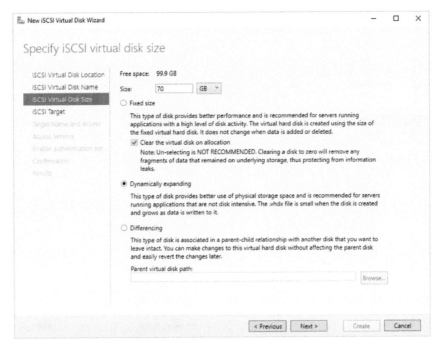

Figure 7-36   Choosing an iSCSI virtual disk size and type

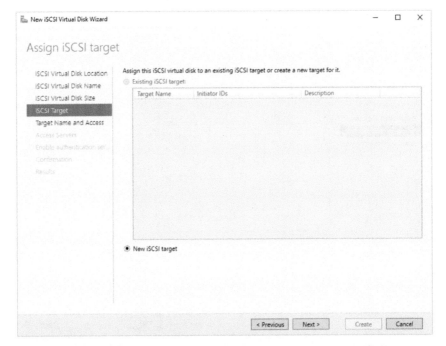

Figure 7-37   Selecting the iSCSI target for a new iSCSI virtual disk

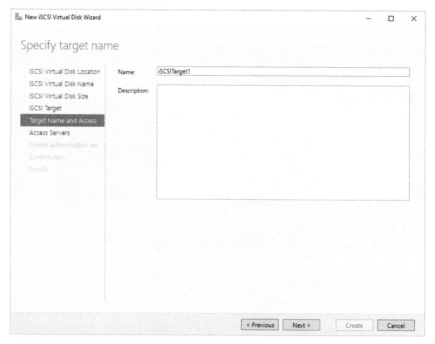

Figure 7-38   Specifying the name for a new iSCSI target

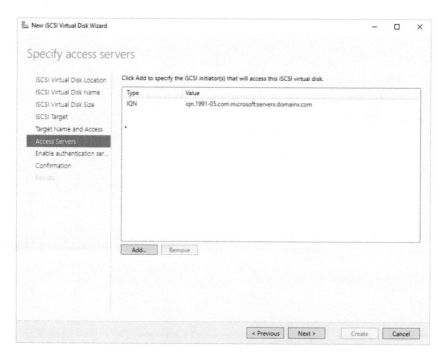

Figure 7-39   Specifying the IQNs of allowed iSCSI initiators

After clicking Next in Figure 7-39, you can optionally enable **Challenge-Handshake Authentication Protocol (CHAP)** authentication, as shown in Figure 7-40. If you enable CHAP authentication, the server administrator must supply the credentials you specify the first time that they configure the iSCSI initiator to connect to the iSCSI target. After you click Next in Figure 7-40, click Create to create the iSCSI virtual disk and target. Figure 7-41 shows the resulting iSCSI target (iscsitarget1) that provides access to the storage in the iSCSI virtual disk (iSCSI Virtual Disk 1).

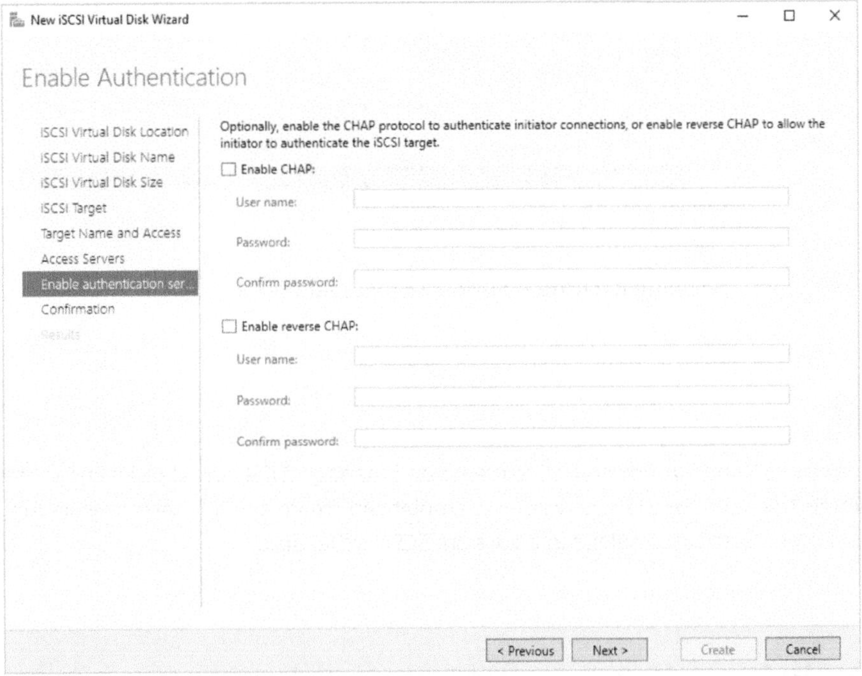

Figure 7-40   Enabling iSCSI target authentication

Over time, you may need to add additional capacity to an iSCSI virtual disk. To do this for iSCSI Virtual Disk 1 in Figure 7-41, right-click iSCSI Virtual Disk 1 in the iSCSI VIRTUAL DISKS pane, click Extend iSCSI Virtual Disk, and specify the new size. You can also use the New iSCSI Virtual Disk Wizard to add additional iSCSI virtual disks that are made available using the existing iSCSI target (iscsitarget1) or a new one.

If you install a new Windows Server 2019 system that requires access to an existing iSCSI target, you will need to add the IQN of the system to the properties of the iSCSI target. To do this for iscsitarget1 in Figure 7-41, right-click iscsitarget1 in the iSCSI TARGETS pane and click Properties. Next, highlight the Initiators tab, click Add, and supply the FQDN of the system in the *Query initiator computer for ID* text box.

Figure 7-41   Viewing iscsitarget1 and iSCSI Virtual Disk 1

Note

You can also use Windows PowerShell to create and manage iSCSI virtual disks and targets. For example, the `New-IscsiServerTarget` cmdlet can create an iSCSI target, while the `New-IscsiVirtualDisk` cmdlet can create an iSCSI virtual disk.

Managing Volume Data

In most cases, data is continually added to the volumes that you configure on a server by applications and users. Consequently, you should regularly monitor the available space on each volume to know when capacity must be added. In addition to monitoring volume usage, server administrators can perform other tasks to manage the data stored on volumes. Common data management tasks include configuring data deduplication, optimizing and repairing volumes, and backing up and restoring data.

Enabling Data Deduplication

Users may store multiple copies of the same document in different folders on the same volume. Say, for example, that your organization creates home directories for each user under a shared folder on the F: volume of one of your Windows Server 2019 file servers. If a file that contains company information is emailed to several users in the organization, each user will likely store their copy of the file in their home directory. As a result, there may be several copies of the same file in the F: volume on your file server, wasting unnecessary space. If you enable **data deduplication** (often shortened to **data dedup**) on the F: volume, then the **Data Deduplication Service** on Windows Server 2019 will periodically scan for duplicate file contents that have not been modified for a certain number of days. If duplicate file contents are found, the underlying filesystem will store a single copy of those contents and ensure that each file name refers to that single copy. If a user modifies the contents of a file that has been deduplicated, a new copy of the modified file is created and associated with the particular file name.

> **Note** 📎
>
> Data deduplication ignores file names when scanning for files to deduplicate. This allows files with the same contents to be deduplicated, even if they have different file names.

> **Note** 📎
>
> While data deduplication requires additional processor calculations, the storage savings provided by data deduplication are significant for many organizations. On a file server that hosts user files, you may find that data deduplication reduces data storage by more than 30 percent.

Windows Server 2019 allows you to enable data deduplication for NTFS and ReFS volumes that are not the boot or system volume, provided that the **Data Deduplication** server role is installed. You can locate this server role in the Add Roles and Features Wizard under the File and iSCSI Services section of File and Storage Services, as shown earlier in Figure 7-32.

After the Data Deduplication server role has been installed, you can use Server Manager to enable data duplication on a volume. For example, to enable data deduplication for the F: volume shown earlier in Figure 7-28, right-click it in the VOLUMES pane, click Configure Data Deduplication, and specify the appropriate options, as shown in Figure 7-42. The options shown in Figure 7-42 will deduplicate data for files that have not been modified for 3 days on the F: volume using default deduplication settings appropriate for a general purpose file server. Moreover, any files that have a .edb, .jrs, .vhd or .vhdx extension, as well as any files in the F:\Databases folder, are excluded from data deduplication.

If you click the Set Deduplication Schedule button in Figure 7-42, you can modify the performance options for the Data Deduplication Service, as shown in Figure 7-43. The options shown in Figure 7-43 will run the Data Deduplication Service during the day

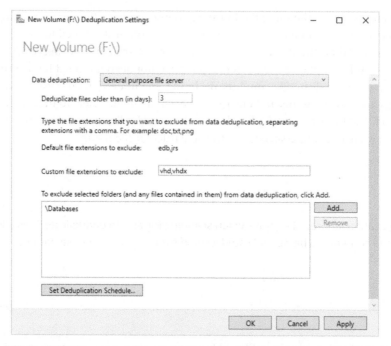

Figure 7-42   Configuring data deduplication for the F: volume

at a low priority to consume few system resources, but will run the Data Deduplication Service with a high priority at 1:45 AM for 6 hours to deduplicate files that could not be deduplicated at other times of the day.

Note

You can also use Windows PowerShell to enable and manage data deduplication. For example, the `Enable-DedupVolume -Volume "F:"` command enables data deduplication for the F: volume using default options, and the `Get-DedupStatus -Volume "F:"` command displays the space saved on the F: volume from data deduplication.

Optimizing Volumes

When you save a file to a filesystem on a hard disk, Windows Server 2019 saves the file to the first area of available space, regardless of whether that area is large enough to store the entire file. Thus, the file might be saved in pieces to several different areas of the hard disk. Over time, this process causes the files on the hard disk to gradually become **fragmented**, particularly as more and more files are created and deleted. When users access a fragmented file, that file is read from different areas on the hard disk, slowing

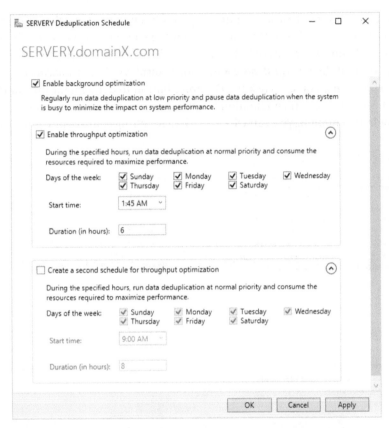

Figure 7-43   Specifying Data Deduplication Service options

access time and creating additional hard disk wear. The process of **defragmenting** locates fragmented files and moves them to a location on the hard disk where they can be stored and read as a single unit.

Because SSDs use non-volatile memory chips for storage, they do not experience the same type of fragmentation that hard disks do. When you save a file to a filesystem on an SSD, that file is saved to a new memory location, even if a previous memory location is no longer used because the associated file was deleted. This is because SSD storage controllers do not automatically remove data from unused memory locations when files are deleted in order to maintain fast performance. Over time, this process forces the SSD to keep track of more memory addresses than it stores data for, slowing access time. Defragmenting an SSD is called **trimming**, and it erases sections of the non-volatile memory chips on the SSD that no longer contain data, consolidating the existing data into fewer memory locations.

By default, all volumes on a Windows Server 2019 system are automatically defragmented or trimmed on a weekly basis during a time of low activity. However, you can modify these options, as well as manually defragment or trim a volume to optimize data access. To do this, right-click a volume (e.g., F:) in File Explorer, click Properties, highlight the Tools tab, and click Optimize to open the Optimize Drives window shown in Figure 7-44. If you click Analyze in Figure 7-44, the selected volume (F:) is analyzed for fragmentation. If the *Current status* column for F: displays *Needs optimization* after the process has completed, you can click the Optimize button to defragment the volume. To modify the automatic defragmentation frequency, or exclude certain volumes from automatic defragmentation, you can click the Change settings button in Figure 7-44.

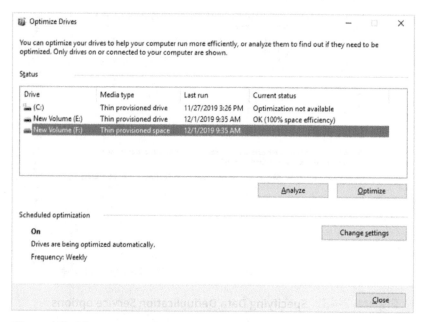

Figure 7-44   The Optimize Drives window

Note

You can also use the `Optimize-Volume` cmdlet to optimize a volume. For example, to optimize the F: volume, you can run the `Optimize-Volume -DriveLetter F` command in Windows PowerShell.

Repairing Volumes

Accessing a volume is performed by the storage subsystem in Windows Server 2019. As the number of applications and users that access and modify data on a volume increases, so does the possibility of storage subsystem errors that result in corrupted data or invalid filesystem information. Volumes that are stored on hard disks may also encounter errors if an area of the hard disk can no longer hold a magnetic charge. This area is called a **bad sector**, and cannot be written to by the storage subsystem. When bad sectors are identified by the storage subsystem, their locations are recorded in a table of bad sectors on the filesystem to ensure that they are no longer used to store data.

If users report errors when trying to save or open files, you should check for, and repair, errors on the volume, such as corrupted data or bad sectors. To do this in File Explorer, right-click a volume (e.g., E:), click Properties, highlight the Tools tab, and click Check to perform a quick check of the volume for errors. If the quick check does not find any errors on the volume, as shown in Figure 7-45, click *Scan drive* in the Error Checking window to perform a full check. Any errors on the volume are repaired automatically, and any data that can be read from bad sectors is written to another location.

Figure 7-45　**The Error Checking window**

You can also check for, and repair, errors on volumes using Server Manager. For example, to check for errors on the F: volume shown earlier in Figure 7-28, right-click the F: volume in the VOLUMES pane, and click Scan File System for Errors. If errors are found, right-click the F: volume and click Repair File System Errors to fix the errors.

Alternatively, you can use commands to check for and repair volume errors. The chkdsk command provides the most functionality and can be run at a Command Prompt or Windows PowerShell window. Table 7-3 lists common options and arguments used with the chkdsk command. To view all of the available chkdsk options and arguments, run the chkdsk /? command.

Table 7-3　**Common chkdsk options and arguments**

Option	Description
volume	Specifies that chkdsk only check the specified *volume* (e.g., C:).
filename	Scans a specified *filename* for errors. You can use wildcards to specify multiple files (e.g., *.dll).
/scan	Scans the volume for errors while it is online.
/spotfix	Automatically fixes errors on the volume previously identified by the Spot Verifier service only, thus saving time.

(continues)

Table 7-3   Common `chkdsk` options and arguments *(continued)*

Option	Description
`/C`	Performs a quick check of the folder structure on a volume.
`/F`	Instructs `chkdsk` to automatically fix errors that it finds.
`/I`	Performs a quick check of indexes on a volume.
`/L:size`	Allows you to specify the *size* of the log file created by `chkdsk`.
`/R`	Searches for bad sectors (on volumes that use hard disks) and attempts to recover information from them.
`/X`	Dismounts or locks a volume before scanning.

To speed up the checking of volumes with `chkdsk`, start the **Spot Verifier** service, which scans for, and identifies, volume errors in the background but does not repair them. Next, you can use the `/spotfix` option to the `chkdsk` command to only fix errors that were previously identified by the Spot Verifier service.

Note 📎

To start the Spot Verifier service, you can run the `net start svsvc` command at a Command Prompt, or the `Start-Service svsvc` command in Windows PowerShell.

Note 📎

The storage subsystem in Windows Server 2019 will automatically start the Spot Verifier service if it encounters filesystem-related errors.

In addition to `chkdsk`, the `Repair-Volume` cmdlet in Windows PowerShell can also scan for, and repair, volume errors. For example, you can run the `Repair-Volume -DriveLetter E -Scan` command in Windows PowerShell to scan the E: volume for errors but not repair them. To repair any errors found on the E: volume, run the `Repair-Volume -DriveLetter E` command. Alternatively, you can repair errors identified by the Spot Verifier service by running the `Repair-Volume -DriveLetter E -SpotFix` command.

Note 📎

The ReFS filesystem prevents corrupted data from being stored. As a result, you cannot check a volume formatted with ReFS for errors.

Backing Up and Restoring Data

As a server administrator, one of your key responsibilities is to ensure that the data on the systems you are responsible for is protected. While fault tolerant RAID volumes protect against storage device failure, they do not protect data when:

- One or more files are deleted or become corrupted
- A filesystem becomes corrupted
- A server fails, and the volumes hosted by the server become unavailable

The most reliable way to protect data is to back the data up on a regular basis. When you back up data, a copy is made to another folder on the system or on another system across the network. If the original data becomes unavailable, it can be restored from the backup copy.

While many organizations purchase third-party backup software to back up the data on multiple systems on the network, Windows Server 2019 provides a free backup tool called **Windows Server Backup** that you can use to back up files on NTFS and ReFS volumes to a dedicated storage device, local volume, or shared folder on the network.

> **Note** 📎
>
> Many organizations back up files to a NAS device on the network. The files on this NAS device are then copied to storage in the cloud. This ensures that systems can be recovered in the event of a catastrophic failure, such as a building fire.

> **Note** 📎
>
> While the Windows Server Backup tool is installed by default on Windows Server 2019, you must install the Windows Server Backup feature before you are able to use it to back up and restore data.

After you have installed the Windows Server Backup feature, click the Tools menu in Server Manager and then click Windows Server Backup to open the Windows Server Backup tool, as shown in Figure 7-46.

Before backing up data, you should choose the type of backup that you wish to perform by clicking Configure Performance Settings in the Actions pane in Figure 7-46. This will open the Optimize Backup Performance window shown in Figure 7-47. The default *Normal backup performance* option shown in Figure 7-47 will back up all of the data that you specify, regardless of whether the files have been modified since the last backup. This is called a **full backup**, and may take a long time to complete, depending on the amount of data that is backed up. To decrease the time it takes to back up data, you can

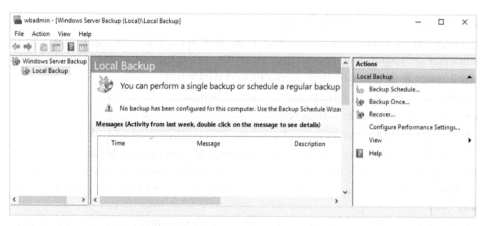

Figure 7-46   The Windows Server Backup tool

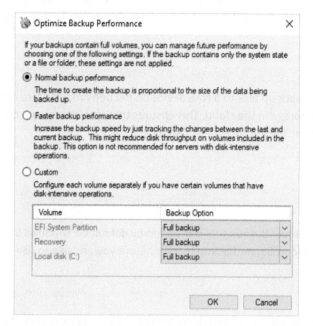

Figure 7-47   The Optimize Backup Performance window

instead select the *Faster backup performance* option. This option performs a full backup the first time that you back up data. However, subsequent backups only back up data that has been modified since the previous backup. These backups are called **incremental backups**, and often take far less time to complete, depending on the number and size of files that were modified since the previous data backup. However, to restore data, you must restore the first full backup, followed by all subsequent incremental backups, in order.

Note

Each full backup performed by the Windows Server Backup tool overwrites the previous full backup.

Note

Recall from Module 5 that the archive attribute is automatically added to a file after creation or modification and automatically removed when the file has been backed up. Full backups ignore the archive attribute when backing up files, whereas incremental backups only back up files that have the archive attribute set.

Note

Windows Server Backup will perform a maximum of 14 incremental backups after a full backup. After 14 incremental backups, another full backup is performed, followed by another 14 incremental backups, and so on.

Note

While full backups take longer to perform, they are the fastest option when you need to restore data.

To schedule a data backup, click Backup Schedule in the Actions pane in Figure 7-46 to open the Backup Schedule Wizard. When you click Next at the first page of the Backup Schedule Wizard, you are prompted to choose the backup configuration, as shown in Figure 7-48. To back up the data on all volumes on the server, select Full server in Figure 7-48. Alternatively, you can select Custom to choose the data that you wish to back up. If you select Custom in Figure 7-48 and click Next, you are prompted to select the data that you wish to back up, as shown in Figure 7-49. The options shown in Figure 7-49 will back up the entire contents of the E: volume, as well as the contents of the C:\Blueprints folder and C:\CompanyForms folder.

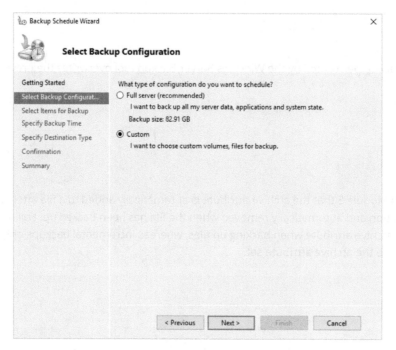

Figure 7-48   Selecting the backup configuration

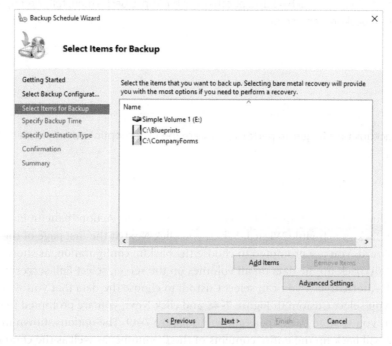

Figure 7-49   Specifying items to back up

When you click Add Items in Figure 7-49, you can choose to back up entire volumes, certain folders or files on a volume, or the contents of the recovery or EFI system partitions. Additionally, you can choose:

- *Bare metal recovery*—This creates a full backup of the entire system. To restore this backup, you must start a Windows Server 2019 installation, click *Repair your computer* (shown earlier in Figure 1-16), and select the *Restore your computer using a system image that you created earlier* option.
- *System state*—This creates a backup of all operating system settings, including the Windows Registry, Active Directory database (for domain controllers), and boot loader files.
- *Hyper-V*—This backs up the configuration and virtual hard disk files for the virtual machines you select and is only available if the Hyper-V role is installed.

By default, the Volume Shadow Copy Service (VSS) is used to back up files that users currently have open by taking a copy of those files that are included in the backup. If you are not using other third-party backup software on your system, you can click Advanced Settings in Figure 7-49, highlight the VSS Settings tab and select the *VSS full Backup* option to ensure that Windows Server Backup keeps a detailed record of the backup.

When you click Next in Figure 7-49, you are prompted to choose the backup schedule, as shown in Figure 7-50. You should choose to perform backups after working hours to minimize the number of open files that the VSS must copy. The default backup schedule shown in Figure 7-50 backs up data each day at 9:00 PM.

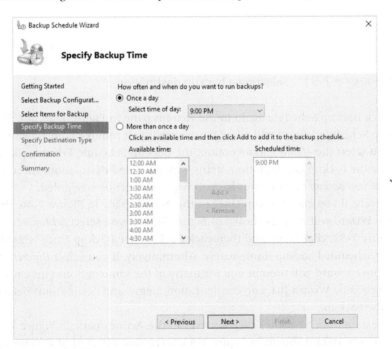

Figure 7-50   Choosing a backup schedule

After you choose a backup schedule in Figure 7-50 and click Next, you are prompted to select the location for the backup, as shown in Figure 7-51. Since *Back up to a volume* is selected in Figure 7-51, you will be prompted to specify the destination volume when you click Next. After you specify the destination volume and click Next, click Finish to complete your scheduled backup.

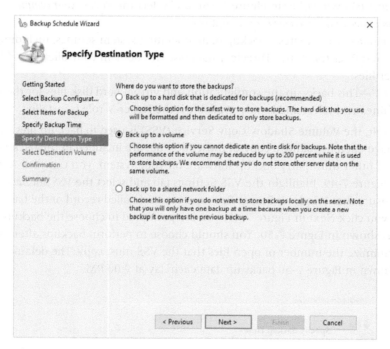

Figure 7-51   Selecting a backup destination

If you click Backup Schedule again in the Actions pane in Figure 7-46, the first page of the Backup Schedule Wizard will allow you to modify or remove your scheduled backup. If you select the *Modify backup* option, the Backup Schedule Wizard will allow you to modify the backup configuration, items, schedule, and destination. Alternatively, if you select the *Stop backup* option, your backup will no longer be scheduled.

Alternatively, if you click Backup Once in the Actions pane in Figure 7-46, the Backup Once Wizard will start, as shown in Figure 7-52. If you select *Scheduled backup options* in Figure 7-52, click Next, and then click Backup, the Backup Once wizard will perform your scheduled backup immediately. Alternatively, if you select *Different options*, the Backup Once wizard will prompt you for many of the same options you chose in the Backup Schedule Wizard (backup configuration, items, and destination) before performing the backup.

To restore data from a backup, click Recover in the Actions pane in Figure 7-46 to open the Recovery Wizard shown in Figure 7-53. To restore a backup that was performed by Windows Server Backup on your server, you should select *This server*. When you click

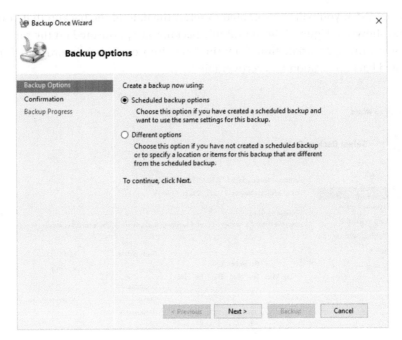

Figure 7-52   The Backup Once Wizard

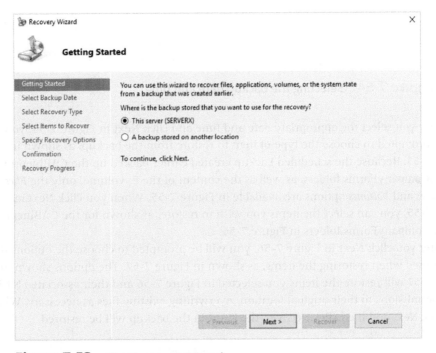

Figure 7-53   The Recovery Wizard

Next in Figure 7-53, you will be prompted to select the date of the backup that you wish to restore as shown in Figure 7-54. If multiple backups are performed on the same day, you must select the appropriate time from the Time drop-down box in order to display the associated backup location and recoverable items.

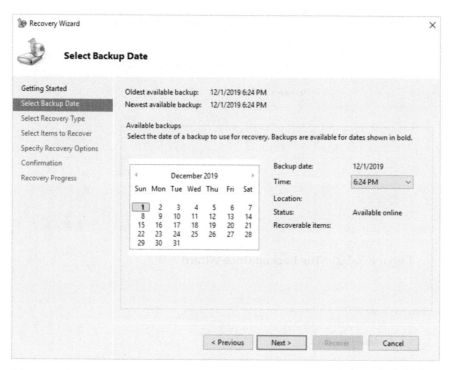

Figure 7-54   **Selecting the backup date and time**

After you select the appropriate date and time and click Next in Figure 7-54, you will be prompted to choose the type of item to restore from the backup, as shown in Figure 7-55. Because the scheduled backup created earlier backed up the C:\Blueprints and C:\CompanyForms folders, as well as the content of the E: volume, only the *Files and folders* and *Volumes* options are available in Figure 7-55. When you click Next in Figure 7-55, you can select the items you wish to restore, as shown for the C:\Blueprints and C:\CompanyForms folders in Figure 7-56.

After you click Next in Figure 7-56, you will be prompted to choose the options that will be used when restoring the items, as shown in Figure 7-57. The options shown in Figure 7-57 will restore the items you selected in Figure 7-56 and their associated NTFS/ReFS permissions to their original location, overwriting existing files as necessary. When you click Next and then click Recover, the items in the backup will be restored.

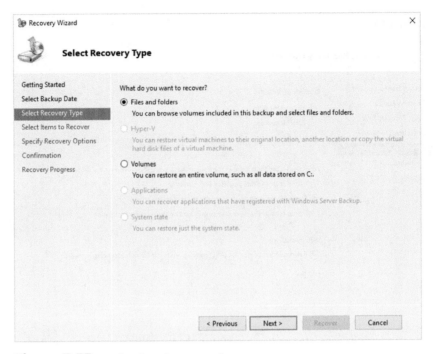

Figure 7-55   Selecting the type of restore

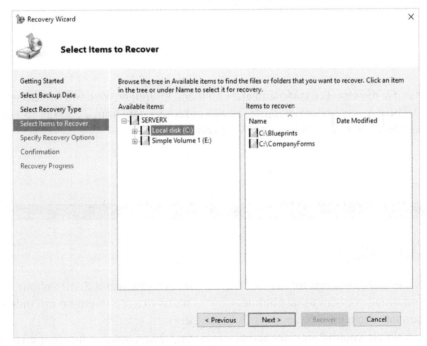

Figure 7-56   Selecting the items to restore

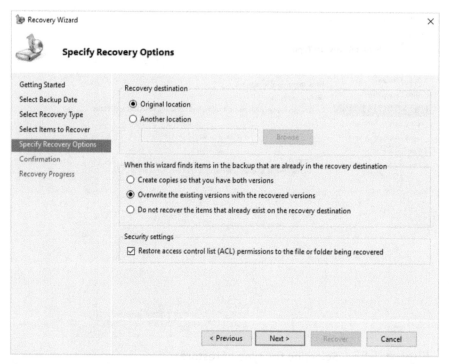

Figure 7-57 Selecting restore options

Note

You can also use the `wbadmin` command at a Command Prompt or Windows PowerShell window to schedule and perform backups, as well as recover data from a backup. To view `wbadmin` options, you can run the `wbadmin /?` command.

Module Summary

- Windows Server 2019 connects to filesystems on storage devices using volumes that are mounted with a drive letter or folder path. A simple volume provides access to a filesystem in a partition on a storage device, whereas a RAID volume provides access to a filesystem on multiple storage devices.

- The most common levels of RAID include 0 (striping or spanning), 1 (mirroring), and

5 (striping with parity). RAID level 0 does not provide fault tolerance in the event of a storage device failure.

- Disk Management can be used to manage simple volumes on basic disks, as well as RAID volumes on dynamic disks.

- In addition to managing simple volumes, Server Manager can manage RAID volumes using the Storage Spaces component of Windows Server 2019. Storage Spaces places storage devices in a storage pool, from which virtual disks and RAID volumes can be created.

- Storage Spaces Direct uses the Failover Clustering feature of Windows Server 2019 to create RAID volumes from storage on multiple servers. It provides volume fault tolerance in the event of a server failure.

- Windows Server 2019 can connect to storage on a remote SAN device using an iSCSI initiator or Fibre Channel HBA. MPIO can optionally be used to provide for multiple, redundant SAN device connections.

- You can allow other systems to access storage on a Windows Server 2019 system using iSCSI by configuring the iSCSI Target Server role.

- In addition to monitoring available storage space, you should regularly optimize and scan volumes for errors. You can also configure data deduplication to save storage space by eliminating duplicate copies of stored data.

- Backing up data to another location is the most reliable way to safeguard data against loss. You can use the Windows Server Backup tool to schedule and perform data backups, as well as to restore data from a backup.

Key Terms

active partition
bad sector
basic disk
boot loader
boot partition
Challenge-Handshake
  Authentication Protocol
  (CHAP)
clustered storage pool
data dedup
data deduplication
Data Deduplication
Data Deduplication Service
defragmenting
Device Specific Module
  (DSM)
Disk Management
duplexing
dynamic disk
EFI system partition
extended partition

Failover Clustering
FC over Ethernet (FCoE)
Fibre Channel (FC)
filesystem
firmware RAID
formatting
fragmented
full backup
GUID Partition Table (GPT)
hardware RAID
Host Bus Adapter (HBA)
IDE (Integrated Drive
  Electronics)
incremental backup
Internet SCSI (iSCSI)
iSCSI initiator
iSCSI Qualified Name (IQN)
iSCSI target
iSCSI Target Server
iSCSI Target Storage
  Provider

iSCSI virtual disk
journaling
Just a Bunch of Disks (JBOD)
logical drive
Master Boot Record (MBR)
Microsoft iSCSI Initiator
  Service
mirroring
mounting
Multipath I/O
Multipath Input Output
  (MPIO)
network-attached storage
  (NAS)
partitions
primary partition
primordial storage pool
RAID volume
recovery partition
remote-direct memory
  access (RDMA)

Serial Advanced Technology Attachment (SATA)	spanning	trimming
Serial Attached SCSI (SAS)	Spot Verifier	UEFI system partition
simple volume	storage pool	virtual disk
Small Computer Systems Interface (SCSI)	striping	Virtual Disk Service (VDS)
	striping with parity	volume
software RAID	system partition	Windows Server Backup
	three-way mirroring	

Review Questions

1. Which of the following RAID volume types provide fault tolerance in the event of a single storage device failure? (Choose all that apply.)
   a. striping
   b. striping with parity
   c. mirroring
   d. JBOD

2. On systems that have a UEFI BIOS, the UEFI system partition is the boot partition. True or False?

3. Which of the following are reasons for creating multiple volumes on a single storage device? (Choose all that apply.)
   a. Allow for the use of more than one type of filesystem
   b. Reduce the chance that filesystem corruption will render all data on the storage device unusable
   c. Segregate different types of data
   d. Speed up access to stored data by keeping filesystems as small as possible

4. When initializing a new storage device that has a capacity larger than 2 TB, you must use a GPT instead of an MBR. True or False?

5. You wish to create a RAID level 5 volume using the Disk Management tool. How many storage devices can you use in the volume?
   a. 3
   b. 7

   c. 32
   d. There is no limit.

6. After noticing a RAID level 5 volume in Disk Management with a status of Failed Redundancy, you located and replaced the failed storage device with a new one. What must you do to return the volume status to Healthy?
   a. Nothing, as the data will automatically be rebuilt on the new storage device
   b. Right-click the RAID volume and click Reactivate Volume
   c. Right-click the RAID volume, click Repair Volume, and select the new storage device
   d. Delete and recreate the RAID volume, and then restore data from a backup

7. When creating a RAID volume using Server Manager, each storage device is automatically converted to a dynamic disk. True or False?

8. When configuring the Storage Spaces component of Windows Server 2019 using Server Manager, which of the following statements is true? (Choose all that apply.)
   a. The primordial storage pool contains all storage devices on a system
   b. RAID volumes are created on a virtual disk that utilizes space in a storage pool comprised of storage devices

c. Virtual disks implement a level of RAID and can use thin or thick provisioning

d. The maximum number of storage devices that you can add to a single storage pool is 32

9. You have configured a new storage pool in Server Manager that contains five storage devices and would like to configure a single virtual disk that uses all of the available capacity from this pool. What RAID type should you select in the New Virtual Disk Wizard if you wish to ensure that your virtual disk remains fault tolerant in the event that two storage devices fail at the same time?

a. Simple

b. Striped

c. Mirror

d. Parity

10. Which of the following are requirements for each server in a Storage Spaces Direct configuration? (Choose all that apply.)

a. Failover Clustering feature installed

b. 64 GB of memory and at least two processors

c. At least six additional storage devices (two or more of which are SSDs)

d. 10 Gb Ethernet interface with RDMA support

11. After storage tiers have been enabled for the storage used by a volume, you can use the `Set-FileStorageTier` cmdlet in Windows PowerShell to ensure that a specific file is always stored on a specified storage tier. True or False?

12. Another server administrator has configured an iSCSI SAN device to provide storage to your Windows Server 2019 system. What must you configure on your Windows Server 2019 system in order to connect to this storage?

a. iSCSI HBA

b. iSCSI initiator

c. iSCSI target

d. MPIO

13. By supplying the device driver for an FC HBA during a Windows Server 2019 installation, you can choose to install Windows Server 2019 on FC SAN storage instead of a local storage device. True or False?

14. What two items must you configure using Server Manager in order to share storage to other systems using iSCSI?

a. iSCSI virtual disk

b. clustered storage pool

c. iSCSI target

d. iSCSI initiator

15. What name format is used to specify the iSCSI initiators that are permitted to connect to an iSCSI target?

a. IQN

b. FQDN

c. IDN

d. UNC

16. You can only run the `chkdsk` command on NTFS and ReFS filesystems. True or False?

17. Which service can you start on a system to reduce the amount of time it takes to repair filesystem errors?

a. Storage Spaces

b. Spot Verifier

c. Volume Repair

d. Data Deduplication

18. When you click the Optimize button for a simple volume in the Optimize Drives window, the underlying storage device is defragmented if it is a hard disk, or trimmed if it is an SSD. True or False?

19. Which of the following statements regarding backup performance options

for Windows Server Backup are true? (Choose all that apply.)

a. Full backups provide the fastest restoration of data

b. Incremental backups take less time to perform than full backups

c. Up to 6 incremental backups can be performed following a full backup

d. Full backups back up files that have the archive attribute set

20. When restoring a backup, you can choose to restore the data to a different location. True or False?

Hands-On Projects

These Hands-On Projects should be completed in the order given and normally take a total of three hours or less to complete. The requirements for these projects include:

- A system with Windows Server 2019 installed according to Hands-On Project 1-1 (Lab Environment 1) or Hands-On Project 1-2 (Lab Environment 2).
- A WindowsServer2019VM2 virtual machine installed according to Hands-On Project 3-5 and configured as a member server according to Hands-On Project 5-2.

Project 7-1: Adding Storage Devices

In this Hands-On Project, you add four virtual hard disks to your WindowsServer2019VM2 virtual machine. You will configure volumes on these virtual hard disks in Hands-On Projects 7-2, 7-3, and 7-4.

1. Boot your Windows Server 2019 host and log into the system as Administrator using the password **Secret555**. Next, click **Start** and then click **Server Manager**.
2. In Server Manager, select the **Tools** menu and then click **Hyper-V Manager**.
3. In Hyper-V Manager, highlight **WindowsServer2019VM2** in the Virtual Machines pane and click **Settings** in the Actions pane.

   a. Highlight **SCSI Controller** under the Hardware section. Click **Add** to add an additional hard drive. Next, click **New** to create a new virtual hard disk file for this additional hard drive.

      i. At the Before You Begin page of the New Virtual Hard Disk Wizard, click **Next**.

      ii. On the Choose Disk Format page, note that VHDX is selected by default and click **Next**.

      iii. On the Choose Disk Type page, note that Dynamically expanding is selected by default and click **Next**.

      iv. On the Specify Name and Location page, type **Disk1.vhdx** in the Name text box and click **Next**.

      v. On the Configure Disk page, type **50** in the Size text box and click **Next**.

      vi. Click **Finish** to create the new virtual hard disk file and associate it with your new SCSI virtual hard disk.

b. Highlight **SCSI Controller** under the Hardware section. Click **Add** to add an additional hard drive. Next, click **New** to create a new virtual hard disk file for this additional hard drive.

    i. At the Before You Begin page of the New Virtual Hard Disk Wizard, click **Next**.

    ii. On the Choose Disk Format page, note that VHDX is selected by default and click **Next**.

    iii. On the Choose Disk Type page, note that Dynamically expanding is selected by default and click **Next**.

    iv. On the Specify Name and Location page, type **Disk2.vhdx** in the Name text box and click **Next**.

    v. On the Configure Disk page, type **50** in the Size text box and click **Next**.

    vi. Click **Finish** to create the new virtual hard disk file and associate it with your new SCSI virtual hard disk.

c. Highlight **SCSI Controller** under the Hardware section. Click **Add** to add an additional hard drive. Next, click **New** to create a new virtual hard disk file for this additional hard drive.

    i. At the Before You Begin page of the New Virtual Hard Disk Wizard, click **Next**.

    ii. On the Choose Disk Format page, note that VHDX is selected by default and click **Next**.

    iii. On the Choose Disk Type page, note that Dynamically expanding is selected by default and click **Next**.

    iv. On the Specify Name and Location page, type **Disk3.vhdx** in the Name text box and click **Next**.

    v. On the Configure Disk page, type **50** in the Size text box and click **Next**.

    vi. Click **Finish** to create the new virtual hard disk file and associate it with your new SCSI virtual hard disk.

d. Highlight **SCSI Controller** under the Hardware section. Click **Add** to add an additional hard drive. Next, click **New** to create a new virtual hard disk file for this additional hard drive.

    i. At the Before You Begin page of the New Virtual Hard Disk Wizard, click **Next**.

    ii. On the Choose Disk Format page, note that VHDX is selected by default and click **Next**.

    iii. On the Choose Disk Type page, note that Dynamically expanding is selected by default and click **Next**.

    iv. On the Specify Name and Location page, type **Disk4.vhdx** in the Name text box and click **Next**.

    v. On the Configure Disk page, type **50** in the Size text box and click **Next**.

    vi. Click **Finish** to create the new virtual hard disk file and associate it with your new SCSI virtual hard disk.

e. Click **OK** to close the Settings window for your WindowsServer2019VM2 virtual machine.

4. Highlight **WindowsServer2019VM2** in the virtual machines pane of Hyper-V Manager and click **Connect** in the Actions pane. In the Virtual Machine Connection window, click **Start** to boot your new virtual machine.

5. At the login screen, click the **Ctrl+Alt+Delete** button in the Virtual Machine Connection window, supply the password **Secret555** for Administrator and press **Enter** to log into the system.

Project 7-2: Disk Management (Simple Volumes)

In this Hands-On Project, you use the Disk Management tool to configure and manage simple volumes on the first virtual hard disk that you added to your WindowsServer2019VM2 virtual machine in Hands-On Project 7-1.

1. On your WindowsServer2019VM2 virtual machine, right-click **Start** and then click **Disk Management**. In the Disk Management tool, view your disk, partition, and volume configuration:

   - The first disk (Disk 0) is a basic disk that contains two primary partitions:
     - A 549 MB NTFS recovery partition that is marked active. This partition is labeled the system partition as it also contains the boot loader.
     - An NTFS partition that uses the remaining available space. This partition is labeled the boot partition as it contains the Windows operating system and is identified as the C: volume.
   - The remaining disks (Disk 1, Disk 2, Disk 3, and Disk 4) are in an Offline state and do not contain any partitions.

2. Right-click **Disk 1** and click **Online**. Next, right-click **Disk 2** and click **Online**, then right-click **Disk 3** and click **Online**. Note that Disk 1, Disk 2, and Disk 3 are labeled as Not Initialized to indicate that they do not have a partition table (either MBR or GPT).

3. Right-click **Disk 1** and click **Initialize Disk**. Note the default options that will place an MBR on Disk 1, Disk 2, and Disk 3, and click **OK**. Note that Disk 1, Disk 2, and Disk 3 are labeled as Basic to indicate that they are now recognized as basic disks in Windows Server 2019.

4. Right-click the **50.00 GB Unallocated** space next to Disk 1 and click **New Simple Volume**.

   a. At the New Simple Volume wizard, click **Next**.

   b. At the Specify Volume Size page, type **5000** in the *Simple volume size in MB* text box and click **Next**.

   c. At the Assign Drive Letter or Path page, note the default E: drive letter assignment and click **Next**. The D: drive letter is reserved for use by the virtual DVD drive in WindowsServer2019VM2.

   d. At the Format Partition page, note the default NTFS formatting options, type **Simple Volume 1** in the Volume label text box, and click **Next**.

   e. Click **Finish** to complete your configuration. Note that your E: volume is associated with the first primary partition on Disk 1. Also note volume size of 5000 MB (4.88 GB).

5. Right-click the **45.12 GB Unallocated** space next to Disk 1 and click **New Simple Volume**.

   a. At the New Simple Volume wizard, click **Next**.

   b. At the Specify Volume Size page, type **5000** in the *Simple volume size in MB* text box and click **Next**.

   c. At the Assign Drive Letter or Path page, note the default F: drive letter assignment and click **Next**.

   d. At the Format Partition page, note the default NTFS formatting options, type **Simple Volume 2** in the Volume label text box, and click **Next**.

   e. Click **Finish** to complete your configuration. Note that your 4.88 GB F: volume is associated with the second primary partition on Disk 1.

6. Right-click the **40.23 GB Unallocated** space next to Disk 1 and click **New Simple Volume**.

   a. At the New Simple Volume wizard, click **Next**.

   b. At the Specify Volume Size page, type **5000** in the *Simple volume size in MB* text box and click **Next**.

   c. At the Assign Drive Letter or Path page, note the default G: drive letter assignment and click **Next**.

   d. At the Format Partition page, note the default NTFS formatting options, type **Simple Volume 3** in the Volume label text box, and click **Next**.

   e. Click **Finish** to complete your configuration. Note that your 4.88 GB G: volume is associated with the third primary partition on Disk 1.

7. Right-click the **35.35 GB Unallocated** space next to Disk 1 and click **New Simple Volume**.

   a. At the New Simple Volume wizard, click **Next**.

   b. At the Specify Volume Size page, type **5000** in the *Simple volume size in MB* text box and click **Next**.

   c. At the Assign Drive Letter or Path page, note the default H: drive letter assignment and click **Next**.

   d. At the Format Partition page, note the default NTFS formatting options, type **Simple Volume 4** in the Volume label text box, and click **Next**.

   e. Click **Finish** to complete your configuration. Note that your 4.88 GB H: volume is associated with the first logical drive in an extended partition that was created from the remaining space on Disk 1.

8. Right-click the **30.47 GB Free space** in the extended partition on Disk 1 and click **New Simple Volume**.

   a. At the New Simple Volume wizard, click **Next**.

   b. At the Specify Volume Size page, note the default value that uses the remaining available space and click **Next**.

   c. At the Assign Drive Letter or Path page, select **Mount in the following empty NTFS folder** and click **Browse**. Click **New Folder**, type **Data**, and press **Enter** to create a new folder called Data on C:\. Click **OK**, note that the new volume will be accessible via the C:\Data folder, and click **Next**.

d. At the Format Partition page, note the default NTFS formatting options, type **Simple Volume 5** in the Volume label text box, and click **Next**.

e. Click **Finish** to complete your configuration. Note that your new volume is associated with the second logical drive in the extended partition. Also note that the I: drive letter was assigned to allow you to easily manage the volume in Disk Management.

9. Click **Start** and then click **File Explorer**.

a. In File Explorer, highlight **This PC** in the navigation pane and note the volume drive letters available and their associated labels.

b. Double-click **Local Disk (C:)** and note that the C:\Data folder is assigned a hard disk icon and has a size defined in the File Explorer window.

c. Double-click **C:\Data** to access the NTFS filesystem in the second logical drive on Disk1.

d. Close File Explorer.

10. In the Disk Management tool, right-click **Simple Volume 5 (I:)** and click **Shrink Volume**. Type **10000** in the *Enter the amount of space to shrink in MB* text box and click **Shrink**. Note that 9.77 GB of free space was made available in the extended partition.

11. Right-click **Simple Volume 5 (I:)**, click **Delete Volume**, and then click **Yes** to remove Simple Volume 5.

12. Right-click **Simple Volume 4 (H:)**, click **Delete Volume**, and then click **Yes** to remove Simple Volume 4.

13. Right-click the extended partition on Disk 1 (**35.35 GB Free space**), click **Delete Partition,** and then click **Yes** to remove the extended partition.

14. Right-click **Simple Volume 3 (G:)**, click **Delete Volume**, and then click **Yes** to remove Simple Volume 3.

15. Right-click **Simple Volume 2 (F:)**, click **Delete Volume**, and then click **Yes** to remove Simple Volume 2.

16. Right-click **Simple Volume 1 (E:)** and click **Extend Volume**.

a. At the Extend Volume Wizard, click **Next**.

b. At the Select Disks page, note that the remaining free space on Disk 1 is selected by default and click **Next**.

c. Click **Finish** to extend Simple Volume 1. Note that Simple Volume 1 now uses all of the 50 GB of available space on Disk 1.

17. Click **Start** and then click **File Explorer**.

a. In File Explorer, highlight **This PC** in the navigation pane and note that only the C: and E: volumes are available.

b. Double-click **Local Disk (C:)** and then double-click the C:\Data folder. Note the error that you receive and click **OK**.

c. Close File Explorer.

18. In the Disk Management tool, right-click **Simple Volume 1 (E:)**, click **Delete Volume,** and then click **Yes** to remove Simple Volume 1.

Project 7-3: Disk Management (RAID)

In this Hands-On Project, you configure and manage RAID volumes on the virtual hard disks that you added to your WindowsServer2019VM2 virtual machine in Hands-On Project 7-1.

1. In the Disk Management tool on WindowsServer2019VM2, right-click **Disk 1** and click **New Spanned Volume**.

    a. At the New Spanned Volume wizard, click **Next**.

    b. At the Select Disks page, note that Disk 1 is selected by default. Select **Disk 2** and click **Add**. Click **Add** again to add the remaining disk (Disk 3). Note that the *Total volume size in megabytes (MB)* lists the combined space available on all three hard disks (153591) and click **Next**.

    c. At the Assign Drive Letter or Path page, note the default E: drive letter assignment and click **Next**.

    d. At the Format Partition page, note the default NTFS formatting options, type **Spanned Volume 1** in the Volume label text box, select **Perform a quick format**, and click **Next**.

    e. Click **Finish**. Click **Yes** when prompted that the operation will convert your disks to dynamic disks. Note that Spanned Volume 1 (E:) is composed of all available space on Disk 1, Disk 2, and Disk 3. Also note that Disk 1, Disk 2, and Disk 3 are assigned a Dynamic disk label.

2. Click **Start** and then click **File Explorer**.

    a. In File Explorer, highlight **This PC** in the navigation pane and note that the Spanned Volume 1 (E:) uses the combined space available on Disk 1, Disk 2, and Disk 3.

    b. Close File Explorer.

3. In the Disk Management tool, right-click **Spanned Volume 1 (E:)**, click **Delete Volume**, and then click **Yes** to remove Spanned Volume 1. Note that Disk 1, Disk 2, and Disk 3 are assigned a Basic disk label.

4. In the Disk Management tool, right-click **Disk 1** and click **New Striped Volume**.

    a. At the New Striped Volume wizard, click **Next**.

    b. At the Select Disks page, note that Disk 1 is selected by default. Select **Disk 2** and click **Add**. Click **Add** again to add the remaining disk (Disk 3). Note that the *Total volume size in megabytes (MB)* lists the combined space available on all three hard disks (153591) and click **Next**.

    c. At the Assign Drive Letter or Path page, note the default E: drive letter assignment and click **Next**.

    d. At the Format Partition page, note the default NTFS formatting options, type **Striped Volume 1** in the Volume label text box, select **Perform a quick format**, and click **Next**.

    e. Click **Finish**. Click **Yes** when prompted that the operation will convert your disks to dynamic disks. Note that Striped Volume 1 (E:) is composed of all available space on Disk 1, Disk 2, and Disk 3.

5. Click **Start** and then click **File Explorer**.

    a. In File Explorer, highlight **This PC** in the navigation pane and note that the Striped Volume 1 (E:) uses the combined space available on Disk 1, Disk 2, and Disk 3.

    b. Close File Explorer.

6. In the Disk Management tool, right-click **Striped Volume 1 (E:)**, click **Delete Volume,** and then click **Yes** to remove Striped Volume 1. Note that Disk 1, Disk 2, and Disk 3 are assigned a Basic disk label.

7. In the Disk Management tool, right-click **Disk 1** and click **New Mirrored Volume**.

    a. At the New Mirrored Volume wizard, click **Next**.

    b. At the Select Disks page, note that Disk 1 is selected by default. Select **Disk 2** and click **Add**. Note that the *Total volume size in megabytes (MB)* lists the space available on a single hard disk (51197) and click **Next**.

    c. At the Assign Drive Letter or Path page, note the default E: drive letter assignment and click **Next**.

    d. At the Format Partition page, note the default NTFS formatting options, type **Mirrored Volume 1** in the Volume label text box, select **Perform a quick format,** and click **Next**.

    e. Click **Finish**. Click **Yes** when prompted that the operation will convert your disks to dynamic disks. Note that Mirrored Volume 1 (E:) uses all available space on Disk 1 and Disk 2.

8. Click **Start** and then click **File Explorer**.

    a. In File Explorer, highlight **This PC** in the navigation pane and note that the Mirrored Volume 1 (E:) lists the space available on Disk 1.

    b. Close File Explorer.

9. In the Disk Management tool, right-click **Mirrored Volume 1 (E:)**, click **Break Mirrored Volume,** and then click **Yes** to break the mirrored volume. Note that you now have two separate simple volumes on Disk 1 and Disk 2 (E: and F:).

    a. Right-click **Mirrored Volume 1 (F:)**, click **Delete Volume,** and then click **Yes** to remove the simple volume.

    b. Right-click **Mirrored Volume 1 (E:)** and click **Add Mirror**. Select **Disk 3**, click **Add Mirror**, and then click **Yes** to copy the data in the *Mirrored Volume 1 (E:)* simple volume to Disk 3 and add a new mirror configuration.

    c. Right-click **Mirrored Volume 1 (E:)**, click **Delete Volume,** and then click **Yes** to remove the mirrored volume. Note that Disk 1, Disk 2, and Disk 3 are assigned a Basic disk label.

10. In the Disk Management tool, right-click **Disk 1** and click **New RAID-5 Volume**.

    a. At the New RAID-5 Volume wizard, click **Next**.

    b. At the Select Disks page, note that Disk 1 is selected by default. Select **Disk 2** and click **Add**. Click **Add** again to add the remaining disk (Disk 3). Note that the *Total volume size in megabytes (MB)* lists the combined space available on two of the three hard disks (102394) to allow for parity and click **Next**.

    c. At the Assign Drive Letter or Path page, note the default E: drive letter assignment and click **Next**.

    d. At the Format Partition page, note the default NTFS formatting options, type **RAID-5 Volume 1** in the Volume label text box, select **Perform a quick format,** and click **Next**.

     e. Click **Finish**. Click **Yes** when prompted that the operation will convert your disks to dynamic disks. After the syncing process has completed, note that RAID-5 Volume 1 (E:) uses all available space on Disk 1, Disk 2, and Disk 3.

11. Click **Start** and then click **File Explorer**.

     a. In File Explorer, highlight **This PC** in the navigation pane and note that the RAID-5 Volume 1 (E:) lists the space available on two of the three disks that make up the volume.

     b. Double-click **RAID-5 Volume 1 (E:)**. Next, right-click the file pane in File Explorer and click **New**, **Text Document** and press **Enter** to accept the default file name of *New Text Document.txt*.

     c. Double-click **New Text Document.txt** to open it in Notepad. Type a line of your choice. Click the **File** menu and click **Save**. Close Notepad when finished.

12. In the Disk Management tool, right-click **Disk 2** and click **Offline**. Note that the status of *RAID-5 Volume 1 (E:)* lists Failed Redundancy.

13. In File Explorer, double-click **New Text Document.txt** to open it in Notepad. Note that you have access to the file contents. Type a line of your choice. Click the **File** menu and click **Save**. Close Notepad and File Explorer when finished.

14. In the Disk Management tool, right-click **Disk 4** and click **Online**. Next, right-click **Disk 4** and click **Initialize Disk**. Note that the default option places an MBR on Disk 4 and click **OK**. Note that Disk 4 is labeled as Basic.

15. Right-click **RAID-5 Volume 1 (E:)** and click **Repair Volume**. Note that Disk 4 is selected by default, click **OK**, and then click **Yes** to generate the data on Disk 4 required to make it a functional member of the RAID-5 volume. After the process has completed, note that Disk 4 is labeled as Dynamic and part of the *RAID-5 Volume 1 (E:)* volume. Also note that the *RAID-5 Volume 1 (E:)* volume lists a Healthy status.

16. Right-click **RAID-5 Volume 1 (E:)**, click **Delete Volume,** and then click **Yes** to remove the RAID volume.

17. Right-click **Disk 2** and click **Online**. Next, right-click the partition on Disk 2, click **Delete Volume,** and then click **Yes** to remove the partition.

18. Close the Disk Management tool.

Project 7-4: Server Manager and Storage Spaces

In this Hands-On Project, you create and manage both simple and RAID volumes in Server Manager on the virtual hard disks that you added to your WindowsServer2019VM2 virtual machine in Hands-On Project 7-1.

1. On your WindowsServer2019VM2 virtual machine, click **Start** and then click **Server Manager**.

2. In Server Manager, highlight **File and Storage Services**, and then highlight **Disks** under the Volumes section. Note the sizes and types of disks shown in the DISKS pane that match the information shown in the Disk Management tool.

3. Highlight disk number **1** in the DISKS pane, select the **TASKS** drop-down box, and click **New Volume**.
   a. At the New Volume Wizard, select **Don't show this page again** and click **Next**.
   b. At the Select the server and disk page, select **Disk 1** and click **Next**.
   c. At the Specify the size of the volume page, type **30** in the Volume size text box and click **Next**.
   d. At the Assign to a drive letter or folder page, note the default drive letter assignment of E: and click **Next**.
   e. At the Select file system settings page, note the default filesystem options, type **Simple Volume 1** in the Volume label text box, and click **Next**.
   f. At the Confirm selections page, click **Create**.
   g. Click **Close** to close the New Volume Wizard.

4. Highlight disk number **1** in the DISKS pane and note the E: volume in the VOLUMES pane.
   a. Right-click the **E:** volume and click **Extend Volume**. Type **50** in the New size text box and click **OK**. After a few moments, note the new size of your E: volume.
   b. Right-click the **E:** volume, click **Scan File System for Errors**, and click **Scan Now**.
   c. Right-click the **E:** volume, click **Delete Volume**, and click **Yes** to remove the E: volume.

5. Highlight **Storage Pools** in the navigation pane of Server Manager and note the default Primordial pool in the STORAGE POOLS pane, and the disks listed in the PHYSICAL DISKS pane.

6. Select the **TASKS** drop-down box in the STORAGE POOLS pane and click **New Storage Pool**.
   a. At the New Storage Pool Wizard, select **Don't show this page again** and click **Next**.
   b. At the Specify a storage pool name and subsystem page, type **Storage Pool 1** in the Name text box and click **Next**.
   c. At the Select physical disks for the storage pool page, place checks in the boxes next to all disks and click **Next**.
   d. At the Confirm selections page, click **Create**.
   e. Click **Close** to close the New Storage Pool Wizard.

7. Highlight **Storage Pool 1** in the STORAGE POOLS pane and note the four disks shown in the PHYSICAL DISKS pane. These disks represent Disk 1, Disk 2, Disk 3, and Disk 4.

8. Highlight **Disks** in the navigation pane of Server Manager and note that only disk 0 is shown in the DISKS pane because disks 1 through 4 are now part of Storage Pool 1.

9. Highlight **Storage Pools** in the navigation pane of Server Manager.

10. Select the **TASKS** drop-down box in the VIRTUAL DISKS pane, and click **New Virtual Disk**. Ensure that Storage Pool 1 is selected and click **OK**.
   a. At the New Virtual Disk Wizard, select **Don't show this page again** and click **Next**.
   b. At the Specify the virtual disk name page, type **Virtual Disk 1** in the Name text box and click **Next**.
   c. At the Specify enclosure resiliency page, click **Next**.
   d. At the Select the storage layout page, select **Parity** and click **Next**.

e. At the Specify the provisioning type page, select **Thin** and click **Next**.

f. At the Specify the size of the virtual disk page, type **100** in the Specify size text box and click **Next**.

g. At the Confirm selections page, click **Create**. If you receive an error at this stage, follow the instructions in the following note.

> **Note** 📎
>
> At the time of this writing, a bug in Storage Spaces in Windows Server 2019 prevents you from adding a virtual disk in Server Manager. If you experience this bug, you can create Virtual Disk 1 using Windows PowerShell. To do this, right-click **Start**, click **Windows PowerShell (Admin)** and run the `New-VirtualDisk -StoragePoolFriendlyName "Storage Pool 1" -FriendlyName "Virtual Disk 1" -ResiliencySettingName Parity -Size 100GB -ProvisioningType Thin` command. Close Windows PowerShell when finished.

h. Click **Close** to close the New Volume Wizard.

11. Click the **Refresh "Storage Pools"** icon in the navigation bar of Server Manager. Note that Virtual Disk 1 appears in the VIRTUAL DISKS pane.

12. Highlight **Disks** in the navigation pane of Server Manager and note that Virtual Disk 1 is set to an Offline state. Right-click **Virtual Disk 1**, click **Bring Online**, and then click **Yes**.

13. Highlight **Storage Pools** in the navigation pane of Server Manager. Next, right-click **Virtual Disk 1** in the VIRTUAL DISKS pane and click **New Volume**.

a. At the Select the server and disk page of the New Volume Wizard, note that Virtual Disk 1 is selected by default and click **Next**. Click **OK** to initialize Virtual Disk 1 with a GPT.

b. At the Specify the size of the volume page, note the default size of 100 MB and click **Next**.

c. At the Assign to a drive letter or folder page, note the default drive letter assignment of E: and click **Next**.

d. At the Select file system settings page, select **ReFS** from the File system drop-down box, type **Storage Space 1** in the Volume label text box, and click **Next**.

e. At the Confirm selections page, click **Create**.

f. Click **Close** to close the New Volume Wizard.

14. Click **Start** and then click **File Explorer**. In File Explorer, highlight **This PC** in the navigation pane and note that *Storage Space 1 (E:)* lists the space available from the virtual disk created from the storage pool. Close File Explorer when finished.

Project 7-5: iSCSI Target Server

In this Hands-On Project, you install and configure the iSCSI Target Server on your WindowsServer2019VM2 virtual machine to provide iSCSI storage to your Windows Server 2019 host. Next, you configure the iSCSI Initiator on your Windows Server 2019 host to connect to the iSCSI storage, as well as create a simple volume in Disk Management to access it.

1. In Server Manager on your WindowsServer2019VM2 virtual machine, click the **Manage** menu and then click **Add Roles and Features**.

   a. At the Select installation type page, click **Next**.

   b. At the Select destination server page, click **Next**.

   c. At the Select server roles page, expand **File and Storage Services**, and then expand **File and iSCSI Services**.

      i. Select **iSCSI Target Server** and click **Add Features** when prompted.

      ii. Select **iSCSI Target Storage Provider** and click **Next**.

   d. At the Select features page, click **Next**.

   e. At the Confirm installation selections page, click **Install**.

   f. At the Installation progress page, click **Close**.

2. In Server Manager, highlight **File and Storage Services**, and then highlight **iSCSI**. Select the **TASKS** drop-down box from the iSCSI VIRTUAL DISKS pane, and click **New iSCSI Virtual Disk**.

   a. At the Select iSCSI virtual disk location page of the New iSCSI Virtual Disk Wizard, select **E:** and click **Next**.

   b. At the Specify iSCSI virtual disk name page, type **iSCSI Virtual Disk 1** in the Name text box and click **Next**.

   c. At the Specify iSCSI virtual disk size page, note the default selection of Dynamically expanding, type **50** in the Size text box, and click **Next**.

   d. At the Assign iSCSI target page, click **Next**.

   e. At the Specify target name page, type **iSCSITarget1** (no spaces) in the Name text box and click **Next**.

   f. At the Specify access servers page, click **Add**.

      i. At the Add initiator ID window, click **Browse**.

      ii. In the *Enter the object name to select text box*, type **serverX** and click **OK**.

      iii. Click **OK** to close the Add initiator ID window. Note the IQN shown for *serverX. domainX.com*.

      iv. Click **Next**.

   g. At the Enable Authentication page, click **Next**.

   h. At the Confirm selections page, click **Create**.

   i. At the View results page, click **Close**. Note that *E:\iSCSI\VirtualDisks\iSCSI Virtual Disk 1.vhdx* is shown in the iSCSI VIRTUAL DISKS pane, and that *iscsitarget1* is shown in the iSCSI TARGETS pane.

   j. Close Server Manager.

3. In Server Manager on your Windows Server 2019 host, click the **Tools** menu and then click **iSCSI Initiator**.

   a. When prompted to start the Microsoft iSCSI service and configure it to start at boot time, click **Yes**.

b. At the iSCSI Initiator Properties window, type the IP address of your WindowsServer2019VM2 virtual machine in the Target text box and click **Quick Connect**.

c. Click **Done** to close the Quick Connect window.

d. Highlight the **Volumes and Devices** tab in the iSCSI Initiator Properties window, click **Auto Configure**, and then click **OK**.

4. Right-click **Start** on your Windows Server 2019 host and click **Disk Management**. Note that a new 50 GB storage device has been added and called Disk 1.

a. Right-click **Disk 1** and click **Online**.

b. Right-click **Disk 1** and click **Initialize Disk**. Note the default options that will place an MBR on Disk 1 and click **OK**.

c. Right-click the **50.00 GB Unallocated** space next to Disk 1 and click **New Simple Volume**.

i. At the New Simple Volume wizard, click **Next**.

ii. At the Specify Volume Size page, click **Next**.

iii. At the Assign Drive Letter or Path page, note the default E: drive letter assignment and click **Next**.

iv. At the Format Partition page, note the default NTFS formatting options, type **Remote iSCSI Volume 1** in the Volume label text box, and click **Next**.

v. Click **Finish** to complete your configuration.

d. Close Disk Management.

5. Click **Start** on your Windows Server 2019 host and then click **File Explorer**.

a. In File Explorer, highlight **This PC** in the navigation pane and note that the Remote iSCSI Volume 1 (E:) lists the space available on the remote iSCSI storage.

b. Double-click **Remote iSCSI Volume 1 (E:)**. Next, right-click the file pane in File Explorer, click **New**, **Text Document,** and press **Enter** to accept the default file name of *New Text Document.txt*.

c. Double-click **New Text Document.txt** to open it in Notepad. Type a line of your choice. Click the **File** menu and click **Save**. Close Notepad when finished.

d. Close File Explorer.

Project 7-6: Managing Volume Data

In this Hands-On Project, you install and configure data deduplication for the E: volume on your WindowsServer2019VM2 virtual machine. Next, you optimize and scan volumes for errors on your WindowsServer2019VM2 virtual machine.

1. In Server Manager on your WindowsServer2019VM2 virtual machine, click the **Manage** menu and then click **Add Roles and Features**.

a. At the Select installation type page, click **Next**.

b. At the Select destination server page, click **Next**.

c. At the Select server roles page, expand **File and Storage Services**, and then expand **File and iSCSI Services**. Select **Data Deduplication** and click **Next**.

    d. At the Select features page, click **Next**.

    e. At the Confirm installation selections page, click **Install**.

    f. At the Installation progress page, click **Close**.

2. In Server Manager, highlight **File and Storage Services**, and then highlight **Disks** under the Volumes section.

3. Highlight **Virtual Disk 1** in the DISKS pane.

4. Right-click **E:** in the VOLUMES pane and click **Configure Data Deduplication**.

    a. At the Storage Space 1 (E:) Deduplication Settings window, select **General purpose file server** from the *Data duplication* drop-down box.

    b. Type **5** in the *Deduplicate files older than (in days)* text box.

    c. Click **Add**. Expand **Storage Space 1 (E:)**, highlight **iscsivirtualdisks**, and click **Select Folder** to exclude the contents of the iscsivirtualdisks folder from data deduplication.

    d. Click **Set Deduplication Schedule** and note the default options. Select **Enable throughput optimization** and click **OK**.

    e. Click **OK** to close the Storage Space 1 (E:) Deduplication Settings window.

5. Right-click **E:** in the VOLUMES pane and note that the *Scan File System for Errors* option is unavailable because the filesystem on E: is ReFS.

6. Highlight **0** (Disk 0) in the DISKS pane.

7. Right-click **C:** in the VOLUMES pane, click **Scan File System for Errors,** and then click **Scan Now**. If the process completes with errors found, right-click **C:** in the VOLUMES pane, click **Repair File System Errors,** and then click **Repair Now**.

8. Right-click **Start** and click **Windows PowerShell (Admin)**.

    a. Type **chkdsk** and press **Enter** to check the filesystem on C: for errors.

    b. Type **E:** and press **Enter** to switch to the E: filesystem provider.

    c. Type **chkdsk** and press **Enter**. Note the message displayed.

    d. Close Windows PowerShell.

9. Click **Start** and then click **File Explorer**.

    a. In File Explorer, highlight **This PC** in the navigation pane.

    b. Right-click **Local Disk (C:)**, click **Properties,** and highlight the **Tools** tab.

    c. Click **Check** and then click **Scan drive**. After the scan has completed, click **Close**.

    d. Click **Optimize** and note that weekly optimization is automatically scheduled. Click **Analyze** to analyze your C: volume for optimization. Next, highlight **Storage Space 1 (E:)** and click **Analyze** to analyze your E: volume for optimization. Click **Close** when finished.

    e. Click **OK**.

    f. Right-click **Storage Space 1 (E:)**, click **Properties,** and highlight the **Tools** tab.

    g. Click **Check**, note the message displayed, and click **Close**.

    h. Click **OK** and then close File Explorer.

Project 7-7: Backup and Restore

In this Hands-On Project, you install the Windows Server Backup feature on your Windows Server 2019 host. Next, you schedule a backup of the C:\MarketingMaterials and C:\MarketingTemplates folders, perform the scheduled backup immediately, as well as restore the backup that was created. Finally, you remove your scheduled backup from the system.

1. In Server Manager on your Windows Server 2019 host, click the **Manage** menu and then click **Add Roles and Features**.

   a. At the Select installation type page, click **Next**.

   b. At the Select destination server page, click **Next**.

   c. At the Select server roles page, click **Next**.

   d. At the Select features page, select **Windows Server Backup** and click **Next**.

   e. At the Confirm installation selections page, click **Install**.

   f. At the Installation progress page, click **Close**.

2. In Server Manager, click the **Tools** menu and then click **Windows Server Backup**.

3. In the navigation pane of the Windows Server Backup tool, highlight **Local Backup** and then click **Backup Schedule** in the Actions pane.

   a. At the Getting Started page of the Backup Schedule Wizard, click **Next**.

   b. At the Select Backup Configuration page, select **Custom** and click **Next**.

   c. At the Select Items for Backup page, click **Add Items**, expand **Local Disk (C:)**, select **MarketingMaterials** and **MarketingTemplates,** and click **OK**. Next, click **Advanced Settings**, highlight the **VSS Settings** tab, select **VSS full Backup,** and click **OK**. Click **Next**.

   d. At the Specify Backup Time page, select **11:30 PM** from the *Select time of day* drop-down box and click **Next**.

   e. At the Specify Destination Type page, select **Back up to a volume** and click **Next**.

   f. At the Select Destination Volume page, click **Add**, highlight **iSCSI Remote Volume 1 (E:),** and click **OK**. Click **Next**.

   g. At the Confirmation page, click **Finish**.

   h. At the Summary page, click **Close**.

4. In the Actions pane of the Windows Server Backup tool, click **Configure Performance**. Note that the default Normal backup performance option performs full backups of all files and click **OK**.

5. In the Actions pane of the Windows Server Backup tool, click **Backup Once**.

   a. At the Backup Options page of the Backup Once Wizard, click **Next**.

   b. At the Confirmation page, note the backup options shown for your scheduled backup and click **Backup**.

   c. After the backup has completed, click **Close**.

6. In the Actions pane of the Windows Server Backup tool, click **Recover**.

   a. At the Getting Started page of the Recovery Wizard, click **Next**.

   b. At the Select Backup Date page, note that your recent backup is selected by default and click **Next**.

c. At the Select Recovery Type page, note that only files and folders in the backup will be restored by default and click **Next**.

d. At the Select Items to Recover page, expand **serverX**, and then select **Local Disk (C:)**. Note that MarketingMaterials and MarketingTemplates are selected and click **Next**.

e. At the Specify Recovery Options page, note the default options. Select **Overwrite the existing versions with the recovered versions** and click **Next**.

f. At the Confirmation page, click **Recover**.

g. At the Recovery Progress page, click **Close** after the folders have been restored.

7. In the Actions pane of the Windows Server Backup tool, click **Backup Schedule**.

a. At the Modify Scheduled Backup page of the Backup Schedule Wizard, select **Stop backup** and click **Next**.

b. At the Confirmation page, click **Finish**.

c. At the Summary page, click **Close**.

d. Close Windows Server Backup.

Discovery Exercises

Exercise 7-1

In Hands-On Project 7-5, you configured a new simple volume (E:) on your Windows Server 2019 host that accesses iSCSI storage provided by your WindowsServer2019VM2 virtual machine. Is this simple volume considered fault tolerant? Explain why or why not in a one-paragraph memo.

Exercise 7-2

The storage capacity provided by a SAN device is often increased over time to meet the needs of the organization. To provide additional capacity for the iSCSI Target Server on your WindowsServer2019VM2 virtual machine, you can extend the existing iSCSI virtual disk, or add an additional iSCSI virtual disk that uses the existing iSCSI target.

- On your WindowsServer2019VM2 virtual machine, extend your existing 50 GB iSCSI Virtual Disk 1 to be 60 GB. Next, access Disk Management on your Windows Server 2019 host and select **Rescan Disks** from the Action menu to view the additional 10 GB unallocated capacity. Finally, extend the E: volume to 60 GB.

- On your WindowsServer2019VM2 virtual machine, add a second 10 GB iSCSI virtual disk called **iSCSI Virtual Disk 2**. Ensure that this iSCSI virtual disk uses the existing iSCSI target (**iSCSITarget1**). Next, access Disk Management on your Windows Server 2019 host and select **Rescan Disks** from the Action menu to view the additional 10 GB disk (Disk 2). Finally, configure a 10 GB ReFS simple volume (F:) on Disk 2.

Exercise 7-3

One of the key benefits of using Storage Spaces to create software RAID volumes is the ability to add capacity to the volume without recreating the volume itself. This can be done by adding more storage devices to the storage pool and then extending the virtual disk and associated volume. Shut down your WindowsServer2019VM2 virtual machine and add another 50 GB disk to the SCSI controller in the settings of the virtual machine. Next, boot your WindowsServer2019VM2 virtual machine and extend **Storage Pool 1** (created in Hands-On Project 7-4) to include the new disk. Following this, extend **Virtual Disk 1** to include the capacity provided by the new disk. Finally, extend your **Storage Space 1 (E:)** volume to include the capacity provided by the new disk, and view your results.

Exercise 7-4

When you schedule a backup, there is no guarantee that the data was backed up successfully. As a result, organizations often perform a test restoration of scheduled backups on a periodic basis (e.g., monthly) to ensure that data is being backed up as expected. In Hands-On Project 7-7, you performed a backup of the MarketingMaterials and MarketingTemplates folders on your Windows Server 2019 host to *Remote Volume 1 (E:)*. Use Windows Server Backup to restore this backup to the C:\TestRestore folder. Next, examine the contents of the C:\TestRestore folder to ensure that your original scheduled backup successfully backed up the data you intended.

Exercise 7-5

Organizations that do not wish to purchase a SAN can configure Storage Spaces Direct to provide fault tolerance for data in the event of a server failure, provided that their servers meet the necessary storage and hardware requirements. You can configure Storage Spaces Direct using either Lab Environment 1 or Lab Environment 2 provided that your physical computer uses SSD storage.

If your physical computer has SSD storage, create two additional Generation 2 virtual machines using Hyper-V Manager on your Windows Server 2019 host called StorageSpacesDirect1 and StorageSpacesDirect2. Each virtual machine should be configured with 4 GB of RAM, seven virtual hard disks, and a network interface connected to the external virtual switch. Next, install Windows Server 2019 on the first virtual hard disk in each virtual machine and join the installed system to your Active Directory domain. Following this, install the Failover Clustering feature on each virtual machine and create a clustered storage pool from the available storage on both virtual machines using Storage Spaces Direct. Finally, create a virtual disk and RAID volume from the space available in the clustered storage pool, shut down the StorageSpacesDirect1 virtual machine and note that the RAID volume is still available on the StorageSpacesDirect2 virtual machine.

CONFIGURING AND MANAGING NETWORK SERVICES

After completing this module, you will be able to:

Describe the process used to resolve FQDNs using DNS

Configure a DNS server

Troubleshoot common DNS issues

Configure a WINS server to provide for NetBIOS name resolution

Describe the process used to obtain IP configuration using DHCP

Configure a DHCP server

Troubleshoot common DHCP issues

Instead of providing access to shared resources, some services resolve names to IP addresses for computers on a network, or provide computers with an IP configuration that can be used to access a network. As a server administrator, you must know how to configure these network services as well as troubleshoot problems related to name resolution and IP configuration. In this module, you'll examine the components and processes used by DNS servers to provide for FQDN name resolution. Following this, you'll learn how to configure DNS zones, resource records, and forwarding, as well as troubleshoot common DNS issues. Next, you'll learn how to configure WINS to provide for NetBIOS name resolution. At the end of this module, you'll explore the DHCP lease process and the procedures used to configure DHCP scopes and learn to troubleshoot DHCP problems.

Understanding DNS

Recall from Module 1 that DNS is a hierarchical namespace used to identify computers on large IP networks such as the Internet. Each part of this namespace is called a **zone**, and DNS servers have **resource records** that contain the FQDN and IP information for computers in a zone. DNS servers typically resolve FQDNs to IP addresses (called a **forward lookup**), but they can also be configured to resolve IP addresses to FQDNs (called a **reverse lookup**).

> **Note** 📎
>
> Before a computer performs forward lookups using DNS servers, it first checks for a line in the **hosts file** that can be used to resolve the FQDN to an IP address. The default hosts file on Windows systems is C:\Windows\system32\drivers\etc\hosts, and the comments at the top of this file provide examples that you can follow to create entries for hosts on your network.

The DNS Lookup Process

When you contact a Web server on the Internet using a Web browser from a home or public network, your Web browser performs a forward lookup of the FQDN which in turn allows it to contact the IP address of the Web server. This forward lookup can be performed by a single DNS server or a series of DNS servers. The whole process used to resolve the FQDN *docs.microsoft.com* is illustrated in Figure 8-1.

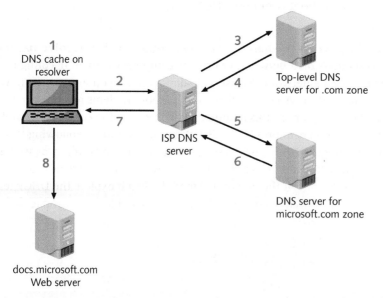

Figure 8-1 The DNS lookup process from a home or public network

In the first step shown in Figure 8-1, the client computer (called the **resolver**) first checks its DNS cache to see if the IP address for *docs.microsoft.com* is listed from a previous forward lookup request. If it is not listed in the DNS cache, the client computer sends a forward lookup request (Step 2) for *docs.microsoft.com* to the Preferred DNS server listed in network interface properties (Figure 1-24), or the Alternate DNS server if the Preferred DNS server cannot be contacted. The Preferred DNS server is typically a DNS server at your ISP. If the ISP DNS server has recently resolved *docs.microsoft.com* and placed the result in its DNS cache, it returns the result immediately to the client computer (called an **iterative query**). If it has not, the ISP DNS server contacts a DNS server for the *.com* top-level zone (Step 3) and repeats the forward lookup request for *docs.microsoft.com* (called a **recursive query**). The *.com* DNS server will not contain the IP address for the *docs.microsoft.com* computer in its zone, but will reply with the IP address of a DNS server for the *microsoft.com* zone (Step 4).

> **Note** 📎
>
> All DNS servers contain a **root hints** file that contains the IP addresses of DNS servers that hold top-level DNS zones.

The ISP DNS server then contacts the DNS server for the *microsoft.com* zone (Step 5) and repeats the forward lookup request for *docs.microsoft.com* (another recursive query). The DNS server for the *microsoft.com* domain contains a resource record that lists the IP address for the *docs.microsoft.com* computer and returns this IP address to the ISP DNS server (Step 6). The ISP DNS server caches the result for future use and then relays it to the client computer (Step 7). The client computer also caches the result for future use before connecting to the IP address of the *docs.microsoft.com* Web server (Step 8).

> **Note** 📎
>
> The amount of time that a computer is able to cache the result of a lookup is determined by the **Time To Live (TTL)** property of the resource record.

> **Note** 📎
>
> A DNS server that contains resource records for one or more zones is said to be **authoritative** for those zones. For example, the microsoft.com DNS server in Figure 8-1 is authoritative for the microsoft.com zone.

> **Note** 📎
>
> A DNS server that does not contain any zones, but instead relays forward lookups and caches the results, is called a **caching-only DNS server**. The ISP DNS server in Figure 8-1 is an example of a caching-only DNS server.

The process illustrated in Figure 8-1 is different when you use a client computer in an organization to resolve *docs.microsoft.com*. This is because organizations often deploy their own DNS servers that host zones needed for Active Directory. Normally, these organization DNS servers are also domain controllers, and each computer joined to the Active Directory domain must be configured to contact an organization DNS server instead of the ISP DNS server to participate in the domain. To allow computers in the domain to resolve FQDNs for computers on the Internet, organization DNS servers are typically configured to relay forward lookup requests for zones that they do not host to ISP DNS servers. As a result, these organization DNS servers are also called **default forwarders**, as they forward requests they cannot resolve to other DNS servers instead of using root hints to perform recursive queries. Figure 8-2 illustrates the typical process used to resolve the FQDN *docs.microsoft.com* from a computer in an organization.

> **Note** 📎
>
> In some environments, an organization DNS server may relay requests to other organization DNS servers before those requests are relayed to an ISP DNS server. Relaying requests to other organization DNS servers increases the likelihood that a lookup is resolved quickly using an entry in the DNS cache on a DNS server in the organization. Consequently, having multiple default forwarders in an organization provides faster name resolution.

In the first step from Figure 8-2, the client computer first checks its DNS cache to see if the IP address for *docs.microsoft.com* was previously resolved before sending a forward lookup request (Step 2) for *docs.microsoft.com* to the organization DNS server listed in network interface properties. If the organization DNS server contains the IP address for *docs.microsoft.com* in its DNS cache from a previous lookup, it returns the result immediately to the client computer. If it does not, the organization DNS server relays the forward lookup request to an ISP DNS server (Step 3). If the ISP DNS server contains the IP address for *docs.microsoft.com* in its DNS cache from a previous lookup, it returns the result immediately to the client computer. If it does not, the ISP DNS server contacts a DNS server for the *.com* top-level zone (Step 4) and repeats the forward lookup request for *docs.microsoft.com*. The *.com* DNS server replies with the IP address of a DNS server for the *microsoft.com* zone (Step 5). The ISP DNS server then contacts the DNS server for the *microsoft.com* zone (Step 6) and repeats the forward lookup request for *docs.microsoft.com*. The DNS server for the *microsoft.com* domain

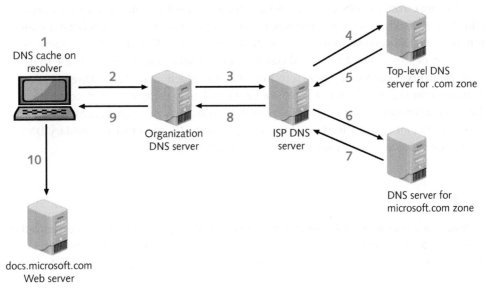

Figure 8-2   **The DNS lookup process in an organization network**

then returns the IP address for the *docs.microsoft.com* computer to the ISP DNS server (Step 7). The ISP DNS server caches the result for future use and then relays it to the organization DNS server (Step 8). The organization DNS server also caches the result for future use and then relays it to the client computer (Step 9). The client computer then caches the result for future use before connecting to the IP address of the *docs.microsoft.com* Web server (Step 10).

Authoritative DNS Server Types

Each zone typically has more than one authoritative DNS server to ensure that names can be resolved if one server is unavailable. The first DNS server in a zone is called the **primary DNS server**, and contains a read-write copy of a **zone file** that stores resource records for the zone. Additional DNS servers are called **secondary DNS servers**, and contain a read-only copy of the zone file from the primary DNS server that they can use to respond to DNS lookup requests. As a result, new resource records are added to the primary DNS server, and secondary DNS servers periodically copy the new records from the primary DNS server in a process known as a **zone transfer**.

Note 📎

In Step 5 of Figure 8-2, the *.com* DNS server will reply with the IP addresses of the primary and secondary DNS servers for microsoft.com. The ISP DNS server will then contact the first IP address in Step 6 or the second IP address if no response is received from the first IP address, and so on.

If the organization DNS server is also a domain controller, zone files can be stored in the Active Directory database and replicated to other domain controllers that are also configured as DNS servers. In this case, each DNS server is called an **Active Directory-integrated primary DNS server** and contains a read-write copy of the zone file in its Active Directory database. If a new resource record is added to an Active Directory-integrated primary DNS server, it is replicated immediately using Active Directory to all other Active Directory-integrated primary DNS servers. New resource records can also be copied from an Active Directory-integrated primary DNS server to a secondary DNS server (that is not a domain controller) using a zone transfer.

> ### Note 📎
>
> To provide fault tolerance for Active Directory and Internet FQDN resolution, an organization should have a minimum of two DNS servers. Moreover, each of these organization DNS servers should also be configured to relay Internet FQDN lookups to at least two different ISP DNS servers.

Accessing DNS Servers in Other Organizations

When an Active Directory domain is implemented, most organizations choose to use a domain name that is not registered with the top-level DNS servers on the Internet. This is considered secure practice as it ensures that the zone used for Active Directory in an organization is not visible to other computers on the Internet using recursive queries. However, there are times when one organization may need to resolve FQDNs for another organization's Active Directory zone, and vice versa. For example, in order to create a trust relationship between two Active Directory domains in different organizations, the DNS servers in each organization must be able to resolve the FQDNs for the other organization's Active Directory zone. Recall from Module 4 that you can configure the existing organization DNS servers in each organization as conditional forwarders that relay forward lookups for the other organization's zone directly to one or more DNS servers in the other organization. Alternatively, you can configure the DNS servers in each organization as **stub DNS servers** for the other organization's zone. As with conditional forwarders, a stub DNS server forwards requests for a target organization's zone directly to a DNS server in the target organization.

Resource Records

Resource records hold information about a service, FQDN, IP address, or zone on an authoritative DNS server. DNS lookups request information contained in specific resource record types. While many different types of resource records are available, the most common are listed in Table 8-1.

Table 8-1	Common DNS resource record types
Resource record	**Purpose**
A (Host)	Resolves an FQDN to an IPv4 address
AAAA (IPv6 Host)	Resolves an FQDN to an IPv6 address
CNAME (Canonical Name)	Also called an alias, it resolves one FQDN to another FQDN. For example, a CNAME record may be used to resolve *www.microsoft.com* to *server05.microsoft.com*.
MX (Mail Exchanger)	Identifies an email server for a zone
NS (Name Server)	Identifies a DNS server that is authoritative for a zone
PTR (Pointer)	Resolves an IP address to an FQDN
SOA (Start of Authority)	Contains zone configuration information, such as zone transfer settings and the default TTL for resource records
SRV (Service Location)	Used to identify the FQDN of a domain controller that provides Active Directory services
WINS Lookup	Used to relay forward lookup requests for a NetBIOS name to a **Windows Internet Name Service (WINS)** server. The configuration of WINS is discussed later in this module.

Host records (A and AAAA) are the most common resource record types configured on a DNS server, as they provide for forward lookups. Although a server administrator can manually create these records on an organization DNS server, they are normally created automatically using the dynamic update feature of DNS to save administrative effort, as discussed in Module 4. If the dynamic update feature is enabled for a zone on the DNS server, Windows 2000 and later systems automatically create (or update) their own host records in that zone on the DNS server at boot time, or when their IP address or FQDN is changed. The dynamic update feature of DNS is also used by domain controllers to automatically create the SRV records that computers use to locate Active Directory services.

Note

The dynamic update feature of DNS is also called **Dynamic DNS (DDNS)**.

Host records can also be used to perform load balancing of services on the network using a feature of DNS called **round robin**. Say, for example, that you have two identically configured Web servers (with IP addresses of 172.16.0.61 and 172.16.0.62) that you would like clients to access using the FQDN *server1.domainX.com*. In this case, you can create two A records for the FQDN *server1.domainX.com*. The first A record associates *server1.domainX.com* with the IP address 172.16.0.61, while the second A record associates *server1.domainX.com* with the IP address 172.16.0.62. In this case, when the first client computer performs a forward lookup of *server1.domainX.com*, the DNS server will return both IP addresses (172.16.0.61 and 172.16.0.62), and the client will contact the first IP address returned (172.16.0.61). However, when the second client computer performs a forward lookup of *server1.domainX.com*, the DNS server will rotate the order of both IP addresses (172.16.0.62 and 172.16.0.61) before returning them to the client to ensure that the second client contacts 172.16.0.62. The order is then rotated again when a third computer performs a forward lookup of *server1.domainX.com* to ensure that the third computer contacts 172.16.0.61, and so on.

If, however, the two identically configured Web servers have IP addresses on different networks (192.168.1.61 and 172.16.0.61), the DNS server will always ensure that the IP address listed first in the returned results most closely matches the IP address of the client making the request. For instance, if a client computer with the IP address 192.168.1.100 performs a forward lookup of *server1.domainX.com*, the DNS server will always respond with the IP address 192.168.1.61 listed first. If a client computer with the IP address 172.16.0.100 performs the same forward lookup of *server1.domainX.com*, the DNS server will always respond with the IP address 172.16.0.61 listed first. This feature, **netmask ordering**, takes precedence over round robin.

Configuring a DNS Server

To configure a Windows Server 2019 computer as a DNS server, you must install and configure the **DNS Server** role. Once installed, this server role functions as a caching-only DNS server that uses root hints and cached entries to respond to lookup requests on all network interfaces. However, you can create forward and reverse lookup zones on the DNS server to provide authoritative responses for lookup requests. If lookup requests cannot be resolved using the zones configured on the server, the DNS server will use its root hints to perform a recursive query. Alternatively, you can configure the DNS server as a default forwarder to relay lookup requests that cannot be resolved to another DNS server, instead of using root hints. To forward lookup requests to another organization's DNS server that is not publicly registered with top-level DNS servers, you can choose to configure either a conditional forwarder or stub zone.

If the DNS Server role was installed by the Active Directory Domain Services role on a new domain controller, then the DNS server is automatically configured as a default forwarder to the Preferred and Alternate DNS servers listed in the properties of the network interface, and the network interface is then modified to ensure that the local server is listed as the Preferred DNS server. Additionally, the DNS server is configured to be authoritative for the Active Directory domain on the domain controller, and resource records for the domain are stored in an Active Directory-integrated primary zone on the DNS server that allows dynamic updates from computers that are joined to the domain.

Regardless of how the DNS Server role was installed, you can manage a DNS server by clicking DNS from the Tools menu in Server Manager to start the DNS Manager tool shown in Figure 8-3. (Note that subsequent discussion in this module refer back to Figure 8-3 repeatedly, so take a moment to familiarize yourself with it.)

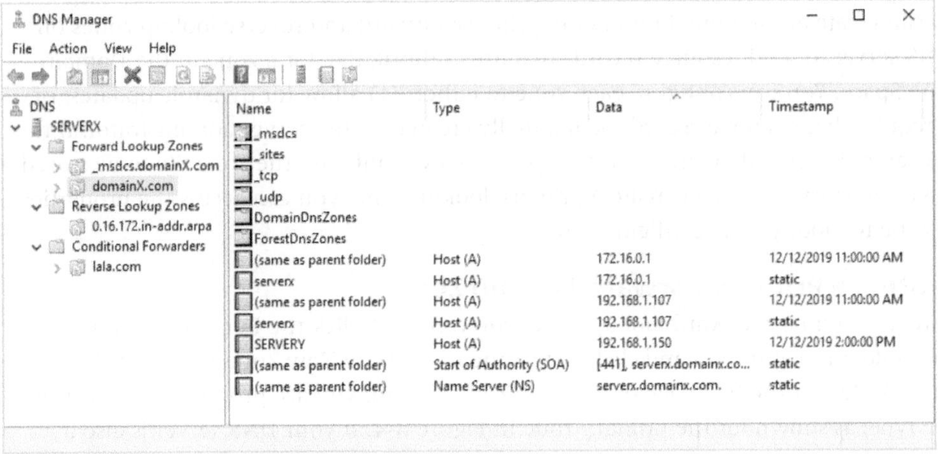

Figure 8-3   **The DNS Manager tool**

The DNS server shown in Figure 8-3 has a forward lookup zone called domainX.com that hosts the resource records for the domainX.com Active Directory domain. There are host (A) records for both network interfaces on serverx (172.16.0.1 and 192.168.1.107) that are associated with the FQDNs *serverx.domainX.com* and *domainX.com* (displayed using *same as parent folder* in Figure 8-3). There is also a host (A) record for SERVERY (192.168.1.150), an SOA record for the zone, and an NS record for the zone that identifies serverx as an authoritative DNS server. The host record for SERVERY and two host records for domainX.com were created by dynamic update as there is a time listed in the Timestamp column. This time indicates the most recent time that the associated computers contacted the DNS server to create or update their resource records, if necessary.

The folders under the domainX.com forward lookup zone contain SRV records that list the location of Active Directory services, such as LDAP, Kerberos, and global catalog. For example, the _tcp folder contains SRV records for use with TCP/IP connections, whereas the _sites folder contains SRV records for domain controllers organized by site. Because SRV records include a priority and weight that are used by computers to locate the nearest domain controller in a domain, they are automatically created by each domain controller using dynamic update to ensure correct location information. Additionally, the _msdcs. domainX.com forward lookup zone shown in Figure 8-3 contains additional host and SRV records that speed the searching of domain controllers across the forest and trusted forests.

The DNS server shown in Figure 8-3 also contains a 0.16.172.in-addr.arpa reverse lookup zone. Because reverse lookup zones are named for the network they represent in reverse order, followed by .in-addr.arpa, this zone contains resource records for the

172.16.0.0/24 network. To forward requests for the lala.com zone to a DNS server in another organization, the DNS server in Figure 8-3 also contains a conditional forwarder for the lala.com zone.

Configuring Primary Zones

You can create an unlimited number of primary forward and reverse lookup zones on a DNS server to hold resource records that are authoritative for a zone in the Domain Name Space. You can configure each zone to either: (1) allow for dynamic updates; or (2) require that resource records be manually created by the server administrator. If the DNS server is also a domain controller, you can also configure the zone file to be stored in Active Directory. After you create a primary lookup zone, you can access the properties of the zone to modify zone configuration.

Creating a Primary Forward Lookup Zone

To create a primary forward lookup zone, you can right-click the Forward Lookup Zones folder in Figure 8-3 and click New Zone to start the New Zone Wizard. When you click Next at the first page of the New Zone Wizard, you are prompted to select the zone type, as shown for the primary zone in Figure 8-4. If your DNS server is also a

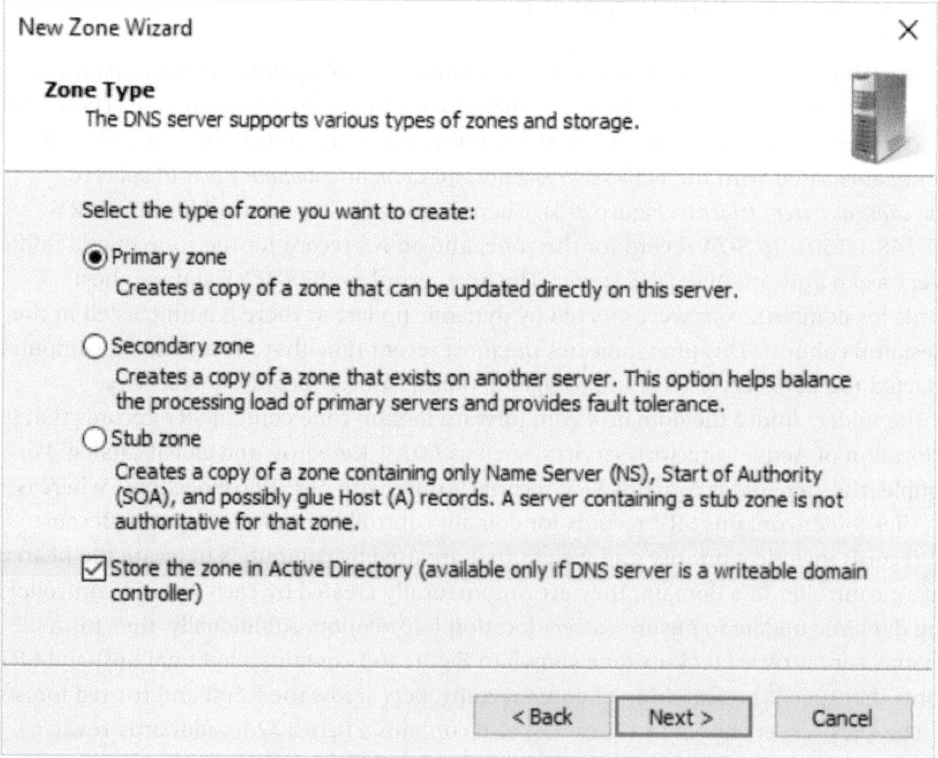

Figure 8-4   Selecting the zone type

domain controller, *Store the zone in Active Directory* is selected by default to create an Active Directory-integrated primary zone, but you can deselect this option to ensure that the zone file is not stored in Active Directory. If you choose to create an Active Directory-integrated primary zone and click Next in Figure 8-4, you are prompted to select the domain controllers to replicate the zone to, as shown in Figure 8-5. The option shown in Figure 8-5 will replicate the zone to all domain controllers in domainX.com that have the DNS Server role installed.

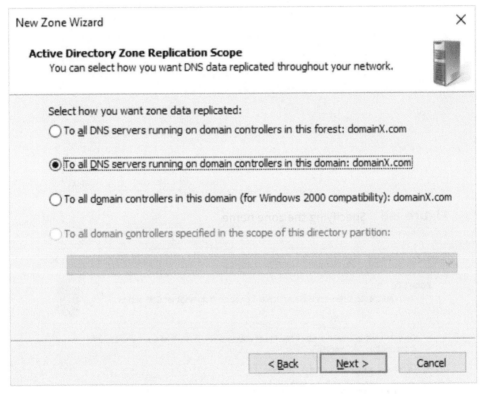

Figure 8-5   Choosing Active Directory-integrated zone replication options

After clicking Next in Figure 8-5 (or after clicking Next in Figure 8-4 if you did not select an Active Directory-integrated primary zone type), you are prompted for the zone name, as shown for zoneX.com in Figure 8-6. If you did not select an Active Directory-integrated primary zone type, you are prompted to choose zone file options when you click Next in Figure 8-6, as shown in Figure 8-7. The options shown in Figure 8-7 will create a zone file under the C:\Windows\system32\dns folder called zoneX.com.dns. Because zone files follow a standard format, instead select *Use this existing file* and specify the path to a zone file that you copied from another DNS server. This allows you to migrate a primary zone from an existing DNS server to your DNS server.

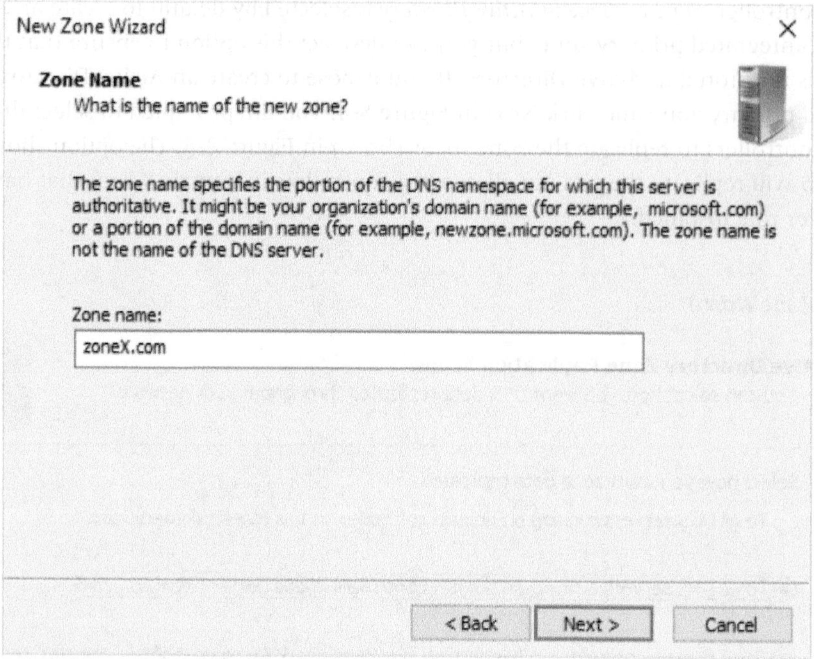

Figure 8-6 Specifying the zone name

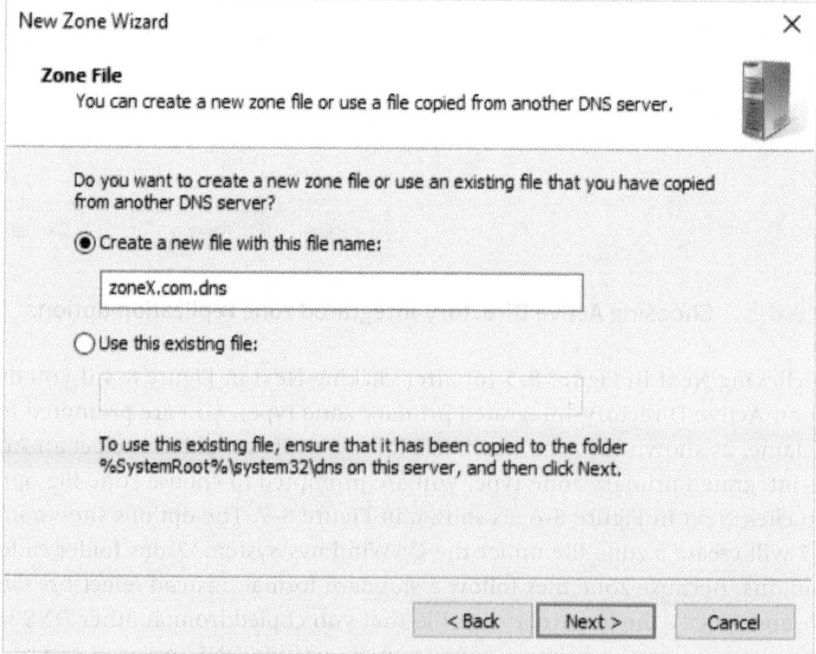

Figure 8-7 Specifying zone file options

After you click Next in Figure 8-7 (or after you click Next in Figure 8-6 if you selected an Active Directory-integrated primary zone type), you are prompted to select the dynamic update configuration for your zone, as shown in Figure 8-8. The option selected in Figure 8-8 allows dynamic updates, but only if·they can be secured using Kerberos. As a result, this option only allows dynamic updates from computers that are joined to the Active Directory domain; it is only available if you selected an Active Directory-integrated primary zone type. If you did not select an Active Directory-integrated primary zone type, only the remaining two options are available in Figure 8-8, which allow for nonsecure dynamic updates, or prevent dynamic updates altogether. After you click Next in Figure 8-8, click Finish to create your primary forward lookup zone.

Note

Allowing nonsecure dynamic updates is considered poor practice as it allows any computer on the network to create resource records in a DNS zone. As a result, most server administrators configure secure dynamic updates or prevent dynamic updates altogether.

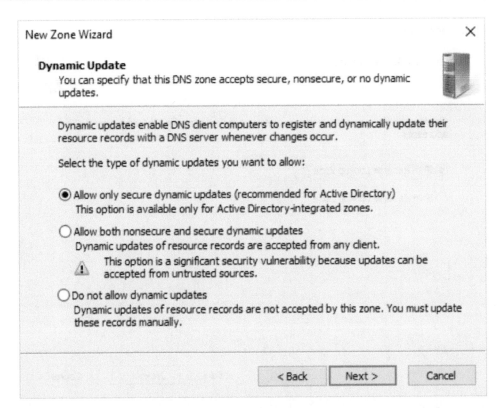

Figure 8-8   Selecting a dynamic update configuration

Creating a Primary Reverse Lookup Zone

To create a primary reverse lookup zone, right-click the Reverse Lookup Zones folder in Figure 8-3 and click New Zone to start the same New Zone Wizard used to create a primary forward lookup zone. When you click Next at the first page of the New Zone Wizard, you are prompted to select the zone type, as shown in Figure 8-4. If you choose to create an Active Directory-integrated primary zone and click Next, you are prompted to select Active Directory-integrated zone replication options, as shown in Figure 8-5. Following this, you are prompted to choose an IPv4 or IPv6 reverse lookup zone, as shown in Figure 8-9. After you click Next in Figure 8-9, you are prompted to specify either the associated network ID that can be used to generate the reverse lookup zone name, or the reverse lookup zone name itself. In Figure 8-10, the Network ID options was used to specify the 172.16.0.0/24 IPv4 network.

After you specify the reverse lookup zone name in Figure 8-10 and click Next, you are prompted for zone file options if you did not select an Active Directory-integrated primary zone type, as shown in Figure 8-11. When you click Next in Figure 8-11, you are prompted to select the dynamic update configuration for the zone, as shown in Figure 8-8. Finally, click Next and Finish to create your primary reverse lookup zone.

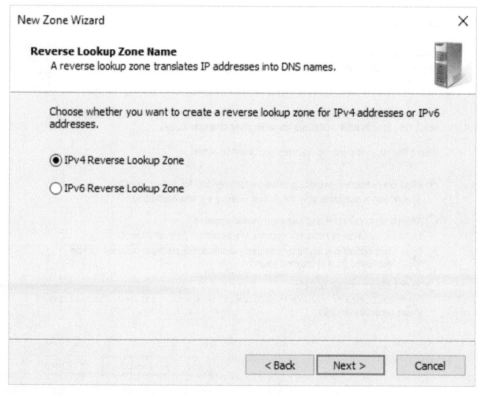

Figure 8-9   Selecting a reverse lookup zone type

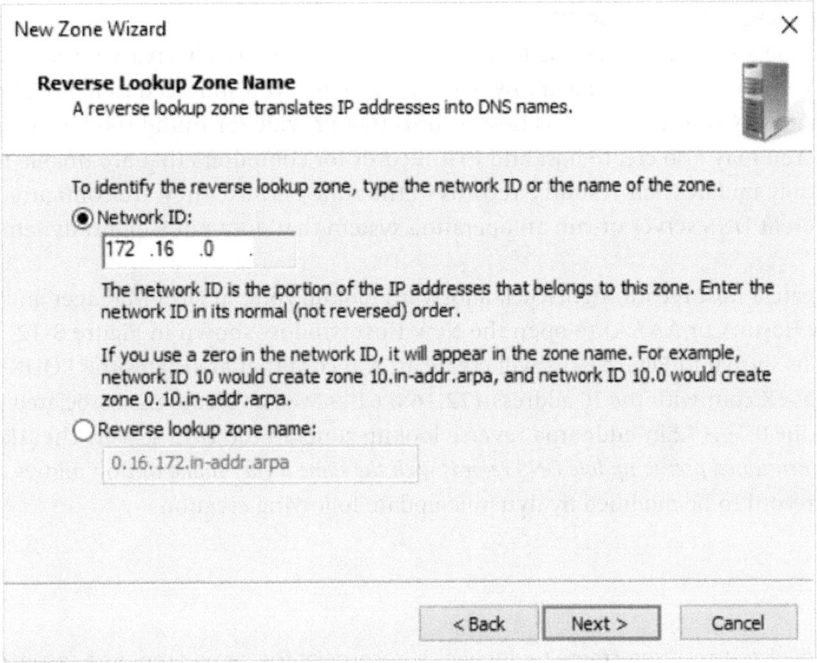

Figure 8-10   Selecting a reverse lookup zone name

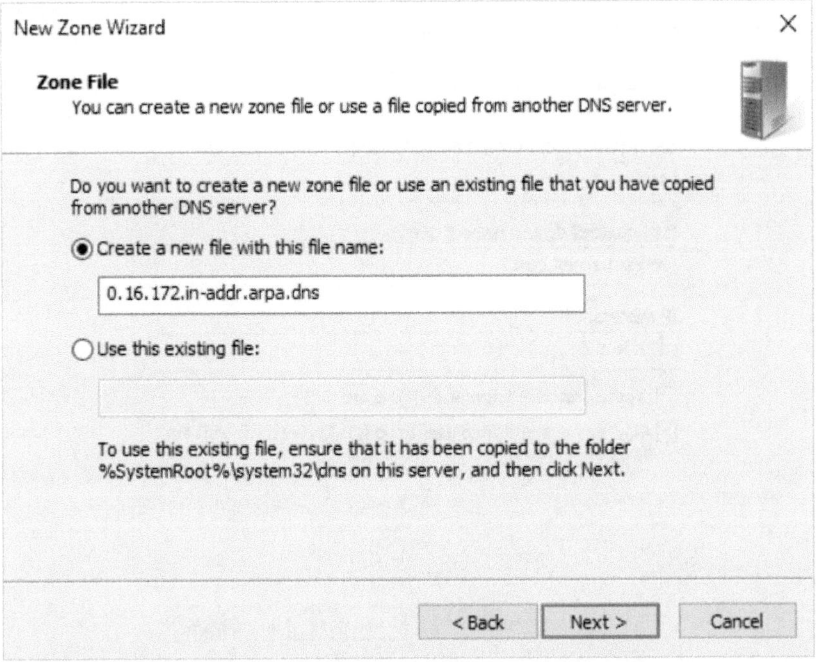

Figure 8-11   Selecting a reverse lookup zone file options

Creating Resource Records

After creating a forward or reverse lookup zone, you can manually create resource records in a zone. For zones that allow dynamic updates, you still need to manually create CNAME and MX records as well as host records that provide for round robin or netmask ordering. You may also create host and PTR records for computers that are unable to automatically update their resource records in the zone because they are configured to use a different DNS server or run an operating system that does not support dynamic update.

To create a host record, right-click a forward lookup zone in DNS Manager and click New Host (A or AAAA) to open the New Host window shown in Figure 8-12. The options shown in Figure 8-12 will create an A record that associates the FQDN server1.zoneX.com with the IP address 172.16.0.61 as well as create the associated PTR record in the 0.16.172.in-addr.arpa reverse lookup zone on the DNS server. The *Allow any unauthenticated user to update DNS records with the same owner name* option allows the resource record to be modified by dynamic update following creation.

Note

Server administrators often create multiple host records at the same time. As a result, when you click Add Host in Figure 8-12, the New Host window remains open to create additional host records.

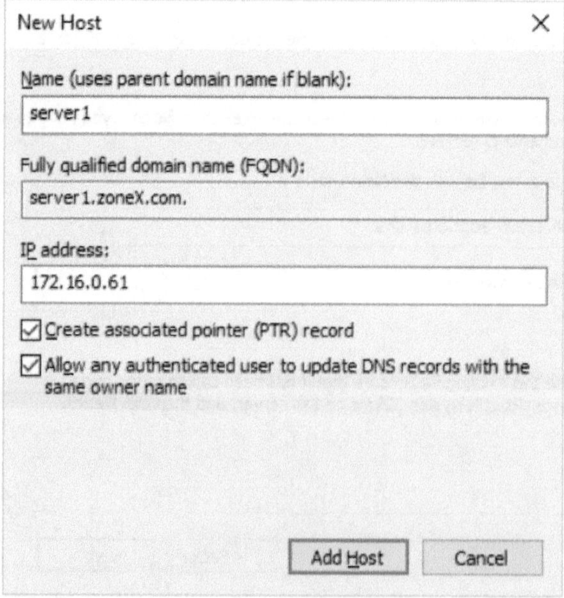

New Host	×

Name (uses parent domain name if blank):

server1

Fully qualified domain name (FQDN):

server1.zoneX.com.

IP address:

172.16.0.61

☑ Create associated pointer (PTR) record

☑ Allow any authenticated user to update DNS records with the same owner name

| Add Host | Cancel |

Figure 8-12 Creating a host record

Host records often represent the computer name that is configured locally on the system. However, for servers that host common network services, you may wish to create a CNAME record that maps a common service name (such as *www* for Web services) to the host record for the server. To create a new CNAME record, right-click a forward lookup zone in DNS Manager and click New Alias (CNAME) to open the New Resource Record window shown in Figure 8-13. The options shown in Figure 8-13 will create a CNAME record that associates the FQDN www.zoneX.com with the FQDN server1.zoneX.com. The *Allow any authenticated user to update all DNS records with the same name* option allows the CNAME record to be updated automatically if the FQDN in the host record for server1.zoneX.com is modified using dynamic update.

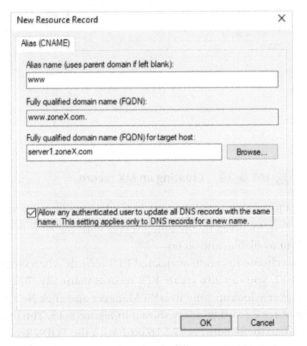

Figure 8-13   Creating a CNAME record

When you send an email, your email server locates the target email server by resolving the MX record for the recipient's zone. For example, to send an email to bob.burtt@zoneX.com, your email server will locate the target email server by resolving the MX record for zoneX.com. To create an MX record for a zone, right-click a forward lookup zone in DNS Manager and click New Mail Exchanger (MX) to open the New Resource Record window shown in Figure 8-14. The options shown in Figure 8-14 identify server1.zoneX.com as the email server for zoneX.com using a priority number of 10. If your organization has multiple email servers, you can create multiple MX records for each one with the same priority number to provide round robin load balancing of email requests. However, if you create multiple MX records with different priority numbers, the list of email servers is returned with the email server that has the lowest

Figure 8-14 Creating an MX record

priority number listed first. This ensures that the email server with the lowest priority number is contacted first, followed by the email server with the second lowest priority number if the first is unavailable, and so on.

Although you can choose to create associated PTR records when creating host records, as shown in Figure 8-12, you can also create PTR records manually. To create a PTR record, right-click a reverse lookup zone in DNS Manager and click New Pointer (PTR) to open the New Resource Record window shown in Figure 8-15. The options shown in Figure 8-15 will associate the IP address 172.16.0.61 with the FQDN server1.zoneX.com and allow the resource record to be modified using dynamic update following creation.

Configuring Zone Properties

After you have created a primary zone, you can right-click it in DNS Manager and click Properties to modify the zone type and options as well as the default zone records. The General tab of zone properties shown in Figure 8-16 allows you to pause lookup responses for the zone as well as change the zone type, the Active Directory-integrated zone replication options (if applicable), and dynamic update configuration. If the zone is configured to accept dynamic updates, resource records are created automatically, but they are not automatically removed by default. As a result, zones that accept dynamic updates often accumulate **stale resource records** that represent computers that are no longer present on the network because they have failed or have been decommissioned or redeployed. To automatically remove stale resource records (a process called **scavenging**), click the Aging button in

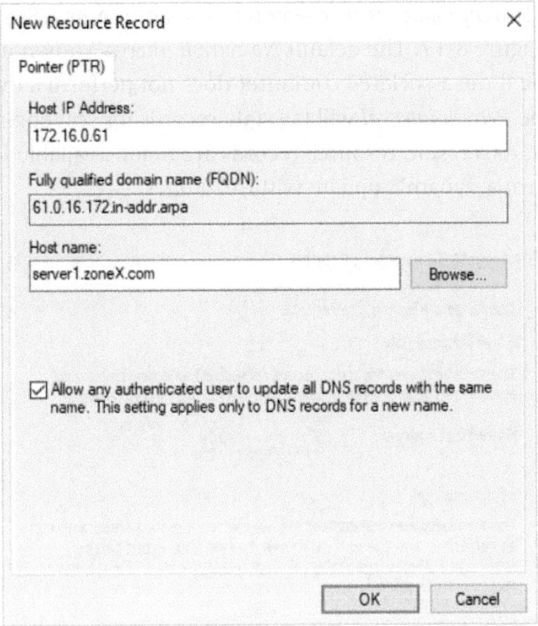

Figure 8-15   Creating a PTR record

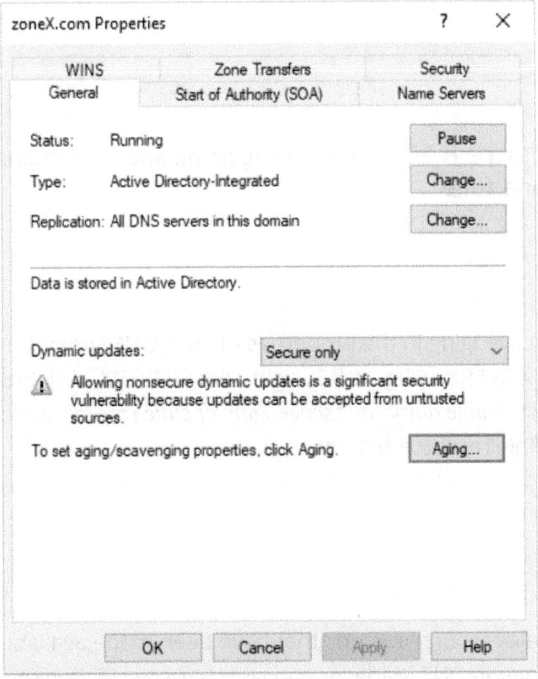

Figure 8-16   The General tab of zone properties

Figure 8-16 and select *Scavenge stale resource records* in the Zone Aging/Scavenging Properties window, as shown in Figure 8-17. The default *No-refresh interval* shown in Figure 8-17 marks resource records as stale if the associated computer does not perform a dynamic update within 7 days, while the *Refresh interval* will tag stale records for scavenging 7 days following the No-refresh interval. As a result, resource records are made available for scavenging if a computer fails to perform a dynamic update within 14 days.

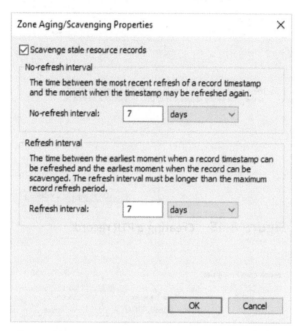

Figure 8-17   Configuring aging and scavenging for a zone

Note 🖉

You must also enable scavenging in the properties of your DNS server for it to function. To enable scavenging for SERVERX in Figure 8-3, right-click SERVERX, click Properties, highlight the Advanced tab, select *Enable automatic scavenging of stale records*, and specify how often you wish to scavenge stale resource records.

Note 🖉

To manually remove stale resource records that have been made available for scavenging, right-click your DNS server in DNS Manager and click *Scavenge Stale Resource Records*.

Note

Scavenging only removes records created using dynamic update. Manually created DNS records are never scavenged.

If you highlight the Start of Authority (SOA) tab of zone properties, you can modify the settings in the SOA resource record for the zone, as shown in Figure 8-18. The serial number of a zone is automatically updated when zone information is changed or resource records are added to the zone. This allows secondary zones to identify when new information is available for zone transfer. A secondary zone requests a zone transfer if the serial number of the primary zone is higher than the serial number of the secondary zone. To force all secondary zones to request a zone transfer, click the Increment button in Figure 8-18. Alternatively, to change the primary zone to another server that is currently hosting a secondary zone, click the Browse button next to the Primary server and select the desired server. The Responsible person in Figure 8-18 is the email address for the server administrator, and it is set to hostmaster@domainx.com by default (the @ symbol is replaced by a period in the SOA record).

Figure 8-18   The Start of Authority (SOA) tab of zone properties

The remaining options in Figure 8-18 specify the settings used for zone transfers as well as the default TTL:

- *Refresh interval* specifies how often secondary zones can attempt to update from the primary zone.
- *Retry interval* specifies how long a secondary zone waits before reattempting to contact the primary zone if an initial attempt fails.
- *Expires after* specifies how long a secondary zone can continue to function without contacting the primary zone, to ensure that its data is accurate.
- *Minimum (default) TTL* provides a default TTL for new resource records created in the zone.

If you highlight the Name Servers tab of zone properties, you can add, remove, or modify NS records for DNS servers that are authoritative for the zone, as shown in Figure 8-19. This is often performed on the primary DNS server prior to configuring secondary DNS zones to ease the configuration of zone transfers.

Figure 8-19 **The Name Servers tab of zone properties**

To create a WINS Lookup resource record, highlight the WINS tab of zone properties, as shown in Figure 8-20. The options shown in Figure 8-20 will relay forward lookup

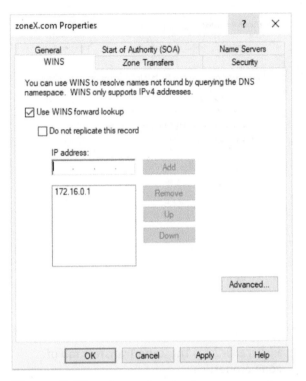

Figure 8-20   The WINS tab of zone properties

requests to the WINS server with the IP address 172.16.0.1 if the FQDN could not be resolved using a host record in the zone. For example, if server4.zoneX.com cannot be resolved using a host record, the DNS server will forward a request for server4 to the WINS server on 172.16.0.1. If the WINS server contains a NetBIOS name record for server4 that it can resolve, the result is returned to the DNS server, where it is cached and then returned to the resolver.

If you highlight the Zone Transfers tab, you enable and configure zone transfers, as shown in Figure 8-21. The options configured in Figure 8-21 allow zone transfers of zoneX.com to DNS servers with IP addresses 172.16.0.2 and 172.16.0.3 only. If you click the Notify button in Figure 8-21, you can optionally choose to notify secondary DNS servers when new records have been created in the zone. This ensures that zone transfers occur immediately following the creation of new records and before the Refresh interval specified on the Start of Authority (SOA) tab.

By default, members of the DnsAdmins, Domain Admins, and Enterprise Admins groups in Active Directory have the ability to manage the settings and resource records in an Active Directory-integrated zone. However, you can modify these permissions or assign permissions to other users or groups by selecting the Security tab, as shown in Figure 8-22.

Figure 8-21 The Zone Transfers tab of zone properties

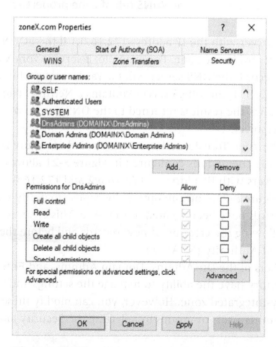

Figure 8-22 The Security tab of zone properties

Note

The Security tab in zone properties is only available for Active Directory-integrated zones.

Creating Secondary Zones

After zone transfers have been allowed to your DNS server in the properties of a primary forward or reverse lookup zone, you can create an associated secondary zone on your DNS server. To create a secondary forward lookup zone, right-click the Forward Lookup Zones folder shown earlier Figure 8-3 and click New Zone to start the New Zone Wizard. When you click Next at the first page of the New Zone Wizard, you must select *Secondary zone* as the zone type in Figure 8-4. This will deselect *Store the zone in Active Directory* as secondary zones cannot be Active Directory-integrated. When you click Next in Figure 8-4, you are prompted for the zone name, as shown for zoneX.com in Figure 8-6. When you click Next in Figure 8-6, you are prompted to specify the IP address of the DNS server that hosts the primary zone, as shown for 172.16.0.1 in Figure 8-23. After you click Next in Figure 8-23, click Finish to create the secondary zone.

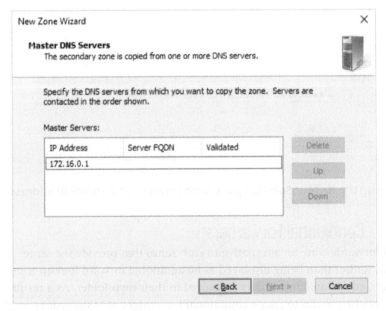

Figure 8-23   Specifying the primary DNS server

Creating Stub Zones

Unlike primary and secondary zones, stub zones are not authoritative. Instead, they contain NS and host records that allow a DNS server to access an authoritative zone on another DNS server. To create a stub zone, right-click the Forward Lookup Zones folder shown earlier in Figure 8-3 and click New Zone to start the New Zone Wizard. When you click Next at the first page of the New Zone Wizard, you must select Stub zone as the zone type in Figure 8-4. If you choose to create an Active Directory-integrated stub zone and click Next, you are prompted to select Active Directory-integrated zone replication options, as shown in Figure 8-5. Following this, you are prompted to choose the name of the zone hosted by the target DNS server, as shown in Figure 8-6. After you click Next in Figure 8-6, you are prompted for zone file options if you did not select an Active Directory-integrated primary zone type, as shown in Figure 8-11. Following this, you are prompted to specify the IP address of a DNS server that is authoritative for the zone, as shown for 4.99.192.1 in Figure 8-24. After you click Next in Figure 8-24, click Next and Finish to create your stub zone.

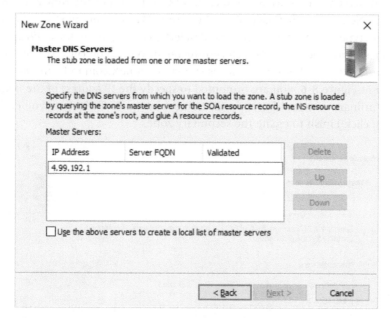

Figure 8-24   Specifying the authoritative DNS server IP address

Configuring Conditional Forwarders

Conditional forwarders are an alternative to stub zones that provide the same functionality. Rather than being displayed as an additional forward lookup zone in DNS Manager, conditional forwarders are stored in their own folder. As a result, server administrators often prefer to create conditional forwarders over stub zones on DNS servers that host many forward lookup zones. To create a conditional forwarder, right-click the Conditional Forwarders folder shown earlier in Figure 8-3 and click New Conditional Forwarder to open the New Conditional Forwarder window shown in Figure 8-25. The options shown in Figure 8-25 will create an Active Directory-integrated conditional forwarder that relays forward lookup requests for the lala.com zone to the DNS server with IP address 4.99.192.1.

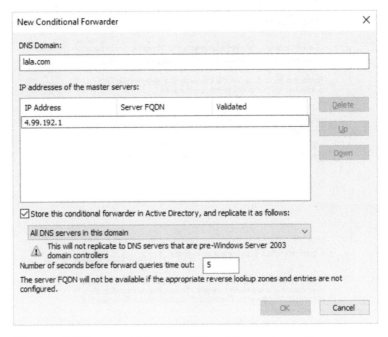

Figure 8-25   Specifying conditional forwarder options

Configuring Default Forwarders

For lookup requests that do not match an authoritative zone or conditional forwarder, DNS servers will use root hints to perform a recursive query in order to resolve the lookup request. However, this can result in a large number of recursive lookup requests in organizations that have many DNS servers. As a result, most organizations will instead configure their DNS servers as default forwarders that relay lookup requests that cannot be resolved to an ISP DNS server or other DNS server in the organization. To configure SERVERX shown earlier in Figure 8-3 as a default forwarder, right-click SERVERX, click Properties, and highlight the Forwarders tab as shown in Figure 8-26. The options shown in Figure 8-26 will forward requests to the DNS server with IP address 192.168.1.1 or the DNS server with IP address 192.168.1.2 if the first DNS server is unavailable. If both DNS servers are unavailable, root hints are used to perform a recursive query.

Figure 8-26   Configuring a default forwarder

Note

You can use the `dnscmd` command to perform the same configuration tasks available in DNS Manager. Type `dnscmd /?` for more information.

Note

There are a wide variety of different PowerShell cmdlets available for configuring zones, resource records, and DNS server settings. Search *PowerShell DnsServer* on docs.microsoft.com for more information.

Troubleshooting DNS

By resolving FQDNs to IP addresses, DNS provides one of the most important services on a network. If a DNS server is unable to perform forward lookups, computers will be unable to contact the services running on other systems on the network or Internet. In many cases, you can solve DNS server-related problems by restarting the DNS Server service on the DNS server. You can restart the DNS Server service using the `Restart-Service dns` command in Windows PowerShell, or by running the `net stop dns` command followed by the `net start dns` command at a Command Prompt window. You can also restart the DNS Server service in DNS Manager by right-clicking your DNS server object and clicking All Tasks, Restart.

Many DNS-related problems are caused by missing or misconfigured resource records. This is especially true for zones that allow dynamic updates, as the dynamic update process runs as a low priority process. Thus, if a DNS client is busy processing a Windows update at boot time, the dynamic update process may not add or update the associated host and PTR record for the computer in the zone on the DNS server. In this case, you can manually run the dynamic update process on the DNS client. To do this, you can execute the `Register-DnsClient` cmdlet in Windows PowerShell, or run the `ipconfig /registerdns` command in a Command Prompt window.

Missing resource records in a secondary zone are often caused by zone transfer issues. Zone transfers may not occur successfully if the network bandwidth is saturated at the time the zone transfer was initiated. To remedy this, you can perform a zone transfer manually. If you right-click a secondary zone in DNS Manager and click *Transfer new copy of zone from Master*, your DNS server will perform a zone transfer of all resource records from the primary zone to the secondary zone. Alternatively, if you right-click a secondary zone and click *Transfer from Master*, your DNS server will perform a zone transfer of any new resource records in the primary zone that have not yet been copied to the secondary zone.

DNS-related problems can also be caused by an invalid entry in the DNS cache. Recall that both the DNS server and resolver cache the result of a DNS lookup request for the time specified in the TTL of the cached record. If a resource record is modified, any DNS servers and resolvers will have invalid information in their DNS cache until the TTL expires. To remedy this, you can clear the entries in the DNS cache to ensure that the correct information is obtained using a DNS lookup. You can run the `Clear-DnsClientCache` cmdlet in Windows PowerShell or the `ipconfig /flushdns` command at a Command Prompt window to clear the DNS cache on a resolver. To clear the DNS cache used by a DNS server, you can run the `Clear-DnsServerCache` cmdlet in Windows PowerShell, or right-click the DNS server object in DNS Manager and click Clear Cache.

Although restarting the DNS Server service, manually performing a dynamic update or zone transfer, and clearing DNS caches are common solutions to many DNS-related problems, they do not work in all situations. As a result, you should troubleshoot each DNS issue based on the information that you can obtain regarding the problem. Moreover, there are several tools that can help you troubleshoot DNS-related problems, including the `nslookup` command, DNS manager, and DNS logs.

Using nslookup

When troubleshooting most DNS-related problems, the first step typically involves testing forward lookups from a resolver using the `nslookup` command at a Command Prompt or Windows PowerShell window. The `nslookup` command can perform both forward and

reverse lookups and will list the DNS server that is used to perform the lookup, as well
as identify whether the result was authoritative (obtained from a zone file on the DNS
server) or non-authoritative (obtained from the DNS server cache). For example, the two
`nslookup` commands shown in Figure 8-27 query the DNS server 192.168.1.107 and
obtain an authoritative result for server1.zoneX.com and a non-authoritative result for
triosdevelopers.com.

Figure 8-27   The nslookup command

Note

If you type `nslookup` with no arguments, it will run in an interactive mode that allows you to
perform multiple lookups.

Note

You can also right-click a DNS server object in DNS Manager and click *Launch nslookup* to start
the `nslookup` command in a Command Prompt window.

The output of `nslookup` provides information that you can use to determine the
nature of the problem and possible solutions. Table 8-2 lists some common solutions to
problems identified by `nslookup`.

Table 8-2	Common solutions to problems identified by nslookup

Problem	Solutions
The DNS server queried by nslookup is incorrect	Configure the IP address of the correct DNS server in network interface properties on the resolver.
No results are returned by a lookup for which the DNS server is authoritative	Ensure that the correct resource records exist in the zone on the DNS server. Create any missing resource records and perform a zone transfer to ensure that they are copied to secondary zones. If the correct resource records exist, restart the DNS Server service.
No results are returned by a lookup for which the DNS server is non-authoritative	First ensure that the configuration of any stub zones and conditional forwarders is correct. Next, ensure that the correct IP addresses are listed on the Forwarders tab of DNS server properties in DNS Manager. If the DNS server is not configured as a default forwarder, ensure that the DNS server is able to contact the top-level DNS servers on the Internet using root hints. Finally, clear the DNS Server cache and restart the DNS Server service.
The DNS server returned incorrect results for which the DNS server is authoritative	Modify the associated records in the zone on the DNS server to include the correct information. Next, clear the DNS cache on the resolver.
The DNS server returned incorrect results for which the DNS server is non-authoritative	Clear the DNS Server cache. Next, clear the DNS cache on the resolver.

Using DNS Manager

To test whether a DNS server is functioning correctly, access the Monitoring tab of DNS server properties in DNS Manager. For example, if you right-click SERVERX in Figure 8-3 (shown earlier), click Properties, and highlight the Monitoring tab, you are able to perform a simple or recursive test, as shown in Figure 8-28.

If you select *A simple query against this DNS server* in Figure 8-28 and click Test Now, the DNS server will perform a DNS lookup in each zone for which it is authoritative. Alternatively, if you select *A recursive query to other DNS servers* and click Test Now, the DNS server will perform a recursive query using its root hints. You can instead select *Perform automatic testing at the following interval* and specify a time interval for repeated tests.

Figure 8-28   The Monitoring tab of DNS server properties

If a simple query test fails, there is likely a misconfigured zone on your DNS server or the DNS Server service needs to be restarted. If a recursive query test fails, your organization firewall may be blocking DNS requests to the top-level DNS servers. If the firewall is not blocking these requests, then the root hints file on the DNS server may have become corrupted. Because every DNS server uses the same root hints file, you can copy the root hints file from another DNS server in your organization to fix the issue. To do this, highlight the Root Hints tab in Figure 8-28, click *Copy from Server*, and specify another DNS server on your network.

Using Log Files

Log files are often used to troubleshoot unusual DNS problems that cannot be resolved using other methods. By default, the DNS Service logs all information to the **DNS Server log**. To view the entries in this log, open Event Viewer, navigate to Applications and Services Logs, and highlight DNS Server. Alternatively, you can select DNS in the navigation pane of Server Manager and view the events in the Events section. You can then reproduce the problem and view the events that occurred immediately afterward to locate information regarding the problem. By searching the event description in a search engine, such as Google, you can often find a remedy to the problem.

If the information in the DNS Server log is not sufficient to locate a solution to the problem, you can enable **debug logging** to obtain more detailed information. Debug logging allows you to record packet-by-packet information about the queries that the DNS server receives. To enable debug logging on your DNS server, access the Debug Logging tab of DNS server properties. For example, if you right-click SERVERX shown earlier in Figure 8-3, click Properties, and highlight the Debug Logging tab, you can select *Log packets for debugging* to enable debug logging, as shown in Figure 8-29. Because debug logging records a large amount of information in the log file that you specify in Figure 8-28, you should only enable it when troubleshooting a DNS-related issue and only for a short period of time.

Figure 8-29   **The Debug Logging tab of DNS server properties**

Configuring WINS

Recall from Module 1 that each Windows system contains a NetBIOS name that is generated from the first 15 characters of the computer name. NetBIOS is a legacy protocol that has been used in Microsoft operating systems since 1985 to identify computers on a network. While FQDNs are the preferred method for identifying computers on networks today, modern Microsoft operating systems such as Windows 10 and Windows Server

2019 still use NetBIOS to identify systems on a network, and many apps still support NetBIOS. For example, if you connect to the data shared folder on server1 using the UNC \\server1\data, File Explorer will assume that server1 is a NetBIOS name as it does not follow FQDN syntax. As with FQDNs, NetBIOS names must be resolved to IP addresses before you are able to connect to them. By default, your computer will send a NetBIOS broadcast on the network to resolve the server1 NetBIOS name. Because broadcasts are interpreted by each computer on the LAN, each NetBIOS name resolution request results in additional processor cycles for each computer as well as increased network traffic. Moreover, routers do not forward NetBIOS broadcast traffic to other LANs. Thus, server1 must be on the same LAN as your computer for the NetBIOS broadcast to reach the server1 computer, which can then reply with its IP address to resolve the NetBIOS name.

To reduce NetBIOS name broadcasts as well as ensure that NetBIOS names can be resolved for computers on other LANs in your organization, you can implement one or more Windows Internet Name Service (WINS) servers to provide centralized NetBIOS name resolution that does not use broadcasts.

> **Note** 📎
>
> While NetBIOS is enabled by default on all Windows systems, some organizations choose to disable it on each computer. These organizations rely entirely on DNS name resolution and do not require a WINS server as a result.

> **Note** 📎
>
> WINS can only be used to resolve NetBIOS names to IPv4 addresses.

Using WINS for NetBIOS Name Resolution

To configure a Windows computer to use a WINS server for NetBIOS name resolution, you can access the properties of the IPv4 protocol for your network interface, as shown earlier in Figure 1-24. Next, click the Advanced button, select the WINS tab, and add the IP address of one or more WINS servers, as shown for 172.16.0.1 in Figure 8-30. During boot time, your computer will contact the first available WINS server listed in the IPv4 configuration of your network interface to create (or update) a **NetBIOS name record** that includes your NetBIOS name and IP address. Following this, your computer will contact the first available WINS server each time a NetBIOS name must be resolved, instead of sending a NetBIOS broadcast on the LAN.

Figure 8-30 Specifying a WINS server in network interface properties

Note

You can also run the `nbtstat -RR` command in a Command Prompt window to create or update the NetBIOS name record for your computer on the WINS server.

Note

If your computer does not contact a WINS server within 6 days, your NetBIOS name record is automatically removed from the WINS server.

Note

To disable NetBIOS for a computer, select *Disable NetBIOS over TCP/IP* in Figure 8-30.

Configuring a WINS Server

To configure a Windows Server 2019 computer as a WINS server, you must install and configure the **WINS Server** feature. After the WINS Server feature has been installed, you can click WINS from the Tools menu in Server Manager to start the WINS tool shown in Figure 8-31.

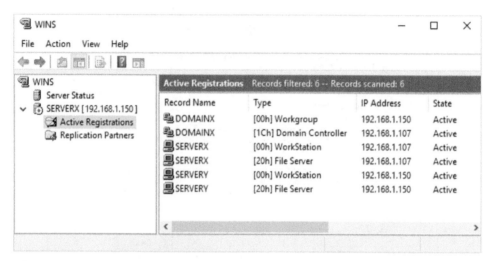

Figure 8-31   The WINS tool

NetBIOS name records can be used to identify unique computers as well as groups (workgroups or domains). In addition to the 15 characters used to identify the NetBIOS name, NetBIOS name records contain a special character that identifies a service that is provided by computer or group. The Active Registrations folder in Figure 8-31 displays two NetBIOS name records for SERVERX (192.168.1.107) and SERVERY (192.168.1.150) indicating that each computer provides the WorkStation and File Server services. Moreover, the two NetBIOS name records for DOMAINX in Figure 8-31 indicate that 192.168.1.150 is a member of the DOMAINX group, and that 192.168.1.107 is a domain controller for the DOMAINX group.

Note 🖉

Group NetBIOS name records are used by legacy (pre-Windows 2000) systems to locate a Windows Server 2019 domain controller. Although these legacy systems are uncommon today, industrial and manufacturing machinery often have a very long useful life. The computers that operate this machinery may contain a legacy operating system that requires access to domain resources, such as shared printers and folders. In these cases, group NetBIOS name records can provide the location for the nearest domain controller.

Because a WINS server typically hosts many NetBIOS name records, the WINS tool does not display NetBIOS name records in the Active Registrations folder shown in Figure 8-31 by default. To display NetBIOS name records, you must right-click the Active Registrations folder, click Display Records, optionally specify criteria to limit the results shown, and click Find Now.

Although NetBIOS name records are normally added to a WINS server automatically, you can also add them manually. To do this, right-click the Active Registrations folder and then click New Static Mapping to open the New Static Mapping window. The New Static Mapping window shown in Figure 8-32 will create a NetBIOS name record for a computer called SERVERZ that has the IP address 192.168.1.90.

Figure 8-32   Creating a NetBIOS name record

If multiple WINS servers are deployed on the network, you can configure them to share their NetBIOS name records. In this case, each WINS server is called a **replication partner** and can resolve all of the NetBIOS names in the organization. To configure a replication partner for the WINS server in Figure 8-31, you can right-click the Replication Partners folder, click New Replication Partner, and supply the IP address of the other WINS server. Next, right-click the replication partner, click Properties, and highlight the Advanced tab to modify the replication configuration, as shown in Figure 8-33. The options shown in Figure 8-33 will pull records from the other WINS server at midnight for up to 30 minutes, and push new records to the other WINS server after 5 records have been created.

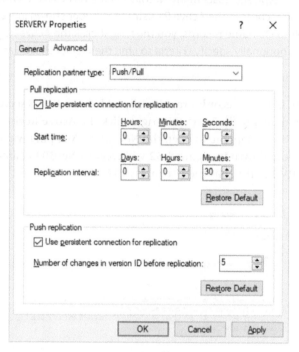

Figure 8-33   **Configuring WINS replication**

Understanding DHCP

Recall from Module 1 that you can configure a network interface manually, or you can use Dynamic Host Configuration Protocol (DHCP) to have it configured automatically. If your network interface is configured using DHCP, it sends a DHCP broadcast on the network requesting IP configuration information. If a DHCP server on the network has a range of IP addresses, it leases an IP address to the client computer for a certain period of time; after this lease has expired, the client computer must send another DHCP request. Because DHCP servers keep track of the IP addresses they lease to client computers, they can ensure that no two computers receive the same IP address. If two computers are accidentally configured manually with the same IP address, neither would be able to communicate successfully using the IP protocol.

In addition to IP addresses, DHCP servers can also send client computers other IP configuration settings, such as a default gateway or DNS server. These IP configuration settings are called **DHCP options** and are identified by number. Table 8-3 lists common DHCP options that are often provided by DHCP servers.

Table 8-3	Common DHCP options
Option name	**Description**
003 Router	Provides the IP address of one or more default gateway routers
004 Time Server	Provides the IP address of one or more **Network Time Protocol (NTP)** servers that can be queried for time and time zone information
006 DNS Servers	Provides the IP address of one or more DNS servers
015 DNS Domain Name	Provides a domain name suffix (e.g., domain*X*.com) that can be used alongside a computer name to provide an FQDN
044 WINS/NBNS Servers	Provides the IP address of one or more WINS servers
046 WINS/NBT Node Type	Configures the order used for NetBIOS name resolution. The default value is 0x8, which ensures that WINS servers are queried before NetBIOS broadcasts are used to resolve NetBIOS names.
060 PXEClient	Lists the FQDN or IP address of a server that hosts a bootable operating system image (e.g.k a WDS server)

Note

DHCP started as a proposal by Microsoft to enhance the BOOTP protocol that provided IP configuration on early IP networks. As a result, DHCP can be configured for backward compatibility to provide BOOTP clients with an IP configuration.

The DHCP Lease Process

The process by which a DHCP client requests IP configuration from a DHCP server involves several stages. First, the client sends a request (DHCPDISCOVER packet) to all hosts on the LAN. In reply, a DHCP server sends an offer (DHCPOFFER packet) that contains a potential IP configuration. The DHCP client then selects (accepts) the offer by sending a DHCPREQUEST packet to the associated DHCP server. Next, the DHCP server sends to the client an acknowledgment indicating the amount of time the client can use the IP configuration (DHCPACK packet). Finally, the client configures itself with the IP configuration. This process is illustrated in Figure 8-34.

Note

If there are multiple DHCP servers on your network, DHCP clients will accept the first offer that they receive and decline all other offers by sending a DHCPDECLINE packet to the other DHCP servers.

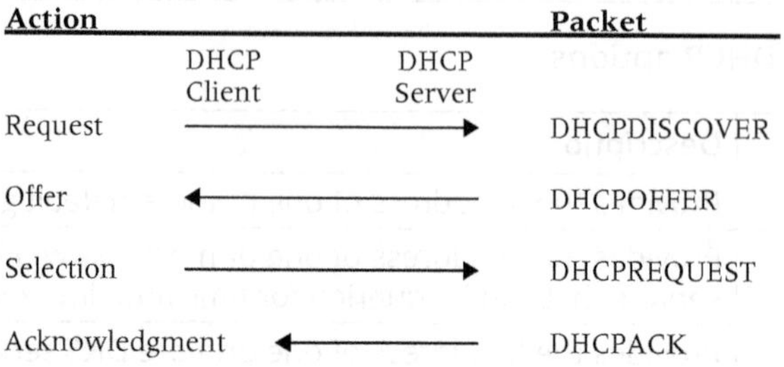

Action			Packet
	DHCP Client	DHCP Server	
Request	⟶		DHCPDISCOVER
Offer	⟵		DHCPOFFER
Selection	⟶		DHCPREQUEST
Acknowledgment	⟵		DHCPACK

Figure 8-34   The DHCP lease process

Halfway through the time period specified by its lease (i.e., at 50 percent of its lease), the DHCP client will send another DHCPREQUEST packet to its DHCP server to renew its IP configuration. If its DHCP server is unreachable, it will try to renew its IP configuration again at 87.5 percent of its lease by sending a DHCPDISCOVER packet to all hosts on the LAN to allow any DHCP server on the LAN to respond with an offer. After the lease is up, the DHCP client discards its IP configuration obtained from the DHCP server and automatically configures the network interface using APIPA (the IPv4 169.254.0.0 network, or IPv6 FE80 network).

Note

IPv6 labels DHCP packets with different names. DHCPDISCOVER, DHCPOFFER, DHCPREQUEST, and DHCPACK packets are labeled as Solicit, Advertise, Request, and Reply, respectively.

DHCP Relay

Because DHCPDISCOVER packets are broadcast to an entire LAN, routers do not forward them to other LANs by default. Thus, if no DHCP server is available on a LAN, DHCP clients will not be able to obtain an IP address lease.

It is costly to place a DHCP server on each LAN in an organization, so each router in an organization is usually configured as a **DHCP relay agent**. When a DHCP relay agent receives a DHCPDISCOVER packet, it forwards it to a DHCP server in the DMZ network, indicating the source IP network on which the DHCPDISCOVER packet originated. The DHCP server then provides a DHCPOFFER for the source IP network to the DHCP relay agent that can be forwarded to the DHCP client. Following this, the DHCP relay agent relays the associated DHCPREQUEST and DHCPACK packets between the DHCP client and server to complete the DHCP lease process.

Note

You must manually enable the DHCP relay agent on the routers in your organization and provide them with the IP address of at least one DHCP server in the DMZ. The process used to do this varies by router model. Consult your router documentation for more information.

Note

In Module 9, we will examine the process used to configure a DHCP relay agent on a Windows Server 2019 software-based router.

Configuring a DHCP Server

To configure Windows Server 2019 as a DHCP server, you must first install and authorize the **DHCP Server** role. Authorizing the DHCP Server role after installation is necessary in an Active Directory environment. This is because the DHCP Server service sends a DHCPINFORM packet on the network each time it starts requesting authorization from a domain controller. If the DHCP Server role has not been previously authorized in the Active Directory domain, the authorization request will be rejected by a domain controller on the network and the DHCP Server service will shut down. If you install the DHCP Server role using the Add Roles and Features Wizard in Server Manager while logged in as user account with domain privileges, you can authorize it on the final page, as shown in Figure 8-35. If you click *Complete DHCP configuration* in Figure 8-35, click Next and Commit to authorize your DHCP server in Active Directory. This also creates the DHCP Administrators and DHCP Users groups in Active Directory, if not already present. Members of the DHCP Administrators group can administer the settings on all DHCP servers in the domain, while members of the DHCP Users group can view DHCP server configuration (often required for help desk staff to aid in providing network support).

After the DHCP Server role is installed, you can manage a DHCP server by clicking DHCP from the Tools menu in Server Manager to start the DHCP tool shown in Figure 8-36.

The DHCP tool uses **scopes** to organize the settings for each IPv4 and IPv6 network that it can provide IP configuration for. The DHCP server shown in Figure 8-36 contains a scope called Accounting LAN that provides IP configuration for the 192.168.100.0 network. To configure a DHCP server, you must create scopes that represent each of the networks for which you wish to provide IP configuration. Following this, you can optionally configure scope and server features that provide additional functionality.

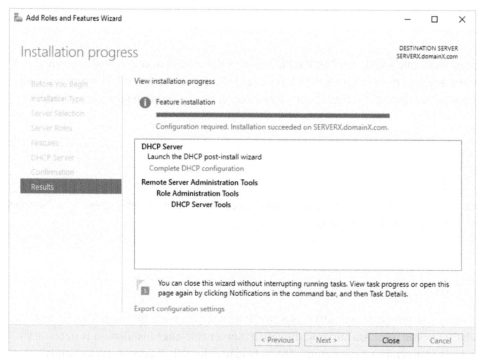

Figure 8-35 Completing the installation of the DHCP Server role

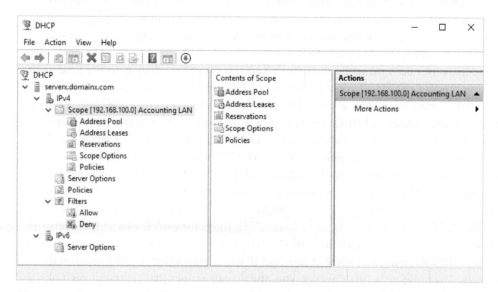

Figure 8-36 The DHCP tool

Creating a New Scope

To create the scope shown in Figure 8-36, highlight IPv4 and select More Actions, New Scope from the Actions pane to start the New Scope Wizard. When you click Next at the welcome page of the New Scope Wizard, you are prompted to supply a name and optional description for your scope, as shown in Figure 8-37. After you click Next in Figure 8-37, you must specify the IP address range and subnet mask, as shown in Figure 8-38.

> **Note**
>
> It is important to select the correct subnet mask during scope creation as it cannot be modified afterward.

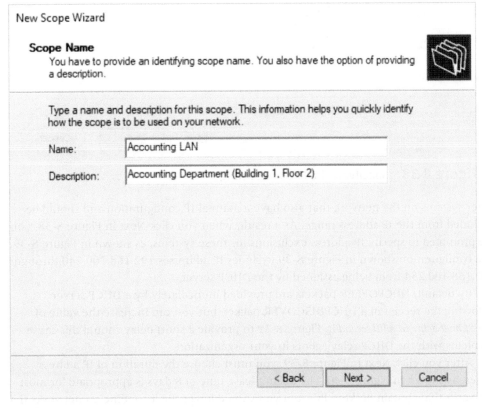

Figure 8-37   **Specifying the scope name**

The range configured in Figure 8-38 provides all usable IP addresses on the 192.168.100.0/24 network. However, one of these IP addresses must be manually configured on the router for the network (the default gateway). Moreover, there may be

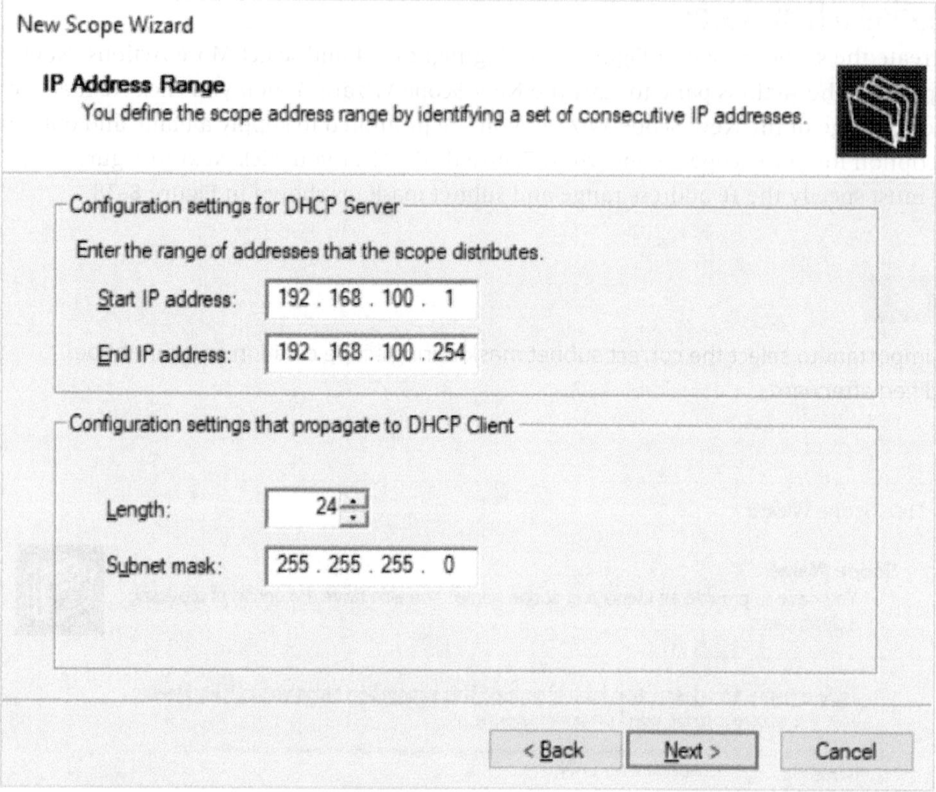

New Scope Wizard

IP Address Range
You define the scope address range by identifying a set of consecutive IP addresses.

Configuration settings for DHCP Server

Enter the range of addresses that the scope distributes.

Start IP address: 192 . 168 . 100 . 1

End IP address: 192 . 168 . 100 . 254

Configuration settings that propagate to DHCP Client

Length: 24 ▲▼

Subnet mask: 255 . 255 . 255 . 0

< Back   Next >   Cancel

Figure 8-38   Specifying the IP address range

other systems on the network that also have a manual IP configuration and should be
excluded from the IP address range. As a result, when you click Next in Figure 8-38, you
are prompted to specify IP address exclusions for these systems, as shown in Figure 8-39.
The configuration shown in Figure 8-39 excludes IP addresses 192.168.100.240 through
192.168.100.254 from being assigned by the DHCP server.

By default, DHCPOFFER packets are provided immediately by a DHCP server
following the receipt of a DHCPDISCOVER packet, but you can increase the value of
the *Subnet delay in milli second* in Figure 8-39 to provide a short delay should this cause
problems with the DHCP relay agents in your organization.

After you click Next in Figure 8-39, you must choose the duration of IP address
leases, as shown in Figure 8-40. The default lease time of 8 days is appropriate for most
networks that contain desktop PCs, but you should lower the lease time on networks that
provide IP address configuration for mobile devices (e.g., laptops, tablets, smartphones),
as those devices often leave the network each day and the IP configuration they obtained
cannot be reused until the associated lease expires.

While you can configure DHCP options following the creation of a scope, the New
Scope Wizard allows you to configure the most common options provided to DHCP

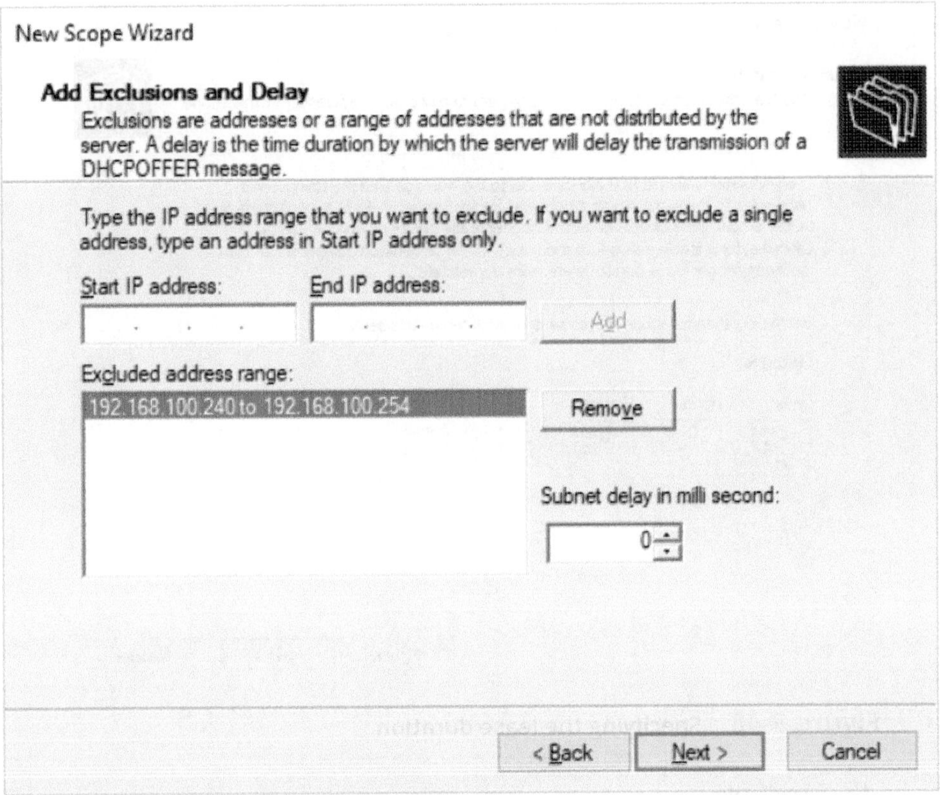

Figure 8-39   Specifying IP address exclusions

clients. When you click Next in Figure 8-40, select the Yes option shown in Figure 8-41 to configure these DHCP options, or the No option to create the scope. If you select the Yes option in Figure 8-41 and click Next, you can optionally specify a default gateway (DHCP option *003 Router*), as shown for 192.168.100.254 in Figure 8-42.

After you click Next in Figure 8-42, you are prompted to optionally specify a domain name suffix (DHCP option *015 DNS Domain Name*) and one or more DNS servers (DHCP option *006 DNS Servers*), as shown in Figure 8-43. The options shown in Figure 8-43 configure a domain name suffix of domainX.com, a preferred DNS server of 192.168.1.107, and an alternate DNS server of 172.16.0.1.

When you click Next in Figure 8-43, you are prompted to optionally specify one or more WINS servers (DHCP option *044 WINS/NBNS Servers*), as shown in Figure 8-44. The options shown in Figure 8-44 configure a preferred WINS server of 192.168.1.107 and an alternate WINS server of 172.16.0.1. If a WINS server is configured in Figure 8-43, the *046 WINS/ NBT Node Type* DHCP option will automatically be configured to the value 0x8 to ensure that the DHCP client uses WINS servers to resolve NetBIOS names before resorting to NetBIOS broadcasts. After you click Next in Figure 8-44, you are prompted to activate the scope, as shown in Figure 8-45. Finally, click Next and Finish to complete the New Scope Wizard.

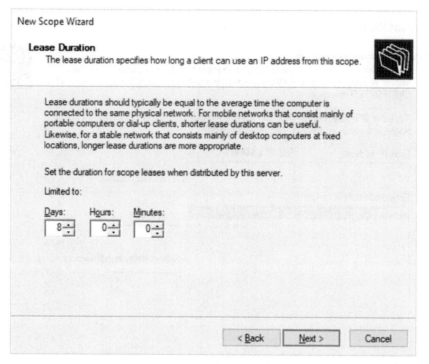

Figure 8-40   Specifying the lease duration

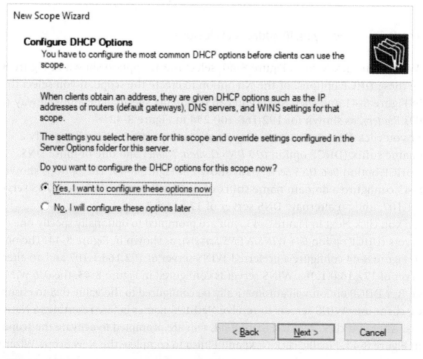

Figure 8-41   Configuring DHCP options

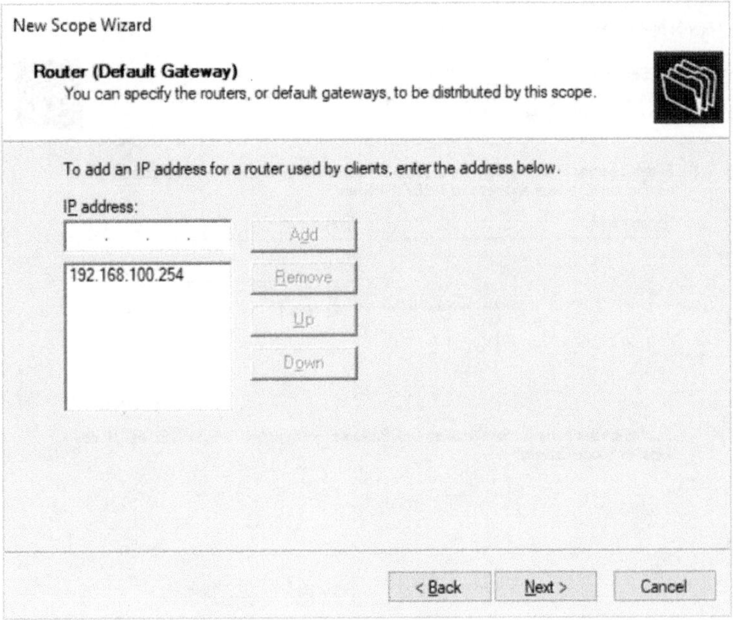

Figure 8-42   Configuring a default gateway option

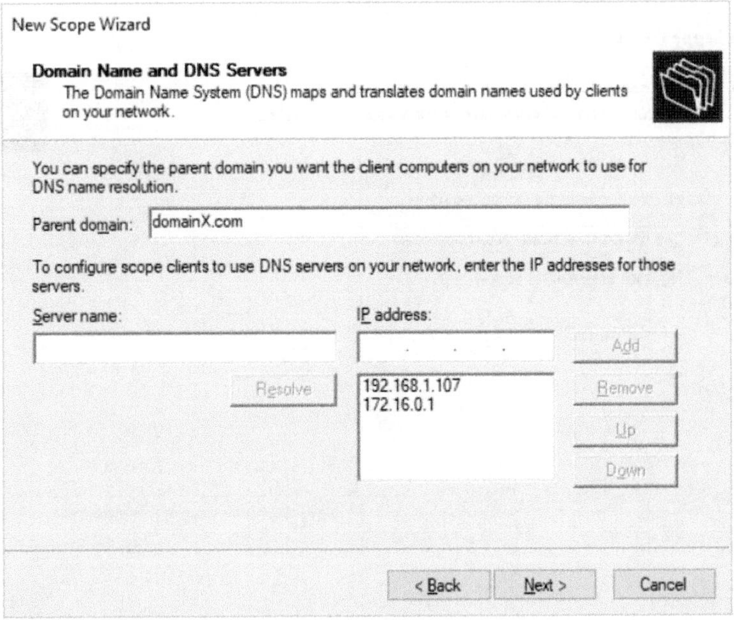

Figure 8-43   Configuring domain name and DNS server options

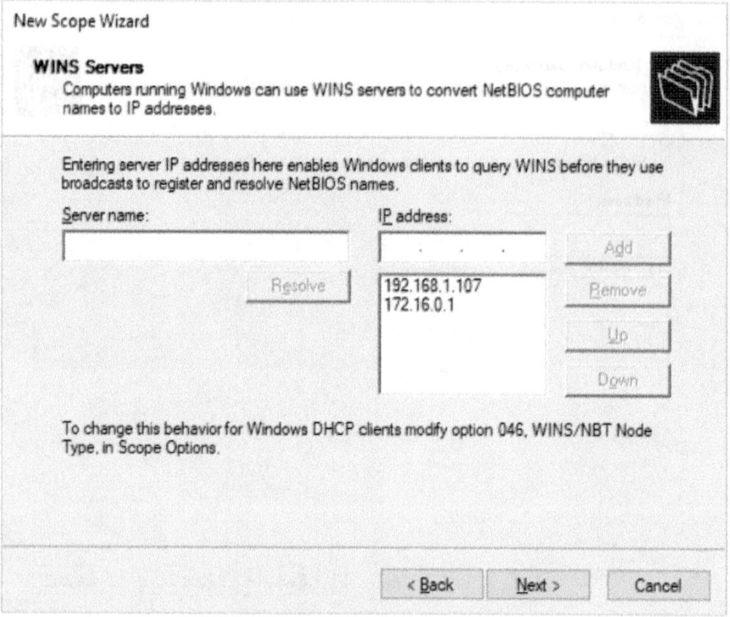

Figure 8-44   Configuring WINS server options

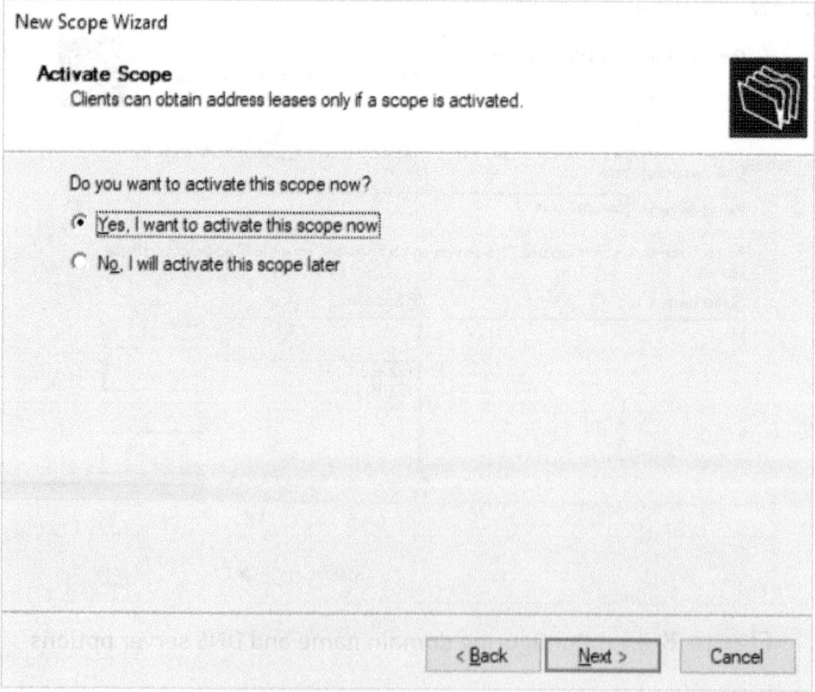

Figure 8-45   Activating the scope

> **Note** 📎
>
> Activating a scope allows the DHCP server to respond to DHCPDISCOVER packets for the associated network. If you do not activate your scope in Figure 8-45, you can activate it afterward. To do this, highlight the scope in the DHCP tool and click More Actions, Activate in the Actions pane.

> **Note** 📎
>
> After scope creation, you can configure DHCP options that cannot be configured in the New Scope Wizard.

> **Note** 📎
>
> The process used to create an IPv6 scope is similar to the process used to create an IPv4 scope. However, you must specify an IPv6 network prefix before specifying the IPv6 address range.

Configuring Scopes

By default, a newly created scope contains several folders, as shown for the Accounting LAN scope in Figure 8-36. Each folder allows you to view or configure certain features of the scope:

- *Address Pool* contains the IP address range and exclusions configured for your scope. To add an exclusion following scope creation, highlight this folder and click More Actions, New Exclusion Range in the Actions pane.
- *Address Leases* lists each lease provided to DHCP clients. To terminate a lease before the lease expiry, highlight it and click More Actions, Delete in the Actions pane. This will send a DHCPNACK packet to the DHCP client. The DHCP client must then send another DHCPDISCOVER packet to obtain a new IP configuration.
- *Scope Options* lists the DHCP options configured for the scope. To modify DHCP options following scope creation, highlight this folder and click More Actions, Configure Options in the Actions pane.
- *Policies* can be used to create **DHCP policies** that provide a specific IP range or DHCP options for DHCP clients based on criteria in the DHCPDISCOVER packet. To create a DHCP policy, highlight this folder and click More Actions, New Policy in the Actions pane.
- *Reservations* allow you to provide the same IP address each time a DHCPDISCOVER is received from a DHCP client that has a certain MAC address. **Reservations** are often created for network-attached printers, servers, and network devices that must

receive an IP address from a DHCP server that does not change over time. To create a reservation that always provides the IP address 192.168.100.100 to a network-attached printer called Ricoh 8220LP (with MAC address 80:a2:f4:77:4f:8b), highlight this folder, click More Actions, New Reservation in the Actions pane, and supply the options shown in Figure 8-46.

Figure 8-46   Creating a reservation

Note

Reservations inherit the DHCP options configured in the Scope Options folder. However, you can highlight a reservation in the Reservations folder and select More Actions, Configure Options from the Actions pane to override inherited DHCP options or configure additional DHCP options for the reservation.

Note

If you highlight the Server Options folder in Figure 8-36 and select More Actions, Configure Options from the Actions pane, you can configure DHCP options that are inherited by each IPv4 scope. Similarly, if you highlight the Policies folder under IPv4 in Figure 8-36 and select More Actions, New Policy from the Actions pane, you can configure a DHCP policy that is inherited by each IPv4 scope.

You can modify other scope features by accessing the properties of the scope. For example, if you highlight the Accounting LAN scope in Figure 8-36 and click More Actions, Properties in the Actions pane, you are able to modify the name, description, IP range, and lease duration, as shown in Figure 8-47.

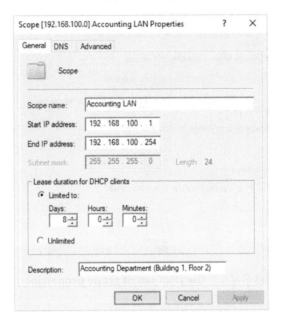

Figure 8-47   The General tab of scope properties

Recall that the DNS dynamic update process runs as a low priority process and may fail to update host and PTR records if a client computer is too busy. Moreover, DHCP clients running legacy (pre-Windows 2000), Linux, or macOS operating systems do not perform dynamic updates unless additional software is configured to deliver this functionality. To provide reliable dynamic updates for all DHCP clients in an organization, you can configure a DHCP server to dynamically update host and PTR records on behalf of each DHCP client when they obtain or renew a DHCP lease. To do this for the Accounting LAN scope, highlight the DNS tab in Figure 8-47, and specify the appropriate options, as shown in Figure 8-48. The options configured in Figure 8-48 allow the DHCP server to perform dynamic updates of A and PTR records for all DHCP clients as well as remove A and PTR records for DHCP clients when their lease expires. To enforce these options as well as ensure that the DHCP server performs a dynamic update only if an existing record for the DHCP client does not already exist on the DNS server, click the Configure button in Figure 8-48 and check the *Enable Name Protection* option.

Recall that DHCP can provide backward compatibility for BOOTP clients. However, this feature is not enabled by default on a new scope. To allow both DHCP and BOOTP clients to obtain an IP configuration from the Accounting LAN scope, highlight the Advanced tab in Figure 8-48, and select the Both option shown in Figure 8-49.

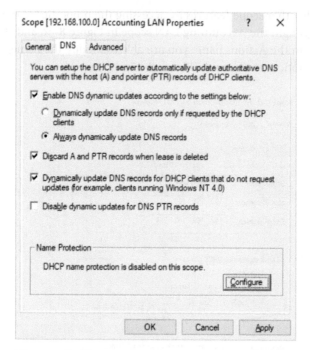

Figure 8-48 The DNS tab of scope properties

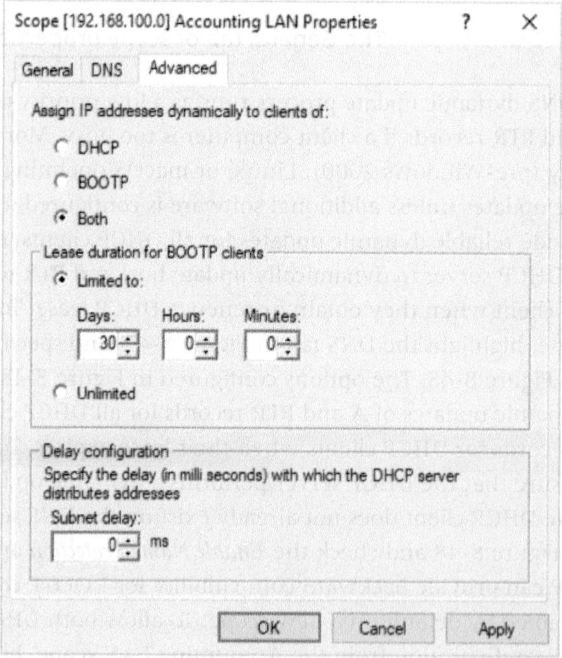

Figure 8-49 The Advanced tab of scope properties

By default, BOOTP clients receive a 30-day lease, but you can modify this lease duration as shown in Figure 8-49. Additionally, you can modify the Subnet delay in Figure 8-49 to provide a delay for DHCPOFFER packets if immediate responses cause problems with the DHCP relay agents in your organization.

Configuring Filters

Some organizations configure **MAC address filtering** on a DHCP server to restrict IP leases to computers that were purchased by the organization. Alternatively, MAC address filtering can be used to prevent one or more computers from obtaining an IP lease from a DHCP server while allowing all others. To configure MAC address filtering in the DHCP tool, access the Filters folder shown in Figure 8-36 and perform one of two procedures:

- To configure the DHCP server to respond only to DHCPDISCOVER packets that contain a MAC address from an organization computer, you select the Allow subfolder and click More Actions, Enable in the Actions pane. Next, you must add the MAC address of each allowed computer to the Actions folder.
- To configure the DHCP server to respond to all DHCPDISCOVER packets except for those that contain a blacklisted MAC address, you select the Deny subfolder and click More Actions Enable in the Actions pane. Next, you must add the MAC address of each blacklisted computer to the Actions folder.

To add a MAC address to an Allow or Deny folder, highlight the folder in the DHCP tool and click More Actions, New Filter in the Actions pane. Next, you must specify a MAC address and description, as shown in Figure 8-50 for Accounting PC001.

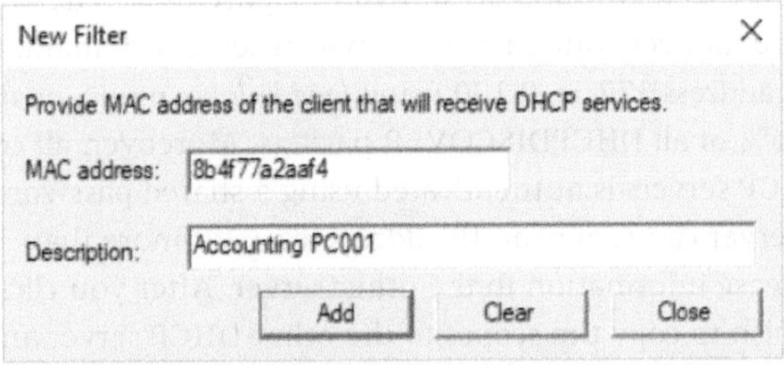

Figure 8-50   Adding a MAC address to a filter

Configuring DHCP Fault Tolerance

To provide fault tolerance for DHCP in an organization, you can configure two DHCP servers in the DMZ with scopes for each network as well as configure the DHCP relay agents in the organization to forward DHCPDISCOVER packets to these DHCP servers. If a DHCP relay agent is configured with the IP address of two DHCP servers, it will forward DHCPDISCOVER packets to the first DHCP server listed and to the second DHCP server if the first is unreachable. Moreover, you can alternate the DHCP server that is listed first in the configuration of each DHCP relay agent to distribute DHCPDISCOVER packets between the two DHCP servers in the DMZ.

However, to prevent these two DHCP servers from independently issuing duplicate IP address leases for a network, the scope on each DHCP server must include a different IP address range for that network. For example, one DHCP server could contain a scope for the 192.168.100.0/24 network that uses the IP address range 192.168.100.1 through 192.168.100.100, and the other DHCP server could contain a scope for the same 192.168.100.0/24 network that uses the IP address range 192.168.100.101 through 192.168.100.200. If one DHCP server fails, the other DHCP server can issue unique IP configuration for the 192.168.100.0/24 network.

Alternatively, you can configure **DHCP failover** to provide fault tolerance for IPv4 scopes on two DHCP servers. DHCP failover works in either *load balance* or *hot standby* mode. In *load balance* mode, each DHCP server contains identical scope and lease information and coordinates all responses to DHCPDISCOVER packets with the other DHCP server to distribute the load. In *hot standby* mode, each DHCP server contains identical scope and lease information, but only the first DHCP server responds to DHCPDISCOVER packets. If the first DHCP server fails, the second DHCP server starts responding to DHCPDISCOVER packets.

To configure DHCP failover, you must first configure scopes for all networks in the DHCP tool on the first DHCP server. Next, highlight IPv4 in the DHCP tool and select More Actions, Configure Failover from the Actions pane to start the Configure Failover wizard. The first two pages of this wizard prompt you to choose the scopes that should be made fault tolerant (all scopes are selected by default) as well as the IP address of the second DHCP server. Following this, the Configure Failover wizard prompts you to select the DHCP failover configuration, as shown in Figure 8-51. The options shown in Figure 8-51 create a failover configuration between serverx.domain.com and the DHCP server with IP address 172.16.0.100 using *load balance* mode, ensuring that each server responds to 50% of all DHCPDISCOVER packets. Moreover, all communication between the two DHCP servers is authenticated using a shared password (*Shared Secret*), and neither server can renew an IP address lease for more than 1 hour without communicating the lease information to the other server. After you click Next in Figure 8-51, click Finish to copy the scopes to the other DHCP server and complete the DHCP failover configuration.

> **Note** 🖉
>
> A wide variety of different PowerShell cmdlets are available for configuring scopes and DHCP server settings. Search *PowerShell DhcpServer* on docs.microsoft.com for more information.

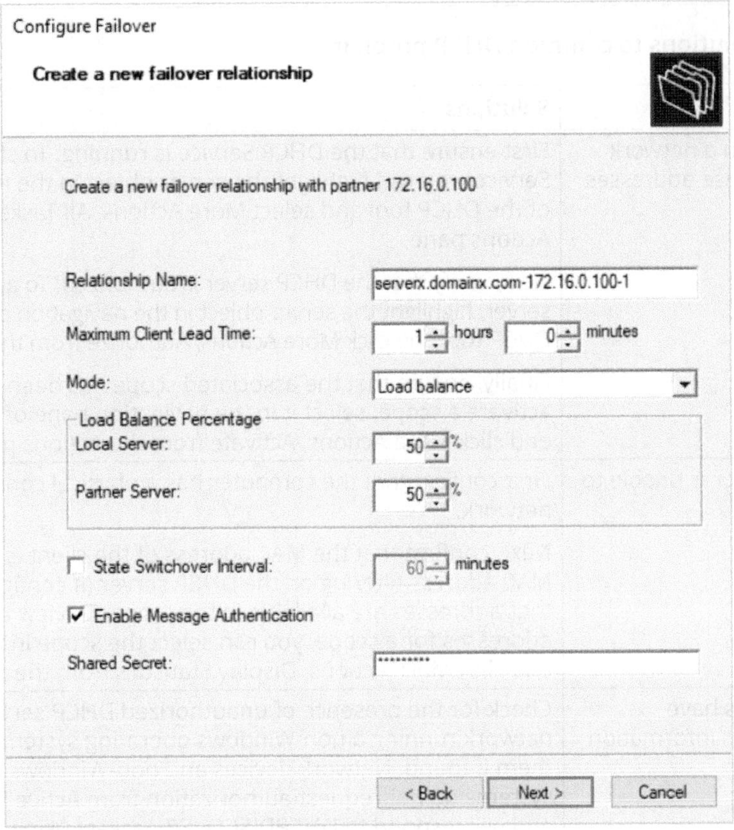

Configure Failover

Create a new failover relationship

Create a new failover relationship with partner 172.16.0.100

Relationship Name:	serverx.domainx.com-172.16.0.100-1
Maximum Client Lead Time:	1 ÷ hours 0 ÷ minutes
Mode:	Load balance ▾

Load Balance Percentage
Local Server: 50 ÷ %

Partner Server: 50 ÷ %

☐ State Switchover Interval: 60 ÷ minutes

☑ Enable Message Authentication

Shared Secret: ••••••••••

< Back   Next >   Cancel

Figure 8-51   Configuring DHCP failover

Note

Large organizations may deploy hundreds of DHCP and DNS servers across many locations to provide for IP configuration and FQDN name resolution. These organizations often deploy an **IP Address Management (IPAM)** software product that provides for centralized management of these servers.

Troubleshooting DHCP

After DHCP scopes have been configured for the networks in your organization, you may need to troubleshoot problems related to the DHCP server configuration as well as problems that prevent DHCP clients from accessing the network or DHCP server. Table 8-4 lists some common problems related to DHCP and possible solutions.

Table 8-4 Solutions to common DHCP problems

Problem	Solutions
All computers on a network are unable to lease addresses	First ensure that the DHCP Service is running. To start the DHCP Service, you can highlight the server object in the navigation pane of the DHCP tool and select More Actions, All Tasks, Start from the Actions pane.
	Next, verify that the DHCP server is authorized. To authorize a DHCP server, highlight the server object in the navigation pane of the DHCP tool and click More Actions, Authorize from the Actions pane.
	Finally, ensure that the associated scope has been activated. To activate a scope, select it in the navigation pane of the DHCP tool and click More Actions, Activate from the Actions pane.
A single computer is unable to lease an address	First confirm that the computer has a physical connection to the network.
	Next, confirm that the MAC address of the client is allowed by MAC address filtering on the DHCP server (if configured), and that addresses are available in the scope. To view available IP addresses for a scope, you can select the scope in the DHCP tool and click More Actions, Display Statistics from the Actions pane.
Some computers have incorrect address information	Check for the presence of unauthorized DHCP servers on the network running a non-Windows operating system and remove them if found. Network devices and non-Windows operating systems do not request authorization from Active Directory and will respond to DHCPDISCOVER packets using their own configuration.
A computer receives an IP conflict error after receiving an IPv4 address	Although DHCP will not lease the same IP address to two different computers, it may lease an IP address that was manually configured on another computer on the network. To prevent this, you can configure the DHCP server to ping an IP address a certain number of times before it is leased to a client computer. If a ping reply is received, the DHCP server will not lease that IP address. To configure this functionality on a DHCP server, highlight IPv4 in the DHCP tool and select More Actions, Properties from the Actions pane. Next, highlight the Advanced tab and enter a number greater than 0 in the *Conflict detection attempts* text box.
The DHCP server is not dynamically updating DNS records for DHCP clients	This can happen if the DNS server is not in the same domain as the DHCP server. In this case, you should specify the credentials for a user account that can be used to perform dynamic updates on your DHCP server. This user account must be a member of the DnsUpdateProxy group in the DNS server's domain. To enter dynamic update credentials on a DHCP server, highlight either IPv4 or IPv6 in the DHCP tool and select More Actions, Properties from the Actions pane. Next, highlight the Advanced tab and click the Credentials button.

After solving a problem that prevents DHCP clients from obtaining an IP address, you may need to manually issue a DHCPDISCOVER packet on the DHCP client to ensure that the client can obtain an IP address. To do this, right-click a network interface in the Network Connections window and click Diagnose. Alternatively, you can run the `ipconfig /renew` command at a Command Prompt window.

Module Summary

- DNS servers provide for FQDN name resolution by hosting zone files that include resource records for each FQDN or by forwarding name resolution requests to other DNS servers.

- Multiple DNS servers are used to provide fault tolerance for zone files. Primary DNS servers contain a read-write copy of a zone file, and secondary DNS servers contain a read-only copy of a zone file. Secondary DNS servers perform a zone transfer to copy new resource records from a primary DNS server.

- The zone file used for Active Directory on organization DNS servers is stored in the Active Directory database and includes resource records that are created by dynamic update.

- A DNS server can be configured to forward name resolution requests to another DNS server using a conditional forwarder, stub zone, default forwarder, or root hints file.

- Most DNS problems are caused by incorrect resource records in a zone or DNS cache and can often be identified using the `nslookup` command.

- You can configure a WINS server to reduce NetBIOS name broadcasts as well as ensure that NetBIOS names can be resolved for computers on other LANs in your organization.

- DHCP can lease IP configuration to other computers on a network that broadcast a DHCPDISCOVER packet. Routers use DHCP relay agents to forward DHCPDISCOVER packets on each LAN to DHCP servers in a DMZ.

- To provide IP configuration for DHCP clients on a network, you must configure a scope on a DHCP server that includes an IP address range and related DHCP options. You can optionally configure DHCP failover to provide fault tolerance for scopes if you have two DHCP servers.

Key Terms

Active Directory-integrated
   primary DNS server
authoritative
caching-only DNS server
debug logging
default forwarder

DHCP failover
DHCP option
DHCP policy
DHCP relay agent
DHCP Server
DNS Server

DNS Server log
Dynamic DNS (DDNS)
forward lookup
hosts file
IP Address Management
   (IPAM)

iterative query	reservation	stale resource records
MAC address filtering	resolver	stub DNS server
NetBIOS name record	resource record	Time To Live (TTL)
netmask ordering	reverse lookup	Windows Internet Name
Network Time Protocol	root hints	Service (WINS)
(NTP)	round robin	WINS Server
primary DNS server	scavenging	zone
recursive query	scope	zone file
replication partner	secondary DNS server	zone transfer

Review Questions

1. Which of the following represents the maximum amount of time that a DNS server or resolver is allowed to cache the result of a forward lookup?
   a. Zone transfer
   b. TTL
   c. Root hints
   d. PTR

2. Windows computers contact their DNS server at boot time to create or update their host resource records. This feature is called zone transfer. True or False?

3. Which of the following are authoritative DNS server types? (Choose all that apply.)
   a. Primary
   b. Active Directory-integrated primary
   c. Secondary
   d. Caching-only

4. If a DNS server does not contain a zone file that contains the resource records for a lookup, and is not configured as a conditional or default forwarder, it will use its root hints file to perform a recursive query. True or False?

5. Which resource record stores zone transfer settings?
   a. NS
   b. PTR
   c. A
   d. SOA

6. You wish to provide access to Web resources in another organization. However, the associated A records for these resources are stored in a zone file on a DNS server in the other organization that is not publicly registered. What can you configure on your organization's DNS server to allow access to these resources? (Choose all that apply.)
   a. A stub zone that forwards requests to the other organization's DNS server
   b. A conditional forwarder that forwards requests to the other organization's DNS server
   c. A primary zone that copies resource records from the zone on the other organization's DNS server
   d. A secondary zone that copies resource records from the zone on the other organization's DNS server

7. Scavenging can be configured to remove stale resource records that were added to a zone using dynamic update. True or False?

8. A user complains that they are unable to contact a specific server in your organization. You remember that you recently modified the A record for this server on your organization's Active Directory-integrated DNS server. Which

troubleshooting step should you try first to remedy the issue?

a. Clear the DNS cache on the DNS server

b. Clear the DNS cache on the user's computer

c. Run the `nslookup` command on the user's computer

d. Restart the DNS Server service

9. Which two resource records can you create in a zone to provide the FQDN of an email server for the zone as well as associate this FQDN with an IPv6 address? (Choose two answers.)

a. MX

b. A

c. CNAME

d. AAAA

10. Which of the following are valid reasons to deploy a WINS server? (Choose all that apply.)

a. To reduce NetBIOS name broadcasts on LANs in an organization

b. To allow computers in one LAN to resolve NetBIOS names in another LAN

c. To resolve NetBIOS names to IPv6 addresses

d. To provide legacy Windows clients access to an Active Directory domain

11. NetBIOS name records are automatically created on a WINS server by computers that are configured to use the WINS server. True or False?

12. Your organization has two WINS servers to provide for NetBIOS name resolution. What can you do to ensure that each WINS server shares its NetBIOS name records with the other server?

a. Configure WINS failover for the two WINS servers

b. Provide the IP address of both WINS servers in IPv4 properties on each WINS client

c. Configure the DNS server to use WINS lookup

d. Configure the two servers as replication partners

13. DHCP servers respond to DHCPDISCOVER packets received from DHCP clients or DHCP relay agents with a DHCPACK packet. True or False?

14. Which of the following are optional components of a DHCP scope?

a. IP address exclusions

b. DHCP options

c. DHCP policy

d. Reservation

15. The default lease time of 8 days for a DHCP scope is appropriate for networks that primarily contain mobile devices, but should be reduce for networks that primarily contain desktop PCs. True or False?

16. DHCP reservations must use the DHCP options from their scope. True or False?

17. Which DHCP option number provides a default gateway router?

a. 003

b. 004

c. 006

d. 015

18. DHCP servers can be configured to dynamically update host and PTR records for legacy DHCP clients and DHCP clients that do not use a Microsoft operating system. True or False?

19. Which two of the following tasks can you perform to provide fault tolerance for two DHCP servers in the DMZ? (Choose two answers.)

a. Ensure that DHCP relay agents in the organization are configured with the IP address of both DHCP servers

b. Ensure that half of the DHCP relay agents in the organization are configured with the IP address of the first DHCP server, and the other half are configured with the IP address of the second DHCP server

c. Configure the two DHCP servers as replication partners

d. Configure DHCP failover in either load balance or hot standby mode for all scopes

20. To prevent a DHCP server from leasing an IPv4 address that has been manually configured on a computer on the network, you can configure a DHCP server to send one or more ping requests to an IPv4 address before leasing it. True or False?

Hands-On Projects

These Hands-On Projects should be completed in the order given. They normally take a total of 3 hours or less to complete. The requirements for these projects include:

- A system with Windows Server 2019 installed according to Hands-On Project 1-1 (Lab Environment 1) or Hands-On Project 1-2 (Lab Environment 2).
- A WindowsServer2019VM2 virtual machine installed according to Hands-On Project 3-5 and configured as a member server according to Hands-On Project 5-2.

Project 8-1: Configuring DNS Zones

In this Hands-On Project, you explore the properties of your DNS server and the Active Directory-integrated primary zone used by Active Directory on your Windows Server 2019 host. Next, you create a primary forward lookup zone as well as a reverse lookup zone that is Active Directory-integrated. Finally, you attempt to create a stub zone for your partner's Active Directory domain that has a conditional forwarder previously configured from Hands-On Project 4-4.

1. Boot your Windows Server 2019 host and log into domain*X*.com as Administrator using the password **Secret555**. Next, click **Start** and then click **Server Manager**.

2. In Server Manager, click the **Tools** menu and then click **DNS**.

3. In the DNS Manager window, right-click the **SERVERX** object in the navigation pane and click **Properties**.

   a. On the Interfaces tab of the SERVER*X* Properties window, note that your DNS server will respond to DNS lookups that are received on all network interfaces by default.

   b. Highlight the **Forwarders** tab. Note that your DNS server is configured as a default forwarder to the IP addresses that you use in your classroom environment and that root hints are used if no forwarders are available.

   c. Highlight the **Advanced** tab and note that round robin and netmask ordering are enabled by default. Select **Enable automatic scavenging of stale records** and note the default value of 7 days.

   d. Highlight the **Root Hints** tab and note the entries that identify the top-level DNS servers and click **OK**.

4. In the navigation pane, expand **Forward Lookup Zones** and highlight **domainX.com**. Note the default A resource records for the computers in your domain. Also note that the SOA, NS, and A resource records for serverX list *static* under the Timestamp column, whereas the A resource records for other computers in your domain list the date and time that they were dynamically updated.

5. In the navigation pane, expand **domainX.com** and highlight **_tcp**. Note the SRV resource records that identify the FQDN of the domain controllers in your domain that host the global catalog (_gc), Kerberos (_kerberos), Kerberos password (_kpasswd), and LDAP (_ldap) services using the TCP/IP protocol.

6. In the navigation pane under domainX.com, expand **sites**, **ChicagoSite** and highlight **_tcp**. Note the SRV resource records for the domain controllers that are part of the ChicagoSite site. Collapse **domainX.com** in the navigation pane when finished.

7. Right-click **domainX.com** in the navigation pane and click **Properties**. Note that the zone type is Active Directory-integrated and that records are replicating to other domain controllers that host DNS in the domain. Also note that the zone accepts secure dynamic updates.

8. Click **Aging**. At the Zone Aging/Scavenging Properties window, select **Scavenge stale resource records**, note the default values for the No-refresh and Refresh intervals, and click **OK**. Click **OK** to close the domainX.com Properties window.

9. Right-click **Forward Lookup Zones** in the navigation pane and click **New Zone**.

    a. At the New Zone Wizard, click **Next**.

    b. At the Zone Type page, note the default selection of Primary zone. Deselect **Store the zone in Active Directory** and click **Next**.

    c. At the Zone Name page, type **zoneX.com** and click **Next**.

    d. At the Zone File page, note that a zone file called zoneX.dns will be created in the C:\Windows\system32\dns folder to store resource records and click **Next**.

    e. At the Dynamic Update page, note the default option that does not allow dynamic updates and click **Next**.

    f. Click **Finish** to create zoneX.com.

10. Right-click **Reverse Lookup Zones** in the navigation pane and click **New Zone**.

    a. At the New Zone Wizard, click **Next**.

    b. At the Zone Type page, note that an Active Directory-integrated primary zone will be created by default and click **Next**.

    c. At the Active Directory Zone Replication Scope page, note the default option that replicates the zone to domain controllers in domainX.com and click **Next**.

    d. At the Reverse Lookup Zone Name page, note the default selection of IPv4 Reverse Lookup Zone and click **Next**.

    e. At the Reverse Lookup Zone Name page, type **172.16.0** in the Network ID text box and click **Next**.

    f. At the Dynamic Update page, note the default option that allows only secure dynamic updates and click **Next**.

    g. Click **Finish** to create the 0.16.172.in-addr.arpa reverse lookup zone.

11. In the navigation pane, highlight **Conditional Forwarders** and note the conditional forwarder that you created earlier in Hands-On Project 4-4 to relay forward lookups for your partner's Active Directory zone to your partner's DNS server.

12. Right-click **Forward Lookup Zones** in the navigation pane and click **New Zone**.

    a. At the New Zone Wizard, click **Next**.

    b. At the Zone Type page, select **Stub zone** and click **Next**.

    c. At the Active Directory Zone Replication Scope page, note the default option that replicates the zone to domain controllers in domain*X*.com and click **Next**.

    d. At the Zone Name page, type the domain name for your partner's Active Directory domain in the Zone name text box and click **Next**.

    e. At the Master DNS Servers page, type the IP address of your partner's DNS server and press **Enter**. Click **Next** when finished.

    f. Click **Finish** and note that you are unable to create the stub zone because a conditional forwarder already exists for your partner's Active Directory domain. This is because conditional forwarders and stub zones perform the same function. Click **OK** and then click **Cancel** to close the New Zone Wizard.

Project 8-2: DNS Zone Properties and Resource Records

In this Hands-On Project, you explore and configure resource records in the zone*X*.com forward lookup zone and 0.16.172.in-addr.arpa reverse lookup zone. Following this, you test name resolution using these resource records.

1. In the navigation pane of DNS Manager on your Windows Server 2019 host, highlight **zone*X*.com** and note the default SOA and NS records that were created.

2. Right-click **zone*X*.com** in the navigation pane and click **Properties**. Note that the zone type is Primary and that dynamic updates are not enabled.

    a. Highlight the **Start of Authority (SOA)** tab and note the default zone transfer intervals and default TTL values in the SOA record.

    b. Highlight the **Name Servers** tab and note that server*X*.domain*X*.com is listed as an authoritative DNS server for the zone.

    c. Highlight the **WINS** tab and select **Use WINS forward lookup**. Enter the IPv4 address of your Windows Server 2019 host in the IP address text box and click **Add**. We will install and configure WINS on your Windows Server 2019 host in Hands-On Project 8-4.

    d. Highlight the **Zone Transfers** tab.

        i. Select **Only to the following servers** and click **Edit**.

        ii. In the Allow Zone Transfers window, type the IP address of your WindowsServer2019VM2 virtual machine and click **OK**.

        iii. Click **Notify**. Select **The following servers**, type the IP address of your WindowsServer2019VM2 virtual machine and click **OK**.

        iv. Click **OK** to close the zone*X* Properties window.

3. Right-click **zone*X*.com** in the navigation pane and click **New Host (A or AAAA)**.

   a. At the New Host window, type **server1** in the Name text box, type **172.16.0.61** in the IP address text box, and select **Create associated pointer (PTR) record**. Click **Add Host** and then click **OK**.

   b. At the New Host window, type **server1** in the Name text box and type **172.16.0.62** in the IP address text box. Click **Add Host** and then click **OK**.

   c. At the New Host window, type **server1** in the Name text box and type **172.16.0.63** in the IP address text box. Click **Add Host** and then click **OK**.

   d. At the New Host window, type **server2** in the Name text box and type **172.16.0.64** in the IP address text box. Click **Add Host** and then click **OK**.

   e. At the New Host window, type **server3** in the Name text box and type **172.16.0.65** in the IP address text box. Click **Add Host** and then click **OK**.

   f. Click **Cancel** to close the New Host window.

4. Right-click **zone*X*.com** in the navigation pane and click **New Alias (CNAME)**. At the New Resource Record window, type **www** in the *Alias name* text box, type **server1.zone*X*.com** in the *Fully qualified domain name (FQDN) for target host* text box and click **OK**.

5. Right-click **zone*X*.com** in the navigation pane and click **New Alias (CNAME)**. At the New Resource Record window, type **ftp** in the *Alias name* text box, type **server2.zone*X*.com** in the *Fully qualified domain name (FQDN) for target host* text box and click **OK**.

6. Right-click **zone*X*.com** in the navigation pane and click **New Mail Exchanger (MX)**. At the New Resource Record window, type **server3.zone*X*.com** in the *Fully qualified domain name (FQDN) of mail server* text box and click **OK**.

7. Highlight **zone*X*.com** in the navigation pane. Note the WINS Lookup, A, CNAME, and MX records that were created.

8. Expand **Reverse Lookup Zones** in the navigation pane and highlight **0.16.172.in-addr. arpa**. Note the PTR resource records that were created in Step 3.

9. Right-click **SERVER*X*** in the navigation pane and click **Launch nslookup**.

   a. At the interactive > prompt in nslookup, type **www.zone*X*.com** and press **Enter**. Note that www.zone*X*.com is an alias to server1.zone*X*.com. Also note that server1.zone*X*.com returns three IP addresses (172.16.0.61, 172.16.0.62, and 172.16.0.63).

   b. Type **www.zone*X*.com** again and press **Enter**. Note that the order of the three IP addresses (172.16.0.62, 172.16.0.63, and 172.16.0.61) has been rotated using round robin.

   c. Type **ftp.zone*X*.com** and press **Enter**. Note that ftp.zone*X*.com is an alias to server2 .zone*X*.com, which has an IP address of 172.16.0.64.

   d. Type **172.16.0.64** and press **Enter**. Note that 172.16.0.4 is associated with the FQDN of server2.zone*X*.com.

   e. Type **set type=mx** and press **Enter**. Next, type **zonex.com** and press **Enter**. Note that the mail server for zonex.com is server3.zone*X*.com, which has an IP address of 172.16.0.65.

   f. Type **exit** and press **Enter** to quit the nslookup utility.

   g. Type **exit** again and press **Enter** to close the Command Prompt window.

10. Close DNS Manager.

Project 8-3: Configuring DNS Secondary Zones

In this Hands-On Project, you install the DNS Server role on your WindowsServer2019VM2 virtual machine, configure a secondary zone for zone*X*.com, and perform a zone transfer.

1. In Server Manager on your Windows Server 2019 host, select the **Tools** menu and then click **Hyper-V Manager**.

   a. Highlight **WindowsServer2019VM2** in the virtual machines pane of Hyper-V Manager and click **Connect** in the Actions pane. In the Virtual Machine Connection window, click **Start** to boot your virtual machine.

   b. At the login screen, click the **Ctrl+Alt+Delete** button in the Virtual Machine Connection window, supply the password **Secret555** for Administrator and press **Enter** to log into the system.

2. On your WindowsServer2019VM2 virtual machine, click **Start** and then click **Server Manager**. Next, click the **Manage** menu and then click **Add Roles and Features**.

   a. At the Select installation type page, click **Next**.

   b. At the Select destination server page, click **Next**.

   c. At the Select server roles page, select **DNS Server** and click **Add Features** when prompted. Click **Next**.

   d. At the Select features page, click **Next**.

   e. At the DNS Server page, click **Next**.

   f. At the Confirm installation selections page, click **Install**.

   g. At the Installation progress page, click **Close**.

3. In Server Manager, click the **Tools** menu and then click **DNS**.

4. In the navigation pane of the DNS Manager window, expand your server object, and expand **Forward Lookup Zones**. Next, right-click **Forward Lookup Zones** and click **New Zone**.

   a. At the New Zone Wizard, click **Next**.

   b. At the Zone Type page, note that the option to store the zone in Active Directory is unavailable because WindowsServer2019VM2 is not a domain controller. Select **Secondary zone** and click **Next**.

   c. At the Zone Name page, type **zone*X*.com** and click **Next**.

   d. At the Master DNS Servers page, type the IP address of your Windows Server 2019 host and press **Enter**. Note that SERVER*X* is shown next to the IP address and click **Next**.

   e. Click **Finish** to create zone*X*.com.

5. Highlight **zone*X*.com** in the navigation pane and note the error indicating that the zone has not been loaded by the DNS server.

6. Right-click **zone*X*.com** in the navigation pane and click **Transfer from Master** to perform the initial zone transfer. Next, right-click **zone*X*.com** in the navigation pane and click **Refresh**. Note that the records you configured in zone*X*.com on your Windows Server 2019 host are present.

7. Right-click **zone*X*.com** in the navigation pane and note that there are no options available to create resource records. Click **Properties** and highlight the **Start of**

Authority (SOA) tab. Note that you are unable to modify the configuration of the secondary zone parameters and click **OK**.

8. Close DNS Manager.

Project 8-4: Installing and Configuring WINS

In this Hands-On Project, you install and configure WINS on your Windows Server 2019 host as well as configure your WindowsServer2019VM2 virtual machine to use WINS for NetBIOS name resolution.

1. In Server Manager on your Windows Server 2019 host, click the **Manage** menu and then click **Add Roles and Features**.

   a. At the Select installation type page, click **Next**.

   b. At the Select destination server page, click **Next**.

   c. At the Select server roles page, click **Next**.

   d. At the Select features page, select **WINS Server** and click **Add Features** when prompted. Click **Next**.

   e. At the Confirm installation selections page, click **Install**.

   f. At the Installation progress page, click **Close**.

2. In Server Manager, click the **Tools** menu and then click **WINS**.

3. In the navigation pane of the WINS tool, expand your server object, right-click **Active Registrations,** and click **New Static Mapping**.

4. At the New Static Mapping window, type **SERVER*X*** in the Computer name text box. Next, type the IP address of your Windows Server 2019 host in the IP address text box and click **OK**.

5. Right-click **Active Registrations**, click **Display Records**, and then click **Find Now**.

6. Highlight **Active Registrations** and note that three NetBIOS name records were created for SERVER*X*, indicating that it is running the WorkStation, Messenger, and File Server services.

7. In Server Manager on your WindowsServer2019VM2 virtual machine, navigate to **Local Server**. In the Properties section, click the hyperlink next to your Ethernet network interface.

   a. In the Network Connections window, right-click your Ethernet adapter and click **Properties**.

   b. In the Ethernet Properties window, highlight **Internet Protocol Version 4 (TCP/IPv4)** and click **Properties**.

   c. Click **Advanced** and highlight the **WINS** tab.

   d. Click **Add**, type the IP address of your Windows Server 2019 host in the WINS server text box, and click **Add**.

   e. Click **OK** to close the Advanced TCP/IP Settings window.

   f. Click **OK** to close the Internet Protocol Version 4 (TCP/IPv4) Properties window.

   g. Click **Close** to close the Ethernet Properties window, and then close the Network Connections window.

8. In the WINS tool on your Windows Server 2019 host, right-click **Active Registrations** in the navigation pane and click **Refresh**. Note that a NetBIOS name record was created for your WindowsServer2019VM2 virtual machine, indicating that it is a File Server.

9. Close the WINS tool.

10. Shut down your WindowsServer2019VM2 virtual machine when finished.

Project 8-5: Installing and Configuring DHCP

In this Hands-On Project, you install the DHCP Server role on your Windows Server 2019 host as well as configure a new DHCP scope, reservation, and policy.

1. In Server Manager on your Windows Server 2019 host, click the **Manage** menu and then click **Add Roles and Features**.

   a. At the Select installation type page, click **Next**.

   b. At the Select destination server page, click **Next**.

   c. At the Select server roles page, select **DHCP Server**, and click **Add Features** when prompted. Click **Next**.

   d. At the Select features page, click **Next**.

   e. At the DHCP Server page, read the information regarding best practices and click **Next**.

   f. Click **Install**.

   g. After the installation has completed, click **Complete DHCP configuration**, click **Next**, click **Commit**, and then click **Close**.

   h. Click **Close** to close the Add Roles and Features Wizard.

2. In Server Manager, select the **Tools** menu and then click **DHCP**.

3. In the DHCP tool, expand your server in the navigation pane and then expand IPv4. Note that the *Scope [172.16.0.0] Internal Network* scope you configured in Hands-On Project 3-3 is available. This is because DHCP configuration is not removed when you remove the DHCP Server role.

   a. Expand **Scope [172.16.0.0] Internal Network** and highlight **Address Pool**. Note the address range of 172.16.0.50 to 172.16.0.100.

   b. Highlight **Scope Options**. Note that the only option configured is 060 PXEClient, used for WDS deployment.

4. Highlight **Scope [172.16.0.0] Internal Network** in the navigation pane and click **More Actions**, **Delete** in the Actions pane. Click **Yes**, and then click **Yes** again to remove your scope.

5. Highlight **Server Options** in the navigation pane and click **More Actions**, **Configure Options** in the Actions pane.

   a. In the Server Options window, check **004 Time Server**.

   b. Type **time.windows.com** in the Server name text box and click **Resolve**.

   c. Click **Add**.

   d. Click **OK** to close the Server Options window. Note that both the 004 Time Server and 060 PXEClient server options are displayed.

6. Highlight **IPv4** in the navigation pane and click **More Actions**, **New Scope** in the Actions pane.

   a. In the Welcome page of the New Scope Wizard, click **Next**.

   b. At the Scope Name page, type **Marketing LAN** in the Name text box and click **Next**.

   c. At the IP Address Range page, supply a Start IP address of **172.16.0.100**. Next, supply an End IP address of **172.16.0.200** and click **Next**.

   d. At the Add Exclusions and Delay page, type **172.16.0.150** in the Start IP address text box, click **Add,** and click **Next**.

   e. At the Lease Duration page, note the default value of 8 days and click **Next**.

   f. At the Configure DHCP Options page, click **Next**.

   g. At the Router (Default Gateway) page, type **172.16.0.1** in the IP address text box, click **Add,** and click **Next**.

   h. At the Domain Name and DNS Servers page, note that the DHCP server is configured to provide the domainX.com domain name suffix and DNS server of 172.16.0.1 to DHCP clients and click **Next**.

   i. At the WINS Servers page, type **172.16.0.1** in the IP address text box, click **Add,** and click **Next**.

   j. At the Activate Scope page, note that the scope will be activated following creation and click **Next**.

   k. Click **Finish** to complete the New Scope Wizard.

7. Expand **Scope [172.16.0.0] Marketing LAN** and highlight **Address Pool**. Note that the address range and exclusion you configured are present.

8. Highlight **Scope Options**. Note the options that were configured during the New Scope Wizard as well as the two options that were inherited from the server.

9. Highlight **Reservations** and click **More Actions**, **New Reservation** in the Actions pane.

   a. At the New Reservation window, type **HPLaserJet_6MP** in the Reservation name text box.

   b. Type **172.16.0.170** in the IP address text box.

   c. Type **f20000ada4d5** in the MAC address text box and click **Add**.

   d. Click **Close**.

10. Expand **Reservations** and highlight **[172.16.0.170] HPLaserJet_6MP**. Note the options inherited from both the scope and server.

11. Highlight **Policies** under Scope [172.16.0.0] Marketing LAN. In the Actions pane, click **More Actions**, **New Policy**.

   a. At the DHCP Policy Configuration Wizard, type **Polycom VoIP phones** in the Policy Name dialog box and click **Next**.

   b. At the Configure Conditions for the policy page, click **Add**. Select **Client Identifier** from the Criteria drop-down box, type **4E00D5** in the Value text box, click **Add,** and then click **OK**. Click **Next** when finished.

> **Note** 📎
>
> Polycom VoIP phones use a client identifier value of 4E00D5 in DHCPDISCOVER packets.

    c. At the Configure settings for the policy page, select **No** and click **Next**.

    d. At the next Configure settings for the policy page, check **003 Router**, type **172.16.0.254** in the IP address text box, and click **Add**. Click **Next**.

> **Note** 📎
>
> The default gateway for VoIP phones should be set to the IP address of the server that provides for VoIP functionality (also called a PBX).

    e. Click **Finish** to create a policy for the scope that provides a different default gateway for Polycom VoIP phones.

12. Highlight **Scope [172.16.0.0] Marketing LAN** and click **More Actions**, **Properties** in the Actions pane.

    a. On the General tab of Scope [172.16.0.0] Marketing LAN Properties, note that you can modify all scope parameters except for the subnet mask as well as set an unlimited lease duration.

    b. Highlight the **DNS** tab and note the default values. Select **Always dynamically update DNS records** and check **Dynamically update DNS records for DHCP clients that do not request updates**.

    c. Click **Configure**, check **Enable Name Protection,** and click **OK**.

    d. Click **OK** to close the Scope [172.16.0.0] Marketing LAN Properties window.

Project 8-6: DHCP Testing and Fault Tolerance

In this Hands-On Project, you install a second network interface on your WindowsServer2019VM2 virtual machine to test the scope you created in Hands-On Project 8-5. Next, you install the DHCP Server role on your WindowsServer2019VM2 virtual machine and configure fault tolerance for the scope.

1. In Hyper-V Manager on your Windows Server 2019 host, highlight **WindowsServer2019VM2** in the Virtual Machines pane and click **Settings** in the Actions pane.

    a. Select **Network Adapter** in the Add Hardware pane and click **Add**.

    b. In the Network Adapter pane, select **Internal Virtual Switch** to connect the new network interface to the internal network and click **OK**.

2. Highlight **WindowsServer2019VM2** in the virtual machines pane of Hyper-V Manager and click **Connect** in the Actions pane.

    a. In the Virtual Machine Connection window, click **Start** to boot your virtual machine.

    b. At the login screen, click the **Ctrl+Alt+Delete** button in the Virtual Machine Connection window, supply the password **Secret555** for Administrator, and press **Enter** to log into the system.

3. On your WindowsServer2019VM2 virtual machine, click **Start** and then click **Server Manager**. Navigate to **Local Server**. In the Properties section, click the hyperlink next to your Ethernet 2 network interface.

   a. In the Network Connections window, right-click your Ethernet 2 network interface and click **Status**.

   b. In the Ethernet 2 Status window, click **Details**. Note that your Ethernet 2 network interface received the first available IP address from the scope configured in Hands-On Project 8-5 (172.16.0.100) as well as the correct default gateway, DNS server, domain name suffix, and WINS server options.

   c. Click **Close** to close the Network Connection Details window.

   d. Click **Close** to close the Ethernet 2 Status window, and then close the Network Connections window.

4. In Server Manager on your WindowsServer2019VM2 virtual machine, click the **Manage** menu and then click **Add Roles and Features**.

   a. At the Select installation type page, click **Next**.

   b. At the Select destination server page, click **Next**.

   c. At the Select server roles page, select **DHCP Server**, and click **Add Features** when prompted. Click **Next**.

   d. At the Select features page, click **Next**.

   e. At the DHCP Server page, read the information regarding best practices and click **Next**.

   f. Click **Install**.

   g. After the installation has completed, click **Complete DHCP configuration**, click **Next**, click **Commit**, and then click **Close**.

   h. Click **Close** to close the Add Roles and Features Wizard.

5. In the DHCP tool on your Windows Server 2019 host, highlight **Address Leases** under Scope [172.16.0.0] Marketing LAN. Note the address lease assigned to your WindowsServer2019VM2 virtual machine. Also note that the reservation for HPLaserJet_6MP is displayed.

6. Highlight **Scope [172.16.0.0] Marketing LAN** and click **More Actions**, **Display Statistics** in the Actions pane. Note that two IP addresses are in use from your scope (equivalent to 2% of your scope). Click **Close** when finished.

7. Highlight **IPv4** and click **More Actions**, **Configure Failover** in the Actions pane.

   a. At the Configure Failover wizard, note that all available scopes are selected and click **Next**.

   b. At the Specify the partner server to use for failover page, type **172.16.0.100** in the Partner Server text box and click **Next**.

   c. At the Create a new failover relationship page, note the default options, type **Secret555** in the Shared Secret text box, and click **Next**.

   d. Click **Finish** to complete the failover configuration.

   e. Click **Close** to close the Configure Failover window.

   f. Close the DHCP tool.

8. In Server Manager on your WindowsServer2019VM2 virtual machine, click the **Tools** menu and then click **DHCP**.

9. In the DHCP tool, expand your server, and then expand **IPv4**. Note that Scope [172.16.0.0] Marketing LAN has automatically been copied from your Windows Server 2019 host.

10. Expand **Scope [172.16.0.0] Marketing LAN** and highlight **Address Leases**. Note that the address lease for your WindowsServer2019VM2 virtual machine is present to ensure that your DHCP server does not lease the 172.16.0.100 address to DHCP clients. Also note that the reservation for HPLaserJet_6MP is displayed to ensure that your DHCP server will provide the correct IP address if a DHCPDISCOVER packet it received from HPLaserJet_6MP printer.

11. Close the DHCP tool.

Discovery Exercises

Exercise 8-1

In Hands-On Project 8-1, you configured an Active Directory-integrated reverse lookup zone for the 172.16.0 network that replicates to all domain controllers in the domainX.com domain. In Discovery Exercise 4-2, you configured WindowsServer2019VM1 as a second domain controller for domainX.com. Boot your WindowsServer2019VM1 virtual machine, open DNS Manager, and verify that the 0.16.172.in-addr.arpa reverse lookup zone exists and contains the appropriate resource records configured in Hands-On Project 8-2. If the 0.16.172.in-addr.arpa reverse lookup zone is not available on WindowsServer2019VM1, use the Active Directory Sites and Services tool to force replication between the TorontoSite and ChicagoSite to ensure that the zone is replicated immediately from your Windows Server 2019 host (in the TorontoSite) to your WindowsServer2019VM1 virtual machine (in the ChicagoSite).

Exercise 8-2

DNS lookup security has been a focus in the technology community for the past decade. Technologies such as *DNS over HTTPS (DoH)* and *DNS over TLS (DoT)* have been recently proposed for widespread use. Once DNS security technology that is currently supported in Windows Server 2019 is *Domain Name System Security Extensions (DNSSEC)*, which can be used to digitally sign resource records using encryption keys to validate their authenticity to clients. In DNS Manager on your Windows Server 2019 host, right-click **zoneX.com** and select **DNSSEC**, **Sign the Zone**. Select the default options as necessary during the wizard to generate encryption keys that are used to digitally sign the records in the zone. Next, refresh the list of resource records in zoneX.com to view your results. Note that each resource record is also assigned a *Resource Record Signature (RRSIG)* resource record. You will also see *Next Secure 3 (NSEC3)* resource records that are used to respond to invalid forward lookup requests as well as *DNSKEY* resource records that hold the encryption keys used to validate the *RRSIG* and *NSEC3* resource records. When finished, right-click **zoneX.com**, select **DNSSEC**, **Unsign the Zone**, and follow the prompts to remove your DNSSEC configuration for zone*X*.com.

Exercise 8-3

Larger organizations often use more than one zone to hold resource records in the organization. Many of these organizations use a domain name for the parent organization (e.g.,domain *X*.com) and subdomains for each division in the organization (e.g., support.domain*X*.com). You can create resource records for support.domain*X*.com on the same DNS server that hosts the zone for domain*X*.com by creating a domain folder under the domain*X*.com zone for support.domain*X*.com. Alternatively, the DNS server that hosts the zone for domain*X*.com can be configured to relay lookup requests to another DNS server in the organization that hosts the zone for support.domain*X*.com (similar to a recursive query involving a top-level DNS server) by creating a delegation for support.domain*X*.com under the domain*X*.com zone.

- In DNS Manager on your Windows Server 2019 host, right-click **domainX.com**, click **New Domain**, and type **support** to create a folder under domain*X*.com called support that can contain resource records for support.domain*X*.com. Next, create some example resource records in this support folder and test your results using the `nslookup` command. Finally, remove the support folder.
- In DNS Manager on your WindowsServer2019VM2 virtual machine, create a new primary zone for support.domain*X*.com and populate it with some example resource records. Next, in DNS Manager on your Windows Server 2019 host, right-click **domainX.com**, click **New Delegation**, and follow the wizard to relay lookup requests for support.domain*X*.com to your WindowsServer2019VM2 virtual machine. Finally, test your results using the `nslookup` command.

Exercise 8-4

In Hands-On Project 8-4, you configured your Windows Server 2019 host as a WINS server and your WindowsServer2019VM2 virtual machine as a WINS client. Most organizations that implement WINS configure multiple WINS servers as replication partners for fault tolerance. Install WINS on your WindowsServer2019VM2 virtual machine and configure it as a replication partner for the WINS server on your Windows Server 2019 host. Finally, verify that the NetBIOS name records on your Windows Server 2019 host were successfully replicated to your WindowsServer2019VM2 virtual machine by examining the Active Registrations folder in the WINS tool on your WindowsServer2019VM2 virtual machine.

Exercise 8-5

Although devices and network interfaces typically use ICMPv6 router discovery to obtain an IPv6 configuration, you can also configure an IPv6 scope on a Windows Server 2019 DHCP server to provide IPv6 addresses on the network. In the DHCP tool on your Windows Server 2019 host, configure a new IPv6 scope that leases addresses on an IPv6 network that uses the prefix **2001:db8:3c4d::** for 8 days. Also ensure that the DHCP server is configured to always update the DNS AAAA and PTR records for each computer that leases an IPv6 address.

CONFIGURING AND MANAGING REMOTE ACCESS SERVICES

After completing this module, you will be able to:

Identify methods used to provide remote access in an organization

Describe the components used to provide for VPN remote access

Configure a remote access server for VPN remote access

Configure RADIUS to support VPN remote access

Describe how DirectAccess can be used to enable automated remote access

Implement remote access using DirectAccess

Identify the components that enable remote access using Remote Desktop and RemoteApp

Configure Remote Desktop Services

In today's mobile landscape, users often require access to organization resources when using a computer outside of the organization network. As a server administrator, you must know how to provide secure remote access to these resources for the users in your organization. In this module, you'll examine the technologies and methods that users can employ to obtain remote access to an organization network. Additionally, you'll learn how to configure VPNs, RADIUS, DirectAccess, and Remote Desktop Services to provide for remote access.

Understanding Organization Networks and Remote Access

Most organizations use a network structure that separates department LANs that contain client PCs from a DMZ network that contains servers, as shown in Figure 9-1.

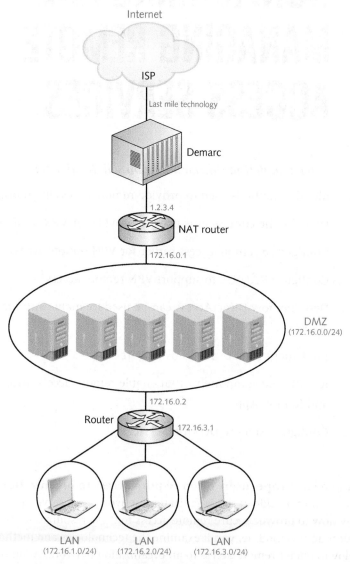

Figure 9-1   A sample network structure

PCs in each department LAN can access the servers in the DMZ via a router that connects the networks, as well as the Internet to which the DMZ is connected. Unless the organization uses IPv6 exclusively, the router that connects the DMZ to the Internet will implement NAT in order to allow networks in the organization to use a reserved IPv4 range and obtain Internet access via a single public IP address. In Figure 9-1, the three department LANs use the 172.16.1.0/24, 172.16.2.0/24, and 172.16.3.0/24 reserved IPv4 ranges, and the DMZ uses the 172.16.0.0/24 reserved IPv4 range. The NAT router connects to the Internet using an external network interface that has a public IP address (1.2.3.4) and connects to the DMZ using an internal network interface that has a reserved IP address (172.16.0.1). Each PC in a department LAN can use its default gateway (set to the associated network interface for the department LAN router) to access the other LANs in the organization. For example, the default gateway for PCs in the 172.16.3.0/24 LAN shown in Figure 9-1 is set to 172.16.3.1 to provide access to the DMZ and other department LANs. To provide Internet access, the department LAN router is configured with a default gateway of 172.16.0.1 to allow packets that are not destined for the DMZ or a department LAN to reach the Internet.

Note

A NAT router like the one shown in Figure 9-1 often contains additional management and security capabilities, such as traffic throttling, intrusion prevention, and malware filtering. In this case, the NAT router is often referred to as a **Next Generation Firewall (NGFW)**.

Although most organizations implement a network structure similar to Figure 9-1, the methods by which organizations connect to the Internet vary by region and technology. Because the Internet is composed of several ISPs that are interconnected by very fast fiber optic connections, the speed at which your organization can transfer information across the Internet is limited by the speed of the technology that connects the organization to the ISP. These technologies are called **last mile technologies** because they often span the "last mile" between the Internet and the organization. Common last mile technologies used to connect to an ISP include:

- **Digital subscriber line (DSL)**, which uses a telephone network.
- **Cable broadband**, which uses a television cable network.
- **Gigabit Passive Optical Network (GPON)**, which uses fiber optic cable.
- **Long-range Wi-Fi**, which uses radio wireless, often using wireless transmitters positioned in a line of sight.

Note

To communicate to an ISP using IP across a telephone network, DSL encloses Ethernet frames in a protocol called **Point-to-Point Protocol over Ethernet (PPPoE)**.

In most cases, the organization NAT router is connected to a **demarcation point** (often shortened to **demarc**) that connects to the ISP using a last mile technology.

The demarc is a translation device or router with a specialized network interface for the last mile technology that passes traffic directly between the ISP and NAT router.

The structure shown in Figure 9-1 allows client computers in the department LANs to access servers in the DMZ and on the Internet. However, there may be times when members of the organization need to connect to resources hosted on servers in the DMZ from outside the organization, for example, when an executive or sales team member needs to access work files on a file server in the organization when on a business trip. In this case, you need to provide access to these resources using a **remote access** technology. To provide for remote access, at least one server in your DMZ must be configured as a **remote access server** that accepts requests from **remote access clients** on the Internet, as shown in Figure 9-2. To access resources on other servers in the DMZ, the remote access client must first connect to the remote access server in the DMZ, using encryption provided by the remote access server. The remote access server then authenticates the user before allowing remote access. In most cases, the remote access server authenticates each remote access user to an Active Directory domain to provide access to the resources in the DMZ network.

To access a remote access server, the remote access client must connect to the public IP of the NAT router (1.2.3.4), which is often resolved using a host record in a DNS zone that is publicly registered with the top-level DNS servers. Additionally, the NAT router must be configured to forward remote access requests to the IP address of the remote access server (172.16.0.50). This forwarding functionality is often called **port forwarding** or **service forwarding**, and allows requests for a particular port or service to be forwarded to an internal server in the DMZ. If the NAT router is also a NGFW, a **reverse proxy** can be configured instead of port forwarding. In addition to forwarding remote access requests, reverse proxies interpret all service requests, and can deny access to traffic it deems malicious as a result.

Note

To configure port forwarding or reverse proxy, consult the documentation for your NAT router or NGFW model.

Alternatively, organizations can connect remote access servers directly to a demarc, as shown in Figure 9-3. In this case, the remote access server must have two network interfaces. One network interface is connected to the demarc and assigned a public IP address (1.2.3.5) that is resolved using a host record in a publicly registered DNS zone, and another network interface is used to connect to the DMZ (172.16.0.50). While no additional configuration is required on the NAT router to allow for this type of remote access, the remote access server is exposed directly to the Internet. As a result, it must have a firewall (and preferably additional security software) enabled to ensure that the security of the remote access server is not compromised.

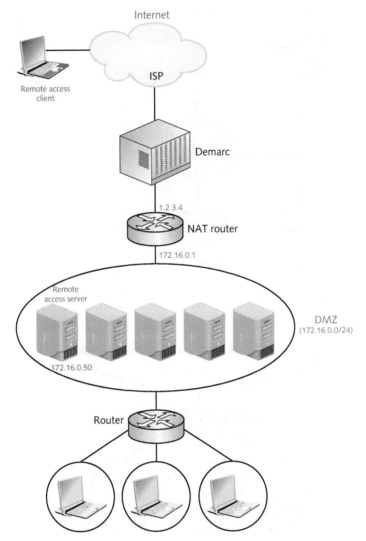

Figure 9-2 Providing remote access via a remote access server in the DMZ

Note 🖉

The design of networks and remote access depends on the needs of the organization and the capabilities of the network hardware implemented. Although the example network structure shown in Figures 9-1 through 9-3 is common to many organizations, it will vary from organization to organization. However, this network structure provides a standard context that we'll use when discussing remote access throughout this module.

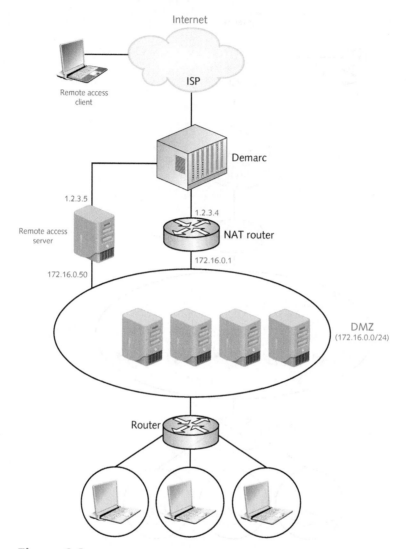

Figure 9-3 Providing remote access via a remote access server connected to the DMZ

Note

Some NGFWs contain built-in remote access server functionality, eliminating the need for a separate remote access server.

> **Note**
>
> Providing remote access may require that you upgrade the available bandwidth on the last mile technology used in the organization.

Microsoft provides three main remote access technologies that can be used to obtain access to servers in a DMZ from across the Internet:

- Virtual private networks (VPNs)
- DirectAccess
- Remote Desktop Services

Each of these remote access technologies provides its own protocols, as well as supports different authentication and encryption types.

> **Note** @
>
> Before Internet access became common, remote access clients used a dial-up modem to dial the telephone number of a modem bank that was connected to a remote access server in the organization. This was called **dial-up remote access**, and used the **Point-to-Point Protocol (PPP)** to relay IP packets across the telephone network instead of the Internet. While Microsoft still supports dial-up remote access across a telephone network, it is rare today. As a result, we will limit our discussion in this module to remote access technologies that use the Internet.

Understanding VPNs

Virtual private networks (VPNs) have been used for remote access across the Internet since the 1990s and continue to be the most widely implemented remote access technology today. Before you implement a VPN solution in your organization, you must first understand how VPNs can be used for remote access. You must also understand the different VPN protocols and authentication types available, as well as how RADIUS can be used to provide for centralized VPN authentication, logging, and policies.

Using VPNs for Remote Access

A virtual private network (VPN) is a remote access technology that provides encryption for data that is sent across the Internet between a remote access client and server. When a remote access client connects to a VPN, a "virtual" network is created between the remote access client and server that is used in addition to the underlying physical network. Data that is sent on the virtual network is encrypted automatically and can only be decrypted by the remote access server or client.

Note

The virtual network that is created by a VPN is also called an **overlay network**, because it must use the underlying physical network for all data transmission.

Because VPNs provide an encrypted channel (or "tunnel") between systems on a network, they are often referred to as **VPN tunnels**. Moreover, each end of the VPN tunnel is represented by a virtual network interface that is configured with an IP address, as shown in Figure 9-4.

In Figure 9-4, the remote access server identifies its side of the VPN tunnel using a virtual network interface that has the IP address 172.16.0.100, while the remote access client identifies its side of the VPN tunnel using a virtual network interface that has the IP address 172.16.0.101. The address range used by the VPN can be manually configured on the remote access server or obtained from a scope on a DHCP server in the DMZ if the remote access server is also configured as a DHCP relay agent.

Note

The IP network used for the VPN does not need to match the IP network used by the DMZ if the remote access server is also configured as a router. For example, if the remote access server in Figure 9-4 uses the IP address 192.168.1.100 for its virtual network interface, and the remote access client uses the IP address 192.168.1.101 for its virtual network interface, the remote access server will automatically route traffic from the VPN network (192.168.1.0/24) to the DMZ network (172.16.0.0/24) if it is also configured as a router.

Furthermore, the default gateway configured in the VPN network interface on the remote access client is automatically set to 0.0.0.0 to ensure that all IP packets generated by the remote access client are encrypted and sent on the VPN to the remote access server. The remote access server then decrypts these IP packets and relays them to the DMZ network to allow users to access resources in the organization.

Because all IP packets are sent to the remote access server across a VPN, requests for Internet resources from remote access clients (e.g., to a webpage such as *www.google.com*) are forwarded by the remote access server to the NAT router or NGFW in the organization, before being sent to the Internet. This allows the NAT router or NGFW in an organization to perform malware scanning or restrict access to certain Internet sites for remote access clients. However, if remote access clients configure **split tunneling** in the properties of their VPN network interface, they will be able to access the resources in their organization's DMZ across the VPN tunnel, but will use the default gateway on their physical network interface to access Internet resources.

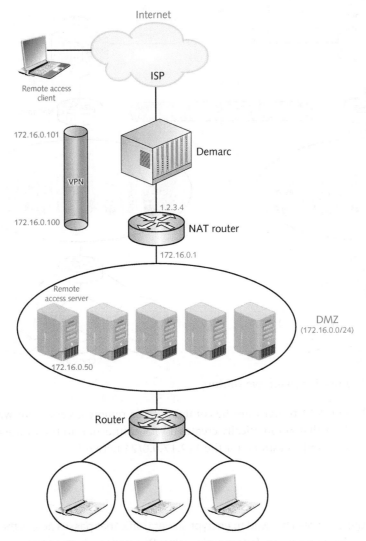

Figure 9-4   A VPN tunnel between a remote access client and server

Using VPNs to Protect Network Traffic

Although VPNs can be used to encrypt IP traffic that passes across the Internet between a remote access client and server, they can also be used to encrypt IP traffic that passes across the Internet between two routers at different locations in an organization, as shown in Figure 9-5. For example, if a computer in Toronto needs to access a resource on a server in the Chicago DMZ, the NAT router in Toronto can create a VPN connection to the NAT router in Chicago to ensure that the traffic is encrypted as it passes over the Internet. In this case, the Chicago NAT router must be configured as a remote access

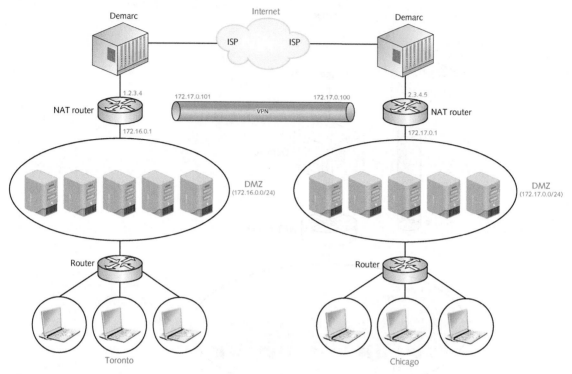

Figure 9-5 A VPN tunnel between two routers

server, and the Toronto NAT router must be configured as a remote access client with a **demand-dial interface** that automatically creates a VPN connection to the Chicago NAT router when it receives traffic destined for the 172.17.0.0/24 network.

> **Note** 🔗
>
> VPNs between routers can also be used to encrypt server traffic that passes across the Internet between different locations, for example, Active Directory replication between domain controllers, or folder content that is synchronized between file servers using DFS replication.

> **Note** 🔗
>
> Most organizations use a hardware-based router or NGFW appliance to provide VPNs between different locations in an organization. However, you can instead configure a Windows Server 2019 system as a router that provides VPNs between locations.

VPN Protocols

Many different VPN technologies have been developed since the 1990s, and each one uses a specific **VPN protocol** to tunnel traffic. When you implement a remote access server using Windows Server 2019, four different VPN protocols are supported:

- **Point-to-Point Tunneling Protocol (PPTP)** is one of the oldest and most widely supported VPN protocols. It was developed by a consortium of vendors including Microsoft and encrypts data using **Microsoft Point-to-Point Encryption (MPPE)**. Although MPPE supports encryption keys varying in length from 40 to 128 bits, modern Windows operating systems such as Windows 10 and Windows Server 2019 contain a registry key that prevent the use of MPPE keys less than 128 bits by default.
- **Layer Two Tunneling Protocol (L2TP)** is a VPN protocol developed by Microsoft and Cisco. It provides for tunneling only and relies on **IP Security (IPSec)** for the encryption of data packets using encryption keys varying in length from 56 to 256 bits. To participate in an L2TP VPN, the remote access client and server must authenticate to each other. To do this, you can configure the same preshared key (password) or install an IPSec encryption certificate on both the remote access client and server.
- **Internet Key Exchange version 2 (IKEv2)** is an enhancement to IPSec that provides VPN tunneling with faster speeds compared to L2TP. It uses 256-bit encryption keys and requires that remote access clients and servers authenticate to each other using an IPSec encryption certificate or preshared key.
- **Secure Socket Tunneling Protocol (SSTP)** is a VPN technology that tunnels data through HTTPS packets on a network. It originally used **Secure Sockets Layer (SSL)** encryption with 128-bit keys. However, modern SSTP implementations use 256-bit keys alongside **Transport Layer Security (TLS)** encryption. To use SSTP, the remote access server must contain an HTTPS encryption certificate.

Note

The configuration of IPSec and HTTPS encryption certificates is discussed in Module 11.

If your remote access server is connected to a NAT router or NGFW, you will need to ensure that the NAT router or NGFW is configured to relay traffic for each supported VPN protocol to the remote access server in the DMZ using port forwarding or reverse proxy. Alternatively, if your remote access server connects directly to the demarc, you must ensure that the firewall on the remote access server allows access to the appropriate VPN protocol. If the configuration tool for the NAT router, NGFW or firewall does not allow you to specify the name of each VPN protocol, you must instead specify the associated port numbers. Table 9-1 lists the port numbers and associated transport protocols (TCP or UDP) used for each VPN protocol supported by Windows Server 2019.

Table 9-1   **VPN protocol port numbers**

VPN Protocol	Port Numbers
Point-to-Point Tunneling Protocol (PPTP)	1723/TCP
Layer Two Tunneling Protocol (L2TP)	1701/TCP, 500/UDP, 4500/UDP (if using NAT)
Internet Key Exchange version 2 (IKEv2)	1701/TCP, 500/UDP, 4500/UDP (if using NAT)
Secure Socket Tunneling Protocol (SSTP)	443/TCP

Note

In addition to port 1723/TCP, PPTP also requires that you allow for the **Generic Routing Encapsulation (GRE)** protocol in a port forwarding, reverse proxy, or firewall configuration. GRE is identified by protocol number 47.

VPN Authentication

Before a VPN tunnel can be established, the remote access client must first authenticate to the remote access server using credentials. The different authentication methods that can be used to protect these credentials as they pass from the remote access client to a Windows Server 2019 remote access server are summarized in Table 9-2.

Note

Remote access clients and servers will use the most secure authentication method that both computers support. The authentication methods summarized in Table 9-2 are listed in order from least secure (PAP) to most secure (EAP).

Table 9-2   **Microsoft VPN authentication methods**

Authentication Method	Description
Password Authentication Protocol (PAP)	Transmits user passwords across the network in plain text (unencrypted). This makes it unsuitable for use except as a last resort for clients that support no other authentication methods.
Challenge Handshake Authentication Protocol (CHAP)	Does not transmit user passwords across the network, but uses the password to generate a hash of a message that is validated by the other system using a challenge and response mechanism. While CHAP is widely supported by many different operating systems and technologies, it cannot be used for PPTP VPNs.

Table 9-2   **Microsoft VPN authentication methods** *(continued)*

Authentication Method	Description
Microsoft Challenge Handshake Authentication Protocol version 2 (MS-CHAP v2)	A version of CHAP supported natively by Microsoft operating systems that provides stronger authentication mechanisms. In addition to authenticating user credentials, MS-CHAP v2 performs authentication for the computers involved in the connection and varies encryption keys with each new connection.
Extensible Authentication Protocol (EAP)	This is not an authentication method as much as it is an authentication system that allows multiple authentication methods to be configured. The client and server can negotiate which EAP authentication method to use. The default EAP authentication methods included with Windows Server 2019 include EAP-MSCHAP v2, Protected EAP (PEAP), and Smart Card or other certificate (also called EAP-TLS).

After the remote access server receives credentials from the remote access client, it must validate them before providing remote access. If the remote access server is joined to an Active Directory domain, it will forward the credentials to a domain controller in the DMZ. If the credentials match those in the user account, and **dial-in permission** is granted in the properties of the user account, the domain controller will allow the remote access connection and return a Kerberos ticket for the user to the remote access server. The remote access server will then create the VPN tunnel, send the Kerberos ticket to the remote access client, and relay traffic from the VPN to the DMZ to allow for resource access.

Using RADIUS

You can optionally configure a remote access server to forward credentials it receives from a remote access client to a **Remote Access Dial-In User Authentication Service (RADIUS)** server instead of a domain controller. RADIUS is a protocol designed to centralize authentication and logging for large distributed networks. Originally intended for dial-up remote access, RADIUS is now used for VPN remote access and other devices that require centralized authentication and logging, such as network switches and wireless access points.

Note

If you configure a remote access server to forward credentials or logging events to a RADIUS server, the remote access server is called a **RADIUS client**.

Note

To provide centralized authentication and logging, you can configure multiple remote access servers as RADIUS clients that forward credentials and logging events to a single RADIUS server.

After a RADIUS server receives credentials from a remote access server, it forwards them to a domain controller for validation. After the domain controller validates the credentials and dial-in permission, it returns the Kerberos ticket for the user to the RADIUS server. The RADIUS server then checks its **remote access policies** to ensure that the user meets necessary requirements before allowing the remote access connection and forwarding the Kerberos ticket to the remote access server. The remote access server will then create the VPN tunnel, send the Kerberos ticket to the remote access client, and relay traffic from the VPN to the DMZ to allow for resource access.

Note

Remote access policies can specify restrictions that must be met prior to obtaining a VPN tunnel, such as time of day, VPN protocol, or authentication method. Additionally, remote access policies can specify restrictions that must be enforced by the remote access server after a VPN connection has been created, such as the maximum time that an idle session can remain connected.

Note

Active Directory user accounts are configured by default to allow a RADIUS server the ability to validate dial-in permission. In this case, the permission specified in a remote access policy is used to allow VPN access instead of the dial-in permission in the Active Directory user account.

Implementing VPNs

To implement remote access using VPNs in your organization, you must install and configure a remote access server, and optionally configure a RADIUS server to provide for centralized authentication and logging, as well as remote access policies. Next, you must configure remote access clients to connect to the remote access server. To protect traffic between two networks using VPNs, you can configure demand-dial interfaces on the routers in your organization.

Configuring a Remote Access Server

To configure Windows Server 2019 as a remote access server for VPN access, you must first install the **Remote Access** server role. When you select this role in the Add Roles and Features Wizard and progress through the wizard, you are prompted to choose the remote access components that you wish to install, as shown in Figure 9-6. At minimum, you should select the *DirectAccess and VPN (RAS)* role service. If you wish to use a different IP network for your VPN and DMZ, or obtain the IP configuration for your VPN using a DHCP relay agent, you must also select the *Routing* role service. Instead of performing remote access, the *Web Application Proxy* role service shown in Figure 9-6 is used to relay Internet requests for Web apps to a Web server in your organization.

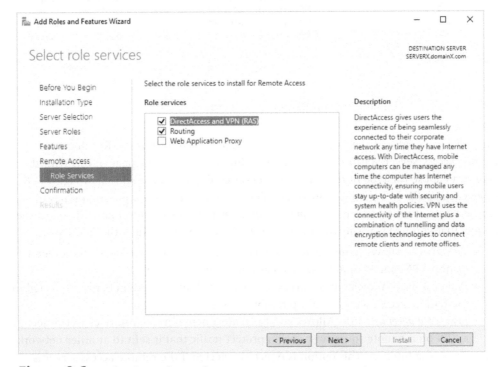

Figure 9-6   **Selecting role services**

After installing the Remote Access server role, you can configure and manage VPN remote access by clicking Routing and Remote Access from the Tools menu in Server Manager to start the **Routing and Remote Access** tool shown in Figure 9-7. Alternatively, you can open the Routing and Remote Access tool from the final page of the Add Roles and Features Wizard. To do this, click *Open the Getting Started Wizard*, and then click *Deploy VPN only*.

When you open the Routing and Remote Access tool following the installation of the Remote Access server role, you must first right-click your server object in the navigation

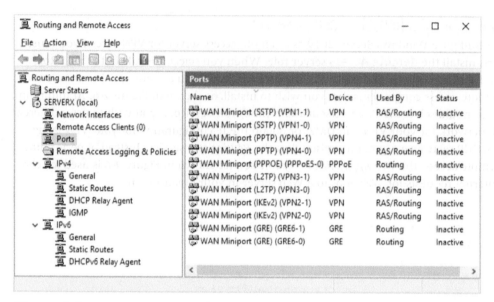

Figure 9-7   The Routing and Remote Access tool

pane and click *Configure and Enable Routing and Remote Access* to start the Routing and Remote Access Server Setup Wizard. After clicking Next at the first page of this wizard, you must choose the type of remote access server configuration, as shown in Figure 9-8. While each option in Figure 9-8 provides a default configuration for different types of remote access, it is best to select *Custom configuration* and click Next to manually select the services that you need, as shown in Figure 9-9. These services include the following:

- *VPN access*—Allows remote access clients to connect to the remote access server using a VPN, and should be selected at minimum.
- *Dial-up access*—Allows remote access clients to dial into a modem bank connected to the remote access server (dial-up remote access).
- *Demand-dial connections*—Allows you to create a demand-dial interface to connect to a VPN on a remote router in order to protect traffic that is sent to another network across the Internet. This option is typically selected if the remote access server is configured as a LAN router or NAT router that is connected to the demarc.
- *NAT*—Allows you to configure the server as a NAT router.
- *LAN routing*— Configures the server as a LAN router. This option should be selected if you plan to use a different IP network for your VPN and DMZ, or if you plan to obtain IP configuration for your VPN using a DHCP relay agent.

After you select the appropriate services in Figure 9-9, you can click Next and then click Finish to complete the wizard. You can then click *Start service* to start your remote access services.

After you have completed the Routing and Remote Access Server Setup Wizard, you may need to perform additional remote access server configuration tasks, depending on

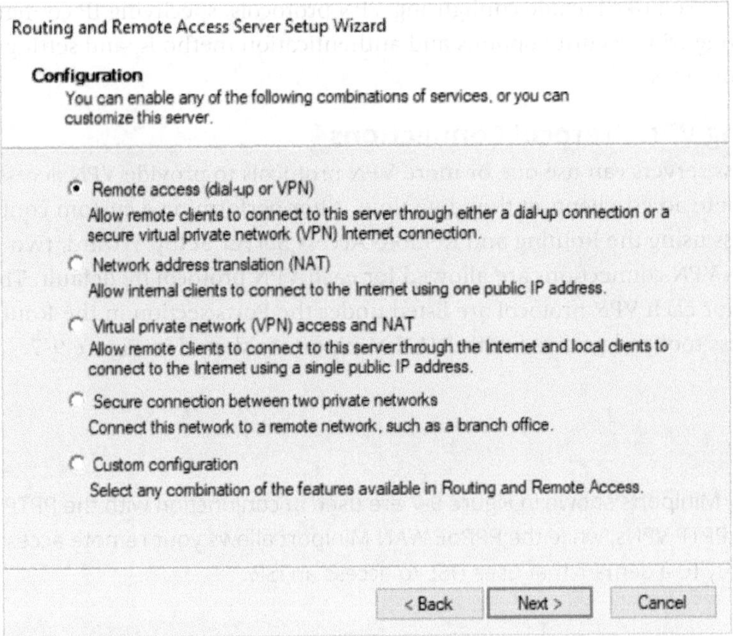

Routing and Remote Access Server Setup Wizard

Configuration
You can enable any of the following combinations of services, or you can
customize this server.

- ⦿ Remote access (dial-up or VPN)
  Allow remote clients to connect to this server through either a dial-up connection or a
  secure virtual private network (VPN) Internet connection.

- ○ Network address translation (NAT)
  Allow internal clients to connect to the Internet using one public IP address.

- ○ Virtual private network (VPN) access and NAT
  Allow remote clients to connect to this server through the Internet and local clients to
  connect to the Internet using a single public IP address.

- ○ Secure connection between two private networks
  Connect this network to a remote network, such as a branch office.

- ○ Custom configuration
  Select any combination of the features available in Routing and Remote Access.

[< Back]   [Next >]   [Cancel]

Figure 9-8   Selecting a remote access server configuration

Routing and Remote Access Server Setup Wizard

Custom Configuration
When this wizard closes, you can configure the selected services in the Routing
and Remote Access console.

Select the services that you want to enable on this server.

- ☑ VPN access
- ☐ Dial-up access
- ☐ Demand-dial connections (used for branch office routing)
- ☐ NAT
- ☑ LAN routing

[< Back]   [Next >]   [Cancel]

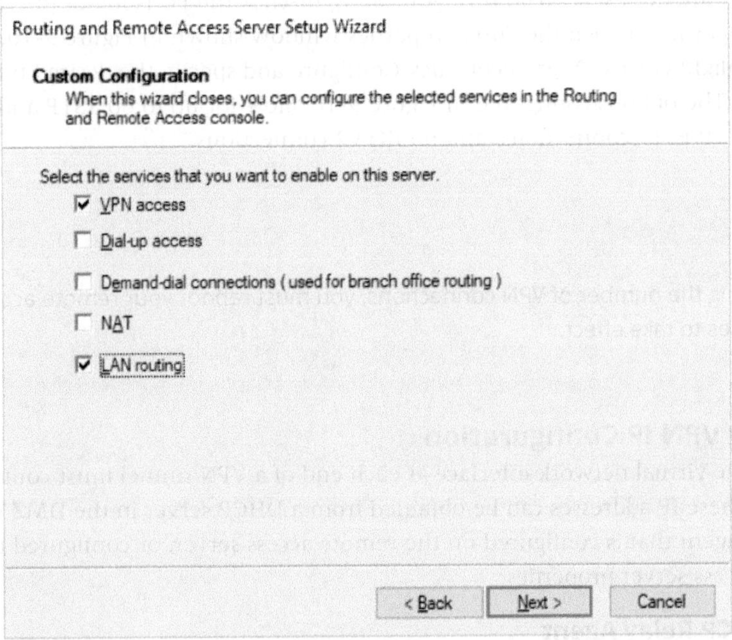

Figure 9-9   Specifying a custom remote access server configuration

your needs. These tasks include configuring VPN protocols, specifying IP configuration for VPNs, configuring security options and authentication methods, and setting dial-in permission for users.

Configuring VPN Protocol Connections

Remote access servers can use one or more VPN protocols to provide VPN access to many different remote access clients at the same time. After performing a custom configuration for VPN access using the Routing and Remote Access Server Setup Wizard, two simultaneous VPN connections are allowed for each VPN protocol by default. The available connections for each VPN protocol are listed under the Ports section in the Routing and Remote Access tool and prefixed with WAN Miniport, as shown in Figure 9-7.

Note

The GRE WAN Miniports shown in Figure 9-7 are used in conjunction with the PPTP WAN Miniports for PPTP VPNs, while the PPPoE WAN Miniport allows your remote access server to connect directly to a demarc that uses DSL to access an ISP.

You should increase the number of connections for each VPN protocol to match the number of remote access clients configured to use the protocol, as well as disable any VPN protocols that are not used. To do this, you can right-click the Ports folder in Figure 9-7, and click Properties to open the Ports Properties window shown in Figure 9-10. Next, you can highlight each VPN protocol, click Configure and specify the desired number of connections. The options configured in Figure 9-10 allow for up to 60 SSTP and L2TP connections, 30 PPTP connections, and no IKEv2 connections.

Note

After modifying the number of VPN connections, you must reboot your remote access server for the changes to take effect.

Specifying VPN IP Configuration

Recall that the virtual network interface at each end of a VPN tunnel must contain an IP address. These IP addresses can be obtained from a DHCP server in the DMZ using a DHCP relay agent that is configured on the remote access server, or configured manually in remote access server properties.

Using a DHCP Relay Agent

DHCP relay agents are located under the IPv4 or IPv6 sections in the Routing and Remote Access tool if the remote access server is also configured as a router. After performing a

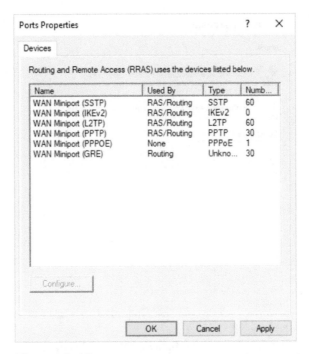

Figure 9-10   Configuring VPN protocol connections

custom configuration for VPN access using the Routing and Remote Access Server Setup Wizard, a DHCP relay agent is added to the IPv4 section only. If you wish to obtain IPv6 addresses for VPN connections, you can right-click the General folder under the IPv6 section in Figure 9-7, click New Routing Protocol, and select DHCPv6 Relay Agent to add the DHCP relay agent for IPv6.

Next, you must configure the DHCP relay agent properties with the IP address of at least one DHCP server that contains a scope for the DMZ network. To do this for IPv4, you right-click DHCP Relay Agent in Figure 9-7, click Properties, and specify the IP address of one or more DHCP servers that contain a scope for your DMZ, as shown in Figure 9-11. The options configured in Figure 9-11 will obtain IP configuration for the VPN from the DHCP server with IP 172.16.0.75, or the DHCP server with IP 172.16.0.76 if the first DHCP server is unavailable. Following this, you must configure the DHCP relay agent to listen for DHCPDISCOVER packets on a network interface. Normally, this is the network interface to which DHCP clients are connected, but for a remote access server, this must be the network interface that is connected to the DMZ. To do this, you right-click DHCP Relay Agent in Figure 9-7 and click New Interface. Next, you select the network interface that connects your remote access server to the DMZ, click OK, and optionally modify the DHCP relay options for the interface, as shown in Figure 9-12. The default options in Figure 9-12 will broadcast DHCPDISCOVER messages on the DMZ network if the DHCP servers configured in the properties of the DHCP relay agent cannot be contacted within 4 seconds. Moreover, these DHCPDISCOVER messages will be allowed to pass through up to 4 additional DHCP relay agents (hops).

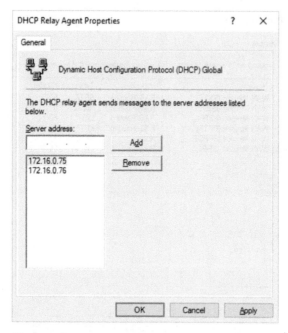

Figure 9-11   Configuring DHCP relay agent properties

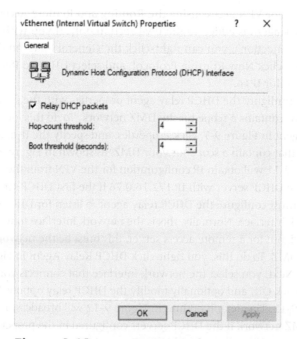

Figure 9-12   Configuring DHCP relay agent interface properties

Using Manual VPN IP Configuration

Instead of obtaining IP configuration from a DHCP server using a DHCP relay agent, you can instead configure an IP address range that is used to assign IP addresses to the virtual network interfaces in a VPN tunnel. To specify an IPv4 configuration for the remote access server in Figure 9-7, you can right-click SERVERX, click Properties, highlight the IPv4 tab, and specify the appropriate options, as shown in Figure 9-13. The options configured in Figure 9-13 assign addresses between 192.168.1.100 and 192.168.1.200 to virtual network interfaces, forward NetBIOS name broadcasts from remote access clients to the DMZ, as well as configure remote access clients with the DNS and WINS servers specified in the configuration of the vEthernet (Internal Virtual Switch) network interface on the remote access server for name resolution. If you highlight the IPv6 tab in Figure 9-13, you can specify a manual IPv6 configuration for IKEv2 and SSTP VPNs, as shown in Figure 9-14. The options configured in Figure 9-14 assign IPv6 addresses that have a 2001:db8:3c4d:: prefix to virtual network interfaces, as well as obtain DNS server and default gateway configuration for remote access clients from the settings in the vEthernet (Internal Virtual Switch) network interface on the remote access server.

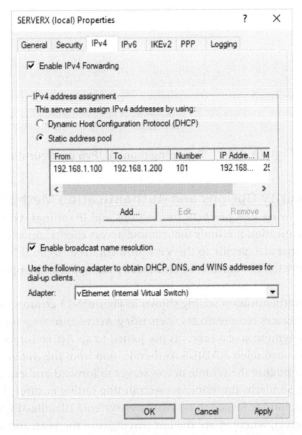

Figure 9-13   Providing manual IPv4 configuration

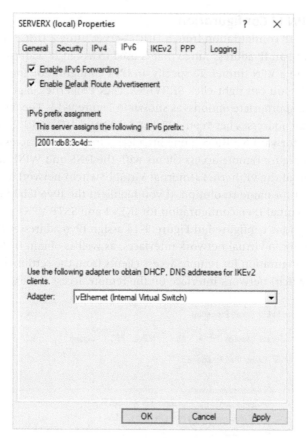

Figure 9-14   Providing manual IPv6 configuration

Configuring Security Options and Authentication Methods

In addition to configuring VPN protocol connections and IP settings, you can also configure the authentication methods that remote access clients can use, as well as security options that are specific to the VPN protocol used. To do this, you must highlight the Security tab in Figure 9-14 and specify the appropriate options, as shown in Figure 9-15.

The Windows Authentication setting shown in Figure 9-15 ensures that the remote access server authenticates remote access users using Active Directory (or the local SAM database if the remote access server is not joined to an Active Directory domain). However, you can instead select RADIUS Authentication from the *Authentication provider* drop-down box to configure the remote access server to forward authentication requests to a RADIUS server. Similarly, the Windows Accounting setting ensures that the details for each VPN connection are logged to C:\Windows\system32\logfiles\IN*yymm*.log on the remote access server, where *yy* are the last two digits of the year, and *mm* are the digits that represent the month of the year. However, you can instead select RADIUS

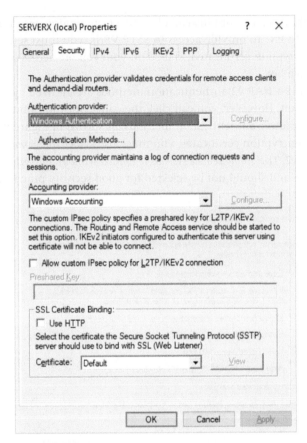

Figure 9-15   The Security tab of remote access server properties

Accounting from the *Accounting provider* drop-down box to configure the remote access server to log VPN connection details to a RADIUS server. Configuring RADIUS authentication and logging is discussed later in this module.

Note

In the early days of computing, the term "accounting" was used to describe the process of recording events. Although remote access and RADIUS servers continue to use this term in their configuration, we will use the term "logging" to refer to the recording of events in this module.

By default, L2TP and IKEv2 VPNs require that each remote access client contains an IPSec encryption certificate. However, if you select *Allow custom IPsec policy for L2TP/IKEv2 connection* in Figure 9-15 and supply a password in the Preshared Key text box, remote access clients can use this password instead of an IPSec encryption certificate to connect to an L2TP or IKEv2 VPN. To provide access to SSTP VPNs, you must select *Use HTTP* and select the HTTPS encryption certificate installed on your remote access server from the Certificate drop-down box.

Only EAP and MS-CHAP v2 authentication methods are allowed by the remote access server by default. However, you can click the Authentication Methods button to provide additional or fewer authentication methods, as shown in Figure 9-16. To allow IKEv2 to use IPSec encryption certificates, you must also select *Allow machine certificate authentication for IKEv2*. The *Allow remote systems to connect without authentication* option only applies to PPTP VPNs and should not be selected for good security practice.

Figure 9-16   Configuring authentication methods

The other tabs in Figure 9-15 contain options that are less frequently configured. The General tab can be used to reconfigure routing and remote access capabilities, the IKEv2 tab can be used to configure IKEv2 parameters (such as idle time-out), the PPP tab can be used to configure dial-up remote access features, and the Logging tab can be used to configure events that are logged by remote access services.

Setting Dial-In Permission

VPN remote access is only granted if the properties of the user account used during authentication allow dial-in permission. For example, to configure dial-in permission for the user Bob Burtt, you can right-click the associated user account in the Active Directory Users and Computers tool, click Properties, and highlight the Dial-in tab, as shown in Figure 9-17. By default, each user account in Active Directory is set to check for dial-in permission in a remote access policy on a RADIUS server using the *Control access through NPS Network Policy* option. If the remote access server is not configured to use RADIUS, you must instead select *Allow access* to ensure that Bob Burtt is able to obtain VPN access from a remote access client. The other options shown in Figure 9-17 apply only to dial-up remote access.

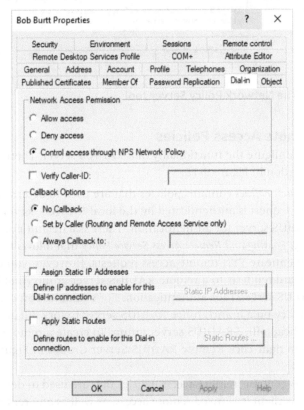

Figure 9-17   Configuring dial-in permission

Configuring RADIUS

To use a Windows Server 2019 system as a RADIUS server, you must first install the **Network Policy and Access Services** role. After this role has been installed, you can use the **Network Policy Server** tool shown in Figure 9-18 to configure the RADIUS server. You can start this tool by selecting Network Policy Server from the tools menu in Server Manager.

If the RADIUS server is joined to an Active Directory domain, it will authenticate remote access user accounts using Active Directory instead of the local SAM database. To allow this functionality, you must right-click NPS (Local) in Figure 9-18 and click *Register server in Active Directory*. Following this, you should configure remote access policies and logging, as well as configure remote access servers as RADIUS clients.

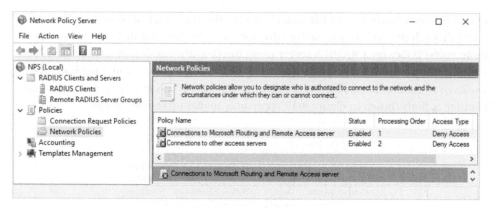

Figure 9-18   The Network Policy Server tool

Configuring Remote Access Policies

Policies are used to configure the functionality of a RADIUS server. There are two folders under the Policies section in Figure 9-18:

- *Connection Request Policies* contains policies that are used to determine whether a remote access request is authenticated by the local RADIUS server or forwarded to a remote RADIUS server for authentication. There is a default policy in this folder called *Microsoft Routing and Remote Access Service Policy* that allows the local RADIUS server to authenticate VPN remote access requests. However, you can modify this policy to forward requests to a remote RADIUS server group (that includes one or more RADIUS servers) for authentication. For example, you could configure the default policy on a branch office RADIUS server to forward authentication requests to a head office RADIUS server group. To create a remote RADIUS server group, you can right-click Remote RADIUS Server Groups in Figure 9-18 and click New.

- *Network Policies* contains remote access policies that are used to determine whether a remote access client is allowed remote access, as well as any remote access characteristics (called **constraints**) that must be met for remote access. You can create multiple remote access policies in this folder that provide unique sets of constraints for different types of remote access clients. Moreover, each remote access policy contains conditions that must be met for the policy to apply to the remote access client. Remote access policies are processed in the order that they are listed in this folder, and remote access clients receive the first policy with conditions they match, ignoring all other remote access policies. The two default remote access policies shown in Figure 9-18 deny remote access requests from Microsoft and other (non-Microsoft) remote access servers, and contain a Processing Order value that ensures they are only processed after other remote access policies.

To create a new remote access policy, right-click the Network Policies folder in Figure 9-18, click New, and specify a policy name and remote access server type, as shown in Figure 9-19. The Accounting Department Remote Access Policy shown in Figure 9-19 applies to VPN and dial-up remote access requests.

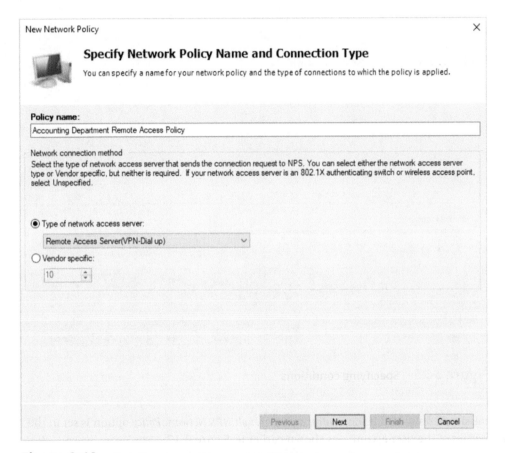

Figure 9-19   Creating a remote access policy

When you click Next in Figure 9-19, you are prompted to add conditions that identify the remote access clients to which the remote access policy applies, as shown in Figure 9-20. The condition added in Figure 9-20 will apply the remote access policy if the remote access user is part of the Accounting-G group. While there are many conditions available for you to choose from when you click the Add button in Figure 9-20, the most commonly configured ones include day and time, authentication type, and VPN protocol (tunnel type).

After you specify the appropriate conditions in Figure 9-20 and click Next, you must select whether to grant or deny access (dial-in) permission, as shown in Figure 9-21. This

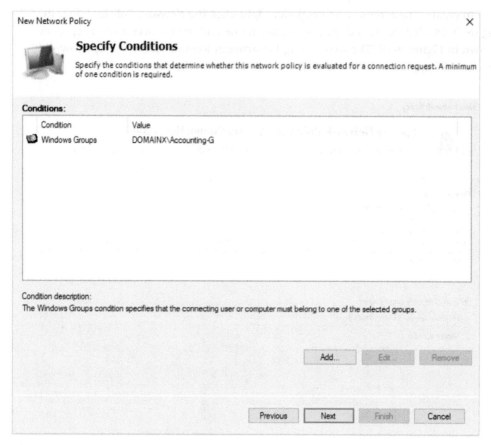

Figure 9-20 Specifying conditions

permission is only used if the *Control access through NPS Network Policy* option is set in the properties of the user account, as shown earlier in Figure 9-17.

After you click Next in Figure 9-21, you are prompted to select the authentication methods that are permitted, as shown in Figure 9-22. The options configured in Figure 9-22 require that remote access clients use either MS-CHAP v2 or EAP-MSCHAP v2.

Note

Although Windows Server 2008 and later remote access servers do not support the first version of MS-CHAP, it is listed in Figure 9-21 in case the remote access client is requesting remote access using a legacy remote access server.

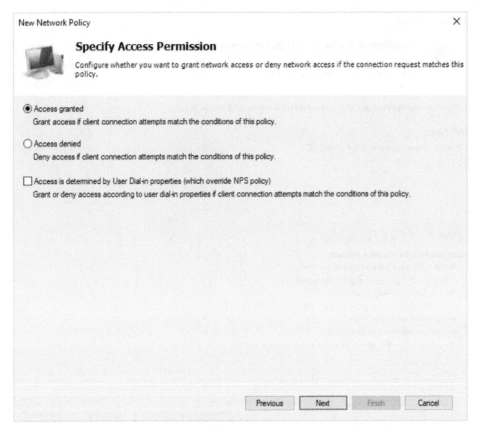

Figure 9-21   Configuring access (dial-in) permission

After you select the appropriate authentication methods and click Next in Figure 9-22, you are prompted to configure the constraints that remote access clients must meet, as shown in Figure 9-23. The available constraints include the following:

- *Idle Timeout* – Specifies the maximum amount of time a remote access session can remain idle before it is disconnected by the remote access server. The option shown in Figure 9-23 disconnects remote access sessions if the remote access client does not send traffic to the remote access server for 5 minutes.
- *Session Timeout* – Specifies the maximum amount of time before an active remote access session is disconnected by the remote access server.
- *Called Station ID* – Specifies the phone number of the dial-up remote access server (only used for dial-up remote access).
- *Day and time restrictions* – Specifies the days and times that remote access sessions are allowed. If an active remote access session persists beyond the allowed time specified, it is disconnected by the remote access server.
- *NAS Port Type* – Specifies the type of network connections (e.g., Ethernet, wireless) that are allowed when connecting to the remote access server.

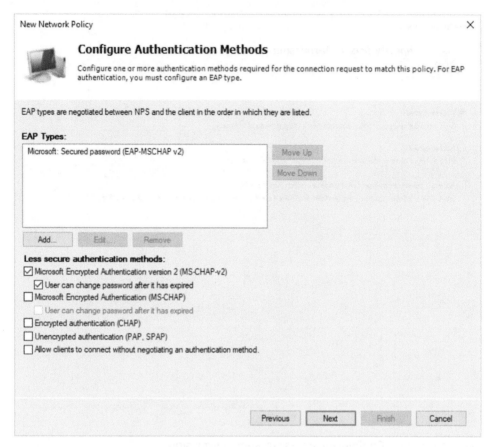

Figure 9-22   Selecting authentication methods

When you click Next in Figure 9-23, you can optionally configure settings for the remote access client, as shown in Figure 9-24. These settings include standard or vendor specific RADIUS attributes that are interpreted by software running on the remote access client, as well as configuration settings used by remote access clients when accessing the remote access server. The available configuration settings include the following:

- *Multilink and Bandwidth Allocation Protocol (BAP)* – Configures settings that allow multiple dial-up remote access connections to be used together in order to increase bandwidth.
- *IP Filters* – Configures custom firewall filters for IPv4 and IPv6 traffic.
- *Encryption* – Configures the encryption levels for MPPE.
- *IP Settings* – Specifies how IP configuration is determined for the remote access client. The default setting shown in Figure 9-24 obtains IP configuration using the method specified on the remote access server.

After you click Next in Figure 9-24, you can click Finish to create the remote access policy. If you create multiple remote access policies, you should ensure that they are listed

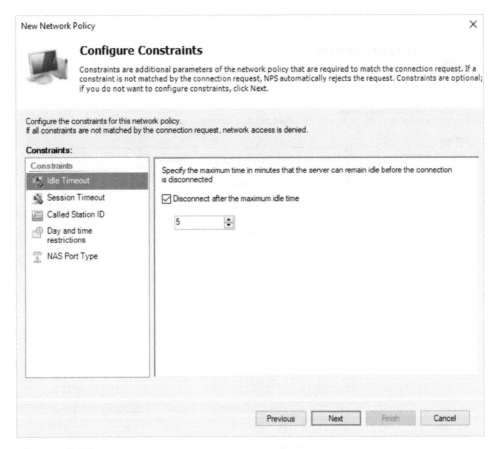

Figure 9-23   Configuring constraints

in the correct processing order under the Network Policies folder. You can right-click a remote access policy under the Network Policies folder and click Move Up or Move Down to move it to a higher or lower position in the processing order, respectively.

Configuring Logging

RADIUS servers log the details of each remote access connection to a text file called C:\ Windows\system32\logfiles\IN*yymm*.log, where *yy* are the last two digits of the year, and *mm* are the digits that represent the month of the year. However, you can highlight the Accounting folder in Figure 9-18 and click one of the following hyperlinks to modify this logging configuration:

- *Change Log File Properties* allows you to modify the events that are logged, as well as the log file format, folder, and rotation (e.g., daily, weekly, monthly).
- *Change SQL Server Logging Properties* allows you to configure the RADIUS server to log events to a table in a database on an SQL server.
- *Configure Accounting* starts a wizard that guides you through the process of configuring log file properties and SQL server logging.

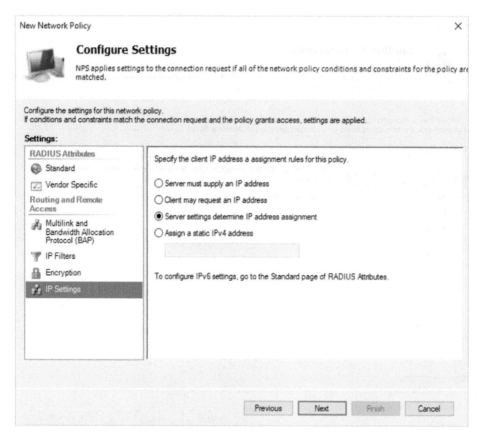

Figure 9-24 Configuring optional settings

Configuring Remote Access Servers to Use RADIUS

Remote access servers do not forward requests to a RADIUS server until they are configured as a RADIUS client. Moreover, RADIUS servers only respond to RADIUS clients that contain the same shared secret (password) in their configuration. As a result, you must add an entry for each RADIUS client on your RADIUS server that includes a shared secret, as well as configure each RADIUS client with the same shared secret.

To add a RADIUS client in the Network Policy Server tool, you can right-click RADIUS Clients in Figure 9-18, click New, and specify the appropriate options, as shown in Figure 9-25. The options configured in Figure 9-25 create a RADIUS client for the SERVERX remote access server (172.16.0.1) that uses a manually specified shared secret. You can optionally highlight the Advanced tab in Figure 9-25 and select *Access-Request messages must contain the Message-Authenticator attribute* to require that RADIUS clients digitally sign traffic that is sent to the RADIUS server.

To configure a remote access server as a RADIUS client, you select RADIUS Authentication from the *Authentication provider* drop-down box in Figure 9-15, click Configure, click Add, and specify the appropriate options, as shown in Figure 9-26.

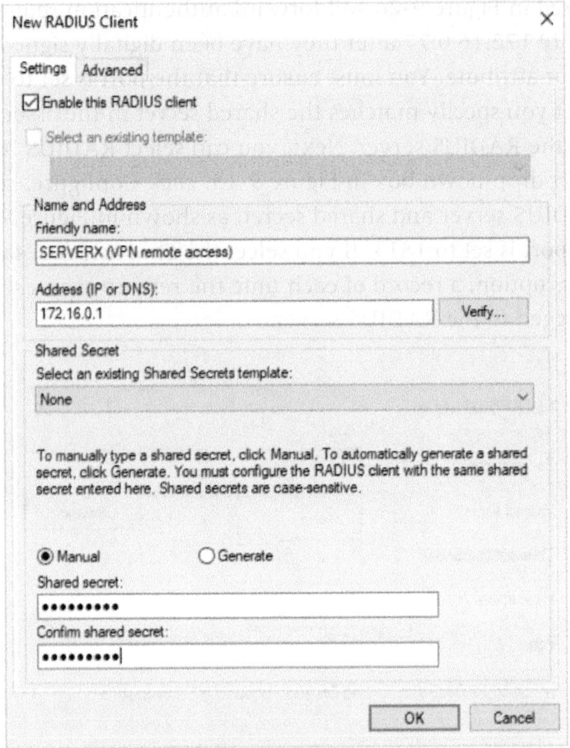

Figure 9-25   Creating a RADIUS client

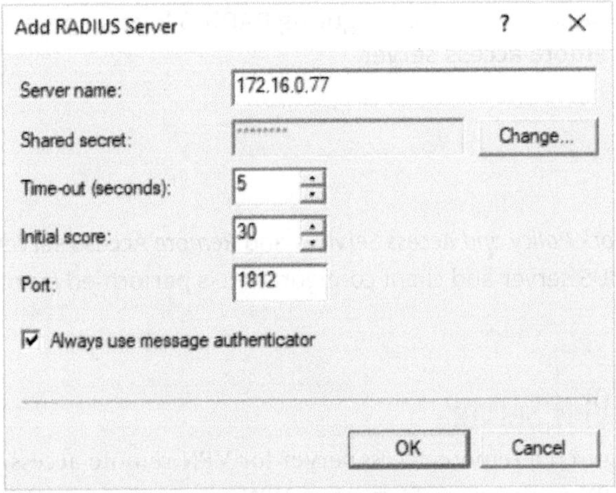

Figure 9-26   Configuring RADIUS
authentication on a remote access server

The options configured in Figure 9-26 will forward authentication requests to the RADIUS server with IP 172.16.0.77 after they have been digitally signed using the message authenticator attribute. You must ensure that the port is set to 1812, and that the shared secret you specify matches the shared secret in the associated RADIUS client configured on the RADIUS server. Next, you can select RADIUS Accounting from the *Accounting provider* drop-down box in Figure 9-15, click Configure, click Add, and specify the same RADIUS server and shared secret, as shown in Figure 9-27. You must also ensure that the port is set to 1813. If you select the *Send RADIUS Accounting On and Accounting Off messages* option, a record of each time the remote access server is started and shut down will be logged to the RADIUS server.

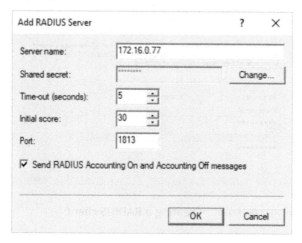

Figure 9-27   Configuring RADIUS logging on a remote access server

Note

If you install the *Network Policy and Access Services* and *Remote* Access server roles on the same computer, RADIUS server and client configuration is performed automatically.

Connecting to a VPN Server

After you have configured a remote access server for VPN remote access, remote access clients can create a VPN connection. To create a VPN connection on a Windows 10 or Windows Server 2019 system, right-click Start, and click Network Connections to open the Settings window. Next, highlight the VPN section, click *Add a VPN connection*, and specify the appropriate options, as shown in Figure 9-28. The options shown in Figure 9-28 create an L2TP VPN connection called *VPN to work* that connects to the public IP address 1.2.3.4.

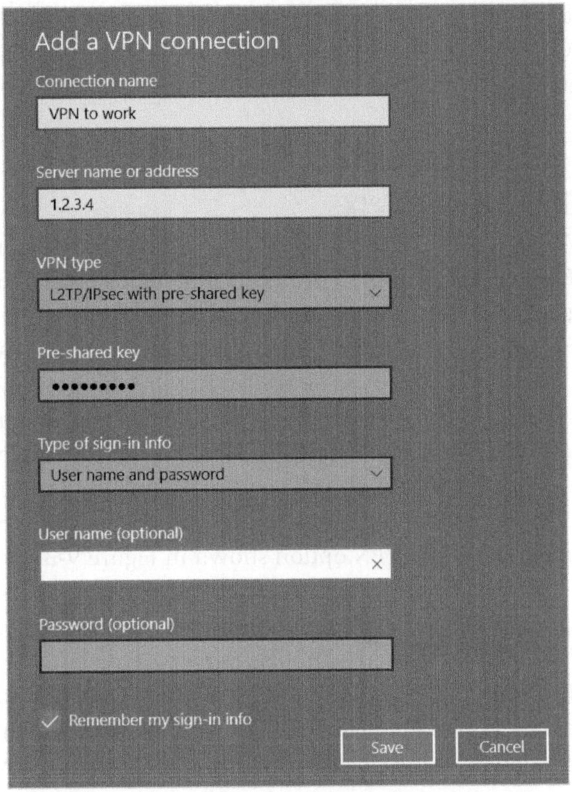

Add a VPN connection

Connection name

VPN to work

Server name or address

1.2.3.4

VPN type

L2TP/IPsec with pre-shared key

Pre-shared key

●●●●●●●●●

Type of sign-in info

User name and password

User name (optional)

×

Password (optional)

✓ Remember my sign-in info

Save   Cancel

Figure 9-28   Creating a VPN connection

When you click Save in Figure 9-28, a new VPN connection is created in the Settings window. To connect to your VPN, click the VPN connection, click Connect, and supply your user credentials, if necessary.

After you have connected to a VPN, you can click the VPN connection and click Disconnect to close the remote access connection. You can also view VPN connections in the Routing and Remote Access tool on your remote access server. Each VPN connection is displayed in the Remote Access Clients folder, and the associated WAN Miniport under the Ports folder is marked Active. You can right-click the VPN connection or associated WAN Miniport and click Status to view remote access statistics, or click Disconnect to close the remote access connection.

Note 📎

After creating a VPN connection, the VPN connection will also be displayed as an additional network interface in the Network Connections section of Control Panel. To configure split tunneling for IPv4 or IPv6, you can right-click this interface, click Properties, and highlight the

Networking tab. Next, you can select either Internet Protocol Version 4 (TCP/IPv4) or Internet Protocol Version 6 (TCP/IPv6), click Properties, click Advanced, and deselect *Use default gateway on remote network*.

Creating a Demand-Dial Interface

If your router is a Windows Server 2019 system, you can create a demand-dial interface in the Routing and Remote Access tool to protect traffic that is passed to another network in your organization. Say, for example, that you wish to configure a demand-dial interface on the Toronto NAT router in Figure 9-5 that creates an IKEv2 VPN to the Chicago NAT router when traffic needs to be routed to the Chicago DMZ (172.17.0.0/24 network). To do this, you could right-click the Network Interfaces folder in Figure 9-7 and click New Demand-dial Interface to start the Demand-Dial Interface Wizard. When you click Next at the first page of this wizard, you are prompted to specify a name for the remote router, as shown for Chicago Router in Figure 9-29. After you click Next in Figure 9-29, you must select the VPN option shown in Figure 9-30. When you click Next in Figure 9-30, you are prompted to select the VPN protocol, as shown for IKEv2 in Figure 9-31. While SSTP VPNs are commonly used between routers, they are not supported for demand-dial interfaces in Windows Server 2019.

After you click Next in Figure 9-31, you must supply the FQDN or associated public IP address of the other router, as shown in Figure 9-32. The IP address shown in Figure 9-32 reflects the public IPv4 address for the Chicago NAT router in Figure 9-5. When you click

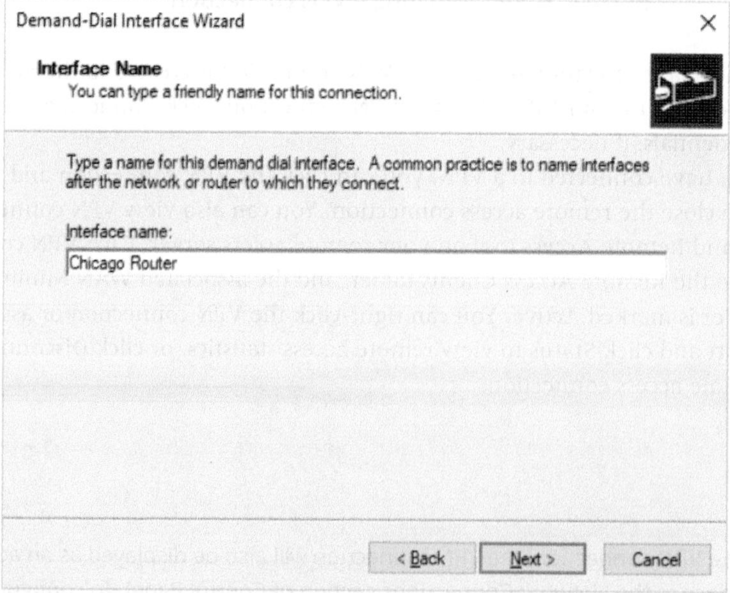

Figure 9-29   Creating a demand-dial interface

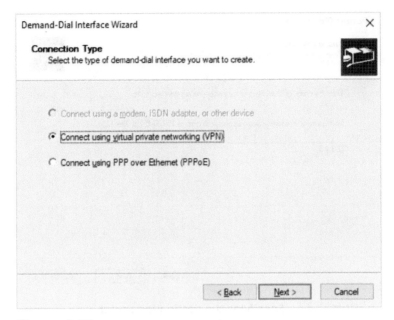

Figure 9-30 Choosing a connection type

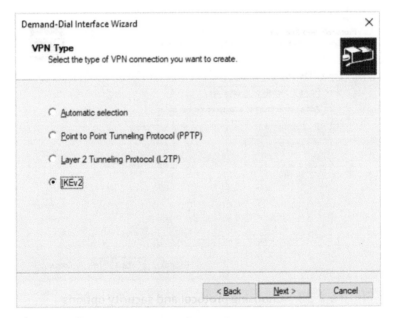

Figure 9-31 Selecting the VPN protocol

Next in Figure 9-32, you must ensure that *Route IP packets on this interface* is selected, as shown in Figure 9-33. If you select *Add a user account so a remote router can dial in*, the Demand-Dial Interface Wizard will additionally prompt you to create a user account

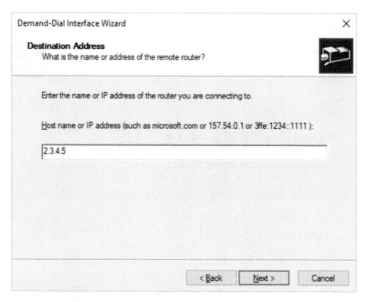

Figure 9-32   Specifying the destination router

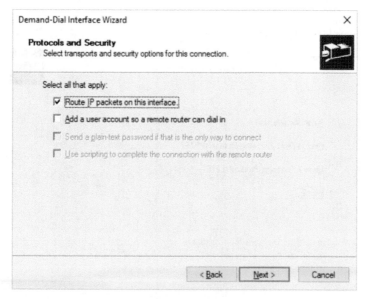

Figure 9-33   Choosing protocol and security options

that can be used when creating a demand-dial interface on the Chicago NAT router that connects to the Toronto DMZ.

After you click Next in Figure 9-33, you must supply the target network to which the demand-dial interface will create a VPN, as shown in Figure 9-34. Because the

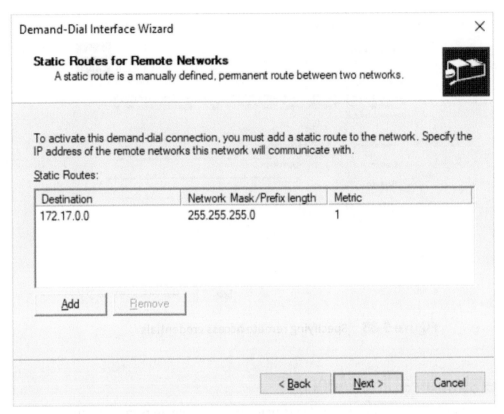

Figure 9-34   Specifying the target network

target network for the demand-dial interface on the Toronto NAT router is the Chicago DMZ, the 172.17.0.0/24 network is configured in Figure 9-34. When you click Next in Figure 9-34, you must supply credentials for a user account that has permission to connect to the remote access server on the Chicago NAT router, as shown for the torontorouter user in Figure 9-35. The domain that you specify in Figure 9-35 should be the NetBIOS name of the Active Directory domain, and is capitalized automatically. After you have specified the appropriate credentials, you can click Next and then Finish to create the demand-dial interface.

If a computer in Toronto forwards packets to the Toronto NAT router that are destined for the 172.17.0.0/24 network, the Toronto NAT router will automatically establish a VPN to the Chicago NAT router before forwarding the packets across the Internet. The length of time that the VPN will remain connected depends on the constraints (Idle Timeout and Session Timeout) configured in the remote access policy used by the Chicago NAT router. However, if the VPN becomes disconnected, it will reconnect when a computer on the Toronto network forwards packets to the Toronto NAT router that are destined for the 172.17.0.0/24 network.

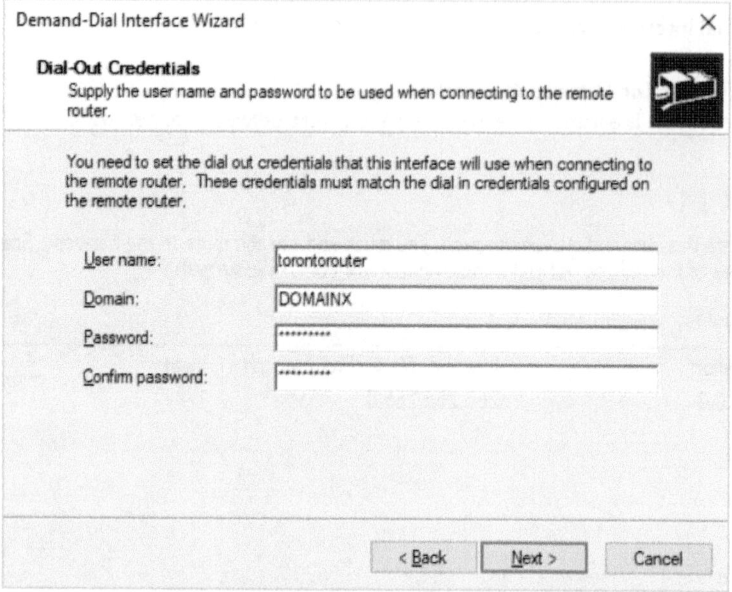

Demand-Dial Interface Wizard   ✕

Dial-Out Credentials
Supply the user name and password to be used when connecting to the remote
router.

You need to set the dial out credentials that this interface will use when connecting to
the remote router. These credentials must match the dial in credentials configured on
the remote router.

User name: torontorouter

Domain: DOMAINX

Password: ••••••••

Confirm password: ••••••••

< Back   Next >   Cancel

Figure 9-35   Specifying remote access credentials

Understanding DirectAccess

Although VPNs can be used to provide remote access, remote users must manually
initiate a VPN connection each time they wish to connect to the resources in their
organization. For organizations that deploy laptop computers that are joined to an Active
Directory domain, secure remote access for these computers can be automated using
DirectAccess. When laptop computers connect to a network outside of the organization,
DirectAccess automatically initiates an IPSec tunnel that functions like a VPN to provide
remote access to the organization DMZ.

To determine whether they are located on a network outside the organization, each
remote access client that participates in DirectAccess contains a **Network Connectivity
Assistant** service that probes a **network location server** using HTTPS each time their
network interface is activated on a network. If the remote access client determines that it is on
a network outside of the organization, it automatically creates an IPSec tunnel to the remote
access server after prompting the user to log into the Active Directory domain, if necessary.

Note

By default, the network location server is installed on the remote access server that is
configured for DirectAccess.

Note

DirectAccess remote access servers use HTTPS to authenticate users to Active Directory. After a user enters their Active Directory credentials, the credentials are cached for use with future remote access connections.

Note

Because DirectAccess uses both HTTPS and IPSec, when configuring firewall exceptions, port forwarding, or reverse proxy, you must specify the port numbers listed in Table 9-1 for SSTP and L2TP/IKEv2 if the configuration tool for the firewall, NAT router, or NGFW does not allow you to specify the DirectAccess protocol by name.

Note

Remote access clients use IPv6 when contacting a network location server or authenticating to a remote access server using DirectAccess. These IPv6 packets are automatically enclosed in IPv4 packets when sent across an IPv4 network.

Note

By default, only Windows 8 Enterprise edition and later computers contain a Network Connectivity Assistant service and are allowed to use DirectAccess. You can optionally configure a remote access server to allow Windows 7 Ultimate and Enterprise edition clients to use DirectAccess. However, you must also install a computer authentication certificate and the **DirectAccess Connectivity Assistant** on each Windows 7 computer. The configuration of computer authentication certificates is discussed in Module 11.

Implementing DirectAccess

To implement DirectAccess, you must first install the Remote Access server role on the Windows Server 2019 system that will function as the remote access server and network location server. Furthermore, you must select the *DirectAccess and VPN (RAS)* role service during the Add Roles and Features Wizard, as shown in Figure 9-6. After you have installed the Remote Access server role, you can configure and manage DirectAccess by clicking Remote Access Management from the Tools menu in Server Manager to start the **Remote Access Management Console** shown in Figure 9-36.

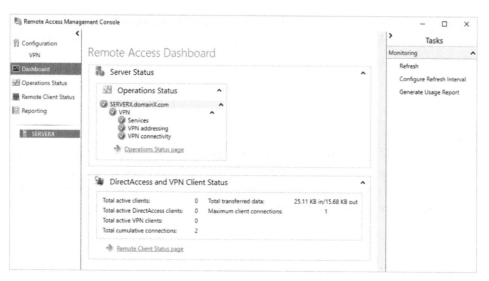

Figure 9-36   The Remote Access Management Console

The Dashboard section is shown by default in Remote Access Management Console and displays the status of remote access services, as well as VPN and DirectAccess client statistics. To view detailed information regarding remote access services, you can highlight Operations Status in the navigation pane. Alternatively, you highlight Remote Client Status in the navigation pane to view detailed client statistics or Reporting to generate reports. To configure DirectAccess, you can highlight VPN under the Configuration section in the navigation pane and click Enable DirectAccess in the Tasks pane to start the Enable DirectAccess Wizard.

Note

You can also open the Enable DirectAccess Wizard from the final page of the Add Roles and Features Wizard. To do this, click *Open the Getting Started Wizard*, and then click either *Deploy DirectAccess only* or *Deploy both DirectAccess and VPN*.

When you click Next at the first page of the Enable DirectAccess Wizard, you are prompted for DirectAccess client configuration options, as shown in Figure 9-37. The options configured in Figure 9-37 will allow all laptop computers in the domain to use DirectAccess to forward traffic to a remote access server when connected to a network outside the organization. To configure remote access clients to use split tunneling for DirectAccess, you can deselect the *Use force tunneling* option shown in Figure 9-37.

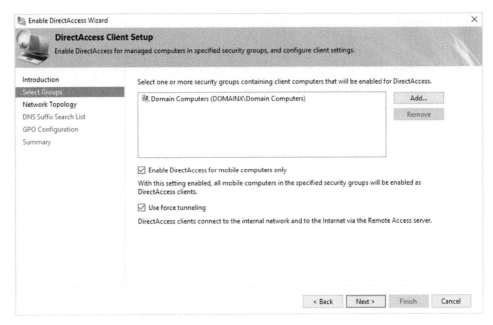

Figure 9-37   Specifying client configuration

After you click Next in Figure 9-37, you are prompted to select the DirectAccess network topology, as shown in Figure 9-38. The *Edge* option shown in Figure 9-38 is used if the DirectAccess remote access server is connected directly to the demarc (Figure 9-3). If your DirectAccess remote access server is located in the DMZ (Figure 9-2), you should select one of the *Behind an edge device* options, depending on the number of network interfaces your server contains. Additionally, you must supply the IP address (or associated FQDN) of the network interface to which remote access clients will connect, as shown for 1.2.3.4 in Figure 9-38. DirectAccess requires that this address be manually configured on the network interface of the remote access server, and not obtained using DHCP.

After you specify the correct network topology options in Figure 9-38 and click Next, you are prompted to configure DirectAccess remote access clients with a list of domain name suffixes, as shown in Figure 9-39. Because DirectAccess remote access clients are joined to a domain, they will use their domain suffix when resolving resource names using DNS, as shown for domainX.com in Figure 9-39. However, if your organization has trust relationships to other organizations that DirectAccess remote access clients must access, you should select *Configure DirectAccess clients with DNS client suffix search list* in Figure 9-39 and add the appropriate domain suffixes to the *Domain suffixes to use* list. This will allow DirectAccess remote access clients to resolve names for resources in other domains without specifying the domain suffix.

Group Policy is used to automatically configure the remote access clients and servers in your organization for DirectAccess. When you click Next in Figure 9-39, you are prompted to optionally modify the default names for the Group Policy objects that will

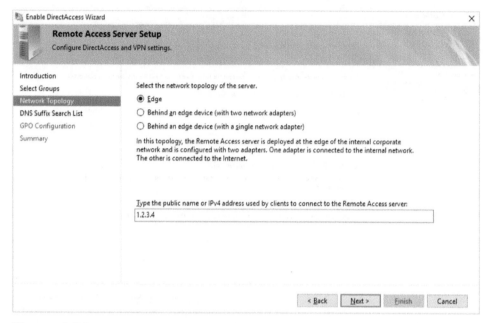

Figure 9-38 Configuring the network topology

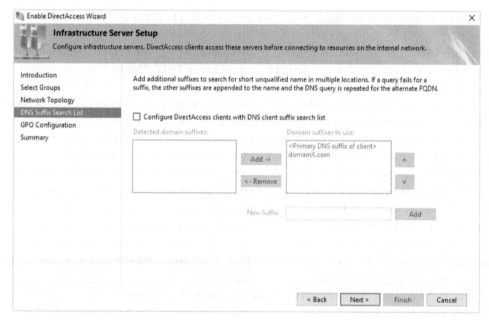

Figure 9-39 Configuring domain suffixes

be created to provide DirectAccess configuration for clients and servers in your domain, as shown in Figure 9-40. Alternatively, if you wish to use an existing Group Policy object to store DirectAccess client or server configuration, you can click the associated Browse button in Figure 9-40 and select the desired Group Policy object.

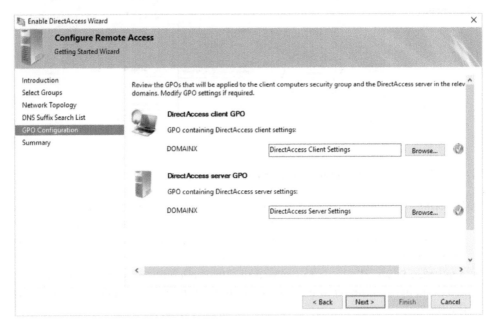

Figure 9-40   Specifying Group Policy object names

When you click Next in Figure 9-40, you can click Finish to configure your server as a DirectAccess remote access server and network location server, as well as ensure that the associated client computers in your domain are enabled for DirectAccess.

To modify your DirectAccess configuration, or specify configuration options that were not available in the Enable DirectAccess Wizard, you can highlight *DirectAccess and VPN* under the Configuration section in the navigation pane of the Remote Access Management Console, as shown in Figure 9-41.

The Remote Access Setup pane shown in Figure 9-41 is divided into four steps that represent the different components of DirectAccess. You can click the Edit button for each component to modify the associated DirectAccess configuration:

- *Remote Clients* allows you to modify the options configured in Figure 9-37, as well as the URL that is used by remote access clients to locate DirectAccess information.
- *Remote Access Server* allows you to modify the options configured in Figure 9-38. Additionally, you can modify the HTTPS certificate used for remote access authentication, allow Windows 7 clients to use DirectAccess, specify a manual IP address range for virtual network interfaces used by the IPSec tunnel (DHCP is used by default), or configure the remote access server to use RADIUS authentication.

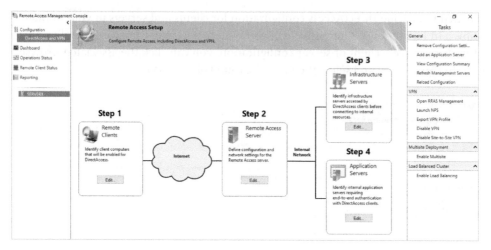

Figure 9-41   Modifying DirectAccess configuration

- *Infrastructure Servers* allows you to modify domain suffix options configured in Figure 9-39. Additionally, you can modify the HTTPS certificate used by the network location server, DNS server settings, and the location of servers that can be used to provide Windows and antivirus updates to remote access clients.
- *Application Servers* allows you to extend the IPSec encryption used between remote access clients and the remote access server to include specific application servers in the DMZ.

Note

There are a wide variety of different PowerShell cmdlets available for configuring VPN and DirectAccess remote access servers. Search *PowerShell RemoteAccess* on docs.microsoft.com for more information.

Understanding Remote Desktop

Remote Desktop uses a different method to achieve remote access compared to VPNs and DirectAccess. Instead of relaying network traffic through an encrypted tunnel to a DMZ, remote access clients use a **Remote Desktop app** to log into a remote access server to obtain a graphical desktop session on the remote access server itself (called **session-based desktop deployment**), or a graphical desktop session from a Hyper-V virtual machine running on the remote access server (called **virtual machine-based desktop deployment**). After a remote access client obtains a graphical desktop session, they can run programs on the remote access server and access resources on the DMZ network to which the remote access server is connected. In other words, Remote Desktop allows remote access clients to access a graphical desktop running in the organization DMZ to provide access to organization resources.

The Remote Desktop app uses **Remote Desktop Protocol (RDP)** to transfer desktop graphics, keystrokes, and mouse movements to and from the remote access server. Programs that are run in a Remote Desktop session are executed on the remote access server and can access shared folders and printers on the organization network as well as volumes and printers installed on the underlying remote access client, if configured. Thus, a remote access user could use File Explorer in their Remote Desktop session to transfer files from the organization to their local computer for later use, or print a document in Microsoft Word on the remote access server to a printer that is installed on their local computer.

Note 🖉

There are Remote Desktop apps available for Windows, macOS, Linux, UNIX, Android, and iOS remote access clients. The Remote Desktop app available by default on Windows systems is called **Remote Desktop Connection**.

Note 🖉

Instead of running a full graphical desktop, remote access clients can use **RemoteApp** to access a single program (e.g., Microsoft Outlook) running on a remote access server using Remote Desktop. This program can also be configured to appear as a shortcut on the Start menu. When remote access clients click this shortcut, the program will execute on the remote access server and transfer the program window, keystrokes, and mouse movements to and from the remote access client.

The collection of services that provide for remote access using Remote Desktop on Windows Server 2019 is called **Remote Desktop Services**, and can be obtained by installing the Remote Desktop Services server role. Table 9-3 summarizes each of these services as well as the ports and transport protocols that they use.

At minimum, you must install either Remote Desktop Session Host or Remote Desktop Virtualization Host, as well as Remote Desktop Licensing on a remote access server to provide for remote access using Remote Desktop. When configuring firewall exceptions, port forwarding, or reverse proxy to the remote access server, you must specify the RDP and HTTPS protocols, or the port numbers listed in Table 9-3 for Remote Desktop Session Host or Remote Desktop Virtualization Host. To provide access to RemoteApp, as well as HTTPS encryption for RDP traffic, you can optionally install Remote Desktop Web Access and Remote Desktop Gateway on the same remote access server, without having to modify the firewall, port forwarding, or reverse proxy configuration.

Table 9-3   Services available for the Remote Desktop services server role

Role service	Description	Ports
Remote Desktop Connection Broker	If multiple Remote Desktop Session Host or Remote Desktop Virtualization Host servers are used, it allows remote access users the ability to reconnect to a disconnected remote desktop session, as well as balances requests for remote desktop sessions across servers.	443/TCP 3389/TCP 3389/UDP
Remote Desktop Gateway	When users connect to a Remote Desktop Session Host or Remote Desktop Virtualization Host server using RDP, this service ensures that all RDP traffic between the remote access server and client is encrypted by enclosing each RDP packet in an HTTPS packet. This role requires that you install an HTTPS certificate.	443/TCP
Remote Desktop Licensing	Allows you to add and manage the licenses required for Remote Desktop Services. Remote Desktop Services provides a 120-day grace period. After this period, you must purchase licenses from Microsoft and configure this service to continue using Remote Desktop Services.	
Remote Desktop Session Host	Provides for session-based desktop deployment and RemoteApp using RDP. This role uses a self-signed HTTPS certificate when authenticating users.	443/TCP 3389/TCP 3389/UDP
Remote Desktop Virtualization Host	Provides for virtual machine-based desktop deployment and RemoteApp using RDP. This role uses a self-signed HTTPS certificate when authenticating users.	443/TCP 3389/TCP 3389/UDP
Remote Desktop Web Access	Provides access to RemoteApp programs configured by the Remote Desktop Session Host or Remote Desktop Virtualization Host, as well as access to Remote Desktop sessions through a Web browser using HTTPS. This role requires that you install an HTTPS certificate.	443/TCP

If you deploy multiple Remote Desktop Session Host or Remote Desktop Virtualization Host remote access servers in your DMZ, then you could install a single server that contains the Remote Desktop Connection Broker to distribute RDP requests across all of the remote access servers. In this case, remote access clients will connect to the Remote Desktop Connection Broker server, and any firewall, port forwarding, or reverse proxy configuration must allow access to this server using the RDP and HTTPS protocols, or the port numbers listed in Table 9-3. Furthermore, the server that hosts the Remote Desktop Connection Broker can also host the Remote Desktop Licensing, Remote Desktop Web Access, and Remote Desktop Gateway role services to provide licensing, RemoteApp, and HTTPS encryption for all remote access servers in the DMZ.

Many server administrators install the Remote Desktop Connection Broker when there is only one remote access server that contains the Remote Desktop Session Host or Remote Desktop Virtualization Host role service. If additional servers are installed with the Remote Desktop Session Host or Remote Desktop Virtualization Host role service afterwards, they are automatically linked with the Remote Desktop Connection Broker, and no additional firewall, port forwarding, or reverse proxy configuration is necessary.

Note

A version of the Remote Desktop Session Host role service is included with every Windows Server 2019 edition installed with the Desktop Experience to allow for graphical remote administration. If enabled, it allows for a maximum of two concurrent Remote Desktop sessions. To enable this version of the Remote Desktop Session Host role service, you can click the Disabled hyperlink next to Remote Desktop in the Local Server section of Server Manager (shown in Figure 1-8).

Implementing Remote Desktop Services

To implement Remote Desktop Services, you must install and configure Remote Desktop Services, as well as create and configure collections that include remote access servers. Following this, you must ensure that users can connect to Remote Desktop sessions, as well as any programs made available using RemoteApp.

Installing Remote Desktop Services

To install Remote Desktop Services, you must install the Remote Desktop Services server role on a Windows Server 2019 system that will function as the remote access server. When you select this role in the Add Roles and Features Wizard and progress through the wizard, you are prompted to choose the role services that you wish to install, as shown in Figure 9-42. The role services selected in Figure 9-42 allow remote access clients to connect to a Remote Desktop Connection Broker on the remote access server to obtain Remote Desktop sessions and RemoteApp programs using session-based desktop deployment.

At the end of the Add Roles and Features Wizard, you must reboot your server before continuing the installation of Remote Desktop Services. After your server has rebooted, you must start the Add Roles and Features Wizard again but instead select *Remote Desktop Services installation* at the Select installation type page, as shown in Figure 9-43.

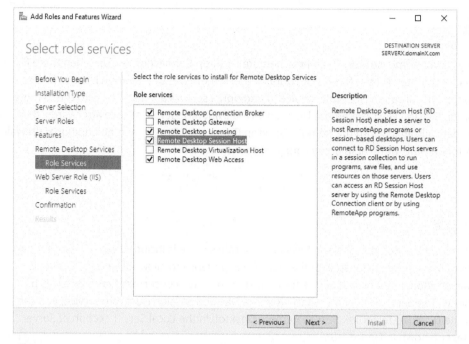

Figure 9-42   Selecting role services

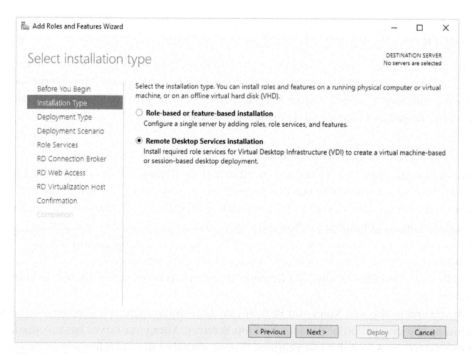

Figure 9-43   Installing Remote Desktop Services

When you click Next in Figure 9-43, you are prompted to select deployment options, as shown in Figure 9-44. Because the Remote Desktop Connection Broker was installed, it is selected as the target for remote access clients. The *Standard deployment* option provides the most flexibility when configuring components and allows you to add multiple existing remote access servers to your Remote Desktop Connection Broker. However, you can instead select *Quick Start* to automatically configure all role services on the local server. When you click Next in Figure 9-44, you must choose whether to configure virtual machine-based desktop deployment or session-based desktop deployment, as shown in Figure 9-45. The option selected in Figure 9-45 matches the Remote Desktop Session Host role service installed earlier.

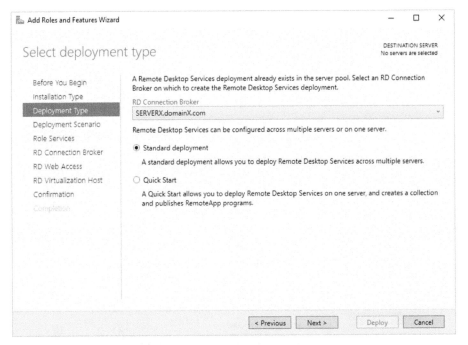

Figure 9-44   Selecting deployment options

After you choose the desktop deployment type in Figure 9-45 and click Next, you will see a summary of the role services that will be installed, as shown in Figure 9-46. This summary should match the role services that you selected earlier, with the exception of Remote Desktop Licensing, which is configured afterward. When you click Next in Figure 9-46, you are prompted to choose a server that hosts the Remote Desktop Connection Broker, as shown in Figure 9-47. Because the local server contains the Remote Desktop Connection Broker, it is selected automatically and you can click Next to specify a server that hosts the Remote Desktop Web Access role service, as shown in Figure 9-48. The options configured in Figure 9-48 will install the Remote Desktop Web Access role service on the local server alongside the Remote Desktop Connection Broker.

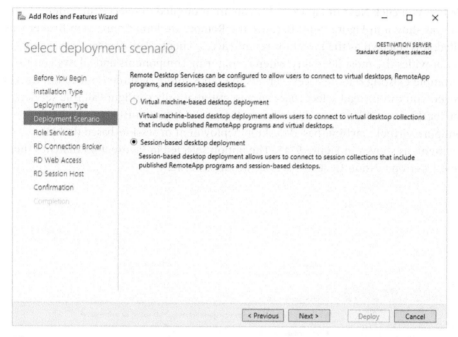

Figure 9-45   Choosing the desktop deployment type

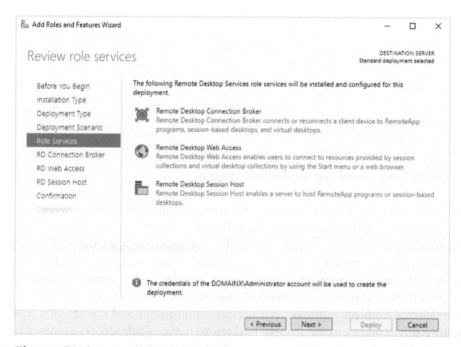

Figure 9-46   Reviewing role services

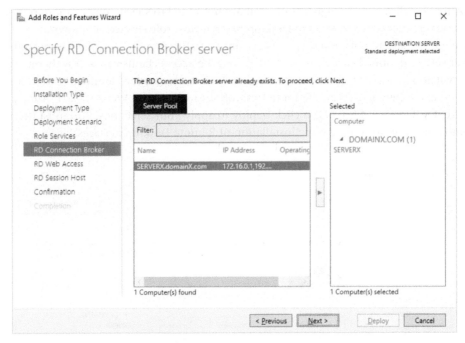

Figure 9-47 Specifying a Remote Desktop Connection Broker server

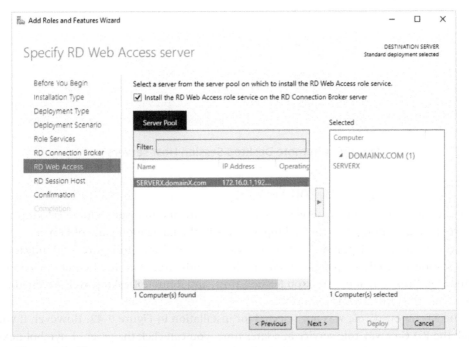

Figure 9-48 Specifying a Remote Desktop Web Access server

After you click Next in Figure 9-48, you are prompted to specify one or more remote access servers that host the Remote Desktop Session Host role service, as shown in Figure 9-49. These remote access servers are linked to the Remote Desktop Connection Broker server identified earlier to ensure that remote access clients can access them. They will also be linked to the Remote Desktop Web Access server identified earlier, to allow access to RemoteApp and Remote Desktop sessions using a Web browser. After you click Next in Figure 9-49, you can click Deploy to apply your selections. You must then reboot your server to complete the installation of Remote Desktop Services.

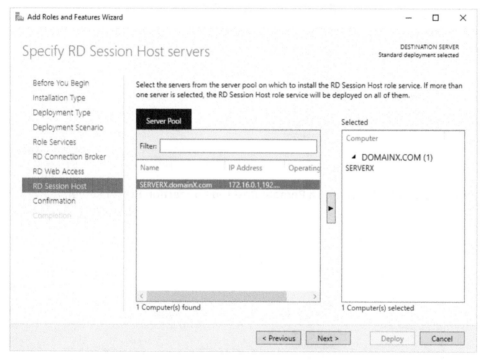

Figure 9-49   Specifying Remote Desktop Session Host servers

Configuring Remote Desktop Services

After you have rebooted your server, you can configure and manage Remote Desktop Services by highlighting Remote Desktop Services in the navigation pane of Server Manager, as shown in Figure 9-50. The Overview section shown in Figure 9-50 indicates that a session-based desktop deployment has been configured with the Remote Desktop Connection Broker, Remote Desktop Session Host, and Remote Desktop Web Access role services on SERVERX.DOMAINX.COM.

The RD Gateway role was not selected for installation in Figure 9-42. However, if you install the RD Gateway role service at a later time, you can click the green + symbol next to RD Gateway in the DEPLOYMENT OVERVIEW section to add it to your configuration.

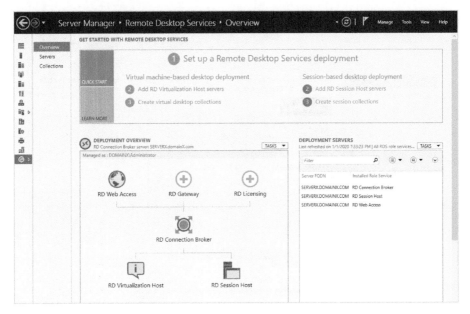

Figure 9-50 The Remote Desktop Services section of Server Manager

Although the Remote Desktop Licensing role service was installed alongside the other role services, it is not configured by default. To configure this role service, click the green + symbol next to RD Licensing and specify the Remote Desktop Licensing server, as shown in Figure 9-51. After you click Next in Figure 9-51, you click Add to complete the configuration. Next, you must specify whether the Remote Desktop licenses that you have purchased from Microsoft are assigned per device or user. To do this, click the TASKS menu in the DEPLOYMENT OVERVIEW section, click Edit Deployment Properties, and highlight the RD Licensing section of Deployment Properties, as shown in Figure 9-52. The Per Device option selected in Figure 9-52 requires that each remote access client have a CAL (as discussed in Module 1). However, the Per User option should be chosen if your organization allows Remote Desktop sessions from remote access clients that are not licensed by the organization, such as home PCs or mobile smartphones.

Recall that the Remote Desktop Web Access and Remote Desktop Gateway role services require that you obtain and install an HTTPS encryption certificate. To configure an existing HTTPS encryption certificate for use with these role services, you can highlight the Certificates section of Deployment Properties in Figure 9-52 and click *Select existing certificate*.

Over time, you may find that a single Remote Desktop Session Host server is not adequate to support the number of Remote Desktop sessions. To add additional remote access servers to your configuration that have the Remote Desktop Session Host role service installed, you can click *Add RD Session Host servers* in the GET STARTED WITH REMOTE DESKTOP SERVICES pane in Figure 9-50. These remote access servers are automatically linked to the Remote Desktop Connection Broker in the existing Remote Access Services configuration.

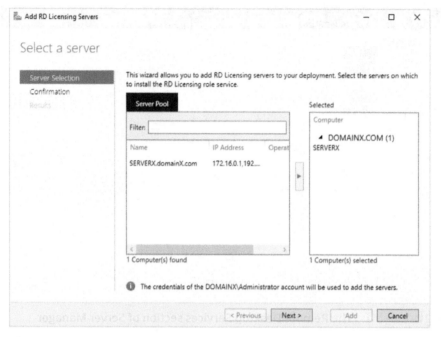

Figure 9-51   Specifying a Remote Desktop Licensing server

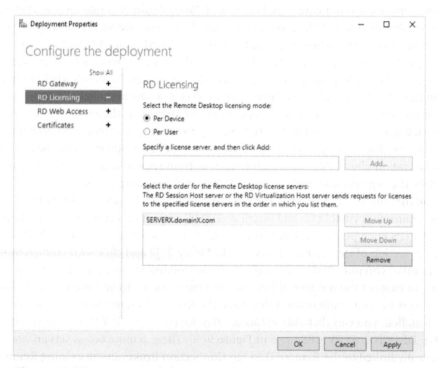

Figure 9-52   Selecting a licensing mode

Configuring Collections

After you have configured the appropriate role services, you must create one or more **collections** that contain remote access servers. Each collection allows specific groups of users in your Active Directory domain access to Remote Desktop, as well as provides configuration for RemoteApp and Remote Desktop sessions. To create a new collection for session-based desktop deployment, you can click *Create session collections* in Figure 9-50 to start the Create Collection wizard. When you click Next at the first page of this wizard, you are prompted for a collection name, as shown for DomainX Collection in Figure 9-53. After you click Next in Figure 9-53, you must specify one or more remote access servers that should be added to the collection, as shown in Figure 9-54. Because the collection in Figure 9-54 is for session-based desktop deployment, only servers that contain the Remote Desktop Session Host role are shown.

When you click Next in Figure 9-54, you are prompted to select the groups that are allowed to access the remote access servers in the collection, as shown in Figure 9-55. The Domain Users group is added by default to allow all domain users access to Remote Desktop, but you can remove this group and add other groups to allow access only to specific job roles or departments in your organization.

If a collection consists of multiple remote access servers, the Remote Desktop Connection Broker may connect a user to a different remote access server when that user requests a

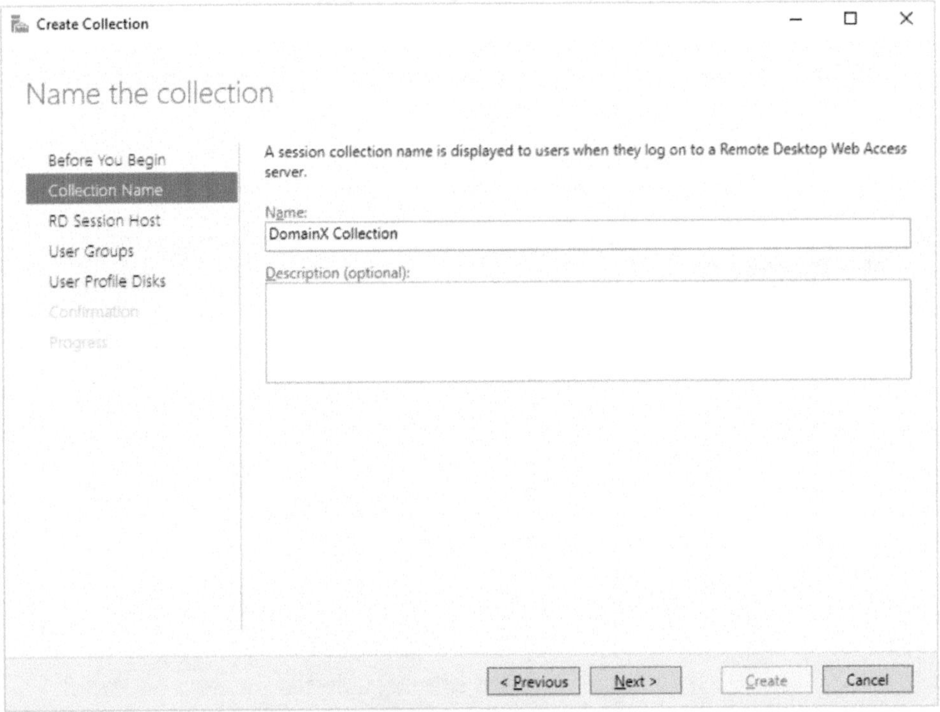

Figure 9-53   Specifying a collection name

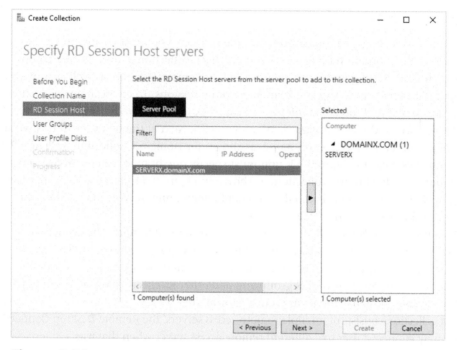

Figure 9-54   Adding remote access servers to a collection

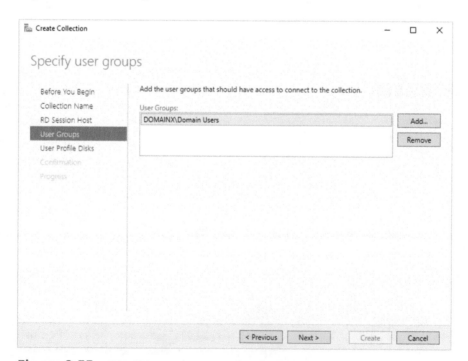

Figure 9-55   Specifying user groups for remote access

new Remote Desktop session. In this case, the desktop customization settings that the user configured on the previous remote access server will not be available. To provide a consistent desktop experience regardless of the remote access server that users connect to, you can configure a collection to store desktop customization settings for users in a shared folder that is accessible to all remote access servers in the collection. When you click Next in Figure 9-55, you are prompted to enable and specify the location and maximum size of this shared folder, as shown in Figure 9-56. The options configured in Figure 9-56 will store up to 20 GB of user desktop customization settings in the ProfileShares shared folder on servery.domainx.com. This folder must also grant the computer accounts for each remote access server Full Control shared folder and NTFS/ReFS permission. After you click Next in Figure 9-56, you can click Create to create your collection.

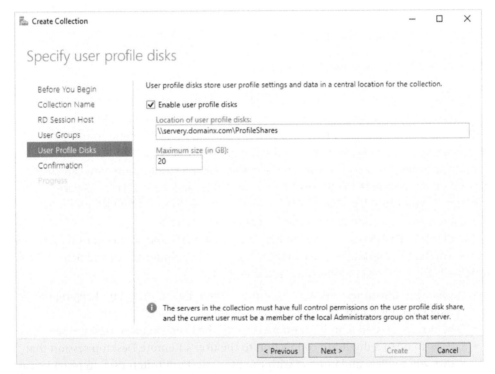

Figure 9-56   Specifying a shared profile location

After creating a collection, you can use Server Manger to configure and manage Remote Desktop for the remote access servers in the collection. To do this, you can highlight the collection under the Collections section in the navigation pane, as shown for the DomainX Collection in Figure 9-57.

If you select the TASKS menu in the PROPERTIES pane of Figure 9-57 and click Edit Properties, you can modify the options you configured when creating the collection, as well as configure session limits, load balancing settings for remote access servers, security settings, and remote access client settings (including the ability to access local volumes and printers).

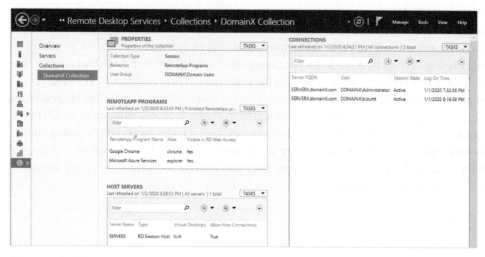

Figure 9-57   The DomainX Collection

The REMOTEAPP PROGRAMS pane displays two programs (Google Chrome and Microsoft Azure Services) made available to remote access clients using RemoteApp. To add additional RemoteApp programs, you can click the TASKS menu in this pane, click *Publish RemoteApp Programs* and specify the desired programs.

To add additional remote access servers to the DomainX Collection, you can click the TASKS menu in the HOST SERVERS pane and click *Add RD Session Host Servers*. Alternatively, you can select *Remove RD Session Host Servers* from the TASKS menu to remove a remote access server from the DomainX Collection.

The CONNECTIONS pane is used to manage Remote Desktop connections. Figure 9-57 displays two Remote Desktop connections in this pane for Administrator and b.burtt. You can right-click one of these connections and then click:

- *Disconnect* to disconnect the user from the Remote Desktop session, keeping the session open for when the user connects again.
- *Send Message* to send a notification message to the user's Remote Desktop session.
- *Shadow* to open a duplicate connection to the user's Remote Desktop session that allows you to view and interact with the user's desktop (often used to provide user support).
- *Log off* to force the user to log off from their Remote Desktop session.

Note

There are a wide variety of different PowerShell cmdlets available for configuring Remote Desktop Services. Search *PowerShell RemoteDesktop* on docs.microsoft.com for more information.

Connecting to Remote Desktop Services

To obtain a Remote Desktop session to a remote access server on a Windows remote access client, you can click Remote Desktop Connection from the Start menu to open the Remote Desktop Connection app shown in Figure 9-58.

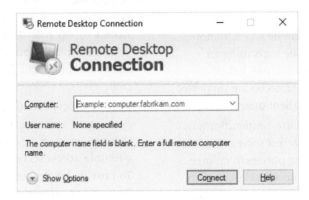

Figure 9-58 **The Remote Desktop Connection app**

The FQDN or IP address that you specify in the Computer text box in Figure 9-58 should match the server that hosts the Remote Desktop Session Host, or the server that hosts Remote Desktop Connection Broker, if used. You can optionally click *Show Options* to modify Remote Desktop session settings, such as display size or local printer availability. Following this, you can click *Connect* and supply your domain credentials to obtain a Remote Desktop session.

If you configured the Remote Desktop Web Access role service, you can also obtain a Remote Desktop session or access RemoteApp programs by navigating to `https://server/RdWeb` in a Web browser, where *server* is the FQDN of the Remote Desktop Web Access server. After you log into this website using domain credentials, you can select options to connect to a Remote Desktop session in the Web browser, download a file that automatically connects to a Remote Desktop session using the Remote Desktop Connection app, as well as access or create Start menu shortcuts for one or more RemoteApp programs that are available on the remote access server. Alternatively, you can open the **RemoteApp and Desktop Connections** tool in Control Panel and click *Access RemoteApp and desktops* to perform the same actions.

Module Summary

- Most organizations connect department LANs to a DMZ network that provides access to servers and the Internet.

- Remote access can be used to provide access to organization resources from a computer outside of the organization. Remote access clients connect to a remote access server that has access to the DMZ.

- VPNs provide remote access by creating an encrypted tunnel between a remote access client and server. Microsoft supports PPTP, L2TP, IKEv2, and SSTP VPN protocols.

- Before providing VPN remote access, remote access servers authenticate users using an authentication protocol. The PAP, CHAP, MS-CHAP v2, and EAP protocols are supported by Microsoft for VPN authentication.

- RADIUS provides centralized authentication and logging for remote access servers. RADIUS servers use remote access policies to enforce characteristics of a remote access connection.

- Demand-dial interfaces on a router are used to provide VPN remote access for packets sent to a remote network.

- DirectAccess automatically creates IPSec tunnels to a remote access server when remote access clients are outside of the organization.

- To provide for VPNs or DirectAccess, you must install and configure the Remote Access server role. To provide for RADIUS, you must install and configure the Network Policy and Access Services server role.

- Remote access clients can obtain a graphical desktop on a remote access server using Remote Desktop, or access a program on a remote access server using RemoteApp. To provide for Remote Desktop and RemoteApp, you must install and configure Remote Desktop Services.

Key Terms

cable broadband
collection
constraint
demand-dial interface
demarc
demarcation point
dial-in permission
dial-up remote access
Digital subscriber line
  (DSL)
DirectAccess
DirectAccess Connectivity
  Assistant
Generic Routing
  Encapsulation (GRE)
Gigabit Passive Optical
  Network (GPON)
Internet Key Exchange
  version 2 (IKEv2)
IP Security (IPSec)

last mile technology
Layer Two Tunneling
  Protocol (L2TP)
long-range Wi-Fi
Microsoft Point-to-Point
  Encryption (MPPE)
Network Connectivity
  Assistant
network location server
Network Policy and Access
  Services
Network Policy Server
Next Generation Firewall
  (NGFW)
overlay network
Point-to-Point Protocol
Point-to-Point Protocol over
  Ethernet (PPPoE)
Point-to-Point Tunneling
  Protocol (PPTP)

port forwarding
RADIUS client
remote access
Remote Access
remote access client
Remote Access Dial-In User
  Authentication Service
  (RADIUS)
Remote Access
  Management Console
remote access policy
remote access server
Remote Desktop
Remote Desktop app
Remote Desktop
  Connection
Remote Desktop Protocol
  (RDP)
Remote Desktop
  Services

RemoteApp
RemoteApp and Desktop
  Connections
reverse proxy
Routing and Remote Access
Secure Socket Tunneling
  Protocol (SSTP)

Secure Sockets Layer (SSL)
service forwarding
session-based desktop
  deployment
split tunneling
Transport Layer Security
  (TLS)

virtual machine-based
  desktop deployment
virtual private networks
  (VPNs)
VPN protocol
VPN tunnels

Review Questions

1. Which of the following is not considered a remote access technology?
   a. DirectAccess
   b. L2TP
   c. PPPoE
   d. Remote Desktop

2. Split tunneling is used to ensure that all network traffic generated by a remote access client passes through a VPN to a remote access server. True or False?

3. Which of the following VPN protocols uses IPSec to encrypt network traffic? (Choose all that apply.)
   a. IKEv2
   b. PPTP
   c. SSTP
   d. L2TP

4. What can you configure on a router to protect traffic destined for another network in the organization as it passes over the Internet?
   a. Port forwarding
   b. Demand-dial interface
   c. Reverse proxy
   d. DirectAccess

5. The Remote Access role service in Windows Server 2019 provides for DirectAccess and VPN remote access, as well as RADIUS. True or False?

6. You have configured a remote access server in your DMZ for IKEv2 VPN access. Which ports on your NAT router must

you configure for port forwarding to this remote access server? (Choose all that apply.)
   a. TCP port 1723
   b. TCP port 1701
   c. UDP port 500
   d. UDP port 4500

7. Which of the following VPN authentication methods is considered the most secure?
   a. EAP
   b. CHAP
   c. MS-CHAPv2
   d. PAP

8. Remote access servers can be configured as RADIUS clients. True or False?

9. What features does RADIUS provide for remote access connections?
   a. Centralized logging
   b. Remote access policies
   c. Centralized authentication
   d. Centralized encryption

10. The user permission necessary for VPN remote access can be granted in the properties of a user account or remote access policy. True or False?

11. What section of a remote access policy contains characteristics that must be met for remote access, such as *Session Timeout*?
    a. Conditions
    b. Criteria
    c. Constraints
    d. Settings

12. DirectAccess uses HTTPS to authenticate remote access users, and IPSec to create an encrypted tunnel for network traffic between the remote access client and server. True or False?

13. Which of the following network topologies should you choose if your DirectAccess remote access server is connected directly to the demarc, as well as to the DMZ?

    a. Edge
    b. Connection Broker
    c. Behind an edge device (with two network adapters)
    d. Behind an edge device (with a single network adapter)

14. DirectAccess supports Windows 7 and later remote access clients by default. True or False?

15. Which of the following Remote Desktop Services role services uses HTTPS to provide encryption for all RDP packets?

    a. Remote Desktop Connection Broker
    b. Remote Desktop Gateway
    c. Remote Desktop Session Host
    d. Remote Desktop Virtualization Host

16. The Remote Desktop Licensing role service cannot be installed on the same computer as the Remote Desktop Session Host service. True or False?

17. Which of the following must you configure to ensure that a particular group of remote access servers grants Remote Desktop access only to members of the Accounting group?

    a. RemoteAccess
    b. RemoteApp
    c. Collection
    d. Connection Broker

18. At minimum, which Remote Desktop Services role services must you install to provide session-based desktop deployment across multiple remote access servers? (Choose all that apply.)

    a. Remote Desktop Session Host
    b. Remote Desktop Connection Broker
    c. Remote Desktop Licensing
    d. Remote Desktop Virtualization Host

19. As a server administrator, which of the following actions can you perform on a Remote Desktop connection to provide interactive user support for the user of the session?

    a. Send Message
    b. Disconnect
    c. Duplicate
    d. Shadow

20. Organizations that allow Remote Desktop sessions from remote access clients that are not licensed by the organization should choose a Per Device licensing mode when configuring Remote Desktop Services. True or False?

Hands-On Projects

These Hands-On Projects should be completed in the order given and normally take a total of three hours or less to complete. The requirements for these projects include:

- A system with Windows Server 2019 installed according to Hands-On Project 1-1 (Lab Environment 1) or Hands-On Project 1-2 (Lab Environment 2).
- A WindowsServer2019VM2 virtual machine installed according to Hands-On Project 3-5 and configured as a member server according to Hands-On Project 5-2.

Project 9-1: Cleanup Tasks

In this Hands-On Project, you perform cleanup tasks on your WindowsServer2019VM2 virtual machine to remove the WindowsServer2019VM2 configuration performed during the Module 8 Hands-On Projects. More specifically, you remove the DHCP, DNS, and WINS servers, as well as the second network interface.

1. Boot your Windows Server 2019 host and log into domain*X*.com as Administrator using the password **Secret555**. Next, click **Start** and then click **Server Manager**.

2. In Server Manager on your Windows Server 2019 host, select the **Tools** menu and then click **Hyper-V Manager**.

   a. Highlight **WindowsServer2019VM2** in the virtual machines pane of Hyper-V Manager and click **Connect** in the Actions pane. In the Virtual Machine Connection window, click **Start** to boot your virtual machine.

   b. At the login screen, click the Ctrl+Alt+Delete button in the Virtual Machine Connection window, supply the password **Secret555** for Administrator and press **Enter** to log into the system.

3. In Server Manager on your Windows Server 2019 host, click the **Tools** menu and then click **WINS**.

4. In the navigation pane of the WINS tool, highlight **Replication Partners**. If you performed Discovery Exercise 8-4, right-click the replication partner for your WindowsServer2019VM2 virtual machine, click **Delete,** and click **Yes** when prompted. Click **Yes** again to complete the removal of the replication partner. Close the WINS tool when finished.

5. In Server Manager, click the **Tools** menu and then click **DHCP**.

6. In the navigation pane of the DHCP tool, highlight **Scope [172.16.0.0] Marketing LAN** and click **More Actions**, **Deconfigure Failover** in the Actions pane. Click **OK**. Click **OK** again to remove the failover configuration. Click **Close** and then close the DHCP tool when finished.

7. On your WindowsServer2019VM2 virtual machine, click **Start** and then click **Server Manager**. Next, click the **Manage** menu and then click **Remove Roles and Features**.

   a. At the Select destination server page, click **Next**.

   b. At the Remove server roles page, de-select **DHCP Server** and click **Remove Features** when prompted. Next, de-select **DNS Server** and click **Remove Features** when prompted. Click **Next** when finished.

   c. At the Remove features page, de-select **WINS Server** and click **Remove Features** when prompted. Click **Next** when finished.

   d. On the Confirm removal selections page, click **Remove** to remove the DHCP, DNS, and WINS servers.

   e. At the Removal progress page, click **Close**.

   f. Shut down your WindowsServer2019VM2 virtual machine.

8. In Hyper-V Manager on your Windows Server 2019 host, highlight **WindowsServer2019VM2** in the Virtual Machines pane and click **Settings** in the Actions pane.

   a. Under the Hardware section in the navigation pane, select **Network Adapter Internal Virtual Switch** and click **Remove**.

   b. Click **OK**.

9. Highlight **WindowsServer2019VM2** in the virtual machines pane of Hyper-V Manager and click **Connect** in the Actions pane.

   a. In the Virtual Machine Connection window, click **Start** to boot your virtual machine.

   b. At the login screen, click the Ctrl+Alt+Delete button in the Virtual Machine Connection window, supply the password **Secret555** for Administrator and press **Enter** to log into the system.

Project 9-2: Configuring a VPN Server

In this Hands-On Project, you configure your Windows Server 2019 host as a VPN server and DHCP relay agent to allow access to the 172.16.0.0/24 network.

1. In Server Manager on your Windows Server 2019 host, click the **Manage** menu and then click **Add Roles and Features**.

   a. At the Select installation type page, click **Next**.

   b. At the Select destination server page, click **Next**.

   c. At the Select server roles page, select **Remote Access** and click **Next**.

   d. At the Select features page, click **Next**.

   e. At the Remote Access page, click **Next**.

   f. At the Select role services page, select **DirectAccess and VPN (RAS)** and click **Add Features** when prompted. Next, select **Routing** and click **Next**.

   g. At the Confirm installation selections page, click **Install**.

   h. At the Installation progress page, click **Open the Getting Started Wizard** and then click **Close** to close the Add the Roles and Features Wizard.

2. At the Configure Remote Access wizard, click **Deploy VPN only** to open the Routing and Remote Access tool.

3. Close the Configure Remote Access window and click **OK** when prompted.

4. In the navigation pane of the Routing and Remote Access tool, right-click **SERVERX** and click **Configure and Enable Routing and Remote Access**.

   a. At the first page of the Routing and Remote Access Server Setup Wizard, click **Next**.

   b. At the Configuration page, select **Custom configuration** and click **Next**.

   c. At the Custom Configuration page, select **VPN access**. Next select **LAN routing** and click **Next**.

   d. Click **Finish**. Next, click **Start service** to start the Routing and Remote Access service.

5. Expand **IPv4** in the navigation pane and highlight **DHCP Relay Agent**. Note that the DHCP relay agent is not configured to listen to DHCPDISCOVER packets on any interface by default.

   a. Right-click **DHCP Relay Agent** and click **New Interface**. Select **vEthernet (Internal Virtual Switch)** and click **OK**. Note the default threshold values and click **OK**.

   b. Right-click **DHCP Relay Agent** again and click **Properties**. Type **172.16.0.1** in the Server address text box and click **Add** to ensure that DHCPDISCOVER requests are forwarded to the DHCP server 172.16.0.1. Click **OK** to close the DHCP Relay Agent Properties window when finished.

6. Right-click **Ports** in the navigation pane and click **Properties**. Note the default number of ports configured for each VPN type by default and click **OK**.

7. Right-click **SERVERX** in the navigation pane and click **Properties**. On the General tab, note that your server is configured for IPv4 routing and remote access.

   a. Highlight the **Security** tab. Note that your VPN server is configured to use Windows Authentication to authenticate remote access clients by default.

   b. Click the **Authentication Methods** button. Note that EAP and MS-CHAP v2 authentication methods are enabled by default, and click **OK**.

   c. Highlight the **IPv4** tab. Note the default options that obtain IP configuration from a DHCP server.

   d. Click **OK**.

8. In Server Manager, click the **Tools** menu and then click **Active Directory Users and Computers**.

   a. Highlight the **Users** folder under domainX.com in the navigation pane.

   b. Right-click the **Administrator** user account and click **Properties**.

   c. Highlight the **Dial-in** tab, select **Allow access,** and click **OK**.

   d. Close the Active Directory Users and Computers tool.

Project 9-3: Connecting to a VPN

In this Hands-On Project, you connect to the VPN server on your Windows Server 2019 host from your WindowsServer2019VM2 virtual machine. Following this, you enable split tunneling on the VPN connection.

1. On your WindowsServer2019VM2 virtual machine, right-click **Start** and click **Network Connections**.

2. In the navigation pane of the Settings window, highlight **VPN** and click **Add a VPN connection**.

   a. Select **Windows (built-in)** from the VPN provider drop-down box.

   b. Type **Sample PPTP VPN Connection** in the Connection name text box.

   c. Type the IP address of your Windows Server 2019 host (on the External Virtual Switch) in the Server name or address box.

   d. Select **Point to Point Tunneling Protocol (PPTP)** from the VPN type drop-down box and click **Save**.

3. Click **Sample PPTP VPN Connection** and then click **Connect**. Type **administrator@ domainX.com** in the User name text box, type **Secret555** in the Password text box, and click **OK**. Note that your VPN displays a Connected status.

4. Right-click **Start** and click **Windows PowerShell**. At the Windows PowerShell prompt, type **ipconfig /all** and press **Enter**. Note that you have two network interfaces:

   - *Ethernet adapter Ethernet* should list the IP configuration for your network connection to the External Virtual Switch.

   - *PPP adapter Sample PPTP VPN Connection* should contain an IP address on the 172.16.0.0/16 network that was obtained from the DHCP server on your Windows

Server 2019 host via the DHCP relay agent. This IP address represents the client side of the PPTP VPN tunnel. Also note that the default gateway for this network interface is set to 0.0.0.0 to ensure that all traffic passes through the VPN connection.

5. On your Windows Server 2019 host, right-click **Start** and click **Windows PowerShell**. At the Windows PowerShell prompt, type **ipconfig /all** and press **Enter**. Note that you have three network interfaces:

   - *Ethernet adapter vEthernet (External Virtual Switch)* should list the IP configuration for your network connection to the External Virtual Switch.
   - *Ethernet adapter vEthernet (Internal Virtual Switch)* should list the IP address 172.16.0.1 that was manually configured for your network connection to the Internal Virtual Switch.
   - *PPP adapter RAS (Dial In) Interface* should contain an IP address on the 172.16.0.0/16 network that matches the server side of the PPTP VPN tunnel to allow VPN clients the ability to connect to the VPN server. Note this IP address for the following step.

6. On your WindowsServer2019VM2 virtual machine, right-click **Start** and click **Run**.

   a. Type ***IPaddress*\\MarketingMaterials** in the Run dialog box and click **OK**, where *IPaddress* is the IP address of your Windows Server 2019 host on the External Virtual Switch. Note that you can continue to access the MarketingMaterials SMB shared folder on your Windows Server 2019 host using an unencrypted connection, as you have previously. Close the File Explorer window.

   b. Right-click **Start** and click **Run**. Type ***IPaddress*\\MarketingMaterials** in the Run dialog box and click **OK**, where *IPaddress* is the IP address of your Windows Server 2019 host on the *PPP adapter RAS (Dial In) Interface* from Step 5. Note that you can now access the MarketingMaterials SMB shared folder on your Windows Server 2019 host using an encrypted connection through the VPN tunnel. Close the File Explorer window.

   c. Right-click **Start** and click **Run**. Type **\\\\172.16.0.1\\MarketingMaterials** in the Run dialog box and click **OK**. Note that the VPN server allows you to access existing hosts on the 172.16.0.0/24 network via the VPN tunnel. Close the File Explorer window.

7. In the Routing and Remote Access tool on your Windows Server 2019 host, highlight **Ports** in the navigation pane. Note that you have one active PPTP port. Right-click this port, click **Status,** and note the statistics and VPN client IP address. Click **Disconnect** to close the VPN tunnel and then click **Close** to close the Port Status window.

8. Open File Explorer and navigate to the **C:\\Windows\\system32\\logfiles** folder. Double-click the **IN*DDMM*.log file** (where *DD* is the day of the month, and *MM* is the month of the year) to open it in Notepad. View the entries for your VPN connection and note that EAP-MSCHAP v2 was used as the authentication method. Close Notepad when finished.

9. In the Settings window on your WindowsServer2019VM2 virtual machine, click **Network and Sharing Center** under the Related settings section.

   a. Click **Change adapter settings** to open the Network Connections section of Control Panel.

   b. Right-click **Sample PPTP VPN Connection**, click **Properties**, and highlight the **Networking** tab.

    c. Select **Internet Protocol Version 4 (TCP/IPv4)** and click **Properties**.

    d. Click **Advanced**.

    e. Deselect **Use default gateway on remote network** and click **OK**.

    f. Click **OK** to close the Internet Protocol Version 4 (TCP/IPv4) Properties window.

    g. Click **OK** to close the Sample PPTP VPN Connection Properties window.

10. Right-click **Sample PPTP VPN Connection** in the Network Connections window and click **Connect / Disconnect**. Next, click **Sample PPTP VPN Connection** and click **Connect**.

11. Right-click **Start** and click **Run**. Type **\\172.16.0.1\MarketingMaterials** at the Run dialog box and click **OK**. Note that you have access to hosts on the 172.16.0.0/24 network via the VPN tunnel. Close the File Explorer window.

12. In the Windows PowerShell window, type **ipconfig /all** and press **Enter**. Note that *Sample PPTP VPN Connection* does not have a default gateway listed. As a result, the default gateway on the *Ethernet* network interface will be used for any traffic that is not destined for the 172.16.0.0/16 network on the remote access client.

13. Right-click **Sample PPTP VPN Connection** in the Network Connections window and click **Connect / Disconnect**. Next, click **Sample PPTP VPN Connection** and click **Disconnect**. Close the Network Connections window when finished.

Project 9-4: RADIUS

In this Hands-On Project, you install and configure the Network Policy and Access Services role on your Windows Server 2019 host, as well as configure a remote access policy for Marketing department users. To test the application of this remote access policy, you configure its settings to disconnect active users after 1 minute and view the results.

1. In Server Manager on your Windows Server 2019 host, click the **Manage** menu and then click **Add Roles and Features**.

    a. At the Select installation type page, click **Next**.

    b. At the Select destination server page, click **Next**.

    c. At the Select server roles page, select **Network Policy and Access Services** and click **Add Features** when prompted. Click **Next**.

    d. At the Select features page, click **Next**.

    e. At the Network Policy and Access Services page, click **Next**.

    f. At the Confirm installation selections page, click **Install**.

    g. At the Installation progress page, click **Close** to close the Add the Roles and Features Wizard.

2. In the navigation pane of the Routing and Remote Access tool, right-click **SERVERX**, click **Properties,** and highlight the **Security** tab. Note that your remote access server is automatically configured to use RADIUS for authentication and logging because the Network Policy and Access Services role was installed on the same computer. Click **OK** when finished.

3. In Server Manager, click the **Tools** menu and then click **Network Policy Server**.

4. In the navigation pane of the Network Policy Server tool, right-click **NPS (Local)** and note that the *Register server in Active Directory* is unavailable. This is because the RADIUS server is installed on a domain controller and automatically registered as a result. Press **Escape**.

5. Expand **Policies** in the navigation pane and highlight **Network Policies**. Note the two default remote access policies that deny dial-in permission for all VPN (Routing and Remote Access server) requests and requests from other servers.

6. Right-click **Network Policies** and click **New** to open the New Network Policy wizard.

   a. At the Specify Network Policy Name and Connection Type page, type **Marketing Remote Access Policy** in the Policy name text box. From the *Type of network access server* drop-down box, select **Remote Access Server (VPN-Dial up)** and click **Next**.

   b. At the Specify Conditions page, click **Add**.

      i. Highlight **User Groups** and click **Add**.

      ii. Click **Add Groups**.

      iii. Type **Marketing-G** in the Select Group dialog box and click **OK**.

      iv. Click **OK** to close the Windows Groups window.

      v. Click **Next**.

   c. At the Specify Access Permission page, note the default option that allows dial-in permission and click **Next**.

   d. At the Configure Authentication Methods page, note the default authentication methods chosen and click **Add**. Select **Microsoft: Secure password (EAP-MSCHAP v2)** and click **OK**. Click **Next**.

   e. At the Configure Constraints page, select **Session Timeout**, check the **Disconnect after the following maximum session time** option and note the default value of 1 minute. Click **Next**.

   f. At the Configure Settings page, select **IP Settings** and note the default value that obtains IP configuration using the method specified on the remote access server. Click **Next**.

   g. Click **Finish**. Note that the Processing Order for the Marketing Remote Access Policy is listed as 1 to ensure that it is processed before the two default remote access policies.

7. Highlight **Accounting** in the navigation pane and note that remote access connections are logged to the C:\Windows\system32\LogFiles folder by default.

   a. Click **Change Log File Properties** and highlight the **Log File** tab. Note the file name format of INyymm.log.

   b. Select **Daily** and note the new file name format of INyymmdd.log.

   c. Click **OK** to close the Log File Properties window.

8. On your WindowsServer2019VM2 virtual machine, right-click **Start** and click **Network Connections**.

   a. In the navigation pane of the Settings window, highlight **VPN**.

   b. Click **Sample PPTP VPN Connection** and then click **Advanced options**.

   c. Click **Clear sign-in info** and then click the back arrow in the upper left of the Settings window.

   d. Click **Sample PPTP VPN Connection** and then click **Connect**. Type **b.burtt@ domainX.com** in the User name text box, type **Secret555** in the Password text box, and click **OK**. Note that your VPN displays a Connected status.

   e. Wait for 1 minute. Note that your VPN is automatically disconnected using the session timeout value you specified in your remote access policy.

   f. Close the Settings window.

9. On your Windows Server 2019 host, open File Explorer and navigate to the **C:\ Windows\system32\logfiles** folder. Note that you now have a IN*ddmmyy*.log file (where *dd* is the day of the month, and *mm* is the month of the year, and *yy* is the year) that was created by your RADIUS server using the daily log format. Double-click this file to open it in Notepad. Note the recent VPN connection from user b.burtt@domain*X*.com and close Notepad when finished.

Project 9-5: DirectAccess

In this Hands-On Project, you configure DirectAccess on your Windows Server 2019 host and examine the results.

1. In Server Manager on your Windows Server 2019 host, click the **Tools** menu and then click **Remote Access Management**.

2. In the navigation pane of the Remote Access Management Console, highlight **VPN** and then click **Enable DirectAccess** in the Tasks pane.

   a. At the Introduction page of the Enable DirectAccess Wizard, click **Next**.

   b. At the DirectAccess Client Setup page, click Add. Type **Domain Computers** in the Select Groups dialog box and click **OK**. Select **Use force tunneling** and click **Next**.

   c. At the Remote Access Server Setup page, select **Behind an edge device (with a single network adapter)**, type **serverX.domainX.com** in the text box and click **Next**.

   d. At the Infrastructure Server Setup page, click **Next**.

   e. At the GPO Configuration page, click **Next**.

   f. At the Summary page, click **Finish**.

3. In the navigation pane, highlight **DirectAccess and VPN**.

4. Click **Edit** under Step 1.

   a. At the Deployment Scenario page of the Remote Access Setup wizard, note that DirectAccess will be used for client access and remote management and click **Next**.

   b. At the Select Groups page, note the selections you chose during the Enable DirectAccess Wizard and click **Next**.

   c. At the Network Connectivity Assistant page, note that clients access http://directaccess-WebProbeHost.domain*X*.com to locate DirectAccess connectivity information and click **Finish**.

5. Click **Edit** under Step 2.

   a. At the Network Topology page of the Remote Access Setup wizard, note the selections you chose during the Enable DirectAccess Wizard and click **Next**.

   b. At the Network Adapters page, note the self-signed HTTPS encryption certificate used for remote access authentication, as well as the network adapter used for remote access requests and click **Next**.

   c. At the Authentication page, note that the remote access server authenticates users using Active Directory and click **Next**.

   d. At the VPN Configuration page, note that the remote access server obtains IP configuration for the IPSec tunnel using a DHCP server but can be assigned a static address range. Highlight the **Authentication** tab and note that DirectAccess uses Windows Authentication by default but can be configured to use a RADIUS Authentication and click **Finish**.

6. Click **Edit** under Step 3.

   a. At the Network Location Server page of the Remote Access Setup wizard, note that the network location server is configured on the remote access server using a self-signed certificate and click **Next**.

   b. At the DNS page, note the default FQDN name resolution settings, as well as the URL for the network location server (DirectAccess-NLS.domain*X*.com) and click **Next**.

   c. At the DNS Suffix Search List page, note that you can modify the DNS suffix list configured during the Enable DirectAccess Wizard and click **Next**.

   d. At the Management page, note that you can optionally add the location of a management server and click **Finish**.

7. Click **Edit** under Step 4. Note that you can optionally extend IPSec encryption to encrypt traffic between remote access clients and specified application servers in the DMZ and click **Finish**.

8. In Server Manager on your Windows Server 2019 host, click the **Tools** menu and then click **DNS**. Highlight **domain*X*.com** under Forward Lookup Zones in the navigation pane. Note the additional A and AAAA resource records created for your DirectAccess configuration. Close DNS Manager when finished.

9. In Server Manager on your Windows Server 2019 host, click the **Tools** menu and then click **Group Policy Management**. In the Group Policy Management tool, expand **Forest: domain*X*.com**, **Domains**, **domain*X*.com** and note the two group policy objects created during the Enable DirectAccess Wizard that hold the settings used to configure DirectAccess clients and servers. Close the Group Policy Management tool when finished.

10. In the Remote Access Management Console, click **Remove Configuration Settings** under the Tasks pane and click **OK**. Click Close to close the Removing Configuration Settings window and close the Remote Access Management Console.

Project 9-6: Remote Desktop Services

In this Hands-On Project, you configure your Windows Server 2019 as a remote access server for Remote Desktop.

1. In Server Manager on your Windows Server 2019 host, click the **Manage** menu and then click **Add Roles and Features**.

   a. At the Select installation type page, click **Next**.

   b. At the Select destination server page, click **Next**.

   c. At the Select server roles page, select **Remote Desktop Services** and click **Next**.

   d. At the Select features page, click **Next**.

   e. At the Remote Desktop Services page, click **Next**.

   f. At the Select role services page, select the **Remote Desktop Connection Broker**.

      i. Select **Remote Desktop Licensing** and click **Add Features** when prompted.

      ii. Select **Remote Desktop Session Host** and click **Add Features** when prompted.

      iii. Select **Remote Desktop Web Access** and click **Add Features** when prompted.

      iv. Click **Next**.

   g. Click **Install**.

   h. Click **Close** to close the Add Roles and Features Wizard.

2. Right-click **Start** and click **Shut down or sign out**, **Restart**. Next, click **Continue** to restart your Windows Server 2019 host.

3. After your Windows Server 2019 host has booted, log into domain*X*.com as Administrator using the password **Secret555**. Next, click **Start** and then click **Server Manager**. After a few moments a notification will appear that you have 120 days to license Remote Desktop Services. You can ignore this notification each time it is displayed.

4. In Server Manager, click the **Manage** menu and then click **Add Roles and Features**.

   a. At the Select installation type page, select **Remote Desktop Services installation** and click **Next**.

   b. At the Select deployment type page, click **Next**.

   c. At the Select deployment scenario page, select **Session-based desktop deployment** and click **Next**.

   d. At the Review role services page, click **Next**.

   e. At the Specify RD Connection Broker server page, click **Next**.

   f. At the Specify RD Web Access server page, select **Install the RD Web Access role service on the RD Connection Broker server** and click **Next**.

   g. At the Specify RD Session Host servers page, click the arrow button to move SERVER*X*.domain*X*.com to the Selected pane and click **Next**.

   h. At the Confirm selections page, select **Restart the destination server automatically if required** and click **Deploy**.

   i. At the View progress page, click **Close**.

5. Right-click **Start** and click **Shut down or sign out**, **Restart**. Next, click **Continue** to restart your Windows Server 2019 host.

6. After your Windows Server 2019 host has booted, log into domain*X*.com as Administrator using the password **Secret555**. Next, click **Start** and then click **Server Manager**.

7. Highlight **Remote Desktop Services** in the navigation pane of Server Manager.

   a. In the DEPLOYMENT OVERVIEW pane, note that Remote Desktop Web Access, Remote Desktop Connection Broker, and Remote Desktop Session Host (used instead of Remote Desktop Virtualization Host) are already configured, but that you can optionally configure Remote Desktop Gateway and Remote Desktop Licensing.

      i. Click the green + symbol next to RD Licensing.

      ii. In the RD Licensing Servers wizard, click the arrow button to move SERVER*X*.domain*X*.com to the Selected pane and click **Next**.

      iii. Click **Add** to add your Remote Desktop Licensing server to your Remote Desktop Services configuration.

   b. In the DEPLOYMENT SERVERS pane, note that SERVER*X*.DOMAIN*X*.COM is configured as a Remote Desktop Connection Broker, Remote Desktop Session Host, Remote Desktop Licensing, and Remote Desktop Web Access server.

   c. In the GETTING STARTED WITH REMOTE DESKTOP SERVICES pane, note that you have the option to add more Remote Desktop Session Host servers, as well as create collections of Remote Desktop Session Host servers.

8. Select the **TASKS** drop-down menu from the DEPLOYMENT OVERVIEW pane and click **Edit Deployment Properties**.

   a. In the Deployment Properties window, note the default option that does not use a Remote Desktop Gateway server.

   b. Highlight **RD Licensing** in the navigation pane and select **Per Device**.

   c. Highlight **RD Web Access** in the navigation pane and note the default URL of https://SERVER*X*.DOMAIN*X*.COM/RdWeb for Remote Desktop Web Access.

   d. Highlight **Certificates** in the navigation pane and note that no certificates have been configured for the Remote Desktop Connection Broker and Remote Desktop Web Access components. Until an HTTPS certificate is configured for these components, they will not be functional.

   e. Click **OK**.

9. In the GET STARTED WITH REMOTE DESKTOP SERVICES pane, click **Create session collections**.

   a. At the first page of the Create Collection wizard, click **Next**.

   b. At the Name the collection page, type **Collection1** in the Name text box and click **Next**.

   c. At the Specify RD Session Host servers page, click the arrow button to move SERVER*X*.domain*X*.com to the Selected pane and click **Next**.

   d. At the Specify user groups page, note the default group of Domain Users and click **Next**.

   e. At the Specify user profile disks page, deselect **Enable user profile disks** and click **Next**.

   f. At the Confirm selections page, click **Create**.

   g. At the View Progress page, click **Close**.

10. In the navigation pane, highlight **Collection1** under the Collections section.
11. Select the **TASKS** drop-down menu from the PROPERTIES pane and click **Edit Properties**.
    a. Highlight **Session** in the Collection1 Collection Properties window and view the available options. Select **5 minutes** from the Idle session limit drop-down box.
    b. Highlight **Load Balancing** and note that SERVER*X*.DOMAIN*X*.COM receives 100 percent of all requests from the Remote Desktop Connection Broker as it is the only remote access server in the collection.
    c. Highlight **Click Settings** and note that users are allowed to access audio devices, volumes (Drives), clipboard (for copy and paste operations), and printers on their remote access client by default and click **OK**.
12. Select the **TASKS** drop-down menu from the REMOTEAPP PROGRAMS pane and click **Public RemoteApp Programs**.
    a. At the Select RemoteApp programs page of the Publish RemoteApp Programs wizard, select **Paint** and click **Next**.
    b. At the Confirmation page, click **Publish**.
    c. At the Completion page, click **Close**. Leave the Collection1 section of Server Manager open for the next Hands-On Project.

Project 9-7: Remote Desktop Connection

In this Hands-On Project, you connect to a partner's remote access server using Remote Desktop and verify your connection.

1. After your partner has completed Hands-On Project 9-6, click **Start** and then click **Remote Desktop Connection**.
2. At the Remote Desktop Connection window, type your partner's IP address on the vEthernet (External Virtual Switch) network interface in the Computer text box and click **Show Options**.
    a. Highlight the **Local Resources** tab and click **More**.
    b. Select **Drives** and click **OK**.
    c. Click **Connect**.
    d. Select **Don't ask me again for connection to this computer** and click **Connect**.
3. At the Windows Security window, click **More choices,** and then click **Use a different account**.
    a. Type **b.burtt@domain*Y*.com** in the User name text box, where *Y* is your partner's number.
    b. Type **Secret555** in the Password text box and click **OK**.
    c. When prompted to validate the self-signed encryption certificate used to protect the credentials, select **Don't ask me again for connections to this computer** and click **Yes**. Note that you now have a Remote Desktop connection to your partner's server.
4. In your Remote Desktop session, click **Start** and then click **Server Manager**. Note that you are prompted for Administrator credentials because you are logged in as a regular user (Bob Burtt). Click **No** to cancel the operation.

5. Right-click **Start** and click **Run**. In the Run dialog box, type **\\172.16.0.1** and click **OK**. Note that you have access to shared resources on your partner's 172.16.0.0/16 internal network.

   a. Spend a few moments browsing your partner's resources. If your partner completed Discovery Exercise 5-1, the contents of the UserGuides, HelpDeskKnowledgebase, and EquipmentRequestForms shared folders should be unique compared to the same shared folders on your server.

   b. In the navigation pane of File Explorer, expand **This PC** and note that you have access to your local volumes. These volumes append the words "on SERVER*X*" following the drive letter. Explore these volumes.

   c. Leave the File Manager window open for a later step.

6. In Server Manager on your partner's Windows Server 2019 host, select the **TASKS** menu in the CONNECTIONS pane for Collection1 and click **Refresh**. Note that an active connection for b.burtt is now listed, as well as a connection for Administrator (that represents your local login). Right-click the connection for **b.burtt** and click **Send Message**. Type a message of your choice in the Send Message dialog box and click **Send**.

7. In the Remote Desktop connection window on your Windows Server 2019 host, note the message that you received.

8. Right-click **Start** and click **Shut down or sign out**, **Disconnect** to disconnect from your Remote Desktop connection.

9. Click **Start** and then click **Remote Desktop Connection**. Note that your partner's IP address is listed in the Computer text box and that b.burtt@domain*Y*.com is listed in the User name field from the previous connection. Click **Connect**. Note that your Remote Desktop connection displays your previous desktop (including File Explorer), because you disconnected from the session previously.

10. Wait 5 minutes. Note that you are warned about reaching your idle time limit. Click **OK** to resume your session and reset this limit.

11. Right-click **Start** and click **Shut down or sign out**, **Sign out** to log out of your Remote Desktop connection.

12. Click **Start** and type **RemoteApp**. Click **RemoteApp and Desktop Connections**.

    a. In the RemoteApp and Desktop Connections window, click **Access RemoteApp and desktops**.

    b. At the Access RemoteApp and desktops window, type **http://*IPaddress*** where *IPaddress* is your partner's IP address on the vEthernet (External Virtual Switch) network interface and click **Next**.

    c. At the Ready to set up the connection page, click **Next**. Note that you are unable to complete the connection as your partner's Remote Desktop Web Access component is not configured with an HTTPS encryption certificate.

    d. Click **Close** to close the Access RemoteApp and desktops window, and then close Control Panel.

Discovery Exercises

Exercise 9-1

In Hands-On Project 9-3, you connected to your Windows Server 2019 host using a PPTP VPN from your WindowsServer2019VM2 virtual machine. Reconfigure your Windows Server 2019 host as a VPN remote access server that allows for L2TP connections using a preshared key of Secret555. Next, configure your remote access server to allow CHAP authentication (this must be performed for the server in the Routing and Remote Access tool as well as in the remote access policy in the Network Policy Server tool). Following this, configure a new VPN connection on your WindowsServer2019VM2 virtual machine that uses L2TP alongside the preshared key of Secret555 to connect to your Windows Server 2019 host. Finally, connect to your Windows Server 2019 host using this VPN connection, and view the active port L2TP port in the Routing and Remote Access tool to verify your configuration.

Exercise 9-2

Recall that demand-dial interfaces are often configured on the router that connects to the demarc in an organization to provide secure access to other networks in the organization across the Internet. You can test this functionality in a classroom environment using a partner. Create a demand-dial interface that automatically connects to a VPN on your partner's router when traffic is sent to the 172.17.0.0/24 network (a fictitious network in our configuration). Next, execute the `ping 172.17.0.1` command in a Command Prompt window on your Windows Server 2019 host. Because the 172.17.0.0/24 network is not configured on your partner's system, you will not receive a response. However, you should notice that your demand-dial interface automatically created a VPN between your router and your partner's router in the Routing and Remote Access tool because you generated traffic destined for the 172.17.0.0/24 network.

Exercise 9-3

In addition to providing remote access to an organization, you can use VPNs to protect personal traffic that is sent to and from the Internet in an untrusted public network, such as the free Wi-Fi network at a fast food restaurant or coffee shop. Consequently, many public VPN providers will allow you to connect to their remote access servers, usually for a monthly or yearly fee. These VPN providers often require that you install a custom VPN client or Web browser plugin that you can use to create a VPN when you are connected to the untrusted public network. One popular example is *Hotspot Shield* (*https://www.hotspotshield.com*). Use an Internet search engine to search for three additional public VPN providers and summarize your findings in a one-page memo. For each provider, list the VPN protocol they use, the cost (if applicable), the method used to connect to the VPN, as well as any other features that differentiate them from other VPN providers.

Exercise 9-4

DirectAccess is not the only method you can use to automatically create remote access connections for laptops in an organization. Windows 10 contains a feature called *AlwaysOn* that automatically connects to a remote access server using an IKEv2 VPN when the computer is located in a network outside of the organization. Use an Internet search engine to research the features and configuration of AlwaysOn. In a one-page memo, compare and contrast the features and configuration of AlwaysOn and DirectAccess.

Exercise 9-5

In addition to providing remote access, Remote Desktop Services can also be used to centralize the location of programs within an organization, as well as allow computers with limited hardware to run programs that require more resources than available. As a result, many manufacturers sell inexpensive computers called *thin clients* that contain only enough resources to run a Remote Desktop app. All other functionality is provided by the programs that are executed in a Remote Desktop connection. Use an Internet search engine to research some thin client products that are available for Microsoft Remote Desktop, as well as some common uses of thin clients in different environments. Summarize your findings in a one-page memo.

Exercise 9-6

Most remote access problems are caused by network-related issues that prevent the remote access client from accessing the remote access server. However, some remote access problems are caused by incorrect configuration on a remote access server. With a partner, brainstorm configuration items to check when a VPN, DirectAccess, or Remote Desktop remote access client is unable to connect to a remote access server. Summarize these configuration items in a one-page memo, organized by remote access type.

CONFIGURING WEB SERVICES AND CLOUD TECHNOLOGIES

After completing this module, you will be able to:

Describe the available cloud components, types, delivery models, and configurations

Provide Web services using Internet Information Services (IIS)

Configure Windows containers

Implement a Linux Web server using the Windows Subsystem for Linux (WSL)

Configure Linux Containers on Windows (LCOW)

Outline scenarios for implementing Windows Server 2019 in a cloud environment

You can choose from many cloud technologies and configurations to host Web apps on Windows Server 2019. To manage Windows Server 2019 systems in a cloud environment, you must understand how to configure Windows Server 2019 Web services, as well as the Windows Server 2019 cloud technologies that support Web apps. In this module, you'll examine key cloud concepts as well as the configuration of Web services on Windows Server 2019. Next, you'll learn how to run Windows Web apps using containers, as well as explore the technologies available for running Linux Web apps on Windows Server 2019. At the end of this module, you'll examine common configuration options used to implement Windows Server 2019 in a cloud environment.

Understanding the Cloud

Many different types of cloud configurations and technologies are available today. In order to configure Windows Server 2019 cloud technologies, you must first have a solid understanding of cloud concepts. More specifically, you should be able to define the cloud, as well as identify various cloud types, delivery models, and storage methods. Additionally, you should understand the process used to deploy new versions of Web apps on cloud servers.

Defining the Cloud

In the early 1990s, the US government–funded **Advanced Research Projects Agency Network (ARPANET)** and **National Science Foundation Network (NSFNET)** infrastructures were sold to different companies to create the commercial Internet. These companies were called Internet Service Providers (ISPs) and provided Internet access to individuals and organizations for a fee.

However, aside from providing physical network access to other computers, ISPs provided no resources. Instead, most resources available on the Internet in the 1990s consisted of websites that contained webpages with information and media (e.g., pictures, music, video) for different topics and organizations. These websites were hosted on Web servers and accessed using the HTTP or HTTPS protocols from a Web browser on a client. As shown in Figure 10-1, the worldwide collection of Web servers on the Internet was called **World Wide Web (WWW)**.

Today, most Web servers contain one or more **Web apps** that process and communicate both data and media to clients in complex ways. Search engines (e.g., Google), Office 365, video streaming services (e.g., Netflix), personal banking

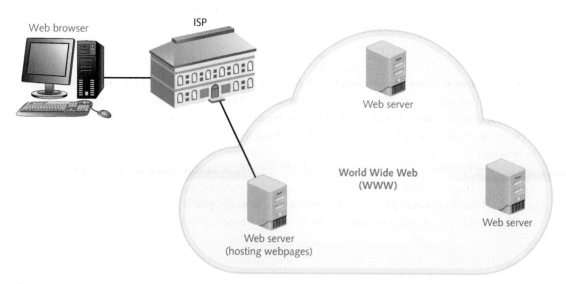

Figure 10-1   **The World Wide Web of the 1990s**

and social media websites, and the software on the Internet that smartphones and smart assistants (e.g., Amazon Alexa) communicate with are all examples of Web apps. Web apps are software programs on Web servers that can be accessed by other computers and IoT devices across the Internet via a client program, Web browser, or mobile app. Each Web server that runs a Web app is called a cloud server, and the worldwide collection of cloud servers is called the cloud, as shown in Figure 10-2.

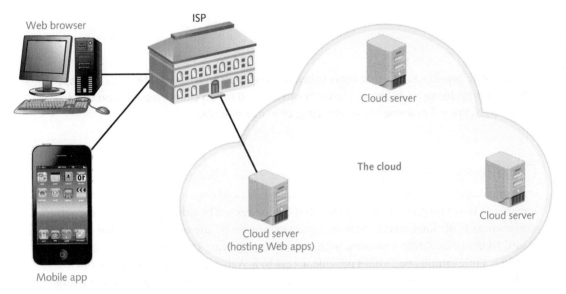

Figure 10-2   **The cloud**

Note

Most Web apps are accessed from a website on a Web server. In this case, the website is said to provide the "front end" for the Web app. Client programs and mobile apps can also be used as the front end for Web apps, either by connecting to a website using the HTTP or HTTPS protocol, or by communicating directly to a Web app on a cloud server using a different TCP/IP protocol.

The rapid growth of the WWW in the 1990s was largely due to the free and open-source **Apache Web server**, which ran on the free and open-source Linux operating system. Apache and Linux allowed anyone with a computer and Internet access to host a Web server to serve webpages without any software costs. Consequently, Web technologies have evolved using the free and open-source ecosystem since the 1990s, and most Web apps in the cloud today run on Linux systems using free and open-source **Web app frameworks**. A Web app framework is a collection of software packages or modules that allow software developers to write Web apps using a **programming language** without having to implement many underlying system functionalities, such as network protocol usage and process/thread management. For example, the Django Web app framework allows programmers to easily write Web apps using the Python programming language, whereas the Microsoft .NET framework allows programmers to easily write Web apps using a wide variety of different programming languages, including C# and Active Server Pages (ASP).

> **Note** 📎
>
> In addition to providing tools that allow software developers to easily create Linux Web apps, Microsoft provides several technologies that can be used to run Linux Web apps on Windows Server 2019. We will examine these technologies in this module.

Cloud Types

Any organization that hosts cloud servers is called a **cloud provider**. A **public cloud** consists of cloud servers on the Internet that can be rented by others, whereas a **private cloud** consists of cloud servers that are used exclusively by the organization that owns them. **Hybrid cloud** refers to using both a public and private cloud together for a specific purpose. For example, you could provide access to a Web app in a private cloud, but redirect users to the same Web app in a public cloud when your Web app receives a large number of requests that consume too many hardware resources.

> **Note** 📎
>
> There are many public clouds available on the Internet, including Amazon Web Services, Google Cloud Platform, Salesforce Cloud, Digital Ocean, and Microsoft Azure.

> **Note** 📎
>
> Each public cloud provider provides a website or configuration tool that allows you to configure cloud servers. These websites and configuration tools are updated frequently and often include terminology and processes that are unique to the cloud provider. As a result, we will not focus on the configuration of a specific public cloud provider in this module. Instead, this module will focus on the Windows Server 2019 technologies and processes that are common in both public and private cloud environments.

Cloud Delivery Models

Regardless of whether you are using a public or private cloud, you can host Web apps on a cloud server using different methods. These methods are called **cloud delivery models** and include **Infrastructure as a Service (IaaS)**, **Platform as a Service (PaaS)**, and **Software as a Service (SaaS)**.

With IaaS, the cloud provider offers a cloud platform that provides Internet access, IP addressing, and FQDN name resolution to virtual machines that you create on their hypervisor. You must manage each virtual machine as you would any other operating system, including installing and managing the Web apps that users will access from across the Internet. This structure is shown in Figure 10-3.

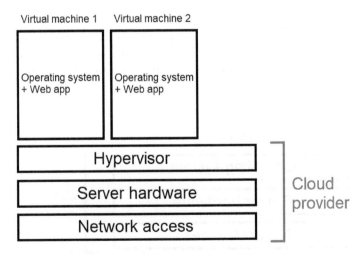

Figure 10-3   A sample IaaS structure

PaaS allows you to run Web app containers in the cloud. Recall from Module 1 that containers do not contain a full operating system. As a result, they must be run using container software that allows access to a kernel and supporting software libraries on an underlying operating system (or "platform"), as shown in Figure 10-4.

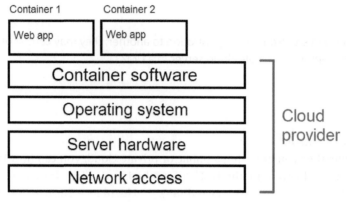

Figure 10-4   A sample PaaS structure

Note

IaaS and PaaS can be used together. In this case, containers are run on the operating system in a virtual machine hosted on a cloud provider.

Unlike IaaS and PaaS, SaaS is not used to configure virtual machines or containers. Instead, the SaaS cloud provider maintains all aspects of the network, hardware, and operating system; it merely executes the Web app that you provide. This structure is shown in Figure 10-5.

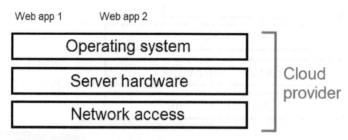

Figure 10-5   A sample SaaS structure

Note

Most public cloud providers allow you to choose between SaaS, PaaS, and IaaS.

> **Note** 📎
>
> The words "as a service" are commonly used for marketing purposes. For example, Mobile as a Service (MaaS) can be used to describe Web apps that manage smartphone devices, whereas Database as a Service (DBaaS) can be used to describe Web apps that provide access to a database. These terms are collectively referred to as **Anything as a Service (XaaS)** and represent specific uses of either SaaS, PaaS, or IaaS.

Cloud Storage

In addition to the storage needed for the Web app, virtual machine, or container, many Web apps need to store large amounts of data on a cloud provider. One option is to store this data on a filesystem on the cloud provider. This type of storage is called **block storage**, and public cloud providers charge you based on the total amount of storage that you select for your filesystem. Because block storage is fast, it is often used for storing database files, but it is normally associated with a single Web app, virtual machine, or container only. Another storage option available with public cloud providers is called **object storage**. Object storage allows Web apps to directly store objects, such as pictures, files, and video using an HTTP request that is sent to an object storage service. Although object storage is slower than block storage, it is often less expensive as the public cloud provider only charges you for the space that is used by the objects you've stored. In addition, object storage can easily be shared by several different Web apps, virtual machines, or containers. Web apps that need to store and share thousands of pictures, files, and video typically use object storage.

> **Note** 📎
>
> When purchasing storage from a public cloud provider, block storage is often referred to as a **persistent volume**, and object storage is often called **Binary Large Object (BLOB) storage**.

> **Note** 📎
>
> Most public cloud providers also charge you **egress fees** to move your data to a private cloud or another public cloud provider.

Understanding Continuous Deployment

Most Web apps that are created by developers in your organization are hosted in a container (PaaS) or virtual machine (IaaS). These Web apps must be revised on a continual basis to fix bugs and incorporate new features. While developers can create new versions of the Web app on their workstation, they need to test these new versions on the cloud provider to ensure that they work as expected before replacing the existing Web app with the new version. As part of the development process, new versions of the Web app may need to be tested on a cloud provider several times per day. Each new version will require that a new container or virtual machine be created with the correct settings for the Web app using **build automation** software. Additional software is required to move the Web app from the developer workstation to the new container or virtual machine on the cloud provider, as well as ensure that the Web app is ready for execution. This entire process is called a **continuous deployment (CD)** workflow, and the server administrators that manage this workflow are called **devops** because they are system operators (ops) that support Web app development (dev). Figure 10-6 illustrates a sample CD workflow that allows developers to push new versions of a Web app to virtual machines in the cloud.

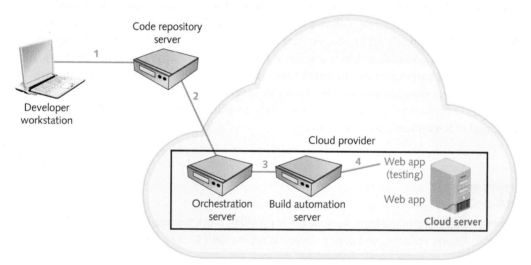

Figure 10-6   A sample CD workflow

The first step shown in Figure 10-6 involves developers pushing a new version of their Web app code to a **code repository** server. Next, **orchestration** software running on a server at the cloud provider obtains the new version of the Web app from the code repository server (step 2), converting it to executable form if necessary (a process called **compiling**). The Web app is then sent to a build automation server (step 3), which creates a new container or virtual machine on the cloud server and adds the Web app to it for testing (step 4). At this point, the new version of the Web app can be tested by the Web app developers. If this new version doesn't work as expected, the container or virtual machine is removed and the whole process is repeated for another new version of the Web app. However, if this new version of the Web app works as expected, the container or virtual machine used to test the Web app will replace the publicly accessible container or virtual machine running the old version of the Web app, and Internet users will immediately have access to the new version.

> **Note** 🖉
>
> Hundreds of different software packages are available for implementing a CD workflow. Today, *Git* is the most commonly used code repository software, while *Jenkins* and *Kubernetes* are commonly used for orchestration. *Ansible, Puppet, Chef,* and *SaltStack* are widely used build automation software packages.

Configuring Web Services

To host websites and Web apps on a Windows Server 2019 system, you can install and configure Microsoft's Internet Information Services (IIS) Web server software. IIS can be used to host websites and Web apps that are used exclusively by organization users, or public websites and Web apps available to Internet users.

We've examined the configuration of several Microsoft Web apps in previous modules, including the Windows Admin Center (https://*servername*), Remote Desktop Web Access (https://*servername*/RdWeb), and the Internet Printing Protocol Web app (http://*printservername*/printers). For each of these Web apps, IIS was automatically installed and configured during the Web app installation. Many third-party Web apps that you install on Windows Server 2019 also require that you install IIS. For example, a help desk ticketing Web app built using the .NET framework will use IIS to provide a website that users can access to submit and track help desk support tickets. If your organization develops a Web app that is used to sell products or provide a service to Internet users, it can be hosted on a Web server in a public or private cloud using IIS. This Web server may be installed directly on server hardware or in a virtual machine or container.

IIS allows any Web app that adheres to the **Common Gateway Interface (CGI)** standard to interface with it. If a Web app supports **Internet Server Application Programming Interface (ISAPI)**, a group of **dynamic-link libraries (DLLs)** can also be generated to provide closer interaction with IIS as well as better performance. However, most Web apps that interface with IIS are written using the ASP or ASP.NET Web app framework. This is because Microsoft provides additional IIS features for ASP and ASP. NET Web apps, including the ability to isolate different Web apps using **application pools** for security and management.

Web app developers will often require access to your Web server to upload and modify website and Web app content. If the Web server is located in your organization, you can share folders using SMB or NFS to provide this access. However, if the Web server is located in a cloud environment across the Internet, **File Transfer Protocol (FTP)** is often used to transfer website and Web app content. As a result, IIS contains an FTP server service that you can optionally install to provide FTP access on your Web server. Alternatively, Web app developers can use **Web Distributed Authoring and Versioning (WebDAV)** to upload and modify website content (but not Web app content). WebDAV uses the standard HTTP and HTTPS protocols to transfer information.

Installing IIS

To configure Windows Server 2019 as a Web server using IIS, you must first install the **Web Server (IIS)** server role. When you select this role in the Add Roles and Features Wizard and progress through the wizard, you are prompted to choose the necessary IIS role services, as shown in Figure 10-7. Each role service shown in Figure 10-7 consists of subcomponents that you can select individually to provide specific Web server features. Table 10-1 describes the components available for each role service.

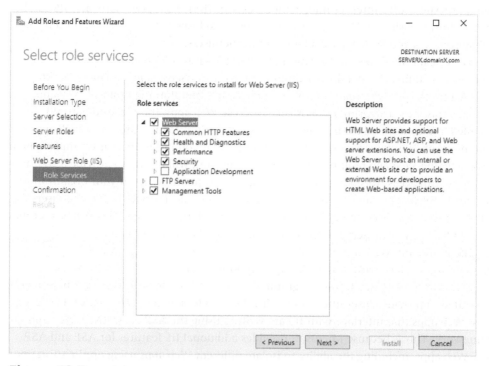

Figure 10-7   Selecting IIS role services

Note

If you install a server role that provides a Web app using the Add Roles and Features Wizard, IIS is also installed (if necessary) and the IIS role services and subcomponents needed by the Web app are automatically selected.

Note

When installing a Web server that will run a Web app created by your organization or a third-party vendor, consult with your organization's Web app developers or the third-party vendor to find out which role services and subcomponents must be installed to support the Web app.

Table 10-1   IIS role services

Role service	Description
Web Server Common HTTP Features	Provides basic Web server functionality, including the ability to serve a default webpage document that uses **Hypertext Markup Language (HTML)**. Additionally, this role service can allow website users to browse file names, view HTTP errors, or use WebDAV.
Web Server Health and Diagnostics	Provides the ability to log website activity using a variety of different formats, including **Open Database Connectivity (ODBC)**. This role service also provides tools monitoring and interpreting server activity and log file contents.
Web Server Performance	Provides compression for both websites (static content) and Web apps (dynamic content) when transmitting data across a network to improve performance.
Web Server Security	Provides for different authentication methods (basic, digest, certificate, and Windows), as well as modules that can be used to restrict access to websites and Web apps based on HTTP/HTTPS packet, IP, domain, and URL.
Web Server Application Development	Provides modules that allow Web apps to interface with the Web server using the .NET framework, ASP, ASP.NET, CGI, and ISAPI. Additionally, this role service allows Web apps to automatically create webpages using **Server Side Includes (SSI)**, as well as allows ASP.NET Web apps to communicate using the **WebSocket** protocol.
FTP Server	Allows users and ASP.NET Web apps to transfer files to and from the Web server using the FTP protocol.
IIS Management Tools	Provides the IIS Management Console tool, IIS management scripts, legacy tool support, as well as a service that allows for remote IIS management.

You can use the Add Roles and Features Wizard to add IIS role services after the Web Server (IIS) server role has been installed. In this case, the existing IIS role services and installed subcomponents will be listed under the Web Server (IIS) server role at the *Select server roles* page, as shown in Figure 10-8. You can then select additional role services or expand the existing role services to select additional subcomponents before progressing through the remainder of the Add Roles and Features Wizard.

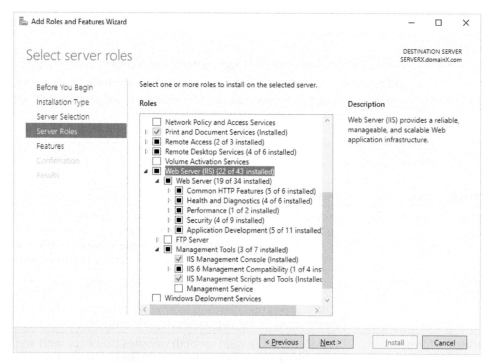

Figure 10-8   **Adding role services to an existing IIS installation**

Configuring IIS

After IIS has been installed, you can manage Web server and website configuration using the **IIS Manager** tool shown in Figure 10-9. To start IIS Manager, you can select Internet Information Services (IIS) Manager from the Tools menu in Server Manager.

As shown in Figure 10-9, a website called *Default Web Site* is created by default under the Sites folder in the Connections pane of IIS Manager. This website responds to HTTP requests on TCP port 80 and allows clients to view the website and Web app content in the C:\inetpub\wwwroot folder. If a user authenticates to the Web server, they receive access to website and Web app files in the C:\inetpub\wwwroot folder according to the NTFS/ReFS permissions assigned to their user account. To allow for public (anonymous) access to *Default Web Site*, the IIS_IUSRS group in your Active Directory domain or workgroup

Figure 10-9   IIS Manager

is granted *Read & Execute* and *List folder contents* NTFS/ReFS permissions to the C:\inetpub\ wwwroot folder. If you click Edit Permissions from the Actions pane in Figure 10-9, you will access the properties of C:\inetpub\wwwroot folder. You can then highlight the Security tab to modify the default NTFS/ReFS permissions. To open the C:\inetpub\wwwroot folder in File Explorer, you can click Explore from the Actions pane in Figure 10-9.

Note @

The IIS_IUSRS group in an Active Directory domain or workgroup is used to provide anonymous access to both website and Web app content. To provide anonymous access to website content only, you can instead assign permissions to the IUSRS group.

You can optionally configure *Default Web Site* to respond to HTTPS requests if an HTTPS encryption certificate is installed on your Web server. To do this, you must click Bindings from the Actions pane in Figure 10-9 and add the HTTPS protocol to the Site Bindings window shown in Figure 10-10. When you click Add in Figure 10-10, you must select the HTTPS protocol and HTTPS encryption certificate, as well as specify the TCP port number (443 is used by default) and host name (FQDN) of the Web server. To ensure that clients do not receive a security warning, the Web server FQDN must match the FQDN listed in the HTTPS certificate.

Figure 10-10   Binding the HTTPS protocol to a website

Note 🔗

You can configure multiple websites on a Web server, but each website must be configured to respond to a unique HTTP or HTTPS port number, and direct clients to a unique folder on the filesystem. To create a website in IIS Manager, you can highlight the Sites folder in the Connections pane and click Add Website from the Actions pane.

The Features View pane in Figure 10-9 displays the *Default Web Site* features that you can configure for each IIS role service subcomponent. To configure a feature, you can select it in the Features View and click Open Feature from the Actions pane. Many of these features can also be configured at the server level if you highlight SERVERX in the Connections pane. In this case, the features will apply to all websites configured on SERVERX. Table 10-2 describes features that are commonly installed on Web servers.

Table 10-2   Common IIS configuration features

Role service	Applies to	Description
Authentication	Server and websites	Specifies the authentication methods required to access a website or Web app. Anonymous authentication is enabled by default to allow for public user access.
Compression	Server and websites	Specifies compression settings for static and dynamic content.

Table 10-2   Common IIS configuration features *(continued)*

Role service	Applies to	Description
Default Document	Server and websites	Specifies the default webpage or Web app file that a client views. By default, clients view the first file in the website folder from the following list: Default.htm, Default.asp, index.htm, index.html, iistart.htm, default.aspx. In the absence of a webpage or Web app file, clients view the file contents of the folder.
Directory Browsing	Server and websites	Specifies information displayed when listing a folder's contents.
Error Pages	Server and websites	Specifies webpages that are shown when a specific error occurs on the Web server (e.g., *404 File Not Found* for an invalid webpage name).
Handler Mappings	Server and websites	Specifies the Web app modules that are used to process files in a website folder.
IP Address and Domain Restrictions	Server and websites	Allows you to create entries for allowed and denied clients based on their IP address or domain name.
Logging	Server and websites	Specifies the format used for logging website requests, as well as the log file location.
Request Filtering	Server and websites	Allows you to configure rules to restrict access to website content, based on the HTTP or HTTPS request.
Server Certificates	Server	Allows you to manage the HTTPS certificates that can be used by websites. You can also use this feature to request an HTTPS certificate from a public or Active Directory Certification Authority, or create a self-signed HTTPS certificate.
SSL Settings	Websites	Specifies whether HTTPS is required for access to a website and whether client certificates can be used for authentication.

The website content used to access Web apps is not normally stored in the C:\inetpub\wwwroot folder of *Default Web Site*. Instead, most server administrators create a **virtual directory** under *Default Web Site* for each Web app on the Web server. A virtual directory associates a directory name in a **Uniform Resource Locator (URL)** to a folder on the filesystem that contains website and Web app content. For example, to access the xcontrol Web app stored in the C:\xcontrolapp directory on serverx.domainx.com, users could enter the `https://serverx.domainx.com/xcontrol` URL in their Web browser. To create this virtual directory under *Default Web Site*, you can click View Virtual Directories from the Actions pane in Figure 10-9, click Add Virtual Directory, and specify the information shown in Figure 10-11.

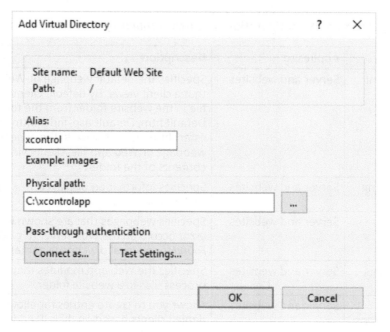

Figure 10-11   Creating a virtual directory

 Note

You can choose from a wide variety of different PowerShell cmdlets for configuring IIS. Search *IISAdministration PowerShell* on docs.microsoft.com for more information.

Configuring Containers

Platform as a Service (PaaS) is the most common method for hosting Web apps in a public or private cloud. In addition to a Web app, most containers include a Web server and one or more Web app frameworks that are required by the Web app.

Recall from Module 1 that Docker is the most common container software used to run containers on operating systems today, and that Windows containers is the component of Windows Server 2019 that allows you to install and use Docker. Docker containers are run and managed by a service called the **Docker daemon** and nearly all Docker configurations are performed using the docker command, which is often referred to as the **Docker client** program.

Docker provides an online repository of preconfigured **container images** that you can download and run on your system to create one or more containers. This repository is called **Docker Hub**, and can be used to host public container images available to anyone, or private container images that are only available to specific user accounts on Docker Hub. Moreover, containers can be customized with settings and software beyond those provided by the container image from which they are created.

> **Note** 📎
>
> You can create a free Docker Hub user account at hub.docker.com.

> **Note** 📎
>
> Organizations can choose to add their Web app to a container created from an existing public container image from Docker Hub, or they can create their own custom container image that includes their Web app. For more information on creating a Docker container image, search *Dockerfile* on docs.docker.com.

Installing Docker

Before you can use Docker to provide for containers on a Windows Server 2019 system, you must first download and install the **Docker Enterprise Edition (EE)** package for Windows Server from either Microsoft or Docker. This package can be obtained using one of two different Windows PowerShell modules:

- *DockerMsftProvider* allows you to obtain a stable (widely tested) version of Docker EE provided by Microsoft.
- *DockerProvider* allows you to obtain the latest version of Docker EE provided by Docker.

> **Note** 📎
>
> At the time of this writing, you must use DockerProvider if you wish to execute Linux containers on Windows Server 2019. Linux containers are discussed later in this module.

To download and install the Docker EE package from Microsoft using the DockerMsftProvider module, you can open a Windows PowerShell window as Administrator and run the following two commands:

```
PS C:\> Install-Module -Name DockerMsftProvider -Repository
psgallery -Force
PS C:\> Install-Package -Name docker -ProviderName
DockerMsftProvider
```

Alternatively, to download and install the latest Docker EE package from Docker using the DockerProvider module, you can open a Windows PowerShell window as Administrator and run the following two commands:

```
PS C:\> Install-Module -Name DockerProvider -Force
PS C:\> Install-Package -Name Docker -ProviderName DockerProvider
-RequiredVersion preview
```

After installing the Docker EE package, you must reboot your system. If you installed Docker EE using the DockerMsftProvider module, the Docker daemon is configured to automatically start at boot time. However, if you installed Docker EE using the DockerProvider module, the Docker daemon is not started by default. You can execute the `Start-Service Docker` command in Windows PowerShell to start the Docker daemon, and the `Set-Service -Name Docker -StartupType Automatic` command to configure it to start automatically at boot time.

Obtaining Container Images

After installing the Docker EE package, you can use the `docker` command at a Windows PowerShell or Command Prompt window to search for and download container images from Docker Hub. First, you must execute the `docker login` command to log into Docker Hub, specifying your Docker Hub credentials when prompted. Next, you can use the `docker search` command to search Docker Hub for container images by keyword. For example, to search Docker Hub for containers that have IIS installed, you can run the following command (partial results shown):

```
PS C:\> docker search iis
NAME                              DESCRIPTION
microsoft/aspnet                  Microsoft IIS images
microsoft/iis                     Microsoft IIS images
nanoserver/iis                    Nano Server + IIS
nanoserver/iis-mysql-php-wordpress Nano Server (v.10.0.14393) + IIS...
nanoserver/iis-php                Windows Nano Server + IIS + PHP 7
compulim/iisnode                  IIS with Node.js
nugardt/iis                       IIS with .NET 4.6 ASP
```

```
jmajoor/iis-aspnetcore              ASP.NET Core on Windows with IIS
iisue/alpine-android-fastlane       A Docker container to build and...
appalachios/iis-hello-world         Simple ASP.NET site build on...
iiska/docker-aws-cli                Docker image providing docker...
...
```

The first two results listed (`microsoft/aspnet` and `microsoft/iis`) are container images that are hosted publicly by the microsoft user on Docker Hub, which indicates that they are provided officially by Microsoft. Most container images provided by the Microsoft user on Docker Hub are modified versions of Server Core.

The next three results are also official container images provided publicly by Microsoft, but hosted using the nanoserver user on Docker Hub to indicate that they were built using Nano Server. Recall from Module 1 that Nano Server is a small footprint Windows Server that can be used to host Web apps. In Windows Server 2016, you can install Nano Server directly on server hardware or generate a Nano Server virtual hard disk file that could be executed as a Hyper-V virtual machine. However, starting with Windows Server 2019, Nano Server is only provided as a base container image (`microsoft/nanoserver`) that you can modify to include additional components such as IIS and Web app frameworks. The nanoserver container images listed in the previous output are Nano Server container images that have been modified to include IIS and other Web app frameworks.

Note 📎

Nano Server container images are often much smaller than other Windows container images and contain fewer components and processes that use system resources. As a result, they are well suited to hosting Web apps in cloud environments where storage and resource utilization must be minimized to save costs.

Note 📎

You should use caution when obtaining publicly available container images hosted by users that you do not recognize, as the container image could contain malicious software.

To download the latest version of the official IIS container image from Docker Hub, you can run the following command:

```
PS C:\> docker pull microsoft/iis
```

Container images on Docker Hub can have different versions. The command shown in the previous output is the same as `docker pull microsoft/iis:latest` (the latest version of the microsoft/iis container). However, you can instead download older versions of a container; for example, the `docker pull microsoft/iis:windowsservercore-1903` command will download an older version of the official IIS container that was created using Server Core build 1903.

> **Note** 📎
>
> You can also download Docker container images directly from Microsoft instead of Docker Hub. For example, to download the latest version of the official IIS container image from Microsoft, you can run the `docker pull mcr.microsoft.com/windows/servercore/iis` command.

Downloaded container images are stored under the C:\ProgramData\docker folder by default. However, you should ensure that container images are stored on a volume that contains enough space for the number and size of container images you wish to use. To modify the default folder used to store container images, you can create the C:\ProgramData\docker\config\daemon.json text file and edit the contents to specify the appropriate path. For example, to store downloaded container images under D:\ProgramData\docker, you can add the following contents to C:\ProgramData\docker\config\daemon.json:

```
{
"graph": "D:\\ProgramData\\docker"
}
```

> **Note** 📎
>
> After modifying the C:\ProgramData\docker\config\daemon.json file, you must restart the Docker daemon for the changes to take effect. To do this, you can use the `Restart-Service Docker` command in Windows PowerShell.

To view downloaded container images, you can use the `docker images` command. The following command output indicates that the latest version of the eckert/xcontrol and microsoft/iis container images have been downloaded:

```
PS C:\> docker images
REPOSITORY        TAG       IMAGE ID        CREATED         SIZE
eckert/xcontrol   latest    ed5286ac7a5e    2 weeks ago     1.33 GB
microsoft/iis     latest    47f923963b92    4 weeks ago     5.01 GB
```

To simplify commands that work with container images, you can create aliases for docker container image names using the docker tag command. For example, to create an alias for the microsoft/iis container image called iis, as well as an alias for the eckert/xcontrol container image called xc and view the results, you can run the following commands:

```
PS C:\> docker tag microsoft/iis iis
PS C:\> docker tag eckert/xcontrol xc
PS C:\> docker images
REPOSITORY        TAG       IMAGE ID        CREATED        SIZE
iis               latest    47f923963b92    4 weeks ago    5.01 GB
xc                latest    ed5286ac7a5e    2 weeks ago    1.33 GB
eckert/xcontrol   latest    ed5286ac7a5e    2 weeks ago    1.33 GB
microsoft/iis     latest    47f923963b92    4 weeks ago    5.01 GB
```

Running Containers

After you have downloaded a container image, you can create containers from it using the docker run command. For example, to create a container that executes the xcontrol Web app in the xc container image on your Windows Server 2019 operating system, you can run the following command:

```
PS C:\> docker run xc xcontrol
```

After the xcontrol Web app has completed executing, Docker stops running the container, releasing any resources it used back to the operating system. You can view currently running containers using the docker ps command, as well as see any previously run containers using the docker ps -a command. The following output demonstrates that the container run in the previous output is no longer running, executed the xcontrol Web app 5 minutes ago on port 80, and exited successfully (exit status = 0) 9 seconds ago:

```
PS C:\> docker ps
CONTAINER ID   IMAGE   COMMAND     CREATED   STATUS              PORTS NAMES
PS C:\> docker ps -a
CONTAINER ID   IMAGE   COMMAND     CREATED   STATUS              PORTS NAMES
162fbe01daf    xc      xcontrol    5m ago    Exited(0)9s ago 80  nice_cray
```

Note from the previous output that a random name was generated for the container during execution (nice_cray) because a name was not specified with the docker run command. Specifying a container name is not mandatory, as all containers also receive a unique container ID when they are run that can be used to identify them afterwards. For example, the 162fbe01daf container ID in the previous output can be used in place of nice_cray when working with the container.

Recall from Module 1 that containers are identified uniquely on the network because they provide a sandboxed Windows environment to the Web apps that they contain. To demonstrate this, the following example creates another container based on the xc container image, but uses an interactive terminal (-it) to execute a Windows Command prompt (cmd) in the container.

This Windows Command prompt allows us to explore the filesystem, hostname, and IP configuration of the container until we close it using the `exit` command:

```
PS C:\> docker run -it xc cmd
d78ac477b654cee0a823a55a8677432743667a432c1084851d85c0e8d20a827c

Microsoft Windows [Version 10.0.17763.914]
(c)2018 Microsoft Corporation. All rights reserved.

C:\> dir
 Volume in drive C has no label.
 Volume Serial Number is 2Ed6-95D9

 Directory of C:\

12/10/2019 04:59 PM <DIR>          inetpub
09/15/2019 04:42 PM          5,510 license.txt
11/28/2019 11:35 PM <DIR>          Program Files
11/28/2019 11:33 PM <DIR>          Program Files (x86)
12/10/2019 04:59 PM        172,328 xcontrol.exe
11/28/2019 04:59 PM <DIR>          Users
12/10/2019 04:59 PM <DIR>          Windows
               2 File(s)        177,838 bytes
               5 Dir(s)  20,702,457,856 bytes free

C:\> hostname
260d4f5b308

C:\> ipconfig
Windows IP Configuration
Ethernet adapter vEthernet (Ethernet) 4:

   Connection-specific DNS Suffix  . :
   Link-local IPv6 Address . . . . . : fe80::1496:1dbe:a825:5727%44
   IPv4 Address  . . . . . . . . . . : 172.24.90.175
   Subnet Mast . . . . . . . . . . . : 255.255.240.0
   Default Gateway . . . . . . . . . : 172.24.80.1

C:\> exit
PS C:\> docker ps
CONTAINER ID  IMAGE  COMMAND   CREATED   STATUS           PORTS NAMES
PS C:\> docker ps -a
CONTAINER ID  IMAGE  COMMAND   CREATED   STATUS           PORTS NAMES
```

```
260d4f5b308    xc    cmd        20s ago   Exited(0)1s ago 80    misty_tom
162fbe01daf    xc    xcontrol   15m ago   Exited(0)5m ago 80    nice_cray
```

The output of the docker ps -a command in the example lists both containers that we have run previously, and output of the hostname command indicates that the container ID is used as the host name. Because the list of previously run containers may grow large over time, you can run the docker container prune command to automatically remove any stopped containers that you don't plan to rerun in the future.

During the installation of Docker EE, a virtual NAT router is created on your Windows Server 2019 system for use by containers. Docker assigns each container it runs a unique IPv4 address on a 172 network behind this virtual NAT router, as shown for the 172.24.90.175 IPv4 address in the output of the ipconfig command. If IPv6 is configured on the underlying network, Docker also assigns a unique IPv6 address to each container behind this virtual router. However, these unique IP addresses are often used to manage individual containers instead of providing client access. Web apps that run in a container are typically made available to the underlying operating system using a unique port number that is associated to the port number used by the Web app. This simplifies the process of connecting to multiple Web apps running on a cloud provider, because clients only need to know the host name of the underlying operating system and the port number for their copy of the Web app.

Say, for example, that you downloaded a private container image from Docker Hub called eckert/js that contains IIS, several Web app frameworks, and a Web app (iot.py) that developers in your organization created. This Web app listens on port 80 and provides a website that allows customers to manage their IoT device from across the Internet. A customer connects to this Web app by first logging into your organization's website. Following this, a unique container is created for the customer based on the eckert/js container image, and the customer is redirected to the port on the cloud server that is associated with their unique container. In the following example, three copies of the eckert/js container are run; each one is named for the customer (cust1, cust2, and cust3), and port 80 is mapped to a unique port number on the underlying operating system for each customer (36001, 36002, and 36003). The end result is illustrated in Figure 10-12.

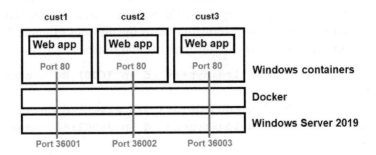

Figure 10-12   The cust1, cust2, and cust3 Windows containers

```
PS C:\> docker run -d -p 36001:80 --name cust1 eckert/js
436be848fefd0da097eb711375a8dbded01d05c979ca944f14dd8ac9ab3fc585
PS C:\> docker run -d -p 36002:80 --name cust2 eckert/js
cfcb44e2d4ce2d1fefd6ba63e051d0a4691b22cae3eb96a01ef9e532fe5fb96e
PS C:\> docker run -d -p 36003:80 --name cust3 eckert/js
55a8677432743667a43d78ac477b654cee0a823a2c1084d85c0e8d20a827c851
PS C:\> docker ps
CONTAINER ID    IMAGE       COMMAND    CREATED    STATUS    PORTS           NAMES
55a867743274    eckert/js   iot.py     37s ago    Up 36s    36003->80/tcp   cust3
cfcb44e2d4ce    eckert/js   iot.py     44s ago    Up 43s    36002->80/tcp   cust2
436be848fefd    eckert/js   iot.py     51s ago    Up 50s    36001->80/tcp   cust1
```

The -d option of the docker run command in the previous example detaches the container from your Windows PowerShell session and keeps it running in the background until you stop it using the docker stop command. For example, running the docker stop cust2 command will stop executing the cust2 container and release its resources to the underlying operating system; this could be performed automatically when customer 2 logs out of the organization's website. Similarly, when customer 2 logs into the organization's website at a later time to manage their IoT device, the website could initiate the docker start cust2 command to run the container again.

You can also obtain an interactive terminal to access a Windows Command prompt (cmd) or Windows PowerShell (powershell) session in a running container using the docker exec command. For example, docker exec -it cust2 powershell would create an interactive terminal to Windows PowerShell in the cust2 container. You can then use this interactive Windows PowerShell session to run PowerShell cmdlets in the running container to manage files, modify IIS configuration, and so on.

Running Hyper-V Containers

The three containers run in the previous example and shown in Figure 10-12 are executed using the same kernel on the underlying Windows Server 2019 system. Recall from Module 1 that you can use Hyper-V to provide each container with a separate copy of the kernel for greater stability, performance, and security. To run a Hyper-V container, you add the --isolation=hyperv option to the docker run command. The following example performs the same container configuration as the previous example, but instead using Hyper-V containers. Figure 10-13 illustrates the end result.

```
PS C:\> docker run --isolation=hyperv -d -p 36001:80 --name cust1
   eckert/js
436be848fefd0da097eb711375a8dbded01d05c979ca944f14dd8ac9ab3fc585
PS C:\> docker run --isolation=hyperv -d -p 36002:80 --name cust2
   eckert/js
```

```
cfcb44e2d4ce2d1fefd6ba63e051d0a4691b22cae3eb96a01ef9e532fe5fb96e
PS C:\> docker run --isolation=hyperv -d -p 36003:80 --name cust3
  eckert/js
55a8677432743667a43d78ac477b654cee0a823a2c1084d85c0e8d20a827c851
```

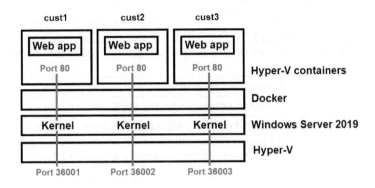

Figure 10-13   The cust1, cust2, and cust3 Hyper-V containers

Container images that are based on Nano Server must be run as Hyper-V containers.

Most software programs that manage cloud servers, including orchestration and build automation software, are made available using Docker container images. After downloading these container images, you can create and run containers from them to execute these software programs on a system.

Common Docker Commands

Nearly all Docker configuration and management is provided by the `docker` command, with many different versions of the `docker` command available. Table 10-3 lists common `docker` commands and their descriptions.

Table 10-3 Common `docker` commands

Command	Description
`docker login`	Logs into Docker Hub (necessary for searching and downloading container images). This login is cached for the remainder of your Windows session.
`docker logout`	Logs out of Docker Hub.
`docker search keyword`	Searches Docker Hub for container images that contain a specific keyword.
`docker pull image`	Downloads a container image.
`docker images`	Lists container images on the local system.
`docker run -it image command`	Creates and runs a container from a container image, executing a command in the container using an interactive terminal. A random name for the container is generated automatically.
`docker run --name name -it image command`	Creates and runs a container from a container image, executing a command in the container using an interactive terminal. The container is assigned the name specified.
`docker run --name name -d image`	Creates and runs a container from a container image. The container runs in the background until stopped manually, and is assigned the name specified.
`docker run --isolation=hyperv --name name -d image`	Creates and runs a Hyper-V container from a container image. The container runs in the background until stopped manually, and is assigned the name specified.
`docker run --isolation=hyperv --name name -p portA:portB -d image`	Creates and runs a Hyper-V container from a container image. The container runs in the background until stopped manually, and is assigned the name specified. The port that the Web app listens on (portB) is mapped to a port on the underlying operating system (portA).
`docker run --isolation=hyperv --name name -P -d image`	Creates and runs a Hyper-V container from a container image. The container runs in the background until stopped manually, and is assigned the name specified. The port that the Web app listens on is automatically mapped to a port above 32767 on the underlying operating system.
`docker start container`	Runs an existing container (by container name or ID).
`docker stop container`	Stops running a container (by container name or ID).
`docker rm container`	Removes a stopped container configuration (by container name or ID).
`docker container prune`	Removes all stopped container configurations.
`docker rmi image`	Removes a container image from the system.
`docker ps`	Displays running containers.

Table 10-2	Common `docker` commands *(continued)*

Command	Description
`docker ps -a`	Displays running and stopped containers.
`docker exec -it` `container command`	Runs a command (often `cmd` or `powershell`) in a running container using an interactive terminal. The container can be specified by container name or ID.
`docker info`	Displays Docker statistics.

Note ✐

You can use the `--help` option for any `docker` command to obtain available options and usage information. For example, `docker --help` will display general options and usage for the `docker` command, and `docker run --help` will display options and usage for the `docker run` command.

Configuring the Windows Subsystem for Linux

Recall that most Web apps that are run on cloud servers today are created for the Linux operating system. In organizations that develop Web apps for Linux systems, you can host those Web apps (and associated Web servers and Web app frameworks) on a Windows Server 2019 server using the **Windows Subsystem for Linux (WSL)**. WSL is a set of operating system components that allows 64-bit Linux programs to execute directly on the Windows kernel without virtualization. Because Linux programs were designed to run in a Linux environment, WSL also provides a Linux filesystem environment that includes the system files from one or more of the following Linux **distributions**:

- Ubuntu
- Debian GNU/Linux
- Kali Linux
- OpenSUSE Leap
- SUSE Linux Enterprise Server
- Fedora

Note ✐

There are many different distributions (or **distros**) of Linux. Each distribution shares the same Linux operating system kernel and libraries but contains different software packages that make up the remainder of the operating system.

Note

WSL is available for Windows 10, Windows Server 2016, and later systems.

Note

WSL 2 is a new version of WSL that was recently released. It runs a Linux kernel alongside the Windows kernel to provide additional performance benefits and features. However, at the time of this writing, WSL 2 is only available for testing purposes to Windows Server Insider Preview members.

Installing and Using WSL

To install WSL on a Windows Server 2019 system, you must install the Windows Subsystem for Linux server feature. After you install this feature, you must reboot your system. Next, download and install at least one package that includes a WSL-supported Linux distribution. To download and install the Ubuntu 18.04 Linux distribution package from Microsoft, you can open a Windows PowerShell window as Administrator, run the following two commands, and reboot your system afterwards:

```
PS C:\> Invoke-WebRequest -Uri https://aka.ms/wsl-ubuntu-1804
-OutFile Ubuntu.appx -UseBasicParsing
PS C:\> Add-AppxPackage Ubuntu.appx
```

After your system has rebooted, you must complete the installation of the Ubuntu Linux distribution. To do this, click Start and then click Ubuntu 18.04 to open a Linux command prompt window that connects you to the Linux filesystem for the Ubuntu 18.04 Linux distribution. The first time that you open this window, you are prompted to create a Linux user account that will be used each time you access the Linux distribution. After supplying a name and password for this Linux user account, you receive a Linux command prompt that allows you to run commands on the Ubuntu Linux distribution, as shown in Figure 10-14. The prompt shown in Figure 10-14 indicates that the user named jason is logged into SERVERX. Table 10-4 lists common Linux commands that you can run on Linux distributions.

Note

You can install multiple Linux distributions for use with WSL. Each distribution can be accessed using the associated icon on the Start menu.

Note

You can also use the `wsl` command at a Windows PowerShell or Command Prompt window to access your Linux distribution. If multiple Linux distributions are installed, you can use `wsl -d distributionname` to access a specific Linux distribution.

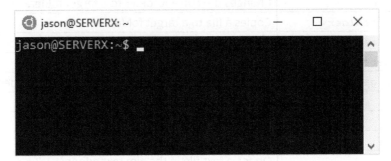

Figure 10-14   **Accessing the Ubuntu Linux Distribution**
Source: The Linux Foundation

The Administrator user on a Linux system is called the super user and assigned a user name of root. As a security precaution, no password is assigned to the root user by default to ensure that users cannot log into the Linux system using the super user account. To allow for system administration, the Linux user account that you create when installing the Ubuntu Linux distribution is automatically granted the ability to run administrative commands as the root user using the `sudo` (super user do) command. Consequently, each administrative command that you type at the Linux command prompt must be prefixed with the `sudo` command by default. Because most commands that install and configure Web servers and Web apps must be run as the root user, you can instead assign a password to the root user using the `sudo passwd root` command. Next, you can run the `su` (substitute user) command to open a Linux command prompt as the root user to run administrative commands without having to prefix them with the `sudo` command.

Unlike Windows systems, Linux systems do not mount filesystems to a drive letter. Instead, the filesystem that contains the Linux operating system files is mounted to a single root folder (/), and additional filesystems can be mounted to folders under this root folder. For example, the C:\folder\subfolder\file.txt pathname on a Windows system would be represented by the /folder/subfolder/file.txt pathname on a Linux system. The actual location of the Linux distribution root folder on your Windows system is C:\Users\Administrator\AppData\Local\Packages\DistributionID\LocalState\rootfs. Moreover, the C:\ folder on your Windows system is automatically mounted to the /mnt/c folder on your Linux distribution, to allow Linux programs to access Windows files.

Table 10-4   Common Linux commands

Command	Description
`uname -a`	Displays system information.
`pwd`	Displays the current folder location.
`ls -l`	Lists files in the current folder, including file details.
`cd targetfolder`	Changes the current folder to a target folder.
`cp file targetfolder`	Copies a file to a target folder.
`cp -R folder targetfolder`	Copies a folder (and its contents) to a target folder.
`mv file targetfolder`	Moves a file to a target folder.
`mv folder targetfolder`	Moves a folder (and its contents) to a target folder.
`rm -f file`	Removes a file.
`rm -Rf folder`	Removes a folder and its contents.
`nano file`	Opens a text file in the nano text editor.
`vim file`	Opens a text file in the vim text editor.
`apt-get update`	Updates the list of online packages available.
`apt-get install package` `apt install package`	Installs a software package from a Linux software repository on an Ubuntu, Debian GNU/Linux, or Kali Linux distribution.
`dnf install package` `yum install package`	Installs a software package from a Linux software repository on a Fedora Linux distribution.
`zypper install package`	Installs a software package from a Linux software repository on an OpenSUSE Leap or SUSE Linux Enterprise Server Linux distribution.
`df -h`	Displays mounted filesystems.
`ps -ef`	Displays all Linux processes running on the system.
`sudo command`	Runs a specified command as the root user.
`sudo passwd root`	Assigns the root user a password.
`su`	Switches the current user to the root user.

Hosting Web Services using WSL

After you have a Linux distribution installed using WSL, you can add software packages
to it from a Linux software repository on the Internet. This can include Web servers, Web
application frameworks, and any other software that may be necessary to run a Web app.
Before installing software packages on the Ubuntu Linux distribution, you should first
run the apt-get update command to ensure that the latest list of packages available
on the Linux software repository is downloaded to your system.

To download and install the Apache Web server, you can run the `apt install apache2` command. Next, you can run the `apachectl start` command to start the Apache Web server, which is configured by default to listen on port 80 for HTTP requests and serve users the webpage in the /var/www/html/index.html file. As with IIS, users can access the FQDN or IP address of your Windows Server 2019 system using a Web browser to view this webpage.

The configuration files for the Apache Web server are stored in the /etc/apache2 folder on the Ubuntu Linux distribution. To modify Web server configuration parameters, such as port number or HTTPS certificate location, you can edit the appropriate file under the /etc/apache2 folder using a text editor such as `nano` or `vim`. After modifying an Apache Web server configuration file, you should check to ensure that you did not make a syntax error by running the `apachectl configtest` command. Finally, you must restart the Apache Web server for the changes to take effect using the `apachectl restart` command. To stop the Apache Web server, you can use the `apachectl stop` command.

> **Note** 🖉
>
> You cannot run on a system multiple services that listen to the same port number. If IIS is already running on your Windows Server 2019 system and listening to port 80, you must modify your Apache configuration to ensure that Apache listens for Web requests on a different port number. Clients must then specify this port number in the URL (e.g., `http://FQDN:port`) to connect to the Apache Web server.

Configuring Linux Containers on Windows

In addition to running Windows containers on a Windows Server 2019 system, you can also run Linux containers using the **Linux Containers on Windows (LCOW)** feature introduced in Windows Server 2019. Linux containers cannot use the WSL for execution, and instead rely on a Linux kernel provided by a Docker component called **LinuxKit**. Moreover, LCOW requires that each Linux container run on a separate Linux kernel. To achieve this, LCOW automatically runs each Linux container as a Hyper-V container to ensure that each Linux container receives a separate Linux kernel provided by LinuxKit. To maximize performance, the Linux kernel provided by LinuxKit executes directly on the Hyper-V hypervisor and independent of the Windows operating system, as shown in Figure 10-15.

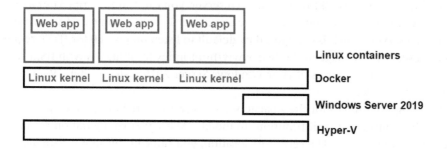

Figure 10-15   Running Linux Containers on Windows

To enable LCOW, open a Windows PowerShell window as Administrator and run the following commands to set the LCOW environment variable and restart the Docker daemon:

```
PS C:\> [Environment]::SetEnvironmentVariable("LCOW_SUPPORTED",
  "1", "Machine")
PS C:\> Restart-Service Docker
```

Next, you can use the same `docker` commands listed in Table 10-3 to obtain Linux container images from Docker Hub, as well as create and manage containers.

For example, after logging into Docker Hub using the `docker login` command, you can search for Linux containers with the Apache Web server using the following command (partial results shown):

```
PS C:\> docker search apache
NAME                        DESCRIPTION
httpd                       The Apache HTTP Server Project
tomcat                      Apache Tomcat is an open source...
cassandra                   Apache Cassandra is an open-source...
maven                       Apache Maven is a software project...
solr                        Solr is the popular blazing-fast open...
apache/nifi                 Unofficial convenience binaries and...
eboraas/apache-php          PHP on Apache (with SSL/TLS support)...
apache/zeppelin             Apache Zeppelin
eboraas/apache              Apache (with SSL/TLS support), built...
groovy                      Apache Groovy is a multi-faceted...
nimmis/apache-php5          This is docker images of Ubuntu 14.04...
apacheignite/ignite         Apache Ignite In-Memory docker image.
...
```

The first result listed (`httpd`) is an official Apache Web server container image provided by Docker as there is no user name prefixing the container name. You can download the latest version of this container image using the `docker pull httpd` command and run containers from it using the `docker run` command. The following example runs three Apache Web server containers (apache1, apache2, and apache3) that associate port 80 in the container to a unique port number on the underlying operating system for each Apache Web server (36001, 36002, and 36003) and displays the results:

```
PS C:\> docker run -d -p 36001:80 --name apache1 httpd
5f96636290b435e4467f9f5ba3ba68d78d8dbecdf2b98468815c3d569d6e59fe
PS C:\> docker run -d -p 36002:80 --name apache2 httpd
372cf6526c45e1129bb647639e0de683d2920dab5cadc49eef7ce939bcc97cb0
PS C:\> docker run -d -p 36003:80 --name apache3 httpd
afb964f00cd7e5c2d6eac7d6f56937aec0676898352512efad5a2d4240587bd4
PS C:\> docker ps
CONTAINER ID   IMAGE   COMMAND   CREATED   STATUS   PORTS          NAMES
afb964f00cd7   httpd   httpd     14s ago   Up 9s    36003->80/tcp  apache3
372cf6526c45   httpd   httpd     24s ago   Up 19s   36002->80/tcp  apache2
5f96636290b4   httpd   httpd     35s ago   Up 30s   36001->80/tcp  apache1
```

The Docker client cannot run and manage Windows and Linux containers simultaneously. As a result, when you run the docker images command, you will only see Linux container images on your system; previously downloaded Windows container images will not be shown and cannot be used to run Windows containers. To run Windows containers, you must first disable LCOW using the following commands:

```
PS C:\> [Environment]::SetEnvironmentVariable("LCOW_SUPPORTED",
 "$null", "Machine")
PS C:\> Restart-Service Docker
```

Following this, the docker images command will list the Windows container images on your system, and you will be able to run Windows containers from them. Linux container images will not be available until you enable LCOW again.

Implementing Windows Server 2019 in a Cloud Environment

You can implement Windows Server 2019 in a cloud environment using many different configuration options. These options vary depending on whether the Web app is hosted in a public or private cloud.

Hosting Web Apps in a Public Cloud

To run a Windows Web app in a public cloud using SaaS, the public cloud provider configures and maintains all aspects of the underlying Windows Server 2019 operating system, including IIS and any Web app frameworks. In this case, you only need to provide the Web app, as well as configure the block or object storage required by the Web app on the public cloud provider. If the Web app was created by your organization, you will also need to implement orchestration and build automation software to provide for continuous deployment. While many public cloud providers provide this software in a SaaS configuration for a fee, you can instead choose to configure virtual machines or containers that provide the necessary orchestration and build automation software packages.

Alternatively, to run a Windows Web app in a public cloud using IaaS, you will need to create, configure, and maintain the associated Windows Server 2019 virtual machine on the public cloud provider's hypervisor. Because public cloud providers charge based on resource usage, you can install a small footprint virtual machine that contains Server Core, IIS, and the necessary Web app frameworks to save cost. If you require more capacity at a later time, you can choose to increase the memory, processor, and block storage resources assigned to this virtual machine or create additional virtual machines. If your Web apps use object storage exclusively, you only need to purchase enough block storage to support the needs of the virtual machines you use because object storage charges are based on consumption. Furthermore, most public cloud providers offer a large selection of virtual machine templates with Windows Server 2019, IIS, and Web app frameworks preinstalled to make the process of creating a new virtual machine easier. To provide continuous deployment for Web apps created by your organization, you will also need to purchase access to orchestration and build automation software from your public cloud provider, or configure additional virtual machines or containers that run the necessary orchestration and build automation software packages.

To run a containerized Windows Web app on a public cloud provider using the PaaS cloud delivery model, you must first configure any block or object storage required by the Web app on the public cloud provider. Next, you must obtain the appropriate Windows container image from a container repository, such as Docker Hub. If the container image contains the Web app and necessary Web app frameworks, you can create containers from it on the cloud provider. However, for Web apps that are created by your organization, orchestration and build automation software are often used to create containers and add the necessary Web app and Web app frameworks.

Note 📎

Because public cloud providers also offer a Linux SaaS platform, as well as the ability to run Linux virtual machines and containers, the same considerations apply when running Web apps created for the Linux operating system on a public cloud provider.

Note 📎

If you run several virtual machines or containers in a public cloud, you should ensure that the virtual machines are shut down and the containers are stopped when not in use to save costs. This can be performed automatically by third-party cloud management software or by configuring the monitoring features made available by the public cloud provider.

Hosting Web Apps in a Private Cloud

Windows Server 2019 provides several different options for running both Windows and Linux Web apps on a private cloud in your organization. For example, you could install Windows Server 2019 on a physical server that is dedicated for running Windows Web apps, or both Windows Web apps and Linux Web apps using the WSL. This configuration uses a SaaS cloud delivery model, and the physical server must contain adequate hardware resources and storage to support the Web apps. Because organizations can use SANs and other storage technologies (e.g., Storage Spaces Direct) to provide fast, scalable, fault-tolerant block storage to cloud servers, private clouds typically use block storage exclusively.

> **Note**
>
> Currently no software package provides object storage on Windows Server 2019. However, Web apps that must use object storage can be hosted in a private cloud. In this case, the Web apps can be configured to access object storage on a public cloud provider, or object storage on a Linux system in the private cloud. *Ceph* is a popular object storage system that can be installed on Linux in a private cloud.

> **Note**
>
> To provide continuous deployment in a private cloud for Web apps that are created by your organization, you must also implement orchestration and build automation software.

You can also use Windows Server 2019 Datacenter Edition or Hyper-V Server to run a large number of virtual machines in a private cloud using the IaaS cloud delivery model. Windows Server 2019 virtual machines can be configured to host Windows Web apps, as well as Linux Web apps using the WSL. Alternatively, you can choose to create Linux virtual machines on Hyper-V to host Linux Web apps. To make the deployment of multiple Windows Server 2019 virtual machines easier, you can create Hyper-V virtual machine templates that contain Windows Server 2019, IIS, and the necessary Web app frameworks, as discussed in Module 3. Similarly, to make the deployment of multiple Linux virtual machines easier, you can create Hyper-V virtual machine templates that contain a Linux distribution as well as the necessary Web server software and Web app frameworks.

> **Note**
>
> The System Preparation Tool cannot be used to prepare a Linux virtual machine template. However, you can use any one of many Linux tools to remove unique system information before creating a Linux virtual machine template, including `virt-sysprep`.

Windows Server 2019 also provides several different options for implementing a PaaS cloud delivery model in a private cloud. To run containerized Windows Web apps, you can install Docker EE on a Windows Server 2019 system that is installed on dedicated server hardware. Alternatively, you can install Docker EE on a Windows Server 2019 Hyper-V host or virtual machine to provide for Hyper-V containers. This configuration also enables you to run containerized Linux Web apps using LCOW, or containerized Windows Web apps that were built using Nano Server for resource efficiency. As with running Web apps in a public cloud, you must obtain the appropriate Windows or Linux container images from a container repository such as Docker Hub, as well as configure the storage needed by the Web app. Container images that contain the Web app and associated Web app frameworks can be run directly using Docker EE. However, Web apps created by your organization are often run on Docker EE using orchestration and build automation software.

Module Summary

- The cloud represents the worldwide collection of cloud servers that host Web apps. Web apps are typically accessed using a Web server on a cloud server.

- Organizations that host cloud servers are called cloud providers, and can host Web apps publicly or privately using one of three delivery models: IaaS, PaaS, or SaaS.

- Web apps can use block or object storage and are often updated to new versions using a continuous deployment workflow.

- You can install and configure the IIS Web server on Windows Server 2019 to provide for websites and Web apps. Most Web apps are accessed using a virtual directory in IIS.

- Before running Windows containers on Windows Server 2019, you must install Docker EE as well as download one or more container images. Container images based on Nano Server must be run as a Hyper-V container.

- Docker container configuration on Windows Server 2019 is performed using the `docker` command.

- WSL can be configured to run Linux Web apps directly on a Windows Server 2019 system using an installed Linux distribution.

- Windows Server 2019 systems can use LCOW to run Linux containers on Docker EE using a Linux kernel provided by LinuxKit.

- The different Windows Server 2019 configurations available in a public or private cloud environment depend on the features of the Web app and cloud delivery model.

Key Terms

Advanced Research
  Projects Agency Network
  (ARPANET)
Anything as a Service (XaaS)
Apache Web server
application pool
Binary Large Object (BLOB)
  storage
block storage
build automation
cloud delivery model
cloud provider
code repository
Common Gateway Interface
  (CGI)
compiling
container image
continuous deployment
  (CD)
devop
distribution
distro
Docker client

Docker daemon
Docker Enterprise Edition
  (EE)
Docker Hub
dynamic-link library (DLL)
egress fee
File Transfer Protocol (FTP)
hybrid cloud
Hypertext Markup
  Language (HTML)
IIS Manager
Infrastructure as a Service
  (IaaS)
Internet Server Application
  Programming Interface
  (ISAPI)
Linux Containers on
  Windows (LCOW)
LinuxKit
National Science
  Foundation Network
  (NSFNET)
object storage

Open Database
  Connectivity (ODBC)
orchestration
persistent volume
Platform as a Service
  (PaaS)
private cloud
programming language
public cloud
Server Side Includes (SSI)
Software as a Service (SaaS)
Uniform Resource Locator
  (URL)
virtual directory
Web app
Web app frameworks
Web Distributed Authoring
  and Versioning (WebDAV)
Web Server (IIS)
WebSocket
Windows Subsystem for
  Linux (WSL)
World Wide Web (WWW)

Review Questions

1. Which of the following cloud delivery
   models uses containers exclusively to run
   Web apps?
   a. SaaS
   b. PaaS
   c. IaaS
   d. XaaS

2. Websites on a Web server provide the front
   end for most Web apps. True or False?

3. In a continuous deployment scenario,
   which software creates a container or
   virtual machine on a cloud server to
   test the functionality of a new Web app
   version?
   a. Orchestration
   b. Code repository
   c. Workflow
   d. Build automation

4. Block storage is a cheaper alternative to object storage on public cloud providers. True or False?

5. To which of the following groups should you assign NTFS/ReFS permissions for Web app content in order to provide anonymous user access?
   a. IUSRS
   b. .NET_USRS
   c. IIS_IUSRS
   d. WWWUSRS

6. What must you configure in IIS Manager to allow users to access a help desk ticketing system Web app using the URL `https://www.sample.com/helpdesk`? (Choose all that apply.)
   a. A help desk virtual directory
   b. Request filtering
   c. An HTTPS protocol binding
   d. The WebSocket protocol

7. Which of the following IIS configuration features is used to specify the default webpage or Web app file that a client views?
   a. Directory Browsing
   b. Handler Mappings
   c. Request Filtering
   d. Default Document

8. The `docker` command is also called the Docker daemon. True or False?

9. Which `docker` command displays container images available on Docker Hub?
   a. `docker images`
   b. `docker container images`
   c. `docker search`
   d. `docker pull`

10. Nano Server containers must be run as a Hyper-V container on Windows Server 2019. True or False?

11. Which command can you execute to create a container from the microsoft/iis container image that runs in the background and automatically maps port 80 in the container to a port above 32767 on the underlying operating system?
    a. `docker run -d -P microsoft/iis`
    b. `docker run -d -p *:80 microsoft/iis`
    c. `docker exec -it -P microsoft/iis`
    d. `docker exec -it -p *:80 microsoft/iis`

12. After a container is running, you cannot configure its contents until the container is stopped. True or False?

13. Which of the following commands can be used to display containers that are no longer running?
    a. `docker ps`
    b. `docker list`
    c. `docker images`
    d. `docker ps -a`

14. The Windows Subsystem for Linux (WSL) allows you to execute Web apps in a virtual machine on Windows Server 2019. True or False?

15. Which of the following Linux distributions are supported for use with WSL? (Choose all that apply.)
    a. Fedora
    b. Ubuntu
    c. OpenSUSE Leap
    d. Debian GNU/Linux

16. The Linux Containers on the Windows (LCOW) feature of Windows Server 2019 allows you to run Linux containers only if Docker EE was obtained using the DockerMsftProvider Windows PowerShell module. True or False?

17. Which of the following commands can be used to start the Apache Web server in a Linux container or WSL Linux distribution on a Windows Server 2019 system?
    a. httpstart
    b. apachectl start
    c. apt-get start apache
    d. apt-get start http

18. Each Linux container run on Windows Server 2019 using LCOW is automatically run as a Hyper-V container that executes on a Linux kernel provided by the LinuxKit component of Docker EE. True or False?

19. You are tasked with deploying a private cloud in your organization that needs to host both Windows and Linux Web apps using a SaaS delivery model on a single Windows Server 2019 system. What technology should you configure on the Windows Server 2019 system?
    a. WSL
    b. LCOW

    c. Hyper-V
    d. Docker EE

20. Your organization develops a containerized Linux Web app that is run on a public cloud provider. To minimize cloud costs, a continuous deployment process is not used. Instead, Web app developers must add new versions of their Linux Web app to a container and test its functionality locally before running it on the public cloud provider. What could you configure on an existing Windows Server 2019 system to allow the Web app developers in your organization to test new versions of their containerized Linux Web app? (Choose all that apply.)
    a. Hyper-V
    b. IIS
    c. Docker EE
    d. LCOW

Hands-On Projects

These Hands-On Projects should be completed in the order given and normally take a total of three hours or less to complete. The requirements for these projects include:

- A system with Windows Server 2019 installed according to Hands-On Project 1-1 (Lab Environment 1) or Hands-On Project 1-2 (Lab Environment 2).
- A WindowsServer2019VM2 virtual machine installed according to Hands-On Project 3-5 and configured as a member server according to Hands-On Project 5-2.

Project 10-1: Configuring IIS

In this Hands-On Project, you install and configure IIS on your WindowsServer2019VM2 virtual machine, as well as explore the Web app configuration on your Windows Server 2019 host.

1. Boot your Windows Server 2019 host and log into domainX.com as Administrator using the password **Secret555**. Next, click **Start** and then click **Server Manager**.

2. In Server Manager on your Windows Server 2019 host, select the **Tools** menu and then click **Hyper-V Manager**.

    a. Highlight **WindowsServer2019VM2** in the virtual machines pane of Hyper-V Manager and click **Connect** in the Actions pane. In the Virtual Machine Connection window, click **Start** to boot your virtual machine.

b. At the login screen, click the Ctrl+Alt+Delete button in the Virtual Machine Connection window, supply the password **Secret555** for Administrator, and press **Enter** to log into the system.

3. On your WindowsServer2019VM2 virtual machine, click **Start** and then click **Server Manager**. Next, click the **Manage** menu and then click **Add Roles and Features**.

   a. At the Select installation type page, click **Next**.

   b. At the Select destination server page, click **Next**.

   c. At the Select server roles page, select **Web Server (IIS)** and click **Add Features** when prompted. Click **Next**.

   d. At the Select features page, click **Next**.

   e. At the Web Server Role (IIS) page, click **Next**.

   f. At the Select role services page, note the default and available selections and click **Next**.

   g. At the Confirm installation selections page, click **Install**.

   h. At the Installation progress page, click **Close** to close the Add the Roles and Features Wizard.

4. In Server Manager, select the **Tools** menu and then click **Internet Information Services (IIS) Manager**. Note the Web server features shown for your server in the Features View pane for your server.

5. Highlight **Authentication** in the Features View pane and click **Open Feature** in the Actions pane. Note that anonymous authentication for Internet users and ASP.NET impersonation for ASP.NET Web apps are configured by default. Click the back button in the title bar when finished.

6. Highlight **Default Document** in the Features View pane and click **Open Feature** in the Actions pane. Note the file names that IIS will search for in order when loading Web content from a document folder. Click the back button in the title bar when finished.

7. Highlight **Logging** in the Features View pane and click **Open Feature** in the Actions pane. Note that one log file is configured for each website and stored in the C:\inetpub\logs\LogFiles folder by default. Click the back button in the title bar when finished.

8. Highlight **Server Certificates** in the Features View pane and click **Open Feature** in the Actions pane. Note that no HTTPS certificates are configured by default.

   a. Click **Create Self-Signed Certificate** in the Actions pane.

   b. In the *Specify a friendly name for the certificate* text box, type the FQDN of your WindowsServer2019VM2 virtual machine.

   c. Select **Web Hosting** from the *Select a certificate store for the new certificate* drop-down box and click **OK**.

9. Expand **Sites** in the Connections pane and highlight **Default Web Site**.

   a. Click **Bindings** in the Actions pane.

      i. At the Site Bindings window, click **Add**.

      ii. At the Add Site Binding window, select **https** from the Type drop-down box and note the default port number of 443. Next, type the FQDN of your WindowsServer2019VM2 virtual machine in the Host name text box, select your self-signed certificate from the SSL certificate drop-down box, and click **OK**.

      iii. Click **Close** to close the Site Bindings window.

b. Highlight **Authentication** in the Features View pane and click **Open Feature** in the Actions pane. Note that anonymous authentication for Internet users is enabled but that ASP.NET impersonation for ASP.NET Web apps is disabled. Click the back button in the title bar when finished.

c. Highlight **Default Document** in the Features View pane and click **Open Feature** in the Actions pane. Note that the file names listed were inherited from the Default Document feature on the server. Click the back button in the title bar when finished.

d. Highlight **SSL Settings** in the Features View pane and click **Open Feature** in the Actions pane. Note that you can optionally require SSL (HTTPS) for all connections to Default Web Site. Click the back button in the title bar when finished.

e. Click **View Virtual Directories** in the Actions pane. Next, click **Add Virtual Directory** in the Actions pane. Type **marketingapp** in the Alias text box and **C:\ MarketingMaterials** in the Physical path text box and click **OK**.

f. Click **Edit Permissions** under the Manage Virtual Directory pane. Highlight the **Security** tab and note the default permissions. Click **Edit** and then click **Add**. Type **IUSR** in the text box and click **OK**.

g. Click **OK** to close the Permissions for MarketingMaterials window, and click **OK** again to close the MarketingMaterials Properties window.

h. Close Internet Information Services (IIS) Manager.

10. Right-click **Start** and click **Run**. Type **notepad** in the Run dialog box and click **OK** to open Notepad.

a. In the Notepad window, type **<html><body><h1>Sample Web Page</h1></body> </html>**.

b. Click the **File** menu and then click **Save As**.

c. In the Save As window, type **"C:\MarketingMaterials\index.htm"** and click **Save** (the double quotes prevent Notepad from appending a .txt extension to the file name).

d. Close Notepad when finished.

11. Open File Explorer and navigate to the **C:\inetpub\wwwroot** folder. Note that there is a default webpage called iisstart.htm as well as an associated iisstart.png graphic file. Close File Explorer when finished.

12. Open a Web browser on your Windows Server 2019 host.

a. Navigate to *http://FQDN*, where *FQDN* is the FQDN of your WindowsServer2019VM2 virtual machine. Note the default IIS webpage displayed from the C:\inetpub\ wwwroot folder.

b. Navigate to *http://FQDN/marketingapp*, where *FQDN* is the FQDN of your WindowsServer2019VM2 virtual machine. Note the website that you configured in the C:\MarketingMaterials folder.

c. Navigate to *https://FQDN*, where *FQDN* is the FQDN of your WindowsServer2019VM2 virtual machine. If a warning appears regarding the self-signed HTTPS certificate, follow the prompts to proceed to the website. Note the default IIS webpage displayed from the C:\inetpub\wwwroot folder using HTTPS.

d. Close your Web browser.

13. In Server Manager on your Windows Server 2019 host, select the **Tools** menu and then click **Internet Information Services (IIS) Manager**. Note the Web server features shown for your server in the Features View pane for your server.

14. Highlight **Application Pools** in the Connections pane and note that four separate application pools are configured. Highlight the RDWebAccess application pool and click Advanced Settings from the Actions pane. Note that CPU usage is not limited for the application pool because 0 is listed next to *Limit (percent)* and click **OK**.

15. Expand **Sites** in the Connections pane. Next, expand **Default Web Site**. Note the Printers virtual directory used to access the Internet Printing Protocol Web app, and the RDWeb virtual directory used to access the Remote Desktop Web Access Web app.

16. Close Internet Information Services (IIS) Manager.

Project 10-2: Windows Containers

In this Hands-On Project, you install Docker on your WindowsServer2019VM2 virtual machine, as well as execute and explore containers that include IIS.

1. On your WindowsServer 2019 host, open your Web browser and navigate to *https://hub.docker.com*. Follow the instructions to create a free Docker Hub account and note your credentials.

2. Right-click **Start** and click **Windows PowerShell (Admin)** to open Windows PowerShell.

3. At the prompt, type `Install-Module -Name DockerMsftProvider -Repository psgallery -Force` and press **Enter**. Type **Y** and press **Enter** to add the Microsoft Docker repository.

4. At the prompt, type `Install-Module -Name DockerProvider` and press **Enter**. Type **Y** and press **Enter** to add the main Docker repository.

5. At the prompt, type `Install-Package -Name Docker -ProviderName DockerProvider -RequiredVersion preview` and press **Enter**. Type **Y** and press **Enter** to download and install Docker Enterprise Edition preview from the Docker repository.

6. At the prompt, type `Restart-Computer -Force` and press **Enter** to restart your Windows Server 2019 host.

7. After your Windows Server 2019 host has booted, log into domain*X*.com as Administrator using the password **Secret555**. Next, right-click **Start** and click **Windows PowerShell (Admin)** to open Windows PowerShell.

   a. Type `Start-Service Docker` and press **Enter** to start the Docker daemon (service).

   b. Type `docker login` and press **Enter**. At the User name prompt, type your Docker Hub user name and press **Enter**. At the Password prompt, type your Docker Hub password and press **Enter**. Note the location of the config.json file that caches your unencrypted Docker Hub password for the duration of your session.

   c. Type `docker search iis` and press **Enter** to search Docker Hub for IIS images and note the results.

   d. Type `docker pull microsoft/iis` and press **Enter** to download the Microsoft container image that includes IIS. This step may take several minutes, depending on the speed of your Internet connection.

e. Type `docker pull httpd` and press **Enter**. Note that there is no matching httpd image available for the windows/amd64 platform.

f. Type `docker images` and press **Enter**. Note your microsoft/iis image, as well as the associated IMAGE ID (the beginning of the hash for the image).

g. Type `docker tag microsoft/iis iis` and press **Enter** to create an alias for your microsoft/iis image called iis.

h. Type `docker images` and press **Enter**. Note your microsoft/iis and iis images have the same IMAGE ID, indicating that they are the same image.

i. Type `docker ps` and press **Enter**. Note that no containers are currently executing.

j. Type `docker run --name iiscontainer1 -P -d iis` and press **Enter** to execute a new container based on your Web server container image that automatically maps a port in the underlying operating system to port 80 in the container. Next, type `docker run --name iiscontainer2 -P -d iis` and press **Enter**, and then type `docker run --name iiscontainer3 -P -d iis` and press **Enter** to execute two more containers from the same container image.

k. Type `docker ps` and press **Enter**. Note that three containers are currently executing (iiscontainer1, iiscontainer2, and iiscontainer3). Also note the port numbers that were chosen for each container on the underlying operating system in the PORTS column (e.g., `0.0.0.0:49537->80/tcp` indicates that port 49537 on the underlying operating system is automatically mapped to port 80 in the container).

8. Open a Web browser.

a. Navigate to `IPaddress:port1`, where *IPaddress* is the IP address of your Windows Server 2019 host and *port1* is the port number you recorded in the previous step for iiscontainer1. Note the default IIS webpage displayed.

b. Navigate to `IPaddress:port2`, where *IPaddress* is the IP address of your Windows Server 2019 host and *port2* is the port number you recorded in the previous step for iiscontainer2. Note the default IIS webpage displayed.

c. Navigate to `IPaddress:port3`, where *IPaddress* is the IP address of your Windows Server 2019 host and *port3* is the port number you recorded in the previous step for iiscontainer3. Note the default IIS webpage displayed. Leave your Web browser open.

9. At the Windows PowerShell prompt, type `docker exec -it iiscontainer3 cmd` and press **Enter** to obtain an interactive Windows command prompt in the iiscontainer3 container.

a. Type `ipconfig` and press **Enter**. Note that your container has a unique IPv4 address on a 172 network chosen by Docker that exists behind a virtual NAT router.

b. Type `cd \inetpub\wwwroot` and press **Enter** to change to the C:\inetpub\wwwroot folder in your container.

c. Type `dir` and press **Enter** to list the folder contents and note the default iisstart.htm webpage.

d. Type `powershell` and press **Enter** to start Windows PowerShell.

e. At the Windows PowerShell prompt, type `Set-Content iisstart.htm` and press **Enter**.

   i. At the Value[0] prompt, type `<html><body><h1>Container 3 Webpage</h1></body></html>` and press **Enter**.

   ii. Press **Enter** again to complete modifying the content of iisstart.htm.

    f. At the Windows PowerShell prompt, type `Get-Content iisstart.htm` and press **Enter**. Note your new website contents.

    g. Type `exit` and press **Enter** to exit Windows PowerShell. Type `exit` again and press **Enter** to exit the interactive command prompt in iiscontainer3 and return to the Windows PowerShell prompt on your Windows Server 2019 host.

10. In your Web browser, refresh your webpage for iiscontainer3 and note the new webpage displayed.

11. At the Windows PowerShell prompt, type `docker stop iiscontainer3` and press **Enter** to stop executing iiscontainer3. Next, type `docker ps` and press **Enter** to verify that iiscontainer3 is no longer running.

12. In your Web browser, refresh your webpage for iiscontainer3 and note the error indicating that the website cannot be reached.

13. At the Windows PowerShell prompt, type `docker ps -a` and press **Enter**. Note that iiscontainer3 is shown. Type `docker start iiscontainer3` and press **Enter** to start iiscontainer3. Next, type `docker ps` and press **Enter** and note the new port number that was chosen for iiscontainer3 on the underlying operating system in the PORTS column.

14. In your Web browser, navigate to `IPaddress:port3`, where *IPaddress* is the IP address of your Windows Server 2019 host and *port3* is the new port number you recorded in the previous step for iiscontainer3. Note that your modified webpage is displayed. Close your Web browser when finished.

15. At the Windows PowerShell prompt, type `docker stop iiscontainer1 iiscontainer2 iiscontainer3` and press **Enter** to stop all of your containers. Next, type `docker container prune` and press **Enter**. Type `y` and press **Enter** to remove all of your containers, without removing the container image from which they were created. Note that only a small amount of space was freed since containers only store the data that is different from their container image, and you only modified one HTML file in iiscontainer3.

16. Close Windows PowerShell when finished.

Project 10-3: WSL

In this Hands-On Project, you install the Windows Subsystem for Linux (WSL) on your Windows Server 2019 host and configure the Ubuntu Linux distribution. Following this, you install the Apache Web server on your Ubuntu Linux distribution, as well as view and modify the default webpage.

1. In Server Manager on your Windows Server 2019 host, click the **Manage** menu and then click **Add Roles and Features**.

    a. At the Select installation type page, click **Next**.

    b. At the Select destination server page, click **Next**.

    c. At the Select server roles page, click **Next**.

    d. At the Select features page, select **Windows Subsystem for Linux** and click **Next**.

e. At the Confirm installation selections page, click **Install**.

f. At the Installation progress page, click **Close** to close the Add the Roles and Features Wizard.

2. Right-click **Start** and click **Shut down or sign out**, **Restart**. Next, click **Continue** to restart your Windows Server 2019 host.

3. After your Windows Server 2019 host has booted, log into domain*X*.com as Administrator using the password **Secret555**. Next, right-click **Start** and click **Windows PowerShell (Admin)** to open Windows PowerShell.

a. Type `Invoke-WebRequest -Uri https://aka.ms/wsl-ubuntu-1804 -OutFile Ubuntu.appx -UseBasicParsing` and press **Enter** to download the Ubuntu Linux 18.04 distribution package. This step may take several minutes, depending on the speed of your Internet connection.

b. At the prompt, type `Add-AppxPackage Ubuntu.appx` and press **Enter** to install the Ubuntu Linux 18.04 distribution package.

c. At the prompt, type `Restart-Computer -Force` and press **Enter** to reboot your Windows Server 2019 host.

4. After your Windows Server 2019 host has booted, log into domain*X*.com as Administrator using the password **Secret555**. Next, click **Start** and then click **Ubuntu 18.04**. After a few moments, you are prompted to create a UNIX user. When prompted for the UNIX user name, type **woot** and press **Enter**. When prompted for the associated password for this user, type **Secret555** and press **Enter**. When prompted to confirm this password, type **Secret555** again and press **Enter**. You now receive a Linux command prompt indicating that you are logged into the system as the woot user with a $ prompt.

a. Type `sudo passwd root` and press **Enter** to assign the root user (equivalent to Administrator in Windows) a password. When prompted to supply your own password to confirm the action, type **Secret555** and press **Enter**. When prompted to specify the root user password, type **Secret555** and press **Enter**. When prompted to confirm this password, type **Secret555** again and press **Enter**.

b. Type `su` and press **Enter** to switch to the root user. When prompted to supply the root user password, type **Secret555** and press **Enter**. Note that your prompt changes to # to indicate that you are a superuser (root) on the Linux system.

c. Type `apt-get update` and press **Enter** to update the Linux software repository files for the Ubuntu Linux distribution.

d. Type `apt install apache2 -y` and press **Enter** to install the Apache Web server. Type **Y** and press **Enter** when prompted to perform the installation.

e. Because IIS is already configured on your Windows Server 2019 host to listen for HTTP requests on port 80, you must ensure that the Apache Web server is configured to listen on a different port number to allow both Web servers to run. Type `nano /etc/apache2/ports.conf` and press **Enter** to open the Apache Web server port configuration file in the nano text editor. Modify the Listen line to read `Listen 8000`. Next, press the **Ctrl** and **O** keys simultaneously on your keyboard to save your settings and press **Enter** to confirm the file location. Next, press the **Ctrl** and **X** keys simultaneously on your keyboard to quit the nano text editor.

f. Type `apachectl start` and press **Enter** to start the Apache Web server.

g. Type `ps -ef` and press **Enter** to view running processes. Note that three apache2 services are running. Leave your Linux command prompt window open.

5. Because the Apache Web server is a Linux program, Windows Firewall is not automatically updated to allow access to it. As a result, you must manually allow access to port 8000 on your Windows Server 2019 host. Right-click **Start** and click **Windows PowerShell (Admin)** to open Windows PowerShell. At the prompt, type `New-NetFirewallRule -DisplayName "Allow HTTP on Port 8000" -Direction Inbound -LocalPort 8000 -Protocol TCP -Action Allow` and press **Enter** to allow port 8000 in Windows Firewall. Close Windows PowerShell when finished.

6. Open a Web browser and navigate to *IPaddress*:8000, where *IPaddress* is the IP address of your Windows Server 2019 host. Note the default Ubuntu Linux webpage.

7. At the Linux command prompt, type `echo "<html><body><h1>Linux Webpage </h1></body></html>" > /var/www/html/index.html` and press **Enter** to overwrite the existing default Ubuntu Linux webpage.

8. Refresh the webpage in your Web browser and note the revised content. Close your Web browser when finished.

9. Close your Linux command prompt window.

Project 10-4: Linux Containers on Windows

In this Hands-On Project, you enable Linux Containers on Windows (LCOW) using Docker on your Windows Server 2019 host. Following this, you obtain and run Linux containers that contain the Apache Web server.

1. On your Windows Server 2019 host, right-click **Start** and click **Windows PowerShell (Admin)** to open Windows PowerShell.

a. Type `[Environment]::SetEnvironmentVariable("LCOW_SUPPORTED", "1", "Machine")` and press **Enter** to enable LCOW.

b. Type `Restart-Service Docker` and press **Enter** to restart the Docker daemon.

c. Type `docker login` and press **Enter**. At the Username prompt, type your Docker Hub user name and press **Enter**. At the Password prompt, type your Docker Hub password and press **Enter**. Note the location of the config.json file that stores your unencrypted Docker Hub password.

d. Type `docker search httpd` and press **Enter** to search Docker Hub for Apache (httpd) images and note the results.

e. Type `docker pull httpd` and press **Enter** to download the official Apache Docker image. This step may take several minutes, depending on the speed of your Internet connection.

f. Type `docker images` and press **Enter**. Note your httpd image, as well as the associated IMAGE ID (the beginning of the hash for the image).

g. Type `docker tag httpd apache` and press **Enter** to create an alias for your httpd image called apache.

    h. Type `docker run --name apachecontainer1 -P -d apache` and press **Enter** to execute a new container based on your Web server container image that automatically maps a port in the underlying operating system to port 80 in the container. Next, type `docker run --name apachecontainer2 -P -d apache` and press **Enter**, and then type `docker run --name apachecontainer3 -P -d apache` and press **Enter** to execute two more containers from the same container image.

    i. Type `docker ps` and press **Enter**. Note that three containers are currently executing (apachecontainer1, apachecontainer2, and apachecontainer3). Also note the port numbers that were chosen for each container on the underlying operating system in the PORTS column.

2. Open a Web browser.

    a. Navigate to `localhost:port1`, where *port1* is the port number you recorded in the previous step for apachecontainer1. Note the default Apache webpage displayed.

    b. Navigate to `localhost:port2`, where *port2* is the port number you recorded in the previous step for apachecontainer2. Note the default Apache webpage displayed.

    c. Navigate to `localhost:port3`, where *port3* is the port number you recorded in the previous step for apachecontainer3. Note the default Apache webpage displayed. Leave your Web browser open.

3. At the Windows PowerShell prompt, type `docker exec -it apachecontainer3 sh` and press **Enter** to obtain an interactive Linux command prompt (shell) in the apachecontainer3 container.

    a. Type `pwd` and press **Enter**. Note the default folder is set to /usr/local/apache2 in the container.

    b. Type `cd htdocs` and press **Enter** to change to the /usr/local/apache2/htdocs folder in your container.

    c. Type `ls` and press **Enter** to list the folder contents and note the default index.html webpage.

    d. Type `echo "<html><body><h1>Container 3 Webpage</h1></body></html>" > index.html` and press **Enter** to modify the contents of the index.html webpage.

    e. Type `cat index.html` and press **Enter** to view the new contents of the index.html webpage.

    f. Type `exit` and press **Enter** to exit the interactive Linux shell and return to the Windows PowerShell prompt on your Windows Server 2019 host.

4. In your Web browser, refresh your webpage for apachecontainer3 and note the new webpage displayed.

5. At the Windows PowerShell prompt, type `docker stop apachecontainer1 apachecontainer2 apachecontainer3` and press **Enter** to stop all of your containers. Next, type `docker container prune` and press **Enter**. Type **y** and press **Enter** to remove all of your containers without removing the container image from which they were created.

6. At the Windows PowerShell prompt, type `[Environment]::SetEnvironmentVariab le("LCOW_SUPPORTED", "$null", "Machine")` and press **Enter** to disable LinuxKit. Next, type `Restart-Service Docker` and press **Enter** to restart the Docker daemon.

7. Close Windows PowerShell when finished.

Project 10-5: Nano Server

In this Hands-On Project, you explore the Nano Server base container image often used to create custom Windows container images that host Web apps.

1. On your Windows Server 2019 host, right-click **Start** and click **Windows PowerShell (Admin)** to open Windows PowerShell.
2. Type `dir \Windows` and press **Enter**. Note the number of contents in the Windows system folder on your Windows Server 2019 host.
3. Type `Get-Service` and press **Enter**. Note the number of services available on your Windows Server 2019 host.
4. Type `docker login` and press **Enter**. At the Username prompt, type your Docker Hub user name and press **Enter**. At the Password prompt, type your Docker Hub password and press **Enter**.
5. Type `docker pull mcr.microsoft.com/nanoserver` and press **Enter** to download the official base Nano Server image. This step may take several minutes, depending on the speed of your Internet connection.
6. Type `docker run --isolation=hyperv --name nanoservertemplate -d mcr.microsoft.com/nanoserver` and press **Enter** to execute a Hyper-V container called nanoservertemplate from your base Nano Server image.
7. Type `docker exec -it nanoservertemplate powershell` and press **Enter** to obtain an interactive Windows PowerShell prompt in your base Nano Server container.
   a. Type `ipconfig` and press **Enter**. Note that the base Nano Server container has an IP address behind the virtual NAT router created by Docker on the 172 network.
   b. Type `dir \Windows` and press **Enter**. Note that the Windows system folder on your Nano Server container has far fewer contents compared to your Windows Server 2019 host.
   c. Type `Get-Service` and press **Enter**. Note that your Nano Server container has far fewer services available compared to your Windows Server 2019 host.
   d. Type `exit` and press **Enter** to exit your Windows PowerShell session in your Nano Server container.
8. Type `docker stop nanoservertemplate` and press **Enter** to stop your Nano Server container.
9. Close Windows PowerShell.

Discovery Exercises

Exercise 10-1

A common analogy used to explain the differences between SaaS, PaaS, and IaaS is called Pizza as a Service. Use an Internet search engine to search for the Pizza as a Service analogy, and summarize how it relates to SaaS, PaaS, and IaaS in a one-page memo.

Exercise 10-2

To allow Web app developers to access content on a cloud server, many server administrators enable the use of FTP. Use the Add Roles and Features Wizard on your WindowsServer2019VM2 virtual machine to add the FTP Server role service to IIS. Next, use IIS Manager to create an FTP site that allows regular FTP access to the C:\MarketingMaterials folder on your WindowsServer2019VM2 virtual machine. Next, download and install the Filezilla FTP client program from *https://filezilla-project.org* on your Windows Server 2019 host and use it to connect to the FTP site on your WindowsServer2019VM2 virtual machine as Administrator. Finally, perform a sample file transfer to your FTP site.

Exercise 10-3

In Hands-On Project 10-2, you downloaded the microsoft/iis container image from Docker Hub and created three containers from it using the same kernel on your Windows Server 2019 host. Perform this configuration again, but instead using Hyper-V containers to ensure that each container uses a unique copy of the Windows Server 2019 kernel. Also ensure that you use the `-p` option alongside the `docker` command to manually associate port 80 in the container to a port number of your choice on your Windows Server 2019 host.

Exercise 10-4

In Hands-On Project 10-3, you installed the Ubuntu Linux distribution on your Windows Server 2019 host using WSL. Install another supported WSL Linux distribution on your Windows Server 2019 host and configure it as an Apache Web server that listens for HTTP requests on port 9000. Test your results when finished.

Exercise 10-5

In Hands-On Project 10-4, you used LCOW to run several Apache containers. Docker Hub contains thousands of different Linux container images that were created for different purposes. Enable LCOW on your Windows Server 2019 host and search Docker Hub for official container images. Download a container image of your choice and run a container based on it. Next, explore the contents of the container while it is running. When finished, stop your container.

Exercise 10-6

Recall that the process of continuous deployment employs complicated orchestration and build automation software that is configured by server administrators called devops. Use an Internet search engine to research the Kubernetes orchestration software product, as well as the Ansible automation software product. In a one-page memo, summarize the features available for each product, as well as the components that they use to perform orchestration or automation for Windows and Linux systems and containers.

MANAGING AND SECURING WINDOWS NETWORKS

After completing this module, you will be able to:

Configure and manage GPOs

Identify the structure and use of public key certificates

Deploy certificates using an enterprise CA

Protect WLAN access using 802.1X Wireless

Use WSUS to manage the distribution of updates

Configure Windows Defender settings, firewall rules, and IPSec

In addition to providing secure access to resources, Windows Server 2019 can manage and secure other systems in an organization. In this module, you'll learn how to manage systems and software in a domain environment using Group Policy. Next, you'll learn how public key certificates are used to protect encryption technologies, as well as the process used to deploy certificates to users and computers in an organization. Following this, you'll learn how to protect wireless networks using 802.1X Wireless, as well as manage updates in an organization using WSUS. At the end of this module, you'll examine the configuration of Windows Defender, firewalls, and IPSec.

Configuring Group Policy

In addition to providing for centralized authentication and single sign-on, recall from Module 4 that Active Directory contains a powerful administrative feature called Group Policy. Group Policy can be used to automatically configure software; Windows features; and security, program, and user interface settings on computers in an Active Directory domain based on the location of a user or computer account in the Active Directory database. To configure Group Policy, you create **Group Policy Objects (GPOs)** that have the appropriate settings. A single GPO can be applied to thousands of users and computers in an organization to reduce the time and effort that it takes to administer a large domain.

> **Note** 📎
>
> To function, GPOs must be linked to a site, domain, or OU object that contains the user or computer accounts that it applies to. Unlike its name suggests, GPOs do not apply to Active Directory groups.

> **Note** 📎
>
> GPO settings are strictly enforced. As a result, users are not able to configure or override settings that are applied by GPOs.

Group Policy settings are stored in two different sections in a GPO:

- Computer Configuration
- User Configuration

At boot time, Windows 2000 and later computers apply the Computer Configuration from all GPOs that are linked to a site, domain, or OU object that contain their computer account. Similarly, when domain users log into a Windows 2000 or later computer, they apply the User Configuration from all GPOs that are linked to a site, domain, or OU object that contains their user account.

> **Note** 📎
>
> Computer Configuration settings are also applied periodically after boot time. By default, workstations and member servers apply their Computer Configuration settings every 90 minutes (plus a random offset between 0 and 30 minutes), whereas domain controllers apply their Computer Configuration settings every 5 minutes.

Depending on the number of GPOs configured and linked to site, domain, and OU objects, a single user or computer account may receive the settings from several GPOs. To prevent conflicts in the event that two or more of these GPOs contain different values for the same setting, GPOs are applied to user and computer accounts based on the link in the following order:

- Site
- Domain
- Parent OU
- Child OUs

Thus, if the User Configuration section of a GPO linked to your domain has a setting that conflicts with the same setting in the User Configuration section of a GPO linked to the OU that contains your user account, you will receive the setting that is configured in the GPO linked to the OU that contains your user account, as it was applied last.

If multiple GPOs are linked to the same site, domain, or OU, they will be applied in link order, with the highest link order applied first and the lowest link order applied last. For example, if GPO1 (link order 1), GPO2 (link order 2), and GPO3 (link order 3) are linked to the same OU that contains your user account, GPO3 will be applied first, followed by GPO2 and then GPO1. If the same settings are configured in all three GPOs, you will receive the settings from GPO1 as it was applied last.

There are two default GPOs in each Active Directory domain that provide default security configuration for computers:

- The *Default Domain Policy* GPO is linked to the domain object and applies to all user and computer accounts in the domain.
- The *Default Domain Controllers Policy* GPO is linked to the Domain Controllers OU and applies to domain controller computer accounts.

Note 📎

For performance reasons, you should only link GPOs to site objects when no alternative options are viable. This is because each client must first match their IP configuration to a subnet that is associated with a site object in order to identify the site of which they are a part.

Note 📎

Each Windows 2000 and later computer also has a local GPO. This GPO is stored in the hidden C:\Windows\system32\grouppolicy folder and contains no configured settings by default. However, if settings are configured in the local GPO, they will be applied before the settings in any GPOs that are linked to site, domain, and OU objects. To edit the local GPO, you can add the Group Policy Object Editor snap-in to the MMC for the local computer, or run the gpedit.msc command at a Windows PowerShell or Command Prompt window.

Configuring GPOs

To configure GPOs in an Active Directory environment, you can click Group Policy Management from the Tools menu in Server Manager to start the **Group Policy Management** tool shown in Figure 11-1.

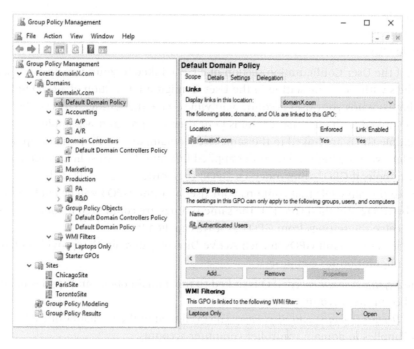

Figure 11-1   The Group Policy Management tool

In addition to three sites (ChicagoSite, ParisSite, and TorontoSite), the domainX.com domain shown in Figure 11-1 contains the OU structure shown earlier in Figure 4-5, as well as the two default GPOs in the Group Policy Objects folder. Furthermore, a link object associates the Default Domain Policy GPO to domainX.com, and another link object associates the Default Domain Controllers Policy GPO to the Domain Controllers OU. Because the link object for the Default Domain Policy GPO is highlighted in the navigation pane in Figure 11-1, the properties of the Default Domain Policy GPO are displayed in the right pane.

Note

Sites are not shown by default in the Group Policy Management Console. To display sites, you must right-click the Sites folder shown in Figure 11-1, click Show Sites, and select the sites that you wish to display.

Blocking and Enforcing GPOs

You can configure the Block Inheritance setting on an OU to prevent user and computer accounts in the OU from applying GPOs that are linked to parent OUs, domains, or sites. Similarly, you can configure the Block Inheritance setting on a domain to prevent domain user and computer accounts from applying GPOs that are linked to sites. However, if a GPO link is configured with the Enforced setting, the associated GPO will be applied to user and computer accounts in domains and OUs that have Block Inheritance configured, and will be applied following other GPOs to ensure that its settings override the same settings in other GPOs. The blue exclamation point icon on the R&D OU in Figure 11-1 indicates that the Block Inheritance setting has been configured. Normally, this would prevent the Default Domain Policy GPO from applying to user and computer accounts in the R&D OU. However, the yellow lock icon on the Default Domain Policy link to domainX.com indicates that it is Enforced to ensure that the Default Domain Policy GPO applies to all OUs, including the R&D OU. To block inheritance on a domain or OU object, you can right-click it in the navigation pane and then click Block Inheritance. Similarly, to enforce a GPO link, you can right-click it in the navigation pane and click Enforced.

Filtering GPOs

The Default Domain Policy in Figure 11-1 applies to all user and computer accounts in domainX.com because the Authenticated Users group (which contains all authenticated user and computer accounts in the domain) is listed in the Security Filtering section of the Scope tab of Default Domain Policy properties. To instead apply the Default Domain Policy GPO to specific users and computers, you can remove the Authenticated Users group from the Security Filtering section and add specific user and computer groups, or specific user and computer accounts.

Recall from Module 2 that you can use WQL (WMI Query Language) statements to obtain information from Windows systems using WMI. To further limit the computers that a GPO applies to, you can configure GPOs with a **WMI filter** that specifies the hardware and software features that must be present on a computer before the GPO is applied. The Laptops Only WMI filter in the properties of the Default Domain Policy GPO in Figure 11-1 applies the GPO to laptop computers in the domain only. To create the Laptops Only WMI filter, you can right-click the WMI Filters folder in the navigation pane of Figure 11-1 and click New. Next, you can specify a name of Laptops Only as well as the following WQL query (laptop computers are identified by having a battery status value):

```
SELECT * FROM Win32_Battery WHERE (BatteryStatus <> 0)
```

Note

Microsoft provides numerous WMI filter examples. Search *GPO WMI* on docs.microsoft.com for more information.

Creating and Linking GPOs

To create a new GPO, you can right-click the Group Policy Objects folder in Figure 11-1, click New, and specify a GPO name. Next, you can link this GPO to one or more site, domain, or OU objects. To do this, you can right-click the object, click *Link an Existing GPO,* and select the GPO you wish to link. You can also right-click a domain or OU object, click *Create a GPO in this domain, and Link it here,* and specify a GPO name to create a new GPO that is linked to the object. After a GPO is linked to a site, domain, or OU object, a link object for the GPO is displayed underneath.

> **Note** @
>
> In addition to supplying a GPO name, you are prompted to optionally select a **starter GPO** when creating a new GPO. A starter GPO is a template GPO that contains Administrative Templates settings (discussed in the next section) that are automatically applied to the new GPO. To create a starter GPO, you can right-click the Starter GPOs folder in Figure 11-1, click New, and specify a GPO name. Following this, you must edit the GPO (discussed in the next section) to include settings that you wish to include in your GPO template.

> **Note** @
>
> If you link multiple GPOs to the same site, domain, or OU, you can modify the link order for the GPOs. To do this, select the site, domain, or OU object in the navigation pane of the Group Policy Management tool, highlight the Linked Group Policy Objects tab, and use the up/down arrow buttons to modify the link order for each GPO.

Configuring GPO Settings

To modify GPO settings, you can right-click a GPO or GPO link in the navigation pane of the Group Policy Management tool and click Edit. For example, if you right-click the Default Domain Policy link shown in Figure 11-1 and click Edit, you will open the **Group Policy Management Editor** tool shown in Figure 11-2.

The Computer Configuration and User Configuration sections of each GPO contain two folders:

- *Policies* contains Group Policy settings, organized into three subfolders:
    - *Software Settings* specifies software packages that are deployed to computers.
    - *Windows Settings* provides operating system configuration.
    - *Administrative Templates* provides configuration for desktop and operating system components.

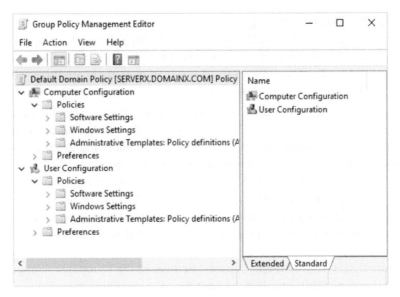

Figure 11-2   The Group Policy Management Editor tool

- *Preferences* contains **Group Policy preferences**. Group Policy preferences can be used to provide configuration for Windows features. Unlike Group Policy settings, Group Policy preference configuration is not strictly enforced and can be modified by users afterward.

There are over 5,000 different individual settings available under the folders and subfolders in a GPO. In the following sections, we'll examine some example settings under the folders shown in Figure 11-2. In the Hands-On Projects and Discovery Exercises for this module, you'll explore and configure additional settings.

Note 📎

Group Policy preferences can only be interpreted by Windows 7 and later clients, as well as Windows Server 2008 and later servers. To allow Windows XP, Windows Vista, and Windows Server 2003 systems to interpret Group Policy preferences, you must install the *Group Policy Preference Client Side Extensions* package from microsoft.com.

Note 📎

If you modify the settings in the *Default Domain Policy* or *Default Domain Controllers Policy* GPOs, you can run the `dcgpofix.exe` command at a Windows PowerShell or Command Prompt window to restore the settings to their default values.

Configuring Software Settings

The Software Settings folder in a GPO allows you to deploy software to computers using Group Policy. This software is typically hosted in a shared folder on a file server and packaged as a **Windows Installer** file (.msi). Moreover, there are three software deployment methods that you can choose from:

- Software that is *Published* under Software Settings in the User Configuration of a GPO can be optionally installed by users. To install published software, users can click *Install a program from the network* in the Programs and Features section of Control Panel, select the software package, and click Install.
- Software that is *Assigned* under Software Settings in the User Configuration of a GPO is made available as a program icon on the Start menu, as well as a file association. This software is automatically installed the first time that a user clicks the program icon on the Start menu, or opens a file that is associated with the program.
- Software that is *Assigned* under Software Settings in the Computer Configuration of a GPO is automatically installed the next time the computer is booted.

For example, the Mozilla Firefox software package shown in Figure 11-3 is published under the Software Settings in the User Configuration of the Default Domain Policy GPO. If users in the domain choose to install this package in the Programs and Features section of Control Panel, the associated `Firefox Setup 72.0.2.msi` file will be downloaded and installed from the software share on server.domainx.com.

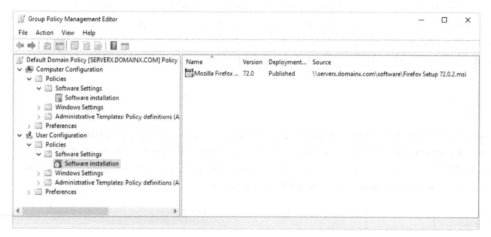

Figure 11-3   Deploying software

To deploy software packages, you can right-click Software Installation under Software Settings in either the Computer Configuration or User Configuration section of Figure 11-3 and click New, Package. Next, you must supply the UNC path to the shared Windows Installer package, click Open, and select the deployment method (Published or Assigned).

Group Policy can also be configured to automatically uninstall software when the GPO no longer applies to the user or computer account to which the software was deployed. A GPO will no longer apply to a user or computer account in the following situations:

- The server administrator removes the software package from the GPO configuration and chooses the *Immediately uninstall the software from users and computers* option when prompted.
- The server administrator removes the GPO.
- The server administrator removes the GPO link to the object that contains the user or computer account.
- The user or computer account is moved to another OU that does not receive the settings from the GPO.

To configure computers to automatically uninstall Mozilla Firefox if the Default Domain Policy GPO in Figure 11-3 no longer applies, you can right-click the Mozilla Firefox package, click Properties, highlight the Deployment tab, and select *Uninstall this application when it falls out of the scope of management.*

Configuring Windows Settings

The Windows Settings folder in a GPO contains subfolders that you can use to configure different Windows settings, as shown in Figure 11-4:

- *Name Resolution Policy* under Computer Configuration allows you to configure DNS settings for use with DNSSEC and DirectAccess.
- *Scripts (Startup/Shutdown)* under Computer Configuration allows you to specify scripts (e.g., PowerShell scripts) that should be executed when a computer boots or is shut down.
- *Scripts (Logon/Logoff)* under User Configuration allows you to specify scripts (e.g., PowerShell scripts) that should be executed when a user logs into or out of their Windows system.
- *Deployed Printers* allows you to deploy shared printers.
- *Security Settings* allows you to configure most Windows security-related settings, such as password and account lockout policies, Kerberos settings, auditing, operating system rights, security options, event log settings, groups membership that is enforced by Group Policy, system service configuration, registry keys, files and folders, wireless LAN configuration, Windows Defender Firewall configuration, certificate configuration, IPSec configuration, as well as policies that can be used to restrict the applications that are allowed to run on a system. Most available security settings are located under Computer Configuration only.
- *Folder Redirection* under User Configuration allows you to store the contents of user folders (e.g., Desktop, Documents, Pictures) in a private shared folder for each user account on a file server. When users access these folders on their PC, they are automatically redirected to the associated folder on the file server. This configuration ensures that user files are only kept on a file server, where they are centrally backed up and protected using fault-tolerant storage.

- *Policy-based QoS* allows you to limit the bandwidth used by TCP, UDP, or HTTP traffic.

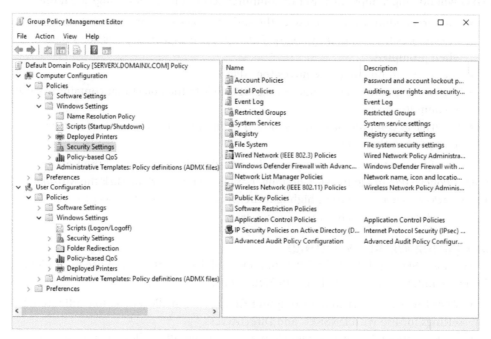

Figure 11-4   Configuring Windows Settings

The Security Settings subfolder of Windows Settings in the Computer Configuration section shown in Figure 11-4 is often the focus for server administrators who wish to secure the computers in the domain. For example, the Account Policies subfolder of Security Settings contains a Password Policy subfolder that holds settings that server administrators use to configure password settings, as shown in Figure 11-5 and described in Table 11-1. The settings configured in Figure 11-5 require complex passwords that contain at least 7 characters, and ensure that users do not reuse their previous 24 passwords. Moreover, users must wait one day following a password change before they are able to change it again, and must change their password every 42 days at minimum.

Note

You can double-click a setting to modify its value, or view its description.

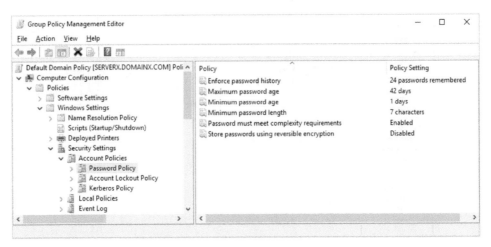

Figure 11-5   Configuring a Password Policy

Table 11-1   Password policy settings

Setting	Description
Enforce password history	Sets the number of passwords (between 0 and 24) that have to be unique before a user can reuse an old password.
Maximum password age	Sets the maximum number of days that a password can be used before the user is required to change it. A value of 0 ensures that passwords do not expire.
Minimum password age	Sets the number of days that a password must be used before a user is allowed to change it.
Minimum password length	Sets the minimum number of characters required in a password (from 0 to 14).
Password must meet complexity requirements	If enabled, requires that passwords be at least six characters in length and have three different character types from the following list: uppercase letters, lowercase letters, numbers, and special characters (e.g., *, %, #).
Store password using reversible encryption	Allows passwords to be stored as text in the Active Directory database and weakly protected using a simple encryption algorithm that can be decrypted by anyone. This setting should only be enabled to support applications that use legacy authentication protocols.

Similarly, the Account Lockout Policy subfolder of Account Policies allows server administrators to automatically lock user accounts after a certain number of invalid login attempts, as shown in Figure 11-6 and described in Table 11-2. The settings configured in Figure 11-6 automatically lock user accounts for 30 minutes when users attempt to log into a computer unsuccessfully 3 times within 5 minutes.

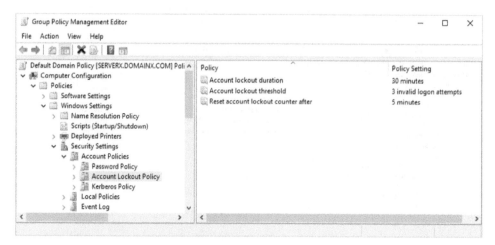

Figure 11-6   Configuring an Account Lockout Policy

Table 11-2   Account Lockout Policy Settings

Setting	Description
Account lockout threshold	Determines the number of failed login attempts that can occur before a user account is locked.
Account lockout duration	Determines the number of minutes that a locked account remains locked before it is automatically unlocked. Specifying a value of 0 ensures that a locked account remains locked until an administrator manually unlocks it.
Reset account lockout counter after	Determines the number of minutes after a failed login attempt before the bad logon counter is reset to zero.

Note

Settings configured under the Account Policies folder only apply if the GPO is linked to a domain object. To configure password and account lockout settings for a particular group of users, you can instead create a **Password Settings Object (PSO)** in the Active Directory Administrative Center. Search Password Settings Object on docs.micrsoft.com for more information.

Configuring Administrative Templates

Most configuration settings in a GPO are stored under the Administrative Templates folder. This folder contains several subfolders that can be used to configure different Windows components, as shown in Figure 11-7:

- *Control Panel* allows you to control access to Control Panel or specific tools and configuration areas in Control Panel, as well as automatically configure Control Panel settings, such as region and language options.

- *Desktop* under User Configuration allows you to provide desktop configuration (e.g., a standard desktop wallpaper), as well as restrict access to desktop features and functionality.
- *Network* allows you configure network-related settings (e.g., DNS), as well as the functionality of network-related technologies (e.g., Offline Files).
- *Printers* under Computer Configuration allows you to configure printing and Print Spooler service features.
- *Server* under Computer Configuration allows you to configure system backup features.
- *Shared Folders* under User Configuration allows you to configure the ability to publish shared folders.
- *Start Menu and Taskbar* allows you to configure or restrict access to Start menu and taskbar features.
- *System* allows you to configure operating system features and functionality, such as power management, shutdown options, and access to removable storage.
- *Windows Components* allows you to configure settings for operating system components and programs, such as Windows Update and File Explorer.
- *All Settings* displays the individual Administrative Templates configuration settings available in the User or Computer Configuration section in alphabetical order. This allows you to quickly locate a setting that you know the name of.

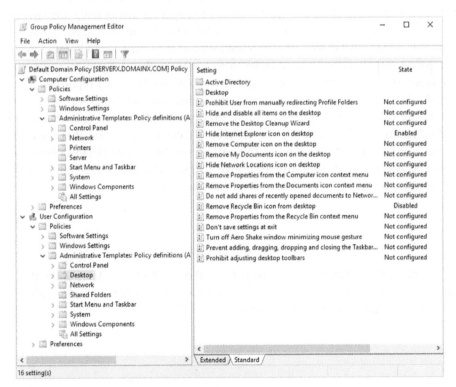

Figure 11-7   Configuring Administrative Templates

Each setting under the Administrative Templates folder describes its function, and can be set to Enabled to provide the function, or Disabled to prevent the function if another GPO processed earlier is configured to provide it. For example, the Desktop configuration shown in Figure 11-7 ensures that the Internet Explorer icon is hidden (*Hide Internet Explorer icon on desktop* = Enabled), but that the Recycle Bin icon is shown (*Remove Recycle Bin icon from desktop* = Disabled).

Moreover, the list of folders available under Administrative Templates can be expanded to include additional configuration settings. Many third party software manufacturers allow you to download and install **administrative template files** that can be imported into a GPO and used to configure settings for their software. Administrative templates files for legacy systems (Windows Vista, Windows Server 2003, and earlier) end in .adm while administrative templates files for Windows Vista SP1, Windows Server 2008, and newer systems end in .admx and may be accompanied by folders that include language customizations. For example, a fr-FR folder will contain French versions of the settings in the English .admx file.

- To import a .adm file into a GPO, you can right-click the Administrative Templates folder under either Computer Configuration or User Configuration in the Group Policy Management Editor, click Add/Remove Templates, and select the .adm file. This will create a Classic Administrative Templates (ADM) folder under the Administrative Templates folder that contains the associated settings.
- To import a .admx file into a GPO, you must copy it (and optionally any language customization folders) to the C:\Windows\PolicyDefinitions folder. Next, you must copy the C:\Windows\PolicyDefinitions folder to the C:\Windows\SYSVOL\ sysvol*domain*\Policies folder in order to ensure that other domain controllers receive the new administrative templates using Active Directory replication. Following this, a new folder containing the configuration settings for the software will be added under the Administrative Templates folders for Computer Configuration and User Configuration in each GPO. For example, after importing the .admx file for Mozilla Firefox, the settings for the Mozilla Firefox Web browser will be available under the Administrative Templates folder, as shown for the User Configuration of Default Domain Policy in Figure 11-8.

Note

If you edit a starter GPO, Administrative Templates is the only folder available under the Computer Configuration and User Configuration sections. The settings in all other GPO folders cannot be configured in a starter GPO.

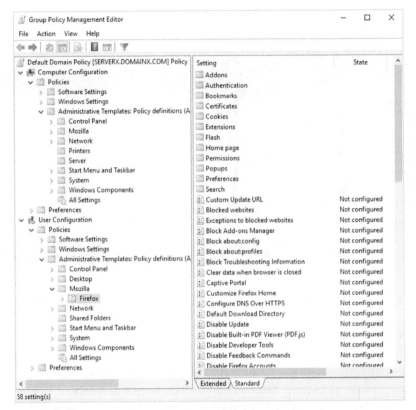

Figure 11-8   Adding settings to Administrative Templates

Configuring Group Policy Preferences

To configure Group Policy preferences, you must specify configuration settings under the Preferences folder in either the Computer Configuration or User Configuration section of a GPO. Moreover, the Preferences folder contains two subfolders that include the features that you can configure, as shown in Figure 11-9:

- *Windows Settings* allows you to add, remove, or modify applications, drive maps, shared folders, environment variables, files, folder, shortcuts, and registry keys.
- *Control Panel Settings* allows you to configure users, groups, settings, and devices in Control Panel.

You can use Group Policy preferences to configure some of the same Windows features that are available in the Windows Settings and Administrative Templates folders under the Policies folder in a GPO. However, Group Policy preferences allows for additional feature configuration options. Most features configured using

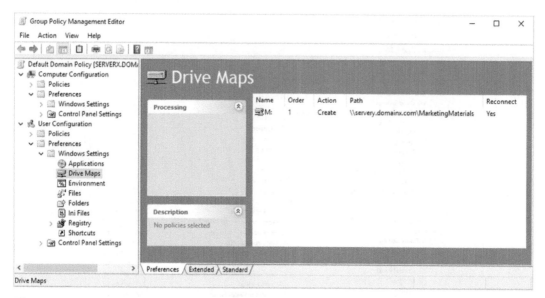

Figure 11-9   Configuring Group Policy preferences

Group Policy preferences allow you to specify the configuration action that must be performed:

- *Create* configures a new feature only if it does not already exist.
- *Replace* replaces an existing feature configuration with a new one.
- *Update* modifies a previously configured feature to include new settings.
- *Delete* removes a feature if it was previously configured.

For example, the Drive Maps feature configured in Figure 11-9 will configure a new M: drive map for \\servery.domainx.com\MarketingMaterials only if it does not already exist. Furthermore, features configured using Group Policy preferences allow you to specify additional processing options, such as whether to apply the configuration once only, or whether the configuration should apply to certain Windows systems (e.g., Windows 7 and newer only). To configure a feature using Group Policy preferences, you can right-click the feature under the Windows Settings or Control Panel Settings folder, click New, *Feature Name*, and specify the appropriate options. For example, to configure a drive map, you can right-click the Drive Maps feature in Figure 11-9 and click New, Mapped Drive.

Note

After you modify a setting in the Group Policy Management Editor, that setting is automatically saved to the GPO object in the Active Directory database as well as copied to the associated file in the SYSVOL share, where it can be accessed by domain computers. As a result, there is no Save button available in the Group Policy Management Editor.

Managing GPOs

After you configure a new GPO, you should review the settings that you configured to ensure that they match your needs, as well as document them for future use. To do this, you can select the GPO or GPO link in the Group Policy Management tool and highlight the Settings tab of GPO properties, as shown for Default Domain Policy in Figure 11-10. You can click the show and hide hyperlinks in the report shown in Figure 11-10 to expand or collapse each configured GPO section, folder, and feature. To save an HTML- or XML-formatted copy of the report, you can right-click any area of the report, click Save Report, and select the format and folder path.

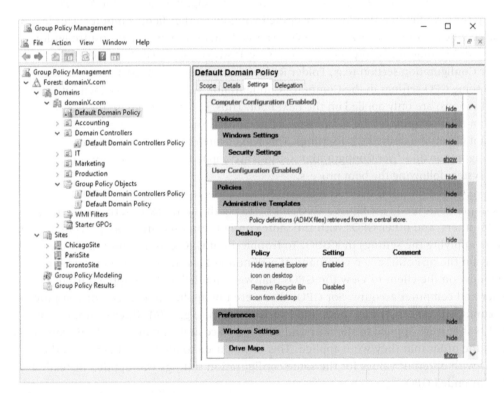

Figure 11-10   **Viewing GPO settings**

Because the Computer Configuration and User Configuration sections of the Default Domain Policy GPO shown in Figure 11-10 contain configured settings, both sections are listed as Enabled. However, you can instead choose to configure settings in only one section in a GPO. In this case, you should disable the unused GPO section to speed up the processing of the GPO by clients. To do this for the Default Domain Policy GPO shown in Figure 11-10, you can highlight the Details tab and either select *Computer configuration settings disabled* or *User configuration settings disabled* from the GPO Status drop-down box.

In general, it is best to minimize the number of settings that you configure in a GPO to ensure that it is processed quickly by clients, as well as reduce the risk of GPO corruption. Backing up the GPOs that you create also ensures that you can quickly restore configuration settings in the event of GPO corruption. To back up all GPOs, you can right-click the Group Policy Objects folder in Figure 11-10, click *Back Up All* and specify a folder path for the backups. Alternatively, to back up a single GPO, you can right-click it under the Group Policy Objects folder and click *Back Up*. To restore a GPO from a backup, you can right-click the corrupted GPO under the Group Policy Objects folder and click *Restore from Backup*.

If clients do not receive the configuration that you specified in a GPO, you can run the gpupdate /force command in a Command Prompt window, or the Invoke-GPUpdate cmdlet in a Windows PowerShell window on the client computer. This forces the client computer to check the SYSVOL shared folder on their domain controller for new GPO settings and apply them, if necessary. However, some GPO settings in the User Configuration section (e.g., Folder Redirection) are only applied at the next login, and some GPO settings in the Computer Configuration section (e.g., Assigned software applications) are only applied on the next boot. Thus, you should advise the user to reboot their computer if the gpupdate /force or Invoke-GPUpdate commands do not obtain the desired GPO settings. This will ensure that both the Computer Configuration and User Configuration settings are applied, because the user must log into the system following the boot process.

GPO configuration issues can also prevent clients from applying a GPO. For example, incorrectly configured GPO links, OUs with the Block Inheritance setting, WMI filters, and other GPOs with the same configuration settings may prevent a client from applying the settings in a GPO. To troubleshoot GPO configuration issues, you can run the gpresult /r command at a Windows PowerShell or Command Prompt window on the client to view the GPOs that were applied and not applied to the user and computer account. For GPOs that were not applied to the user or computer account, the output of this command lists the reason (e.g., WMI filter settings). For GPOs that were applied to the user and computer account, the output of this command lists the order that they were applied. This can be used to identify whether another GPO with different values for the same configuration settings was applied instead of the intended GPO.

Alternatively, you can use the **Group Policy Results Wizard** in the Group Policy Management tool to troubleshoot the application of Group Policy. The Group Policy Results Wizard provides the same information as the gpresult /r command, but in a graphical report that can be saved to an HTML- or XML-formatted file. To start the Group Policy Results Wizard, you can right-click the Group Policy Results folder shown in Figure 11-10 and click Group Policy Results Wizard. During this wizard, you must specify the appropriate user and computer accounts before the results are displayed.

> **Note** @
>
> You can also use `Get-GPResultantSetOfPolicy` cmdlet to troubleshoot the application of Group Policy. Like the Group Policy Results Wizard, this cmdlet generates a graphical report that lists GPOs that were applied and not applied to a user and computer account. For example, to generate an HTML report called C:\reports\b.burttGPO.html that lists the GPOs that were applied and not applied to the b.burtt user on the MKTG-PC-01 computer, you can run the `Get-GPResultantSetOfPolicy -user b.burtt -computer MKTG-PC-01 -reporttype html -path c:\reports\b.burttGPO.html` command in Windows PowerShell on a domain controller.

Deploying Public Key Certificates

Many different technologies rely on the use of public key certificates for the encryption of data. To support the use of these technologies in an organization, you must understand the function of public key certificates, as well as the process used to deploy them to users and computers in an organization.

Understanding Public Key Certificates

Recall from Module 5 that EFS uses both symmetric and asymmetric encryption to protect the contents of files. When you encrypt a file using EFS, a randomly generated symmetric encryption key is used to encrypt the file contents. This symmetric encryption key is then stored in the file's metadata and encrypted using your asymmetric public key to ensure that other users are unable to decrypt the data.

Most technologies that encrypt data across a network use both symmetric and asymmetric encryption together in a similar way. For example, when you access a website using HTTPS, your Web browser first downloads the public key of the Web server, as shown in step 1 of Figure 11-11. Next, the Web browser generates a symmetric key that it will use to encrypt traffic to and from the Web server. However, the Web server must also have a copy of this symmetric key to decrypt traffic from the Web browser. To ensure that a copy of this symmetric key can be sent securely across the network to the Web server, the Web browser encrypts the symmetric key using the Web server's public key (step 2). Next, the Web browser sends the encrypted symmetric key across the network to the Web server (step 3). The Web server then uses its private key to decrypt the symmetric key that was encrypted using its public key (step 4). At this point, both the Web browser and Web server hold a copy of the same symmetric key and use it to encrypt all traffic that passes between them using symmetric encryption exclusively (step 5).

> **Note** 📎
>
> The process described in Figure 11-11 is performed quickly at the beginning of each HTTPS session. If HTTPS is displayed in the URL of your Web browser, and the target webpage is shown, step 5 has already occurred.

> **Note** 📎
>
> Most symmetric encryption keys are 256 bits in length and are regenerated at the beginning of each new connection. Each additional bit in the length of an encryption key doubles the strength of the encryption against key guessing attacks. For example, a 257-bit key is twice as difficult to guess compared to a 256-bit key. Because asymmetric keys are not regenerated frequently, they are typically 2048 bits in length to provide additional protection against key guessing attacks.

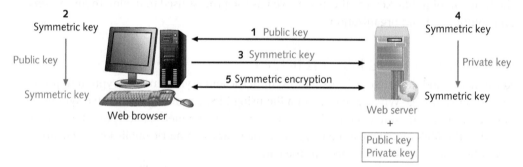

Figure 11-11   Accessing a website using HTTPS

Unfortunately, there is one security weakness to the process shown in Figure 11-11. A hacker could intercept the public key as it is sent from the Web server to the Web browser and substitute their own public key in its place. The Web browser would have no way of knowing whether the public key it received was from the Web server or the hacker. After the Web browser generates a symmetric encryption key, encrypts it using the hacker's public key, and sends it on the network, the hacker could intercept the communication and decrypt the symmetric encryption key using their private key. This is called a **man-in-the-middle attack** and is often used by hackers when redirecting HTTPS traffic to a malicious website for the purposes of stealing information.

To prevent man-in-the-middle attacks, public keys are sent to a trusted third-party computer called a **Certification Authority (CA)** for endorsement before they are used for secure technologies, such as HTTPS. This process is called **enrollment** and is usually performed immediately after a public/private key pair has been generated. After the CA verifies the identity of the user or computer that generated the public key, it creates a **public key certificate** (often shortened to **certificate**) that includes:

- A serial number
- A certificate name
- Intended certificate uses and technologies (e.g., EFS, HTTPS, IPSec, L2TP, IKEv2, email encryption, secure authentication, and so on.)
- A public key
- A **digital signature** of the public key
- A time period for which the certificate is valid (typically 1 year)
- The location of the **Certificate Revocation List (CRL)**
- The location of the CA's public key (called the **trusted root**)

The most important part of a certificate is the digital signature. The digital signature in the certificate is a hash of the public key that is encrypted using the private key of the CA. To decrypt data that is encrypted using a private key, you must use the associated public key. Because any computer or user can request the public key of the CA, they can decrypt the digital signature. If a digital signature can be decrypted by using the CA's public key, it proves that the CA's private key must have been used to create the digital signature. Additionally, this also proves that the CA verified the identity of the computer or user that generated the public key.

> **Note** 📎
>
> A **hash** (also called a **checksum**), is a calculation performed on the contents of a file or set of data. As a result, hashes are often used to determine whether data has been modified in transit.

> **Note** 📎
>
> After decrypting the digital signature in a certificate, the public key hash within is verified against another hash calculation on the public key to ensure that the contents of the public key have not been modified by a hacker.

After a CA creates a certificate, it returns it to the computer that generated the public key such that it can be used for secure technologies, such as HTTPS. Because the CA only issues certificates and does not directly participate in the encryption process, it maintains a list of any issued certificate serial numbers that should not be used in the CRL. The location of the CRL (typically a website) is listed in the certificate itself so that client computers can check the CRL before using the public key in the certificate. Certificates are added to the CRL when they are no longer used, or in the event that the public key is compromised by a hacker.

> **Note** 📎
>
> Remember that CAs do not generate public/private key pairs. They only issue certificates that are used to validate a public key that was generated by another computer.

After a Web server has a certificate, Web browsers will download the certificate instead of the public key, as shown in step 1 of Figure 11-12. Next, the Web browser will perform the following tasks to validate the certificate (step 2):

- Confirm that the certificate has not expired
- Ensure that the CRL does not list the certificate serial number
- Decrypt the digital signature using the trusted root
- Verify that the hash in the digital signature matches the hash of the public key in the certificate

Next, the Web browser generates a symmetric key that is encrypted using the public key in the certificate (step 3). The Web browser then sends the encrypted symmetric key to the Web server (step 4) where it is decrypted using the Web server's private key (step 5) before being used to perform symmetric encryption (step 6).

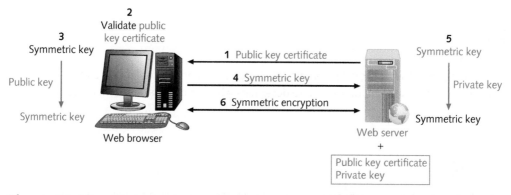

Figure 11-12   Using a public key certificate to protect HTTPS

There are many technologies in an organization that use certificates for secure access, including Web servers and Web apps (using HTTPS), IPSec, VPNs (SSTP, L2TP, IKEv2), DirectAccess, IPP (using HTTPS), EAP authentication, and EFS. Some technologies do not require certificates to function, but will use them to prevent man-in-the-middle attacks if available. For example, if your user account has an EFS certificate, it is used when encrypting files. This practice prevents cryptolocker malware from using EFS to encrypt files using a memory-based EFS man-in-the-middle attack that replaces your public key with the public key used by the cryptolocker malware. Moreover, if each domain controller has a certificate, Active Directory will encrypt LDAP and replication traffic using it to provide additional security for the domain.

> **Note**
>
> Some technologies (e.g., Windows Admin Center and DirectAccess) generate a self-signed certificate for use during installation. This self-signed certificate does not protect against man-in-the-middle attacks and should be replaced with a CA-signed certificate.

To provide secure access to technologies that support certificates, you must provide the associated certificates for the users and computers in your organization. There are many **public CAs** on the Internet that issue certificates for a fee, as well as some that issue certificates for free (e.g., LetsEncrypt). Nearly all computers and mobile devices receive the trusted roots of these public CAs alongside Web browser and operating system updates and can validate certificates that were issued from them as a result. Consequently, public CAs are often used to obtain HTTPS certificates for Web servers and Web apps that are accessed by Internet users that are not part of your organization. To obtain a certificate from a public CA, you must generate a public/private key pair using the appropriate settings, upload the public key to the public CA's website, and then download the certificate after the public CA validates your identity (which usually takes more than 24 hours).

> **Note**
>
> Public CAs are also called **commercial CAs**.

Because obtaining certificates from a public CA for each user and computer in your organization is impractical, you can instead configure a Windows Server 2019 system as an **enterprise CA** in your organization that can be used to issue certificates automatically to users and computers using **certificate templates** and Group Policy. This process is called **auto-enrollment** and simplifies the management of certificates in your organization. Because the trusted root of an enterprise CA is normally provided to organization computers only, only users and computers in your organization can validate certificates that were issued by an enterprise CA.

> **Note**
>
> When auto-enrollment is configured, the trusted root of an enterprise CA is automatically distributed to each domain computer using Group Policy.

Note

Organizations that use an enterprise CA to issue certificates to their users and computers are said to have a **public key infrastructure (PKI)**.

Note

Large organizations can have several CAs configured in a **CA hierarchy**. The first CA deployed in a hierarchy is called the **root CA** and other CAs that participate in the hierarchy are called **subordinate CAs**. In most organizations, only a single enterprise root CA is necessary.

Installing an Enterprise CA

To configure Windows Server 2019 as an enterprise CA, you must first install the **Active Directory Certificate Services** server role. When you select this role in the Add Roles and Features Wizard and progress through the wizard, you are prompted to choose the role services that you wish to install, as shown in Figure 11-13. At minimum, you should select the *Certification Authority* role service. The *Certificate Enrollment Policy Web Service*,

```
Add Roles and Features Wizard                                      —    □    ×

Select role services                              DESTINATION SERVER
                                                  SERVERX.domainX.com

Before You Begin        Select the role services to install for Active Directory Certificate Services
Installation Type
Server Selection        Role services                         Description
Server Roles            ☑ Certification Authority             Certification Authority (CA) is used
Features                ☐ Certificate Enrollment Policy Web Service   to issue and manage certificates.
                        ☐ Certificate Enrollment Web Service   Multiple CAs can be linked to form a
AD CS                   ☐ Certification Authority Web Enrollment   public key infrastructure.
   Role Services        ☐ Network Device Enrollment Service
Confirmation            ☐ Online Responder
Results

                                        < Previous    Next >      Install      Cancel
```

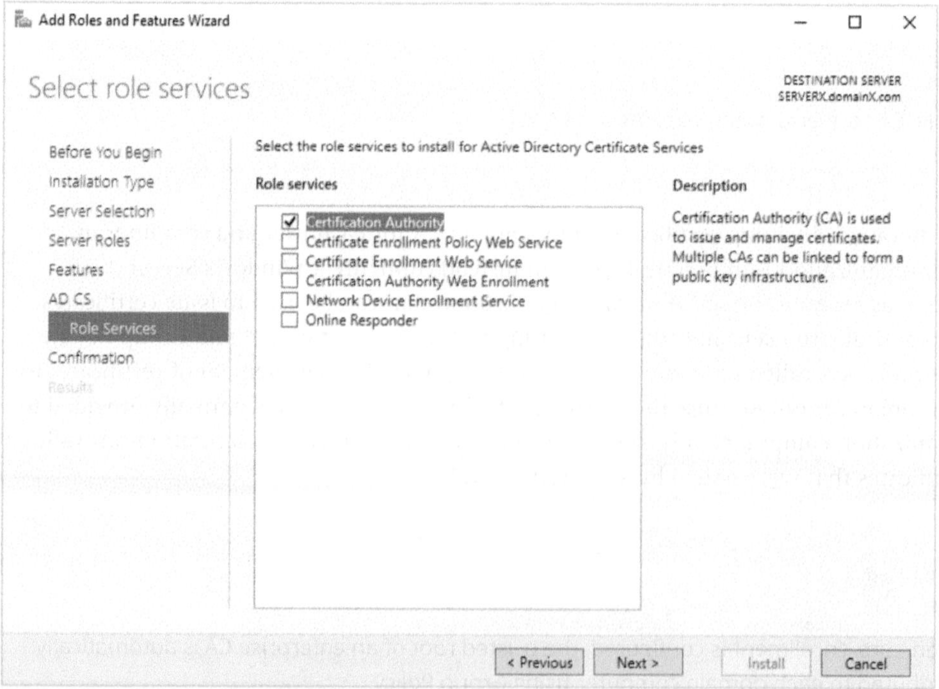

Figure 11-13   Selecting role services

Certificate Enrollment Web Service, and *Certification Authority Web Enrollment* role services provide a Web app that allows users to request certificates for their computer, even if their computer is not joined to the Active Directory domain. The *Network Device Enrollment Service* role service allows routers and other network devices to obtain certificates, and the *Online Responder* role service allows clients to use the **Online Certificate Status Protocol (OCSP)** to view CRL information.

After the necessary role services have been installed, you can click *Configure Active Directory Certificate Services on the destination server* on the final page of the Add Roles and Features Wizard to open the AD CS Configuration wizard. The default selections shown during this wizard configure an enterprise root CA called *domain-server-CA* that contains a new 2048-bit public/private key pair, and uses the SHA-256 algorithm to hash public keys when generating digital signatures for certificates. These settings are appropriate for most environments.

> **Note** 📎
>
> The CA public/private key pair expires every 5 years by default to minimize the chance that a hacker could guess it. At this time, a new CA public/private key pair is generated automatically. This new key pair is functionally equivalent to the previous public/private key pair when used with the same asymmetric encryption algorithm in order to guarantee the validity of previously signed certificates.

> **Note** 📎
>
> After you install Active Directory Certificate Services on a computer, the computer name and domain membership cannot be modified. This is because the name and domain membership of the CA computer are included in each certificate issued by the CA and used by other computers to locate the CRL.

Configuring an Enterprise CA for Certificate Enrollment

After you have installed an enterprise CA on a Windows Server 2019 system, you can configure it using the **Certification Authority tool** shown in Figure 11-14. To open this tool, you can select Certification Authority from the Tools menu in Server Manager.

The folders under the domainX-SERVERX-CA server object in Figure 11-14 are used to manage and configure most CA functionality:

- *Revoked Certificates* lists certificates that have a future expiry date but should not be used. These certificates are automatically added to the CRL after one week. To add these certificates to the CRL immediately, you can right-click this folder and select All Tasks, Publish.

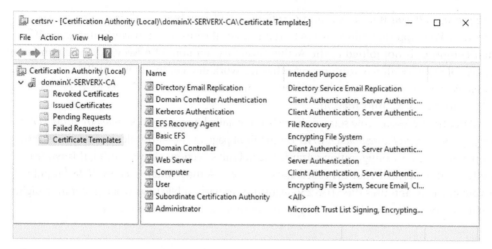

Figure 11-14   The Certification Authority tool

- *Issued Certificates* lists all certificates that have been issued to users and computers. You can right-click a certificate in this folder and click All Tasks, Revoke Certificate to move it to the Revoked Certificates folder.
- *Pending Requests* lists certificate enrollment requests that must be manually approved by a server administrator before they are issued to a user or computer. To approve an enrollment request in this folder, you can right-click it and click All Tasks, Issue.
- *Failed Requests* lists certificate enrollment requests that cannot be completed because the request did not match the criteria in the certificate template.
- *Certificate Templates* lists the certificate templates that are used by the CA to process certificate enrollment requests. To add a certificate template to this folder, you can right-click it and click New, Certificate Template to Issue.

Before users and computers in your domain can obtain certificates, you must configure certificate templates that contain the appropriate settings and permissions. To configure certificate templates, you can right-click the Certificate Templates folder in Figure 11-14 and click Manage. This will open the **Certificate Templates Console** shown in Figure 11-15.

Each certificate template available in the Certificate Templates Console contains settings that the CA can use to issue certificates for a particular use or technology. For example, the Web Server certificate template can be used to issue certificates to computers for use with HTTPS and SSTP VPNs, whereas the IPSec certificate template can be used to issue certificates to computers for use with IPSec, as well as IKEv2 and L2TP VPNs. The Computer certificate template is a general-purpose template that can be used to issue certificates to computers for use with any technology that requires client or server authentication. Similarly, the User certificate template is a general-purpose template that can be used to issue certificates to users for use with EFS, secure email, and any technology that uses certificates for user authentication.

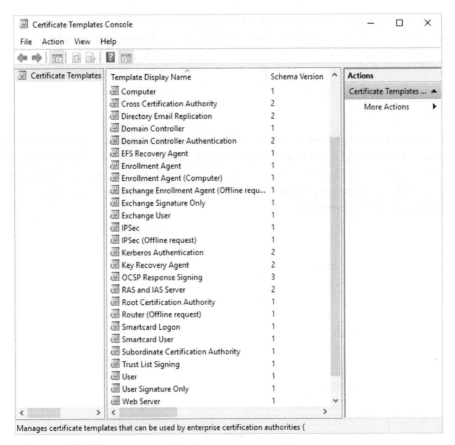

Figure 11-15   The Certificate Templates Console

The number in the Schema Version column in Figure 11-15 reflects the minimum computer version that can use the template. Templates that list schema version 1 can be used by Windows 2000 and later computers but have limited configuration options and cannot be used for auto-enrollment. Schema version 2 templates allow for the latest configuration options and auto-enrollment, but only apply to Windows XP and Windows Server 2003 or later computers. Schema version 3 templates are used to issue certificates that provide CA services only. For backward compatibility, most certificate templates are provided using schema version 1. However, you can right-click any schema version 1 certificate template and click Duplicate Template to create a copy of it that uses schema version 2. You can then modify this new template to suit your needs before adding it to your CA.

For example, to create a schema version 2 copy of the User certificate template in Figure 11-15, you can right-click it, click Duplicate Template, and then specify the appropriate template display name on the General tab, as shown for DomainX User Certificate in Figure 11-16 (spaces are removed to generate the actual template name). The configuration shown in Figure 11-16 ensures that certificates issued using the template are published in Active Directory for quick access by applications and are valid for 1 year. Moreover, certificates that are auto-enrolled using this template are automatically renewed 6 weeks prior to the end of the validity period.

Note

When a certificate is renewed using auto-enrollment, the user or computer generates a new public/private key pair that is functionally equivalent to the previous public/private key pair when used with the same asymmetric encryption algorithm. The new public key is then sent to the CA, where it is digitally signed and issued to the user or computer as a new certificate that replaces the existing certificate.

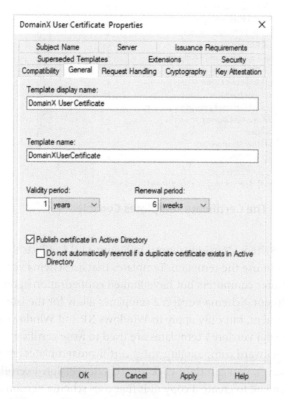

Figure 11-16   The General tab of certificate template properties

If you highlight the Subject Name tab in Figure 11-16, you can specify the information and format used when generating names for certificates that are issued using the certificate template, as shown in Figure 11-17. The configuration shown in

Figure 11-17 will name issued certificates using the LDAP distinguished name and UPN of the associated user account in Active Directory. The *E-mail name* and *Include e-mail name in subject name* options should only be selected if your organization uses Microsoft Exchange Server or Office 365 to assign email attributes to user accounts. Otherwise, enrollment requests will fail and be listed under the Failed Requests folder shown in Figure 11-14.

Figure 11-17   The Subject Name tab of certificate template properties

After configuring the options on the General and Subject Name tabs, you should configure the certificate template permissions on the Security tab, as shown in Figure 11-18. To manually enroll for a certificate based on a certificate template, a user or computer must have Read and Enroll permission. For a GPO to auto-enroll users or computers for certificates, those users or computers must have Read, Enroll, and Autoenroll permissions to the certificate template. Because the Authenticated Users group is granted Read, Enroll, and Autoenroll permissions in Figure 11-18, all users in the domain will be able to manually enroll for a certificate as well as receive a certificate using auto-enrollment.

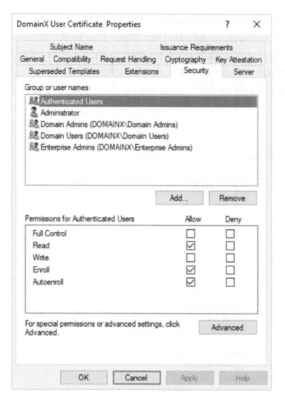

Figure 11-18   The Security tab of certificate template properties

You can use the other tabs shown in 11-18 to optionally configure other certificate template settings:

- *Issuance Requirements* allows you to specify options for manual certificate request approval. If these options are configured, certificate requests are placed in the Pending Requests folder shown in Figure 11-14 until a server administrator approves them.
- *Compatibility* allows you to configure the minimum client and CA version to which the template applies.
- *Request Handling* allows you to specify the purpose of the certificate (e.g., encryption) as well as the software library (provider) that is used to perform the encryption.
- *Cryptography* allows you to specify encryption options, such as the minimum asymmetric key size.
- *Key Attestation* allows you to add TPM validation to certificates.
- *Superseded Templates* allows you to specify legacy certificate templates that the certificate template should replace. Users and computers that have previously received certificates based on legacy certificate templates will automatically receive a new certificate to use in its place.

- *Extensions* allows you to specify certificate usage information.
- *Server* allows you to control the certificate and certificate request information that is stored on the CA.

After you have configured the appropriate certificate template options, you can click OK in Figure 11-18 to create the DomainX User Certificate. To allow DomainX User Certificate to be used by your CA, you must also add it to the Certificate Templates folder in the Certification Authority tool.

Enrolling for Certificates

The method that you use to deploy certificates in an organization using an enterprise CA depends on the number of users or computers that require certificates. For example, if computers in the Marketing department require a certificate for use with IKEv2, you can configure the appropriate certificate template to allow Read, Enroll, and Autoenroll permissions to a group that contains the Marketing department computers. Next, you can enable auto-enrollment in a GPO linked to an OU that contains the Marketing department computers to ensure that Marketing department computers receive an IKEv2 certificate. Alternatively, if a single user requires a certificate for use with EFS, you can configure the appropriate certificate template to allow Read and Enroll permissions for the user account, and advise the user to manually enroll for a certificate.

Configuring Auto-Enrollment

To configure auto-enrollment, you must first ensure the appropriate certificate templates have been configured to allow Read, Enroll, and Autoenroll permissions to users or computers in your organization. Next, you can enable auto-enrollment settings in a GPO that applies to the associated user and computer accounts.

To enable auto-enrollment for user certificates in a GPO, you must navigate to *User Configuration, Policies, Windows Settings, Security Settings, Public Key Policies*. Next, you must edit the *Certificate Services Client – Certificate Enrollment Policy* setting and select Enabled in the Configuration Model drop-down box, as shown in Figure 11-19.

Following this, you must edit the *Certificate Services Client – Auto-Enrollment* setting, select Enabled in the Configuration Model drop-down box and select *Update certificates that use certificate templates*, as shown in Figure 11-20. The other options shown in Figure 11-20 allow Group Policy to automatically manage and renew expired certificates, as well as log and display certificate expiry notices 10% before the end of its lifetime, according to the expiry date.

To enable auto-enrollment for computer certificates in a GPO, you must navigate to *Computer Configuration, Policies, Windows Settings, Security Settings, Public Key Policies*. Next, you must edit the *Certificate Services Client – Certificate Enrollment Policy* and *Certificate Services Client – Auto-Enrollment* settings, as shown in Figures 11-19 and 11-20.

When a user applies a GPO that has auto-enrollment configured, a public/private key pair is generated in the user account for each new certificate template that grants the user Read, Enroll, and Autoenroll permissions. The public key from each public/private

Figure 11-19 Enabling the certificate enrollment policy

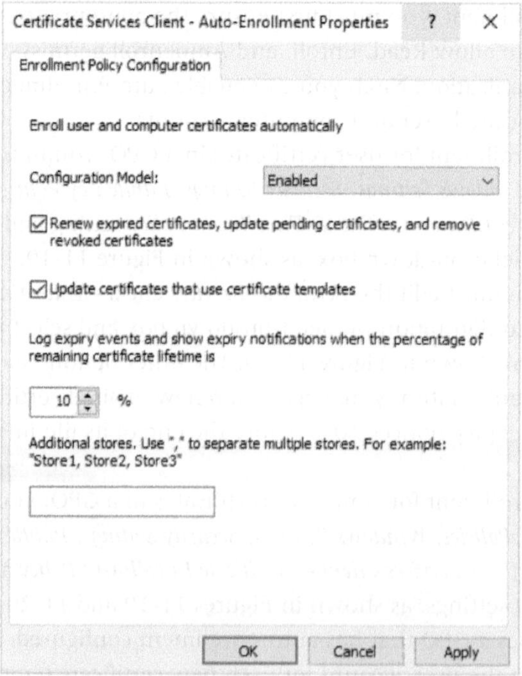

Figure 11-20 Enabling auto-enrollment

key pair is then sent to the CA for digital signing and returned to the user account as a certificate. Alternatively, when a computer applies a GPO that has auto-enrollment configured, a public/private key pair is generated in the Windows Registry on the computer for each new certificate template that grants the computer Read, Enroll, and Autoenroll permissions. The public key from each public/private key pair is then sent to the CA for digital signing and returned to the Windows Registry on the computer as a certificate.

Enrolling for a Certificate Manually

To manually enroll for a user certificate from an enterprise CA, you can run the `certmgr.msc` command in a Windows PowerShell, Run, or Command Prompt window to open the Certificates MMC snap-in for your user account, as shown in Figure 11-21.

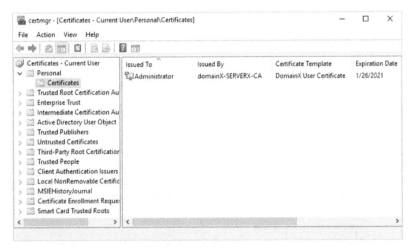

Figure 11-21   The Certificates MMC snap-in for a user account

Next, you can right-click Certificates under the Personal folder and click All Tasks, Request New Certificate to start the Certificate Enrollment wizard. When you click Next at this wizard, you must ensure that Active Directory Enrollment Policy is selected, as shown in Figure 11-22. Following this, you can click Next and select the appropriate certificate template, as shown for DomainX User Certificate in Figure 11-23. Only certificate templates that grant your user account Read and Enroll permissions are shown. When you click Enroll in Figure 11-23, a public/private key pair is generated in your user account. The public key is then sent to the CA, where it is digitally signed and returned to your user account as a certificate.

The process you use to manually enroll for a computer certificate from an enterprise CA is nearly identical to that used to enroll for a user certificate. However, you instead run the `certlm.msc` command in a Windows PowerShell, Run, or Command Prompt window to open the Certificates MMC snap-in for your local computer account. Next, you can right-click Certificates under the Personal folder and click All Tasks, Request New

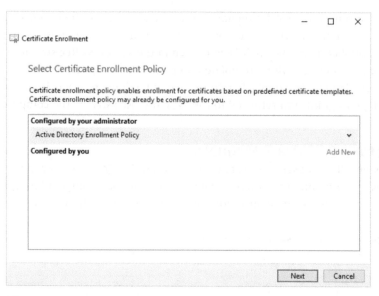

Figure 11-22   Selecting the certificate enrollment policy

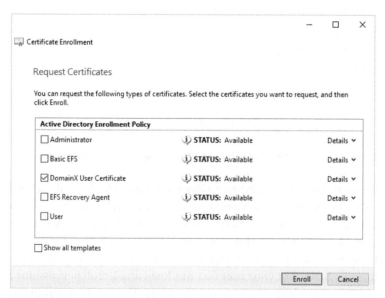

Figure 11-23   Selecting the certificate template

Certificate to start the Certificate Enrollment wizard. After selecting the Active Directory Enrollment Policy and appropriate certificate template during this wizard, you can click Enroll to generate a public/private key pair in the Windows Registry on your local computer. The public key is then sent to the CA, where it is digitally signed and returned to the Windows Registry on your local computer as a certificate.

Recall from Module 10 that you can use IIS Manager to enroll a computer for an HTTPS certificate. To enroll for an HTTPS certificate from an enterprise CA, you must first configure an appropriate certificate template that grants your computer account Read and Enroll permission. Next, you can navigate to the Server Certificates feature in IIS Manager, click Create Domain Certificate from the Actions pane and specify the appropriate information in the Create Certificate wizard, as shown in Figure 11-24. The name specified in the *Common name* text box shown in Figure 11-24 must match the FQDN of the website or Web app, while all other information is provided for description purposes only. When you click Next in Figure 11-24, you must select your enterprise CA and supply a friendly name for your certificate that will be displayed alongside

> **Note**
>
> You can also use the Server Certificates feature in IIS Manager to enroll for an HTTPS certificate from a public CA. To do this, you can click Create Certificate Request from the Actions pane, supply the appropriate website or Web app information, and specify a file to save the certificate request to. Next, you must upload this certificate request file to the public CA's website and download the certificate file after it is made available. Following this, you can return to the Server Certificates features in IIS Manager, click Complete Certificate Request from the Actions pane, and specify the certificate file to complete the process.

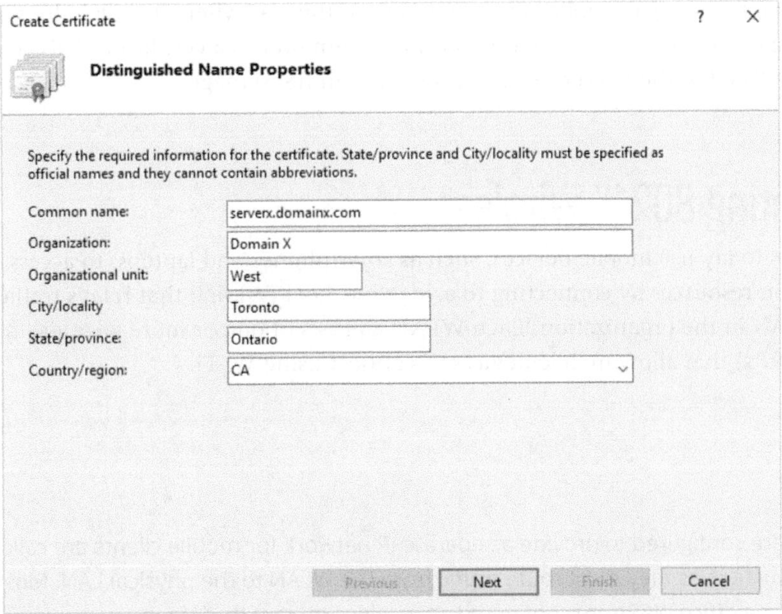

Create Certificate   ?   ✕

Distinguished Name Properties

Specify the required information for the certificate. State/province and City/locality must be specified as official names and they cannot contain abbreviations.

Common name:	serverx.domainx.com
Organization:	Domain X
Organizational unit:	West
City/locality:	Toronto
State/province:	Ontario
Country/region:	CA

Previous   Next   Finish   Cancel

Figure 11-24   Enrolling for an HTTPS certificate using IIS Manager

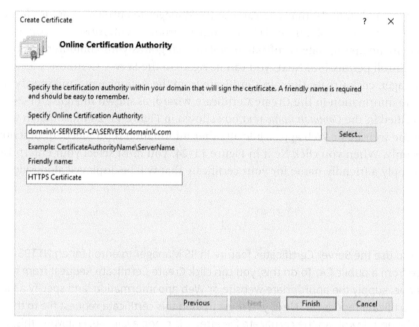

Figure 11-25   Specifying the enterprise CA and friendly name

the certificate in IIS Manager, as shown in Figure 11-25. When you click Finish in Figure 11-25, a public/private key pair will be generated in the Windows Registry on your local computer. The public key is then sent to the CA, where it is digitally signed and returned to the Windows Registry on your local computer as a certificate. This certificate will also be listed in the Server Certificates feature in IIS Manager.

Implementing 802.1X Wireless

Many users today use mobile devices, such as smartphones and laptops, to access organization resources by connecting to a **wireless LAN (WLAN)** that relays traffic to a physical LAN in the organization. Each WLAN consists of one or more **wireless access points (WAPs)** that allow mobile devices to connect using Wi-Fi.

Note

WAPs that are configured to provide a separate IP network for mobile clients are called **wireless routers** as they must route traffic from the WLAN to the physical LAN. Most small office or home office WAPs are configured as wireless routers by default.

To keep data confidential as it passes over the WLAN, most WAPs are configured to encrypt traffic between the mobile device and the WAP using **Wi-Fi Protected Access (WPA)**, which uses symmetric encryption exclusively. **Wi-Fi Protected Access II (WPA2)** is the most common version of WPA implemented by WLANs. To access most WPA2 WLANs, you must specify the Wi-Fi password for the WLAN (also called the pre-shared key, or PSK). This Wi-Fi password is then used to generate a symmetric encryption key for the Wi-Fi connection between the mobile device and the WAP. Because all WLAN users use the same Wi-Fi password, there are many wireless cracking tools available that can decrypt WPA2 WLAN traffic by comparing it to hash tables of known wireless patterns. To prevent this, some WAPs allow you to configure a VPN connection for each mobile device. However, most organizations instead use a RADIUS server to randomly generate symmetric encryption keys for each mobile client. This technology is called **802.1X Wireless** and prevents wireless cracking tools from decrypting WLAN traffic.

When a mobile device user connects to a WAP that is configured to use 802.1X Wireless, their mobile device automatically downloads a certificate from a RADIUS server, as shown in step 1 of Figure 11-26. This certificate is used to create a secure tunnel between the mobile device, WAP, and RADIUS server. Next, the user is prompted to log into the RADIUS server using Active Directory domain credentials that are passed to the RADIUS server across the secure tunnel (step 2) and authenticated to a domain controller (step 3). If the credentials match those in a user account, the RADIUS server randomly generates a symmetric encryption key for use with WPA2 and sends this key to both the mobile device and WAP (steps 4 and 5) for use when encrypting traffic. To provide additional security against wireless cracking tools, the RADIUS server periodically generates a new symmetric encryption key and repeats steps 4 and 5. Moreover, each mobile device that connects to the WAP using 802.1X Wireless receives a different symmetric encryption key that it uses to encrypt traffic.

> **Note**
>
> **Wi-Fi Protected Access III (WPA3)** is a recent technology that is supported by some WAPs. While WPA3 does not use a Wi-Fi password in the same way that WPA2 does, it can still be compromised by wireless cracking tools. As a result, organizations also use 802.1X Wireless to protect WPA3 WLANs.

> **Note**
>
> Most organizations implement a separate WLAN for guest access that does not use 802.1X Wireless. This WLAN is configured to allow access to Internet resources only, and not organization resources.

> **Note** 📎
>
> While less common, 802.1X can also be used to protect access to Ethernet network switches that support it. This technology is called **802.1X Wired**.

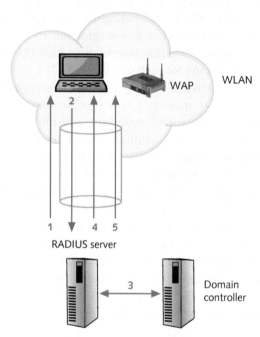

Figure 11-26   Using 802.1X Wireless to protect WLAN access

Configuring RADIUS for 802.1X Wireless

To configure a Windows Server 2019 system as a RADIUS server for use with 802.1X Wireless, you must first configure the Network Policy and Access Services server role, as discussed previously in Module 9. After this server role has been installed, you must use the Network Policy Server tool to activate the server in Active Directory, as well as create RADIUS clients for each WAP in your organization, noting the shared secret that you configure for each one.

Next, you must open the Certification Authority tool on your enterprise CA and add the *RAS and IAS Server* certificate template to the Certificate Templates folder. The *RAS and IAS Server* certificate template uses schema version 2 and assigns Read permission to all domain computers, as well as Enroll permission to servers that have the Network Policy and Access Services server role installed. After this certificate template has been added to the enterprise CA, you must use the Certificates MMC snap-in on the RADIUS server to manually enroll for a certificate using it.

Following this, you can highlight NPS (Local) in the Network Policy Server tool, select *RADIUS server for 802.1X Wireless and Wired Connections* and click *Configure 802.1X* to start the Configure 802.1X wizard shown in Figure 11-27. The options shown in Figure 11-27 will create connection request and network policies on the RADIUS server called Secure Wireless Connections for WAP RADIUS clients.

Figure 11-27   The Configure 802.1X wizard

When you click Next in Figure 11-27, the list of RADIUS clients that you have previously configured on the RADIUS server are displayed, as shown in Figure 11-28. You can add additional RADIUS clients at this page as well as edit or remove existing RADIUS clients. Because the network policy for 802.1X Wireless will only apply to WAP RADIUS clients, it is safe to leave existing VPN RADIUS clients in this list.

After you configure the appropriate RADIUS clients in Figure 11-28 and click Next, you must choose the EAP authentication method as shown in Figure 11-29. The **Protected Extensible Authentication Protocol (PEAP)** method selected in Figure 11-29 is required

Figure 11-28   Specifying RADIUS clients

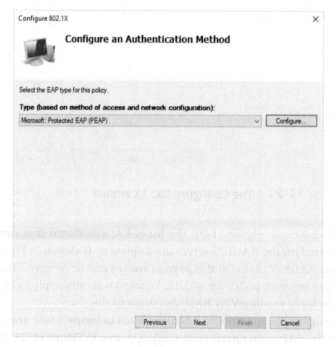

Figure 11-29   Selecting the authentication method

by most WAPs for use with 802.1X Wireless. You can view the certificate used for PEAP by clicking the Configure button in Figure 11-29. If no certificate is shown, you must enroll your RADIUS server for a certificate that uses the *RAS and IAS Server* certificate template.

After you click Next in Figure 11-29, you must specify the user groups that are allowed to authenticate to the RADIUS server using 802.1X Wireless, as shown in Figure 11-30. The Domain Users group shown in Figure 11-30 allows all users in DOMAINX to authenticate to WAPs in the organization using 802.1X Wireless. When you click Next in Figure 11-30, you can optionally specify RADIUS attributes before clicking Next and Finish to complete your configuration.

Figure 11-30   Specifying user groups

Configuring a WAP for 802.1X Wireless

After you have configured a RADIUS server for 802.1X Wireless, you must configure each WAP to use forward authentication requests to the FQDN or IP address of your RADIUS server on port 1812 using the shared secret configured in the associated WAP RADIUS client. To do this, you can access the configuration tool for the WAPs in your organization. Because WAP vendors provide different interfaces for their configuration tools, you must consult your vendor documentation for the process used to configure 802.1X Wireless.

Most WAPs identify 802.1X Wireless using the word "RADIUS" or "Enterprise" in their configuration tool. For example, the configuration tool for the TP-LINK WAP shown in Figure 11-31 configures 802.1X Wireless for WPA2 connections by forwarding authentication requests to the RADIUS server with IP address 172.16.0.77 on port 1812 using the shared secret Shared%Secret.

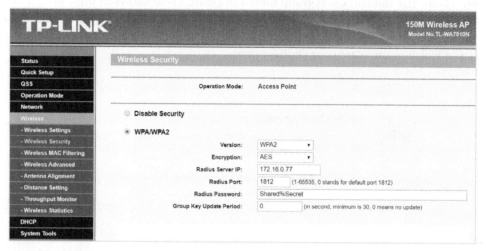

Figure 11-31   Configuring a TP-LINK WAP for 802.1X Wireless

Configuring Windows Server Update Services

When flaws and security weaknesses are discovered in operating systems and other software products, the software vendor releases an associated software **update** to remedy the issue. As a server administrator, you should ensure that the software products in your organization are regularly updated to provide stability and security. **Microsoft Update** servers on the Internet provide the latest updates for Microsoft software products, and Windows users can use the **Windows Update** section of Control Panel or Settings (Windows 10, Windows Server 2016, and later) to search for and install these updates, or schedule automatic update installation.

Note

Windows computers contact the Microsoft Update servers on the Internet using HTTPS (TCP port 443), which is allowed on firewalls by default.

If several computers in an organization obtain updates from Microsoft Update at the same time, the bandwidth on the organization's Internet connection could become saturated, preventing access to Microsoft Update and other Internet resources. Moreover, by allowing computers in the domain to obtain updates from Microsoft Update directly, you cannot easily identify computers that have installed a particular update, or prevent the installation of updates that cause problems with other software applications.

To solve these problems, you can implement a **Windows Server Update Services (WSUS)** server in your organization. This WSUS server can be configured to regularly download updates from Microsoft Update for each software product that you have in your organization (a process called **synchronization**), as well as distribute them to the computers in your organization. To ensure that computers obtain updates from the WSUS server instead of Microsoft Update, you must configure a GPO that provides the appropriate settings.

> **Note** 📎
>
> Computers that are configured to obtain updates from a WSUS server use HTTP on TCP port 8530, or HTTPS on TCP port 8531 (if IIS on the WSUS server is configured to use an HTTPS certificate issued by an enterprise CA).

> **Note** 📎
>
> Updates must be approved on the WSUS server before they can be installed on computers. You can also decline updates that should not be installed, as well as configure WSUS to force the removal of previously installed updates.

> **Note** 📎
>
> In large organizations, you can implement multiple WSUS servers to balance the load of update requests. These WSUS servers can be configured to obtain updates from a central WSUS server that synchronizes with Microsoft Update.

Installing WSUS

To configure Windows Server 2019 as a WSUS server, you must first install the Windows Server Update Services server role. When you select this role in the Add Roles and Features Wizard and progress through the wizard, you are prompted to choose the role services that you wish to install, as shown in Figure 11-32. The configuration shown in Figure 11-32 installs the necessary WSUS services as well as the **Windows Internal Database (WID)** that is used to store information about each update, such as the computers that have successfully installed it. You can select *SQL Server Connectivity* in place of *WID Connectivity* in Figure 11-32 to instead store information about each update in a database on a Microsoft SQL Server that you specify. When you click Next in Figure 11-32, you are prompted to supply the folder that should store synchronized updates, as shown for D:\WindowsUpdates in Figure 11-33. To explore the functionality

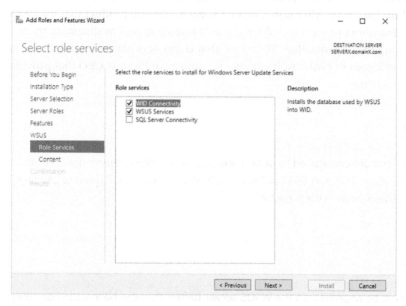

Figure 11-32 **Configuring role services**

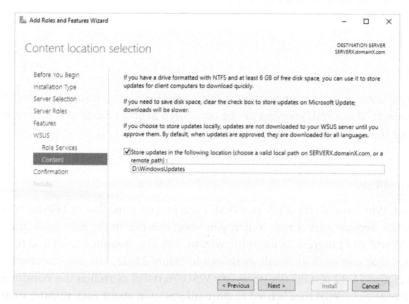

Figure 11-33 **Specifying the location of update content**

of WSUS in an IT lab environment, you can deselect *Store updates in the following location* in Figure 11-33. In this case, WSUS will not store the update content, but instead redirect computers to the Microsoft Update servers on the Internet to obtain updates. When you click Next in Figure 11-33, you can click Install to install the WSUS role services. On the final page of the Add Roles and Features Wizard, you must click *Launch Post-Installation tasks* to create the database used by WSUS.

Configuring WSUS

After you have installed the necessary WSUS role services, you can click Windows Server Update Services from the Tools menu in Server Manager to start the Windows Server Updates Services Configuration Wizard. After clicking Next on the first two pages of this wizard, you are prompted to specify the location from which to synchronize updates, as shown in Figure 11-34. By default, updates are synchronized from Microsoft Update servers on the Internet, but you can instead select *Synchronize from another Windows Server Update Services server* in Figure 11-34 and specify another WSUS server in your organization. When you click Next in Figure 11-34, you are prompted to specify a proxy server configuration, as shown in Figure 11-35. This configuration is only necessary if your organization obtains Internet access using a proxy server instead of a NAT router.

After you click Next in Figure 11-35, you can click Start Connecting in Figure 11-36 to download the list of available updates from Microsoft Update. After this list has been

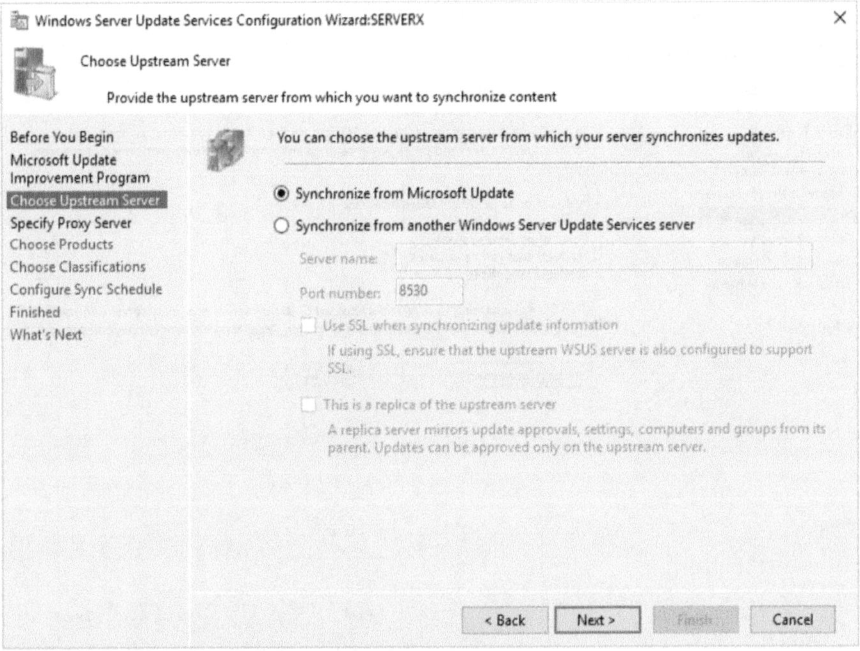

Figure 11-34 Choosing the update source

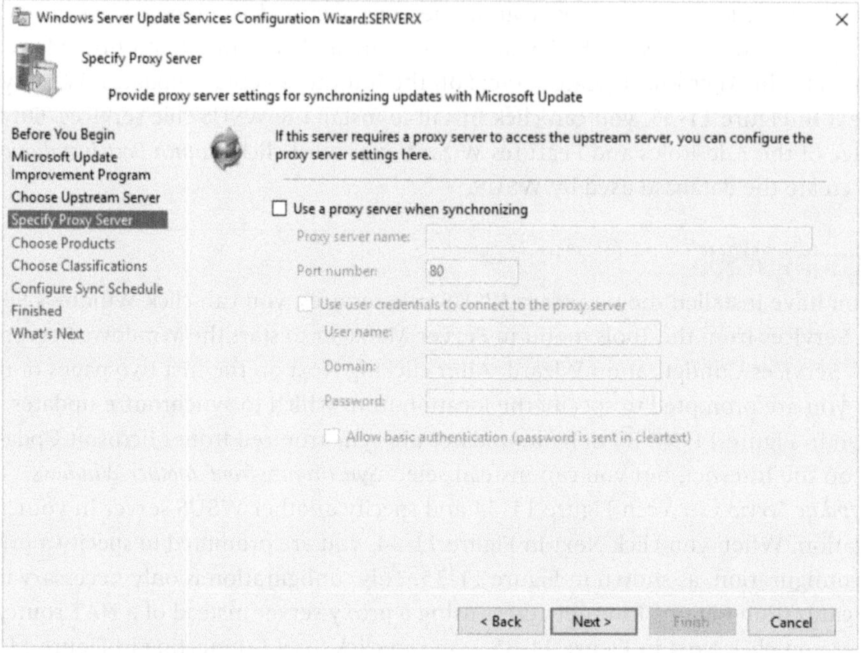

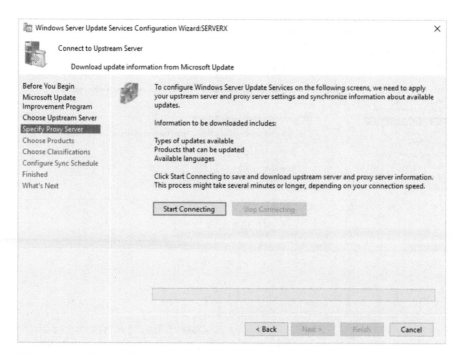

Figure 11-35   Specifying proxy server configuration

Figure 11-36   Downloading update information

downloaded, you can click Next and select the operating system and software product versions for which updates should be synchronized, as shown in Figure 11-37. To prevent updates from consuming too much storage on your WSUS server, you should only select the operating systems and software products that are deployed in your organization.

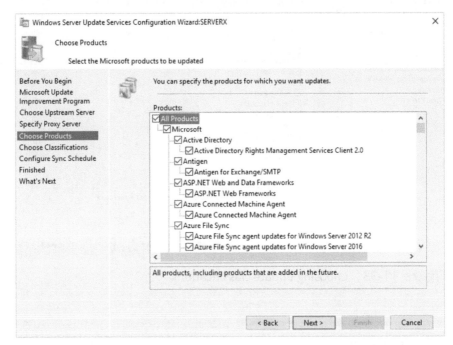

Figure 11-37   Choosing products

When you click Next in Figure 11-37, you must select the type of updates to synchronize for each operating system version and software product, as shown in Figure 11-38. To provide stability and security for the Microsoft software products in your organization, you should select *Critical Updates* and *Security Updates* at minimum. After you click Next in Figure 11-38, you are prompted to choose synchronization options, as shown in Figure 11-39. The options configured in Figure 11-39 automatically synchronize updates each day at 1:00 am. After you select the appropriate synchronization options and click Next, you can select *Begin initial synchronization* and click Finish to start synchronizing updates and open the **Update Services tool** shown in Figure 11-40.

Note

After completing the Windows Server Updates Services Configuration Wizard, the Update Services tool is opened each time you click Windows Server Update Services from the Tools menu in Server Manager.

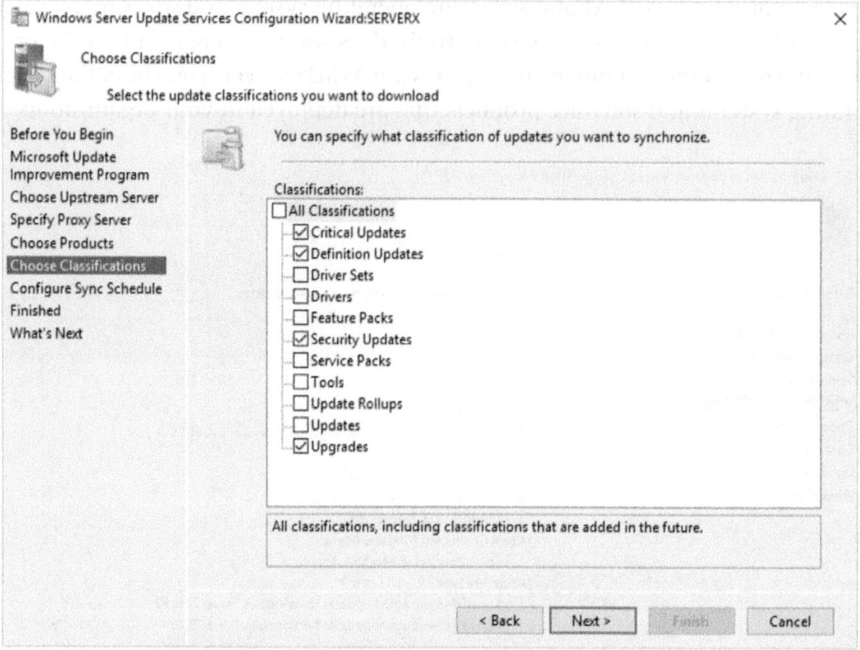

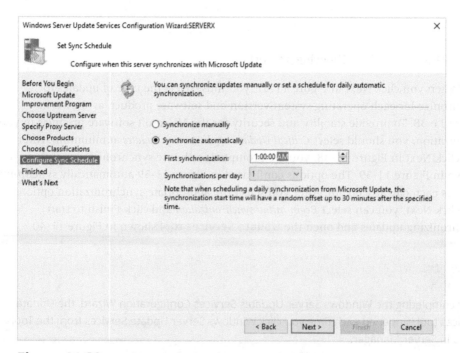

Figure 11-38   Choosing update classifications

Figure 11-39   Configuring synchronization options

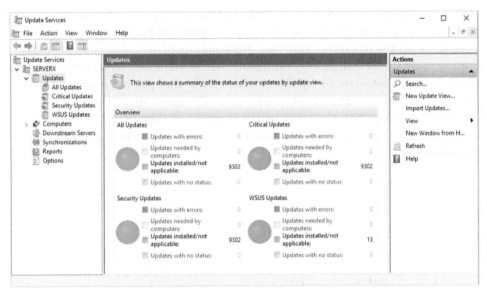

Figure 11-40   The Update Services tool

You can access the different features under your server in the navigation pane of the Update Services tool in Figure 11-40 to manage WSUS:

- *Updates* allows you to view an update summary. You must highlight the appropriate update category under this feature (e.g., Critical Updates) to display the individual updates that have been synchronized on your WSUS server. To allow an update to be installed, you can right-click it, click *Approve*, select the appropriate computer group, and click *Approved for Install*. To prevent an update from being installed, you can right-click it and click *Decline*. To force the removal of a previously installed update, you can right-click it, click *Approve*, select the appropriate computer group, and click *Approved for Removal*.
- *Computers* allows you to view the computers that have installed updates, as well as create computer groups to organize them for reporting and update approval. The default *All Computers* group in this feature includes all computers in your organization.
- *Downstream Servers* lists other WSUS servers that are configured to synchronize updates from the WSUS server.
- *Synchronizations* lists previous synchronizations, as well as allows you to perform a manual synchronization or modify synchronization options.
- *Reports* allows you to generate reports that list the status of updates and synchronizations, as well as computers that have installed or not installed updates.
- *Options* allows you to modify the same options configured in the Windows Server Updates Services Configuration Wizard, as well as configure additional WSUS features and perform server maintenance tasks.

In some organizations, server administrators install new updates on a single computer in each department to ensure that they do not cause problems before they are approved for installation on a WSUS server. However, problems caused by updates are rare today and can be easily solved by removing the update. As a result, many server administrators configure WSUS to automatically approve updates. To do this, you can highlight Options in the navigation pane of Figure 11-40, click Automatic Approvals, and configure one or more automatic approval rules, as shown in Figure 11-41. The Default Automatic Approval Rule shown in Figure 11-41 automatically approves critical and security updates for all computers.

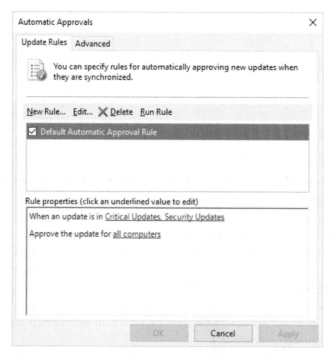

Figure 11-41   Configuring automatic approval rules

Configuring a WSUS GPO

To ensure that computers in your organization obtain updates from your WSUS server instead of Microsoft Update, you must edit the settings of a GPO that applies to the associated computer accounts. For example, to ensure that all computers in the domain obtain updates from your WSUS server, you could edit a GPO that is linked to the domain and navigate to *Computer Configuration, Policies, Administrative Templates, Windows Components, Windows Update*. Next, you must edit the *Configure Automatic Updates* setting, as shown in Figure 11-42. The options configured in Figure 11-42 require that computers automatically download and install updates at 3:00 am every day. To ensure that these updates are installed from a WSUS server instead of Microsoft Update, you must edit the *Specify intranet Microsoft update service location* setting, as shown in Figure 11-43. The options configured in Figure 11-43 ensure that computers install updates from the WSUS. domainX.com server using HTTP on TCP port 8530, as well as advise the server of updates that were successfully installed.

Note

Because modern PCs automatically enter power saving mode when not in use, most organizations require that users leave their computer powered on at the end of the day. This allows GPOs to provide for the automatic installation of updates and other software after working hours.

Note

If the WSUS server has an HTTPS certificate issued by an enterprise CA, you can specify https in place of http, and 8531 in place of 8530 in Figure 11-43.

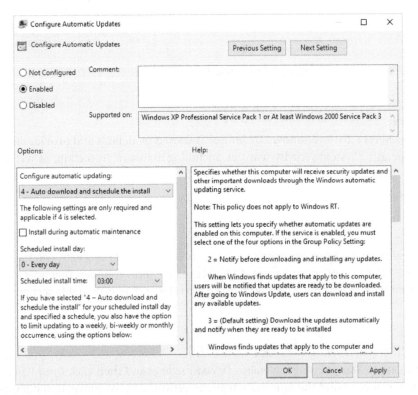

Figure 11-42   Configuring automatic updates

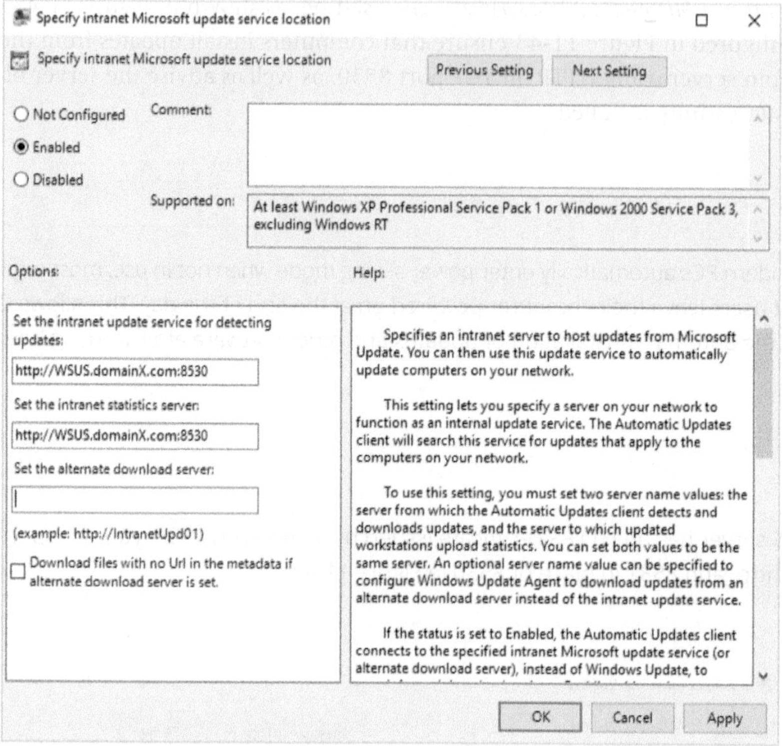

Figure 11-43   Specifying a WSUS server

Configuring Windows Defender

In Windows Server 2019, **Windows Defender** is started by default and provides many different operating system security features, including malware protection, as well as firewall and IPSec functionality.

> **Note** @
>
> Windows Defender has been renamed to **Microsoft Defender** starting with Windows 10 build 1909. Because Windows Server 2019 still uses the term Windows Defender in configuration tools at the time of this writing, we will refer to it as such in this section.

Configuring Windows Defender Features

If you navigate to Start, Settings, *Windows Defender settings* and then click *Open Windows Security*, you can configure the four main features provided by Windows Defender, as shown in Figure 11-44:

- *Virus & threat protection* allows you to perform a malware scan on your system, schedule periodic malware scans, as well as enable real-time and cloud-delivered malware protection. You can also enable **controlled folder access** to prevent ransomware from modifying files, folders, and memory on your system.
- *Firewall & network protection* allows you to enable or disable the firewall for your computer when connected to a domain, public, or private network. Computers that can contact a domain controller on the network are automatically part of a domain network. However, when you connect to a new network outside of your organization, you are prompted to select whether the network is a public network (e.g., a public WLAN at a coffee shop) or a private network (e.g., a home network). Windows Defender provides default **firewall rules** that specify appropriate restrictions for each network type (called a **firewall profile**) and automatically applies them when you connect to the associated network. You can optionally modify the default firewall rules in this section.
- *App & browser control* allows you to configure the action taken when new apps are accessed from the Internet (the default action is to warn the user), as well as configure app exploit protection features.
- *Device security* displays whether your computer uses UEFI secure boot and supports the **core isolation** feature provided by processor virtualization extensions. If core isolation is supported, you can enable the **memory integrity** setting to prevent malware and network attacks from accessing high-security processes.

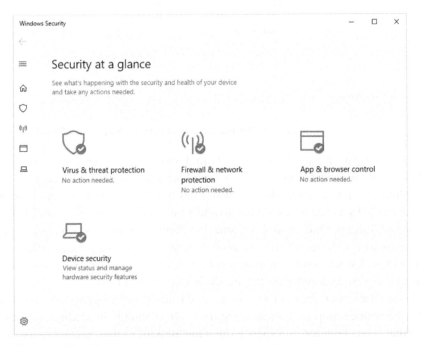

Figure 11-44 Configuring Windows Defender features

Configuring Windows Defender Firewall with Advanced Security

When you install and configure roles or features in Windows Server 2019, Windows Defender automatically adds a firewall rule to allow inbound and outbound access to the associated programs. Furthermore, most third-party software automatically configures Windows Defender firewall rules to provide for inbound and outbound access to the associated programs. However, some third-party software requires that you manually add or modify existing firewall rules to provide program access. You can use the **Windows Defender Firewall with Advanced Security** tool shown in Figure 11-45 to manage firewall rules. To open this tool, you can run the `wf.msc` command in a Windows PowerShell, Run, or Command Prompt window.

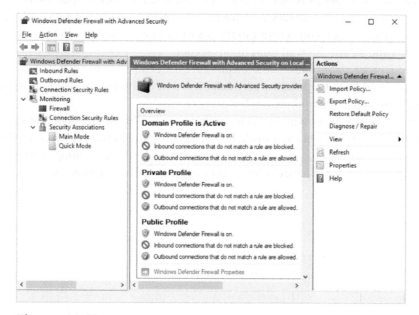

Figure 11-45 **Windows Defender Firewall with Advanced Security**

You can highlight Inbound Rules or Outbound Rules in the navigation pane of Figure 11-45 to view available firewall rules for inbound and outbound access, or highlight Monitoring, Firewall to view firewall rules that have been recently enforced on network traffic by Windows Defender. To add a new firewall rule, you can highlight either Inbound Rules or Outbound Rules and click New Rule in the Actions pane. For example, to create a new firewall rule to allow inbound access to a program that listens to TCP port 5678 and 5680, you can highlight Inbound Rules in Figure 11-45 and click New Rule to start the New Inbound Rule Wizard shown in Figure 11-46.

If Windows Defender already has a predefined rule for the program, you can select it from the Predefined drop-down box in Figure 11-46 to modify its settings. Otherwise, you can either select Program and specify the name or path of the executable file on the following page, or select Port and specify the TCP or UDP ports used by the program

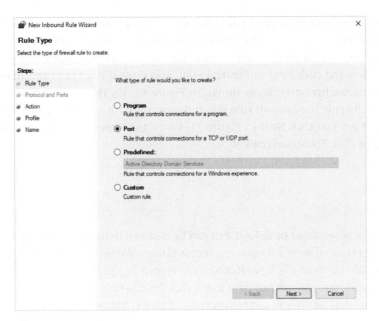

Figure 11-46   Creating a new firewall rule for inbound access

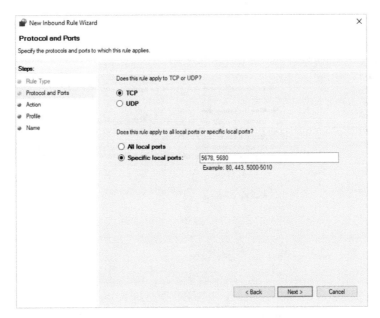

Figure 11-47   Specifying protocols and ports

on the following page. Because Port is selected in Figure 11-46, the next page of the New Inbound Rule Wizard prompts you to specify the associated protocol and port configuration, as shown for TCP port 5678 and 5680 in Figure 11-47.

When you click Next in Figure 11-47, you are prompted to select the firewall rule action, as shown in Figure 11-48. The action configured in Figure 11-48 allows access to the program, even if the connection is not encrypted using IPSec. After you select the appropriate action and click Next in Figure 11-48, you must specify the firewall profiles that should apply the firewall rule, as shown in Figure 11-49. The options configured in Figure 11-49 will apply the firewall rule when the computer is connected to a domain network only. After you click Next in Figure 11-49, you can specify a name for your new firewall rule and click Finish to create it.

Note

New firewall rules are enabled by default, but can be disabled temporarily to help when troubleshooting resource access. If resource access is unavailable after disabling the associated firewall rule, then the firewall can be eliminated as a potential cause of the issue. To disable a firewall rule, you can highlight it and click Disable Rule from the Actions pane. To enable the firewall rule again, you can highlight it and click Enable Rule from the Actions pane.

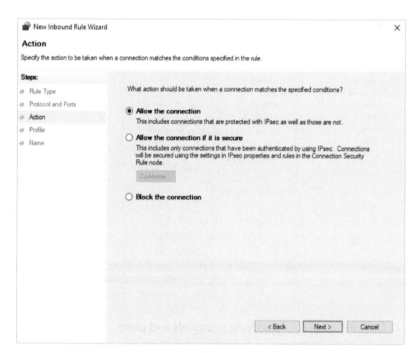

Figure 11-48   Choosing the action

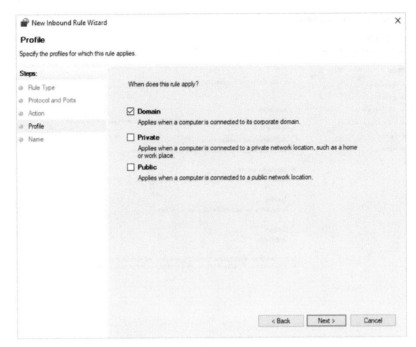

Figure 11-49   Selecting firewall profiles for the firewall rule

In addition to configuring firewall rules, the Windows Defender with Advanced Security tool allows you to configure **connection security rules** to automatically encrypt IP traffic on the network using IPSec. To prevent man-in-the-middle attacks, each computer that the connection security rule applies to should have an IPSec certificate issued by an enterprise CA.

Say, for example, that you wish to use IPSec to encrypt traffic that is destined for a database server (IP address = 172.16.0.99). To do this, you can highlight Connection Security Rules under the navigation pane in Figure 11-45, click New Rule from the Actions pane, and select *Server-to-server* at the New Connection Security Rule Wizard shown in Figure 11-50. When you click Next in Figure 11-50, you are prompted to specify the IP address of the computers in the connection, as shown in Figure 11-51. The options configured in Figure 11-51 ensure that the connection security rule applies to all traffic destined for 172.16.0.99.

After you click Next in Figure 11-51, you must select the authentication requirements, as shown in Figure 11-52. The option shown in Figure 11-52 requires that both computers perform IPSec authentication for their connection to succeed and be encrypted using IPSec. When you click Next in Figure 11-52, you must choose the method used to authenticate the computers, as shown in Figure 11-53. The options configured in Figure 11-53 require that both computers have an IPSec certificate issued by domainX-SERVERX-CA. To configure Kerberos or NTLM authentication methods, or to use two authentication methods, you can select Advanced in Figure 11-53 and then click Customize.

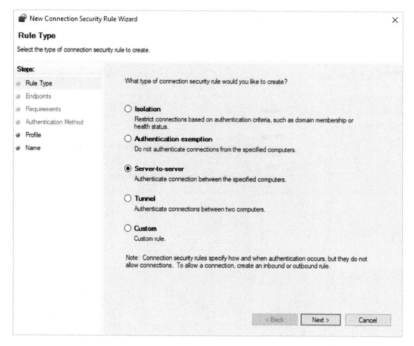

Figure 11-50   Creating a new connection security rule

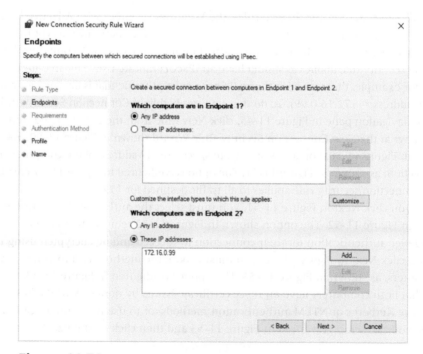

Figure 11-51   Specifying endpoint IP addresses

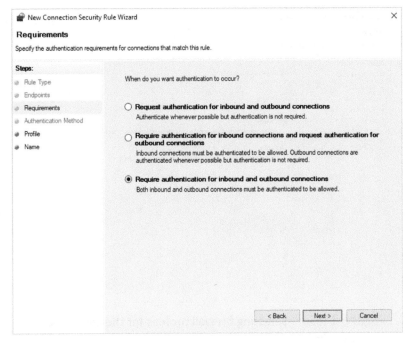

Figure 11-52   Choosing connection requirements

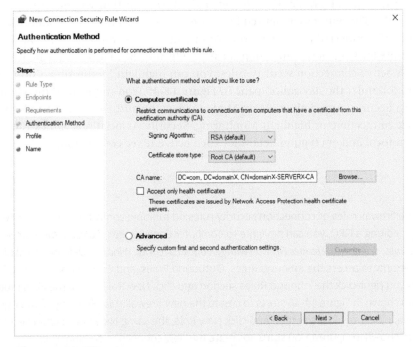

Figure 11-53   Specifying the authentication method

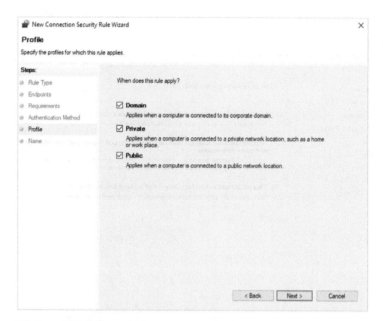

Figure 11-54 Selecting firewall profiles for the connection security rule

After you configure the authentication method and click Next in Figure 11-53, you must specify the firewall profiles that should apply the connection security rule, as shown in Figure 11-54. The options configured in Figure 11-54 will apply the firewall rule when the computer is connected to any network. After you click Next in Figure 11-54, you can specify a name for your new connection security rule and click Finish to create it.

To view active connection security rules, you can highlight Monitoring, Connection Security Rules under the navigation pane in Figure 11-45. You can instead highlight Monitoring, Security Associations, Main Mode to view the authentication details for each active IPSec connection, or highlight Monitoring, Security Associations, Quick Mode to view the protocol and encryption details for each active IPSec connection.

Note

To configure firewall rules or connection security rules on multiple computers, you can use Group Policy. After editing a GPO, you can navigate to *Computer Configuration, Policies, Windows Settings, Security Settings, Windows Defender Firewall with Advanced Security, Windows Defender Firewall with Advanced Security* to access the Inbound Rules, Outbound Rules, and Connection Security Rules sections. If you right-click the Inbound Rules section and click New Rule, the same New Inbound Rule Wizard shown in Figure 11-46 starts to create the new firewall rule. Similarly, if you right-click the Connection Security Rules section and click New Rule, the same New Connection Security Rule Wizard shown in Figure 11-50 starts to create the new connection security rule.

> **Note** 📎
>
> Recall from Module 2 that you can use the `New-NetFirewallRule` cmdlet in Windows PowerShell to create new firewall rules, or the `Set-NetFirewallProfile` cmdlet to enable or disable a firewall for one or more firewall profiles. To create a new connection security rule using Windows PowerShell, you can use the `New-NetIPsecRule` cmdlet.

Module Summary

- Group Policy can be used to configure settings and software on Windows computers in an Active Directory environment. To configure Group Policy, you create GPOs that are linked to site, domain, or OU objects.

- GPOs organize Group Policy settings into Software Settings, Windows Settings, and Administrative Templates, as well as contain Group Policy preferences for configuring Windows features.

- The Computer Configuration of a GPO applies to computers at boot time and periodically afterward, whereas the User Configuration of a GPO applies to users at login.

- Certificates are issued by a CA. They prevent man-in-the-middle attacks by validating the authenticity of public keys.

- You can configure an enterprise CA to issue certificates to users and computers within an organization by installing Active Directory Certificate Services.

- Group Policy can be used to auto-enroll users and computers for certificates based on the permissions within a certificate template on an enterprise CA.

- To protect the encryption used by WLANs in your organization using 802.1X Wireless, you can configure a RADIUS server to generate the encryption keys for wireless clients and WAPs.

- You can deploy a WSUS server in your organization to manage the distribution of updates for Microsoft products. Updates are downloaded and approved on a WSUS server for installation by domain computers that install them according to the settings within a GPO.

- Windows Defender protects the Windows operating system from malware and other security threats, as well as provides for firewall and IPSec functionality.

Key Terms

802.1X Wired
802.1X Wireless
Active Directory Certificate
 Services

administrative template
 file
auto-enrollment
CA hierarchy

certificate
Certificate Revocation List
 (CRL)
certificate template

Certificate Templates
  Console
Certification Authority (CA)
Certification Authority tool
checksum
commercial CA
connection security rule
controlled folder access
core isolation
digital signature
enrollment
enterprise CA
firewall profile
firewall rule
Group Policy Management
Group Policy Management
  Editor
Group Policy Object (GPO)
Group Policy preferences
Group Policy Results Wizard
hash

man-in-the-middle attack
memory integrity
Microsoft Defender
Microsoft Update
Online Certificate Status
  Protocol (OCSP)
Password Settings Object
  (PSO)
Protected Extensible
  Authentication Protocol
  (PEAP)
public CA
public key certificate
public key infrastructure
  (PKI)
root CA
subordinate CA
starter GPO
synchronization
trusted root
update

Update Services tool
Wi-Fi Protected Access
  (WPA)
Wi-Fi Protected Access II
  (WPA2)
Wi-Fi Protected Access III
  (WPA3)
Windows Defender
Windows Defender Firewall
  with Advanced Security
Windows Installer
Windows Internal Database
  (WID)
Windows Server Update
  Services (WSUS)
Windows Update
wireless access point
  (WAP)
wireless LAN (WLAN)
wireless router
WMI filter

Review Questions

1. Group Policy settings apply to which of the following objects? (Choose all that apply.)
   a. Users
   b. Computers
   c. Groups
   d. OUs

2. There are no GPOs created in an Active Directory domain by default. True or False?

3. You have created a new Group Policy Object (GPO). To which of the following objects can this GPO be linked? (Choose all that apply.)
   a. OU
   b. Group
   c. Site
   d. Domain

4. Group Policy preferences can be used to configure Windows features, but are only interpreted by Windows 7, Windows Server 2008, and later computers by default. True or False?

5. You wish to configure a GPO that allows users in your organization to install a package using the Programs and Features section of Control Panel. Which software deployment method should you choose when configuring the Software Settings section of a GPO?
   a. Publish the software in the User Configuration
   b. Assign the software in the User Configuration
   c. Publish the software in the Computer Configuration

    d. Assign the software in the Computer Configuration

6. Which section of a GPO contains the most security-related settings for the Windows operating system?

    a. User Configuration, Windows Settings

    b. Computer Configuration, Windows Settings

    c. User Configuration, Administrative Templates

    d. Computer Configuration, Administrative Templates

7. You can import administrative template files into a GPO to allow Group Policy to configure third-party software settings. True or False?

8. Which of the following is not included in a certificate?

    a. Public key

    b. Private key

    c. Digital signature

    d. CRL location

9. Which term refers to the process whereby a user or computer obtains a certificate from a CA?

    a. PKI

    b. enrollment

    c. revocation

    d. hashing

10. Group Policy can be configured to auto-enroll certificates for users and computers based on the permissions in a certificate template on an enterprise CA. True or False?

11. Which certificate template permissions must you grant to a user or computer before they are auto-enrolled for a certificate using Group Policy? (Choose all that apply.)

    a. Read

    b. Write

    c. Enroll

    d. Autoenroll

12. Only schema version 1 certificate templates can be configured for auto-enrollment. True or False?

13. In an 802.1X Wireless configuration, which component generates the encryption keys used for WPA?

    a. WAP

    b. Wireless client

    c. RADIUS server

    d. Domain controller

14. You must enroll each WAP for a certificate based on the *RAS and IAS Server* certificate template before they can be configured for 802.1X Wireless. True or False?

15. Which of the following statements regarding the functionality of WSUS are true? (Choose all that apply.)

    a. WSUS prevents Microsoft Update traffic from saturating the bandwidth on an organization's Internet connection.

    b. Group Policy is used to direct domain computers to a WSUS server for updates.

    c. Updates can be manually or automatically approved for distribution on a WSUS server.

    d. A WSUS server can be configured to remove updates from computers that have installed them.

16. To reduce the amount of storage that is consumed by updates on a WSUS server, you should configure the WSUS server to only synchronize updates for products that are deployed in your organization. True or False?

17. Which of the following port numbers is used to obtain updates from a WSUS server using HTTPS?

    a. 80

    b. 443

    c. 8530

    d. 8531

18. Firewall profiles contain a series of firewall rules that apply to a computer when it is connected to a particular type of network (public, private, domain). True or False?

19. Which of the following Windows Defender features can be used to limit the files, folders, and processes that ransomware can modify?
    a. Core isolation
    b. Memory integrity

    c. Controlled folder access
    d. Secure boot

20. What can you configure in the Windows Defender Firewall with Advanced Security tool to automatically protect network traffic between computers using IPSec?
    a. Firewall profiles
    b. Connection security rules
    c. IPSec rules
    d. Security Associations

Hands-On Projects

These Hands-On Projects should be completed in the order given and normally take a total of three hours or less to complete. The requirements for these projects include:

- A system with Windows Server 2019 installed according to Hands-On Project 1-1 (Lab Environment 1) or Hands-On Project 1-2 (Lab Environment 2).
- A WindowsServer2019VM2 virtual machine installed according to Hands-On Project 3-5 and configured as a member server according to Hands-On Project 5-2.
- Access to a physical WAP and mobile smartphone (both are optional but recommended).

Project 11-1: Configuring Group Policy

In this Hands-On Project, you configure GPOs on your Windows Server 2019 host, as well as test their application on your WindowsServer2019VM2 virtual machine.

1. Boot your Windows Server 2019 host and log into domain*X*.com as Administrator using the password **Secret555**. Next, click **Start** and then click **File Explorer**.
2. In the navigation pane of File Explorer, expand **This PC**, and highlight **Local Disk (C:)**.
3. Click the **Home** menu and then click **New folder**. Type **Software** and press **Enter**. Click the **Home** menu again and then click **New folder**. Type **UserData** and press **Enter**.
4. Right-click the **Software** folder and click **Properties**.
   a. Highlight the **Sharing** tab in the Software Properties window, and click **Advanced Sharing**.
   b. In the Advanced Sharing window, select **Share this folder**.
   c. Click **OK** to close the Advanced Sharing window and click **Close** to close the Software Properties window.
5. Right-click the **UserData** folder and click **Properties**.
   a. Highlight the **Sharing** tab in the UserData Properties window, and click **Advanced Sharing**.
   b. In the Advanced Sharing window, select **Share this folder**.

   c. Click **Permissions**, select **Full Control** under the Allow column and click **OK**.

   d. Click **OK** to close the Advanced Sharing window and click **Close** to close the UserData Properties window.

   e. Close File Explorer.

6. Open a Web browser and navigate to **https://sourceforge.net/projects/msi-installers/**. Follow the website instructions to download the latest version of the Notepad++ program. This will download a compressed (.zip) file.

   a. When the download has completed, double-click the downloaded .zip file from your Web browser to open it in File Explorer.

   b. Right-click the Notepad++ Windows Installer (.msi) file and click **Copy**.

   c. In the navigation pane of File Explorer, expand **This PC**, **Local Disk (C:)**, right-click **Software,** and click **Paste**.

   d. Close File Explorer.

7. Click **Start** and then click **Server Manager**. Next, click the **Tools** menu and then click **Group Policy Management**.

8. In the navigation pane of the Group Policy Management window, expand **Forest: domain*X*.com**, **Domains**, **domain*X*.com**.

9. Right-click **Default Domain Policy** and click **Edit**.

   a. In the navigation pane of the Group Policy Management Editor window, expand **Computer Configuration**, **Policies**, **Software Settings**.

      i. Right-click **Software installation** and click **New**, **Package**.

      ii. Type **\\server*X*.domain*X*.com\software** in the File name text box and click Open.

      iii. Select the **Notepad++*version*.msi** file and click **Open**.

      iv. At the Deploy Software window, note the default selection of Assigned and click **OK**.

      v. Right-click **Notepad++**, click **Properties,** and highlight the **Deployment** tab.

      vi. Select **Uninstall this application when it falls out of the scope of management** and click **OK**.

   b. In the navigation pane, expand **Computer Configuration**, **Policies**, **Windows Settings**, **Security Settings**, **Account Policies** and highlight **Password Policy**. Note the default values.

   c. Under Account Policies, highlight **Account Lockout Policy**.

      i. Double-click **Account lockout threshold**, select **Define this policy setting**, type **3** in the text box, and click **OK**. At the Suggested Value Changes window, click **OK**.

      ii. Double-click **Reset Account lockout counter after**, type **10** in the text box, and click **OK**.

      iii. Double-click **Account lockout duration**, type **60** in the text box, and click **OK**. Note that your configuration locks user accounts for 60 minutes after 3 invalid logins within 10 minutes.

   d. In the navigation pane, expand **User Configuration**, **Policies**, **Administrative Templates** and highlight **Desktop**. Double-click **Hide and disable all items on the desktop**, select **Enabled,** and click **OK**.

e. In the navigation pane, expand **User Configuration**, **Preferences**, **Windows Settings**.

    i. Right-click **Drive Maps** and click **New**, **Mapped Drive**.

    ii. Select **Create** from the Action drop-down box.

    iii. Type **\\domainX.com\warehouse** in the Location text box.

    iv. Select **Reconnect** and type **Data Warehouse** in the Label as text box

    v. Select **W** from the Use drop-down box and click **OK**. Note the new drive map configuration shown.

f. Close the Group Policy Management Editor window.

10. In the navigation pane of the Group Policy Management window, right-click **Marketing** and click **Block Inheritance**.

11. Right-click **Marketing** and click **Create a GPO in this domain, and Link it here**. Type **Marketing Group Policy** in the Name text box and click **OK**.

12. Expand **Marketing** in the navigation pane and note the GPO link for the Marketing Group Policy.

13. Right-click **Marketing Group Policy** and click **Edit**.

a. In the navigation pane of the Group Policy Management Editor window, expand **User Configuration**, **Policies**, **Windows Settings**, **Folder Redirection**.

    i. Right-click **Documents** and click **Properties**.

    ii. At the Documents Properties window, select **Basic – Redirect everyone's folder to the same location** from the Setting drop-down box.

    iii. Type **\\serverX.domainX.com\UserData** in the Root Path text box, and note that a target folder will be created for each user under this path using the example shown.

    iv. Highlight the **Settings** tab, note the default option that grants the user exclusive permissions to the folder, and click **OK**.

    v. Note the warning and click **Yes** to add the configuration.

b. In the navigation pane, expand **User Configuration**, **Policies**, **Administrative Templates** and highlight **Control Panel**. Double-click **Prohibit access to Control Panel and PC settings**, select **Enabled,** and click **OK**.

c. Close the Group Policy Management Editor window.

14. In the navigation pane of the Group Policy Management window, select **Marketing Group Policy** and then highlight the **Settings** tab. Note that Computer Configuration settings have not been configured. Highlight the **Details** tab, select **Computer configuration settings disabled** from the GPO Status drop-down box, and click **OK**.

15. Close the Group Policy Management window.

16. In Server Manager, select the **Tools** menu and then click **Hyper-V Manager**.

17. Highlight **WindowsServer2019VM2** in the virtual machines pane of Hyper-V Manager and click **Connect** in the Actions pane. In the Virtual Machine Connection window, click **Start** to boot your virtual machine.

18. At the login screen, click the **Ctrl+Alt+Delete** button in the Virtual Machine Connection window, supply the password **Secret555** for Administrator, and press **Enter** to log into the system.

   a. Note that no items appear on your desktop. This is because the User Configuration of the Default Domain Policy GPO was applied to the Administrator user account located under the default Users folder in the domain.

   b. Click **Start** and note that Notepad++ is listed under the *Recently added* section. This is because the Computer Configuration of the Default Domain Policy GPO was applied to the computer account for the WindowsServer2019VM2 virtual machine located under the default Computers folder in the domain.

   c. Select **File Explorer** from the Start menu, expand **This PC**, and note that you have a mapped drive (W:\) for Domain*X* Warehouse. This is because the Group Policy preferences from the User Configuration of the Default Domain Policy GPO was applied to Administrator.

   d. Right-click **Start**, click **Shut down or sign out**, **Sign out**.

19. At the login screen, click the **Ctrl+Alt+Delete** button in the Virtual Machine Connection window, click **Other user**, and supply a user name of **b.burtt@domain*X*.com**. Supply the password **Secret555** and press **Enter** to log into the system.

   a. Note that the Recycle Bin appears on your desktop. This is because the User Configuration of the Default Domain Policy GPO was not applied to the Bob Burtt user account located under the Marketing OU due to the Block Inheritance setting.

   b. Right-click **Start** and click **Settings**. Note that you are unable to access the Settings window. This is because the User Configuration of the Marketing Group Policy GPO was applied to the Bob Burtt user account located under the Marketing OU.

   c. Click **Start** and click **Control Panel**. Note the error message that you receive and click **OK**.

   d. Click **Start** and click **File Explorer**. Right-click Documents and click Properties. Note that Bob Burtt's documents folder has been redirected to \\server*X*.domain*X*.com\ UserData\b.burtt and click **OK**.

   e. Right-click **Start**, click **Shut down or sign out**, **Sign out**.

20. At the login screen, click the **Ctrl+Alt+Delete** button in the Virtual Machine Connection window, supply an invalid password for Bob Burtt and press **Enter**. Repeat this process three more times and note the message indicating that the Bob Burtt user account has been locked.

21. In Server Manager on your Windows Server 2019 host, click the **Tools** menu and then click **Active Directory Users and Computers**.

   a. Highlight the **Marketing** OU under domain*X*.com.

   b. Right-click **Bob Burtt**, click **Properties**, and highlight the **Account** tab. Note that the account is currently locked.

   c. Select **Unlock account** and click **OK**.

   d. Close Active Directory Users and Computers.

22. On your WindowsServer2019VM2 virtual machine, click the **Ctrl+Alt+Delete** button in the Virtual Machine Connection window, click **Other user** and supply the user name **administrator@domain*X*.com**. Supply the password **Secret555** and press **Enter** to log into the system.

23. Right-click **Start** and click **Windows PowerShell (Admin)**. At the prompt, type `gpresult /r` and press **Enter**. Note that the User Configuration and Computer Configuration of the Default Domain Policy GPO was applied, but that the Local Group Policy was not applied because it contained no settings. Close Windows PowerShell when finished.

Project 11-2: Configuring Active Directory Certificate Services

In this Hands-On Project, you install and configure Active Directory Certificate Services on your Windows Server 2019 host, as well as configure certificate templates and enroll for certificates.

1. In Server Manager on your Windows Server 2019 host, click the **Manage** menu and then click **Add Roles and Features**.

   a. At the Select installation type page, click **Next**.

   b. At the Select destination server page, click **Next**.

   c. At the Select server roles page, select **Active Directory Certificate Services** and click **Add Features** when prompted. Click **Next**.

   d. At the Select features page, click **Next**.

   e. At the Active Directory Certificate Services page, click **Next**.

   f. At the Select role services page, note the default selection (Certification Authority) and click **Next**.

   g. At the Confirm installation selections page, click **Install**.

   h. At the Installation progress page, click **Configure Active Directory Certificate Services on the destination server** to open the AD CS Configuration wizard.

      i. At the Credentials page of the AD CS Configuration wizard, click **Next**.

      ii. At the Role Services page, select **Certification Authority** and click **Next**.

      iii. At the Setup Type page, note the default selection (Enterprise CA) and click **Next**.

      iv. At the CA Type page, note the default selection (Root CA) and click **Next**.

      v. At the Private Key page, note the default selection (Create a new private key) and click **Next**.

      vi. At the Cryptography for CA page, note the default key length for the CA public/ private key pair (2048 bits) and hashing algorithm (SHA256) and click **Next**.

      vii. At the CA Name page, note the default name for your CA (domain*X*-SERVER*X*-CA) and click **Next**.

      viii. At the Validity Period page, note the default validity period for the CA public/ private key pair (5 years) and click **Next**.

      ix. At the Certificate Database page, note the default location for the CA database (C:\Windows\system32\CertLog) and click **Next**.

    x. At the Confirmation page, click **Configure**.

    xi. At the Results page, click **Close**.

  i. At the Installation progress page of the Add Roles and Features Wizard, click **Close**.

2. In Server Manager, select the **Tools** menu and then click **Certification Authority**.

  a. In the Certification Authority tool, expand **domain*X*-SERVER*X*-CA** in the navigation pane and highlight **Certificate Templates**. Note the default certificate templates that have been added to the CA.

  b. Right-click **Certificate Templates** and click **Manage**.

  c. In the Certificate Templates Console, right-click **Computer** and click **Duplicate Template**.

    i. Click the **General** tab and type **Domain*X* Computer** in the Template display name text box.

    ii. Click the **Subject Name** tab and note that the name of each issued certificate will match the DNS name of the associated computer.

    iii. Click the **Extensions** tab and note that the certificate template is intended for client and server authentication.

    iv. Click the **Security** tab, select **Enroll** and **Autoenroll** in the Allow column for Authenticated Users to allow all computers in the domain to auto-enroll for certificates based on this template, and click **OK**. Note that the Domain*X* Computer certificate template uses schema version 2.

  d. Right-click **User** and click **Duplicate Template**.

    i. Click the **General** tab and type **Domain*X* User** in the Template display name text box.

    ii. Click the **Subject Name** tab and deselect the **Include e-mail name in subject name** and **E-mail name** options.

    iii. Click the **Extensions** tab and note that the certificate template is intended for EFS, secure email, and client authentication.

    iv. Click the **Security** tab, select **Enroll** and **Autoenroll** in the Allow column for Authenticated Users to allow all users in the domain to auto-enroll for certificates based on this template, and click **OK**. Note that the Domain*X* User certificate template uses schema version 2.

  e. Close the Certificate Templates Console.

  f. In the Certification Authority tool, right-click **Certificate Templates** and click **New, Certificate Template to Issue**. Select **Domain*X* Computer** and click **OK**.

  g. Right-click **Certificate Templates** and click **New, Certificate Template to Issue**. Select **Domain*X* User** and click **OK**.

  h. Right-click **Certificate Templates** and click **New, Certificate Template to Issue**. Select **RAS & IAS Server** and click **OK**.

  i. Highlight **Certificate Templates** and note that your certificate templates have been added to the CA.

3. Right-click **Start** and click **Run**. Type `certlm.msc` and press **Enter** to open the Certificates MMC snap-in for the local computer.

  a. Expand **Personal** in the navigation pane, right-click **Certificates**, and click **All Tasks, Request New Certificate**.

      i. At the Certificate Enrollment wizard, click **Next**.

      ii. At the Select Certificate Enrollment Policy page, click **Next**.

      iii. At the Request Certificates page, select **RAS and IAS Server** and click Enroll.

      iv. Click **Finish** to close the Certificate Enrollment wizard.

    b. Highlight **Certificates** in the navigation pane of the Certificates MMC snap-in and note that you have a certificate that is based on the *RAS and IAS Server* certificate template.

    c. Close the Certificates MMC snap-in.

4. In Server Manager, click the **Tools** menu and then click **Group Policy Management**.

5. In the navigation pane of the Group Policy Management window, expand **Forest: domainX.com**, **Domains**, **domainX.com**.

6. Right-click **Default Domain Policy** and click **Edit**.

    a. In the navigation pane of the Group Policy Management Editor window, expand **Computer Configuration**, **Policies**, **Windows Settings**, **Security Settings** and highlight **Public Key Policies**.

      i. Double-click **Certificate Services Client – Certificate Enrollment Policy**, select **Enabled** from the Configuration Model drop-down box, and click **OK**.

      ii. Double-click **Certificate Services Client – Auto-Enrollment** and select **Enabled** from the Configuration Model drop-down box. Next, select the **Renew expired certificates, update pending certificates, and remove revoked certificates** and **Update certificates that use certificate templates** options and click **OK**.

    b. In the navigation pane of the Group Policy Management Editor window, expand **User Configuration**, **Policies**, **Windows Settings**, **Security Settings** and highlight **Public Key Policies**.

      i. Double-click **Certificate Services Client – Certificate Enrollment Policy**, select **Enabled** from the Configuration Model drop-down box and click **OK**.

      ii. Double-click **Certificate Services Client – Auto-Enrollment** and select **Enabled** from the Configuration Model drop-down box. Next, select the **Renew expired certificates, update pending certificates, and remove revoked certificates** and **Update certificates that use certificate templates** options and click **OK**.

    c. Close the Group Policy Management Editor window.

    d. Close the Group Policy Management window.

7. On your WindowsServer2019VM2 virtual machine, right-click **Start** and click **Shut down or sign out**, **Restart**. Click **Continue** to reboot your WindowsServer2019VM2 virtual machine.

8. At the login screen of your WindowsServer2019VM2 virtual machine, click the **Ctrl+Alt+Delete** button in the Virtual Machine Connection window, supply the password **Secret555** for Administrator and press **Enter** to log into the system.

9. Right-click **Start** and click **Run**. Type `certlm.msc` and press **Enter** to open the Certificates MMC snap-in for the local computer. Expand **Personal** in the navigation pane and highlight **Certificates**. Note that your computer has an auto-enrolled

certificate based on the Domain*X* Computer certificate template. Close the Certificates MMC snap-in when finished.

10. Right-click **Start** and click **Run**. Type `certmgr.msc` and press **Enter** to open the Certificates MMC snap-in for your user account. Expand **Personal** in the navigation pane and highlight **Certificates**. Note that your user account has an auto-enrolled certificate based on the Domain*X* User certificate template. Close the Certificates MMC snap-in when finished.

11. In the Certification Authority tool on your Windows Server 2019 host, highlight the **Issued Certificates** folder and note the certificates that were issued by your CA. Close the Certification Authority tool when finished.

Project 11-3: Configuring 802.1X Wireless

In this Hands-On Project, you configure RADIUS for 802.1X, and optionally test your configuration using a WAP.

1. In Server Manager on your Windows Server 2019 host, click the **Tools** menu and then click **Network Policy Server**.

2. In the navigation pane of the Network Policy Server tool highlight **NPS (Local)**.

3. Select **RADIUS server for 802.1X Wireless or Wired Connections** from the Standard Configuration drop-down box and click **Configure 802.1X**.

   a. At the Configure 802.1X wizard, select **Secure Wireless Connections**, note the default policy name, and click **Next**.

   b. At the Specify 802.1X Switches page, click **Add**.

      i. Type **Lab WAP** in the Friendly name text box.

      ii. Type the IP address of your WAP in the Address text box. If you are performing this configuration without access to a physical WAP, supply the sample IP address **1.2.3.4**.

      iii. Type **Secret555** in the *Shared secret* and *Confirm shared secret* text boxes and click **OK**.

   c. Click **Next**.

   d. At the Configure an Authentication Method page, select **Microsoft: Protected EAP (PEAP)** from the Type drop-down box and click **Configure**. Note that you have a certificate that can be used for PEAP. This certificate was issued using the *RAS & IAS Server* certificate template in Hands-On Project 11-2. Click **OK** and then click **Next**.

   e. At the Specify User Groups page, click **Add**, type **Domain Users,** and click **OK**. Click **Next**.

   f. At the Configure Traffic Controls page, click **Next**.

   g. Click **Finish**.

4. Expand **Policies** in the navigation pane of the Network Policy Server tool, highlight **Connection Request Policies,** and note the Secure Wireless Connections policy that was created. Next, highlight **Network Policies** and note the Secure Wireless Connections policy that was created.

5. Close the Network Policy Server tool.

6. In the configuration tool for your physical WAP, navigate to the area that allows you to configure WPA security, supply the following information, and apply your changes when finished:
   - RADIUS (or Enterprise) server = **IP address of your Windows Server 2019 host**
   - Shared Secret = **Secret555**
   - Port = **TCP port 1812**

7. Use a smartphone to connect to the physical WAP and accept the identity of the enterprise CA when prompted. Following this, you are prompted to supply credentials for a domain user account. Provide the user name **Administrator@domainX.com** and password **Secret555** to gain access to the WLAN.

Project 11-4: Configuring WSUS

In this Hands-On Project, you install and configure WSUS to provide critical and security updates for Windows systems in your Active Directory domain.

1. In Server Manager on your Windows Server 2019 host, click the **Manage** menu and then click **Add Roles and Features**.
   a. At the Select installation type page, click **Next**.
   b. At the Select destination server page, click **Next**.
   c. At the Select server roles page, select **Windows Server Update Services** and click **Add Features** when prompted. Click **Next**.
   d. At the Select features page, click **Next**.
   e. At the Windows Server Update Services page, note the default selections and click **Next**.
   f. At the Content location selection page, deselect **Store updates in the following location** and click **Next**.
   g. At the Confirm installation selections page, click **Install**.
   h. At the Installation progress page, click **Launch Post-Installation tasks** and then click **Close** to close the Add Roles and Features Wizard.

2. In Server Manager, select the **Tools** menu and then click **Windows Server Update Services** to start the Windows Server Updates Services Configuration Wizard.
   a. At the Before You Begin page, click **Next**.
   b. At the Microsoft Update Improvement Program page, deselect **Yes, I would like to join the Microsoft Update Improvement Program** and click **Next**.
   c. At the Choose Upstream Server page, note the default selection that synchronizes from Microsoft Update and click **Next**.
   d. At the Specify Proxy Server page, click **Next** if your organization does not use a proxy server for Internet access. If your organization uses a proxy server for Internet access, select **Use a proxy server when synchronizing**, specify the appropriate proxy server configuration information, and click **Next**.
   e. At the Connect to Upstream Server page, click **Start Connecting**. This will download the Windows Catalog and may take several minutes, depending on the speed of your Internet connection. When finished click **Next**.

f. At the Choose Products page, note the default selections for Windows operating system products and click **Next**.

g. At the Choose Classifications page, deselect **Definition Updates** and **Upgrades** and click **Next**.

h. At the Configure Sync Schedule page, select **Synchronize automatically**, specify **1:00:00 AM** in the First synchronization text box, and click **Next**.

i. At the Finished page, select **Begin initial synchronization** and click **Finish** to close the Windows Server Updates Services Configuration Wizard, and open the Update Services tool.

3. In the Update Services tool, expand **SERVER***X* in the navigation pane and highlight **Options**.

a. Click **Automatic Approvals** in the Options pane and check the **Default Automatic Approval Rule**.

b. Click **Run rule** to approve critical and security updates that have already been synchronized on the WSUS server.

c. Click **Close** to close the Running Rule window.

d. Click **OK** to close the Automatic Approvals window.

4. Close the Update Services tool.

5. In Server Manager, click the **Tools** menu and then click **Group Policy Management**.

6. In the navigation pane of the Group Policy Management window, expand **Forest: domain***X***.com**, **Domains**, **domain***X***.com**.

7. Right-click **Default Domain Policy** and click **Edit**.

a. In the navigation pane of the Group Policy Management Editor window, expand **Computer Configuration**, **Policies**, **Administrative Templates**, **Windows Components,** and highlight **Windows Update**.

b. Double-click **Configure Automatic Updates**, select **Enabled,** and then select **4 – Auto download and schedule the install** from the *Configure automatic updating* drop-down box. Next, specify **1:00** in the *Scheduled install time* drop-down box and click **OK**.

c. Double-click **Specify intranet Microsoft update service location** and select **Enabled**. Next, type **http://server***X***.domain***X***.com:8530** in both the *Set the intranet update service for detecting updates* and *Set the intranet statistic server* text boxes and click **OK**.

8. Close the Group Policy Management Editor window.

9. Close the Group Policy Management window.

Project 11-5: Configuring Windows Defender

In this Hands-On Project, you explore Windows Defender settings, as well as configure a firewall rule using the Windows Defender Firewall with Advanced Security tool.

1. On your Windows Server 2019 host, click **Start**, type **Windows Defender settings,** and press **Enter** to open the Windows Security section of Settings.

2. Click **Open Windows Security** and note that all areas of your system are protected by default.

   a. Click **Virus & threat protection**.

      i. Click **Quick scan** to perform a malware scan on your system.

      ii. Click **Threat history** and view the results. Click the back arrow in the upper left of the Windows Security window.

      iii. Click **Manage ransomware protection** and note that Controlled folder access is not enabled by default. Click the back arrow twice in the upper left of the Windows Security window.

   b. Click **Firewall & network protection**.

      i. Note that the firewall is enabled for the active (Domain network) profile.

      ii. Click **Allow an app through firewall** and note the default firewall rules that you can configure.

      iii. Click **Cancel** and then click the back arrow in the upper left of the Windows Security window.

   c. Click **App & browser control**.

      i. Note the default action that warns users of unrecognized apps.

      ii. Click **Exploit protection settings** and note that all system settings are enabled by default.

      iii. Click **Program settings** and note that you can modify protection settings for programs on the system. Click the back arrow twice in the upper left of the Windows Security window.

   d. Click **Device security**.

      i. Note whether core isolation and secure boot are enabled on your Windows Server 2019 host.

      ii. Click **Core isolation details** and note that core isolation is disabled by default.

      iii. Close the Windows Security window, and then close the Settings window.

3. Right-click **Start** and click **Run**. Type `wf.msc` in the Run dialog box and click **OK** to open Windows Defender Firewall with Advanced Security.

4. Highlight **Inbound Rules** in the navigation pane and note the default rules available for each firewall profile.

5. Click **New Rule** in the Actions pane.

   a. At the New Inbound Rule Wizard, select **Port** and click **Next**.

   b. At the Protocols and Ports page, note the default selection of TCP, type **27950, 27952, 27960, 27965** in the *Specific local ports* text box, and click **Next**.

   c. At the Action page, note the default action that allows the connection and click **Next**.

   d. At the Profile page, note the default selection of all firewall profiles and click **Next**.

   e. At the Name page, type **IT Network Load Testing Software** in the Name text box and click **Finish**. Note that your new inbound rule is enabled for all profiles.

6. Close Windows Defender Firewall with Advanced Security.

Discovery Exercises

Exercise 11-1

In Hands-On Project 11-1, you configured and tested the application of Group Policy. However, there are many different GPO configurations and settings available that you can explore. Open the Group Policy Management tool on your Windows Server 2019 host and perform the following tasks:

a. Create a new GPO that is linked to the Marketing OU that disables the *Prohibit access to Control Panel and PC settings* for users. Ensure that the GPO has a higher link order than the Marketing Group Policy. Next, log into your WindowsServer2019VM2 virtual machine as Bob Burtt to verify that Control Panel and Settings are accessible.

b. Remove the Notepad++ configuration in your Default Domain Policy, choosing the option to remove the installed application from computers. Reboot your WindowsServer2019VM2 virtual machine and verify that Notepad++ was automatically removed.

c. Create a starter GPO that contains five different User Configuration settings of your choice that have not been previously configured during Hands-On Projects. Next, create a new GPO that uses this starter GPO and link it to the Marketing OU. Finally, verify your configuration by logging into your WindowsServer2019VM2 virtual machine as Bob Burtt.

d. Create a new GPO that is linked to your domain that disables the *Hide and disable all items on the desktop* setting for users. Next, enforce the GPO link to ensure that it is applied to all users in the domain. Verify your results by logging into your WindowsServer2019VM2 virtual machine as Bob Burtt.

e. Use the Group Policy Results wizard to verify the application of the GPOs you configured in the previous steps for the Bob Burtt user on your WindowsServer2019VM2 virtual machine.

Exercise 11-2

Configuring and managing software is a common use for Group Policy in most organizations. Download the Windows Installer file and associated administrative template files for the Google Chrome Web browser from **https://cloud.google.com/chrome-enterprise/browser/download**. Next, create a GPO that deploys the Google Chrome Web browser to all computers in your domain. Following this, import the administrative template files for the Google Chrome Web browser and configure the GPO to provide all users with a default Chrome homepage of **http://serverX.domainX.com**. Test your results when finished.

Exercise 11-3

In Hands-On Project 11-2, you configured an enterprise CA to issue certificates based on certificate templates. To provide for many of the technologies discussed in Modules 9 and 10, you can configure your enterprise CA to issue certificates based on the Web Server and IPSec certificate templates.

a. Create a copy of the IPSec certificate template that is issued to all computers in your domain using auto-enrollment. Next, configure a VPN server on your Windows Server 2019 host for use with IKEv2. Finally, create a new IKEv2 VPN connection on your WindowsServer2019VM2 virtual machine to test your results.

b. Create a copy of the Web Server certificate template. Next, manually enroll your Windows Server 2019 host for a certificate based on this template using IIS Manager. Following this, configure the Default Web Site in IIS Manager to use this certificate for HTTPS instead of the self-signed certificate configured in Hands-On Project 10-1 and test your results by accessing **https://serverX.domainX.com** from a Web browser. Finally, configure the VPN server on your Windows Server 2019 host for use with SSTP and create a new SSTP VPN connection on your WindowsServer2019VM2 virtual machine to test your results.

Exercise 11-4

In addition to providing updates for Microsoft products, WSUS can also be used to deploy software (either .exe or .msi) in an organization using the free and open source WSUS Package Publisher tool. Follow the instructions at **https://github.com/DCourtel/ Wsus_Package_Publisher/wiki/Installation** to download and configure the WSUS Package Publisher tool on your Windows Server 2019 host. Next, configure it to deploy the Notepad++ program to the computers in your domain and test your results.

Exercise 11-5

In Discovery Exercise 11-3 a), you deployed an IPSec certificate to each computer in your domain using auto-enrollment. Now, configure a connection security rule under the Windows Defender Firewall with Advanced Security section of the Default Domain Policy GPO that requires IPSec for systems that communicate with your WindowsServer2019VM2 virtual machine. When finished, connect to a shared resource on your WindowsServer2019VM2 virtual machine from your Windows Server 2019 host and use the Windows Defender Firewall with Advanced Security tool to view the IPSec connection.

MONITORING AND TROUBLESHOOTING WINDOWS SERVER 2019

After completing this module, you will be able to:

Outline the process used to monitor and troubleshoot systems

Use common monitoring and troubleshooting tools

Troubleshoot common hardware, software, operating system, performance, and network problems

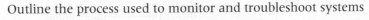

Throughout this textbook, you have examined the components that make up a Windows Server 2019 system. In this module, you learn how to monitor and troubleshoot these components. You'll explore monitoring and troubleshooting practices, as well as the tools that can be used to monitor server performance and troubleshoot system problems. At the end of this module, you'll examine common troubleshooting procedures for resolving different types of problems on a Windows Server 2019 system.

Monitoring and Troubleshooting Methodology

After you have successfully installed Windows Server 2019, configured and secured server roles, and documented settings, you must maintain the system's integrity over time. This includes monitoring, proactive maintenance, and reactive maintenance, as illustrated in Figure 12-1.

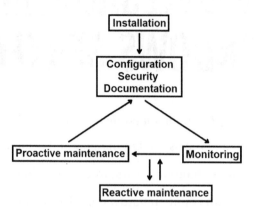

Figure 12-1   The monitoring and maintenance cycle

Monitoring is one of a system administrator's most time-consuming tasks; it involves examining network connectivity, viewing log files, and running performance utilities periodically to identify problems and their causes. **Proactive maintenance** involves taking the required steps to minimize the chance of future problems as well as their impact. Performing regular system backups, monitoring available storage, creating **baselines** and analyzing performance trends to identify problems before they occur are examples of proactive maintenance. All proactive maintenance tasks should be documented for future reference. This information, along with any data backups, is vital to the reconstruction of your system, should it suffer catastrophic failure.

Note

A baseline is a set of performance measurements taken during periods of normal system activity. When performance issues arise, you can compare current performance measurements to those in the baseline. Values that have changed dramatically from the baseline can help you pinpoint the source of the performance problem.

Reactive maintenance is used to correct problems when they arise during monitoring. When a problem is solved, it needs to be documented and the system adjusted proactively to reduce the likelihood that the same problem will occur in the future. Furthermore, documenting the solution to problems creates a template for action, allowing subsequent or similar problems to be remedied faster.

> **Note** 🔗
>
> Any system documentation should be stored in a folder on a separate computer so it is not lost during a system failure. Many organizations store system documentation in their help desk ticketing software, which is backed up regularly to ensure that the documentation is not lost during a system failure.

Reactive maintenance is further composed of many tasks known as **troubleshooting procedures**, which can be used to efficiently solve a problem in a systematic manner.

When a problem occurs, you need to gather as much information about the problem as possible. This might include examining system log files, viewing configuration settings, as well as running monitoring programs and comparing current performance results to baseline values. In addition, you might research the symptoms of the problem on the Internet; many technology-related websites list procedures that can be used to check for certain problems.

Following this, you need to try to isolate the problem by examining the information gathered. Determine whether the problem is persistent or intermittent and whether it affects all users or just one.

Given this information, you might then generate a list of possible causes and solutions organized by placing the most probable solution at the top of the list and the least probable solution at the bottom of the list. Using the Internet at this stage is beneficial because solutions for many Windows Server 2019 problems are posted at docs.microsoft.com and other websites that can be found by performing a Google search for keywords related to the problem. In addition, posting the problem on a Windows-related forum website will likely generate many possible solutions.

Next, you need to implement and test each possible solution for results until the problem is resolved. When implementing possible solutions, it is very important that you only apply one change at a time. If you make multiple modifications, it will be unclear as to what worked and why.

After the problem has been solved, document the solution for future reference and proceed to take proactive maintenance measures to reduce the chance of the same problem recurring in the future. These troubleshooting procedures are outlined in Figure 12-2.

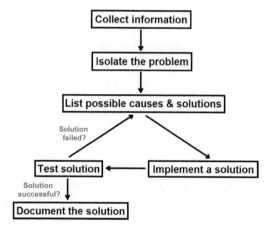

Figure 12-2   Common troubleshooting procedures

The troubleshooting procedures listed in Figure 12-2 serve as a guideline only. You might need to alter your approach for certain problems. Remember, troubleshooting is an art that you will begin to master only with practice. However, two golden rules will guide you during any troubleshooting process:

- Prioritize problems—If you need to solve multiple problems, prioritize the problems according to severity and spend the most time on the most severe problems. Becoming fixated on a small problem and ignoring larger issues results in much lower productivity. If a problem is too difficult to solve in a given period of time, it is good practice to ask for help.
- Try to solve the root of the problem—Some solutions might appear successful in the short term yet fail over the long term because of an underlying problem. Effective troubleshooting requires good instincts, which in turn comes from a solid knowledge of the system hardware and software configuration. To avoid missing the underlying cause of any problem, try to justify why a certain solution was successful. If it is unclear why a certain solution was successful, it is likely that you have missed an underlying cause to the problem that must be remedied in order to prevent the same problem from recurring.

Monitoring and Troubleshooting Tools

Recall from Module 2 that Server Manager and the Windows Admin Center can be used to monitor system events and performance. However, Windows Server 2019 comes with several additional tools that server administrators can use to obtain more detailed system and performance information. The most common of these include the following:

- Task Manager
- Resource Monitor

- Performance Monitor
- Data Collector Sets
- Event Viewer
- Reliability Monitor

We will explore these tools in the following sections, as well as discuss how they can be used to monitor and troubleshoot a Windows Server 2019 system.

Task Manager

In addition to viewing and managing **processes**, **Task Manager** can be used to quickly analyze the performance of a system, and it is often the first tool that server administrators open when reacting to a performance problem. Here are some methods for opening Task Manager:

- Right-click the Start menu or taskbar and then click Task Manager.
- Run the `taskmgr.exe` command from a Windows Run, PowerShell, or Command Prompt window.
- Press the Ctrl+Alt+Del key combination and then click Task Manager.
- Press the Ctrl+Shift+Esc key combination.

Note 🖉

While the terms "program" and "process" are often used interchangeably by server administrators, they are two different things. A program is an executable file on a filesystem, whereas a process is a program that is currently loaded into memory and executing on the system.

By default, Task Manager only displays a short list of processes started by the current user. To view performance information, you must click *More details* and highlight the Performance tab as shown in Figure 12-3. By default, the Performance tab displays hardware utilization information regarding your processor (CPU), including the number of processes, threads, and handles. A **thread** is a unique sequence of instructions that is executed by a process. In general, processes that consume large amounts of processor time often contain numerous threads. These processes perform better on processors that have more logical processors (or virtual processors for a virtual machine), as threads can execute simultaneously on different processor cores. A **handle** is a resource (often a file) that is connected to a process. Processes that use storage frequently often use a large number of handles.

Selecting Memory in Figure 12-3 will display memory utilization information, as shown in Figure 12-4. The values shown in Figure 12-4 indicate that the system has 32 GB of physical memory, with 1.5 GB of uncompressed memory currently being used (leaving 30.5 GB available). Applications have currently requested 1.4 GB of virtual memory from the paging file (called **committed memory**), and the adjacent value of

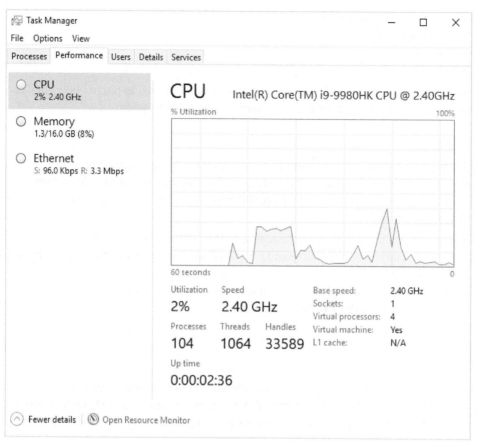

Figure 12-3   Viewing processor performance

34.9 GB represents the total virtual and physical memory. Because the system has 32 GB of physical memory, this indicates that the paging file is 2.9 GB in size. While up to 10% of physical memory can be used to speed filesystem access for processes (called **cached memory**), the system shown in Figure 12-4 indicates that only 0.4 GB of physical memory is currently being used for this purpose. Moreover, 79.6 MB of memory used by device drivers and the Windows kernel can be transferred to the paging file if necessary (called the **paged pool**), while 61.3 MB cannot be transferred (the **non-paged pool**).

Selecting Ethernet in Figure 12-4 will display network statistics for the associated network interface, as shown in Figure 12-5. The send and receive values shown in Figure 12-5 will vary depending on the number of clients connected to the server and the amount of data that they are transferring. High sustained send and receive values could indicate a large number of connections transferring data, or a **Distributed Denial of Service (DDoS)** network attack that is flooding the server with traffic in an attempt to disrupt service.

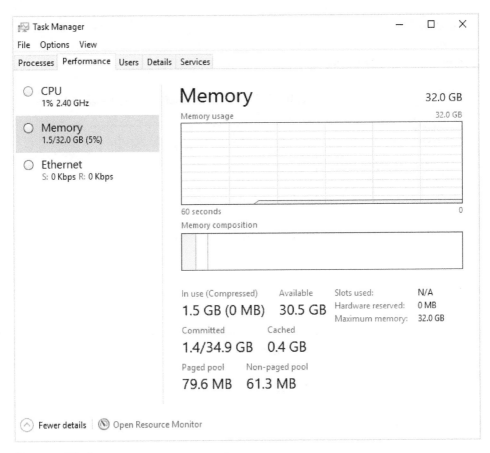

Figure 12-4 Viewing memory performance

High processor or memory utilization values can be the result of too many processes running on the system, but can also be caused by rogue processes and memory leaks. **Rogue processes** are processes that have encountered an error that forces them to use an unusually high amount of processor time. **Memory leaks** cause processes to enter a state that allows them to continually use more memory, until the memory in the system is exhausted. To identify rogue processes, you can highlight the Processes tab, click the CPU column to sort the processes by processor utilization and examine the results, as shown in Figure 12-6. It is not unusual for large processes, such as a database engine, to have a high processor utilization. However, if a smaller process (e.g., File Explorer or Notepad) uses a high processor utilization, it may have become a rogue process. Similarly, to identify memory leaks, you can click the Memory column in Figure 12-6 to sort the processes by memory utilization and examine the results. A process with a high memory utilization that continues to grow could indicate a memory leak. After you identify a rogue process or memory leak, you

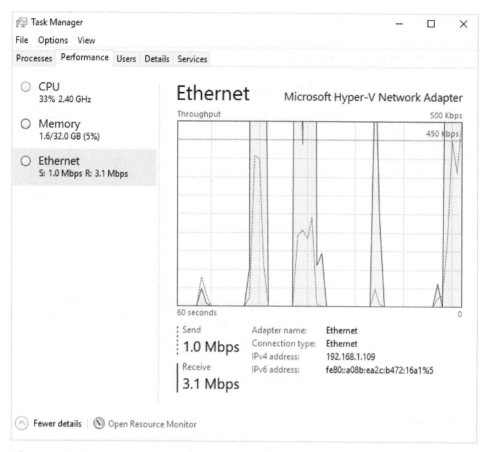

Figure 12-5   Viewing network performance

should right-click the process in Figure 12-6 and click *End task*. If the problem reoccurs after the associated process is started again, you should search for an update from the program vendor as most rogue processes and memory leaks are caused by an error in the program logic.

Note

If you encounter a rogue process or memory leak for a program developed by your organization, you should first right-click the process in Figure 12-6 and click *Create dump file* to create a file that contains the memory contents of the process. This **dump file** can then be used to help the developer team in your organization identify and fix the program logic problem.

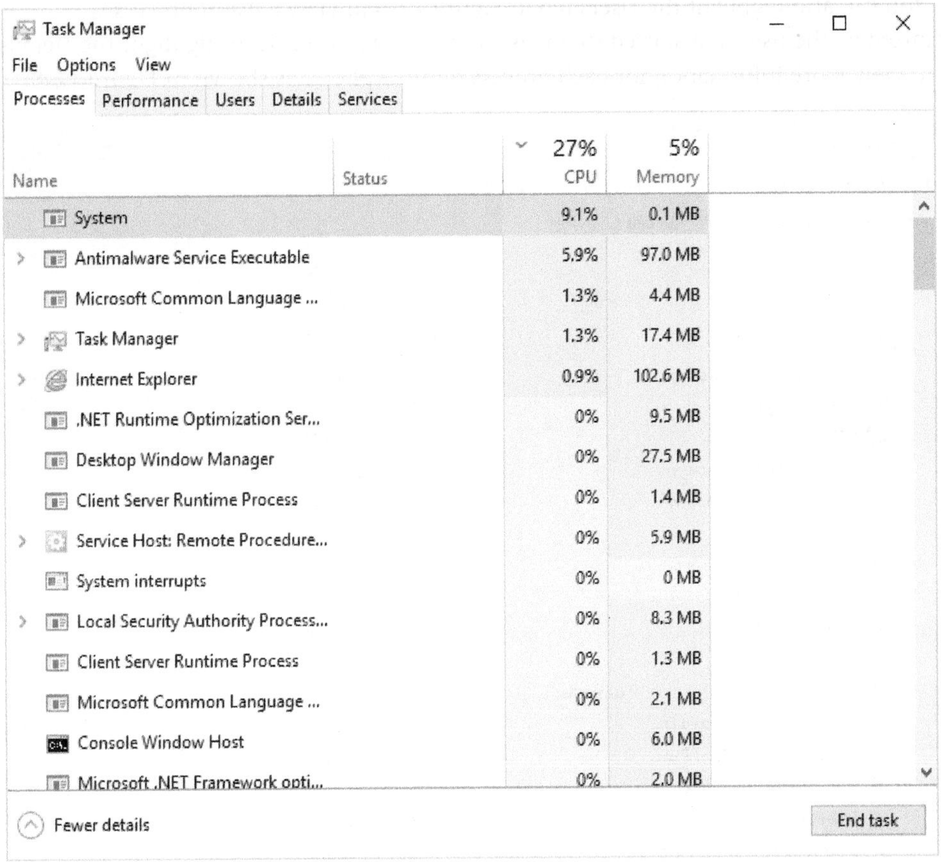

Task Manager	— □ ×

File   Options   View

Processes   Performance   Users   Details   Services

Name	Status	⌄ 27% CPU	5% Memory	
▦ System		9.1%	0.1 MB	^
> ▦ Antimalware Service Executable		5.9%	97.0 MB	
▦ Microsoft Common Language ...		1.3%	4.4 MB	
> 📄 Task Manager		1.3%	17.4 MB	
> 🌐 Internet Explorer		0.9%	102.6 MB	
▦ .NET Runtime Optimization Ser...		0%	9.5 MB	
▦ Desktop Window Manager		0%	27.5 MB	
▦ Client Server Runtime Process		0%	1.4 MB	
> ⚙ Service Host: Remote Procedure...		0%	5.9 MB	
▦ System interrupts		0%	0 MB	
> ▦ Local Security Authority Process...		0%	8.3 MB	
▦ Client Server Runtime Process		0%	1.3 MB	
▦ Microsoft Common Language ...		0%	2.1 MB	
▦ Console Window Host		0%	6.0 MB	
▦ Microsoft .NET Framework opti...		0%	2.0 MB	∨

⌃ Fewer details   End task

Figure 12-6   Viewing processes

Note 📎

You can also right-click a process in Figure 12-6 and click *Search online* to search for information regarding the process in your default search engine, or *Open file location* to open the folder that contains the associated program.

Note 📎

Many processes shown in Figure 12-6 consist of subprocesses (e.g., Antimalware Service Executable). You can display these subprocesses by expanding the process using the arrow icon to the left of the process name.

You can also highlight the Users tab in Figure 12-6 to view a list of processes organized by the user that started them, as shown in Figure 12-7, or highlight the Details tab to view more information for each process on the system, as shown in Figure 12-8.

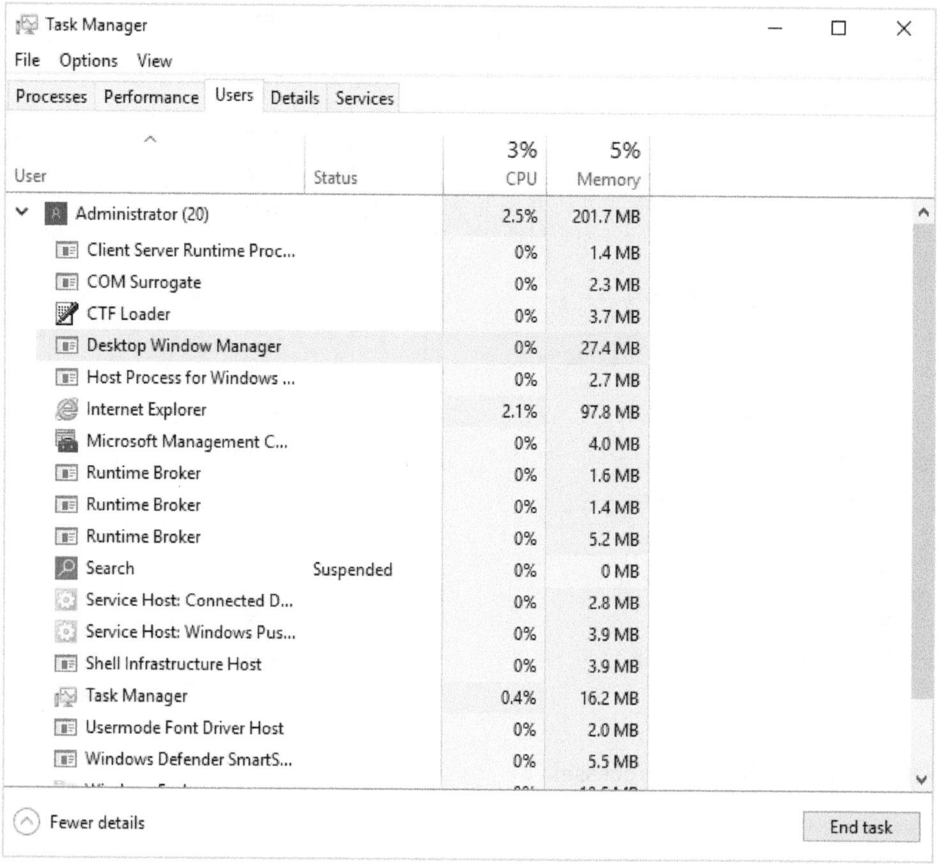
Task Manager
File Options View
Processes Performance Users Details Services
User
Status
3% CPU
5% Memory
Administrator (20) 2.5% 201.7 MB
Client Server Runtime Proc... 0% 1.4 MB
COM Surrogate 0% 2.3 MB
CTF Loader 0% 3.7 MB
Desktop Window Manager 0% 27.4 MB
Host Process for Windows ... 0% 2.7 MB
Internet Explorer 2.1% 97.8 MB
Microsoft Management C... 0% 4.0 MB
Runtime Broker 0% 1.6 MB
Runtime Broker 0% 1.4 MB
Runtime Broker 0% 5.2 MB
Search Suspended 0% 0 MB
Service Host: Connected D... 0% 2.8 MB
Service Host: Windows Pus... 0% 3.9 MB
Shell Infrastructure Host 0% 3.9 MB
Task Manager 0.4% 16.2 MB
Usermode Font Driver Host 0% 2.0 MB
Windows Defender SmartS... 0% 5.5 MB
Fewer details
End task

Figure 12-7 Viewing processes by user

In addition to showing the process ID (PID), status, user name, and CPU and memory utilization for each process, the Details tab shown in Figure 12-8 provides additional actions when you right-click a process:

- *End process tree* ends the process and all associated subprocesses.
- *Set priority* can be used to increase or reduce the amount of processor time that the system dedicates to running the process.
- *Set affinity* allows you to specify the physical and logical processors on which to run the process.
- *Analyze wait chain* shows the threads or processes that are blocking the process.
- *UAC virtualization* allows you to run the process as a standard user, while still allowing the process to perform privileged tasks on the system.

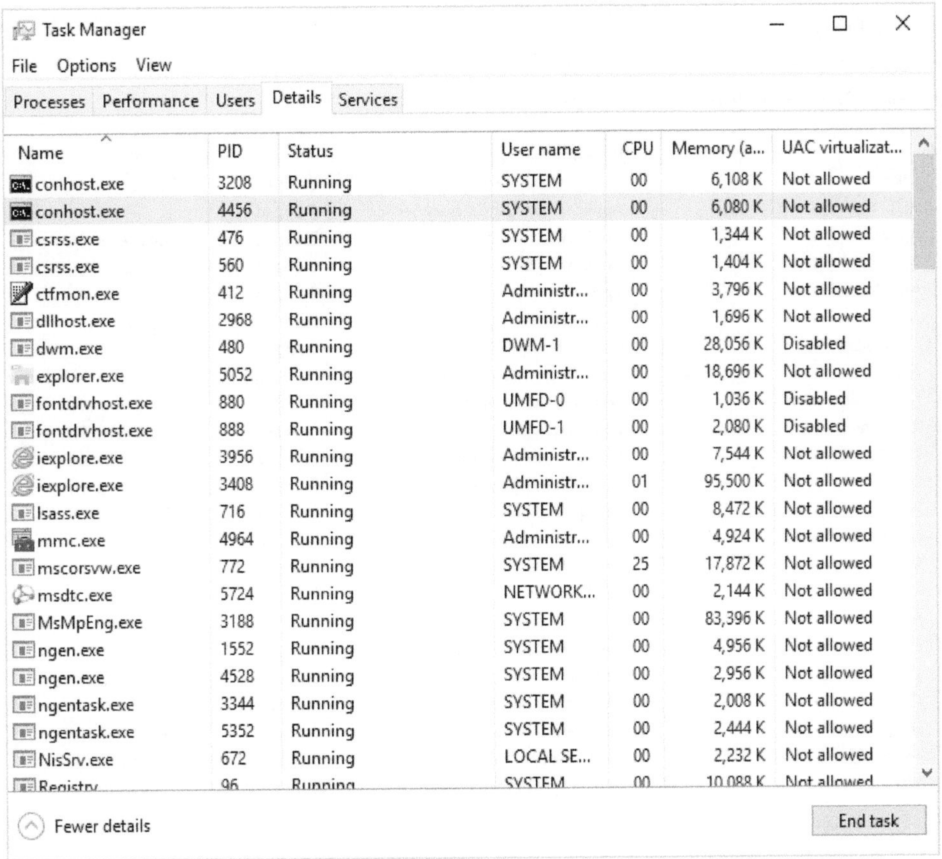

Name	PID	Status	User name	CPU	Memory (a...	UAC virtualizat...
conhost.exe	3208	Running	SYSTEM	00	6,108 K	Not allowed
conhost.exe	4456	Running	SYSTEM	00	6,080 K	Not allowed
csrss.exe	476	Running	SYSTEM	00	1,344 K	Not allowed
csrss.exe	560	Running	SYSTEM	00	1,404 K	Not allowed
ctfmon.exe	412	Running	Administr...	00	3,796 K	Not allowed
dllhost.exe	2968	Running	Administr...	00	1,696 K	Not allowed
dwm.exe	480	Running	DWM-1	00	28,056 K	Disabled
explorer.exe	5052	Running	Administr...	00	18,696 K	Not allowed
fontdrvhost.exe	880	Running	UMFD-0	00	1,036 K	Disabled
fontdrvhost.exe	888	Running	UMFD-1	00	2,080 K	Disabled
iexplore.exe	3956	Running	Administr...	00	7,544 K	Not allowed
iexplore.exe	3408	Running	Administr...	01	95,500 K	Not allowed
lsass.exe	716	Running	SYSTEM	00	8,472 K	Not allowed
mmc.exe	4964	Running	Administr...	00	4,924 K	Not allowed
mscorsvw.exe	772	Running	SYSTEM	25	17,872 K	Not allowed
msdtc.exe	5724	Running	NETWORK...	00	2,144 K	Not allowed
MsMpEng.exe	3188	Running	SYSTEM	00	83,396 K	Not allowed
ngen.exe	1552	Running	SYSTEM	00	4,956 K	Not allowed
ngen.exe	4528	Running	SYSTEM	00	2,956 K	Not allowed
ngentask.exe	3344	Running	SYSTEM	00	2,008 K	Not allowed
ngentask.exe	5352	Running	SYSTEM	00	2,444 K	Not allowed
NisSrv.exe	672	Running	LOCAL SE...	00	2,232 K	Not allowed
Registry	96	Running	SYSTEM	00	10,088 K	Not allowed

Fewer details

End task

Figure 12-8   Viewing process details

Note

You can right-click a process on the Processes tab (Figure 12-6) and click *Go to details* to quickly navigate to the associated process on the Details tab (Figure 12-8).

Some processes are part of a Windows service that runs in the background and does not interact with the desktop. You can highlight the Services tab in Figure 12-8 to view the services on your system, as shown in Figure 12-9. Most problems related to unresponsive services can be resolved by restarting the service, or starting it if it is stopped. You can right-click a service in Figure 12-9 and click *Restart* to restart it, or *Start* to start it.

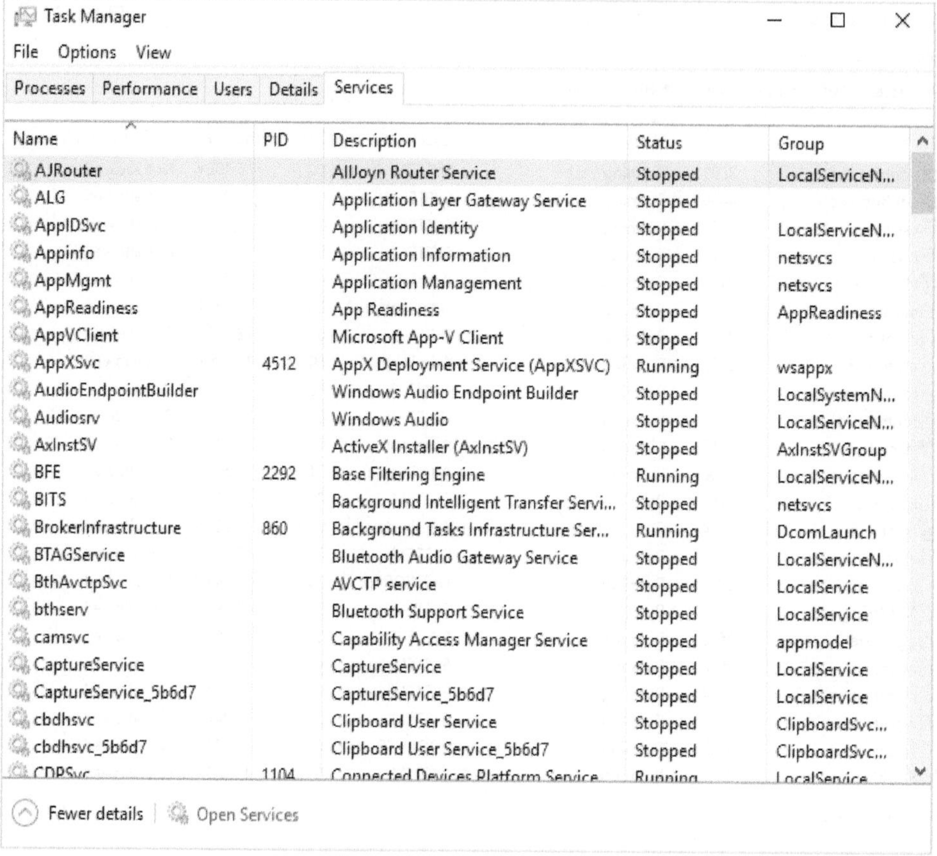

Figure 12-9   Viewing services

Resource Monitor

If you need more information than Task Manager offers in order to troubleshoot a performance problem such as a process that is writing to a particular file, you can run the **Resource Monitor**, as shown in Figure 12-10. To start Resource Monitor, you can select Resource Monitor from the Tools menu in Server Manager. Alternatively, you can click Open Resource Monitor on the Performance tab of Task Manager (shown earlier in Figure 12-3), or run the `resmon.exe` command from a Windows Run, PowerShell, or Command Prompt window.

In addition to a graph showing CPU, disk, network, and memory utilization, the CPU section on the Overview tab of Resource Monitor displays a list of processes that you can select to display the associated detailed storage, network, and memory information. Because the `sqlserver.exe` process was selected in the CPU section of Figure 12-10, the Disk section displays read and write information for the three files that the process is using. To view the network and memory utilization for the `sqlserver.exe` process, you can expand the Network and Memory sections, respectively.

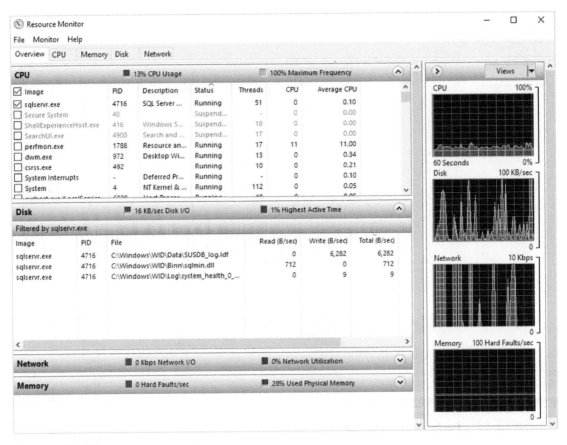

Figure 12-10   Resource Monitor

The other tabs shown in Figure 12-10 display specific information for each process selected in the CPU section of the Overview tab:

- The CPU tab displays related services and file handles.
- The Memory tab displays physical and virtual memory usage.
- The Disk tab displays the disks and files used.
- The Network tab displays network activity, TCP connections, and ports.

Performance Monitor

Performance Monitor is Windows Server's most comprehensive tool for collecting data on real-time system performance; it allows you to track how individual system resources are being used and how they are behaving under the current workload. You can access this tool by navigating to Performance Monitor under the Monitoring Tools folder in the Performance MMC snap-in, as shown in Figure 12-11. To start the Performance MMC snap-in, you can click Performance Monitor from the Tools

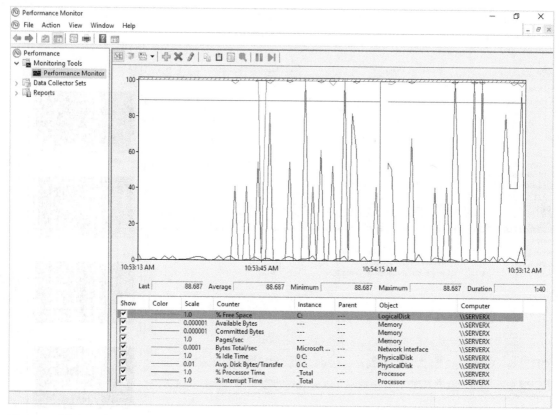

Figure 12-11 Performance Monitor

menu in Server Manager, or run the `perfmon.exe` command from a Windows Run, PowerShell, or Command Prompt window.

The performance information shown in Figure 12-11 is composed of three components:

- **Performance objects** are the areas of the system that can be monitored. Common examples of performance objects include Processor, Memory, Physical Disk, Logical Disk (for volumes), and Network Interface.
- **Performance counters** are the components of a performance object that monitor a specific type of event.
- **Instances** represent a specific hardware device or software component. For example, if your system has two network interfaces, you can choose to monitor the first network interface only (the first instance).

For example, the first line graphed in Figure 12-11 displays the output from the *% Free Space* performance counter in the *LogicalDisk* performance object for the *C:* instance. Some of the many different performance objects and counters are described in Table 12-1.

Table 12-1   Common performance objects and counters

Object	Counter	Descriptions
Processor	% Processor Time	The percentage of time the processor spends executing processes
	% Privileged Time	The percentage of time the processor spends executing processes that require privileged access to the system
	% User Time	The percentage of time the processor spends executing processes that do not require privileged access to the system
	% Interrupt Time	The percentage of time that the processor is responding to interrupts
Memory	Available Bytes	The bytes of physical memory currently available for use
	Committed Bytes	The bytes of virtual memory currently reserved by applications
	Pages/sec	The number of times that virtual memory is accessed by the system (each access is called a **page fault**)
PhysicalDisk	% Idle Time	The percentage of time that the storage device was not performing read or write operations
	Avg. Disk Bytes/Transfer	The average number of bytes transferred between memory and disk during read and write operations.
	Disk Bytes/sec	The rate at which bytes are transferred to and from the storage device
	Avg. Disk Queue Length	The average number of requests waiting in memory to be processed by the storage device
LogicalDisk	% Free Space	The percentage of free space on the volume.
Network Interface	Bytes Total/sec	The rate at which bytes are transferred to and from the network interface
	Packets/sec	The rate at which packets are sent to and from the network interface

Note

Each server role and feature also adds objects and counters to the system that can be used in Performance Monitor. For example, the *Total Query Received/sec* performance counter in the *DNS* performance object can be used to monitor the average number of name resolution lookups that a DNS server receives each second.

To add a performance counter to Performance Monitor, you can click the Add icon (+) from the Performance Monitor toolbar in Figure 12-11. This will open the Add Counters window shown in Figure 12-12, where you can add the appropriate performance counters and instances. In Figure 12-12, the *% Free Space* performance counter under the *LogicalDisk* object for the *C:* instance on the local computer was added. You can optionally select *Show description* in Figure 12-12 to view a pane that describes the function of each counter that you select.

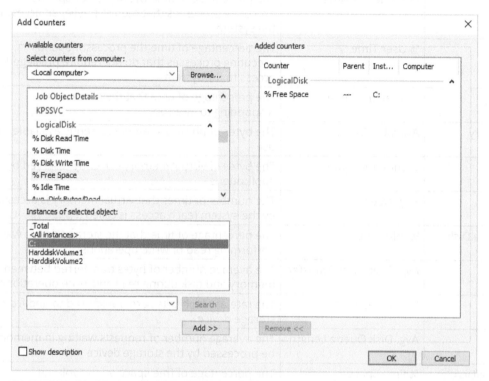

Figure 12-12   Adding a performance counter

Because it is difficult to view the output of multiple performance counters in the default line graph view of Performance Monitor, you can select the *Change graph type* drop-down box from the Performance Monitor toolbar in Figure 12-11 (third icon from the left) and select *Histogram bar* to view current performance counter values as a bar chart, or *Report* to view a report of the current performance counter values, as shown in Figure 12-13.

The report shown in Figure 12-13 is appropriate for creating a simple performance baseline, as it lists the values for each performance counter. You can right-click the report and click *Save Settings As* to save the report as a webpage (.htm file) that can be stored in a central location for documentation purposes. When performance problems occur at a later time, you can open this .htm file in a Microsoft Web browser on the same computer to view the baseline values. You can also click the Unfreeze Display icon in the webpage to view the current values of each performance counter interactively using the Performance Monitor. Performance

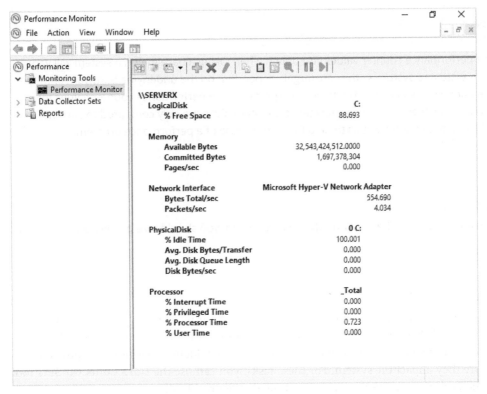

Figure 12-13   Performance Monitor report view

counters with current values that differ greatly from the baseline values can help identify the cause of the performance problem. Say, for example, that the *Pages/sec* performance counter in the *Memory* object has a current value of 49982 compared to a baseline value of 290. The large difference between the current and baseline value indicates that the paging file is being used far more compared to a time of normal performance. As a result, the performance problem may be the result of one or more processes that are currently consuming too much memory, or inadequate physical memory for the processes that the system is running. To remedy this problem, you could add more physical memory to the system, or move some programs or server roles to another system that has adequate resource capacity.

> **Note**
>
> You can also use the `Get-Counter` cmdlet in Windows PowerShell to view the value for a performance counter. Consequently, you could add several `Get-Counter` commands to a PowerShell Script that can be executed to create a baseline or view current performance information.

Note 📎

The performance counter values you obtain when taking a baseline on a system will vary from system to system as they are largely dependent on the underlying hardware and software. As a result, you should not interpret baseline performance counter values for a system. Instead, baseline performance counter values are only compared to current performance counter values to help locate the cause of a performance problem.

Note 📎

Any time you add software or hardware to a system, you should take a new baseline for that system.

Data Collector Sets

While the Performance Monitor allows you to monitor real-time system performance and create simple baselines, it is not suitable for creating baselines that span a period of time, or for analyzing trends that can be used to proactively identify performance problems before they impact the system. For these tasks, you can use the **Data Collector Sets** tool in the Performance MMC snap-in, as shown in Figure 12-14.

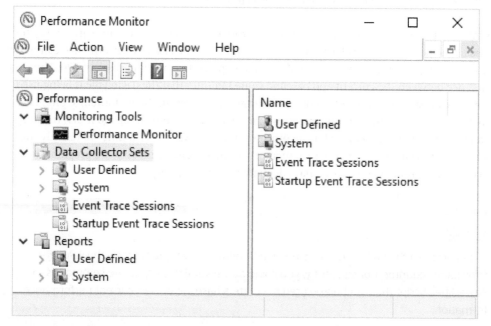

Figure 12-14   The Data Collector Sets tool

Using the Data Collector Sets tool, you can create a **data collector set** to collect and log data from performance counters, **event trace providers**, or system configuration information in the Windows Registry. Event trace providers are Windows components that report detailed information about the Windows kernel and system applications. Alternatively, you can create a data collector set to monitor a performance counter and log the associated data only when the performance counter exceeds or falls below a certain value. This data collector set configuration is called a **performance counter alert**.

Creating a Data Collector Set to Log Data

To create a new data collector set, you can right-click the User Defined folder under the Data Collector Sets folder in Figure 12-14 and click New, Data Collector Set to start the Create new Data Collector Set wizard shown in Figure 12-15. The options configured in Figure 12-15 will manually create a data collector set called *SERVERX Data Collector Set*, but you can instead select *Create from a template* to use one of the following preconfigured data collector sets:

- *Active Directory Diagnostics*—Collects data about Active Directory activity using both performance counters and event trace providers.

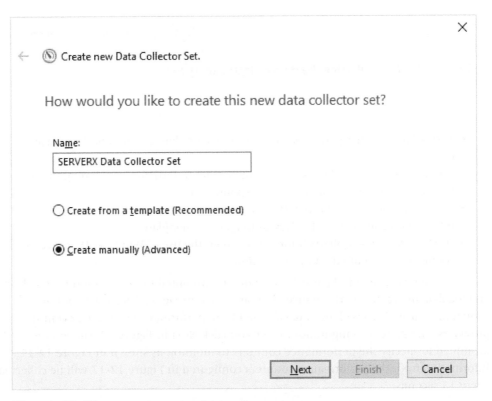

Figure 12-15   Creating a new data collector set

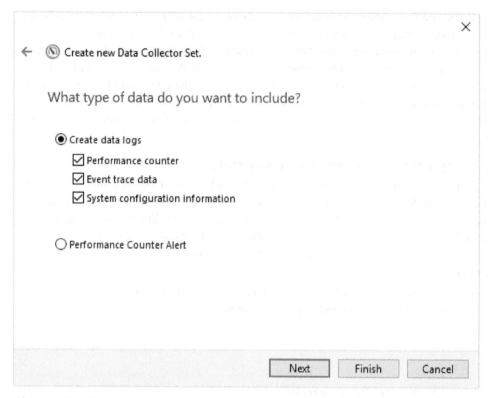

Figure 12-16   Selecting the data collector set type

- *Basic*—Collects basic performance data using a predefined set of performance counters.
- *System Diagnostics*—Collects system configuration information, including the status of processes, hardware, and system response times.
- *System Performance*—Collects system performance information alongside the information collected by the System Diagnostics template.
- *WDAC Diagnostics*—Collects information about the use of Windows Data Access components that are used by applications.

After you click Next in Figure 12-15, you are prompted to select whether to collect and log data or create a performance alert, as shown in Figure 12-16. The options shown in Figure 12-16 will log data collected from performance counters, event trace providers, and system configuration. After you click Next in Figure 12-16, you are prompted to specify the performance counters to monitor, as shown in Figure 12-17. Information from the performance counters configured in Figure 12-17 will be collected every 15 seconds.

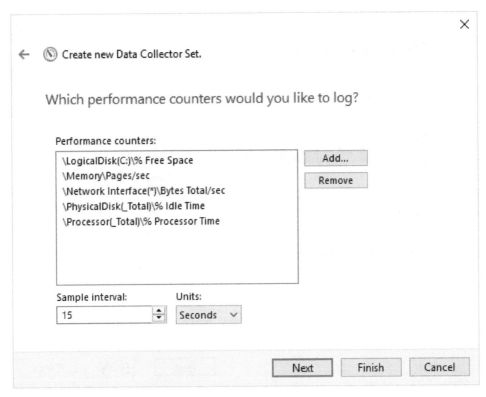

Figure 12-17   Specifying performance counters

When you click Next in Figure 12-17, you are prompted to specify the event trace providers to monitor, as shown in Figure 12-18. The event trace provider configured in Figure 12-18 will log events generated by all Windows services. After you click Next in Figure 12-18, you are prompted to specify the Windows Registry keys to collect system configuration data from, as shown for the SOFTWARE key under HKEY_LOCAL_ MACHINE (HKLM) in Figure 12-19.

After you click Next in Figure 12-19, you can optionally modify the default folder to store the collected data, as shown in Figure 12-20. After you click Next in Figure 12-20, you must specify data collector set options, as shown in Figure 12-21. The options configured in Figure 12-21 will run the data collector set as the Administrator user account and start collecting data after you click Finish.

After creating a data collector set, you can right-click it under the User Defined folder in Figure 12-14 and click *Start* to start collecting data, *Stop* to stop collecting data, or *Properties* to modify its configuration. The properties dialog box for a data collector set has the following six tabs:

- *General* allows you to specify a data collector set description and searchable keywords, as well as modify the user that it should run as.

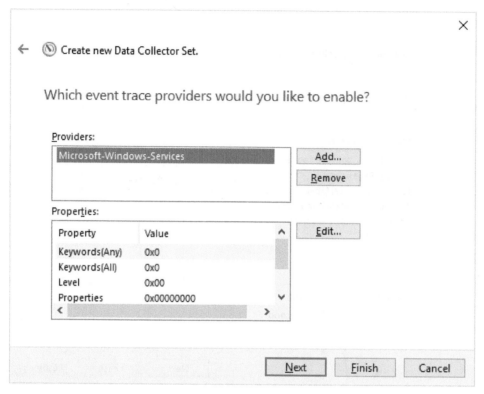

Figure 12-18   Specifying event trace providers

- *Directory* allows you to specify the directory path and naming convention for log files.
- *Security* allows you to specify permissions that allow other users to manage and view results for the data collector set.
- *Schedule* allows you to create a regular schedule on which to run the data collector set, such as at 10:00am every weekday.
- *Stop Condition* allows you to specify conditions that are used to automatically stop a data collector set, such as a maximum time duration or log file size.
- *Task* allows you to run a specified task each time the data collector set is stopped.

Note

The System folder shown in Figure 12-14 contains several predefined data collector sets that you can start in order to monitor system performance and configuration.

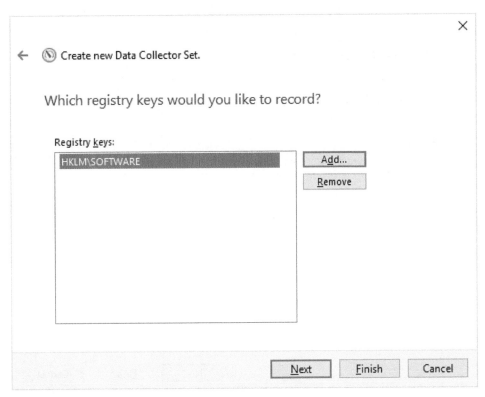

Figure 12-19   Specifying Windows Registry keys

 Note

The Startup Event Trace Sessions folder in Figure 12-14 contains several predefined data collector sets that monitor event trace providers on the system. If you right-click one of these data collector sets, click Properties, highlight the Trace Session tab and select Enabled, it will automatically start next time your system is booted and be displayed under the Event Trace Sessions folder.

Creating a Performance Counter Alert

The process used to create a performance counter alert is almost identical to the process used to create a data collector set for collecting and logging data. If you select Performance Counter Alert in Figure 12-16 and click Next, you are prompted to specify performance counters and the associated alert values, as shown in Figure 12-22. The configuration shown in Figure 12-22 will log data only when the *% Free Space* performance counter under the *LogicalDisk* object for the *C:* instance falls below a value of 30. After you click

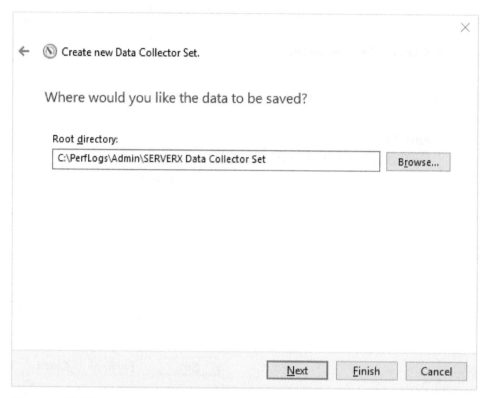

Figure 12-20   Specifying the log folder path

Next in Figure 12-22, you are prompted to configure the same data collector set options shown in Figure 12-21. After you click Finish in Figure 12-21, you can manage the performance counter alert as you would any other data collector set.

Viewing the Results of a Data Collector Set

After you stop a data collector set, you can view the data that has been collected. To view the data collected from performance counters, you can expand the User Defined folder under the Reports folder and select the appropriate report under the folder for your data collector set, as shown in Figure 12-23. Each report is named for the date that the data collector set was started using the Computername_*YYYYMMDD*-SerialNumber format, where *YYYY* is the year, *MM* is the month, and *DD* is the day.

The log file that stores the data shown in Figure 12-23 is located in a folder called SERVERX_20200206-000001 under the folder path specified in Figure 12-20. To view the contents of this folder, you can right-click SERVERX_20200206-000001 in Figure 12-23 and click View, Folder as shown in Figure 12-24:

- *DataCollector01.blg* contains data collected from performance counters and can be opened using the Performance MMC snap-in (Figure 12-23).

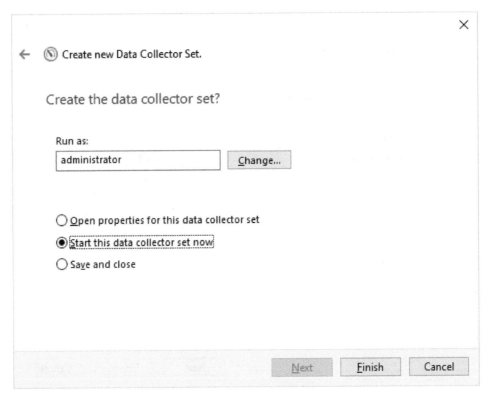

Figure 12-21   Specifying data collector set options

- *DataCollector02.etl* contains data collected from event trace providers and can be opened by one of many different third-party programs, as well as the **PerfView** program available from Microsoft.
- *DataCollector03.xml* contains system information from the Windows Registry and can be opened using any program that can read XML data, such as a Web browser or Microsoft Word.

Event Viewer

When troubleshooting problems that affect a particular system component, service, or application, you can often obtain details regarding the nature of the problem by examining event information stored in **event logs**. You can use the **Event Viewer** tool

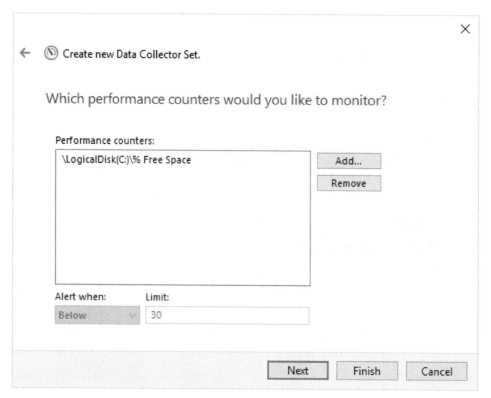

Figure 12-22   Configuring a performance counter alert

shown in Figure 12-25 to view event logs and the events they contain. To start Event Viewer, you can click Event Viewer from the Tools menu in Server Manager, right-click the Start menu and click Event Viewer, or run the `eventvwr.exe` command from a Windows Run, PowerShell, or Command Prompt window.

Five standard Windows event logs are available under the Windows Logs folder in the Event Viewer navigation pane shown in Figure 12-25:

- *Application* stores events from software applications on the system.
- *Security* stores auditing events, such as a successful or failed attempt to access a file.
- *Setup* stores events from the installation of server roles and features.
- *System* stores operating system-related events, including service startup, hardware errors, and events related to authorization and authentication.
- *Forwarded Events* stores events that were obtained from computers on the network using an **event subscription**. To create an event subscription, you can right-click the Subscriptions folder in Figure 12-25 and click Create Subscription.

To limit the number of events recorded in the Application and System event logs, Windows creates additional event logs for system and software components that normally

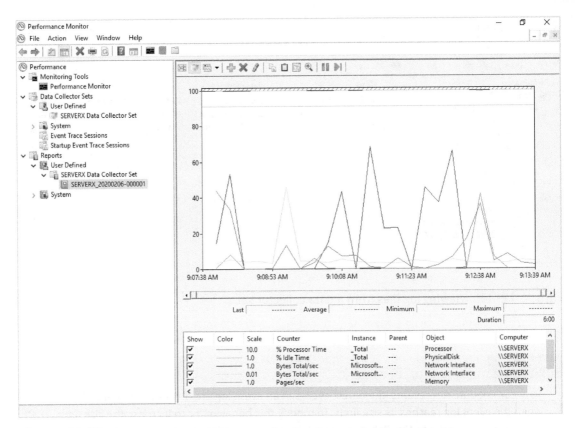

Figure 12-23   Viewing performance counter data from a data collector set

contain a large number of events. These events are located under the *Applications and Services Logs* folder in the navigation pane of Event Viewer shown in Figure 12-25. For example, hardware-related events are stored in the *Hardware Events* event log, whereas events from the DNS Server service are stored in the *DNS Server* event log. Moreover, the *Microsoft* folder under *Applications and Services Logs* in Figure 12-25 contains several subfolders that contain event logs for individual Windows components.

> **Note** 📎
>
> To save the events in an event log to a file for documentation purposes, you can select the event log in the navigation pane, click Save All Events As from the Actions pane, and specify the file location and format. After you have saved the contents of an event log, you can click Clear Log from the Actions pane to clear its contents.

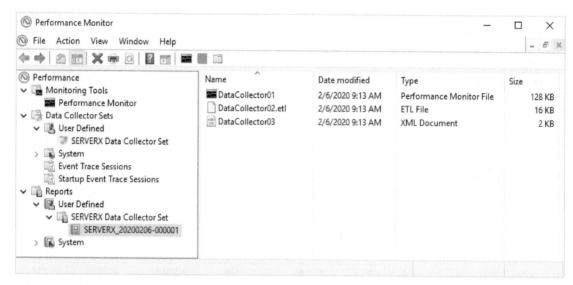

Figure 12-24   Viewing log files from a data collector set

To accommodate new events, the oldest events in an event log are deleted automatically when the event log reaches its size limit. To modify this behavior, or to increase the size limit for an event log, you can highlight the event log in the navigation pane of Event Viewer and click Properties in the Actions pane.

Viewing Events

Each event displayed in Event Viewer contains a level that indicates the type or severity of the event. Six different event levels are available:

- *Information*—Indicates that a component or application successfully performed an operation. These events are identified by a blue "i" icon.
- *Warning*—Indicates a problem that may interrupt the functionality of an application, service, or system. These events are identified by a yellow exclamation point icon.
- *Error*—Indicates a problem that prevents an application, service, or system from functioning properly. These events are identified by a red exclamation point icon.
- *Critical*—Indicates a problem that prevents system access or causes system instability. These events are identified by a red "x" icon.
- *Audit Success*—Indicates a successful auditing event. These events are only available in the Security event log and are identified by a yellow key icon.

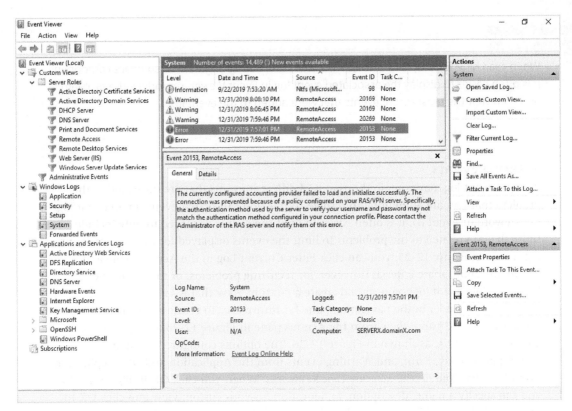

Figure 12-25 Event Viewer

- *Audit Failure*—Indicates a failed auditing event. These events are only available in the Security event log and are identified by a yellow key icon.

The System event log selected in the navigation pane of Figure 12-25 displays Information, Warning, and Error level events in the System pane. Furthermore, the event selected in the System pane in Figure 12-25 displays the event description, as well as other properties, including an event ID number and the date that the event was logged. You can copy the event description or ID number into a search engine (e.g., Google) or the search text box at docs.microsoft.com to locate possible solutions to problems identified by the event.

Note 🖉

To search for the next occurrence of a certain event in an event log, you can click Find from the Actions pane in Event Viewer and specify an event ID or keyword.

Note 📎

When searching for events related to a problem that affects a system or software component, it is often easier to display the associated event log in Event Viewer, reproduce the problem, and then view the most recent events that were added to the event log.

Filtering Events

A single event log may contain thousands of different events that are unrelated to the problem that you are attempting to resolve. While you can search events in an event log by keyword or event ID, it is often easier to limit the events displayed to only include those that are related to the problem. To limit the events displayed for the System event log shown in Figure 12-25, you can click Filter Current Log in the Actions pane and specify the appropriate criteria. However, for recurring problems, or to display events from multiple event logs, you should create a **custom view** that is saved under the Custom Views folder in the navigation pane for future use. To create a custom view, you can click Create Custom View from the Actions pane in Figure 12-25 and specify the appropriate criteria, as shown in Figure 12-26. The options configured in Figure 12-26 will display Critical, Error, and Warning events from the Application and DFS Replication event logs that contain the *Response Time* keywords. When you click OK in Figure 12-26, you can specify a name, description, and location for your custom view and click OK to create it. Following this, you can select the custom view in the navigation pane of Event Viewer to display the associated events.

Each time you install a new server role, a custom view that displays the associated events is automatically created in the Server Roles folder under the Custom Views folder in the navigation pane, as shown earlier in Figure 12-25. These custom views can be used to quickly locate problems related to a server role. For example, the RemoteAccess event from the System event log shown in Figure 12-25 would be easier to locate by selecting the Remote Access custom view. Furthermore, the Administrative Events custom view shown in Figure 12-25 displays only Critical, Error, and Warning events for each event log on the system, and can be used to quickly locate events after reproducing a problem.

Note 📎

You can also use the Get-EventLog cmdlet in Windows PowerShell to view the events in an event log.

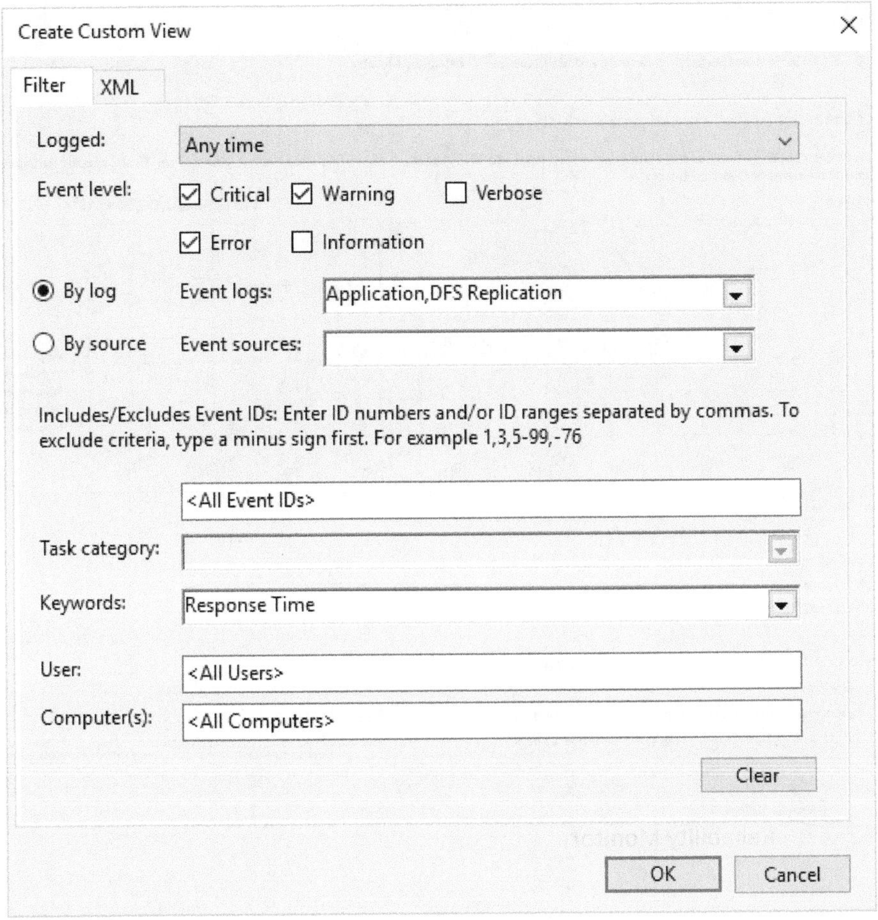

Figure 12-26   Creating a custom view

Reliability Monitor

While custom views in Event Viewer are often useful when troubleshooting a specific problem, they do not easily indicate event trends over a period of time in order to proactively identify system stability or performance problems. To do this, you can use the **Reliability Monitor** shown in Figure 12-27. You can start the Reliability Monitor by navigating to *System and Security, Security and Maintenance* in Event Viewer and clicking *View reliability history* under the Maintenance section. Alternatively, you can run the perfmon.exe /rel command from a Windows Run, PowerShell, or Command Prompt window to start the Reliability Monitor.

The highlighted day on the graph shown in Figure 12-27 indicates that there were critical application failures, warnings, and information events during that time

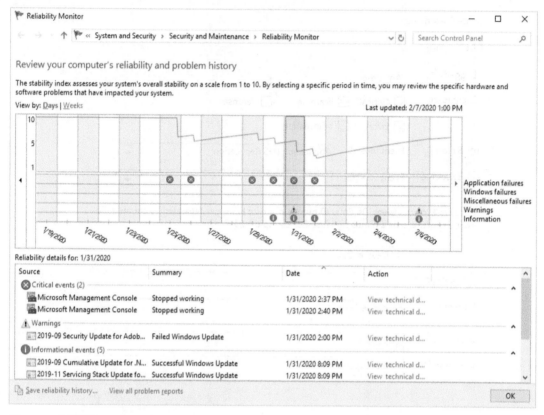

Figure 12-27   Reliability Monitor

that resulted in a lower system stability index value (blue line). If the stability index in Reliability Monitor value drops over a period of time, you can take steps to resolve the associated issues before system performance and stability is affected. To view more information about an event shown in the Reliability Monitor, you can double-click it under the *Reliability details for* pane.

Resolving Common System Problems

The possible problems that can arise on Windows Server 2019 systems are too numerous to list here. However, as a troubleshooter, you'll most often face a set of the common problems described in this section. Most Windows Server 2019 problems can be divided into five categories: hardware-related, performance-related, software-related, operating system-related, and network-related.

Hardware-Related Problems

Failure of hardware components is common in environments where servers are continually under heavy load. In some cases, the hardware component fails entirely, preventing the system from using it. However, in other cases, hardware components may fail intermittently, or malfunction by sending large amounts of information to the processor when not in use. This process, known as **jabbering**, can slow down a processor and, hence, the rest of the Windows system. You can detect jabbering by monitoring the *% Interrupt Time* performance counter in the *Processor* performance object. Hardware device failures of any kind will be recorded in the Hardware Events event log. System components, services, and applications will also generate Error events in other event logs when they are unable to access the hardware device. Together, these events will result in a lower stability index in Reliability Monitor.

Because hard disks and SSDs are used frequently, they are the most common hardware component to fail. If the Windows system uses a fault tolerant storage configuration (e.g., RAID level 1, 5, or 6), the data on the failed storage device can be regenerated after you replace it with a new one, as discussed in Module 7.

If, however, the Windows system does not use a fault tolerant storage configuration and the failed storage device does not contain the system or boot volume, you can perform the following steps to recover the data:

1. Power down the system and replace the failed storage device.
2. Boot the Windows system.
3. Recreate the volumes on the replaced storage device.
4. Restore the original data from a backup.

Alternatively, if the failed storage device contained the system or boot partition, and you have a full backup of the operating system (the *Bare metal backup* option in Windows Server Backup), you can perform the following steps to restore the full backup:

1. Power down the system and replace the failed storage device.
2. Boot the system using Windows Server 2019 installation media and click *Repair your computer* at the Windows Server 2019 installation page (shown earlier in Figure 1-16).
3. Click *Troubleshoot*, and then click *System Image Recovery*.
4. Click *Windows Server* and supply the location of the full system backup in the *Re-image your computer wizard*.

If the failed storage device contained the system or boot partition, and you don't have a full backup of the operating system, you can perform the following steps to rebuild the system:

1. Power down the system and replace the failed storage device.
2. Boot the system using Windows Server 2019 installation media, recreating the same volumes that were on the original system and perform a new Windows Server 2019 installation.
3. Configure the system with the original computer name.

4. Reset the existing Active Directory computer account.
5. Join the system to the Active Directory domain. If the failed system was a domain controller, you can install and configure Active Directory Domain Services again.
6. Restore the original user data from backup.

Note

To reduce problems caused by hardware malfunction, most organizations retire computer equipment after three to five years of use (the warranty period for most hardware).

Performance-Related Problems

Performance problems occur when the software on a system requires more hardware resources than is currently available. As a result, resolving performance problems often involves reducing the amount of software that is run on a system or adding additional hardware resources.

To minimize the change of performance problems, you should first examine the services that are running on a system and remove or disable any unnecessary ones to prevent them from consuming system resources. For example, if you have installed the DHCP service on a server for test purposes and then no longer require it, the service should be uninstalled, or disabled. You can click the Status column on the Services tab of Task Manager shown in Figure 12-9 to sort the available service list, and then review those that are currently running. If you identify an unnecessary service, you can right-click the service and click Stop. Next, you must prevent the service from starting at boot time. To do this, you can click Open Services in Figure 12-9 to open the Services tool. Next, you can right-click the service in the Services tool, click Properties, and select Disabled from the *Startup type* drop-down box, as shown in Figure 12-28 for the Application Layer Gateway Service.

Note

You can also use Windows PowerShell to stop and disable services. For example, to stop and disable the Application Layer Gateway Service shown in Figure 12-28, you could run the `Stop-Service ALG ; Set-Service ALG -StartupType disabled` command in Windows PowerShell.

If the performance information shown by Task Manager or Resource Monitor indicate that necessary processes are consuming too many resources on a system, or current performance counters for hardware components vary greatly from their baseline values, you can adjust the number of processes competing for hardware resources to resolve

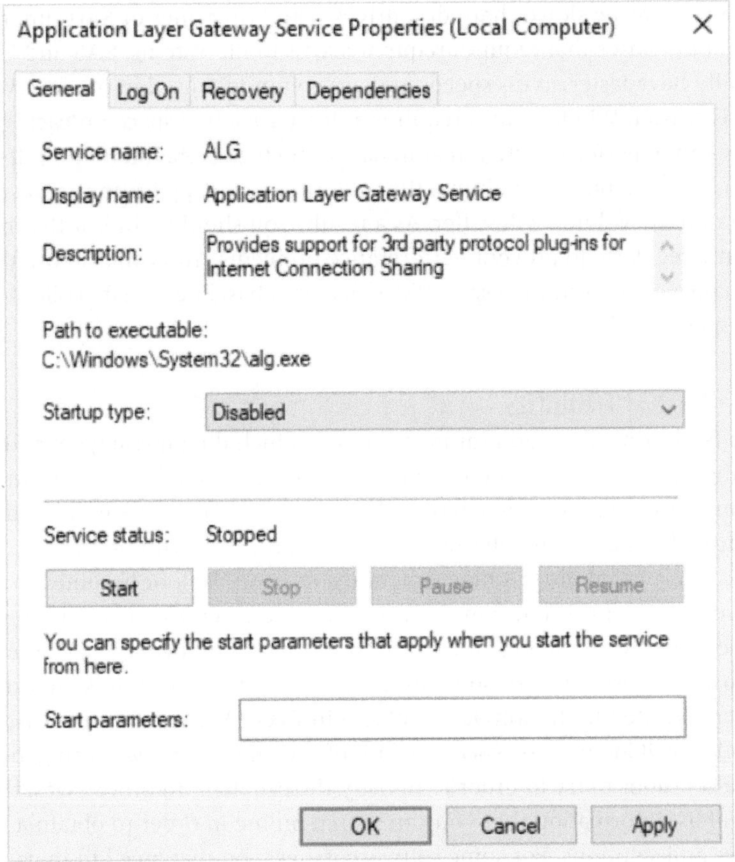

Figure 12-28   Disabling a service

the performance problem. For example, if other systems in your organization are under-utilized, you can move some applications and server roles to those systems to provide adequate resources for existing applications and sever roles.

Performance problems can also be remedied by altering the hardware. Upgrading or adding another processor allows the Windows system to execute processes faster and reduce the number of processes running concurrently on the processor. Some devices can perform processing tasks that are normally performed by the processor; this is known as **bus mastering**. Upgrading hardware components to include bus mastering reduces the amount of processing the processor must perform and, hence, increases system speed. Most modern server systems use bus mastering disk controllers and network interfaces as a result.

Adding physical memory to the computer also increases system speed because it gives processes more working space in memory and reduces the use of the paging file. Because the operating system, hardware devices, and processes use memory constantly, adding physical memory to any system often has a profound impact on system performance.

In addition, replacing slower hard disk drives with faster ones or SSDs improves the performance of programs that require frequent access to filesystems. SAS and NVMe devices typically have faster access speeds and are commonly used in modern Windows servers for this reason. Windows also requires at least 20% free space on each volume for file caches and to perform system maintenance, such as defragmentation. If less than 20% free space is available on a volume, the performance of applications and services that store data on the volume will suffer. As a result, you should monitor the free space on each volume regularly to prevent performance problems. You can also use the *% Free Space* performance counter in the *LogicalDisk* object in a baseline or data collector set to monitor free space.

Software-Related Problems

Processes can fail during execution for many reasons, including missing dependencies, incorrect configuration settings, software bugs, or conflicting applications. Restrictive file permissions, incorrect file ownership, and missing environment variables may also prevent a process from accessing files needed for the process to run properly.

In some cases, a failed process may generate a memory leak or become a rogue process that you can identify and remove using Task Manager. However, in most cases, the failed process will stop and log an event to the Application event log, or the event log for the particular server role or software component. As a result, it is important to search for events related to the software problem in Event Viewer. In some cases, the event description will identify the specific cause of the failure, and you can generate a list of possible solutions to try in order to remedy the problem. In other cases, the event description will list information that you can search online in order to obtain a list of possible causes and solutions. For some software issues, you may need to update or reinstall the software to remedy the problem.

Operating System-Related Problems

The Windows operating system can also encounter problems that prevent it from running properly. For example, system file corruption or an incorrect device driver or configuration change in the Windows Registry can cause the system to crash, or prevent the system from booting successfully. In the case of a system crash, you should first ensure that you have the latest critical updates for the software on your system. Next, you should examine the contents of the System event log in Event Viewer at the time of the system crash to identify possible causes and solutions. If the system fails to boot following a crash, you can access the **Advanced Boot Options** menu at boot time to remedy the problem. To enable the Advanced Boot Options menu, you must perform the following tasks:

1. Boot the system using Windows Server 2019 installation media and click *Repair your computer* at the Windows Server 2019 installation page (shown earlier in Figure 1-16).
2. Click *Troubleshoot*, and then click *Command Prompt*.

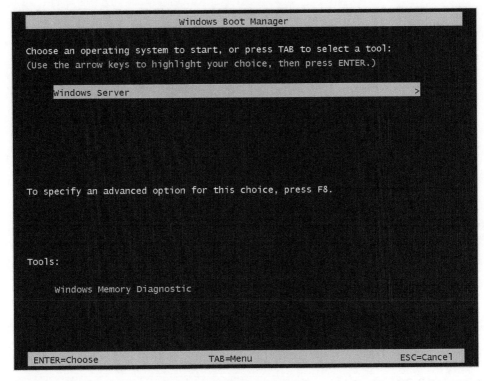

Figure 12-29   The Windows Boot Manager screen

3. Execute the `bcdedit.exe /set {bootmgr} displaybootmenu yes timeout 15` command to configure the Windows boot loader to display the Windows Boot Manager screen at boot time for 15 seconds. Press **Enter**.
4. Shut down your system and remove the Windows Server 2019 installation media.
5. Restart your Windows Server 2019 system.
6. When you see the Windows Boot Manager screen shown in Figure 12-29, press the **F8** key to access the Advanced Boot Options menu shown in Figure 12-30 and described in Table 12-2.

Network-Related Problems

Problems related to the network are common in most environments. The most common network issues that server administrators encounter relate to network connectivity, service access, and network latency.

Network Connectivity Issues

If you are unable to connect to other computers on the network from a Windows Server 2019 system, first determine if the associated network interface has a valid IP configuration and is connected properly to the LAN. You can run the `ipconfig /all`

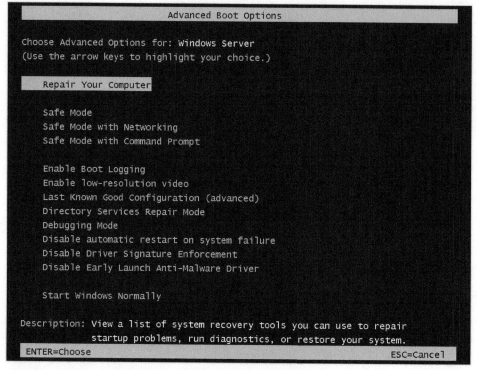

Figure 12-30   The Advanced Boot Options menu

Table 12-2   Advanced Boot Options menu options

Option	Description
Repair Your Computer	Allows you to access tools that can automatically repair boot issues or recover a system from backup. Choose this option first when troubleshooting a problem that prevents the system from booting.
Safe Mode	Boots the system without network connectivity using the minimum configuration of devices and drivers. You can enter **Safe Mode** to access files and programs that allow you to resolve an issue that prevents the system from booting.
Safe Mode with Networking	Boots the system with network connectivity using the minimum configuration of devices and drivers.
Safe Mode with Command Prompt	Boots the system without network connectivity or a graphical desktop using the minimum configuration of devices and drivers. Access to a command prompt is provided in this mode only.
Enable Boot Logging	Creates a record of device drivers and software components that were loaded at boot time (C:\Windows\ntbtlog.txt). The last line of this file indicates the device driver or software component that prevented the system from successfully booting.

Table 12-2   Advanced Boot Options menu options *(continued)*

Option	Description
Enable low-resolution video	Boots the system using basic video drivers. Choosing this option allows you to start a system that failed to boot due to an incorrect video driver.
Last Known Good Configuration (advanced)	Boots the system using the information in the Windows Registry used for the last successful boot. Choosing this option allows you to start a system that failed to boot previously due to incorrect settings in the Windows Registry or a recently added device driver.
Directory Services Repair Mode	Boots a domain controller into Safe Mode with Networking, without loading Active Directory services. You can access this mode to restore a System State backup (which includes the Active Directory database) on a domain controller that has a corrupted Active Directory database.
Debugging Mode	Boots the system while transmitting detailed event data to another computer over a serial or USB connection.
Disable automatic restart on system failure	Prevents the system from automatically restarting if it fails.
Disable Driver Signature Enforcement	Allows unsigned device drivers to be installed. This option allows you to install drivers from trusted vendors that do not have a valid digital signature.
Disable Early Launch Anti-Malware Driver	Prevents Microsoft Defender from scanning drivers for malware at boot time. This option allows you to start a system that cannot boot due to a device driver that Microsoft Defender deems suspicious.
Start Windows Normally	Starts the system without any special options.

command at Windows PowerShell or Command Prompt window to view the IP configuration of each network interface on the system. If a network interface uses DHCP to obtain IP settings, also ensure that the DHCP server is available on the network and has not exhausted its range of IP addresses.

Following this, you should test connectivity to the IP address of your network interface using the `ping` *IPaddress* command at a Command Prompt window, or the `Test-NetConnection` *IPaddress* command in Windows PowerShell. If you do not receive a successful response, then the device driver for your network interface has experienced a failure that can be solved by rebooting the system.

Next, you should test connectivity to an IP address on the same LAN as your network interface using the `ping` or `Test-NetConnection` command. If you are unable to connect to other computers on your LAN, you may need to reboot your network switch.

After testing local LAN access, you should test connectivity to an IP address on another LAN, or a public IP address on the Internet using the `ping` or `Test-NetConnection` command. If you are unable to connect to computers outside of your LAN, you may not have the correct default gateway configured on your network interface, or a router between your computer and the target IP address has failed, contains incorrect configuration, or is experiencing high load. You can supply the target IP address as an argument to the `tracert` or `Test-NetConnection -TraceRoute` command to determine which router is the source of the problem.

If you can access both local and remote LANs from your system by IP address, then the issue is likely due to name resolution. Test connectivity to the FQDN of a computer on network (e.g., using the `ping FQDN` or `Test-NetConnection FQDN` command). If connectivity to the computer's FQDN fails, then ensure that your network interface lists the correct DNS server for name resolution, and that the DNS server is available on the network. If the DNS server is unavailable, you can specify an alternate DNS server in your network interface configuration to obtain network connectivity.

Note

When using `ping` or `Test-NetConnection`, it is best to choose a target computer that does not have a firewall enabled. Firewalls often block ICMP, preventing these commands from receiving a successful response. In this case, you can determine whether the target computer was contacted successfully by looking for the target computer's IP address in the MAC address cache on your computer. You can use the `arp -a` command to display the MAC address cache.

Service Access Issues

If clients are unable to contact a particular service running on your server from across the network, you should start troubleshooting at the server itself. First, use Task Manager to determine if the network service is running, and start the service if necessary. If the network service fails to start, then check the associated event in the System event log to determine why the service failed to start, searching the description online if necessary. Incorrect configuration settings, restrictive folder or file permissions, and other programs that are listening to the same TCP or UDP port number can prevent a service from starting successfully.

Next, determine if the service is listening on the correct port number using the `netstat -a` command at a Command Prompt window, or the `Get-NetTCPConnection` and `Get-NetUDPEndpoint` commands in Windows PowerShell. If the network service is configured to listen to a non-standard port number, then client programs will also need to specify the non-standard port number for a connection to be successful.

Following this, attempt to interact with the network service locally to see if it is responding to requests on the correct port number. For example, to interact with the local Web server listening on port 80, you could run the `Test-NetConnection -Port 80 localhost` command and see if it responds successfully. If there is no response, you may need to restart the Web server service or verify that it has the correct settings in its configuration files.

If the network service is responding to requests, you should attempt to access the network service from the local computer using an appropriate client program. For example, to obtain the default Web page from the local Web server, you could access the URL `http://localhost` from a local Web browser or run the `Invoke-WebRequest localhost` command in Windows PowerShell. If you are unable to obtain the default Web page, then local file permissions on the Web page file or incorrect Web server configuration could be the cause.

Next, you should attempt to access the service from another computer on the network by connecting to the service by IP address. If you are able to access a service locally, but are unable to access the same service from across a network by IP address, then a firewall on the server or network is likely preventing the access. To remedy the issue, you can allow the protocol name or port number in the appropriate firewall configuration.

Finally, you should attempt to access the service from another computer on the network by connecting to the service using the FQDN. If you can access the service from another computer by IP address but not by FQDN, then name resolution is the issue. Check to ensure that the other computer lists the correct DNS server and that the DNS server is online and contains the appropriate resource records (if authoritative), or cached records (if non-authoritative). You may need to clear the DNS cache on both the resolver and DNS server to remove incorrect records. Most problems that prevent clients from accessing services on a server are caused by incorrect resource records in a DNS zone file or DNS cache. This is often reflected by posts on websites and social media sites, such as the DNS haiku shown in Figure 12-31.

Figure 12-31 A popular DNS haiku from Reddit

Network Latency Issues

Sometimes, a network is properly configured, but the time it takes for services to respond to network requests is very high or users receive occasional timeout errors when attempting to connect to a service. This problem is called **network latency** and can occur when a network is saturated with traffic or has limited bandwidth.

To determine if a particular service or application is saturating the network, you can examine the traffic that is passing to and from your network interface using a third-party **packet sniffer** program. If, for example, you notice a very large number of DHCPDISCOVER or DHCPREQUEST packets on the network, then the DHCP server service is likely unavailable, and the client computers attempting to renew their IP configuration are saturating the network with DHCP requests.

> **Note** 📎
>
> Many third-party packet sniffer programs are available. **Wireshark** is a free packet sniffer program that you can download from *https://wireshark.org*.

You can also test the network latency between your computer and other computers on the network to identify bandwidth problems. To test the latency (in milliseconds) to a target computer by IP address, you can use the `pathping IPaddress` command at a Command Prompt window, or the `Test-NetConnection -InformationLevel Detailed IPaddress` command in Windows PowerShell.

In some cases, network latency can be caused by firewall devices that are restricting network throughput, or by a malfunctioning network interface, switch, or router that is dropping IP packets instead of processing them. In this case, rebooting the affected device often remedies the problem. If network latency affects a single computer, then an application on that computer is probably sending or receiving a large amount of data on the network interface. Using Resource Monitor to list the top processes accessing the network can help you identify which one is causing the problem.

Module Summary

- Maintaining the integrity of a Windows server involves monitoring, proactive maintenance, and reactive maintenance. Reactive maintenance is further composed of troubleshooting procedures.

- Task Manager can be used to quickly analyze the performance of a system, as well as identify and stop rogue processes and memory leaks.

- Resource Monitor can be used to display the specific hardware resources used by processes on the system.
- Performance counters can be added to Performance Monitor to obtain detailed system performance information.
- You can configure data collector sets to collect and log data from performance counters, event trace providers, or system configuration information in the Windows Registry.
- Baselines document normal activity. You can use Performance Monitor or data collector sets to create baselines that can be used to identify possible causes of performance problems.
- Event logs store a detailed record of system and application notifications organized by event level and can be viewed using Event Viewer or Reliability Monitor.
- Different troubleshooting procedures are used to solve hardware-related, performance-related, software-related, operating system-related, and network-related problems.

Key Terms

Advanced Boot Optionsbaseline	Event Viewer	performance object
bus mastering	handle	PerfView
cached memory	instance	proactive maintenance
committed memory	jabbering	process
custom view	memory leak	reactive maintenance
data collector set	monitoring	Reliability Monitor
Data Collector Sets	network latency	Resource Monitor
Distributed Denial of Service (DDoS)	non-paged pool	rogue process
dump file	packet sniffer	Safe Mode
event log	page fault	Task Manager
event subscription	paged pool	thread
event trace provider	performance counter	troubleshooting procedure
	performance counter alert	Wireshark
	Performance Monitor	

Review Questions

1. On which part of the maintenance cycle do server administrators spend the most time?
   a. Monitoring
   b. Proactive maintenance
   c. Reactive maintenance
   d. Documentation

2. Many organizations store system documentation in help desk ticketing software. True or False?

3. Which of the following steps is not a common troubleshooting procedure?
   a. Test possible solutions
   b. Isolate the problem
   c. Delegate responsibility
   d. Collect information

4. A baseline is a set of performance information for a system during normal times of operation. True or False?

5. Which of the following can be easily identified on the Processes tab of Task Manager? (Choose all that apply.)
   a. Rogue processes
   b. The number of bytes a process is sending to and from the network
   c. The files that a process is using
   d. Memory leaks

6. Committed memory refers to the memory that is used by the Windows kernel and device drivers. True or False?

7. Which task should you perform in Task Manager before stopping a problematic process for a program that was created by your organization?
   a. Right-click the process and click *Create dump file*
   b. Right-click the process and click *Search online*
   c. Right-click the process and click *Analyze wait chain*
   d. Right-click the process and click *UAC virtualization*

8. Resource Monitor allows you to identify the storage devices and files that a single process is accessing. True or False?

9. Which of the following components represents a specific hardware device or software component that can be monitored?
   a. Performance object
   b. Performance alert
   c. Performance counter
   d. Instance

10. Which of the following performance counters can be used to identify jabbering hardware?
    a. Pages/sec
    b. % Interrrupt Time
    c. Committed Bytes
    d. Bytes Total/sec

11. Each server role and feature that is added to a Windows Server 2019 system also adds additional performance objects and counters. True or False?

12. Which two tools are commonly used to create performance baselines? (Choose two answers.)
    a. Performance Monitor
    b. Task Manager
    c. Data Collector Sets
    d. Event Viewer

13. Performance baselines are typically created only after installing a new Windows Server 2019 system. True or False?

14. Which of the following can be included in a data collector set? (Choose all that apply.)
    a. Performance counter
    b. Dump files
    c. Event trace provider
    d. Windows Registry key

15. There are five event levels available in an event log: Information, Warning, Error, Audit Success and Audit Failure. True or False?

16. What can you create in Event Viewer to display specific types of events from one or more event logs?
    a. Event filter
    b. Custom view
    c. Data collector set
    d. Event alert

17. Reliability Monitor displays a system stability index value for each day based on the values of specific performance counters. True or False?

18. Which of the following actions can be performed to solve a performance problem? (Choose all that apply.)
    a. Stop and disable unnecessary services
    b. Move applications to other systems

c. Add additional hardware

d. Upgrade hardware devices with bus mastering versions

19. Searching an event description or event ID online can generate a list of possible causes and associated solutions for a problem. True or False?

20. Which of the following options on the Advanced Boot Options menu can be used to start a system that failed to boot previously due to incorrect settings in the Windows Registry, or a recently added device driver?

a. Safe Mode

b. Debugging Module

c. Disable Driver Signature Enforcement

d. Last Known Good Configuration (advanced)

Hands-On Projects

These Hands-On Projects should be completed in the order given and normally take a total of three hours or less to complete. The requirements for these projects include:

- A system with Windows Server 2019 installed according to Hands-On Project 1-1 (Lab Environment 1) or Hands-On Project 1-2 (Lab Environment 2).
- A WindowsServer2019VM2 virtual machine installed according to Hands-On Project 3-5 and configured as a member server according to Hands-On Project 5-2.

Project 12-1: Monitoring Performance and Processes

In this Hands-On Project, you use Task Manager on your Windows Server 2019 host to monitor system performance, as well as monitor and manage processes and services. Following this, you examine process resources using Resource Monitor.

1. Boot your Windows Server 2019 host and log into domain*X*.com as Administrator using the password **Secret555**.

2. Right-click the taskbar and then click **Task Manager**.

3. Highlight the **Performance** tab and note the information regarding your processor, as well as the current utilization and number of processes, threads, and handles.

    a. Select **Memory** and note the physical memory that is in use, as well as the committed, cached, paged, and non-paged memory.

    b. Select the first **Ethernet** network interface and note the speed at which traffic is sent and received on the interface.

    c. Select the second **Ethernet** network interface and note the speed at which traffic is sent and received on the interface.

4. Highlight the **Processes** tab.

    a. Click **CPU** to sort the process list by processor utilization and note the top processes using the processor.

    b. Click **Memory** to sort the process list by memory utilization and note the top processes using system memory.

    c. Right-click the **Windows Explorer** process and note the options available. Click **Restart** to restart Windows Explorer.

5. Highlight the **Users** tab and expand **Administrator** to view the processes started as the Administrator user. Note that both Windows Explorer and Task Manager are started.

   a. Right-click the **Windows Explorer** process and note the options available. Click **Go to details** to view the Windows Explorer process on the Details tab. Note the PID, status, user name, CPU utilization, memory utilization, and UAC virtualization value for the explorer.exe (Windows Explorer) process.

   b. Right-click the **explorer.exe** process and note the options available. Click **Set priority** and then click **Above normal**. Click **Change priority** to run the process with a higher priority.

6. Highlight the **Services** tab and click **Status** to sort the list of available services by status. Right-click **EventLog** and note the options available. Click **Restart** to restart the Windows Event Log service.

7. Highlight the **Performance** tab and click **Open Resource Monitor**.

8. On the Overview tab of Resource Monitor, expand the **Disk** section and note the processes that are currently writing to files on the system. More active processes are listed first.

9. Expand the **Network** section and note the processes that are currently sending and receiving data on the network. Processes that are sending more data are listed first.

10. Expand the **Memory** section and note the processes that are currently sending and receiving bytes on the network. Processes that use more physical and virtual memory are listed first.

11. In the CPU section, select the **System** process (which represents the Windows kernel and operating system services). Note the files that are currently being accessed by the System process under the Disk section, the data being transferred in the Network section, and the physical and virtual memory used in the Memory section.

12. Highlight the **CPU** tab.

    a. Expand the **Associated Handles** section and note the handles used by the System process.

    b. Expand the **Associated Modules** section, and the shared libraries (.dll files) used by the System process.

13. Highlight the **Memory** tab and note the graphical breakdown of your memory usage.

14. Highlight the **Disk** tab.

    a. Expand the **Disk Activity** section and note the files that are currently being accessed by the System process, as well as the speed at which bytes are read from and written to each one.

    b. Expand the **Storage** section and note the volumes used by the System process, as well as the available space on each volume.

15. Highlight the **Network** tab.

    a. Expand the **Network Activity** section and note the computers on the network that the System process is communicating with, as well as the number of bytes that are sent and received per second for each network connection.

b. Expand the **TCP Connections** section and note the TCP ports and latency value for each network connection used by the System process.

c. Expand the **Listening Ports** section and note the TCP and UDP ports to which the System process is listening for network connections.

16. Close Resource Monitor and Task Manager.

Project 12-2: Creating a Baseline

In this Hands-On Project, you use Performance Monitor to create and view a baseline of system performance on your Windows Server 2019 host.

1. On your Windows Server 2019 host, click **Start** and then click **Server Manager**. Next, click the **Tools** menu and click **Performance Monitor** to open the Performance MMC snap-in.

2. In the Performance MMC snap-in, highlight **Performance Monitor** in the navigation pane.

3. Click the **X** icon in the toolbar to remove the default performance counter that was added.

4. Click the **+** icon in the toolbar to open the Add Counters window.

a. In the Available counters pane, expand the **Processor** performance object and select the **% Idle Time** performance counter. Next, select <**All instances**> and click Add to add the performance counter.

b. Repeat the previous step for all other performance counters listed in Table 12-1. Also ensure that you add a copy of the *% Free Space* performance counter for each volume instance on your system (e.g., C:, E:).

c. Click **OK** to add the performance counters to the Performance Monitor.

5. Select the drop-down box next to the **Change graph type** icon in the toolbar (third icon from the left) and select **Histogram bar** to view a bar chart of each performance counter.

6. Select the drop-down box next to the **Change graph type** icon in the toolbar again and select **Report** to view the values of each performance counter.

7. Right-click any area of the report and click **Save Settings As**. Type **C:\Perflogs\Baseline-SERVERX-*date*** in the File name text box and click Save, where *date* is the current date.

8. Right-click **Start** and then click **Run**. Type **C:\Perflogs** in the Run dialog box and click **OK** to open the C:\Perflogs folder in File Explorer.

9. Double-click the **Baseline-SERVERX-*date*.htm** file to open it with Internet Explorer and click **Allow blocked content** when prompted. Note the values in your baseline. Next, click **Unfreeze Display** in the website toolbar (represented by a green play icon) and click Yes to view the current values for each performance counter in your baseline.

10. Close Internet Explorer when finished.

Project 12-3: Creating Data Collector Sets

In this Hands-On Project, you create and start data collector sets on your Windows Server 2019 host, as well as create a performance alert. Following this, you view the performance data collected by your data collector sets.

1. In the Performance MMC snap-in on your Windows Server 2019 host, expand **Data Collector Sets** in the navigation pane and then expand **User Defined**. Note the default data collector set that can be started to monitor performance counters. Next, expand **System** and note the default system data collector sets that can be started to monitor Active Directory and system information.

2. Right-click **User Defined** and click **New**, **Data Collector Set**.

   a. At the Create new Data Collector Set wizard, type **Performance Baseline Data Collector Set** in the Name text box and click **Next**.

   b. On the *Which template would you like to use?* page, select **System Performance** and click **Next**.

   c. On the *Where would you like the data to be saved?* page, note the default folder path and click **Next**.

   d. On the *Create the data collector set?* page, click the **Change** button, supply a User name of **Administrator** and Password of **Secret555** and click OK. Select **Start this data collector set now** and click **Finish**. Note that your data collector set is now running.

3. Right-click **Performance Baseline Data Collector Set**, click **Properties**, and highlight the **Stop Condition** tab. Note that the data collector set will run for 1 minute to collect performance information by default and click **Cancel**. In the right pane, note that the System Performance template used to create the data collector set added both performance counters and event trace providers.

4. Right-click **User Defined** and click **New**, **Data Collector Set**.

   a. At the Create new Data Collector Set wizard, type **Active Directory Monitoring Data Collector Set** in the Name text box, select **Create manually (advanced)**, and click **Next**.

   b. On the *What type of data do you want to include?* page, select **Performance counter** and **Event trace data** and click **Next**.

   c. On the *What performance counters would you like to log?* page, click **Add**.

      i. In the Available counters pane, expand the **DirectoryServices** performance object, select the **DS Directory Searches/sec** performance counter and click **Add**.

      ii. Next, select the **LDAP Searches/sec** performance counter and click **Add**.

      iii. Click **OK** to add the two performance counters to the data collector set.

   d. Note the default sample interval of 15 seconds and click **Next**.

   e. On the *What event trace providers would you like to enable?* page, click **Add**. Select **Active Directory Domain Services: Core** and click **OK**. Click **Next**.

    f. On the *Where would you like the data to be saved?* page, note the default folder path and click **Next**.

    g. On the *Create the data collector set?* page, click the **Change** button, supply a User name of **Administrator** and Password of **Secret555** and click OK. Select **Start this data collector set now** and click **Finish**. Note that your data collector set is now running.

5. Right-click **User Defined** and click **New**, **Data Collector Set**.

    a. At the Create new Data Collector Set wizard, type **Hardware Failure Monitoring Data Collector Set** in the Name text box, select **Create manually (advanced)**, and click **Next**.

    b. On the *What type of data do you want to include?* page, select **Performance Counter Alert** and click **Next**.

    c. On the *What performance counters would you like to log?* page, click **Add**. In the Available counters pane, expand the **Processor** performance object, select the **% Interrupt Time** performance counter, click **Add**, and then click **OK**.

    d. Type **80** in the Limit text box to ensure that the *% Interrupt Time* performance counter is logged only if its value exceeds 80% and click **Next**.

    e. On the *Create the data collector set?* page, click the **Change** button, supply a User name of **Administrator** and Password of **Secret555** and click OK. Select **Start this data collector set now** and click **Finish**. Note that your data collector set is now running.

6. Right-click **Hardware Failure Monitoring Data Collector Set**, click **Properties**, and highlight the **Directory** tab. Note the default location used to store data for the performance alert and click **Cancel**.

7. Right-click **Active Directory Monitoring Data Collector Set** and click **Stop**.

8. Expand **Reports** in the navigation pane and then expand **User Defined**.

9. Expand **Performance Baseline Data Collector Set** and select **SERVERX_*date*-000001**.

    a. View the performance summary and resource overview in the right pane. Next, expand the **CPU, Network, Disk, Memory,** and **Report Statistics** sections in turn and note the results shown.

    b. Right-click **SERVERX_*date*-000001** and click **View**, **Performance Monitor**. Note the performance counters that were monitored by the data collector set for the 1 minute it was run.

10. Expand **Active Directory Monitoring Data Collector Set** and select **SERVERX_*date*-000001**.

    a. View the performance counter data collected in the Performance Monitor interface in the right pane.

    b. Right-click **SERVERX_*date*-000001** and click **View**, **Folder**. Note the DataCollector01. blg file that contains the performance counter data, as well as the DataCollector02.etl file that contains the event trace provider data.

11. Close the Performance MMC snap-in.

Project 12-4: Viewing Events

In this Hands-On Project, you explore events in Event Viewer on your Windows Server 2019 host, as well as create a custom view. Following this, you view the system stability index and associated events in the Reliability Monitor.

1. In Server Manager on your Windows Server 2019 host, click the **Tools** menu and then click **Event Viewer**.

2. Expand **Windows Logs** in the navigation pane and select the **Application** event log.

    a. In the Application pane, click the **Level** column to sort events by event level and note any Error events.

    b. Select an Error or Warning event of your choice and view the event description in the lower pane, as well as the event ID and keywords.

    c. Double-click the event description to select all of the event description text and click **Copy** in the Actions pane.

    d. Open a Web browser, navigate to **https://google.com** and paste your event description into the search text box by pressing the **Ctrl+v** key combination on your keyboard. Explore the results to locate possible causes and solutions to your Error event.

3. Repeat the tasks under the previous step for the following event logs:

    a. **System** under Windows Logs

    b. **DFS Replication** under Applications and Services Logs

    c. **DNS Server** under Applications and Services Logs

    d. **Hardware Events** under Applications and Services Logs

4. Select the **Application** event log in the navigation pane and click **Properties** in the Actions pane. Note the maximum log size of 20480 KB, and default action that overwrites events as needed and click **OK**.

5. Expand **Custom Views** in the navigation pane and select the **Administrative Events** custom view. Note that no Information level events are displayed in this custom view.

6. Expand the **Server Roles** folder under Custom Views and note the custom views created for each server role on your system. Select the **Print and Document Services** custom view and repeat the tasks under step 2.

7. Click **Create Custom View** in the Actions pane.

    a. At the Create Custom View window, select **Critical**, **Warning**, and **Error** in the Event level section.

    b. Click the Event logs drop-down box, expand **Applications and Services Logs**, **Microsoft**, **Windows**, select **Backup**, and press **Enter**.

    c. Click **OK**.

    d. At the Save Filter to Custom View window, type **Backup Events** in the Name text box and click **OK**. Note any Critical, Error, or Warning events related to backups in the Backup Events pane.

8. Close Event Viewer.

9. Right-click **Start** and click **Run**. Type **perfmon.exe /rel** in the Run dialog box and click **OK** to start the Reliability Monitor.

   a. Observe the stability index value for your system over the past three weeks.

   b. Highlight the day that had the lowest stability index value and note the events shown.

   c. Double-click the most serious event by event level, view the event information, and click **OK**.

10. Close Reliability Monitor.

Project 12-5: Testing Connectivity and Service Access

In this Hands-On Project, you use commands on your Windows Server 2019 host to test connectivity and service access.

1. On your Windows Server 2019 host, right-click **Start** and click **Windows PowerShell (Admin)**.

2. At the prompt, type **ipconfig /all** and press **Enter**. Note the IP configuration of each of your network interfaces.

3. At the prompt, type **ping IPaddress** and press **Enter**, where *IPaddress* is the IP address of the network interface connected to your classroom LAN. Note that you receive replies from your network interface.

4. At the prompt, type **ping IPaddress** and press **Enter**, where *IPaddress* is the IP address of your partner's network interface. If you do not receive replies from your partner's network interface, type **arp -a** and press **Enter**. You should see your partner's network interface listed in the MAC address table, indicating that a firewall on your partner's system has blocked ICMP traffic from the ping command.

5. At the prompt, type **ping 1.1.1.1** and press **Enter** to contact the one.one.one.one host on the Internet. If you do not receive replies, your organization's firewall may be blocking ICMP requests.

6. At the prompt, type **ping one.one.one.one** and press **Enter** to contact the one.one.one.one host on the Internet by FQDN. If you do not receive replies, the forwarding configuration on your DNS server configuration may be incorrect, or you may need to clear the DNS cache on your DNS server or client.

7. At the prompt, type **Test-NetConnection one.one.one.one** and press **Enter**. Note the results and latency value.

8. At the prompt, type **Test-NetConnection one.one.one.one -TraceRoute** and press **Enter**. Note the IP address of the routers that your request passed through to reach its destination.

9. At the prompt, type **tracert one.one.one.one** and press **Enter**. Note the IP address of the routers that your request passed through to reach its destination, as well as the latency values recorded for each one.

10. At the prompt, type **Get-NetTCPConnection** and press **Enter**. Note the TCP ports for which your system is listening.

11. At the prompt, type **Get-NetUDPEndpoint** and press **Enter**. Note the UDP ports for which your system is listening.

12. At the prompt, type **netstat -a** and press **Enter**. Note the TCP and UDP ports for which your system is listening.

13. At the prompt, type **Test-NetConnection -Port 53 localhost** and press **Enter**. Note that your server is responding to DNS requests on TCP port 53.

14. At the prompt, type **Test-NetConnection -Port 53 *IPaddress*** and press **Enter**, where *IPaddress* is the IP address of your partner's network interface. If the test fails, your partner's firewall is preventing access.

15. At the prompt, type **nslookup one.one.one.one *IPaddress*** and press **Enter**, where *IPaddress* is the IP address of your partner's network interface to resolve the FQDN of the one.one.one.one host using your partner's DNS server.

16. Close Windows PowerShell.

Project 12-6: Accessing Advanced Boot Options

In this Hands-On Project, you enable and access the Advanced Boot Options menu on your Windows Server 2019 host and use it to enable boot logging.

1. If you are using Lab Environment 1, insert the Windows Server 2019 DVD installation media into your DVD drive on your Windows Server 2019 host and proceed to step 3.

2. If you are using Lab Environment 2, click the **File** menu in your Virtual Machine Connection window and click **Settings**.

   a. Highlight **Firmware** under the Hardware section, select **DVD Drive** and click **Move Up** until it is listed first in the Boot order section.

   b. Highlight **DVD Drive** under the Hardware section, select **Image file** and click **Browse**. Navigate to the ISO image file for Windows Server 2019 and click **Open**.

   c. Click **OK**.

3. Right-click **Start**, click **Shut down or sign out**, **Restart**. Click Continue to reboot your system.

4. When prompted to Press any key to boot from CD or DVD, press **Enter** to boot from the Windows Server 2019 installation media.

5. Click **Next** and then click **Repair your computer**.

6. At the Choose an option screen, click **Troubleshoot**.

7. At the Advanced options screen, click **Command Prompt**.

8. At the prompt, type **bcdedit.exe /set {bootmgr} displaybootmenu yes timeout 15** and press **Enter**.

9. Close the command prompt window and click **Turn off your PC**.

10. Boot your Windows Server 2019 host. At the Windows Boot Manager screen, press the **F8** key and examine the different options on the Advanced Boot Options menu.

11. Navigate to the **Enable Boot Logging** option and press **Enter**.

12. After your system has booted, log into domain*X*.com as Administrator using the password **Secret555**.

13. Right-click **Start** and click **Run**. Type **notepad C:\Windows\ntbtlog.txt** in the Run dialog box and click **OK**. View the components loaded during your previous boot. Close Notepad when finished.

Exercise 12-1

Many free "stress test" programs are available for you to download and use to generate activity on a Windows system. Most of these stress test programs generate activity for a single area of the system (processor, storage I/O, memory, network). Use a search engine to locate and download a free stress test program available for Windows and execute it afterwards. Next, open the performance baseline that you created in Hands-On Project 12-2, view the current values for each performance counter and compare them to the values in the performance baseline. Note the differences between the current and baseline values in the system areas for which the stress test program generates activity.

Exercise 12-2

Recall that each server role that you install adds additional performance objects and counters to a system that can be used to take baseline measurements for the associated server services. In Hands-On Project 12-2, you created a performance baseline using Performance Monitor using the performance counters listed in Table 12-1. Create a new performance baseline using Performance Monitor that contains two counters of your choice from each of the following server roles: Active Directory Domain Services, Active Directory Certificate Services, DHCP Server, DNS Server, File and Storage Services, Hyper-V, Print and Document Services, Remote Access, Remote Desktop Services, Web Server (IIS), and Windows Server Update Services.

Exercise 12-3

In Hands-On Project 12-3, you created a data collector set called *Active Directory Monitoring Data Collector Set* that monitored the *Active Directory Domain Services: Core* event trace provider. Navigate to **https://github.com/Microsoft/perfview** in your Web browser and follow the instructions to download and run the **PerfView.exe** program. Next, open the **C:\Perflogs\Admin\Active Directory Monitoring Data Collector Set\SERVERX_date-000001\ DataCollector02.etl** file in PerfView and examine the trace information that was recorded.

Exercise 12-4

In Hands-On Project 12-4, you used Event Viewer to explore events on your Windows Server 2019 host. Event Viewer can also be used to retrieve events from other systems on the network using event subscriptions. Boot your WindowsServer2019VM2 virtual machine. Next, create an event subscription in Event Viewer on your Windows Server 2019 host that obtains Critical, Error, and Warning events from the System and Application logs on your WindowsServer2019VM2 virtual machine. Ensure that the event subscription is run as the Administrator user and stores events from the WindowsServer2019VM2 virtual machine in the Forwarded Events event log. Finally, create a custom view in Event Viewer on your Windows Server 2019 host that displays Critical, Error, and Warning events from the System and Application logs on both your Windows Server 2019 host and WindowsServer2019VM2 virtual machine.

Exercise 12-5

Recall that packet sniffer programs can be used to examine the traffic on a LAN to determine if a particular service or application is saturating the network. Open a Web browser, navigate to **https://wireshark.org** and follow the instructions to download and install the free Wireshark packet sniffer program. Next, open Wireshark and follow the instructions to capture and view the network traffic on your classroom LAN.

GLOSSARY

1U server—A rackmount server with a height of 1.75 inches. Larger rackmount servers have a height that is a multiple of a 1U server.

802.1X Wired—A standard that enhances the security of physical LANs through the use of RADIUS.

802.1X Wireless—A standard that enhances the security of WLANs through the use of RADIUS.

A

Access Control List (ACL)—A list of users and groups that identifies the permissions they have been granted to a resource.

access-based enumeration—An SMB feature that only displays shared folders that users have Read share and NTFS/ReFS permission to.

Active Directory—The Microsoft components and software that are used to provide single sign-on and centralized management of computers on a network.

Active Directory Administrative Center—A graphical tool that can configure objects within an Active Directory domain.

Active Directory Certificate Services—A component of Active Directory that provides centralized management of encryption certificates within a domain.

Active Directory Certificate Services—The Windows Server 2019 server role that implements a Certification Authority.

Active Directory Domains and Trusts—A graphical tool that can configure Active Directory functional levels and trust relationships.

Active Directory Recycle Bin—An Active Directory feature that allows deleted objects to be recovered easily.

Active Directory Sites and Services—A graphical tool that can configure Active Directory sites and global catalog services.

Active Directory Users and Computers—A graphical tool that can configure objects within an Active Directory domain.

Active Directory-based Activation role—A role that can be installed on a domain controller to provide automatic activation for computers that are joined to the same Active Directory domain.

Active Directory-integrated primary DNS server—A primary DNS server that stores its zone file in the Active Directory database.

active partition—The partition on which a standard BIOS searches for a boot loader.

active screening—A file screen configuration that is strictly enforced.

administrative template file—A file that can be imported into a GPO to provide administrative template settings for third party software.

ADSI Edit—A tool that can be used to view objects and attributes within the Active Directory database.

Advanced Boot Options—A menu that allows you to access troubleshooting tools and alternate startup methods at the beginning of a Windows boot process.

Advanced Encryption Standard (AES)—A symmetric encryption algorithm used by many different technologies.

Advanced Research Projects Agency Network (ARPANET)—The first network to implement the TCP/IP protocol.

Advanced Threat Protection (ATP)—An optional component of Microsoft Defender that can be used to provide cloud-based inspection for malware and network traffic.

alias provider—The PowerShell provider that is used to manage aliases within Windows PowerShell.

alias—A shortcut to a cmdlet within Windows PowerShell.

AMD-V—Hardware-assisted virtualization support available in some AMD processors.

ANDing—The process by which binary bits are compared to calculate the network and host IDs from an IP address and subnet mask.

Anything as a Service (XaaS)—A blanket term that refers to cloud services that are not specifically identified as SaaS, PaaS. or IaaS.

Apache Web server—A free and open-source Web server that is commonly run on Linux systems.

application pool—A feature of IIS that allows for the isolation and management of ASP and ASP.NET Web apps.

application programming interface (API)—A software interface that allows applications to access functions provided by an operating system.

AppSocket—An improved version of the HP JetDirect protocol used for printing to network-attached printers using TCP.

array variable—A variable that contains multiple, distinct values.

asymmetric encryption—A type of encryption that uses two keys. One key is used to encrypt data, while the other key is used to decrypt data.

attack surface—The sum total of all avenues that attackers can potentially use to obtain access to a system.

attribute—A property of an object within Windows PowerShell.

attribute—A property within an Active Directory object.

attribute—A setting within a folder or file that provides a particular filesystem feature.

audit policy—A series of settings within a Group Policy that can be used to configure auditing.

authentication—The process of proving your identity to a computer (often with a user name and password).

authoritative—A DNS server that contains resource records for a portion of the Domain Name Space.

auto-enrollment—A feature of Active Directory Certificate Services and Group Policy that allows users and computers to automatically enroll for certificates based on the permissions in a certificate template.

Automatic Private IP Addressing (APIPA)—A feature that automatically configures a network interface using an IPv4 address on the 169.254.0.0 network, or an IPv6 address on the FE80 network.

Azure Active Directory—Active Directory services provided by Microsoft's Azure cloud.

Azure Backup—A feature that allows you to back up on-premises data to Microsoft's Azure cloud.

Azure Site Recovery—A feature that allows you to provide services within Microsoft's Azure cloud in the event of an on-premises server failure.

Azure Update Management—A feature that allows you to manage Windows updates from Microsoft's Azure cloud.

B

backup domain controller (BDC)—A domain controller within a Windows NT domain that holds a read-only copy of the domain SAM database.

bad sector—An area of a hard disk that no longer stores data.

baseline—A measure of normal system activity.

basic disk—A disk configured in the Disk Management tool that does not contain a software RAID volume.

Basic Input/Output System (BIOS)—The program stored on the hardware of a computer that is used to start an operating system after the computer is powered on.

Best Practices Analyzer (BPA)—A tool built into Server Manager that scans a server or role for configuration that does not follow Microsoft best practices.

bidirectional printing—A printing feature that allows print devices to communicate status information to print servers and print clients in addition to receiving print jobs.

Binary Large Object (BLOB) storage—*See* object storage.

blade server—A server that can be housed within a single rackmount server.

block storage—Filesystem storage made available by a cloud provider.

boot image—A bootable WIM image that contains a Windows installation program.

boot loader—A program that loads an operating system.

boot partition—The partition that contains a Windows boot loader.

Boot Protocol (BOOTP)—A legacy protocol that is used to automatically obtain IP configuration from a server on the network.

Branch Office Direct Printing (BODP)—A feature that allows print servers to redirect print job requests from print clients within a remote office directly to a network-attached print device within the remote office.

BranchCache—A modern replacement for offline file caching that provides additional features and performance.

bridgehead server—The domain controller within each Active Directory site that replicates Active Directory information to other sites.

broadcast—A TCP/IP communication destined for all computers on a network.

build automation—A process used within cloud environments that allows containers and virtual machines to be created quickly.

Burnaware—A free software program that can be used to write the contents of an ISO image to a DVD.

bus mastering—The process by which hardware components perform tasks normally executed by the processor.

C

CA hierarchy—A series of CAs that maintain a parent–child relationship.

cable broadband—A last mile technology that transfers data across a cable television network.

cached credential—An encrypted password for a domain user that is stored on a computer. It is used to provide local system access for a user if Active Directory is unavailable.

cached memory—Physical memory that is used for speeding system access to filesystems.

caching-only DNS server—A DNS server that uses its DNS cache and recursion to respond to lookup requests.

capacity planning—The process used to determine hardware and software requirements based on the current and future needs of users within an organization.

capture image—A bootable WIM image that contains a modified installation program designed to create a WIM installation image from an installed operating system.

certificate provider—The PowerShell provider that is used to manage encryption certificates within Windows.

Certificate Revocation List (CRL)—A list of certificate serial numbers that should not be used for encryption.

Certificate Store—The location on a Windows system that stores encryption certificates.

certificate template—A series of settings that define the policies and rules that a CA uses when issuing a certificate.

Certificate Templates Console—A graphical tool used to manage certificate templates on a Windows Server 2019 CA.

certificate—*See* public key certificate.

Certification Authority (CA)—An entity that issues public key certificates to users and computers.

Certification Authority tool—A graphical tool used to manage a Windows Server 2019 CA.

Certification Authority—A trusted computer that digitally signs encryption certificates for other computers.

Challenge-Handshake Authentication Protocol (CHAP)—An authentication protocol used to validate the identity of remote systems and users.

checkpoints—*See* snapshots.

checksum—*See* hash.

child domain—An Active Directory domain that has a parent domain. For example, child. domain.com is a child domain of domain.com.

child OU—An OU that has been created within another OU in the Active Directory database.

class—An object type within Active Directory.

classless interdomain routing (CIDR) notation—A notation that is often used to represent an IP address and its subnet mask.

Client Access License (CAL)—A license for a network connection to a server.

Client for NFS—The feature that allows a Windows system to connect to a shared folder using NFS.

client—A computer on a network that accesses resources on other computers.

cloud delivery model—The method that can be used by a cloud provider to host Web apps in their network and server infrastructure.

cloud provider—An organization that hosts one or more cloud servers.

cloud server—A server that is located within a data center on the Internet.

cloud—A term that refers to the worldwide collection of publicly accessible servers on the Internet.

clustered storage pool—A storage pool that includes storage from multiple servers using Storage Spaces Direct.

clustering—A process whereby several different servers can respond to client requests as a single entity.

cmdlet—A command within Windows PowerShell.

code repository—A service that provides for the storage of software source code.

collection—A group of remote access servers that provide Remote Desktop.

command chaining— A feature of MS-DOS and Windows PowerShell that allows you to run multiple commands on the same command line, one after another.

comment—A line within a PowerShell script that is not executed, but instead used to document the purpose or key features of PowerShell script contents.

commercial CA—*See* public CA.

committed memory—The virtual memory in a paging file that has been reserved for use by applications.

Common Gateway Interface (CGI)—A specification used by a Web server for running and communicating information to Web apps.

Common Internet File System (CIFS)—*See* Server Message Block (SMB).

common name (CN)—An LDAP identifier that represents the name of an object within an Active Directory database.

compiling—A process used to convert source code created by a programming language into an executable program.

Component Object Model (COM)—A framework that allows Windows apps to communication with each other and the operating system.

compound authentication—An Active Directory feature that provides for additional information within Kerberos tickets for use by network services.

computer account—An object within an Active Directory database that represents a computer that is joined to an Active Directory domain.

computer name—A name that you specify on a Windows computer that is used to generate the computer's host name and NetBIOS name.

conditional forwarder—A DNS server feature that forwards requests for a particular domain to a target DNS server.

configuration partition—The section of the Active Directory database that stores the list of domains and trust relationships.

connection security rule—A rule that defines network traffic that must be protected using IPSec.

constant—A variable whose value cannot be changed after creation.

constraint—A remote access characteristic that is enforced by a remote access policy.

container image—A template from which containers can be created.

container object—An Active Directory object that functions to group other Active Directory objects.

container—A subset of an operating system that provides a unique service on the network.

contiguous namespace—A term that refers to two or more DNS names that share the same domain name.

continuous deployment (CD)—A process whereby new versions of Web apps are regularly sent to a cloud provider for testing and deployment.

controlled folder access—A Microsoft Defender feature that helps protect documents and files from modification by ransomware.

core isolation—A Microsoft Defender feature that uses processor virtualization extensions to isolate processes on an operating system.

Credential Security Support Provider (CredSSP)—An authentication protocol used by applications that relays local user credentials to a remote system.

custom filters—Search filters that are available within the Print Management tool that can list printers and printer drivers that match predefined criteria.

custom view—An Event Viewer filter that displays events from one or more event logs that match specified criteria.

D

data collector set—A group containing one or more performance counters, trace providers, or Windows Registry keys that can be monitored and logged.

Data Collector Sets—A graphical tool that can be used to create data collector sets.

Data Deduplication Service—The Windows Server 2019 service that provides data deduplication.

data deduplication—A filesystem feature that ensures that duplicate files are only stored once on the physical storage device.

data deduplication—A technology that eliminates duplicate file contents on a filesystem without removing files.

Data Deduplication—The Windows Server 2019 server role that provides the Data Deduplication Service.

data dedup—*See* data deduplication.

Data Execution Prevention (DEP)—A Windows component that monitors memory usage and prevents malicious programs from accessing other programs on the system.

debug logging—A process that involves logging packet-by-packet information for DNS queries received by a DNS server.

decision construct—A statement that can be used to modify how commands are processed within a PowerShell script.

default forwarder—A DNS server that relays lookup requests it cannot resolve (using zone files or conditional forwarders) to another DNS server.

default gateway—The IP address of the router on the network used to send packets to remote networks.

defragmenting—A process that optimizes hard disk storage by relocating fragmented files to a contiguous area of the hard disk.

demand-dial interface—A virtual network interface on a router that can be used to create a VPN to another router to protect traffic passing to a destination network.

demarcation point—A device or router in an organization that uses a last mile technology to connect to an ISP.

demarc—*See* demarcation point.

demilitarized zone (DMZ)—*See* perimeter network.

Deployment Server—The core component of WDS. It provides all WDS functionality that is not related to transporting packets across the network.

Desired State Configuration—A Windows feature that allows you to configure computers based on a template.

Device Manager utility—A tool within the Windows Control Panel that allows you to manage all hardware device settings on a Windows system.

Device naming—A virtual network interface feature that allows the underlying physical network adapter name to be shown within the virtual machine.

Device Specific Module (DSM)—A component that defines MPIO capabilities for a SAN device.

Devices and Printers utility—A tool within the Windows Control Panel that allows you to add and manage hardware devices and printers.

devop—A server administrator that manages the software that provides a CD workflow.

DFS Management—The graphical management tool used to manage DFS on Windows Server systems.

DFS namespace—A shared folder that contains links to other shared folders on the network.

DFS Namespaces—The server role that provides the ability to create a DFS namespace on Windows Server systems.

DFS replication group—A group of servers that synchronize the file contents within a folder.

DFS Replication—The server role that allows Windows Server systems to synchronize folder contents with other Windows Server systems on the network.

DFS staging folder—A folder that stores files and file changes that are replicated to other systems using DFS.

DHCP failover—A DHCP Service feature that coordinates DHCP configuration and response between two DHCP servers for load balancing and fault tolerance.

DHCP guard—A feature that prevents a virtual machine from accepting IP configuration from an unknown DHCP server on the network.

DHCP option—A configuration setting that is provided by a DHCP server, in addition to an IP address.

DHCP policy—An IP configuration that is applied to DHCP clients that match specific criteria.

DHCP relay agent—A component that can be configured on a router to forward DHCP requests from one network to a DHCP server on another network.

DHCP Server—The Windows Server 2019 server role that provides for DHCP server services.

dial-in permission—The permission that is required for access to dial-up or VPN remote access. It can be granted in the properties of a user account or remote access policy.

dial-up remote access—A form of remote access in which a remote access client uses a modem to connect to a modem bank on a remote access server, using PPP.

differencing disk—A virtual hard disk file that references another virtual hard disk file that contains an operating system. Any changes made to a virtual machine that uses a differencing disk are stored within the differencing disk only.

digital signature—A hash that is encrypted using a private key.

Digital subscriber line (DSL)—A last mile technology that transfers data across a telephone network.

DirectAccess Connectivity Assistant—The DirectAccess component on a Windows 7 Ultimate or Enterprise edition computer.

DirectAccess—A remote access technology that automatically creates IPSec tunnels to a remote access server when remote access clients are outside of the organization.

directory partition—A section of the Active Directory database.

Directory Services Restore Mode (DSRM)—A mode to which you can boot a domain controller in order to restore or repair the Active Directory database.

discretionary access control list (DACL)—A list of groups and users that have been assigned permissions to a resource, such as a folder or file.

disjointed namespace—A term that refers to two or more DNS names that have dissimilar domain names.

Disk Management—A graphical utility that can be used to configure simple and RAID volumes on a Windows system.

distinguished name (DN)—An LDAP identifier that includes the name and location of an object within an Active Directory database.

Distributed Denial of Service (DDoS)—A network attack in which multiple attackers flood a system with network traffic in order to prevent other systems from accessing it.

Distributed File System (DFS)—A replication service used on modern Windows Server systems.

distribution group—An Active Directory group object that is used by an email system.

distribution—An operating system that is made up of a Linux kernel and supporting software.

distro—*See* distribution.

DNS Server log—The Windows Server 2019 log that stores events from the DNS Server service.

DNS Server—The Windows Server 2019 server role that provides for DNS server services.

Docker client—A program that can be used to create and manage Docker containers.

Docker daemon—The Docker service that provides for container functionality.

Docker Enterprise Edition (EE)—The version of Docker that is supported by Windows Server 2019.

Docker Hub—An online repository of container images that can be used with Docker.

Docker—A common software that allows operating systems to host containers.

domain controller—A server within a domain that authenticates other computers and provides for centralized management.

domain functional level—A mode that dictates the minimum allowed domain controller version within a domain.

domain group account—A group account that is stored within an Active Directory database.

domain local—A group scope that allows a group to be used within the domain to which it belongs, but allows members from any domain in the forest.

Domain Name Space (DNS)—A hierarchical namespace used for host names.

Domain Naming Master—An FSMO used to coordinate the modification of Active Directory domains and trust relationships within a forest.

domain partition—The section of the Active Directory database that stores the objects within a single domain.

domain registrar—An organization that publicly registers domain names on the Internet.

domain user account—A user account that is stored within an Active Directory database.

domain—A logical grouping of computers on a network that provides centralized management and single sign-on.

driver signing—The process by which a device driver is digitally signed by a trusted third party, such as Microsoft.

dump file—A file that is used to save the memory contents of a process.

duplexing—A mirroring configuration in which each storage device is connected to a different storage controller.

dynamic disk—A disk that contains a software RAID volume configured in the Disk Management tool.

Dynamic DNS (DDNS)—*See* dynamic update.

Dynamic Host Configuration Protocol (DHCP)—A protocol that is used to automatically obtain IP configuration from a server on the network.

dynamic memory—A Hyper-V feature that allows a virtual machine to increase or decrease the memory it uses following boot, based on the available memory in the physical server.

dynamic update—A feature that allows computers to automatically create records on a DNS server.

dynamic-link library (DLL)—A set of functions that can be shared by multiple Windows programs.

E

edition—A specific version of Windows Server that contains a unique set of features designed for a particular environment.

EFI system partition—*See* UEFI system partition.

egress fee—A cost that organizations pay to move data from a public cloud provider to another public or private cloud provider.

Encrypting File System (EFS)—A feature of NTFS that allows for the encryption of individual files and folders.

encryption algorithm—A mathematical procedure for encrypting data.

Enhanced Metafile (EMF)—The default format that the GDI uses when storing documents within a spool folder.

enrollment—The process whereby a computer or user requests a certificate from a CA.

enterprise CA—A CA that issues certificates to users and computers within an organization.

entry—A component of the Windows Registry that stores hardware, software, or user settings.

environment provider—The PowerShell provider that is used to manage environment variables within Windows.

environment variables—Information that is stored in memory that is used by programs to locate settings and other information.

escape character—A character that represents a text separator, such as a newline or tab.

event log—A detailed record of system and application notifications that is stored by the Windows operating system.

event subscription—A configuration in Event Viewer that obtains events from other computers.

event trace provider—Components of the Windows operating system that provide information about the Windows kernel and system applications.

Event Viewer—A graphical log viewer tool within Windows operating systems.

Event Viewer—A graphical tool that can be used to view the contents of event logs.

exit status—A number that is returned by a command that indicates whether it executed successfully or not.

extended partition—A primary partition that can be subdivided into logical drives on a storage device that uses an MBR.

external trust—A trust relationship between an Active Directory domain and another domain outside of the Active Directory forest.

external virtual switch—A virtual switch that allows virtual machines to communicate with the underlying physical wired or wireless network.

F

Failover Clustering—A Windows Server 2019 feature that provides for server clustering.

failover—The process whereby a server within a cluster assumes the role of another server within the cluster that has failed.

FC over Ethernet (FCoE)—An FC SAN technology that transfers information using Ethernet cables.

Fibre Channel (FC)—A SAN technology that allows systems with an FC HBA to access a FC SAN.

file caching—A Windows feature that uses memory to speed the transfer of information to and from physical storage devices.

File Explorer—A graphical file browsing tool within Windows.

file group—A file category that is used by file screens.

file screens—A feature that prevents users from storing files of certain types within a folder on an NTFS filesystem.

File Server Resource Manager—A server role and associated graphical tool that can be used to implement additional features on a Windows file server, such as folder quotas and file screens.

File Signature Verification tool (Sigverif)—A tool that can be used to search for unsigned system and device driver files.

File System Freeze (fsfreeze)—A Linux service that is used to back up open files.

File Transfer Protocol (FTP)—A common protocol used to transfer files across networks, such as the Internet.

filesystem provider—The PowerShell provider that is used to manage filesystems on storage devices. It is the default PowerShell provider.

filesystem—A format that defines how an operating system uses a storage device.

firewall profile—A series of firewall rules that apply to a computer when it is connected to a particular type of network (public, private, domain).

firewall rule—A rule that defines network traffic that is allowed or blocked.

firmware RAID—A RAID configuration provided by the system BIOS.

Flexible Single Master Operations (FSMO)—A domain controller function that cannot be shared by all domain controllers within a domain or forest.

flushing—A Windows feature that removes file caching information from memory after the information has been written to a physical storage device.

folder quota—A storage limit that applies to a folder on an NTFS filesystem.

forest functional level—A mode that dictates the minimum allowed domain controller version within a forest.

forest root domain—The first domain installed within an Active Directory forest.

forest trust—A trust relationship between two Active Directory forests.

forest wide authentication—A setting within a forest trust that authenticates users prior to resource access.

forest—The largest container object within Active Directory.

formatting—The process of placing a filesystem on a storage device.

forward lookup—A DNS lookup that resolves a FQDN to an IP address.

fragmented—A term that describes a file that is stored in a non-contiguous area of a storage device.

full backup—A backup type that backs up all data that you specify.

Fully Qualified Domain Name (FQDN)—A host name that follows DNS naming convention.

function provider—The PowerShell provider that is used to manage functions within Windows PowerShell.

function—A shortcut to a series of commands within Windows PowerShell.

G

gateway server mode—The mode that the Windows Admin Center functions within when installed on a Windows Server 2016 or 2019 system.

Generation 1 virtual machine—A Hyper-V virtual machine that emulates older hardware.

Generation 2 virtual machine—A Hyper-V virtual machine that emulates newer hardware and performs faster than a Generation 1 virtual machine.

Generic Routing Encapsulation (GRE)—A protocol that provides for the tunneling of other protocols.

Generic Volume License Key (GVLK)—A license key that is purchased for use within an organization and often embedded into the installation media.

Gigabit Passive Optical Network (GPON)—A last mile technology that transfers data across a fiber optic network.

global catalog—A list of all objects within an Active Directory forest.

global—A group scope that allows a group to be used within any domain in the forest, but restricts membership to local domain objects.

globally-unique identifier (GUID)—An attribute that uniquely identifies an Active Directory object within a forest.

Graphics Device Interface (GDI)—A print API that is supported by legacy and modern Windows systems.

group ID (GID)—A number assigned to a UNIX group account.

group nesting—The process of adding a group object as a member of another group object.

Group Policy Management Editor—A graphical tool that can be used to configure the settings within a Group Policy object.

Group Policy Management—A graphical tool that can be used to manage Group Policy.

Group Policy Object (GPO)—An Active Directory object that contains Group Policy settings and preferences.

Group Policy preferences—The part of a GPO that can be used to configure Windows features.

Group Policy Results Wizard—A component of the Group Policy Management tool used to troubleshoot the application of Group Policy.

Group Policy—A component of Active Directory that provides centralized management of Windows computers within a domain.

group scope—The property of an Active Directory group that determines where a group can be used and the objects it can contain.

guest operating system—A virtual operating system that is run on a hypervisor.

GUID Partition Table (GPT)—A modern partition table used on storage devices.

H

handle—A resource that is connected to a process.

hard quota—A folder quota that is strictly enforced.

hardware RAID—A RAID configuration provided by storage controller hardware.

hash—A calculation that is based on the size and contents of data.

Host Bus Adapter (HBA)—A hardware interface that provides for communication to an external device.

host ID—The portion of an IP address that denotes the host.

host operating system—The operating system used to host a Type 2 hypervisor.

hosts file—A file on a local computer that contains entries that can be used to resolve FQDNs to IP addresses.

HP JetDirect—A protocol used for printing to network-attached printers using TCP.

hybrid cloud—An environment that integrates services that run on-premises to services within the cloud.

Hypertext Markup Language (HTML)—The standard format used for displaying websites in a Web browser.

Hyper-V container—A container that is provided a separate copy of the Windows Server 2019 kernel via components provided by Hyper-V.

Hyper-V Extensible Virtual Switch—The protocol within network interface properties that allows the network interface to be shared by multiple virtual machines that are connected to the associated external virtual switch.

Hyper-V Manager—A graphical tool that can be used to install, manage, and interact with Hyper-V virtual machines.

Hyper-V—A Type 1 hypervisor created by Microsoft.

hypervisor—The software component that provides for virtualization.

I

IDE (Integrated Drive Electronics)—A legacy storage technology used to interface with IDE hard disks on a system.

IIS Manager—The graphical tool used to manage Internet Information Services (IIS) on a Windows Server 2019 system.

incremental backup—A backup type that backs up data that you specify, but only if that data has been modified since the previous backup.

index—An organized list of files and folders on a system.

Infrastructure as a Service (IaaS)—A cloud delivery model that uses virtualization to provide access to Web apps.

Infrastructure Master—An FSMO used to coordinate group membership, GUID, and DN information within an Active Directory domain and forest.

Input/Output (I/O) address—An area of memory dedicated for the transfer of information to and from a hardware device.

Input/Output Operations Per Second (IOPS)—The number of storage requests sent to and from a storage device per second.

install image—A WIM image that contains the files that comprise an operating system.

instance—A specific hardware device or software component.

Intel VT—Hardware-assisted virtualization support available in some Intel processors.

internal trust—A default trust relationship created between domains within an Active Directory forest.

internal virtual switch—A virtual switch that allows virtual machines to communicate amongst themselves and the host operating system.

Internet Control Message Protocol (ICMP)—A protocol used on the Internet to provide error messages and network-related information.

Internet Control Message Protocol version 6 (ICMPv6)—A protocol used by computers to obtain an IPv6 configuration from a router on the network.

Internet Explorer Enhanced Security Configuration (IE ESC)—A feature on Windows Server that prevents the Internet Explorer Web browser from connecting to websites that are not within its trusted sites list.

Internet Information Services (IIS)—The Web server software included in Windows Server.

Internet Key Exchange version 2 (IKEv2)—A VPN protocol that uses IPSec to encrypt data transfer on networks.

Internet of Things (IoT)—A term that refers to the worldwide collection of small Internet-connected devices.

Internet Printing Client—The Windows feature that provides the ability to print to shared printers using IPP.

Internet Printing Protocol (IPP)—A protocol that is used to print documents to a print server using HTTP or HTTPS.

Internet Protocol (IP) address—A series of four 8-bit numbers that represent a computer on a network.

Internet SCSI (iSCSI)—A SAN technology that allows systems to access a SAN device using an Ethernet network connection.

Internet Server Application Programming Interface (ISAPI)—A set of Windows functions that provides a faster interaction between Web apps and IIS compared to CGI.

Internet Service Provider (ISP)—A company that provides Internet access.

Interrupt Request (IRQ) line—A channel of communication used between a hardware device and a processor.

IP Address Management (IPAM)—A software technology that is used to manage many DNS and DHCP servers.

IP Security (IPSec)—A suite of protocols that can be used to provide data encryption for IPv4 and IPv6 packets.

IP version 4 (IPv4)—The most common version of IP used on the Internet. It uses a 32-bit addressing scheme organized into different classes.

IP version 6 (IPv6)—A recent version of IP that is used by some hosts on the Internet. It uses a 128-bit addressing scheme.

IPsec task offloading—A feature of network interfaces that allows IPsec calculation to be performed by the physical network interface instead of the operating system.

iSCSI initiator—A software component that enables an operating system to connect to an iSCSI target.

iSCSI Qualified Name (IQN)—A name format used to identify iSCSI initiators.

iSCSI Target Server—The server role that allows Windows Server 2019 to provide storage to other systems using iSCSI.

iSCSI Target Storage Provider—The server role that allows the iSCSI Target Server to back up open files and support legacy management tools.

iSCSI target—A storage area on a SAN device that is made available to other systems.

iSCSI virtual disk—A special .vhdx file that the iSCSI Target Server uses to provide storage.

ISO image file—A file that stores a virtual filesystem that can be written to a removable media device such as a DVD or USB flash drive.

iterative query—A DNS lookup that is resolved using an entry in the cache on a DNS server.

J

jabbering—The process by which failing hardware components send large amounts of information to the processor.

journaling—A filesystem feature that allows for quick file recovery following a power failure.

journaling—A filesystem feature that records filesystem operations.

Just a Bunch of Disks (JBOD)—*See* spanning.

K

Kerberos armoring—An Active Directory feature that protects the initial stages of Kerberos authentication against common network attacks.

Kerberos—A UNIX authentication protocol. Also, the protocol used by computers within an Active Directory domain.

kernel—The core component of an operating system that executes processes on the computer hardware.

Key Management Services (KMS)—A service that runs on a Windows Server computer that allows for activation of other computers on an organization's network.

key—A major section within the Windows Registry. For example, HKEY_LOCAL_MACHINE.

key—A random string of bits that can be used alongside an encryption algorithm.

keyboard-video-mouse (KVM) switch—A device often used on server racks that allows a single keyboard, mouse, and monitor to be shared by all of the rackmount servers.

Kubernetes—A set of software components that can be used to centrally manage containers within a cloud or on-premises environment.

L

last mile technology—A technology that connects an organization network to an ISP.

Layer Two Tunneling Protocol (L2TP)—A VPN protocol that uses IPSec to encrypt data transfer.

leaf object—An Active Directory object that represents a unique entity and does not contain other objects.

Lightweight Directory Access Protocol (LDAP)—A protocol that is used to obtain information from a directory service, such as Active Directory.

Line Printer Daemon (LPD)—A UNIX protocol that is used to print documents to a print server.

Line Printer Request (LPR)—A port type that is used when printing to a shared printer using LPD.

Linux Containers on Windows (LCOW)—A Docker feature that allows Linux containers to run on Windows Server 2019 using Hyper-V and LinuxKit.

LinuxKit—A Docker component that provides a Linux kernel and minimal Linux distribution for executing Linux containers.

live migration—A feature of Hyper-V that allows you to move a running virtual machine from one Hyper-V host to another.

Local Area Network (LAN)—A network in which the computers are all in close physical proximity.

local group account—A group account that is stored within the SAM database on a Windows system.

local user account—A user account that is stored within the SAM database on a Windows system.

Local Users and Groups—An MMC snap-in tool that can be used to create and manage local users and groups on a system.

locally attached print devices—Print devices that are connected to the computer using a physical cable, such as parallel, serial, or USB.

locally attached printers—Printers that print to a locally attached print device.

logical drive—A partition that exists within an extended partition.

logical processor—A component (or core) within a physical processor that acts as a standalone processor.

logon script—A script that is executed immediately after a user logs into a system.

long-range Wi-Fi—A last mile technology that uses modified antenna or signaling methods to achieve a longer Wi-Fi signal range between two devices or computers.

loop construct—A statement that can be used to repetitively process commands within a PowerShell script.

loopback IP address—An IP address that refers to the local computer only.

LPR Port Monitor—The Windows feature that provides the ability to print to shared printers using LPD.

M

MAC address filtering—A process that restricts access to a service based on the client MAC address.

MAC address spoofing—The process of modifying the MAC address on a physical or virtual network adapter.

man-in-the-middle attack—An exploit that involves a hacker altering communication between two parties without them knowing.

Master Boot Record (MBR)—The legacy partition table used on storage devices that are 2 TB or smaller.

Media Access Control (MAC) address—A unique 48-bit hexadecimal number that manufacturers add to each physical network interface they manufacture.

member server—A Windows Server system that is joined to an Active Directory domain but does not function as a domain controller or hold a copy of the AD database.

memory integrity—A Microsoft Defender feature that prevents malicious applications from accessing Windows processes.

memory leak—A condition whereby a process continually uses more and more memory within a system, until there is no more memory available.

metacharacter—A character that has special meaning within PowerShell.

metadata—The section of a folder or file that stores permissions, attributes, and other information regarding the folder or file.

method—A function that can be performed on an object within Windows PowerShell.

Microsoft Azure—The suite of cloud services that are provided by Microsoft.

Microsoft Defender—A Windows component that provides malware protection as well as firewall and IPSec functionality.

Microsoft Identity Manager (MIM)—A software product that manages the digital identities of users.

Microsoft iSCSI Initiator Service—The Windows Server 2019 service that provides iSCSI initiator functionality.

Microsoft Management Console (MMC)—A graphical management console that provides a series of snap-ins that can be used to manage components of Windows.

Microsoft Point-to-Point Encryption (MPPE)—A protocol that provides data encryption for traffic that passes through a PPTP VPN.

Microsoft Update—A service provided by Microsoft that allows Windows systems to download updates for software products across the Internet.

mirroring—A fault tolerant RAID level 1 configuration that stores identical copies of data on two different storage devices.

monitoring—The process by which system areas are observed for problems or irregularities.

mounting—The process of associating a filesystem with a drive letter or folder.

multicast—A feature of IP that allows data to be transmitted to a group of destination computers simultaneously.

Multipath I/O—The Windows Server 2019 feature that provides for MPIO.

Multipath Input Output (MPIO)—A technology that provides multiple, redundant paths to a storage device.

Multiple Activation Key (MAK)—A license key that can be activated on the Internet for a set number of Windows computers.

multitasking—The ability to run multiple processes simultaneously on a system.

N

named pipe—A file that represents a persistent connection to a process.

Nano Server—A small footprint Windows Server installation option that provides a bare minimum set of services for running Web apps and a small number of server services.

National Science Foundation Network (NSFNET)—A historical network that connected to other TCP/IP networks used by academic and research organizations.

nested virtualization—A feature of Hyper-V that allows you to run virtual machines within other virtual machines.

NetBIOS name record—A record on a WINS server that is used to resolve a NetBIOS name to an IP address.

NetBIOS name—A unique name for a Windows computer that is broadcast to other computers on the LAN.

netmask ordering—A feature of DNS that ensures the first result returned in a list closely matches the IP address of the resolver.

Network Address Translation (NAT)—A technology that allows a router to obtain Internet resources on behalf of computers on the network.

Network Connectivity Assistant—The DirectAccess service on a Windows 8 Enterprise or later computer that connects to the network location server.

Network File System (NFS)—A UNIX file sharing protocol.

network ID—The portion of an IP address that denotes the network.

network latency—Slow or intermittent replies to network requests.

network location server—A DirectAccess server that is probed by remote access clients to determine whether they are inside or outside of the organization.

Network Policy and Access Services—The Windows Server 2019 server role that provides RADIUS services.

Network Policy Server—The graphical tool that configures and manages RADIUS.

Network Time Protocol (NTP)—A protocol used to obtain time and time zone information across a network, such as the Internet.

network-attached print devices—Print devices that have a network interface (e.g., Ethernet, Wi-Fi, Bluetooth) and accept print jobs from computers on the network.

network-attached printers—Printers that print to a network-attached print device.

network-attached storage (NAS)—A file server that allows other systems on the network to store files using a file sharing protocol such as SMB, NFS, or FTP.

network—Two or more computers joined together via network media and able to exchange information.

New Technology File System (NTFS)—The traditional file system used on Windows Server systems.

Next Generation Firewall (NGFW)—A router that provides additional security capabilities, such as malware filtering and intrusion prevention.

NIC Teaming—A technology that allows multiple network interfaces to function as a single unit for load balancing and fault tolerance.

non-paged pool—Physical memory used by device drivers and the Windows kernel that cannot be moved to the paging file.

non-uniform memory access (NUMA)—A technology used on multi-processor systems that allows memory to be shared between processors directly for greater performance and scalability.

Non-Volatile Memory Express (NVMe)—An SSD technology that provides fast transfer speeds within a small form factor.

N-tier—A software design in which clients must pass through several different systems or applications before obtaining access to data.

O

object storage—Storage made available to Web apps run within a cloud provider. Web apps access object storage using an HTTP request.

object—A basic element of Active Directory that represents an individual item within the Active Directory database, such as a user or computer.

object—An item representation within Windows PowerShell.

octet—A single, 8-bit section of an IPv4 address.

offline file caching—An SMB shared folder feature that allows users to download copies of files and programs to a cache on their local computer for reliable modification.

Online Certificate Status Protocol (OCSP)—A protocol that can be used to obtain the status of a certificate in a CRL.

on-premises server—A server that is located within an organization.

Open Database Connectivity (ODBC)—A standard format that allows Web apps and other programs to access a database.

orchestration—The process of coordinating multiple, separate CD tasks.

organizational unit (OU)—A container object within Active Directory that serves to organize leaf objects.

Out-of-Box Experience (OOBE)—The initial setup wizard that is run following a Windows installation.

output redirection—A feature of MS-DOS and Windows PowerShell that allows you to save the output of a command to a file.

overlay network—A logical network that functions on an existing physical network.

P

packet sniffer—A program that displays the traffic passing through a network interface.

packet—A package of data formatted by a network protocol.

page description language (PDL)—The format used by PostScript printers to describe the appearance of a printed page.

page fault—The process whereby data is read from or written to a paging file.

page—A block of information that is written to memory.

paged pool—Physical memory used by device drivers and the Windows kernel that can be moved to the paging file, if necessary.

paging file—A file on a Windows system that provides virtual memory.

parent domain—An Active Directory domain that has one or more child domains.

partitions—Divisions of a storage device that can contain a filesystem.

passive screening—A file screen configuration that provides warnings only.

pass-through disk—A physical hard disk or SSD that is used exclusively by a virtual machine for storage.

Password Settings Object (PSO)—An Active Directory object that stores password and account policy settings.

PDC Emulator—An FSMO used to coordinate password changes and provide time synchronization within an Active Directory domain.

peer-to-peer networking—A network design in which each computer manages access to its own resources independently.

performance counter alert—A data collector set that logs performance counter data when the value of a performance counter exceeds or falls below a set value.

performance counter—A specific type of event that can be monitored in a performance object.

Performance Monitor—A graphical tool that can be used to view and graph the values of performance counters.

performance object—An area of the system for which performance can be monitored.

PerfView—A graphical program that can be used to view files that contain data collected from event trace providers.

perimeter network—A network that uses network-based firewalls to protect access to the servers that are contained within.

permission—A term that refers to a privilege granted to a resource, such as a shared folder or printer.

persistent volume—*See* block storage.

physical processor—A processor that is represented by a single piece of hardware.

piping—The process of sending output from one command to another within Windows PowerShell using the pipe symbol on your keyboard (|).

Platform as a Service (PaaS)—A cloud delivery model that provides access to containerized Web apps.

Plug and Play (PnP)—A technology that allows new hardware devices to be configured automatically for use within an operating system.

Point-to-Point Protocol over Ethernet (PPPoE)—A protocol used to transfer data using DSL.

Point-to-Point Protocol—A protocol used to transfer data between two devices, often across a telephone network. Dial-up remote access and PPPoE use PPP to transfer data.

Point-to-Point Tunneling Protocol (PPTP)—A VPN protocol that uses MPPE to encrypt data transfer.

port forwarding—The process whereby a NAT router forwards requests it receives on its external network interface to a server on the internal network by service name or port number.

port mirroring—A feature of physical and virtual switches that sends a copy of all network traffic to a specific network interface for inspection.

Portable Document Format (PDF)—A standard file format for text and graphical images that can be read by most software applications.

PostScript—A standard printing and imaging technology that uses PDL to describe the appearance of a printed page.

power plan—A set of power settings that you can choose to use for a Windows system.

PowerShell console file—A file that can be used to store customizations for a Windows PowerShell session, such as background color and font size.

PowerShell profile script—A PowerShell script that is automatically executed when you open Windows PowerShell.

PowerShell provider—A PowerShell plug-in that can be used to manage a particular area of the system or Windows PowerShell.

PowerShell script—A text file with a .ps1 extension that contains PowerShell cmdlets and control structures for later execution.

Preboot Execution Environment (PXE)—A technology that allows a network interface to boot an operating system or operating system installation program from a server on the network.

preemptive multitasking—A type of multitasking in which each process is isolated from the other processes on the system.

prestaging—The process whereby a computer account is created within Active Directory before the associated computer is joined to an Active Directory domain.

primary DNS server—A DNS server that contains a read-write copy of a zone file.

primary domain controller (PDC)—A domain controller within a Windows NT domain that holds a read-write copy of the domain SAM database.

primary partition—A major partition on a storage device.

primordial storage pool—A placeholder in Storage Spaces that lists storage devices in the system that have not been configured as part of a storage pool.

Print and Document Services—The server role within Windows Server 2019 that provides the Print Management tool as well as the IPP and LPD printer sharing protocols.

print client—A computer that prints to a shared printer.

print device—A physical device that prints a print job onto paper.

print job—A document that has been formatted to the specifications of a print device.

Print Management—A Windows Server 2019 tool that can be used to manage and monitor print servers within an organization.

print processor—A software component within Windows that provides for the formatting of documents within a spool folder.

print queue—*See* spool folder.

print server—A computer that shares one or more printers.

Print Spooler—The service on Windows systems that provides nearly all print functionality.

Printer Control Language (PCL)—The format used by most non-PostScript printers to describe the appearance of a printed page.

printer driver—A software component that allows the Print Spooler service to format and render jobs for a particular print device model.

printer pool—A configuration that consists of a printer that prints to more than one print device of the same model.

printer—The software representation of a print device on a Windows system.

private cloud—A set of one or more cloud servers that are used exclusively by the organization that owns them.

private key—An asymmetric encryption key that is not shared to other entities. It is often used to decrypt data that was encrypted using the matching public key.

private virtual switch—A virtual switch that allows virtual machines to communicate amongst themselves.

privileged access management (PAM)—A set of software features that restrict the capabilities of privileged users within an Active Directory environment.

privileged mode—A mode that is given the highest priority on a system.

proactive maintenance—The measures taken to reduce future system problems.

process—A program that is currently executing on the system.

processor scheduling—A Windows performance setting that specifies how processor resources are allocated to programs.

production checkpoint—A checkpoint provided by a backup service within a guest operating system.

programming language—A set of syntax rules that can be used to produce the instructions needed to create a computer program.

Protected Extensible Authentication Protocol (PEAP)—A version of EAP that is commonly used to authenticate wireless computers that use 802.1X wireless.

protected network—A Hyper-V feature that automatically moves a virtual machine that is part of a cluster to another computer within the cluster in the event of an underlying system failure.

protected process—A process that is isolated from other processes on a system.

protocol—A set of rules of communication used between computers on a network.

proxy server—A network server that accepts Internet requests from other computers on the same LAN and obtains the desired resource on their behalf.

public CA—A CA that issues certificates to users and computers publicly on the Internet.

public cloud—A set of one or more cloud servers that can be publicly rented.

public key certificate—A document that verifies the identity of an enclosed public key.

public key infrastructure (PKI)—A set of software components in an organization that allow for the issuing of certificates to users and computers.

public key—An asymmetric encryption key that can be used by other users, software, or computers on the network. It is often used to encrypt data.

publishing—The process of creating Active Directory objects that represent network resources, such as shared folders.

Q

Quality of Service (QoS)—A term that refers to any technology that manages or limits the flow of data.

queuing—*See* spooling.

R

rackmount server—A thin form factor used to house server hardware that is installed in a server rack.

RADIUS client—A network device or server that forwards authentication and logging requests to a RADIUS server for validation.

RAID volume—A volume that accesses a filesystem stored on multiple storage devices.

rapid server deployment—The process of installing one or more server operating systems within a short period of time.

reactive maintenance—The measures taken when system problems arise.

Read-only Domain Controller (RODC)—A domain controller that has a read-only copy of the Active Directory database which contains a reduced number of password attributes.

realm trust—A trust relationship between an Active Directory domain and a UNIX Kerberos realm.

recovery agent—A user or group that can be used to access EFS-encrypted files.

recovery partition—A partition that is created during the Windows Server 2019 installation that stores programs and files used to repair or recover the operating system following operating system corruption.

recursive query—A DNS lookup that is resolved by first contacting a top-level DNS server.

Redundant Array of Independent Disks (RAID)—The process of combining the storage spaces of several hard disk drives into one larger, logical storage unit.

Registry Editor—A graphical MMC tool that can be used to edit the Windows Registry.

registry provider—The PowerShell provider that is used to manage the HKEY_LOCAL_MACHINE and HKEY_CURRENT_USER keys within the Windows Registry.

Relative Identifier (RID)—The unique portion of a SID for an Active Directory object.

Reliability Monitor—A graphical tool that allows you to view the stability history of your computer.

remote access client—A computer that accesses a network using remote access.

Remote Access Dial-In User Authentication Service (RADIUS)—A protocol used to centralize authentication and logging for remote access and other technologies.

Remote Access Management Console—A graphical configuration tool for managing DirectAccess, as well as monitoring DirectAccess and VPN connections.

remote access policy—A policy used by a RADIUS server to allow or prevent remote access based on characteristics of the remote access connection.

remote access server—A computer or device that provides remote access to a network.

remote access—The process whereby a client accesses resources in an organization's network (e.g., DMZ) from outside of the organization.

Remote Access—The Windows Server 2019 server role that provides for routing, as well as dial-up, VPN, and DirectAccess remote access.

Remote Desktop app—The app on a remote access client that creates a Remote Desktop session to a remote access server using RDP.

Remote Desktop Connection—The default Remote Desktop app used on Windows systems.

Remote Desktop Protocol (RDP)—The protocol used by Remote Desktop to transfer information between a remote access client and server.

Remote Desktop Protocol (RDP)—The protocol used by the Remote Desktop Connection app on Windows computers when accessing a graphical desktop on another Windows computer.

Remote Desktop Services—The services on a Windows Sever 2019 system that provide for Remote Desktop.

Remote Desktop—A method of remote access that provides remote access clients with a graphical desktop on a remote access server.

remote differential compression (RDC)—A DFS replication feature that only replicates changes made to files.

Remote Server Administration Tools (RSAT)—Tools that you can download to a Windows 10 PC to allow for the remote administration of Windows Server systems on a network.

RemoteApp and Desktop Connections—A Control Panel tool that can be used to connect to Remote Desktop sessions and RemoteApp programs.

RemoteApp—A Remote Desktop feature that allows individual programs to be accessed on a remote access client using RDP.

remote-direct memory access (RDMA)—A technology that allows hardware on one system to access hardware on another system without the help of an operating system.

rendering—The process of converting a document within a spool folder into a format that a print device can understand.

replication partner—A WINS server that shares its NetBIOS name records with another WINS server.

reservation—A unique IP configuration that is always provided to a DHCP client that has a particular MAC address.

Resilient File System (ReFS)—A new file system used on Windows Server systems that has additional reliability features and support for Storage Spaces.

resolver—The computer that requests a DNS lookup.

Resource Monitor—A graphical tool the displays the utilization of hardware and software resources.

resource record—A record stored in a zone file.

reverse lookup—A DNS lookup that resolves an IP address to a FQDN.

reverse proxy—A technology that obtains server resources on behalf of a client.

RID Master—An FSMO used to provide unique RIDs to domain controllers within an Active Directory domain.

right—A term that refers to a privilege that grants access to the Windows operating system.

rogue process—A process that monopolizes processor time unnecessarily.

role seizure—The process whereby an FSMO is forcefully transferred to another domain controller.

root CA—The top-most parent CA in a CA hierarchy.

root hints—A file that contains the IP addresses of the top-level DNS servers for the Domain Name Space.

round robin—A feature of DNS that rotates a list of returned results for load balancing purposes.

router guard—A feature that prevents a virtual machine from accepting route information from an unknown router on the network.

router—A device capable of transferring packets from one network to another.

Routing and Remote Access—The graphical tool that configures and manages routing, as well as dial-up and VPN remote access.

Rufus—A free software program that can be used to write the contents of an ISO image to a bootable USB flash drive.

S

Safe Mode—A Windows diagnostic mode that only allows essential system programs to start.

sandboxing—The process of running separate Web apps within separate containers.

scavenging—The process of removing stale resource records on a DNS server.

Schema Master—An FSMO used to coordinate the modification of the Active Directory schema within a forest.

schema partition—The section of the Active Directory database that stores the schema.

schema—A list of all classes and attributes that can be defined within Active Directory.

scope—An object in the DHCP tool that represents the IP configuration for a particular network.

Second Level Address Translation (SLAT)—A hardware-assisted virtualization technology available in modern processors that coordinates the use of memory between virtual machines and physical memory.

secondary DNS server—A DNS server that contains a read-only copy of a zone file that was obtained from a primary DNS server.

Secure Socket Tunneling Protocol (SSTP)—A VPN protocol that uses HTTPS packets to transfer data on networks.

Secure Sockets Layer (SSL)—A legacy protocol that provides data encryption for network traffic.

Security Accounts Manager (SAM)—A database that stores local user and group accounts.

security group—An Active Directory group object that is used to assign rights and permissions to group members.

security identifier (SID)—An attribute that identifies an Active Directory object within an ACL.

Security log—A Windows log file that stores auditing events.

security principal—An entity, such as a group or user, that can be listed within a DACL or SACL.

selective authentication—A setting within a forest trust that authenticates users after determining that a desired resource is available to the user.

self-signed certificate—An encryption certificate that is digitally signed by the computer that created it, instead of a trusted third-party Certification Authority.

separator page—An optional first page of a print job that provides the name of the document and the user that submitted the print job.

Serial Advanced Technology Attachment (SATA)—A modern version of IDE that uses serial communication to interface with SATA hard disks and SSDs on a system.

Serial Attached SCSI (SAS)—A modern version of SCSI that uses serial communication to interface with SAS hard disks and SSDs on a system.

Server Core App Compatibility Feature on Demand (FOD)—An optional package that can be installed on Server Core to provide additional frameworks required for certain applications.

Server Core—A small footprint Windows Server installation option that does not provide a graphical desktop.

Server for NFS—The server role that provides NFS file sharing capability within Windows Server.

Server Manager—A graphical management tool included within Windows Server.

Server Message Block (SMB)—The default file sharing protocol used by Windows systems.

Server Side Includes (SSI)—A programming language used by Web apps to generate website content.

server—A computer on a network that shares resources to other computers.

service forwarding—*See* port forwarding.

Service Principle Name (SPN)—A name that can be used to uniquely identify a network service within Active Directory.

service record—A record stored on a DNS server that identifies the location of an Active Directory service.

Services tool—A graphical utility that can start, stop, restart, and configure services on a Windows system.

session-based desktop deployment—A Remote Desktop Services deployment type that provides Remote Desktop sessions to a remote access server.

shared folder permission—A permission that grants or denies a connection to a shared folder.

shared printer—A printer that is shared to other systems on the network.

shell—A command-line interface.

shielded virtual machines—A Hyper-V feature that allows virtual machine hard disk files to be encrypted.

Shielding—A Hyper-V feature that encrypts the contents of a virtual hard disk file.

shortcut trust—A trust relationship between two domains within the same Active Directory forest.

Simple Mail Transfer Protocol (SMTP)—The protocol used to transmit email across the Internet.

simple volume—A volume that accesses a filesystem stored on a single storage device.

single sign-on—The process whereby users authenticate once to a domain controller to prove their identity to other computers within the same domain.

single-root I/O virtualization (SR-IOV)—A technology that allows a network interface to provide a separate communication channel for each virtual machine that uses it.

site link object—An Active Directory object that represents an Internet connection between two sites.

site object—An Active Directory object that represents a physical location within a LAN.

site—*See* site object.

Small Computer Systems Interface (SCSI)—A legacy storage technology used to interface with SCSI hard disks on a system.

small footprint—A minimal operating system installation.

smart paging file—A paging file that is used by a virtual machine should available memory become exhausted.

snapshots—A feature of many hypervisors that allows you to restore a virtual machine to a previous point in time.

soft quota—A folder quota that provides warnings only.

Software as a Service (SaaS)—A cloud delivery model that provide access to Web apps without requiring the configuration of virtual machines or containers.

Software Defined Networking (SDN)—A term that refers to the software components and frameworks that provides network functionality for virtual machines and containers.

software RAID—A RAID configuration provided by software in an operating system.

solid state disk (SSD)—A storage device that is comprised of non-volatile memory chips.

spanning—A RAID-like technology that accumulates multiple storage devices into a single unit.

split tunneling—A VPN configuration that prevents the remote access client from forwarding all network traffic to the VPN.

spool folder—The folder that stores documents and print jobs during the printing process.

spooling—The process whereby a print API stores a document within a spool folder.

Spot Verifier—A Windows Server 2019 service that scans for filesystem errors and stores the location of any errors found.

stale resource records—A resource record that was created using dynamic update, but has not been refreshed by the computer for which the record was created for a long period of time.

standalone server—A Windows Server system that is part of a workgroup.

standard checkpoint—A checkpoint provided by Hyper-V that additionally captures the running state of programs.

starter GPO—A template that can be used to simplify the configuration of Administrative Templates in new GPOs.

storage area network (SAN)—A storage array that is accessed by one or more servers on a server rack.

Storage Migration Service—A Windows Server feature that allows you to move data between servers and the cloud.

storage pinning—A feature that allows you to specify the physical location of different types of data within a volume that spans multiple storage devices.

storage pool—A collection of storage devices in Storage Spaces.

Storage Replicas—A Windows Server feature that allows you to replicate data between different Windows Server systems.

Storage Spaces Direct—A Windows Server feature that allows the combined storage within a cluster to be made available as a single volume to users on the network.

Storage Spaces—A Windows Server feature that allows you to create and manage volumes from multiple storage devices.

storage tiers—A feature that allows an operating system to store more frequently accessed data on faster storage devices within a volume that spans multiple storage devices.

striping with parity—A fault-tolerant RAID level 5 configuration that distributes file contents and associated parity information across multiple storage devices.

striping—A type of RAID level 0 that distributes file contents evenly across multiple storage devices.

stub DNS server—A DNS server that forwards requests for a zone directly to an authoritative DNS server.

subkey—A part of the Windows Registry that exists within a key.

subnet mask—A series of four 8-bit numbers that determine the network and host portions of an IP address.

subnet object—An Active Directory object that represents an IP network.

subordinate CA—A CA that exists underneath the root CA in a CA hierarchy.

switch—A device that allows computers to communicate on a wired network.

symmetric encryption—A type of encryption where a single key is responsible for both encrypting and decrypting data.

synchronization—The process whereby a WSUS server downloads the latest updates from Microsoft Update.

system access control list (SACL)—A list of groups and users that are audited when they use certain permissions to access a resource.

system environment variables—Environment variables that apply to all users on the system.

System File Checker—A tool that can be used to detect damaged, overwritten, or unsigned Windows files and replace them with the proper version.

System log—A Windows log file that stores system events.

system partition—The partition that contains a Windows operating system.

System Preparation Tool—A utility that can be used to remove unique information from an operating system prior to duplication.

T

target—A link to another shared folder on the network.

Task Manager—A graphical tool that can be used to view and manage processes, as well as view system performance information.

template user account—A user account that is only used to create other user accounts with common settings.

Teredo—A protocol used to encapsulate IPv6 packets within an IPv4 network.

thick provisioning—The process of using a virtual hard disk file that has a fixed size.

thin provisioning—The process of using a virtual hard disk file that dynamically expands as needed up to a maximum size.

thread—A single unit of execution within a process.

thread—A unique sequence of instructions that is executed by a process.

three-way mirroring—A mirroring configuration that stores identical copies of data on three different storage devices.

ticket—A token that is used by the Kerberos authentication protocol.

Time To Live (TTL)—The amount of time that a computer is allowed to cache the results of a DNS lookup.

token—A collection of data that is used to validate the identity of a user to systems on a network.

tracing—The process of reading through an existing script to understand its contents.

transitive—A property that allows a trust relationship to apply to other trust relationships.

Transmission Control Protocol/Internet Protocol (TCP/IP)—The most common network protocol used on the Internet. It provides for reliable communication.

Transport Layer Security (TLS)—A protocol that provides data encryption for network traffic.

Transport Server—The component of WDS that responds to PXE requests and sends WIM image data to computers on the network.

tree—A collection of domains within an Active Directory forest that share a DNS domain name.

trimming—A process that optimizes SSD storage by erasing memory locations that no longer store data.

troubleshooting procedure—A task performed when solving a system problem.

trust relationship—An association between Active Directory domains that provides for resource access.

Trusted Platform Module (TPM)—A hardware component within a computer BIOS that contains encryption keys and related information.

trusted root—The public key of a CA or CA hierarchy.

trust—*See* trust relationship.

Type 1 hypervisor—A hypervisor that runs directly on computer hardware.

Type 2 hypervisor—A hypervisor that runs as a program within an operating system.

type cast—A notation that is used to indicate the type of data that should be stored within a variable or constant.

U

UEFI system partition—The partition that stores operating system boot loaders on a system that has a UEFI BIOS.

unattended answer file—An XML-formatted text file that contains default selections to be used during a Windows installation.

unicast—IP communication that is destined for a single computer.

Unified Extensible Firmware Interface (UEFI)—A BIOS standard that is used on modern computers.

Uniform Resource Locator (URL)—The name used to identify a World Wide Web resource, such as a webpage.

uninterruptible power supply (UPS)—A device that contains battery storage and is used to supply power to computers in the event of a power outage.

Universal Group Membership Caching (UGMC)—An Active Directory site property that allows domain controllers to cache universal group membership information for authenticated users.

Universal Naming Convention (UNC)—The format used to specify the location of shared folders on Windows systems.

Universal PnP (UPnP)—An extension of PnP that can be used to automatically configure hardware, services, and network protocols.

universal—A group scope that allows a group to be used within any domain in the forest and contain any forest objects.

Update Services tool—The graphical tool used to manage WSUS.

update—A downloadable program that provides fixes or enhancements for software.

User Datagram Protocol/Internet Protocol (UDP/IP)—A less-reliable, but faster version of the TCP/IP protocol.

user environment variables—Environment variables that apply to the current user on the system.

user ID (UID)—A number assigned to a UNIX user account.

User Principle Name (UPN)—An Active Directory user name format (username@ domainname) that is stored in the global catalog.

user quota—A storage limit that applies to a user or group on an NTFS filesystem.

V

variable provider—The PowerShell provider that is used to manage variables within Windows PowerShell.

variable—A small location in memory that stores a piece of information used by a program, such as Windows PowerShell.

Virtual Desktop Infrastructure (VDI)—A tool built into Server Manager that scans a server or role for configuration that does not follow Microsoft best practices.

virtual directory—A directory name in a URL that allows clients to access website and Web app content in a specific folder on a Web server.

Virtual Disk Service (VDS)—A storage framework used by Windows systems prior to Windows 8 and Windows Server 2012.

virtual disk—A portion of a storage pool in Storage Spaces that can be used for creating RAID volumes.

virtual LAN (VLAN)—A portion of a switch that is treated as an independent switch. Each VLAN on a switch has a unique VLAN number to identify it.

virtual machine bus (VMBus)—The Hyper-V component that provides communication between virtual and physical devices.

virtual machine queue—A technology that optimizes traffic sent between a virtual machine and a hypervisor.

virtual machine template—A virtual machine that is copied to create additional virtual machines.

virtual machine-based desktop deployment—A Remote Desktop Services deployment type that provides Remote Desktop sessions to a Hyper-V virtual machine running on a remote access server.

virtual machine—*See* guest operating system.

virtual memory—An area of physical storage that is used to store information normally found in physical memory.

virtual private network (VPN)—A software-defined network that is used to provide secure access to computers across an existing network.

virtual private networks (VPN)—An overlay network that provides encryption for network traffic that passes from a remote access client to a remote access server.

virtual processor—A software-defined logical processor within a virtual machine.

virtual switch—A software component that allows virtual machines to communicate on a virtual network.

virtualization—The process of running several separate operating systems concurrently on a single computer.

Volume Shadow Copy Service (VSS)—A Windows service that is used to back up open files.

volume—A filesystem that can be accessed using a drive letter or folder in the Windows operating system.

VPN protocol—A protocol that provides VPN functionality between a remote access client and server.

VPN tunnels—*See* virtual private networks (VPN).

W

Web app frameworks—A collection of software packages or modules that allow software developers to write Web apps.

Web app—An application that runs on a cloud server.

Web Distributed Authoring and Versioning (WebDAV)—A standard that allows clients to modify website content on a Web server using HTTP or HTTPS.

Web Server (IIS)—The Windows Server 2019 server role used to install Internet Information Services (IIS).

Web Services Discovery (WS-Discovery)—A packet that is used by WSD-enabled printers to advertise printer availability and status information.

Web Services for Devices (WSD)—A technology that is used by some network-attached print devices to allow print clients and print servers to easily locate the print device on the network.

WebSocket—An alternative to the HTTP protocol that can be used by Web apps when communicating with other Web apps or client programs.

Wi-Fi Protected Access (WPA)—A security standard used for computers that send data on a WLAN.

Wi-Fi Protected Access II (WPA2)—A version of WPA that is commonly used on networks today.

Wi-Fi Protected Access III (WPA3)—A recent WPA version that provides stronger data protection.

Windows Internet Name Service (WINS)—A Windows Server 2019 service used to resolve NetBIOS names to IP addresses.

Windows Admin Center—A Web-based graphical management tool available for Windows Server.

Windows Assessment and Deployment Kit (ADK)—A package of utilities that can be used to aid in the deployment of Windows systems.

Windows Containers—The components that allow Docker to provide containers on the Windows Server 2019 operating system.

Windows Defender Firewall with Advanced Security—A graphical tool that can be used to manage firewall and connection security rules.

Windows Defender—*See* Microsoft Defender.

Windows Deployment Services (WDS)—A Windows Server role that can be used to install operating systems on computers that boot from the network.

Windows Deployment Services tool—The graphical utility that is used to configure WDS.

Windows Explorer—*See* File Explorer.

Windows Imaging Format (WIM)—A file-based image format that contains the installation files used to install a Windows operating system.

Windows Indexing Service—The service on Windows systems that builds an index of files for fast searching.

Windows Installer—The package manager used by the Windows operating system.

Windows Internal Database (WID)—A database system that is included with many free Microsoft products, such as WSUS.

Windows Management Instrumentation (WMI)—A set of specifications and frameworks that can be used to view and manage Windows operating system settings.

Windows PowerShell Integrated Scripting Environment (ISE)—A graphical tool that can be used to create and test PowerShell scripts.

Windows PowerShell—A shell included within Windows operating systems that has scripting features and can be used to perform system management.

Windows Presentation Foundation (WPF)—A graphical subsystem that Windows applications can use to provide a user interface.

Windows Registry—A central database that stores most hardware and software settings on a Windows system.

Windows Search Service—A modern file indexing service that can be installed on Windows systems.

Windows Server Azure Network Adapter—A service that allows you to integrate on-premises servers with servers and services hosted within Microsoft's Azure cloud.

Windows Server Backup—The Windows Server 2019 feature and tool used to back up and restore data.

Windows Server Catalog—A website that lists hardware devices that are supported by Windows operating systems.

Windows Server Configuration Wizard (sconfig.cmd)—A management tool included within Server Core that can be used to manage server settings.

Windows Server Update Services (WSUS)—A Windows Server 2019 service that allows server administrators the ability to manage the distribution of updates for Microsoft products.

Windows Subsystem for Linux (WSL)—A component of Windows 10 and Windows Server 2019 that allows you to run Linux applications on the Windows kernel.

Windows Subsystem for Linux (WSL)—A Windows Server 2019 server role that allows 64-bit Linux programs to execute using the Windows Server 2019 kernel.

Windows System Image Manager—A graphical utility that can be used to create an unattended answer file.

Windows Update—The component of a Windows operating system that obtains updates from Microsoft Update.

winRM—The component of Windows that allows remote management from other systems using Windows PowerShell.

WINS Server—The Windows Server 2019 feature that provides for WINS server functionality.

wireless access point (WAP)—A device that allows computers on a WLAN to connect to a physical LAN.

wireless access point (WAP)—A device that allows wireless devices to communicate on a wireless network.

wireless LAN (WLAN)—A network that links computers together using wireless communication.

wireless router—A WAP that routes IP packets from wireless computers to another IP network on a physical LAN.

Wireshark—A common packet sniffer program.

WMI class—A type of data referenced by WMI.

WMI consumers—Programs, such as Windows PowerShell, that can query WMI.

WMI filter—A filter that uses WQL to limit the computers that can apply a GPO.

WMI infrastructure—The components within Windows that provide WMI.

WMI namespace—A WMI component that provides a type of access to the system.

WMI provider—A WMI component that provides a set of WMI classes that identify specific areas of the system.

workgroup—A logical grouping of computers on a network that implement peer-to-peer networking.

World Wide Web (WWW)—The worldwide collection of Web servers.

WQL (WMI Query Language)—A SQL database-like format that you can use within Windows PowerShell to access WMI.

X

X.500—A widely-adopted standard for directory services defined by the International Telecommunication Union (ITU).

XML Paper Specification (XPS)—A print API and associated document format that is supported by modern Windows systems and print devices.

Z

zone file—A file that contains the resource records for a DNS zone.

zone transfer—The process of copying resource records from a primary DNS server to a secondary DNS server.

zone—A portion of the Domain Name Space.

INDEX